North
Brittany

Managing editor: Liz Coghill
English translation: Atlas Translations, Eileen Townsend-Jones
Editorial: Jane Franklin, Eileen Townsend-Jones, Zoe Ross

Additional research and assistance: Jane Moseley, Sofi Mogensen, Kate Williams, Michael Summers
Index: Dorothy Frame

Series director: Philippe Gloaguen
Series creators: Philippe Gloaguen, Michel Duval
Chief editor: Pierre Josse
Assistant chief editor: Benoît Lucchini
Coordination director: Florence Charmetant

Editorial team: Yves Couprie, Olivier Page, Véronique de Chardon, Amanda Keravel, Isabelle Al Subaihi, Anne-Caroline Dumas, Carole Bordes, Bénédicte Bazaille, André Poncelet, Jérôme de Gubernatis, Marie Burin des Roziers and Thierry Brouard.

Our guides provide independent advice. The authors and compilers do not accept any remuneration for the inclusion of addresses in this guide. Please note that we cannot accept any responsibility for any loss, injury or inconvenience sustained by anyone as a result of any information or advice contained in this guide.

Feedback

We have done our best to ensure the accuracy of the information contained in this guide. However, addresses, phone numbers, opening times etc. do invariably change from time to time, so if you find a discrepancy please do let us know and help us update the guides. As prices may change so may other circumstances – a restaurant may change hands or the standard of service at a hotel may deteriorate since our researchers made their visit. Again, we do our best to ensure information is accurate, but if you notice any discrepancy, please let us know. You can contact us at: hachetteuk@orionbooks.co.uk or write to us at Cassell & Co, address below.

Price guide

Because of rapid inflation in many countries, it is impossible to give an accurate indication of prices in hotels and restaurants. Prices can change enormously from one year to the next. As a result we have adopted a system of categories for the prices in the guides: 'Budget', 'Moderate', 'Chic' and 'Très Chic' (in the guides to France), otherwise 'Expensive' and 'Splash out' in the others.

First published in the United Kingdom in 2002 by Cassell & Co
© English Translation Cassell & Co 2002
© Hachette Livre (Hachette Tourisme) 2001
© Cartography Hachette Tourisme

Distributed in the United States of America by Sterling Publishing Co., Inc.
387 Park Avenue South, New York, NY 10016-8810.

A CIP catalogue for this book is available from the British Library.

ISBN 1 84202 020 X

Typeset at The Spartan Press Ltd, Lymington, Hants.
Printed and bound by Aubin, France. E-mail: sales@aubin-imprimeur.fr

Cover design by Emmanuel Le Vallois (Hachette Livre) and Paul Cooper.
Cover photo © Hachette Tourisme. Back cover photo © Hachette Tourisme.

Cassell & Co, Wellington House, 125 Strand, London WC2R 0BB

routard

North
Brittany

**The ultimate
food, drink and
accommodation guide**

HACHETTE

Contents

NORTH FINISTÈRE 360

Just Exactly Who or What is a Routard?

You are. Yes, you! The fact that you are reading this book means that you are a Routard. You are probably still none the wiser, so to explain we will take you back to the origin of the guides. Routard was the brainchild of a Frenchman named Philippe Gloaguen, who compiled the first guide some 25 years ago with his friend Michel Duval. They simply could not find the kind of guide book they wanted and so the solution was clear – they would just have to write it themselves. When it came to naming the guide, Philippe came up with the term Routard, which at the time did not exist as a bona fide word – at least, not in conventional dictionary terms. Today, if you look the word up in a French-English dictionary you will find that it means 'traveller' or 'globetrotter' – so there you have it, that's what you are!

From this humble beginning has grown a vast collection of some 100 titles to destinations all over the world. Routard is now the bestselling guide book series in France. The guides have been translated into five different languages, so keep an eye out for fellow Routard readers on your travels.

What exactly do the guides do?

The short answer is that they provide all the information you need to enable you to have a successful holiday or trip. Routards' great strength however, lies in their listings. The guides provide comprehensive listings for accommodation, eating and drinking – ranging from campsites and youth hostels through to four star hotels – and from bars, clubs and greasy spoons to tearooms, cafés and restaurants. Each entry is accompanied by a detailed and frank appraisal of the address, rather like a friend coming back from holiday who is recommending all the good places to go (or even the places to avoid!). The guides aim to help you find the best addresses and the best value for money within your price range, whilst giving you invaluable insider advice at the same time.

Anything else?

Routard also provides oceans of practical advice on how to get along in the country or city you are visiting plus an insight into the character and customs of the people. How do you negotiate your way around the transport system? Will you offend if you bare your knees in the temple? And so on. In addition, you will find plenty of sightseeing information, backed up by historical and cultural detail, interesting facts and figures, addresses and opening times. The humanitarian aspect is also of great importance, with the guides commenting freely and often pithily, and most titles contain a section on human rights.

Routard are truly useful guides that are convivial, irreverent, down-to-earth and honest. We very much hope you enjoy them and that they will serve you well during your stay.

Happy travelling.

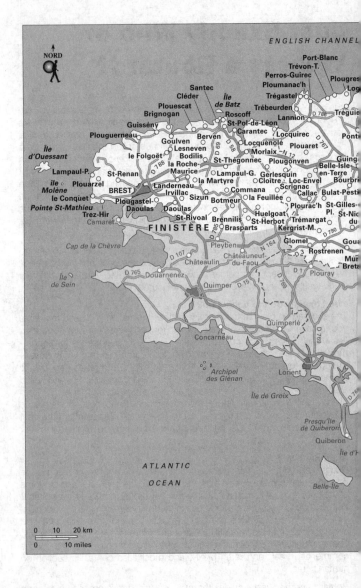

| Paimpol | Places covered in guide |
| Pontivy | Locator only |

de Bréhat
te de l'Arcouest
aazlanec
pol

nloup
Saint-Quay-   Sables-   *Cap*
Portrieux   d'Or   *Fréhel*
Binic   Erquy   Fort la Latte   Cancale   le Mont-
laudren   Dinard   Saint-Michel   Avranches
    D 786   St-Cast   Saint-Malo
Pléneuf-   D 768   Ploubalay   St-Suliac   N 176
Val-André   Plancoët   Dol-de-
nt-Brieuc   Lamballe   Bretagne
uintin   Dinan   Combourg
TES - D'ARMOR
Moncontour   ILLE - ET -   Fougères
             Tinténiac
Bécherel   Hédé
Loudéac   Montauban-
de-Bretagne
Montfort-   Champeaux
sur-Meu   Vitré
Forêt de   RENNES
Paimpont
Ploërmel   VILAINE   la Roche
         aux Fées   la Guerche-
MORBIHAN   de-Bretagne

Châteaubriant

Redon
la Roche-
Bernard   LOIRE -
le Croisic   Saint-Nazaire   ATLANTIQUE
la Baule   Loire
               NANTES
Pornic

Îles Chausey

MANCHE

MAYENNE

NORTH BRITTANY

Map List

Symbols Used in the Guide

Please note that not all the symbols below appear in every guide.

- ■ Useful addresses
- 🛈 Tourist office
- ✉ Post office
- ☎ Telephone
- 🚆 Railway station
- 🚌 Bus station
- 🚐 Shared taxi
- 🚊 Tram
- River transport
- Sea transport
- ✈ Airport
- ⌂ Where to stay

- ✕ Where to eat
- ♟ Where to go for a drink
- ♪ Where to listen to music
- ♦ Where to go for an ice-cream
- ★ To see
- 🛍 Shopping
- • 'Other'
- 🅿 Parking
- ✕ Castle
- ⁂ Ruins

- ⚓ Diving site
- ⌂ Shelter
- ⛺ Camp site
- ▲ Peak
- ● Site
- ○ Town
- ✕ Hill
- ⛪ Abbey, chapel
- ≪ Lookout
- ⇗ Beach
- ✕ Lighthouse
- ⚒ Facilities for the disabled

Getting There

By Air

FROM BRITAIN

Air France flies to Nantes three times daily and Brest twice daily from London Gatwick. Air France also flies to Rennes twice daily from London City. **British Airways** flies regularly from Gatwick to Nantes. **Ryanair** makes a daily flight to Dinard from London Stanstead.

Domestic flights from Paris with **Air France** fly into airports at Brest, Lorient, Quimper, Rennes and Nantes. Flights with **Air Liberté** fly from Strasbourg, Lille and Mulhouse via Rennes and from Paris-Orly to Lannion.

Brit Air (☎ 0-802-802-802) is based at Morlaix-Ploujean airport. Their flights leave from Brest, Nantes and Rennes to London and the French cities of Le Havre, Lyon, Marseille, Nice, Paris, Strasbourg and Toulouse.

Finistair is a little company running a seasonal daily link (not in winter) between Lorient and Belle-Île, using 9-seater planes: ☎ 02-97-31-41-14 and another link between Brest and the Île d'Ouessant: ☎ 02-98-84-64-87. Their prices are reasonable.

Journey times vary from 1 hour 10 minutes to 1 hour 30 minutes. Expect to pay around £150 to £200, with slightly higher prices for weekend departures or departures from a regional airport, but be aware that ticket prices can reach over £400. There can, however, be some real bargains, even in July and August, through travel agents or airline price promotions. The travel pages of the weekend broadsheet newspapers and websites such as www.cheapflights.com, www.expedia.com and www.lastminute.com are also good hunting grounds for flight deals.

Good bets for tickets to Paris include **British Airways**, **buzz** and **bmi British Midland**. Air France and SNCF also offer combined air and rail deals via Paris. Travelling from the UK to Brittany via Paris may seem a roundabout route, but fares to Paris are often the cheapest, particularly if travelling in high season and can be more convenient if you would prefer to travel from a regional airport.

Always ensure that your chosen airline is endorsed by ABTA. Contact the Air Travel Advisory Bureau for advice on airlines and prices.

✪ **Air France** 10 Warwick Street, First Floor, London W1B 5LZ. ☎ (0845) 084 5111. Website: www.airfrance.com

✪ **bmi British Midland** Donington Hall, Castle Donington, Derby DE74 2SB. ☎ (0870) 607 0555. Website: iflybmi.com

✪ **British Airways** Waterside, PO Box 365, Harmondsworth UB7 0GB. ☎ (0845) 773 3377. Website: www.britishairways.com

⊕ buzz Endeavour House, Stansted Airport, Essex CM24 1RS. ☎ (0870) 240 7070. www.buzzaway.com

⊕ Ryanair Dublin Airport, County Dublin. ☎ (0870) 333 1231. Website: www.ryanair.com

⊕ The Air Travel Advisory Bureau Columbus House, 28 Charles Square, London N1 6HT. ☎ (020) 7635 5000. Website: www.atab.co.uk

TRAVEL AGENTS IN BRITAIN

■ **Airline Network** (discount flights by phone only): ☎ (0870) 241 0019

■ **Bridge the World** (discount flights and packages): 47 Chalk Farm Road, London NW1 8AJ. ☎ (0870) 444 7474. Website: www.bridgetheworld.com

■ **Council Travel** (discount flights): 28a Poland Street, London W1V 3DB. ☎ (020) 7287 9410. Website: www.counciltravel.com

■ **Flightbookers** (discount flights and packages): 177–178 Tottenham Court Road, London W1P 0LX. ☎ (0870) 010 7000. Website: www.ebookers.com

■ **STA Travel** (students and people under 26): 86 Old Brompton Road, London SW7 3LQ. 37 branches nationwide. ☎ (0870) 160 0599. Website: www.statravel.co.uk

■ **Thomas Cook** (flights and packages): Branches nationwide. ☎ (0990) 666 222. Website: www.thomascook.com

■ **Trailfinders** (discounts and specialist itineraries): 215 Kensington High Street, London W8 6BD. Six branches nationwide. ☎ (020) 7937 1234. Website: www.trailfinders.com

■ **USIT Campus Travel** (students and people under 26): Mayflower House, Armada Way, Plymouth PL1 1LD. 51 branches nationwide. ☎ (0870) 240 1010. Website: www.usitcampus.co.uk

Specialist Travel Agents

The travel sections of the Sunday broadsheets are particularly good sources of information on travel agents providing specialist packages to Brittany, and many travel agents in the UK can arrange package tours that include flights and Channel crossings.

■ **Brittany Direct Holidays** (walking, cycling, boating and self-catering tours): 362–364 Sutton Common Road, Sutton SM3 9PL. ☎ (020) 8641 6060.

■ **Brittany Ferries Holidays** (accommodation, mid-range and general packages): Wharf Road, Portsmouth PO2 8RU. ☎ (0870) 901 2400. Website: www.brittanyferries.com

■ **Brittany Travel Ltd** (self-catering, cottages and gîtes for hire in Brittany): 10 Little Acres, Ware SG12 9JW. ☎ (01920) 413013. Website: www.brittany.co.uk

■ **The French Holiday Service** (properties to rent, tours and activity holidays): 178 Piccadilly, London W1 0B8. ☎ (020) 8324 4007. Website: www.leisuredirection.co.uk

■ **French Life Holidays** (cottages, camping and villas across Brittany): Leeds LS18 4AW. ☎ (0113) 281 9998. Website: www.frenchlife.co.uk

■ **Matthews Holidays** (self-drive and mobile home holidays in Brittany): 8 Bishopmead Parade, East Horsley KT24 6RP. ☎ (01483) 284044. Website: www.matthewsfrance.co.uk

■ **Vacances en Campagne** (self-catering and general accommodation, including chateaux for rent): Bignor, near Pulborough RH20 1QD. ☎ (01798) 869433. Website: www.indiv-travellers.com/holiday-properties-in-france

■ **VFB Holidays** (Cottage holidays, packages and villas): Normandy House, High Street, Cheltenham, GL50 3FB. ☎ (01242) 240340. Website: www.vfbholidays.co.uk

For a comprehensive list of tour operators and travel agents, contact:

⊟ The French Government Tourist Office 178 Piccadilly, London W1 0B8. ☎ (0900) 124 4123. Website: www.francetourism.com

FROM IRELAND

There are no direct flights between Ireland and Brittany. Travellers will need to fly to Paris and take a train or connecting flight, or travel via London. Dublin is the busiest international airport in Ireland and flights between Paris and Ireland are short and usually inexpensive. **British European**, **bmi British Midland** and **British Airways** all fly from Belfast International and Dublin to Paris. **Air France** flies from Dublin to Paris, **Aer Lingus** flies from Cork and Dublin to Paris and **Ryanair** flies from Dublin to Paris Beauvais-Tille.

Expect to pay about IR£130–200 for a return flight from Dublin to Paris. Look out for special deals via travel agents, the Internet, the travel pages of the weekend broadsheets and the airlines themselves.

✪ **Aer Lingus** 40–41 Upper O'Connell Street, Dublin 1. ☎ (01) 886 8888. Website: www.flyaerlingus.com

✪ **Air France** Dublin Airport, County Dublin. ☎ (01) 605 0383. Website: www.airfrance.com

✪ **bmi British Midland** Donington Hall, Castle Donington, Derby DE74 2SB. ☎ (01) 283 8833. For enquiries from Northern Ireland ☎ (0870) 607 0555. Website: www.iflybmi.com

✪ **British Airways** 13 St Stephen's Green, Dublin 1. ☎ 1-800-626-747. For enquiries from Northern Ireland: ☎ (0345) 222 111. Website: www.britishairways.com

✪ **British European Airlines** Exeter Airport, Exeter CX5 2BD. ☎ (01890) 925532. Website: www.british-european.com

✪ **Ryanair** Dublin Airport, County Dublin. ☎ (01) 609 7800. Website: www.ryanair.ie

TRAVEL AGENTS IN IRELAND

- **American Express Travel** 116 Grafton Street, Dublin 2. ☎ (01) 677 2874
- **Budget Travel** 134 Lower Baggot Street, Dublin 2. ☎ (01) 661 3122
- **Budget Travel Shops** 63 Main Street, Finglas 11, Dublin (seven offices in Dublin and throughout Ireland). ☎ (01) 834 0637
- **Go Holidays** 28 North Great George Street, Dublin 1. ☎ (01) 874 4126
- **Hello France** The Mill Centre, Crosses Green, Cork ☎ (021) 378 404
- **Irish Ferries** 2–4 Merrion Row, Dublin 2. ☎ (01) 661 0511. Website: www.irishferries.ie
- **Neenan Travel** 12 South Leinster Street, Dublin 2. ☎ (01) 676 5181
- **Thomas Cook** 11 Donegal Place, Belfast BT1 6ET. ☎ (01232) 554 455. 118 Grafton Street, Dublin. ☎ (01) 677 1721. Website: www.thomascook.com
- **Trailfinders** 4–5 Dawson Street, Dublin 2. ☎ (01) 677 7888. Website: www.trailfinders.com
- **USITNOW** 19–21 Aston Quay, O'Donnell Bridge, Dublin. ☎ (01) 602 1700. 13B Fountain Centre, College Street, Belfast BT61 6ET. ☎ (01232) 324 4073. Website: www.usitnow.ie

For a comprehensive list of tour operators and travel agents, contact:

⓭ The French Government Tourist Office 35 Lower Abbey St, Dublin 1. ☎ (01) 703 4046

Travellers from Ireland may find it worthwhile flying to London and connecting with a Eurostar service or flight to Brittany, or booking a package tour.

FROM THE UNITED STATES

There are no direct flights from the United States to Brittany. Travellers from the US will need to fly to Paris, and then take a connecting internal flight from Paris to Brittany (for example, to Brest, for about $150 extra). Another option is to fly to Paris, then take a TGV high-speed train from Paris to Brittany. Many airlines also often offer inexpensive fares to European cities such as London, Amsterdam and Frankfurt from where travellers can connect to Brittany by air or train.

Most of the lowest fares to Europe depart from the east coast. Flight times last about 7 to 9 hours from the east coast gateways, rising to 10 to 12 hours from cities on the west coast. If booking in advance, expect to pay about $600 for a return flight to Paris from New York in high season.

The US airline industry is highly competitive and travellers should be able to find excellent deals on fares to Brittany. Discount travel agents sell tickets offloaded by airlines, often on an 'open jaw' basis that will enable you to fly into one European city and fly out of another. Such travel agencies also sell railcards and tours. Travel clubs can also be worthwhile if you're planning to do a bit of travelling. The travel sections of Sunday broadsheets are good for bargain hunting, as are Internet travel sites such as www.lowestfare.com, www.priceline.com and www.previewtravel.com. Always ensure that your travel agent is endorsed by ASTA. Airlines themselves can often be as competitive as agencies, especially if you are booking APEX (Advanced Purchase Excursion) tickets or winter Super APEX tickets.

✪ **Air France** 125 West 55th Street, New York, NY 10019. ☎ 1-800-237-2747. Website: www.airfrance.com

✪ **American Airlines** 4200 Amon Carter, PD 2400, Fort Worth, TX 76155. ☎ 1-800-433-7300. Website: www.aa.com

✪ **Cathay Pacific** 590 Fifth Avenue, Fifth Floor, New York, NY 10036. ☎ 1-800-223-2742. Website: www.cathaypacific.com

✪ **Continental Airlines** 2929 Alan Parkway, PO Box 4607, Houston,TX 77210. ☎ 1-800-525-0280. Website: www.continental.com

✪ **Delta Airlines** Atlanta International Airport, Atlanta, GA 30320. ☎ 1-800-221-1212. Website: www.delta-air.com

✪ **Northwest Airlines** 100 East 42nd Street, Second Floor, New York, NY 10017. ☎ 1-800-447-4747. Websites: www.nwa.com or www.klm.com

✪ **TWA** 650 Anton Boulevard, Suite F, Costa Mesa, CA 91364. ☎ 1-800-982-4141. Website: www.twa.com

✪ **United Airlines** ☎ 1-800-241-6522. Website: www.ual.com.

✪ **US Air** 10 Eyck Plaza, 40 North Pearl Street, Albany, New York, NY 12207. ☎ 1-800-428-432. Website: www.usairways.com

TRAVEL AGENTS IN THE UNITED STATES

■ **Air Courier Association** 191 University Boulevard, Suite 300, Denver, CO 80206. ☎ (303) 278 8810

■ **Last Minute Travel Club** (standby deals): 132 Brookline Avenue, Boston, MA 02215. ☎ 1-800-LAST MIN

■ **STA Travel** (students and people under 26): 48 East 11th Street, New York, NY 10003. ☎ 1-800-781-4040. Branches nationwide. Website: www.statravel.com

■ **USIT (Council Travel) USA** (students and people under 26): 931 West-wood Boulevard, Westwood, Los Angeles, CA 90024. ☎ 1-800-226-8624. Over 60 branches nationwide. Website: www.counciltravel.com

Specialist Travel Agents in the United States

When arranging a package deal, make sure the agent is a member of USTOA or is approved by the ASTA.

Companies specializing in tours to Brittany from the USA include:

■ **Eurobike Tours** (bicycle and walking tours around Brittany): PO Box 990, DeKalb, IL 60115. ☎ 1-800-321-6060. Website: www.eurobike.com

■ **New Frontiers** (tours and packages): 6 East 46th Street, New York, NY 10017. ☎ (212) 986 6006 or 1-800-677-0720. Website: www.newfrontiers. com

■ **The French Experience** (tours, car rental, and accommodation in cottages and chateaux in Brittany): 370 Lexington Avenue, New York, NY 10017. ☎ 1-800-28-FRANCE. Website: www.frenchexperience.com

■ **Tour de France** (general and theme tours around Brittany): 738 Dakota Trail, PO Box 379, Franklin Lakes, NJ 07417. ☎ (201) 891 0076

■ **Ville et Village** (cottages, villas and properties to rent in Brittany and across France): 2124 Kittredge Street, Suite 200, Berkeley, CA 94704. ☎ (510) 559 8080. www.villeetvillage.com

For a comprehensive list of tour operators and travel agents, contact:

🚹 **The French Government Tourist Office** 444 Madison Avenue, 16th Floor, New York, NY 10022. ☎ (212) 838 7855. Website: www.france tourism.com

TRAIN TRAVEL FOR NORTH AMERICAN CITIZENS

Eurail passes for European-wide train travel have to be bought in the United States before departure.

🚄 **Rail Europe** 226 Westchester Avenue, White Plains, New York, NY 10604. ☎ 1-800-438-7345

FROM CANADA

There are no direct flights from Canada to destinations in Brittany and all journeys will need to be made via Paris. The main European airlines fly at least once daily to Paris from Montreal or Toronto, while the smaller ones offer between two and four flights a week.

Expect to pay around CAN$700 for a return to Paris in the winter (more at Christmas), and CAN$800 during the peak summer months. Keep an eye out for reductions on Internet sites or the weekend travel sections of the broadsheet newspapers. There is less international competition on flights from Canada than from the United States, so prices are less likely to be keen. Canadian travellers might consider flying from one of the northern US cities. A flight from Buffalo to Paris, for example, could be as low as US$400.

The flight time from Montreal to Paris is about 6 hours 30 minutes and from Toronto to Paris takes about 7 hours 30 minutes. The flight time from Vancouver is about 12 hours 30 minutes.

✈ **Air Canada** 979 de Maisonneuve Boulevard West, Montreal H4A 3T2. ☎ 1-888-247-2262. Website: www.aircanada.ca

✈ **Air France** Suite 810, 151 Bloor Street West, Toronto, M56 1T6 ☎ 1-800-667-2747. Website: www.airfrance.com

✈ **British Airways** 4120 Yonge Street, Suite 100, Toronto M2P 2B8. ☎ 1-800-AIRWAYS / 1-800-247-9297. Website: www.britishairways.com

✈ **Canadian Airlines** 165–168 18 Street South East, Calgary T2E 6J5. ☎ 1-800-466-7000. Website: www.cdnair.ca

✈ **Northwest/KLM** Toronto Pearson International Airport, Toronto. ☎ 1-800-374-7747. Website: www.nwa.com / www.klm.com

TRAVEL AGENTS IN CANADA

■ **Collacutt Travel** (general travel services): The Bayview Village Centre, 2901 Bayview Avenue, Toronto M2K 1E6. ☎ 1-888-225-9811. Website: www.collacutt-travel.com

■ **New Frontiers/Nouvelles Frontières** 1001 Sherbrook Street East, Suite 720, Montreal H2I 1L3. ☎ (514) 526 8444

■ **Sears Travel** (general services): ☎ 1-888-884-2359. More than 80 offices throughout Canada. Website: www.sears.ca

■ **Travel Cuts** (student travel organization): 187 College Street, Toronto M5T 1P7. ☎ (416) 979 2406 or 1-800-667-2887. Website: www.travelcuts.com

■ **Travel House** (tours, packages, discount travel): 1491 Yonge Street, Suite 401, Toronto M4T 1ZR. ☎ (416) 925 6322. Branches country-wide. Website: www.travel-house.com

Many of the travel agents listed in 'Travel Agents in the United States' are also happy to organize trips for travellers from Canada.

Specialist Travel Agents in Canada

■ **Butterfield and Robinson** 70 Bond St, Toronto M5B 1X3. ☎ 1-800-678-1147. Website: www.butterfieldandrobinson.com

■ **Randonnée Tours** Room 100, 62 Albert Street, Winnipeg, Manitoba R38 1E9. ☎ (204) 475 6939 or 1-800-465-6488. Website: www.randonnee tours.com

For a list of tour operators and travel agents, contact:

🏢 **The French Government Tourist Office** 30 St Patrick's Street, Suite 700, Toronto M5T 3A3. ☎ (416) 593 4723, or 1981 Avenue McGill College, Suite 490, Montreal H3A 2W9. ☎ (514) 288 2026.

FROM AUSTRALIA AND NEW ZEALAND

There are no direct flights from Australia or New Zealand to Brittany. Travellers from these parts will have to fly to Paris or another European city and pick up a connection to Brittany from there by air or land.

Direct flights go to Paris and other cities in Europe from the major cities in Australia and New Zealand. These flights will usually include a stopover in an Asian city and flight times vary from 19 to 25 hours. Many passengers expand their holiday by extending their stopover by one or two nights, for a small extra charge. This needs to be set up with the airline in advance.

The most inexpensive fares are frequently with Asian airlines such as **Garuda** although the most frequent flights to Europe are made by **British Airways** and **Qantas**. Travellers should expect to pay around AUD$1,500 to $2,000 for a return fare in low season. Return tickets increase by about AUD$500 to $1,000 in high season.

Return flights from New Zealand begin at around NZ$2200 in low season. Travellers should find good deals through travel agents, particularly on flights to London and extended itinerary travel.

● **Air France** 64 York Street, Sydney 2000. ☎ (02) 932-1000. Dataset House, 143 Nelson Street, Auckland. ☎ (09) 303-3521. Website: www.air france.com

● **Air New Zealand** 5 Elizabeth Street, Sydney 2000. ☎ (02) 13 24 76. Air New Zealand House, 72 Oxford Terrace, Christchurch. ☎ (0800) 737-000. Website: www.airnz.co.nz

● **British Airways** Chifley Square, 70 Hunter Street, Sydney 2000. ☎ (02) 9258-3300. Auckland International Airport (09) 356-8690. Website: www.britishairways.com

● **Cathay Pacific** 3/F International Terminal, Sydney International Airport, Mascot, Sydney 2020. ☎ 13 26 27. 11th Floor, Arthur Andersen Tower, 205–209 Queen Street, PO Box 1313, Auckland. ☎ (09) 379-0861. Website: www.cathaypacific.com

● **Malaysia Airlines** MAS, 16th Spring Street, Sydney 2000. ☎ (02) 913-2627. MAS, 12th Floor, The Swanson Centre, 12–26 Swanson Street, Auckland, PO Box 3729. Auckland. ☎ (09) 373-2741. Website: www. malaysiaairlines.com

● **Qantas** Qantas Centre, 203 Coward Street, Mascot, Sydney 2020. ☎ 13-12-11 or (02) 9691-3636. 191 Queen Street, Auckland 1. ☎ (09) 357-8900 or 0800-808-967. Website: www.qantas.com

● **Singapore Airlines** Singapore Airlines House, 17–19 Bridge Street, Sydney 2000. ☎ (02) 9350-0100. Tenth Floor, West Plaza Building, Corner Albert and Fanshawe Streets, Auckland 1. ☎ (0800) 808-909. Website: www.singaporeair.com.au

TRAVEL AGENTS IN AUSTRALIA AND NEW ZEALAND

■ **Flight Centres** Level 13, 33 Berry Street, North Sydney 2060. ☎ (02) 924-2422. 205 Queen Street, Auckland 1. ☎ (09) 309-6171. ☎ 1-1300-131-600 for nearest branch.

■ **STA Travel** 855 George Street, Sydney 2000. ☎ (02) 9212-1255 (72 branches). 90 Cashel Street, Christchurch, New Zealand. ☎ (03) 379-9098 (13 branches). For nearest branch ☎ 13-17-76. Website: www.statravel.com.au

■ **Thomas Cook** 175 Pitt Street, Sydney. ☎ 1-300-728-748 (branches nationwide) 96 Anzac Avenue, Auckland. ☎ 0800-500-600 (branches nationwide). Websites: www.thomascook.com.au and www.thomascook.com.nz

■ **Trailfinders** 91 Elizabeth Street, Brisbane, Queensland 4000. ☎ (07) 3229-0887. Website: www.trailfinder.com/australia

FROM SOUTH AFRICA

There are no direct flights from South Africa to Brittany, and South African visitors will have to travel to the region via Paris or London, making the onward connection either on an internal flight or a TGV high-speed train.

Flights from Johannesburg go direct to Paris, but flights from Cape Town stop over in Johannesburg. Currently, **Air France** and **South African Airways** operate daily direct flights to Paris. **British Airways** has 18 flights a week from South Africa (Johannesburg and Cape Town), all via London. Standard return tickets should cost between R3,300 and R5,000, depending on the season.

✛ **Air France** 196 Oxford Road, Oxford Manor, Illovo, Johannesburg 2196. ☎ (011) 880-8040. Website: www.airfrance.com

✛ **British Airways** Grosvenor Court, 195 Grosvenor, Rosebank, Johannesburg 2196. ☎ (0860) 011-747 or (011) 441-8600. Website: www.british airways.com

✛ **South African Airways** Airways Park, Jones Road, Johannesburg International Airport, Johannesburg 1627. ☎ (011) 978-1763. Website: www. saa.co.za

TRAVEL AGENTS IN SOUTH AFRICA

■ **STA Travel** Level 3, Leslie Social Sciences Building, University of Cape Town, Rondebosch 7700, Cape Town. ☎ (021) 685-1808. Website: www.sta-travel.co.za

■ **USIT Adventures** Rondebosch Shopping Centre, Rondebosch Main Road, Rondebosch, Cape Town. ☎ (021) 685-2226. Website: www.usit-adventures.co.za

By Train

FROM BRITAIN

Eurostar runs trains from London Waterloo or Ashford in Kent to Lille almost hourly throughout the day, connecting with French SNCF network trains to cities in Brittany. Travellers should find easy connections from Lille through to Nantes or Rennes on a TGV (high-speed train).

Expect to pay anything from £70 to £270 for a standard second-class return from London. A first-class return can cost over £400. Reduced fares are available for students, senior citizens and groups, and discounts are also offered for advance bookings. Eurostar often offers promotions that can bring the price of a return to as low as £30. It is often best to book tickets with Eurostar direct, as many travel agents will charge a booking fee. Be sure to arrive at your Eurostar station at least 25 minutes before departure.

Tickets for SNCF services can be bought at stations in France, but travellers with Internet access may prefer to book through their website, which allows you to specify the speed, departure time and price that you require.

Travellers thinking of longer itineraries in France may find the Interrail pass good value. For as little as £160, students and people under 26 can enjoy 22 days of travel on French railways. The pass includes half-price travel on British trains and free passage with some of the cross-channel ferry companies, although you do have to pay supplements on high-speed trains. Contact travel agents specializing in student travel, such as STA Travel or USIT Campus Travel (*see* 'Travel Agents in Britain').

Eurostar (London Waterloo–Paris Gare du Nord), Waterloo International Terminal, London SE1 (Waterloo tube). Also: Eurostar Ticket Office, 102–104 Victoria Street, London SW1 5JL. ☎ (0870) 518 6186 (7am–10pm). Website: www.eurostar.co.uk

SNCF Rail Europe Ltd French Railways House, 179 Piccadilly, London W1 0B8. ☎ (0870) 584 8848. Websites: www.sncf.com or www.raileurope. com

FROM PARIS

TGV high-speed trains leave Paris for Brittany from the Gare Montparnasse. On the Paris–Rennes route there are about 16 return journeys each day, with a travel time of 2 hours 3 minutes. For Paris–Brest there are about eight return trips daily; the best journey time is 4 hours 6 minutes.

Paris–St-Malo has ten journeys daily. Including a change at Rennes, the journey time is 3 hours 6 minutes. Paris–St-Brieuc has 8 journeys each day and the trip takes 2 hours 52 minutes.

FROM ELSEWHERE IN FRANCE

The TGV also comes into Rennes direct from Lille (3 hours 50 minutes) and from Lyon (4 hours 30 minutes) and it's also possible to pick up the train at Paris-Charles-de-Gaulle airport, at Marne-la-Vallée-Chessy and at Massy-TGV station.

By Sea

FROM BRITAIN

Several cross-Channel ferries sail direct from the UK to Brittany. **Brittany Ferries** sails from Portsmouth to St-Malo and from Plymouth to Roscoff. **Condor Ferries** sails from Poole to St-Malo. However, the Dover–Calais crossing is often the most popular since it is short and usually the cheapest.

Expect to pay from £40 to £100 for a car and two passengers between Dover and Calais and from £70 to upwards of £200 for the longer crossings. The foot-passenger fare starts at £20. Foot-passengers can also travel on coaches through the Eurotunnel.

A wide range of discounts is available, including package deals, off-peak reductions, deals for five-day trips, and special prices are offered to members of motoring organizations. Discounts are also offered if you book well in advance.

The **Seacat** travels from Dover to Calais in 45 minutes and from Newhaven to Dieppe in 4 hours, although journey and departure times can be affected by bad weather. Prices start at about £100 for a single.

⚓ **Brittany Ferries** (Plymouth–Roscoff, Poole–Cherbourg, Portsmouth–Caen, Portsmouth–St-Malo) Wharf Road, Portsmouth PO2 8RU. ☎ (0870) 901 2400. Website: www.brittanyferries.com

⚓ **Condor Ferries** (Poole–Cherbourg, Poole–St-Malo) Condor House, New Harbour Road South, Hamworthy, Poole, Dorset BH15 4AJ. ☎ (0845) 345 2000. Website: www.condorferries.co.uk

⚓ **P&O Portsmouth** (Portsmouth–Cherbourg, Portsmouth–Le Havre), Peninsula House, Wharf Road, Portsmouth PO2 8TA. ☎ (0870) 598 0555. Website: www.poef.com

⚓ **Seacat** (Dover–Calais, Folkestone–Boulogne, Newhaven–Dieppe) International Hoverport, Dover CT17 9TG. ☎ (0870) 240 8070 or (0870) 524 0241. Website: www.hoverspeed.co.uk

FROM IRELAND

Brittany Ferries runs a once-weekly service from Cork to Roscoff, which takes around 15–17 hours. **Irish Ferries** runs boats from Rosslare to Roscoff and to Cherbourg, with the journey taking upwards of 15 hours. Both companies also offer package tours.

One-way fares for foot passengers start at about IR£30–60 on Brittany Ferries, and IR£75 on Irish Ferries. Expect to pay at least double this price if you are taking a car.

Direct ferry services between Ireland and France can be long and infrequent, so Irish travellers, especially those taking a car, sometimes chose to travel via the UK. **P&O Irish Sea Ferries** sail from Larne to Fleetwood and from Dublin to Liverpool. **Irish Ferries** and **Stena Line** sail from Dublin to Holyhead. The Stena Line service from Rosslare to Fishguard can prove especially convenient for those travelling by car.

For more information on routes to France from the UK *see* 'By Sea from Britain' and 'By Train from Britain'.

⚓ **Brittany Ferries** (Cork–Roscoff) Wharf Road, Portsmouth, PO2 8RU. ☎ (021) 427 7801. Website: www.brittanyferries.com

⚓ **Irish Ferries** (Dublin–Holyhead, Rosslare–Cherbourg, Rosslare–Roscoff) 2–4 Merrion Row, Dublin 2. ☎ (01) 638 3333. Rosslare ☎ (053) 33158. Cork ☎ (01) 661 0511. Enquiries from Northern Ireland: ☎ (0800) 018 2211. Website: www.irishferries.ie

⚓ **P&O Irish Sea Ferries** (Dublin Port–Liverpool, Larne–Fleetwood) Peninsula House, Wharf Road, Portsmouth PO2 8TA. ☎ (0870) 242 4777. Website: www.poirishsea.com

⚓ **Stena Line** (Dublin Port–Holyhead, Rosslare–Fishguard) The Ferry Terminal, Dun Laoghaire, Co. Dublin. ☎ (01) 204 7777. Website: www. stenaline.co.uk

Travellers from Ireland without cars can travel by train through the UK. This either means catching another ferry from the south coast of England, or catching a Eurostar service that connects through Calais, where there will be connections through to Brittany. The Continental Rail Desk of **Iarnrodd Éireann** in Dublin can arrange journeys to France for you. Most travellers sail from Dublin to connect with a **Virgin Trains** service from Holyhead that reaches London Euston in about 3 hours 30 minutes.

🚆 **Iarnrodd Éireann** (Continental Rail Desk) 35 Lower Abbey Street, Dublin 1. ☎ (01) 677 1871.

🚆 **SNCF Britrail Ltd** Third Floor, 123 Lower Baggot Street, Dublin 2. ☎ (01) 661 2866. Website: www.sncf.com

🚆 **Virgin Trains** (Holyhead–London Euston) ☎ (0845) 722 2333. Website: www.virgintrains.co.uk

By Car

FROM BRITAIN

UK driving licences are valid in France and you will need at least third-party insurance to drive on French roads. All drivers should carry their insurance documents, as well as the required car kit of spare bulbs, red triangle and headlight deflectors.

French motorways (*autoroutes*) are well maintained, but tolls can be very expensive. The speed limit on motorways is 130kph (80mph). For more information about driving in France, *see* 'Getting Around'.

If you decide to take a car to France, you can travel by sea or you can put the car on the train and go with **Eurotunnel**. The ferry is usually the cheapest option, but there are sometimes special deals on Eurotunnel tickets to be picked up on the company's website, as well as through travel agents and in the Sunday newspapers.

Eurotunnel's auto-train shuttle service to Calais transports cars and their passengers across the Channel in about 35 minutes. The auto-trains run 24 hours a day. Departures are roughly every half-hour in daytime and once an hour at night. Expect to pay upwards of £200 for a return ticket including a car and passengers. Advance booking can sometimes bring the price down and is advisable in any case in high season. Be sure to arrive at least 25 minutes before departure time.

🚆 **Eurotunnel** (Folkestone–Calais), Customer Service Centre, Junction 12 of the M20, PO Box 300, Folkestone CT19 4DQ. ☎ (0870) 535 3535. 24-hour recorded information: ☎ (0891) 555 566. Website: www.eurotunnel.co.uk

By Coach

FROM BRITAIN

Eurolines operate daily coach services from London Victoria to St-Malo via Portsmouth and to Roscoff via Plymouth in summer. There are four or five services every week, all year round, to Nantes, via Dover or Calais. The journey time to St-Malo and Roscoff is about 13 hours and prices begin at about £50 for an adult return. The journey time to Nantes is 14 hours and prices begin at about £95.

Eurolines runs in partnership with National Express, which also runs buses to London from all over the UK. Throughout the year, there are regular services to Paris and destinations in Normandy such as Cherbourg, from where travellers can connect to Brittany on local bus or train.

🚌 **Eurolines** (London Victoria–Paris), Eurolines Travel Shops, 52 Grosvenor Gardens, London SW1W 0AG (Victoria tube). ☎ (0870) 514 3219. Website: www.eurolines.co.uk

FROM IRELAND

The Irish bus service **Bus Éireann** (based in Dublin) runs regular buses to connect with Eurolines services to France. There is a twice-daily service from Dublin to Paris (via London) that takes 22 hours. Bus Éireann can also arrange your journey so that you can connect through the UK with a service to Brittany.

There is no direct service from Belfast to Paris. Eurolines runs a direct twice-daily service from Belfast to London Victoria, from where travellers can connect on to Brittany.

GETTING THERE

Bus Éireann (coach services throughout Ireland via Dublin to Paris-Bagnolet), Central Bus Station (Busaras), Store Street, Dublin 1. ☎ (01) 830-2222. Website: www.buseireann.ie

General Information

ACCOMMODATION

Brittany offers a huge range of accommodation for those on a budget, from youth hostels and hotels for young people to classic one- and two-star hotels. There are also more luxurious three- and four-star establishments for those on larger budgets. The hotels included here have been chosen using the criteria of value for money, central position, charm and attractiveness. Some have all of these qualities, or most of them.

See 'Tourist Offices' for details.

Booking

Brittany is a popular destination, particularly in July and August, around Easter and over the French May bank holidays, so you're strongly advised to make a reservation in advance if you're going then. When you're sure of your dates, phone first to make the booking and then send a letter to confirm your reservation details, along with the required guarantee, which can be a credit card number. Ring before you arrive to double-check that everything is confirmed and to ensure that the place where you'll be staying will accept your chosen method of payment. If you're going to Brittany out of season, it's advisable to call the hotel you have chosen and check that it's open during that period.

It's also worth thinking about the facilities you're looking for. Some three-star hotels have swimming pools in which to relax after a hot day on the road or beach. Parking is usually readily available in country hotels, but it's worth checking in advance, and some city hotels offer underground or lock-up garages. This is important in some of the larger cities, where car crime is on the increase.

Facilities and Ratings

French tourist authorities classify hotels into five categories, ranging from one- to four-stars, plus a four-star deluxe rating. They indicate the level of facilities offered, but can't tell you anything about the warmth, friendliness and charm of the establishments. For many Routard readers, the family-run hotel will be a good option and they can be found in most villages. Relaxed and friendly, they often have a dining room that is open to both residents and non-residents.

Prices and facilities vary greatly from hotel to hotel and within the establishments themselves, depending on the quality and attributes of the room. For example, a balcony, sea-view or en-suite complete bathroom (rather than shower) will add to the room price. You can discuss the different prices and facilities with the proprietor, who should have a list of the various tariffs. Single occupancy rates are only marginally cheaper than double occupancy, since prices are normally per room rather than per person. Triple or quad rooms are often available, with extra beds added to a double room, and this is usually cheaper than staying in two rooms. Double beds are common, but again you should specify a *grand lit* (double bed) if you'd prefer one. You do need to stipulate an en-suite bathroom or shower, as these aren't available in every room and cost extra.

Tariffs

Breakfast (usually coffee, a croissant, bread and jam) is often optional (at a cost of around 20F to 35F). Remember to stipulate whether you want to have breakfast, as it is frequently cheaper to go to a bar or café. Tax and service are included in the price except if you are staying on a half board (*demi-pension*) or full board (*pension*) basis. Half board includes breakfast and a set lunch or dinner and can be compulsory in the busy season, in some hotels with restaurants. Full board includes all meals. These options can be good value, particularly if the hotel turns out to have the only restaurant in the village!

LOGIS DE FRANCE, AUBERGES AND RELAIS

The Maison de la France shop (*address above*) has free copies for personal callers of the *Logis de France* guide, which details one- and two-star establishments with restaurants (*auberges*). These are usually found outside the larger towns and cities in smaller towns and villages. Other hotels, located mostly on the roadside outside built-up areas, are designated as *Relais* (the word actually means posting house, where horses were changed). Independently run, they provide good, frequently excellent, accommodation with regional cuisine, mostly in rustic surroundings. For those seeking accommodation in tranquil surroundings, the free *Relais du Silence* guide features hotels in chateaux or houses of character, located in peaceful environments. A useful website is: www.silencehotel.com.

Historic independent hotels and chateaux in all price ranges are detailed in the *Châteaux & Hotels de France Guide*. The *Relais et Châteaux Guide* lists some of the best hotels in France and is also available free of charge from the Maison de la France shop or can be sent within the UK by calling the publishers on ☎ (020) 7630 7667. The only charge is for postage and packing. Freephone information is available on ☎ 00 800 2000 0002, or visit the website: www.relaischateaux.com.

CHAMBRES D'HÔTE

In rural areas there are plenty of opportunities for a stay in a private home or farm in what are known as *chambres d'hôte* (the nearest equivalent to British bed and breakfasts). Mostly situated in farmhouses or villages, they can range in what they offer, but it's usually from one to several bedrooms. They will often provide dinner (*table d'hôte*) on request. Listed separately in tourist office brochures, many are inspected and registered by the *Gîtes de France* organization. Watch out for the distinctive *chambre d'hôte* road signs. Prices vary but they are often an opportunity to enjoy traditional home cooking, French company and local information.

GÎTES

Self-catering is also an option and companies rent different types of accommodation, ranging from rural farm cottages to beach apartments. The *Gîtes de France* organization provides brochures and detailed lists of accommodation. Contact the Maison de Gîtes de France, 59 rue St-Lazare, 75439 Paris Cedex 09. ☎ 01-49-70-75-75. Fax: 01 42-81-28- 53. Website: www.gites-de-france.fr. Reservations should be made with the Gîtes de France office in each *département*. A brochure of *gîtes* is also available in the UK from Brittany Ferries: ☎ (0990) 360 360.

You'll find that the owners of the *gîte* often live nearby and they are usually very welcoming, although rarely in English! Facilities range in standard, but this is a great way to experience Breton life.

GÎTES D'ÉTAPE

A *gîte d'étape* is a simple walking shelter with bunk beds (minus bedding) and a basic self-catering kitchen, established by the local village or municipality along GR (*Grande Randonnée*) walking paths or scenic bike routes. These are attractively priced (usually from 40F to 50F per night) and are listed in the individual Topoguides.

YOUTH HOSTELS

The good news is that there's no age limit for staying in a youth hostel in France. The French youth hostel federation, FUAJ, is a non-profit-making organization, and it produces a free guide listing the addresses of all the hostels in France.

Services offered include reservations for a maximum of six nights, as much as six months in advance in certain youth hostels. Hostels are often very busy (or even full), but the organization can make a booking for you (in a dormitory only) well ahead of your trip. You pay for the bed, plus a reservation fee of about 17F. In return, you receive a voucher confirming your reservation, which you present at the youth hostel on arrival. You may cancel (the cancellation period varies from one hostel to another), but you will pay a cancellation charge of about 33F.

FUAJ membership cards are 70F for under-26s and 100F for over-26s. A family card, valid for families with two adults and one or more children under 14, costs 150F. You will need to prove your family's identity with some form of documentation.

To obtain a membership card, contact the FUAJ national office in Paris. For on-the-spot purchases you will need to show some ID, such as a passport. By post, send a photocopy of your passport together with a cheque/money order for the above amounts plus 5F handling charge.

Information is available in all youth hostels and at all FUAJ centres in France.

■ **La Fédération Unie des Auberges de Jeunesse** (FUAJ) (national office of French youth hostel association): 27 rue Pajol, 75018 Paris. ☎ 01-44-89-

87-27. Fax: 01-44-89-87-10. Recorded information: ☎ 08-36-683-693 (2.23F per min). Website: www.fuaj.org

Joining in Britain

For information about joining before you leave, contact the **Youth Hostels Association (YHA)** for membership details and other information. An international YHA card costs £12 for adults for a year and is valid worldwide. The **International Youth Hostel Federation (IYHF)** will issue the card. They also produce guidebooks to hostels overseas and run an international booking network from the same number.

■ **YHA**: Trevalyan House, Matlock, Derbyshire DE4 3YH. ☎ (0870) 870 8808. Fax: (01727) 844126. Email: customerservices@yha.org.uk. Website: www.yha.org.uk

■ **IYHF**: First Floor, Fountain House, Parkway, Welwyn Garden City, Herts AL1 6JH. ☎ (01707) 324170. Email: iyhf@iyhf.org. Website: www.iyhf.org

■ International booking site: www.hostelbooking.com

■ Irish website: www.irelandyha.org

■ French website: www.fuaj.org

■ Scottish website: www.syha.org.uk

CAMPING

Camping is an extremely popular pastime in France, almost a national passion, and nearly every village and town has at least one campsite to cater for all those who choose to spend their holiday under canvas. There are more than 11,000 campsites in France and they are officially graded by the Fédération Française de Camping/Caravanning (☎ 01-42-72-84-08. Fax: 01-42-72-70-21). There are four grades of sites to choose from, with facilities varying from a (deliberately) basic one- and two-star farm or vineyard site for back-to-nature campers to three- or four-star superior categories of camp-sites, equipped with hot showers, bar, restaurant, grocer's shop, washing machines and swimming pool. There are many beach-side campsites in Brittany, but do note that they get very busy at the height of summer.

Camping à la ferme (camping on a private farm) generally offers few or no facilities but it's an invitingly cheap and often atmospheric way of seeing the area. The *camping municipal*, or town campsite, is run by the local municipality and is another cheap option. You can generally rely on these campsites to be clean and to have plenty of hot water. They frequently occupy prime local positions. In the busy months it's advisable to book ahead, as sites become very crowded.

One little word of caution: don't ever indulge in camping rough (*camping sauvage*) on anyone's land without asking permission, or you'll risk facing the wrath of a furious farmer, his dog or perhaps even the police. Check the addresses listed under 'Tourist Offices' in this section, or use a tourist offices' listing. Also look out for *Le Guide Officiel Camping/Caravanning*, available in bookshops in France.

BUDGET

ACCOMMODATION

Your daily budget will depend largely on the location and standard of accommodation you select and your form of transport. Self-catering is obviously a good way of keeping your costs down and half or full board can be a good option. This guide offers a wide selection of accommodation throughout the area and the prices vary so much, it would be hard to give exact prices here.

Accommodation is listed in this guide in four price categories:

Budget

Moderate

Chic

Très Chic

FOOD AND DRINK

Good quality, inexpensive food is available in many local restaurants and most offer fixed-price menus that are generally better value than if you eat à la carte. Lunch is often very reasonable – you can enjoy a meal with wine for under 70F. The celebrated Breton *crêpe* or pancake is generally a cheap and delicious option, thin and delicate with a wide choice of fillings. *Crêperies* are on just about every corner in Brittany. For picnics and self-catering, head to the local markets where you'll find fresh, delicious and tempting produce. Other good sources for picnic food are the *charcuteries* or *traiteurs,* both of which sell prepared dishes sold by weight in cartons or tubs.

If your hotel tariff doesn't include breakfast, it is often cheaper to venture out to a bar or café for your coffee and croissant. Hotel breakfasts charged separately tend to be rather pricey.

Wine and beer are generally very cheap in supermarkets, but the mark-up on wine in restaurants is high so if you're watching your francs, go for the house wine, which is usually acceptable and quite a bit cheaper. Alternatively, you can often order wine by the glass.

It's easy to make a big dent in your pocket spending money on drinks in cafés and bars – stick to black coffee, wine and draught lager, which are the safest options.

CLIMATE

Brittany's weather is renowned for its whims – some say that's why the Breton word for climate (*amzer*) is feminine. The sky changes remarkably quickly: from grey and stormy one day to clear blue the next. It can be misty at dawn, clear at midday and perfect in the evening, with the sky frequently taking on gorgeous hues.

Misconceptions, clichés and prejudice have affected the reputation of the Breton climate in western Europe. People say that it always rains here, and of course, it does sometimes, but Brittany gets its fair share of sun, too. When the wind is in clement mood, the weather can be beautiful. Summer days in Brittany are longer than in any other spot in France, with almost an hour's extra daylight in midsummer. The further north you go, the longer the days are.

Predictably, summer is the time when most visitors come to Brittany, and popular tourist sites can be very busy, with sun worshippers packed onto the beaches like sardines. May is a lovely month, with the countryside at its best, but the French enjoy a series of long weekends in this month and it can be surprisingly crowded. June is less crowded but the wind can be rather fresh. The first half of July and the last half of August are warm and sunny, and less crowded than the peak time of mid-July to mid-August. If September is warm it can be the most delightful time to visit. The school children are safely behind their desks and the beaches relatively empty. In October the autumnal colours are lovely, and if the weather is behaving, it can be a lovely month to see Brittany. If you're looking for dramatic weather, November to March are the months to go.

Strangely enough, there is less rainfall in Rennes than in Toulouse, less in Carnac than in Nice, less in Brest than Biarritz. Brittany is cradled by two seas, the English Channel and the Atlantic, and the Breton peninsula has a gentle and invigorating ocean climate. It never gets stiflingly hot or unpleasantly cold. The coastal air is so rich in iodine, it's a real tonic.

The north coast, under the protective influence of the Gulf Stream, has fewer than 15 frosts a year. The prevailing winds are north-westerly on the Finistère coast, with sheltered areas, such as the Île de Bréhat, which has an average of 639 millimetres (25 inches) of rain in 163 days. In the south of France, Toulouse has an average of 665 millimetres (26 inches) in 139 days.

The south coast has a sunnier, warmer and drier climate. Carnac (Morbihan) has an average of 128 days of rain per year and 2,055 hours of sunshine. Biarritz, by comparison, has 177 days of rain per year. The average temperature in Morbihan is 18°C (65°F) in summer. The south coast of Finistère also enjoys good weather, with microclimates in the Fouesnant and Bigouden regions.

Recorded weather information is available by telephone, if your French is up to it.

Regional forecast: ☎ 08-36-68-02-29

Finistère: ☎ 08-36-68-02-29

Morbihan: ☎ 08-36-68-02-56

Côtes d'Armor: ☎ 08-36-68-02-22

Ille-et-Vilaine: ☎ 08-36-68-02-35

Shipping forecast: ☎ 08-36-68-08-08, for forecasts for up to 20 nautical miles off the coasts.

Brittany's classified weather stations are located at: Perros-Guirec, Sables-d'Or-les-Pins, St-Quay-Portrieux, Le Val-André, Dinard, Paramé, St-Briac-sur-Mer, St-Lunaire, St-Malo, Carnac and Quiberon.

CLOTHING

Having read the entry on Brittany's climate, you have probably already decided to pack accordingly. Take warm clothes for unpredictable days and wet weather gear just in case. If you plan to enjoy some of the delightful trails, make sure you have a good pair of walking shoes and a rucksack. Don't forget your swimwear. If you do, there are a few nudist beaches in Brittany, but there are also plenty of shops in which to remedy the situation!

COMMUNICATIONS

POST

Stamps are available at post offices (*la poste*, closed after 12 noon Saturday and all day Sunday), at newsagents (*tabacs*) and sometimes in souvenir or postcard shops. Postcards and letters up to 20g to the UK cost 3F. Post offices are listed in this guide where relevant; last pick-up is around 6pm or 7pm. Outgoing post can usually be left at the reception desk of larger hotels.

You can receive mail at the central post offices of most towns through the *Poste Restante* system. Letters should be addressed to you (preferably with the surname first and in capitals) at 'Poste Restante, Poste Centrale', followed by the name of the town and its postcode, if possible (detailed in this guide for all the main cities). Remember to ask the staff to check the sorting box under the initial of your first name as well as your surname. To collect your mail you will need a passport or other identification. There may be a charge of a couple of francs.

French post-boxes are yellow and often have three slots – one for the town you are in, one for the surrounding *département* and one for other destinations.

Town Names and Postcodes

For each town the French name and the Breton name is given, where there is one. Each town has its own postcode, which is indicated next to the town name e.g.: RENNES (*ROAZHON*) 35000.

TELEPHONE

Telephone calls in France cost roughly the same as in the US and UK. Not many telephone boxes take coins, and phone cards (*télécartes*) are far more widely used. These cards, which represent good value for money, are available from *tabacs*, or from post offices. Phoning from a hotel is expensive, as it is in most countries.

GENERAL INFORMATION

GENERAL INFORMATION (side tab)

CONVERSION TABLES

Men's sizes

Shirts

UK	USA	EUROPE
14	14	36
14½	14½	37
15	15	38
15½	15½	39
16	16	41
16½	16½	42
17	17	43
17½	17½	44
18	18	46

Suits

UK	USA	EUROPE
36	36	46
38	38	48
40	40	50
42	42	52
44	44	54
46	46	56

Shoes

UK	USA	EUROPE
8	9	42
9	10	43
10	11	44
11	12	46
12	13	47

Women's sizes

Shirts/dresses

UK	USA	EUROPE
8	6	36
10	8	38
12	10	40
14	12	42
16	14	44
18	16	46
20	18	48

Sweaters

UK	USA	EUROPE
8	6	44
10	8	46
12	10	48
14	12	50
16	14	52
18	16	54
20	18	56

Shoes

UK	USA	EUROPE
3	5	36
4	6	37
5	7	38
6	8	39
7	9	40
8	10	42

Temperature

- To convert °C to °F, multiply by 1.8 and add 32.
- To convert °F to °C, subtract 32 and multiply by 5/9 (0.55). 0°C=32°F

US weights and measures

1 centimetre	0.39 inches	1 inch	2.54 centimetres
1 metre	3.28 feet	1 foot	0.30 metres
1 metre	1.09 yards	1 yard	0.91 metres
1 kilometre	0.62 miles	1 mile	1.61 kilometres
1 hectare	2.47 acres	1 acre	0.40 hectares
1 litre	1.76 pints	1 pint	0.57 litres
1 litre	0.26 gallons	1 gallon	3.79 litres
1 gram	0.035 ounces	1 ounce	28.35 grams
1 kilogram	2.2 pounds	1 pound	0.45 kilograms

One particular card, *carte France Télécom*, can be used on any telephone, whether it's in a public booth or at a friend's house, without you having to worry about immediate payment. All charges go on your card, with which you can phone within France and to over 80 countries. All calls are charged according to French prices. To obtain a *carte France Télécom*, dial: ☎ 0-800-202-202. You pay an advance of 40F when you first use the card.

To use the card, dial the number on the card that allows you to initiate access, followed by your pass code and then the number of the person whom you are dialling. Press the # key and you'll be connected. No coins are required.

For all calls within France – both local and long-distance – dial all 10 digits of the phone number. Phone numbers are broken up into five sets of two, and each set is spoken as a whole number. The number 02-25-30-55-68, for example, would be said 'zero-two, twenty-five, thirty, fifty-five, sixty-eight'. If you do say it as individual numbers, however, you will be understood!

Area Codes

France is divided up into five telephone regions, using the area codes 01 to 05. The regions have been allocated as follows:

- 01   Paris and environs
- 02   Northwest France (Nantes, Rouen, and including Brittany)
- 03   Northeast France (including Lille and Strasbourg)
- 04   Southeast France (including Lyon, Grenoble and Marseille)
- 05   Southwest France (including Bordeaux and Toulouse)

Tollfree numbers in France begin with 0-800.

Dialling Codes to France

Dial the international code given below, then the nine-digit number, omitting the initial zero of the area code.

From United Kingdom	00 33
From Republic of Ireland	00 33
From USA	011 33
From Canada	011 33
From Australia	0011 33
From New Zealand	00 33
From South Africa	09 33

Dialling Codes from France

To call overseas from France, dial 00, wait for the tone, then dial the country code, and then the desired number, omitting any initial zero of the area code.

For United Kingdom	00 44
For Republic of Ireland	00 353
For USA	00 1
For Canada	00 1
For Australia	00 61

| For New Zealand | 00 64 |
| For South Africa | 00 27 |

Most people in French cities seem to live by (and through) their mobile phones. Many British-registered mobile phones will be usable in France, but most mobile phones from the US don't work in Europe, so check with your supplier before you leave.

INTERNET

The French are mad about technology – indeed, they have had access to online information for more than 15 years, with France Télécom's Minitel service – and you're bound to come across some cybercafés as you travel around Brittany. Many serve coffee and other drinks, and sometimes sandwiches and snacks, and all provide computer terminals by the hour, so that you can pick up and send e-mails, and surf the Net at your leisure. More are opening all the time. Those already established include:

■ **Les Années Bleues**: 23 rue Bruat, Brest. ☎ 02-98-44-48-19. Website: www.mygale.org/03/brestnet/ableues

■ **Le Macao**: 2 rue Basse, Morlaix. ☎ 02-98-88-47-26

■ **O'Brasil**: 2 rue St-Georges, Rennes. ☎ 02-99-78-17-81

You'll also find terminals for public use in post offices in many of the larger towns.

TRAVELLERS WITH DISABILITIES

The international ♿ logo is used to indicate those establishments offering disabled access or rooms that are suitable for guests with disabilities. Some places are fully equipped in this respect and meet the latest requirements. Others are older or less sophisticated and, as a result, are unable to fulfil the most recent requirements. However, they still welcome all travellers and manage to provide access to bedrooms or to the restaurant. As always, it is advisable to check in advance if a hotel or restaurant is able to cater for your personal mobility needs.

A number of groups and associations continue to try to integrate people with disabilities into everyday life in France and in Europe in general.

Useful information on access and facilities for the disabled is available from the **Comité National Français de Liaison pour la Réadaptation des Handicapés** (CNRH), 236 *bis* rue de Tolbiac, 75013 Paris. ☎ 01-53-80-66-44. They will send you a catalogue of publications.

Other helpful information can be found at the following websites:

www.access-able.com

www.handitel.org

EATING OUT

Restaurants generally serve lunch from noon until 2pm, with dinner from 7pm to 10pm. Bretons tend to eat quite early in restaurants, at noon or 12.30pm for lunch, and between 7pm and 9pm in the evening. Breton meals can go on for a long time, particularly if you have a large seafood platter to start.

Cafés and bars in towns are open later than restaurants, and brasseries in the cities tend to keep their doors open continuously. Eating your main meal at lunchtime can be a good way of saving money, since many places offer special lunch menus that are considerably cheaper than those on offer in the evening. You may find that the village or small town you are in comes to a virtual standstill during lunch or dinner – the mealtime is an important daily event all over France. Hotel restaurants are often a good choice if they serve residents and regular non-residents. The prices are generally reasonable and the atmosphere friendly and interesting.

If you are staying in *chambres d'hôte* in the country, you can enjoy good and inexpensive meals with your hosts, who will normally be using local, fresh, home-grown produce. In rural areas, you'll find bars and cafés that are right at the centre of village life, sometimes with terraces or gardens. The cafés can be good spots for lunch, which will usually include a *plat du jour* (daily special) and a dessert plus a quarter litre of wine (for around 50F) as well as sandwiches, omelettes and salads. In some rural areas, the local café may serve dinner too.

The bars will serve sandwiches or a *croque monsieur* (toasted ham-and-cheese sandwich) rather than a full meal. There's also a wide selection of portable and picnic food in the shops of Breton villages and towns, and the cities are full of snack-food opportunities, with no shortage of outdoor kiosks and *crêperies*. Vegetarians will find the local *crêpes* to be one of the best options in Brittany.

Prices, and what they include, are usually posted outside the establishment and you'll often see a choice of set-price menus (*menus fixes*), where the number of courses is determined and the choice relatively limited. If prices are not listed, you may find they are quite high, so do check. *Menus fixes* are often the best option for those on a budget and can sometimes include the house wine (*vin compris*). At the cheaper end, the menus tend to focus on standard dishes, including *steak frites* (steak and chips). However, at the more expensive end, they are a good way of enjoying regional dishes and meals of up to five courses, and a set-price gourmet *menu dégustation* can be a great treat, offering a range of the chef's specialities. If you just want one course, go for the *plat du jour* (daily special), often served in bars and brasseries. The other alternative is the no-choice *formule* menu, where what you read is what you get.

If you decide to eat à la carte, you'll enjoy a much greater choice, unlimited access to the chef's specialities and a larger bill! However, you can just go for one course instead of three or four. You can choose several starters or share dishes, and it's a good option for vegetarians who can select a number of dishes from the starters (*entrées*). If service is included, it will say *service* compris (or *s.c.*) on the menu; if it is not included, you'll see the words *service non compris* (or just *s.n.c.*) and this means that you will have to add on the tip when you settle the bill.

DRINKS

Wine (*vin*) or a drink (*boisson*) is occasionally included in the cost of a *menu fixe*. When ordering house wine (*réserve* or *cuvée*), which is usually produced locally and is always the cheapest option, ask for *un quart* (0.25 litres or two glasses), sometimes called *un pichet*, which is the word for a small jug, *un demi-litre* (0.5 litre) or *une carafe* (1 litre). This is a good and inexpensive way of sampling the region's wines. If you just fancy a glass of wine ask for *un verre*. If you're anxious about cost, ask for *vin ordinaire* or *vin de table*.

You need to know a few adjectives: *rouge* is red, *blanc* is white and *rosé* is pink. *Brut* is very dry, *sec* is dry, *demi-sec* and *moelleux* are sweetish, *doux* is sweet, and *méthode champenoise* denotes a sparkling wine. Mineral water (*eau minérale*) comes either sparkling (*eau gazeuse* or *pétillante*) or still (*non-gazeuse* or *plat*). If you would prefer tap water ask for *l'eau du robinet*, which will be brought free to your table. Draught beer (*bière à la pression*) is cheaper than bottled varieties. Ask for *une pression* or *une demi* (0.33 litre).

COURSES IN A FRENCH MEAL

You don't have to 'do as the Romans do' and indulge in a full-scale meal. Just in case you're tempted, remember that a meal can consist of some or all of the following:

Apéritif: a pre-meal drink, such as *kir* (white wine with a dash of blackcurrant liqueur or *cassis*). You may be offered a *kir Breton* (cider mixed with blackberry or blackcurrant liqueur) or a *pommeau* (an alcoholic apple apéritif).

Hors d'oeuvres: usually soup, pâté or charcuterie.

Entrée: starter or first course, usually fish, salad or an omelette. Shellfish often features in Breton starters.

Plat principal (main course): usually meat, poultry, game or offal, *garni de* (accompanied by) vegetables, rice or potatoes. In Brittany, you could try a *plateau de fruits de mer* as your main course although it is quite often seen on the menu as a starter.

Salade verte (green salad): to refresh the stomach

Fromage (cheese)

Dessert (also known as *entremets*)

Café, chocolats or *mignardises* (coffee and chocolates or petit-fours)

Digestif: an after-dinner drink, such as brandy. Lambig is the Breton equivalent of the apple-based Calvados from Normandy, which is a well-kept secret. It makes a delicious digestif.

L'addition (the bill): also known as *la douleureuse* (literally translated as 'the painful one', which it can sometimes be).

EATING WITH THE KIDS (OR THE DOG)

The French welcome children in most places. You may find special facilities hard to come by, such as high chairs and baby seats, and specific children's menus are also rare. However, many establishments will be happy to provide smaller dishes at a reduced price. It is not uncommon to discover dogs hidden under the table or even on their own chair, concealed in a smart handbag.

ELECTRICITY

Voltage is 220V and sockets accept plugs with two round pins. Adaptors can be bought at the airport before you leave, but you can also buy them at most department stores. Some of the more expensive hotels have built-in adaptors – for shavers only.

EMBASSIES AND CONSULATES

FRENCH EMBASSIES AND CONSULATES ABROAD

United Kingdom: French Embassy, 58 Knightsbridge, London SW1X 7JT. ☎ (020) 7201 1000. Website: www.ambafrance.org.uk

French Consulate-General (visas) 6 Cromwell Place, London SW7 7EN. ☎ (020) 7838 2050. 24-hour visa information: ☎ (0891) 887733 (premium rate).

Scotland: French Consulate, 11 Randolph Crescent, Edinburgh EH3 7TT. ☎ (0131) 220-6324. 24-hour visa information: ☎ (0891) 600215 (premium rate).

Republic of Ireland: French Embassy, 36 Ailesbury Road, Dublin 4. ☎ (01) 260 1666

United States: French Embassy, 4101 Reservoir Road NW, Washington, DC 20007. ☎ (202) 944-6000 or 6212. Website: www.info-france-usa.org. There are also French Consulates in Atlanta, Boston, Chicago, Houston, Los Angeles, Miami, New Orleans, New York, San Francisco and Washington, DC.

Canada: French Embassy, 42 Sussex Drive, Ottawa K1M 2C9. ☎ (613) 789-1795. Fax: (613) 562-3704. Website: www.ambafrance-ca.org. There are also French Consulates-General in Moncton, Montreal, Quebec, Toronto and Vancouver.

Australia: French Embassy, 6 Perth Avenue, Yarralumla, Canberra, ACT 2600. ☎ (43) 2216-0100. Fax: (43) 2216-0156. E-mail: embassy@france. net.au. Website: www.france.net.au. There are also French Consulates-General in Sydney and Melbourne.

New Zealand: French Embassy, 34–42 Manners Street, PO Box 11-343, Wellington. ☎ (04) 384-2555 or 2577. Website: www.ambafrance.net.nz. There is also a French Consulate in Auckland.

GENERAL INFORMATION

South Africa: French Embassy, 807 George Avenue, Arcadia, Pretoria 0083, Gauteng. ☎ (12) 429-7000 or 7029. Website: www.france.co.za. There are also French Consulates in Johannesburg and Cape Town.

FOREIGN CONSULATES IN PARIS

United Kingdom: 35 rue du Faubourg-St-Honoré, 75383 Paris. ☎ 01-44-51-31-00. Fax: 01-42-66-91-42. Consulate: ☎ 01-44-51-31-02. Fax: 01-44-51-31-27. Website: www.amb-grandebretagne.fr. There are also Consulates-General in Bordeaux, Lille, Lyon, Marseille and Paris.

Republic of Ireland: 12 avenue Foch, 75116 Paris. ☎ 01-44-17-67-00. Fax: 01-44-17-67-60.

United States: 2 avenue Gabriel, 75008 Paris. ☎ (Embassy and Consulate) 01-43-12-22-22. Fax: 01-42-55-97-83. Website: www.amb-usa.fr. There are also US Consulates in Marseille and Strasbourg.

Canada: 35 avenue Montaigne, 75008 Paris. ☎ 01-44-43-29-94. Fax: 01-44-43-29-99. Website: www.amba-canada.fr

Australia: 4 rue Jean Rey, 75724 Paris Cedex 15. ☎ 01-40-59-33-00. Fax: 01-40-59-33-10. Website: www.austgov.fr

New Zealand: 7 *ter*, rue Léonardo-de-Vinci, 75116 Paris. ☎ 01-45-00-24-11. Fax: 01-45-01-26-39.

South Africa: 59 quai d'Orsay, 75007 Paris. ☎ 01-45-55-92-37. Fax: 01-47-05-51-28. There are also South African Consulates in Le Havre, Lille and Marseille.

FOREIGN CONSULATES IN BRITTANY

United Kingdom: British Consulate, 25 rue Ingenieur Verriere, 56100 Lorient. ☎ 02-97-87-36-36. Fax: 02-97-87-36-49. Honorary Consul: 8 boulevard des Maréchaux, 35800 Dinard. ☎ 02-99-46-26-64. Fax: 02-99-16-09-26.

United States: American Presence Post, Rennes. Limited consular services for US citizens only. ☎ 02-23-44-09-60.

EMERGENCIES

- **Police**: ☎ 17
- **Fire Brigade** (Sapeurs Pompiers): ☎ 18
- **Emergency medical advice – Ambulance service (SAMU),** information on nearest hospital, doctor or pharmacy: ☎ 15
- **SOS Médecins** (emergency doctors) and **SOS Dentistes** (emergency dentists): call the local number in the phone book under '*Médecins/Dentistes qualifiés*' or ☎ 12 for directory enquiries and ask for help.
- **24-hour pharmacies**: look up local numbers in the phone book under *Pharmacies*.

ENTRY FORMALITIES

PASSPORTS AND VISAS

France signed an international agreement in 1985, since which time a visa issued by a French Embassy has included entry not only to France, but also to Austria, Belgium, Germany, Italy, Luxembourg, The Netherlands, Portugal and Spain. There is no longer any formal border between these countries, and flights between them now take off and land from domestic terminals.

The UK did not sign this agreement and as a consequence has maintained inter-EU immigration control. However, many UK ports of entry have a separate passenger exit, marked by a blue sign with yellow stars, where EU members can simply wave their passport at an immigration officer.

Citizens of the UK and any other EU country, who hold a valid passport, may remain in France for as long as they wish without a visa and may also be employed while abroad.

Citizens of the United States, Australia and New Zealand do not require a visa for short stays (up to three months), but they must apply to their nearest consulate or embassy for long-stay visas or a *Carte de Commerçant*, which permits employment in France.

Canadian citizens do not need a visa to visit France; they are at liberty to remain in the country for a period of up to three months providing they are in possession of a passport valid up to six months after the end of the intended visit. For longer (and working) stays a visa will be required and may be obtained at the French embassy or consulate.

Citizens of South Africa need a visa to enter France and must apply at least three weeks before leaving South Africa. Out of season, visas can be obtained relatively quickly at the nearest consulate or embassy, but queues can be long in summer. Applicants must have a passport that is valid for at least three months after the expiry date of the visa. Short-stay visas are valid for 90 days from the day of issue, and can be used for multiple entries. Transit visas are valid for two months, and long-stay visas are valid for continuous periods of up to 90 days for three years, but are only issued after consideration of each individual case. Students, diplomats or those who have business interests in France should contact their nearest French embassy before departure.

CUSTOMS AND DUTY-FREE

No matter where you are travelling from, the importing of narcotics, copyright infringements, fakes and counterfeit goods is strictly prohibited for anyone travelling to France. Firearms and ammunition are also forbidden unless accompanied by specific authorization from the appropriate ministry in Paris.

When returning to the UK, obscene material and offensive weapons are prohibited in addition to those items listed by French customs.

GENERAL INFORMATION

UK (EU) citizens: any goods that are for personal use are free from both French and UK customs duty. To meet the criteria of 'personal use' there is a set of guidelines that are used by all EU customs officers. These allow up to 800 cigarettes or 1kg of loose tobacco, 10 litres of spirits, 90 litres of wine and 110 litres of beer. Despite the liberalized restrictions on importing and exporting tobacco and alcohol, the removal of duty-free allowances for EU visitors means that prices in France now include duty, which cannot be recuperated.

At any port of entry, those with nothing to declare should use the 'Green Channel' and those with goods in excess of their allowance should use the 'Red Channel', both marked clearly after passport control. There is a separate 'Blue Channel' for EU residents (*see* 'Passports and Visas').

For further information and clarification, in the UK contact the Excise and Inland Customs Advice Centre ☎ (020) 7202 4227, or visit their website at www.hmce.gov.uk. The UK Customs Office (☎ (020) 7919 6700) publishes a leaflet called *A Guide for Travellers*, detailing regulations and duty-free allowances. In France, call the customs information centre in Paris: ☎ 01-40-01-02-06.

Non-EU citizens: the limitations on import and export outside the EU are far more stringent than within it, but visitors from outside the EU may take home goods free of duty or tax. To qualify, you must spend more than 1,200F at a single store; the retailer will supply a Retail Export Form, called a *bordereau de détaxe*, which must be endorsed by customs and will be returned by them to the retailer, who will in turn refund the tax portion (20.6 per cent) of your purchase.

Visitors over 15 may take up to 1,200F worth of articles back home with them free of duty or tax. In addition they may leave France with 200 cigarettes or 250g of smoking tobacco, 2 litres of wine, 1 litre of spirits and 50g of perfume. Those under 17 may not export tobacco or alcohol from France.

The US Customs Service (PO Box 7407, Washington, DC 20044; ☎ (202) 927-5580) publishes a free leaflet entitled *Know Before You Go*.

GETTING A JOB

See 'Working in France' *below*.

FESTIVALS AND EVENTS

The following calendar includes some (but by no means all) of the Breton festivals and *pardons*. *Pardons* are simple chapel fêtes and processions that flourished in Brittany towards the end of the Middle Ages. Most have their roots in ancient rites and centre on particular rituals, involving blessing the sea or a dedication to a saint after whom a church is named. Each *pardon* begins with a mass followed by a procession where coloured banners are carried, along with statues and relics of the saint or saints that are being honoured. Almost every community church and chapel will have its own *pardon*.

In summer, many Breton communities organise a *fest-noz,* a traditional evening festival of Breton music and dance, lubricated with cider or other alcohol.

Remember that dates will often change from year to year. For precise information, check with the annual lists held by local tourist offices.

January
Fête des Rois (Epiphany) 6 January. This religious date is celebrated by the eating of the *Galette des Rois*, a traditional cake with a crown and a hidden charm. The child who finds the charm wears the crown and becomes king or queen for a day.

Traveling Rennes: film festival on the theme of cities, held during a week in late January.

March
Carnaval naval Brest: carnival held in the commercial port at the end of March, celebrating the sea, together with a large dance.

April
Fête de la Coquille Erquy: this festival celebrates the *coquille St-Jacques* (scallop) and is held every three years (next event to be held in April 2002). Also takes place in years two and three at St-Quay-Portrieux and Loguivy-de-la-Mer.

Fête du Livre (book festival) Bécherel: Easter weekend.

May
Labour Day: 1 May. Processions and marches organized by trade unions, and gifts of bouquets of lily-of-the-valley.

Pardon de Notre-Dame-de-Délivrance Quintin: first Sunday in May.

Pardon de St-Yves Tréguier: third Sunday in May. This is an important event in honour of the patron saint of lawyers and defender of the poor.

Pardon des Chevaux St-Herbot (Finistère): third Sunday in May.

Étonnants Voyageurs (Amazing Explorers) St-Malo: a celebration of travel writing held in May each year and lasting for three or four days.

Fête de la St-Michel Mont St-Michel: spring folk festival held in May (autumn festival held in September).

Pardon des Chevaux St-Herbot: third Sunday in May.

Grand Pardon de St-Mathurin, Moncontour-de-Bretagne Whit Sunday and Whit Monday.

Pardon de Notre-Dame-de-Tout-Remède Rumengol: Trinity Sunday.

Pardon de Notre-Dame-de-Callot Carantec: Trinity Sunday.

June
Fête de la Musique throughout France: takes place in midsummer (around 21 June). On the evening of the longest day, musicians take to the streets and stages of France, to take part in this government-inspired annual festival. This social phenomenon dates back to 1981.

Voix des Pays Fougères: concerts are held in the chateau during a weekend in early June.

Pardon de St-Pierre-St-Paul Plouguerneau: last Sunday in June.

Art Rock Festival St Brieuc: 1–3 June. International musicians.

Fête de la morue (cod festival) Binic: 25, 26 and 27 June. Traditional rigged boats, sea shanties and a Breton pipe band.

Mont St-Michel Bay Marathon between Cancale and Mont St-Michel: mid-June. Details on the website: www.mont-st-michel-marathon.com

July
Pardon de Notre Dame de Bon Secours Guingamp: a major festival held on the first Saturday in July.

Folklore du Monde St-Malo: world folk music is enjoyed for a week at the beginning of July.

Bastille Day July 14. The most important day in French revolutionary history is celebrated all over France, with parties and fireworks.

Tombées de la Nuit (Breton arts festival) Rennes: theatre and music festival held during first ten days in July.

Festival harpe celtique (Celtic harp festival) Dinan: concerts and exhibitions are held, with the greatest players in Brittany performing during a week around 14 July.

Pardon de l'Île de Goudelin Finistère: 13, 14 and 15 July.

Pardon de St-Carantec Carantec: third Sunday in July.

Fêtes du Bocage vitréen Vitré: held during first two weeks in July with locals enjoying folk dancing and songs of the sea.

Fête des Remparts Dinan: locals dress in medieval costume for this hugely popular festival held in mid-July every second year in even years (next in 2002).

Festival de Musique sacrée St-Malo: held in the cathedral from mid-July to mid-August.

Grande fête des bateaux (boat festival) Brest: a huge festival celebrating all things marine, held in July every four years (next in 2004).

Jeudis du Port (Harbour Thursdays) Brest: free festival of song held every Thursday evening in July and August.

Estivales photographiques (photographic summer season) Lannion: July and August.

Festival des Arts dans la rue (street art festival) Morlaix: held from mid-July to mid-August.

Les Nocturiales Redon: a medieval, baroque and Celtic music festival held from early July to end August.

Pardon Islamo-Chrétien (Islamic-Christian pilgrimage) Le Vieux-Marché: fourth Sunday in July.

Breton dancing classes, Redon: held on Thursday evenings at 9pm, in July and August, in front of the St-Saveur church.

August
Fête de la mer (Festival of the Sea) Dahouët port: held annually in mid-August, with folk dancing and sea shanties.

Fête du Chant de Marin (maritime festival) Paimpol: a three-day festival celebrating the life of sailors and the great age of wooden sailing ships. Lots of music, concerts and sea shanties.

Fête de la St-Loup Guingamp: a week-long festival of Breton dancing that starts the Sunday following 15 August, featuring the 'Dérobée de Guingamp' dance.

Pardon de Notre-Dame-de-la-Garde Dahouët: 20 August. A procession makes its way from the chapel to the port.

Pardon de Notre-Dame-de-Roncier Rostrenen: 14, 15 and 16 August.

Pardon de Notre-Dame-de-la-Clarté Perros-Guirec: 15 August.

Route du Rock St-Malo: the most important rock festival in Brittany, held mid-August for three days with big international groups.

Fête médiévale Moncontour-de-Bretagne: a medieval festival held during the second half of August (less important than the Fête des Remparts in Dinan but more historically accurate).

Fête folklorique des Hortensias (hydrangea festival) Perros-Guirec: throughout the month.

September
Fête de la St-Michel Mont St-Michel autumn festival held on the Sunday nearest to 20 September (the spring festival is held in May).

Grand pardon de Notre-Dame-du-Folgoët Le Folgoët: held on the Sunday closest to 8 September.

Pardon de la St-Michel Plouguerneau: last Sunday in the month.

October
Pardon de Notre-Dame-des-Marais Fougères: 13 and 14 October.

Quai des Bulles St-Malo: a comic strip festival held during the last weekend of October.

Festival de musique baroque Lavellec: this festival of ancient music owes its origins to the restoration in 1986 of the Lavellec organ built by Dallam, the 17th-century organ builder.

December
Transmusicales Rennes: an international rock festival held during the first week in December. Enjoy rock, jungle, hip-hop, techno and more.

24 December (Christmas Eve) throughout France: many French families have a big meal on the evening before Christmas Day, rather than on the day itself. For some, Christmas Midnight Mass at their local church is more of a priority.

HEALTH AND INSURANCE

France has a very good public health service, and standards are comparable with those found in other western European countries and the US. For minor ailments, go in the first instance to a pharmacy (look out for the green cross), where highly qualified pharmacists should be able to give you valuable advice. Many medicines are available over the counter in France. There are no compulsory inoculations for visitors to France.

In an emergency, doctors' and dentists' services are available at the end of the phone (see 'Emergencies'). Hospitalized visitors will be expected to make immediate payment for any treatment, but hospital staff will help with arrangements with insurance companies.

Statistically speaking, you are far more likely to encounter accidents or fall victim to some form of crime when abroad than at home. Travel insurance is therefore highly recommended. It is available through credit card companies, travel agents and student and senior-affiliated organisations (such as STA and SAGA). Insurance may be included in the price of your ticket or package, or you may be covered by your credit card company (particularly American Express) if your ticket was purchased with that card.

For South Africans coming to France, the French Embassy will insist on proof of insurance before issuing a visa.

British and Irish Visitors
Form E111 entitles the holder to free or reduced-cost emergency medical treatment when in France. If a visitor is hospitalized, he or she can expect the same level of care and treatment as in the UK. Available at any main post office, E111s must be filled out and stamped by the post office before you leave the UK; they are issued free of charge and are valid indefinitely, or until used to claim treatment.

North American Visitors
Whereas Canada's public health service will pay a proportion of its citizens' medical costs while abroad, the US Medicare/Medicaid programme does not cover health expenses outside the US, and US medical insurance is not always valid in France. It is advisable to check the nature and extent of foreign coverage with individual insurance companies; often, the visitor will have to pay first and claim reimbursement later.

Australians, New Zealanders and South African Visitors
Citizens of these countries are on their own if they need treatment and do not have health insurance. French hospitals demand on-the-spot payment for medical care, so getting insurance cover is vital.

IF YOU NEED TREATMENT

Local hospitals are the place to go in an emergency (*urgence*). Even French citizens have to pay for ambulances. Doctors take turns being on duty at night and on holidays, even in rural areas. Their telephone numbers normally carry a recorded message with instructions on what to do, so try to get a French speaker to help you understand these. It's worth carrying a phone card with you for just such an occasion. You can ask for a doctor's details at a pharmacy (*pharmacie*) or look them up under '*Médecins qualifiés*'. *See also* 'Emergencies'.

If it isn't an emergency, visit a pharmacy. There's a rota of pharmacies in cities and information is available in the local newspaper or in the windows of the pharmacies themselves.

LANGUAGE

France has an enviable education system, which puts a good emphasis on the learning of English. As a result, especially in the larger cities, you should be able to communicate successfully with most people under a certain age. Hotel reception staff will almost always be able to speak English. Waiters and waitresses will usually know enough to take your order in English, but it is fun to attempt to get to grips with the menu in French and in Brittany you should meet with a more encouraging response than you do in Paris, so give it a try. Even speaking just a few words or putting together a few sentences will make you popular with the natives, so it is worth swotting up on your rusty school French before you leave.

See also 'The Languages of Brittany' in 'Background'.

Over the next few pages you'll find a selection of very basic French vocabulary and many apologies if the word you are looking for is missing. For those struggling with French menus, there is more help at the back of the book in the detailed menu decoder.

Finally, if you do not know the right French word, try using the English one with a French accent – it is surprising how often this works.

BASIC GRAMMAR

The French language is closely linked to its grammar and a grasp of the basics is useful.

Nouns and Adjectives

All French nouns are either masculine or feminine and gender is denoted as follows: 'the' singular is translated by le (m), la (f) or l' (used only before a word beginning with a vowel or a mute 'h'; 'the' plural = les (whatever gender and in front of a vowel or mute 'h'). 'A' = un (m), une (f) (there are no exceptions for vowels or mute 'h').

Adjectives agree with the gender of the accompanying noun. A singular masculine noun uses the adjective with no change; for a singular feminine noun, an 'e' is added. In the plural, in either case, add an 's' to whatever you had in the singular. Don't worry too much about gender agreement when talking, although if you wish to perfect your pronunciation, remember that as 'e' or 'es' usually makes the final consonant hard. The 's' in the plural is not pronounced. When you are in a hurry, worrying about the correct gender can complicate things – just say 'le' or 'la', whichever comes into your head first. Sometimes you will get it right and you'll usually be understood.

In the listings that follow, the feminine versions of nouns and adjectives, where applicable, are given simply to help you to understand written French. The words are either written out in full or shown as '(e)'.

Pronouns

There are two forms of the word 'you' – tu is 'you' in the singular, very informal and used with people you know, vous is 'you' in the singular but is used in formal situations and when you don't know the person, vous is also the plural form. Young people often address each other as 'tu' automatically, but when in doubt and to avoid offence, always use 'vous'.

Verbs

Just three verbs are the foundation of all verb forms in French: the verbs 'être' ('to be'), 'avoir' ('to have') and 'aller' ('to go'). However sketchy your knowledge of French may be, you can get a long way by just knowing these. The past tenses of verbs are constructed using the verb 'to have' (a small number of exceptions use the verb 'to be') and the future tense is built using the verb 'to go' (as 'I am going to . . .'). Be familiar with them and you're halfway there!

The verb 'to be' ('être'):

I am	je suis
you are (informal/sing.)	tu es
he/she/it is	il(m)/elle(f)/il est
we are	nous sommes
you are (formal/plural)	vous êtes
they are	ils(m)/elles(f) sont

To say 'it is'/'that is'/'this is' use 'c'est'; the plural is 'ce sont'. It is not gender-specific.

The verb 'to have' ('avoir'):

I have	j'ai
you have (informal/sing.)	tu as
he/she/it has	il(m)/elle(f)/il a
we have	nous avons
you have (formal/plural)	vous avez
they have	ils(m)/elles(f) ont

The verb 'to go' ('aller'):

I go	je vais
you go (informal/sing.)	tu vas
he/she/it goes	il(m)/elle(f)/il va
we go	nous allons
you go (formal/plural)	vous allez
they go	ils(m)/elles(f) vont

ESSENTIAL VOCABULARY

Yes/No	Oui/Non
OK	D'accord
That's fine	C'est bon
Please	S'il vous plaît
Thank you	Merci
Good morning/Hello during the day)	Bonjour
Good evening/night/Hello (during the evening)	Bonsoir
Hello/Goodbye (very informal)	Salut
Goodbye	Au revoir
See you soon	A bientôt
Excuse me	Excusez-moi
I am sorry	Je suis désolé(m)/désolée(f)
Pardon?	Comment?

Handy Phrases

Do you speak English?	Parlez-vous anglais?
I don't speak French	Je ne parle pas français
I don't understand	Je ne comprends pas
Could you speak more slowly please?	Pouvez-vous parler moins vite, s'il vous plaît?
Could you repeat that, please?	Pouvez-vous répéter, s'il vous plaît?
again/once again	encore/encore une fois
I am English/Scottish/ Welsh/Irish/American/ Canadian/Australian/ a New Zealander	Je suis anglais(e)/écossais(e)/ gallois(e)/irlandais(e)/américain(e)/ canadien(ne)/australien(ne)/ néo-zélandais(e)
My name is . . .	Je m'appelle . . .
What is your name?	Comment vous appelez-vous?
How are you?	Comment allez-vous?
Very well, thank you	Très bien, merci
Pleased to meet you	Enchanté(e)
Mr/Mrs	Monsieur/Madame
Miss/Ms	Mademoiselle/Madame
How?	Comment?
What?	Quel (m)/Quelle (f)?
When?	Quand?
Where (is/are)?	Où (est/sont)?

Which?	Quel (m)/Quelle (f)?
Who?	Qui?
Why?	Pourquoi?

Essential Words

good	bon/bonne
bad	mauvais/mauvaise
big	grand/grande
small	petit/petite
hot	chaud/chaude
cold	froid/froide
open	ouvert/ouverte
closed	fermé/fermée
toilets	les toilettes/les W.C.
women	dames
men	hommes
free (unoccupied)	libre
occupied	occupé/occupée
free (no charge)	gratuit/gratuite
entrance	l'entrée
exit	la sortie
prohibited	interdit/interdite
no smoking	défense de fumer

TIME AND SPACE

Periods of Time

a minute	une minute
half an hour	une demie-heure
an hour	une heure
week	une semaine
fortnight	une quinzaine
month	un mois
year	un an/une année
today	aujourd'hui
yesterday/tomorrow	hier/demain
morning	le matin
afternoon	l'après-midi
evening/night	le soir/la nuit
during (the night)	pendant (la nuit)
early/late	tôt/tard

Telling the Time

What time is it?	Quelle heure est-il?
At what time?	A quelle heure?
(at) 1 o'clock/2 o'clock etc.	(à) une heure/deux heures etc.
half past one	une heure et demie
quarter past two	deux heures et quart

quarter to three	trois heures moins le quart
(at) midday	à midi
(at) midnight	à minuit
See also 'Numbers'	

GETTING AROUND

by bicycle	à bicyclette/en vélo
by bus	en bus
by car	en voiture
by coach	en car
on foot	à pied
by plane	en avion
by taxi	en taxi
by train	en train

In Town

map of the city	un plan de la ville
I am going to . . .	Je vais à . . .
I want to go to . . .	Je voudrais aller à . . .
I want to get off at . . .	Je voudrais descendre à . . .
platform	le quai
return ticket	un aller-retour
single ticket	un aller simple
ticket	le billet
timetable	l'horaire
airport	l'aéroport
bus/coach station	la gare routière
bus stop	l'arrêt de bus
district	le quartier/l'arrondissement
street	la rue
taxi rank	la station de taxi
tourist information office	l'office du tourisme
train station	la gare
underground	le métro
underground station	la station de métro
bag/handbag	le sac/le sac-à-main
case	la valise
left luggage	la consigne
luggage	les bagages

Directions

Is it far?	Est-ce que c'est loin?
How far is it (from here) to . . . ?	Combien de kilomètres (d'ici) à . . . ?
Is it near?	Est-ce que c'est près d'ici?
here/there	ici/là
near/far	près/loin
left/right	gauche/droite
on the left/right	à gauche/à droite

straight on	tout droit
at the end of	au bout de
up	en haut
down	en bas
above (the shop)	au-dessus (du magasin)
below (the bed)	au-dessous (le lit)
opposite (the bank)	en face (de la banque)
next to (the window)	à côté (de la fenêtre)

DRIVING

Please fill the tank (car)	Le plein, s'il vous plaît
car hire	la location de voitures
driver's licence	le permis de conduire
petrol	l'essence
to rent/hire a car	louer une voiture
unleaded	sans plomb

IN THE HOTEL

I have a reservation	J'ai une réservation
for 2 nights	pour 2 nuits
I leave . . .	Je pars . . .
I'd like a room.	Je voudrais une chambre.
Is breakfast included?	le petit-déjeuner est inclus/compris?
single room	une chambre à un lit/Une chambre simple
room with double bed	une chambre à lit double/ une chambre à grand lit
twin room	une chambre à deux lits
room with bathroom	une chambre avec salle de bains
and toilet	et toilette/W.C.
a quiet room	une chambre calme
bath	le bain
shower	la douche
with air conditioning	avec climatisation
1st/2nd floor	premier/deuxième étage
breakfast	le petit-déjeuner
dining room	la salle à manger
ground floor	le rez-de-chaussée (RC)
key	la clef
lift/elevator	l'ascenseur

Paying

How much?	C'est combien, s'il vous plaît?/ Quel est le prix?
Do you accept credit cards?	Est-ce que vous acceptez les cartes de crédit?
Do you have any change?	Avez-vous de la monnaie?

(in) cash	(en) espèces
coin	la pièce de monnaie
money	l'argent
notes	les billets
price	le prix
travellers' cheques	les chèques de voyage

EATING OUT

See also 'Understanding the Menu' at the end of the book.

General

Do you have a table?	Avez-vous une table libre?
I would like to reserve a table.	Je voudrais réserver une table.
I would like to eat.	Je voudrais manger.
I would like something to drink.	Je voudrais boire quelque-chose.
I would like to order, please.	Je voudrais commander, s'il vous plaît.
The bill, please.	L'addition, s'il vous plaît.
I am a vegetarian.	Je suis végétarien (ne).

Meals and Mealtimes

breakfast	le petit-déjeuner
cover charge	le couvert
dessert	le dessert
dinner	le dîner
dish of the day	le plat du jour
fixed price menu	la formule/le menu à prix fixe
fork	la fourchette
knife	le couteau
lunch	le déjeuner
main course	le plat principal
menu	le menu/la carte
(Is the) service included?	Est-ce que le service est compris?
soup	la soupe/le potage
spoon	la cuillère
starter	l'entrée/le hors-d'oeuvre
waiter	Monsieur
waitress	Madame, Mademoiselle
wine list	la carte des vins

Cooking Styles

baked	cuit/cuite au four
boiled	bouilli/bouillie
fried	à la poêle
grilled	grillé/grillée
medium	cuit/cuite à point
poached	poché/pochée

rare	saignant
steamed	à la vapeur
very rare	bleu
well done	bien cuit/cuite

Meat, Poultry, Game and Offal

bacon	le bacon
beef	le boeuf
chicken	le poulet
duck	le canard
frogs' legs	les cuisses de grenouilles
game	le gibier
ham	le jambon
kidneys	les rognons
lamb	l'agneau
meat	la viande
pork	le porc
rabbit	le lapin
salami style sausage (dry)	le saucisson-sec
sausage	la saucisse
snails	les escargots
steak	l'entrecôte/le steak/le bifteck
veal	le veau

Fish and Seafood

cod	le cabillaud/la morue
Dublin bay prawn/scampi	la langoustine
fish	le poisson
herring	le hareng
lobster	le homard
mullet	le rouget
mussels	les moules
oysters	les huîtres
pike	le brochet
prawns	les crevettes
salmon (smoked)	le saumon (fumé)
sea bass	le bar
seafood	les fruits de mer
shellfish	les crustacés
skate	le raie
squid	le calmar
trout	la truite
tuna	le thon

Vegetables, Pasta and Rice

cabbage	le chou
cauliflower	le chou-fleur
chips/french fries	les frites

garlic	l'ail
green beans	les haricots verts
leeks	les poireaux
onions	les oignons
pasta	les pâtes
peas	les petits pois
potatoes	les pommes-de-terre
rice	le riz
sauerkraut	la choucroute
spinach	les épinards
vegetables	les légumes

Salad Items

beetroot	la betterave
cucumber	le concombre
curly endive	la salade frisée
egg	un oeuf
green pepper/red pepper	le poivron/poivron rouge
green salad	la salade verte
lettuce	la laitue
tomato	la tomate

Fruit

apple	la pomme
banana	la banane
blackberries	les mûres
blackcurrants	les cassis
cherries	les cerises
fresh fruit	le fruit frais
grapefruit	le pamplemousse
grapes	les raisins
lemon/lime	le citron/le citron vert
orange	l'orange
peach	la pêche
pear	la poire
plums	les prunes/les mirabelles (type of plum)
raspberries	les framboises
red/whitecurrants	les groseilles
strawberries	les fraises

Desserts and Cheese

apple tart	la tarte aux pommes
cake	le gâteau
cheese	le fromage
cream	la crème fraîche
goat's cheese	le fromage de chèvre
ice cream	la glace

Sundries

ashtray	un cendrier
bread	le pain
bread roll	le petit pain
butter	le beurre
crisps	les chips
mustard	la moutarde
napkin	la serviette
oil	l'huile
peanuts	les cacahuètes
salt/pepper	le sel/le poivre
toast	le toast
vinegar	le vinaigre

DRINKS

beer	la bière
a bottle of . . .	une bouteille de . . .
black coffee	un café noir
coffee	un café
with cream	un café-crème
with milk	un café au lait
a cup of . . .	une tasse de . . .
decaffeinated coffee	un café décaféiné/un déca
espresso coffee	un express
freshly-squeezed lemon/orange juice	un citron pressé/une orange pressée
a glass of . . .	un verre de . . .
herbal tea	une tisane/infusion
with lime/verbena	au tilleul/à la verveine
with mint	à la menthe
with milk/lemon	au lait/au citron
milk	le lait
(some) mineral water	de l'eau minérale
orange juice	un jus d'orange
(some) tap water	de l'eau du robinet
(some) sugar	du sucre
tea	un thé
wine (red/white)	le vin (rouge/blanc)

SHOPPING

See also 'Paying'

Useful Shopping Vocabulary

I'd like to buy . . .	Je voudrais acheter . . .
Do you have . . . ?	Avez-vous . . . ?
How much, please?	C'est combien, s'il vous plaît?
I'm just looking, thank you.	Je regarde, merci.
It's for a gift.	C'est pour un cadeau/C'est pour offrir.

Shops

antique shop	le magasin d'antiquités
baker	la boulangerie
bank	la banque
book shop	la librairie
cake shop	la pâtisserie
cheese shop	la fromagerie
chemist/drugstore	la pharmacie
clothes shop	le magasin de vêtements
delicatessen	la charcuterie
department store	le grand magasin
gift shop	le magasin de cadeaux
the market	le marché
newsagent	le magasin de journaux
post office	la poste/le PTT
shoe shop	le magasin de chaussures
the shops	les boutiques/magasins
tobacconist	le tabac
travel agent	l'agence de voyages
expensive	cher
cheap	pas cher, bon marché
sales	les soldes
size (in clothes)	la taille
size (in shoes)	la pointure
too expensive	trop cher

TELEPHONING

telephone/phone booth	le téléphone/la cabine téléphonique
phone card	la carte téléphonique
post card	la carte postale
stamps	les timbres

DAYS OF THE WEEK

Monday	lundi
Tuesday	mardi
Wednesday	mercredi
Thursday	jeudi
Friday	vendredi
Saturday	samedi
Sunday	dimanche

COLOURS

black	noir/noire
blue	bleu/bleue
brown	brun/brune
green	vert/verte
orange	orange

pink	rose
red	rouge
white	blanc/blanche
yellow	jaune

NUMBERS

enough	assez
zero	zéro
one/first	un/une; premier/première
two/second	deux/deuxième
three/third	trois/troisième
four/fourth	quatre/quatrième
five/fifth	cinq/cinquième
six/sixth	six/sixième
seven/seventh	sept/septième
eight/eighth	huit/huitième
nine/nineth	neuf/neuvième
ten/tenth etc	dix/dixième etc
eleven	onze
twelve	douze
thirteen	treize
fourteen	quatorze
fifteen	quinze
sixteen	seize
seventeen	dix-sept
eighteen	dix-huit
nineteen	dix-neuf
twenty	vingt
twenty-one	vingt-et-un
twenty-two/three etc	vingt-deux/vingt-trois etc
thirty	trente
forty	quarante
fifty	cinquante
sixty	soixante
seventy	soixante-dix
eighty	quatre-vingts
ninety	quatre-vingt-dix
hundred	cent
thousand	mille

MEDIA

NEWSPAPERS AND MAGAZINES

For those of you who want to keep in touch, English-language newspapers (UK and US) are on sale on the day after publication in most large cities and resorts. They cost quite a bit more than at home, though. If you fancy reading a French newspaper, *Le Monde* is the most widely respected of these but is rather highbrow (no photos!). You can even read it online (in French) at www.lemonde.fr. *Le Figaro* is also quite conservative in its views, whereas *Libération* (known as Libé) is more left-wing. The top-selling national is *L'Équipe*, dedicated to sports coverage, but there are numerous magazines, covering health, nature, travel, cycling, gossip and more. These are for sale in shops and in traditional *kiosques* (newsstands). The regional dailies have a wide circulation, and the regional paper with the largest circulation is the very serious Rennes-based publication, *Ouest-France*. *Le Télégramme* is popular in western Brittany, but for travellers, these papers are probably only of relevance for their listings. Two interesting magazines published in Brittany (in Douarnenez) are *Chasse Marée*, focussing on matters marine, and *Ar Men*, which covers Breton cultural matters.

RADIO AND TV

France has four television channels in the public sector (France 2, France 3, Arté and La 5eme) together with three private channels (TF1, M6 and Canal Plus). Viewing reaches its peak at 8pm, when the French gather round their sets to watch the day's news, either on TF1 or France 2. There are 250 channels available on cable or via satellite and some hotels offer these facilities, as do a few of the more luxurious campsites. The cable networks include CNN, BBC World Service, BBC Prime, MTV and Paris Première, which shows a selection of VO (*version originale*) films.

If you've got a radio, you can tune into the English-language news on the BBC World Service on 648kHz AM or 198kHz long wave from midnight to 5am and BBC Radio 4 during the day. You can listen to Voice of America on 90.5, 98.8 and 102.4 FM. For radio news in French, listen to France Inter on 87.8 FM, Europe 1 on 104.7 FM or France Infos, the national rolling news station, on 105.5 FM.

French and international news is accessible online at www.afp.com.

MONEY

THE EURO

TIP Euro coins and notes are due to be introduced in January 2002 and the euro will be the sole currency in France from 17 February 2002. At the time of writing we were unable to include the equivalent euro prices alongside prices in francs, however those readers familiar with the French franc should find the franc prices a useful guide.

To convert franc prices into euros, divide the amount in francs by 6.56; so for example, 1,000F = 152.43€. The official euro/franc conversion rate has been fixed at 6.56 French francs to one euro. The euro/£ conversion rate stands at about 63 pence to one euro. Check the currency website **www.oanda.com** for up-to-date Sterling/euro conversion rates.

1 euro = 6.56 FF
1 euro = circa 63 pence

CHANGING MONEY

Foreign currency or travellers' cheques can be exchanged at banks displaying a *Change* sign (closed Saturday and Sunday) or at Bureaux de Change at all French airports, in train stations of big cities and in town centres. They are likely to stay open on Sundays in popular tourist areas, but their rates will not be as favourable as the banks'. American Express cheques are widely accepted in France and if they are exchanged at an Amex office, you won't pay commission. You can also obtain travellers' cheques from Thomas Cook or your bank.

CREDIT CARDS

Credit cards are widely accepted in France, but do check the window stickers in the hotels, shops or restaurants to determine if your card is acceptable before making a purchase. Visa is known as Carte Bleue in France and is almost universally recognized, with Access, Mastercard (also known as Eurocard), Diners Club and American Express also commonly accepted. Do note that some businesses don't accept American Express, and you should check that your hotel or restaurant takes cards, as the smaller ones often don't.

You can also use credit cards for cash advances at banks and in automatic teller machines (ATMs) and you'll be given the choice of instructions in French and English. You will need a PIN – it should be the same as the one you use at home but do check before you leave. Since all French credit cards are now smart cards (containing a microchip capable of storing data, known as a *puce*), your request may be denied. Try another machine if so. If this happens in a restaurant or hotel, explain that it is a foreign card with a magnetic strip (*piste magnétique*). You may have to tap in your PIN and press the green key (*validez*) on a keypad or the staff may make a call to clear it.

When paying by credit card, do check the amount that appears on the slip – there's no decimal point between 'francs' and 'centimes'. Note also that most French banks no long accept Eurocheques.

Lost or Stolen Cards

If your card is lost or stolen, you should cancel it as soon as possible by calling the number in your own country. Cardholders should travel with their bank's 24-hour contact number. British Visa and Barclaycard holders can simply call (a freephone number) from France for assistance. Barclaycard's number is ☎ (01604) 234234 (24 hours); Visa's number is ☎ (01383) 621166 (24 hours).

In France, numbers are as follows:

Mastercard: ☎ 01-45-67-84-84

American Express Cards: ☎ 01-47-77-72-00

Diners Club: ☎ 01-49-06-17-50

American Express (lost or stolen travellers' cheques): ☎ 08-00-90-86-00 (a freephone call if made from inside France only)

MUSEUMS

A museum pass from the *Centre des Monuments Nationaux* (Centre for National Monuments) is valid for one year and gives entry to 107 public monuments throughout France. The benefits include free access to temporary exhibitions in the listed locations and no queueing. In north Brittany, you can use the pass at Ernest Renan's birthplace in Tréguier.

The pass costs 280F and can be purchased at the sites mentioned, or by post from the *Centre des Monuments Nationaux,* Centre d'Informations, 62 rue St-Antoine, 75186 Paris Cedex 04. ☎ 01-44-61-21-50.

The following are some of the best museums in north Brittany:

Brest (Finistère): Océanopolis, aquarium and technical and scientific marine centre.

Dinan (Côtes d'Armor): Donjon du Château (castle keep). The site and the furniture are worth seeing, as are the mementoes of Anne of Brittany.

Montfort-sur-Meu: Écomusée du Pays de Montfort en Brocéliande (open-air museum). Highly eclectic museum covering everything from mineralogy to architecture with real flair.

Pleumeur-Bodou (Côtes d'Armor): Cosmopolis, for high-tech tourism, where visitors can relive the history of telecommunications.

Rennes (Ille-et-Vilaine): Musée de Bretagne (museum of Brittany). Regional history and prehistory, furniture, costume, objects, paintings. Recently modernized.

Rennes-Sud (Ille-et-Vilaine): Écomusée du Pays de Rennes (the Ferme de la Bintinais open-air museum, on the road to Châtillon-sur-Seiche). Large museum depicting the agriculture of the past and of today.

National museums and art galleries are closed on Tuesdays while municipal museums are generally closed on Mondays.

POLICE

If you're unlucky enough to be the victim of a theft, head to the nearest police station or *gendarmerie* with your identity (and vehicle papers). You need a police statement for insurance purposes. You may need to be patient, and it is also helpful to speak some French. In the event of losing your passport, inform both the police and the nearest consulate.

By law, the French police can stop anyone and demand to see their ID; the French are obliged to carry their identity cards with them at all times. The police don't often pick on respectable-looking tourists, but be polite and patient if they do choose to stop you.

The emergency number to call for the police is ☎ 17.

PUBLIC HOLIDAYS

Banks, shops and museums will be closed on the following public holidays, but most restaurants will stay open.

1 January (New Year's Day – *le jour de l'An*); Easter Monday – *le lundi de Pâques* (March or April); 1 May (Labour Day – *la fête du Travail*); 8 May (VE Day); last Thursday in May (Ascension Day – *l'Ascension*); Whit Sunday (*Pentecôte*) and Whit Monday (May or early June); 14 July, National Day (Bastille Day); 15 August (Assumption – *l'Assomption*); 1 November (All Saints' Day – *la Toussaint*); 11 November (Armistice Day – *l'Armistice*); 25 December (Christmas Day – *le jour de Noël*).

Where a national holiday falls on a Sunday, the next day is taken as a holiday instead, if a national holiday falls on a Thursday, the French often take the Thursday and the Friday off, making a four-day weekend. This is known as *faire le pont*, 'to make the bridge' over the Friday.

SAFETY

It is difficult to generalize on the subject of personal safety, but on the whole Brittany is a safe destination for visitors. However, it's always wise to take all the usual precautions, particularly in the larger cities. Try to park your car in underground or covered parking if possible and avoid leaving your car in remote spots. Don't take your valuables to the beach or, worse still, leave them unattended.

If you're unlucky enough to be the victim of a theft, head to the nearest police station or *gendarmerie* with your identity (and vehicle papers). You will need a police statement for insurance purposes. In the event of losing your passport, inform both the police and the nearest consulate.

SHOPPING

France offers a great shopping experience, both for day-to-day needs and for things to take home, and Brittany is no exception.

OPENING HOURS

Department stores are open Monday to Saturday, 9am to 6.30pm or 7.30pm. They don't close for lunch and stay open late one night a week and on Sunday too in the few weeks leading up to Christmas. If you don't have cash, you can usually pay by credit card, but you should check first in the smaller shops. Few outlets accept travellers' cheques or Eurocheques, although the larger department stores probably will.

Smaller, more specialized shops are open from around 7am to noon and then from after lunch to 7pm, sometimes later in larger towns. They normally close on Sunday afternoon and al day Monday, although some grocers and supermarkets are open on Monday nowadays. Bakers often close by about

1pm. A Sunday morning can be a busy shopping time in many towns and villages.

Hypermarkets usually stay open until 9pm or 10pm.

FROM HYPERMARKETS TO SPECIALIST FOOD STORES

The massive hypermarkets (*hypermarchés*) are usually located on the outskirts of sizeable towns – look out for signs indicating the *Centre Commercial*. Casino, Carrefour and Auchan are the largest of the hypermarkets, and stores such as Monoprix and Prisunic, which are usually to be found in town centres, are more like department stores. Buying your petrol at a hypermarket will definitely save money.

However, if you buy all your provisions in these larger stores, you will miss out on the delights of shopping in the specialist food shops. The *boulangeries* and *pâtisseries* sell delicious bread and pastries, while a *fromagerie* offers a tempting choice of cheeses, and the *charcuteries* and *traiteurs* have done all the work by preparing and selling dishes by weight – all perfect for picnics.

MARKETS

In Brittany, market day means fête day. Once you've managed to park the car, you're in for a treat. The markets (*marchés*) selling regional and seasonal produce are wonderfully colourful and fragrant places to explore, with their flowers and fabulously fresh seafood, including oysters and coquilles St-Jacques (scallops). The markets also sell a vast range of vegetables and fruits, such as cauliflower, globe artichokes and strawberries, which you are usually buying direct from the growers.

Food markets take place daily in larger cities and weekly in smaller towns and villages. They are social occasions for the locals and mostly finish around noon. Try the *saucisse galette* (a Breton sausage crêpe) or an *andouille fumée* (smoked chitterling sausage) as you explore. You may be tempted to try some oysters or take some home (depending on which country you are returning to). Vintage oyster-producing centres include Canacale, Paimpol, Tréguier river, Morlaix-Penzé and Brest bay, and they have their own distinctive qualities. Oysters are full of flavour particularly when there's an 'r' in the month.

Breton fish markets and auctions, known as *criées*, are well worth a visit. Increasingly, they are becoming computerized and open only to those in the business, but some fishing ports still maintain their traditions and allow the public the chance to glimpse their fascinating world. Ask for information at the nearest tourist office. Some of the main fish markets that you can visit are at Erquy, Loguivy-de-la-Mer, Ploubazlanec, Roscoff and St-Quay-Portrieux. The buyers arrive at daybreak and make their selections from fish displayed in boxes, divided by type and size. An auctioneer conducts proceedings and keeps a close eye on gestures and smiles to bring the sales to conclusion. It's a sort of open-air Stock Exchange!

Don't forget to taste the Breton cakes and biscuits, including *kouign amann* (the most traditional cake made with a good deal of butter as its name 'butter-cake' suggests). *Gâteau Breton* is also buttery but denser and melts in the mouth. Not surprisingly, you won't have to look far to find a crêpe if you're feeling peckish.

What to Buy

Having enjoyed the markets, you may want to buy a few Breton specialities to take home and there's quite a choice.

Garments, crafts and household items

The Breton pure wool striped fisherman's jumpers (also available in children's sizes) make lovely gifts, along with the fishermen's hats (*casquettes*) or traditional jackets. Other potential presents include beautiful lace shawls, embroidered aprons and clogs (*sabots*). Quimper *faïence* (pottery) is a wonderful souvenir and is quite unlike anything else. Quimper, on the south coast of Brittany, has been a leading centre for the production of traditional Breton pottery for almost 200 years. In the mid-19th century, the characteristic hand-painted Breton peasant figure (the 'Petit Breton') began to appear on pottery ware with his traditional baggy pants, bright breeches and waistcoat, plus a black Breton hat, gradually usurping the more traditional motifs. This design has formed the basis of the success of Quimper pottery ever since.

Throughout Brittany you will find numerous examples of Breton lace, known as *picot*. Lace-making techniques were originally brought over to the Pays Bigouden from Ireland by a nun searching for a way for the locals to earn much-need money after the disappearance of sardine shoals that they used to fish. The souvenir shops also display attractive original jewellery, often in silver, including necklaces, rings and Celtic crosses.

Drinks

You could always take a bottle or two of local cider home. Look out for the terms *cidre fermier* or *cidre traditionnel*, signs that it has been made on a small-holding or using a traditional method. Morlaix makes a delicious cider. Lambig, the local equivalent of Calvados from Normandy, is much rarer than its counterpart and makes a delicious *digestif*, gift or souvenir. Muscadet is the famous wine made in the Loire Atlantique, in south Brittany and its fresh and crisp taste makes it the perfect wine for Breton fish and seafood. A couple of Breton breweries still produce *cervoise,* the name of the beer drunk by the Gauls and often ordered by the cartoon Gaul Astérix and his friends. *Chouchen*, a sweet alcoholic mead, is also delicious – it's made using fermented honey and water. It can be drunk as an apéritif or digestif and is also used in regional cooking. Beer has been brewed in Brittany since the 17th century, and a glass of Coreff from Morlaix is worth a try.

SMOKING

Cigarettes are still relatively inexpensive in France, and the French remain inveterate smokers, despite laws passed ten years ago that banned smoking in many public areas. Smoking is even quite common in business meetings, and you will still often come across that familiar image of the archetypal Frenchman, Gauloise stuck to his bottom lip, eyes screwed up against the blue smoke. Some restaurants offer non-smoking (*non fumeur*) areas, but the rules are not always observed. If you need an ashtray, ask for a *cendrier*, and if you need a light, simply say '*Vous avez du feu*?'

SPORTS AND LEISURE ACTIVITIES

CANAL TRIPS

Brittany has an extensive network of 500 kilometres (310 miles) of navigable canals and rivers, which criss-cross the whole region. Everything seems more colourful from the perspective of a canal boat. The waterways run their course through speckled granite, grey sandstone and crimson schist, making the contrast with the flower-decorated locks even more striking.

■ **Paris Canal-Quiztour**: Bassin de La Villette, 19–21 quai de la Loire, 75019 Paris. ☎ 01-42-40-81-60. Fax: 01-42-40-77-30.

A branch of Paris Canal-Quiztour at Messac, on the Vilaine, rents out boats suitable for anything from two to twelve people.

CYCLING

Brittany is a great place to go cycling, whether you stick to the roads or go across country. The following organizations give you any information you need about cycling and mountain biking in Brittany.

– **Côtes-d'Armor**: Comité Départemental de Cyclotourisme (regional organization for cycling holidays) ☎ 02-96-43-76-67.

– **Finistère**: Comité Départemental de Cyclotourisme, 47 rue F Leroy, 29000 Quimper. ☎ 02-98-95-33-24.

– **Ille-et-Vilaine**: Comité Départemental de Cyclotourisme, Maison des Sports, 13 *bis* avenue de Cucillé, 35065 Rennes Cedex. ☎ 02-99-54-67-67.

FISHING

Despite some horrendous pollution of the waterways, work done by groups such as Eaux et Rivières (Waterways and Rivers), based in Lorient, means that it is still possible to fish in Brittany for salmon and trout.

For salmon fishing, the river Élorn (Finistère) comes top, followed by the Trieux (Côtes-d'Armor), which is currently undergoing a re-population operation and scientific monitoring, the Ellé and the Blavet (Morbihan), the lower reaches of the Aulne, and the Steir and the Odet (Finistère). For trout, the rivers mentioned above are good, plus the Scorff (Morbihan), the Penzé (Finistère) and the Léguer (Côtes-d'Armor).

■ **French fishing hotline service**: ☎ 08-36-68-88-80. This premium-rate recorded message service provides information (in French) on fishing sites and on the price and validity of fishing cards.

HORSE-RIDING

If you want to go out on horseback, it's useful to know that using marked footpaths is not forbidden. The following organizations can provide information on any aspect of riding:

■ **Ligue Équestre de Bretagne** (Breton equestrian association): 17 rue du 62e-RI, 56103 Lorient Cedex. ☎ 02-97-84-44-00.

■ **Délégation Régionale d'Équitation sur Poney Bretagne** (regional organization for pony-trekking in Brittany): P.C. de Fenicat, 35170 Bruz. ☎ 02-99-41-16-30. Fax: 02-99-41-29-13.

■ **Association de Tourisme Équestre de Bretagne** (association for equestrian holidays in Brittany): 33 rue Laennec, 29710 Ploneis. ☎ 02-98-91-02-02.

■ **Comité Breton d'Endurance** (Breton group for endurance riding): M. Lebaud, Kernabo, 56520 Guidel. ☎ 02-97-65-37-80.

■ **Association des Cavaliers d'Extérieur des Côtes-d'Armor** (Côtes-d'Armor association for trekking on horseback): Kertau, 22190 Plérin. ☎ 02-96-74-68-05.

WALKING

In the Middle Ages, in honour of the seven saints who brought Christianity to Brittany, the practice spread of making a tour of Brittany, with a spell of contemplation at each of their tombs along the way. Pilgrims would visit the tombs of St Samson at Dol-de-Bretagne, St Patern at Vannes, St Corentin at Quimper, St Aurélien at St-Pol-de-Léon, St Tugdual at Tréguier and St Brieuc and St Malo in their respective towns. This pilgrimage around Brittany (or 'Tro Breizh' in Breton) was a 500-kilometre journey (310 miles) and anyone who completed the whole circuit was sure of a place in heaven. The route was known as the 'pilgrimage of the seven saints' and is a beautiful trip, to be thoroughly recommended – although these days it won't necessarily guarantee you a place in paradise. The practice died out at the end of the Middle Ages but has been revived since 1994 by two associations:

Route Historique du Tro Breizh: boulevard Hérault, 22000 St-Brieuc. ☎ 02-96-33-10-22.

Chemins du Tro Breizh: St-Pol-de-Léon. ☎ 02-98-69-16-53. This organization arranges an annual pilgrimage between two of the seven towns.

France has a superb national and regional network of long-distance marked footpaths called the *Grande Randonnée* (or GR) routes. They are all numbered, using the prefix *GR*. Brittany alone has 5,000 kilometres (3,125 miles) of footpaths. You can walk (almost) round the Breton coast, on the path known variously in the locality as the *Sentier du Littoral* (coastal path), the Grande Randonnée 34 (or GR34), or the *Sentier des Douaniers* (customs officers' path). There are a number of different types of routes, including regional tours, denoted by the prefix *GRP*; and walks and strolls (prefixed *PR*) lasting a day or less. Some of these are circular walks that follow the old towpaths along the canals in the Trois Rivières or Redon regions.

All the French Grande Randonnée paths are described in a Topoguide, which has maps and gives details about campsites, refuge huts and where to buy provisions. These are available in local bookshops in Brittany or in the UK from Stanfords, 12–14 Long Acre, London WC2E 9LP. ☎ (020) 7836 1321. Fax: (020) 7836 0189. Website: www.stanfords.co.uk. They are published by the principal French walkers' organization, **Fédération française de la Randonnée Pédestre** (*see below* for details). Most tourist information centres will also be able to supply maps and leaflets on the walks in their area. Some of the GRs are detailed in this guide.

– **The coastal path** or **customs officers' path** (GR34) was defined by a law of 31 December 1976 and certain sections of it are specially protected by the Conservatoire du Littoral (coastal conservation organization). It is subject to particular regulations when it crosses bird sanctuaries, such as those at Cap Fréhel or Cap Sizun, where the local residents are obliged to leave at least 3 metres (10 feet) between the edge of their property and the highest level reached by the water.

– **Brittany's Grande Randonnée routes** (GR3, 34, 341, 342, 37, 38 and 39) are marked in red and white. The routes are all described one-way, but you can always retrace your steps and discover the countryside from a different perspective, especially along the coast. The E5, a European path, crosses France and runs down into Italy, from the Pointe du Raz in western Brittany all the way to Venice.

– **The regional paths** (GRP) are marked in yellow and red. The routes are circular and give you chance to get a deeper cultural knowledge of the region over the course of a walk lasting about a week. Examples are the tour of the Gallo region around Loudéac; the tour of the Monts d'Arrée leaving from Huelgoat; the tour of the Montagnes Noires around Gourin; and the tour of the Forêt de Brocéliande near Rennes.

– The **Fédération des Parcs Naturels Régionaux de France** (the co-ordinating body for the French regional parks) can give plenty of information about the location and types of France's regional parks. Visit their website: www.parcs-naturels-regionaux.tm.fr.

– There are many **paths for walks and strolls** (PR), usually marked out in yellow, but sometimes in other colours. The routes start either at tourist attractions or at walkers' shelters. They last from about an hour to one day at the most, and are ideal for family groups or children. The time taken to do the walk is estimated on the basis of a walking speed of 4 kilometres (2.5 miles) an hour with no stops.

■ **Comité Régional du Tourisme de Bretagne** (regional tourist association): 1 rue Raoul-Ponchon, 35069 Rennes Cedex. ☎ 02-99-28-44-30. Fax: 02-99-28-44-40.

■ **Fédération française de la Randonnée Pédestre (FFRP)** (French walkers' federation): produces a number of guides on marked footpaths throughout France. Their information centre is at 14 rue Riquet, 75019 Paris. ☎ 01-44-89-93-93. Fax: 01-40-35-85-67. Website: www.ffrp.asso.fr

■ **Association Bretonne des Relais et Itinéraires** (Breton association for tourist routes and places to stay): co-ordinates nearly 130 shelters along the route of the marked footpaths, and produces a number of guides. Contact them at: ABRI, 4 rue Ronsard, 35000 Rennes. ☎ 02-99-31-13-50. Fax: 02-99-26-13-54.

■ **France Randonnée**: 9 rue des Portes Mordelaises, 35000 Rennes. ☎ 02-99-67-42-21. Fax: 02-99-67-42-23. This company runs fully organized tours that you can do with or without a guide. They're real specialists, using local people for the inside track on what there is to see and do. Gastronomic tours, too.

■ There is no shortage of local walking associations along the routes. Walks are also organized by the **Parc naturel régional d'Armorique**, which can be contacted via Menez-Meur, BP 35, 29460 Hanvec Cedex. ☎ 02-98-68-81-71. They offer walking routes in the countryside and in the forests.

WIND-BASED SPORTS

The wind along Brittany's north coast is no longer needed for turning the sails of windmills, but instead, it has become a hugely valuable commodity for the leisure industry and is used to power the numerous land- and water-based machines that are enjoyed by the fans of 'sliding and gliding sports', especially at the water speed base at Brest harbour. The vast stretches of beach that are exposed at low tide are ideal for a whole new range of sports. You can go sand-yachting or windsurfing at Cherrueix, Erquy or St-Michel-en Grève and surfing is possible at Plouescat or at Sables d'Or.

DIVING

Why not make the most of being in a region that's full of opportunities to go diving? Being down there among the creatures of the sea and experiencing those totally unexpected brilliant colours is quite amazing. You don't even need to be a wonderful swimmer or even particularly sporty – the only requirement is to be at least eight years old and to be in good health. If you take any kind of medication, then diving is probably best avoided, and it's definitely not on if you're pregnant. Once you have got beyond the introductory lesson, you will need to provide a medical certificate and of course, this is in your interest. Introductory lessons for children, by the way, are given in a specially adapted environment, with warm water and no currents.

It's a myth that diving is bad for the ears and you soon learn how to breathe with your nose blocked. It turns out that this kind of 'positive' breathing is one of the best forms of relaxation going.

The whole experience is being underwater transforms your perceptions of time and space – it can only be described as 'other-worldly'. Still, it's a good idea not to get too carried away. Safety regulations are there to be observed as you go along.

Remember that it's advisable to leave at least 24 hours before travelling by aeroplane, as you need to be sure that your system is fully decompressed.

Diving centres

In France, the vast majority of diving clubs are affiliated to the FFESSM (Fédération Française d'Études et de Sports Sous-Marins). The rest belong to the ANMP (Association Nationale des Moniteurs de Plongée) or the SNMP (Syndicat National des Moniteurs de Plongée). Whichever is their affiliated body, the clubs all operate with fully qualified trainers, who oversee all the dives and know their own spots like the back of their hands.

A good diving club is somewhere where you know you can have a good time but where you know that safety comes first. Beware of any club that will take you down without a thorough understanding of your level, because being too laid back is just plain dangerous.

It makes sense to double-check that everything seems to be well maintained (look out for signs of rust as well as general cleanliness) and that all the standard, compulsory safety equipment is on board (oxygen, safety belts, radio and so on). Staff qualification certificates should also be on display. Don't be afraid to ask – after all, you're paying for the dive and it's your safety that's at stake. Beyond that, all you need to decide on is whether to go with a larger club, where everything runs along tried and tested lines or a smaller one, where arrangements might be much more flexible.

Expect to pay an average of 150F to 220F per dive, and remember that you will also need an annual permit, which costs about 250F.

Your first time?

What happens first of all is your initiation (the French call it a *baptême* or 'baptism'). This costs between 150F and 220F and takes just half an hour, during which time your instructor will show you the basics. Just let yourself go! Even if you feel dressed up rather like a Christmas tree in the middle of summer, remember that once you're underwater, you won't notice the weight of all that gear. You won't be allowed to go any deeper than 5 metres (16 feet). If the wetsuit feels tight, well, it should be. Any pockets of air that stay inside the suit will reduce your body temperature.

Once you're initiated, you're in for a period of apprenticeship.

Levels of skill

Learning to dive is a matter of moving gradually up through the ability levels.

– At Level I you can go down to a depth of 20 metres (65 feet), accompanied by an instructor. This costs upwards of 1,500F.

– At Level II you are allowed out unaccompanied to a depth of 20 metres (65 feet). Your maximum permitted depth is 40 metres (130 feet) but this will be with an instructor. Prices start at 1,800F.

– You then move on to Level III, where you are completely unsupervised and can dive to the maximum safe limit of 65 metres (213 feet). This costs about 1,500F.

– Level IV is the stage you reach in order to become professionally qualified.

Obviously enough, you should expect to progress through the levels with plenty of time between each, in order to get enough experience under your belt. Ask the instructors about this – after all, they've already been through it!

All divers are given a diving passport, which records their progress and level of ability achieved.

International diving standards

If you expect to be diving in other countries, it's essential to ask for the international equivalent of your diploma. These international standards are set by either CMAS (Confédération Mondiale des Activités Subaquatiques) or CEDIP (European Committee of Professional Diving Instructors). The best thing to do is to get your level of ability assessed by a PADI-qualified instructor (Professional Association for Diving Instructors), as this will be recognized worldwide. It's worth knowing that diplomas issued by NAUI (National Association of Underwater Instructors) and SSI (Scuba Diving International) are also recognized throughout the world.

On the other hand, if you have already dived elsewhere, your level of ability will be assessed by an instructor, who will test your skills and give you an appropriate level in the French system.

Diving in Northern Brittany

The Atlantic coast is a favourite place for divers, and the coast of Brittany offers an incredible wealth of underwater sights. However, it's a place to approach with the right amount of humility and caution, because the storms, high tides and dangerous currents along these shores are extreme and unforgiving. If you plan to do a lot of diving in Brittany, you will need to carry out a serious programme of training.

– **Weather**: you need good weather to dive. The ideal time of year is from June to September, when the surface temperature is 17°C (62°F) (it's colder the further down you go). Some regions have diving spots that are sheltered from the extremes of the weather. You need to watch out for the strong swell from the west.

– **Meteorological forecasts**: ☎ 08-36-68-08- followed by the two-digit department number (Côtes d'Armor = 22; Finistère = 29; Ille-et-Villaine = 35). *See also* 'Climate' for fuller details on recorded weather forecasts.

– **Depths**: the average depth is 15–20 metres (49–65 feet) and diving is rarely available below 30 metres (98 feet). This reduces the risk of decompression problems.

– **Visibility**: the average visibility is 5–6 metres (16–20 feet), and is frequently reduced along the coast because of sediment moved about by the tides. Visibility comparable to that in the Mediterranean (20 metres or 65 feet) is common when you dive down to rocks that are out at sea. All the same, the water is clearer around the islands (Ouessant and Les Sept-Îles) than along the coast. Visibility on wrecks is limited.

– **Tides**: the state of the tides is an all-important factor. The best time to dive is at slack water, when the tide is neither coming in nor going out, as you then avoid the strong currents. Slack water at high tide gives the best visibility conditions, as the clear water comes from out at sea and the fish are there in abundance. Slack water at low tide allows you to go down at least 5 metres (16 feet) to a diving spot and decompression levels are reduced.

– **Currents**: dangerous currents exist in the waters off Brittany, caused by the strong tides and increased by the geography of the place, especially around the island of Ouessant and the Brest peninsula.

– **Recommended equipment**: you will need a hooded wetsuit with a minimum thickness of 5mm, plus gloves that will protect you from protruding metal on the wrecks and give you a grip on the rocks if you meet a strong current. A compass is essential, as is a lamp, which will allow you to see the brilliant colours as well as to explore down in the rock crevices and be visible to your co-divers. Some form of security warning system is also advisable, either a visible smoke alarm or one that produces an audible signal.

– **Marine life**: there is a rich and wide variety. Your instructor will introduce you to all the beautiful things and all the traps that lurk in Breton waters. Some plant and animal species can be found reliably in each of the diving spots, from kelp (laminaria), anemones and sponges to whiting, conger eels, bass, coley and wrasse, right down to common crabs and sea urchins. The golden rule, of course, is to treat this fragile environment with all the respect that it deserves. Don't take anything away and be careful where you put your hands.

– **Last words of advice**: when you're diving, don't ever allow yourself to lose contact with the rest of your group. Watch out for abandoned nets on the rocks or in wrecks. Make sure that your diving boat is properly equipped with oxygen (which is obligatory) and remember that the decompression chamber, if you ever need it, is located at Brest.

GENERAL INFORMATION

TIME

France is one hour ahead of GMT (Greenwich Mean Time) and changes its clock in spring and autumn. In France, 'am' and 'pm' are not used – the 24-hour clock is widely applied.

TIPPING

There are no strict rules for tipping in France, as there are in the USA, for example. In **bars**, it's quite common to leave the smallest bits of change for the waiter, but it's not necessarily expected. Waiting at restaurant tables in France is a respected profession, with special colleges and exams, and waiting staff are paid properly, and do not have to rely on tips (which is not always the case in some countries). Unscrupulous waiters may, however, return your change to you on a saucer with the coins hidden on the bottom, then the bill, then the notes. Remember to check underneath your bill or you could be leaving a very generous tip indeed.

In **restaurants**, a 15 per cent service charge is already included in the price, but it is customary to tip the waiter or waitress, especially if the food or service was exceptional (up to 10F in a bistrot, more in a nice restaurant). It's a similar situation in hotels, where a standard service charge is included on the bill by law, and a tip is proffered only for very special service. **Taxi drivers** do expect a tip – give 10 per cent.

Until recently, there was a long-held tradition in France of tipping cinema ushers or usherettes 1 or 2F after they had shown you to your seat, but this has finally gone out of fashion.

TOILETS

The infamous French *toilettes à la Turque* – two footplates, a hole in the ground and a ferocious flushing system that always splashes your shoes and often quite a lot more – can still be found in a number of places in Brittany, although you are more likely to find a conventional and familiar arrangement today than you would a few years back. It's very common for a bar or restaurant to have only one toilet, used by men and women. Female readers might like to know that you often have to walk past a urinal to get to the private facilities.

Bear in mind that it's considered impolite to use an establishment's toilets without being a customer. If you're desperate, the polite thing to do is to put 1F on the counter, uttering a smiling '*Merci, Monsieur*' as you leave. Otherwise, the facilities in museums or department stores might be a better bet.

If you're travelling on main roads, it's advisable to use the free facilities at service stations and roadside stopping places (*aires de repos*). Watch out for the occasional public toilets where you have to pay to enter – or exit! And it's normal to leave a small tip for the caretaker of the toilets if you see that there is one.

TOURIST INFORMATION

TOURIST OFfiCES ABROAD

■ The French Government Tourist Office (known as Maison de la France) is at 178 Piccadilly, London W1V OAL. ☎ (020) 7399 3500. Their information line is ☎ (0906) 824 4123 (premium rate). E-mail: info@mdlf.co.uk.

International offices include:

United States: ☎ (410) 286-8310 and ☎ (312) 751-7800

Canada: ☎ (514) 288 4264

Australia: ☎ (02) 92 31 52 44

TOURIST INFORMATION IN PARIS

冃 Office du tourisme et des congrès de Paris: Central Office, 127 avenue des Champs-Élysées, 75008 Paris. ☎ 01-49-52-53-54 or (premium rate) 08-36-68-31-12. Metro: George-V or Charles-de-Gaulle-Étoile. Website: www.paris-touristoffice.com. This main tourist office is staffed by a multilingual team, who can supply information on all the French regions.

■ **Maison de la Bretagne**: 203 boulevard St-Germain, 75007 Paris. ☎ 01-53-63-11-50. Nearest metro: Rue-du-Bac. In this regional tourist information office there's an excellent library on Brittany.

■ **Ti Ar Vretoned** (previously known as the *Mission Bretonne*): 22 rue Delambre, 75014 Paris. ☎ 01-43-35-26-41. Fax: 01-43-35-26-41. Website: www.gwalarn.org. Metro: Montparnasse-Bienvenüe, Vavin or Edgar-Quinet. This is the most active Breton association in Paris, promoting the Breton language and information on aspects of Celtic culture.

■ **Ministère des Transports, direction des transports terrestres** (ministry of transport):Arche de la Défense, Pilier sud, 92055 La Défense Cedex. ☎ 01-40-81-17-16. Metro: Arche de la Défense. For information on the canals of Brittany.

■ **Gîtes de France**: 59 rue St-Lazare, 75009. ☎ 01-49-70-75-75. Metro: Trinité.

TOURIST OFFICES IN BRITTANY

Ⓑ Bretagne INFOS: 1 rue Raoul-Ponchon, 35069 Rennes Cedex. ☎ 302-99-36-25-25. Fax: 02-99-28-44-40. E-mail: tourism-crtb@tourismebretagne.com. This is the official regional tourist service.

See individual town entries for details of local tourist offices.

USEFUL TOURISM WEBSITES

www.visiteurope.com – the European Travel Commission provides useful information on travelling to and around 27 European countries, with links to commercial booking services such as car hire; also rail schedules and weather reports.

www.franceguide.com – gives useful listings.

www.bretagne.com – for information on Brittany, with over 3,000 useful links.

www.brittanytourism.com – discover Breton heritage, festivals and events and information on accommodation.

www.brittany-shops.com – the best of local Breton products, from food and drink to gifts.

www.chez.com/bretagneceltique – gives all the details on Breton beliefs, druids and dolmens, with plenty of maps and drawings.

www.kervarker.org – a site dedicated to the Breton language with an online dictionary and grammar and a self-teaching course.

www.tvbreizh.com – the website of Brittany's own TV station, TV Breizh.

Local tourist office websites and e-mail addresses:

Binic:	officedetourismedebinic@wanadoo.fr
Combourg:	www.combourg.org; OT@combourg.org
Côtes d'Armor:	www.cotes-darmor.com
Étables-sur-Mer:	otsi.etablesurmer@wanadoo.fr
Fougères:	www.ot-fougeres.fr;
	ot.fougeres@wanadoo.fr
Lamballe:	otsi.lamballe@netcourrier.com
Morlaix and Haut Finistère:	cint-292@morlaix.cci.fr
Plérin:	ot.plerin@wanadoo.fr
Pleumeur-Bodou:	pleumeur.office@leradome.com
Rennes:	www.bretagne35.com; tourisme35.cdt
	@wanadoo.fr; www.ville-rennes.fr
St-Malo:	www.bretagne-4villes.com
St-Quay-Portrieux:	saintquayportrieux@wanadoo.fr
Vitré:	www.ot-vitre.fr; info@ot-vitre.fr

TRANSPORTATION

Local information on train and bus connections is provided in the various sections of this guide.

CAR HIRE

There are several car hire companies in France, but competitive prices on pre-paid cars in the UK and US make it worth checking with local agents before you leave. Try to take advantage of fly-drive offers. Car rental in France is relatively expensive. The big firms – Hertz, Avis, Europcar and Budget – are at most airports and in most big cities. Local firms can be cheaper but check the small print and confirm where you can drop off the car. Most rental firms will only deal with people over 25 (without a hefty extra insurance premium) and all drivers must be over 21 with one year's experience. Most cars are manual, so if you really want to drive an automatic transmission vehicle, book well ahead. Keep your fuel levels topped up as petrol stations keep shop hours and most close on Sunday and/or Monday. They are few and far between in some rural areas.

Driving

Speed limits in France are 130kph (80mph) on motorways, 110kph (68mph) on dual carriageways and 50 kph (30 mph) in towns. On other roads keep to 90 kph (56 mph). Instant (and hefty) fines are issued for speeding and drink-driving. The police must issue a receipt showing the amount paid.

Useful websites and telephone numbers include:

Motorway information: www.autoroutes.fr

Road conditions: www.bison-fute.equipement.gouv.fr

Route planner: www.iti.fr

Traffic and road conditions: ☎ 08-36-68-20-00 (outside Paris and Île de France)

BY TRAIN

The **TGV Atlantique** (high-speed rail service) from Paris–Gare Montparnasse will take you to Rennes in two hours and Brest in four. Paris–Quimper serves Rennes and Redon (among other destinations) and the Paris–Brest line stops at Rennes and St-Brieuc.

Within Brittany, there is a network of much slower trains serving further destinations, in particular towns on the coast. Inland Brittany is not served particularly well by trains and the local bus network is more extensive.

Train tickets in France must be validated and you need to *composter votre billet* (stamp your ticket) in the little orange machines by the entrance to the lines. This dates and validates your ticket. After a break of more than 24 hours, you must *composter* your ticket again.

The **SNCF** website is at www.sncf.com. SNCF also operates a telephone information, reservation and prepayment service in English (7am–10pm French time). In France ☎ 08-36-35-35-39.

BY BUS

Buses are run by the SNCF (replacing discontinued rail routes) or private companies. They can be useful for local and some cross-country journeys. The timetable in rural areas is designed to suit working, market and school hours. Buses often leave very early in the morning and return during the afternoon. Private bus firms tend to charge more than trains. Some towns have a coach station (*gare routière*), which is usually located near the train station, but often the line will start near the main square. Check with the local tourist office for departure points.

WORKING IN FRANCE

Working in France is theoretically possible for all EU nationals, who also have the right to receive the French Jobseeker's Allowance, and are entitled to the minimum French wage. In practice, high unemployment levels mean that finding a job can be difficult, and foreigners employed at the lower end of the scale (as nannies, bar staff or fruit pickers, for example) are likely to be poorly paid. Non-EU citizens must obtain a work permit, which is given on the spot to students with at least one term left to complete in France, on application.

If you are planning to work in France, you need to bear a few things in mind. Anyone staying in France for over three months must have a *carte de séjour*, or residency permit. EU citizens are entitled to one automatically. Despite the high unemployment levels, you may find jobs in the cities doing bar or club work, freelance translating, teaching English, fixing software or data processing or working as an au pair. In the countryside, seasonal fruit picking or teaching English are other options.

If you speak good French, working in the travel industry is a possibility – working on bus tours or in summer campsites. Write to tour operators in early spring and keep an eye out in travel magazines.

Eurocamp recruits staff for its holidays and campsites. To contact them in the UK ☎ (01606) 787522, or visit their website: www.eurocamp.co.uk

If you are already in France, check the job section of local newspapers and of *Le Monde*, *Le Figaro* and *International Herald Tribune*. The notice boards in English-language bookshops are worth looking at.

Also try **CIDJ** (Centre d'Information et de Documentation Jeunesse), 101 quai Branly, 75740 Paris, Cedex 15. ☎ 01-44-49-12-00. Email: cidj@cidj. asso.fr. Website: www.cidj.asso.fr. Alternatively, contact **CRIJ** (Centre Régional Information Jeunesse): CRIJ Côte d'Azur, 19 rue Gioffrédo, 06000 Nice. ☎ 04-93-80-93-93. Email: CRIJ.COTE.DAZUR@wanadoo.fr. Website: www.crij.org/nice

For those who want to find out more about rural life, there are opportunities to work on **organic farms** as working guests. For more information, send a stamped addressed envelope to Organic Farms at:

WWOOF UK, Fran Whittle, PO Box 2675, Lewes BN7 1RB

WWOOF Canada, RR 2, S.18, C.9, Nelson, British Columbia VIL 5P5

WWOOF Australia, RSD, Buchan, VIC 3885

WWOOF New Zealand, Jane and Andrew Strange, PO Box 1172, Nelson

Also check out their website at: www.wwoof.org

If you are looking for something more secure, you should do some research and plan in advance. The following contact points may be useful.

TEACHING

www.britcoun.org/english/engvacs.htm – this British Council website gives listings of English teaching vacancies.

Teaching English Abroad: a useful book published by Vacation Work, 9 Park End Street, Oxford OX1 1HJ. ☎ (01865) 241978. Fax: (01865) 790885.

WORKING AS AN AU PAIR

UK: Avalon Au Pairs ☎ (01344) 778246

United States: American Institute for Foreign Study: ☎ (203) 869-9090

France: Accueil Familial des Jeunes Étrangers ☎ 01-42-22-50-34

VOLUNTARY WORK

If you're interested in history and archaeology (and are over 18), there's a whole range of restoration projects and archaeological digs in which to get involved. In exchange for your labour, you get board and lodging. Contact: **Cotravaux**, 11 rue de Clichy, 75009 Paris. ☎ 01-48-74-79-20. Fax: 01-48-74 14-01 or **CHAM**, 5 and 7 rue Guilleminot, 75014 Paris. ☎ 01-43-35-15-51. Fax: 01-43-20-46-82.

Another organization to contact for voluntary work is **Concordia**, 1 rue de Metz, 75010 Paris. ☎ 01-45-23-00-23.

Useful Reading

Emplois d'Été en France (Summer Jobs in France): Vac-Job, 46 avenue Réné-Coty, 75014 Paris. ☎ 01-43-20-70-51.

Living and Working in France by Victoria Pybus, published by Vacation Work (*see* 'Teaching' *above*).

Background

Brittany is like nowhere else on earth – an oddly-shaped peninsula jutting out into the Atlantic with the busy waters of the English Channel to the north.

Wherever you go in North or South Brittany, you can see the close connection between the land and the sea. From the *abers* or tongues of water that reach deep inland at Lannilis and the Aber-Ildut in North Finistère, to the islands dotted around the Golfe du Morbihan in the south near Vannes, across to the Penmarc'h peninsula and the Pays Bigouden in the west of Finistère, the sea encroaches twice a day into the ancient tidal estuaries leaving strange arrows of sand and rock that project out into the sea.

In the eyes of writers and historians alike, Brittany is seen as the 'tough' part of France. This is perhaps evidenced both by the historically difficult times to which the region has been subjected and the violent extremes of nature that have been and always will remain a constant factor. Over the centuries, the people and the land itself have been subjected to a combination of both.

HISTORY AND POLITICS

Breton Nationalism

Breton nationalists come in a number of different guises. They might be militant autonomists striving for independence for Brittany or simply defenders of the Breton language and culture. They might even be daubers of road signs or bombers of tax offices and electric pylons. Whatever form they take, they are united by a single rallying symbol: the *gwenn ha du* or black and white flag. During nationalist protest marches it can be seen held aloft, at arm's length.

Breton militancy defies definition – it is by nature fragmented, taking many forms. In essence it is a rather nebulous turmoil made up of small, sometimes rival groups. The political side of things is essentially represented by the Union Démocratique Bretonne (UDB), a group that has often flirted with the socialist party. At the other end of the scale, the Armée Révolutionnaire Bretonne (ARB, now officially disbanded) was the radical bastion of the armed struggle. Between these two exist a variety of different groups, including Diwan, which organizes schooling in Breton; Stourm-ar-Brezhoneg, which advocates official bilingualism; Emgann, a group dedicated to reform; and Kendalc'h, which teaches Breton music and dance.

The Breton language has a strong presence throughout Brittany. Both television and radio stations offer programmes in Breton. Road signs are given in both French and Breton in the *départements* of Finistère, Morbihan and the Côtes-d'Armor, and the Breton flag can be seen fluttering above some official buildings. Plenty of cars carry a 'BZH' badge – this stands for Breizh, the Breton word for 'Brittany'. Other expressions of Breton nationalism can be seen in the regional press, its literature and its cultural movements, although the degree of political commitment seems to vary considerably. It is difficult to see where the boundary lies between simple regionalism and aggressive nationalism.

Clearly, in the prevailing economic climate, Brittany has witnessed a move towards a more independent identity over the last few years. To illustrate this point, 1996 saw the creation, in Rennes, of the Comité Consultatif de l'Identité Bretonne (consultative committee on Breton identity), whose aim is to promote all forms of regional expression.

Breton Emblems

The ermine became the emblem for Brittany at the beginning of the 12th century, as a result of the marriage of Alix, heiress to the Duchy of Brittany, to Pierre de Dreux (known as 'Mauclerc'), a duke of the House of Capet. In addition to his family coat of arms, Mauclerc wore a heraldic ermine, to distinguish himself from other members of his family. Surprisingly, Alix took her husband's coat of arms, including the ermine, instead of using her own, and before long, coins in Brittany bore the device of an ermine.

Brittany has taken the ermine as its motto, in the phrase *Plutôt la mort que la souillure*, which means 'death before dishonour'. The immaculate white ermine is believed to choose death in preference to getting itself dirty, a story thought to have originated with Anne of Brittany. One day when she was out riding, an ermine being pursued by huntsmen was seen to stand its ground and prepare to die rather than run across a wide stretch of mud. Naturally, Anne saved the ermine's life by pleading with the huntsmen and from that time onwards, used its image on her coat of arms. The ermine is also represented on the Breton flag.

The Breton Flag

The striped Breton flag is known as the *gwenn ha du* – the 'black and white'. Created in 1923 by Morvan Marchal, the founder of the militant nationalist movement known as *Breizh Atao*, the flag was declared to be the Breton national flag in 1927. Its five black stripes symbolize the dioceses in Upper Brittany that speak French (Rennes, Nantes, Dol, St-Malo and Penthièvre) while the four white stripes represent the parts of Lower Brittany (Cornouaille, Léon, Trégor and Vannetais) where Breton is spoken. The 11 black ermines on the flag are thought to denote the 11 dukes and duchesses who ruled over Brittany.

The first Breton flag dates from 1188. Crusaders on the Third Crusade were asked to wear their national flag by way of identity, and at that time, the Bretons were fighting under a banner that bore a black cross on a white background – the *Kroaz Du*. In the 13th century, in the reign of Pierre Mauclerc, the flag of the Duchy consisted of black ermines on a white background.

This traditional design was rejected by Marchal's militant movement in the 1920s due to its rather medieval appearance and the fact that the ermines bore too much resemblance to the *fleurs-de-lis* that were scattered on a white background on the French royalist flag. The nationalists were, of course, mostly Republicans.

Banned after World War II, the flag nevertheless became the emblem of the nationalist revival in the 1970s. Today it has proper recognition as the Breton flag and is widely used. Jean-Loup Chrétien, a French astronaut of Breton origins, even took it into space.

BACKGROUND

The *Triskèle* (or *triskell*)

Apart from the striped flag, the ermine and the *triskèle* are the two main emblems of Brittany. This is a kind of cross made up of three spiralling legs, joined up by a triangle. The three branches represent the three natural elements of air, fire and water and this was used by the Celts as a motif on their helmets and shields. Its use revived at the end of the medieval period, and is seen in religious art and on country furniture. During the 20th century, it took on a nationalist connotation, with several political groups and druidic sects using it as their emblem. It is also now a common motif to be found on the Celtic jewellery that is produced in Brittany, especially rings and pendants.

The Celtic Cross

The cross is the basic symbol of Christian belief and is usually depicted by the Celtic races within a circle. Circles were significant for the druids, and their rites were always held within the protection of a circle. The wheel also played a part in Celtic tradition, as it epitomized the notion that 'time turns but does not pass'. This belief is still common in Brittany today.

The Brittany–Wales Connection

Originally, the Bretons were 'boat-people' – refugees driven out of their own country of Britain (now Great Britain) during wartime and forced to set sail in rickety boats to seek a better world. There is much evidence to show us that Brittany was, in fact, largely founded by emigrants from Wales.

This influx began around the 5th century. At that time, Britain was largely populated by Britons, who had lived there for hundreds of years. The last legions of the Roman Empire were no longer able to withstand the pressure from the Barbarians around the extensive borders of their Empire and were abandoning their most far-flung territories. As the Romans departed, they left the way clear for the Picts and the Scots, in the north, and the Saxons in the east. Little by little, the invaders forced the Britons into the mountainous regions of Cambria (the old name for Wales) and into Devon and Cornwall. Many preferred to flee across the Channel to seek refuge in Armorique, or what is now the Brittany peninsula.

Other waves of emigrants were to follow, primarily adventurers looking for virgin land to settle. This mass exodus lasted for more than 150 years, from 450 to about 600. The Christians who landed in Armorique, the vast majority of whom had come from Cornwall or South Wales, named their new land 'Bretagne' or 'Brittany', after the country they had left behind.

The emigrants in Brittany followed the natural instinct of people who had converted to Christianity – they built the first monasteries, constructed hermitages and founded churches, naming them all as they would have done had they still been in Wales. This explains the striking similarity between place names in Brittany and in Wales. Many of the names of places in Wales start with 'Llan', 'Tre' or 'Aber', as they do in Brittany (especially in Finistère, Morbihan and the Côtes-d'Armor). The 5th-century migrants all spoke the same language: Breton. Today, linguistic development means that a Breton will understand little Welsh, although a Welshman may well get the gist of a phrase in Breton. There are many similarities in the written words.

The spiritual elite were brought over from the Welsh monasteries in order to keep the religious flame burning. Many monks and adventurers became the most famous saints in Brittany: David (the patron saint of Wales), Samson ('Samzun' in Breton), Malo (who founded the town of St-Malo), Brieuc (St-Brieuc), and Guirec (who gave his name to Perros-Guirec). And there were also adventurer saints: Gwenolé, Tugdual (one of the seven founding saints of the Breton dioceses), Goueznou, Iltud (the discoverer of l'Aber-Ildut), Goneri, Gildas (Gweltaz), Méen and Thelo (there is more than one place called Llandeilo in Wales).

The linguistic similarities between so many of the place names make it clear that a significant number of Breton towns and villages were originally founded by emigrants from Wales in the 6th century AD. There are plenty of interesting examples:

– In St-Malo, there is a road called rue Mac-Law (which later became 'Malo'), named after the town's founder. **St Malo** lived in what is now Gwent in southeast Wales in the second half of the 5th century. He attended the monastic school in Llancarfan in Glamorgan, a monastery from which large numbers of saints left for Armorique.

– L'Aber-Ildut (Finistère) is derived from the name of **St Iltud**, who was born in Wales in the 5th century. He founded the monastic school in Llantwit (now Llantwit Major – the Welsh name for this town is Llanilltud Fawr: 'Llan' means 'church' and 'fawr' is a mutated form of 'mawr' or 'major') in Glamorgan, where many of the Breton saints were educated, before emigrating to Armorique. One of his disciples, who went by the name of Lunaire, arrived in 535 near to what is now Dinard. This is the origin of the place name St-Lunaire.

– St-Pol-de-Léon (Finistère) is derived from the name of **Paul** (nicknamed Aurélien) who was born around 492 in Penohen (meaning 'cow's head') in Glamorgan. He emigrated to Armorique, together with many of his disciples, including Tégonec (Coneg or Conog).

– The seaside resort of Perros-Guirec (Côtes-d'Armor) owes its name to **St Guirec** (Kireg), a poor Briton who lived in Wales and crossed the seas with a group of 60 selected monks.

– The town of St-Brieuc (Côtes-d'Armor) was founded by **Brieg** (Brigomaglos) who was born near Aberystwyth in Mid-Wales.

– **St Cado**, who is very famous in Morbihan, was born in Wales in about 522. The son of one of the kings of Glamorgan, he emigrated to Brittany after spending 12 years in Llancarfan monastery.

– **St David** (Dewi) is the most popular saint in Wales (and the patron saint). Although he never actually crossed the sea to Brittany, he still lends his name to St-Divy (Finistère).

– **St Gunthiern** (or Gurthiern), one of the Briton kings of Cambria, left his country and landed on the island of Groix where he adopted the lifestyle of a hermit.

– The town of Landerneau (Finistère) was founded in the 5th century by a Welshman called **Ténénan** or Tinidor. He arrived by boat, sailed up the river (now the Elorn), and christened his new world 'Lan-Tenedor'.

IMPORTANT DATES

– **c. 2200 BC**: the local people, of whom we know very little, begin to erect megaliths, menhirs, dolmens and covered walkways.

– **4th to 1st century BC**: expansion of the Celts into what was then called Armorique. The country is divided among a number of tribes: Osismes and Curiosolites in the north; Venetes, Redones and Namnetes in the south.

– **56 BC**: Julius Caesar's troops defeat the Venetes; Roman occupation of Armorica begins.

– **c. 400**: pursued by the Angles and the Saxons, the Britons from Britain (as opposed to Bretons from Brittany) cross the Channel and set up their own Little Britain (Brittany), where they found hermitages. These would later turn into the walled parish enclosures that became typical in the region.

– **831**: deposition of Wido, the Comte de Vannes; he is replaced by Nominoë.

– **846**: constitution of the monarchy. Charles le Chauve (Charles the Bald) recognizes the independence of Brittany, of which Nominoë is pronounced king.

– **939**: last Norman invasions, led by Alain Barbe-Torte. By now, Breton is spoken throughout Armorique.

– **1341–65**: Brittany is ravaged by a war of succession between the Blois and the Montfort families. The outcome is the accession of a Montfort, Jean IV, to the ducal throne.

– **1399–1442**: reign of Duke Jean V, the father of a splendid period in Brittany when its navy was one of the most powerful in the world. He is crowned in Rennes, and reigns from a magnificent castle in Nantes. He names ambassadors to the Pope, raises his own army and gives his homeland a tremendous boost.

– **1406**: birth of Gilles de Rais, in Machecoul. Known as 'Bluebeard', who became infamous for heinous crimes that it is now thought he never actually committed.

– **1488**: defeat of the Breton army at St-Aubin-du-Cormier, Ille-et-Vilaine, and signing of the regrettable 'Verger' Treaty, which subjected Brittany to the rule of a France still reeling from the Hundred Years War.

– **1491**: Anne of Brittany becomes the queen of France by marrying Charles VIII.

– **1498**: Charles VIII dies; Anne remarries, with King Louis XII.

– **1514**: death of Anne of Brittany. Her daughter, Claude of France, inherits the duchy and marries the Comte d'Angoulême and Duc de Valois, who later becomes King François I.

– **1532**: in Vannes in August, the state of Brittany signs the act that unites Brittany and France. The act undertakes to respect Breton privileges, but fails to meets many of its promises.

– **1675**: revolt by the *bonnets rouges* in response to the tax imposed on stamped paper. The revolt is brutally suppressed by the governor of the province, the Duc de Chaulnes.

– **16th, 17th and 18th centuries**: Brittany enjoys the height of religious and popular art. Numerous churches, chapels, crosses and fountains are built, using local granite.

– **1718**: the Marquis de Pontcallec takes part in a plot to 'defend the freedom of Brittany'. He is beheaded in 1720.

– **1768**: birth in St-Malo of Chateaubriand, who becomes a writer, a diplomat and a minister.

– **1789**: year of revolution in France and in Brittany. Representatives of the province found the Club Breton, which later becomes the Club des Jacobins, the radical faction of the Revolution.

– **1793–99**: the Chouan movement develops around its historical leaders, Cadoudal, La Rouërie and du Boisguy. The episode concludes with a massacre at Savenay, near Pontchâteau.

– **1828**: birth of writer Jules Verne in Nantes.

– **1919–39**: revival of the Breton nationalist movement. Foundation of the *Breizh Atao* newspaper, the Breton autonomist party (1927) and the Breton nationalist party (1932). First terrorist attacks by autonomists (1932).

– **1957**: formation of the Mouvement pour l'Organisation de la Bretagne (MOB) (movement for the organization of Brittany), and the Comité d'étude et de Liaison des Intérêts Bretons (committee for the study of and for liaison on Breton interests).

– **1966**: first bomb attacks by the Front de Libération de la Bretagne (FLB) – the Breton Liberation Front.

– **1970–80**: complete cultural and economic revolution. Breton musicians Alan Stivell and Pierre Jakez Helias reach a wide audience.

– **1972**: questionable decision to re-amalgamate the department of Loire-Atlantique into the Pays de la Loire region.

– **7 May 1989**: explosion at the regional headquarters in Nantes.

– **March 1992**: local elections. The Greens enter the political arena with a combination of ecology and cultural identity in preparation for the 'eleventh plan'.

– **1996**: Creation in Rennes of the Comité Consultatif de l'Identité Bretonne (consultative committee on Breton identity).

– **September 1996**: Pope John Paul II celebrates a mass at Ste-Anne d'Auray in front of more than 100,000 people. The event confirms the recent religious revival in Brittany.

– **12 December 1999**: the Fina petrol-tanker *Erika* is wrecked off the coast of Finistère. The resulting oil slick stretches down the Breton coastline as far as the Vendée, with serious consequences for the ecological balance of the

BACKGROUND

whole region. Attempts to alleviate the problem are hampered by violent storms at the end of the month.

– **October 2000**: one year on, the beaches are finally pronounced clean after a massive effort by the military, working with teams of volunteers.

GEOGRAPHY

The Breton peninsula is about the same size as Belgium. Its highest point lies at a height of a mere 384 metres (1,260 feet) – this is at the top of Tuchen Gador, in the mountain range (using 'mountain' in the loosest sense of the word) that extends from Brest to Lamballe. Parallel to the south coast are the Montagnes Noires ('Black Mountains'), which stretch from Locronan in the Baie de Douarnenez across to Malestroit, northeast of Vannes, gently flattening out as they go. Between the two is a series of basins, at Châteaulin, Loudéac and Rennes.

The Armorican Massif is as old as the Vosges or the Ardennes, in the east of France. Two-thirds of its surface is shale, with granite and gneiss, micas-chists and quartzites making up the rest, and giving the region its rounded yet distinctive shapes. The tortuous route travelled by the River Argoat, for example, is one result of this unusual geological formation. Even in the very depths of the Breton countryside, nowhere is ever more than 100 kilometres (60 miles) from the sea and its influence is felt everywhere.

What is perhaps most remarkable about the coastline of Brittany is the way that, from one end of the region to the other, its rugged promontories alternate with charming beaches. Constantly battered by the tides, the sea has a tidal range of 10–12 metres (30–40 feet) along the English Channel and one of 5–6 metres (16–20 feet) on the Atlantic coast.

The sea level has changed a number of times and the last major event, known as the 'Flanders movement' encroached into areas that had already been settled by man. Examples of this exist in the cromlech of Er Lanic in the Golfe du Morbihan in the south and at Le Conquet, to the west of Brest. The low-lying land around the Mont-St-Michel was submerged during this period, as, it is thought, was the town of Ys in the Baie de Douarnenez. As the sea penetrated deeper into the land, it invaded the river estuaries, changing the shape of the landscape yet again.

ECONOMY

The Breton economy operates at two levels. After a decline in the 1970s and early 1980s, prosperity is now, finally, on the increase in the east, in larger towns such as Rennes, Vitré and Redon, and in Upper Brittany in general.

Bounded by the sea on three sides, the Breton peninsula has 1,200 kilometres (745 miles) of coastline, which contribute substantially towards providing the environment and the economy with an interesting mixture of rural and maritime interests. Improved roads and fast rail connections have played a part in making Brittany appear much more accessible, especially with the construction of the autoroute all the way to Brest and with the introduction, too, of the TGV high-speed trains along a route from Paris to Brest via Rennes.

The regional capital of Rennes is soon to benefit from an automatic metro service, with completion due in 2002. Within the sphere of industry, Brittany is home to a number of research projects. As much as 34 per cent of electronic research carried out in France is done in the region, as well as 14 per cent of the medical research and 8 per cent of the research relating to food crops. Overall, with unemployment figures slightly below the national average, Brittany has very little to complain about, except perhaps the lack of qualified or experienced workers in areas such as building, where demand has outstripped supply.

AGRICULTURE AND FISHING

Brittany is France's main agricultural area, although nationally, the industry now represents only 10 per cent of the population. Livestock farming accounts for three-quarters of the agricultural output of the region, with Brittany leading the way in the production of French pork, beef, veal and chicken.

All along the Atlantic coast of North Brittany are areas that are blessed with good-quality soil and a favourable climate, notably the strip between St-Malo and Cancale, and the *ceinture dorée* ('golden belt') around Roscoff. The farmers here have an excellent reputation for producing first-class vegetables, including artichokes, cauliflower, potatoes, tomatoes and French beans and many of them have now gone over to organic methods.

Fishing in North Brittany takes place all along the coast between St-Malo and Brest and is very much of a traditional nature except at the industrial port of St-Malo itself. In season, the market is supplied with stocks of sea bass, sole, pollock and angler fish as well as spider crabs, common crabs, prawns and the much-prized scallops and oysters.

INDUSTRY

Salting plants, dairies, slaughterhouses and factories where fish and vegetables are canned and ready meals and animal feeds are prepared, are all natural by-products of the agricultural production in the region. These industries have kept their head above water even in spite of the difficulties presented by BSE.

Ille-et-Vilaine is best known for its dairy produce and for its beef, pork and poultry, while pork is the mainstay in Côtes d'Armor, centred around Lamballe. Agri-food production in North Finistère is concentrated in fish canneries and the production of biscuits.

The electronics and telecommunications sector in Brittany is reinforced by a strong research industry. The Atalante technical centre in Rennes has been a breeding ground for a number of cutting-edge developments that are important in France. These have included the development of the Minitel system, a kind of primitive Internet system used for looking up information on directories and databases, and Transpac, a data transfer package. Similar

BACKGROUND

centres are located at Lannion (Anticipa) and at Brest (Iroise), which has become the European capital for maritime science.

North Brittany also has its share of major industrial names, with a Citroën car factory at Rennes, and a shipbuilding industry at Brest as well as Alcatel, Mitsubishi and Canon.

THE SERVICE SECTOR

The service sector, which encompasses administration, the army, commerce, transport, services and tourism, now provides the largest number of jobs in Brittany, and some 60 per cent of the working population now work in this sector. In the past five years, retail outlets have increased hugely in number, with numerous developments outside the main centres of population. The Leclerc chain of hypermarkets started out in Finistère at Landerneau.

Tourism in North Brittany is also thriving, with the greatest number of visitors travelling to the Côtes d'Armor. It is hardly surprising that Brittany as a whole has become France's second most popular summer holiday destination, attracting large numbers of visitors from elsewhere in Europe.

THE PEOPLE

THE BRETONS AND THE SEA

It seems strange that in many of the coastal regions of Brittany, the local people for a long time had no more connection with the sea than people living inland. Even now, very few of the islands off the Breton coast derive their livelihood from fishing. The little island of Batz, where the only traditional activity is agriculture, is a classic example. Many of the notorious inhabitants of this infamous stretch of North Finistère coastline only ever got their feet wet when they went scavenging wrecked ships or collecting seaweed to turn into fertilizer.

Many Bretons believe that the sea will only bring bad luck, and the best way to live a quiet life is to avoid it. Some Breton towns, such as St-Malo and Cancale, have always relied on the sea for their livelihood, but they are not in the majority.

When watersports, and particularly sailing, came into fashion at the beginning of the 20th century, it was hardly a major populist movement. Only middle-class families with second homes on the coast were likely to devote themselves to messing about on the water. In the 1950s, hobby sailing and dinghies became the real craze, and trendy young things from Carnac to St-Malo went mad about anything to do with sailing or surfing, though this largely passed the older natives of Brittany by.

The turning point came in 1964, when a young Breton navy officer thought up the crazy idea of beating the British at their own game and invented the famous 'Transat' sailing race. Éric Tabarly become not only a national celebrity, but also came to be seen by the media as the symbol of Breton identity. The Bretons in their little cottages took this to heart, and began to look out towards wider horizons. Further glory was to follow for Brittany, as others were swept along by Tabarly's success. In the 1970s and 80s, many Breton sailors went on to gain celebrity, winning Transats, making round-the-world voyages and putting their names into the record-books.

From that time onwards, even the smallest sailing clubs in the remotest parts have been inundated by young Bretons dreaming of glory. Some have even gone on to win Olympic medals, apparently driven on by a desire to conquer the ocean.

It makes no sense to talk about Bretons and the sea without mentioning fishing. Once only a means of subsistence, fishing has now become a leisure activity for local people and tourists alike. In Brittany, children on holiday go hunting for shrimps or crabs in little rock pools. But even leisure fishing is not a simple task and it requires some experience. Every port or village has its own 'champion' who knows all the rocks in his area and uses his tide-table in order to be in the right place at the right time. Like the expert mushroom-picker, he will guard his secrets jealously. Good fishermen are sparing in what they take from nature; they maintain their 'patch' by allowing the shellfish to grow before fishing them, and putting back any rocks they overturn along the way.

See also 'Seaweed and Seaweed Farming' in 'Food and Drink'.

BACKGROUND

FAMOUS BRETONS

Anne, Duchess of Brittany was the most famous woman in the history of the province, which formed part of her dowry when she married the French king. Many writers can claim Breton ancestry, from the 18th-century diplomat and writer Chateaubriand to 'Beat Generation' novelist and poet Jack Kerouac. The following selection is completely subjective.

Gérard d'Aboville: solo rower who has crossed the Atlantic and the Pacific. When he is not off on one of his extraordinary adventures, he lives near Auray, where he was born in 1945.

Fulgence Bienvenüe: born in 1852 in Uzel (Côtes d'Armor), this engineer invented the Paris Métro system and oversaw its creation. He is the only person to have had a metro station named after him (Montparnasse-Bienvenüe) in his own lifetime.

Bernard Hinault: born in 1954 in Yffiniac, *the* star of world cycling between 1975 and 1986. Now working in industry, and very much back in his homeland, he can still be seen pedalling from one meeting to another.

Jack Kerouac (real name Jacques Lebris de Kerouac): the author of *On the Road*, and one of the leading lights of the 'Beat Generation', came from a Breton family that emigrated to Canada.

Alfred Jarry: born in Laval, this forerunner of surrealism spent his childhood at St-Brieuc, where the folklore of Brittany provided his early poetic inspiration. Best remembered for his Theatre of the Absurd piece *Roi Ubu*.

Louis Jouvet: born in Crozon in 1887, Jouvet was a master comedian and provided the inspiration for generations of comedians to come.

Miou Miou: the actress known as Miou Miou was born in 1950 in Plouenan near Morlaix. She made a sensational film debut in *Les Valseuses*, with Gérard Depardieu.

Anne Quéffelec: this virtuoso pianist was born in Brest. Her brother **Yann** won the French literary Prix Goncourt for his *Noces barbares*.

Alain Resnais: from Vannes, a director who has often filmed in his native country.

Yves Rocher: world-famous producer of plant-based cosmetic products in La Gacilly, a town with 2,100 inhabitants, of which he is also the mayor and the chief benefactor.

Alan Stivell: born Alain Cochevelou in Langonnet, creator of ethno-modern Breton music over a period of more than 20 years. With 15 hit albums, he is one of the few Breton-speaking singers/musicians to have reached the French Top 50.

BRETONS IN CARICATURE

Astérix and Obelix: despite their Frenchness, this cartoon series featuring two Armorican 'Gauls' have brought pleasure to people of all ages and cultures all over the world. They were created as a result of the collaborative genius of writer, Uderzo, and illustrator, Goscinny. The personality of Astérix is an example of how the French consider a typical Breton to be – a bolshie, loud-mouthed libertarian.

Bécassine: created in 1905 by the writer Caumery working with the illustrator Pichon, Bécassine was a lifelong inhabitant of Clocher-les-Bécasses, a fictional village near Quimper in southern Brittany. An old-fashioned governess, she was always full of ideas and bursting with common sense. Much loved by the nation for years, particularly during the pre-World War II period, Bécassine's popularity is enduring and she is still on sale in many bookshops today.

THE BRETONS IN PARIS

There was a mass exodus of Bretons to Paris in the early 20th century, leaving behind the countryside that could no longer support them. Arriving by train at the large Montparnasse station in the centre of Paris they frequently settled down where they landed, close to the station. These poor migrants formed their own little groups, opened cafés named after their native towns and set up social and traditional associations (now known as cultural associations) to keep the spirit of their region alive.

It was a Breton from Uzel, the engineer Fulgence Bienvenüe, who made it possible for the Paris Métro to be built under the city. (*See* 'Famous Bretons'.)

THE LANGUAGES OF BRITTANY

Breton is spoken in the west and a dialect called 'Gallo' in the east. It's not as simple as that though, as the Breton-speaking region is divided into the Vannetais and the Léonard, and there are even further subdivisions.

Brittany has its roots in the colonies of emigrants who came from Great Britain in the 5th century (see 'The Brittany–Wales Connection' in 'History and Politics'). Like Welsh and Cornish, Breton is also derived from the language of the Britons, which itself has its roots in Celtic.

Modern place names and family names date back to some time between the 5th and the 9th century, when the old Breton language was spoken. In 1464, the first Breton/French/Latin dictionary was produced. Curiously, Breton was never spoken in Nantes or in Rennes, even though the latter was the historical capital of the old duchy. However, between the 9th and the 11th centuries, it was spoken virtually right across Upper Brittany, west of a line running from Mont-St-Michel in the north down to Pornic (in the Vendée). There were also Breton settlers in the *département* of Mayenne, in Normandy and on the island of Jersey.

The 'Gallo' dialect was also spoken (the Bretons refer to the French as *gallecs*, or 'foreigners'). Like the Frankish, Picardy and Norman dialects, this was a romance language derived from popular Latin and a branch of the old medieval French dialects.

Since the Third Republic (in the latter half of the 19th century), which dictated that French must be taught everywhere, both Breton and Gallo have declined both in terms of numbers of speakers and influence. Today, there are about 665,000 people who claim that they can understand Breton, most of these living to the west of a line running from Paimpol on the north coast to Vannes in the south. Breton speakers today are generally confined to those aged over 40, or with a farming background, and live in Côtes-d'Armor or Finistère.

There is also an academic variation of Breton, which is taught in Rennes and Brest. Out of the 32,700 students in this region taking their Baccalauréat (high school-leaving) exams at the age of 18, around a thousand candidates sit an exam in Breton, compared with only 800 who take an exam in Gallo.

Bilingual road signs have become a part of life. Private Breton schools sponsored by the Diwan ('the seed') organization have been integrated into the national education system and there are newspapers and rock songs in Breton. In addition, the recent rediscovery of *Barzaz-Breizh*, a collection of popular songs immortalized as long ago as 1839, has provided material for programmes on regional television, but there are, however, no programmes in Gallo.

Spoken Breton sounds like a cross between lisping English and more guttural German. Some of the sounds are quite harsh to the ear and the grammar and vocabulary are difficult to pick up unless you are a linguist. Listed below are some words that will be useful in understanding signs as well as food and place names.

See also 'The Brittany–Wales Connection'.

BACKGROUND

COMMON WORDS IN BRETON

aber	estuary (in north Finistère; *see also 'aven'*)
amann	butter
argoat	land
armor	sea
avel	wind
aven	estuary (in south Finistère); *see also 'aber'*
bara	bread (*bara mar plij*: some bread, please)
bihan	small (Le Bihan is a common surname)
braz	big (*Mor-Braz*: ocean). See also '*mor*' and '*bihan*'.
Breizh	Brittany (*Mor-Breizh*: the English Channel)
coat	wood, forest
coz	old (*ar tad koz*: grandfather)
dol	table (*dolmen*: stone table) (also seen as '*taol*' and '*tol*')
dour	water
enez	island
feunteun	fountain
gast!	shit! (the most common swear word)
gwin	wine (*gwin ru*: red wine)
heol	sun
hir	long (*menhir*: long stone)
huel	high
iliz	church
izel	low (*Breizh izel*: eastern Brittany)
kastell	castle
kenavo	goodbye
ker	village, hamlet, group of houses – 18,000 place names in Brittany begin with 'Ker', making it the most common prefix in the region.
kouign	cake (*kouign-amann*: cake made with a lot of butter)
lan	sacred place, monastery, hermitage
lann	moor, gorse
loc	isolated place, hermitage, religious foundation
mad	good (*Bloavez Mad*: Happy New Year; *digemer mad*: welcome)
men	stone, rock
menez *or* méné	eroded hill with a rounded top
meur	large, vast (*botmeur*: large bush)
mor	sea (*ar moraer*: sailor; *ar morzen*: siren). See also '*bihan*', '*braz*' and '*Breizh*'.
nevez	new
penn	end, head (*Penn Ar Bed*: the end of the land = Finistère)
pesk	fish (*ar toul pesked*: fish soup).
plou, pleu, plo, plu	parish. The most popular place name prefix after *Ker*. *Plou*: an organization of cultivated land (cf *plough* in English), grouping together numerous hamlets scattered across the countryside. (*See also* * *below*.)
roc'h	ridge, schist rock; the opposite of *menez*
taol, tol	root of *dol*: table

ti	individual house (*pen ti*: small house; *ti an aod*: coastal house)
tref, *trev*, *tre*	place or parish division
traez henn	beach (*an draezhenn*: the shore)
war-raok	in front
war sav	standing up
Yar-mat!	Cheers!

* The pejorative French expression *une bande de ploucs* ('a bunch of country bumpkins') was coined by non-Bretons to describe unsophisticated people. *Plouc* is derived from the Breton place name *plou* (*see above*).

COMMON FAMILY NAMES

Briand:	this name means 'elevation' or 'privilege' and is very common in Brittany
Le Gall	from *gallus*, meaning Gaulish
Le Goff	'blacksmith', or 'person with magic powers'
Morvan	from *meur man*, which means 'great spirit'

TRADITION AND CUSTOMS

THE DRUIDS

The heart of ancient druidism lay on the island of Anglesey (formerly Mona) in Wales. Although Julius Caesar was sufficiently interested to mention it in his chronicle *The Gallic Wars,* this did not seem to have stopped him massacring the druids who lived there. Druids, along with poets and bards, existed in all the Celtic countries: Ireland, Scotland, Wales, Cornwall, Devon, the Isle of Man and, of course, in the peninsula of Brittany.

A druid was at the very top of the social hierarchy, superior even to the Celtic king. A priest, judge and teacher all in one, his name originated from the word *druwi-des,* which means 'very far-sighted, very wise'. Druids were seen as interpreters of divine wishes, and made sacrifices to Ésus, Teutatès, Taranis and Bélénus (the god of the sun), as well as to the other main gods in the druid pantheon.

For the druid, nature, trees and plants were sacred and he worshipped the oak – the king of the trees – as the Celtic representation of Jupiter. Dressed in a white robe, a druid would climb an oak tree and use a golden sickle to gather magical mistletoe in a white cloth.

The assumption that it was the druids who erected dolmens and menhirs is wrong. These megaliths existed long before the arrival of the Celts, although it is possible that the druids used them for their rituals.

The druid still exists today. It is thought that there are as many as a million in Great Britain and 60,000 in France, counting all the different sects. In modern Brittany, the traditional *Gorsedd* branch of druidism is still active.

STORIES AND LEGENDS

The concept of Brittany as a 'land of legends' has been much exploited by marketing people, who never seem to pass up the opportunity to dwell on the region's 'mysterious' dimension in their bid to entice visitors. What this superficial approach tends to conceal, however, is a genuine Breton tendency to make up stories and legends. The following are just some of the more common characters from Breton legend:

Ankou: something you wouldn't want to meet on a dark night – a skeleton armed with a scythe, this is the traditional Breton herald of death. He rides around at night on his *karrig an Ankou* ('Ankou's chariot'), carrying off the dead to the 'other side'. People believe that if you hear the wheels of the chariot creaking, then a loved one is soon to die. In certain coastal areas, Ankou is said to carry out his deadly job aboard the *bag noz* ('night boat'). No one ever returns from an encounter with this grim reaper.

King Arthur and the Arthurian legends: in medieval times, many Breton tales revolved around the legends connected with King Arthur. The stories of King Arthur and the Knights of the Round Table are common to both Brittany and Britain, with both countries claiming Arthur and his court as their own. In Brittany, the existence of Arthur has been localized to the Forêt de Brocéliande in the 11th century, some people believing that the spirits of Arthur, Lancelot, Percival, Merlin the Magician, Guinevere and Morgan Le Fay still haunt the old forest at Brocéliande. (*See* 'Forêt de Paimpont', in Ille-et-Vilaine.)

The Korrigans: These little dwarves (*korr* means 'dwarf' and the suffix *ig* means 'little') crop up all the time in traditional stories. They live in the countryside and generally make their dens in caves or dolmens, where they collect immense riches, which they bestow on humans from time to time. They are also capable of handing out severe punishments to those who do not believe in them.

PARDONS

Brittany seems to have more religious monuments than any other region in Europe. For centuries, the local people demonstrated their faith in God by building elaborate churches and by creating beautiful sculpted calvaries and crosses.

It was against this background of religious fervour that the *pardons* developed. These are annual festivals organized with the aim of paying collective homage to the local saint, and provide a tangible intermediary between man and eternal life. Almost every community church and chapel has its own *pardon*, each beginning with a mass followed by a costumed procession during which coloured embroidered banners and flags are carried, along with statues and relics of the saint or saints that are being honoured.

Every parish had a shrine, or sometimes many shrines, to its own saint, located in little chapels dotted around the countryside, and a *pardon* will sometimes progress around the local shrines, making a splendid visual treat for visitors.

Today, the *pardons* are many and varied and, while some of them retain a religious flavour, others do not. Whatever form they take, all the *pardons* in Brittany have witnessed a revival over the last few years.

For an extensive list of *pardons* in North Brittany, *see* 'Festivals and Events' in 'General Information'. Although *pardons* take place annually, be aware that the actual dates often change from one year to the next. For precise information, check with the annual lists held by local tourist offices.

THE *TRO BREIZH* ('TOUR OF BRITTANY')

The *Tro Breizh*, or 'Tour of Brittany', is in fact a pilgrimage through the seven towns that were founded by the seven founders of Christianity in Brittany: the route covers Vannes and Quimper, in South Brittany to St-Pol-de-Léon, Tréguier, St-Brieuc, St-Malo and Dol-de-Bretagne in North Brittany. The tradition of the tour goes back to the 9th century, when those who completed the pilgrimage were guaranteed entry into heaven; those who did not were forced to cover the same distance in purgatory after their death, moving forward slowly, by the length of their coffin every seven years! Although the pilgrimage was very popular in the 12th and 13th centuries, it had almost disappeared by the end of the Middle Ages. It was resurrected again in 1994, by the two organizations, detailed below.

■ **La route historique du Tro Breizh**: Boulevard Hérault, 22000 St-Brieuc. ☎ 02-96-33-10-22. This organization's main aim is to renovate all the sites associated with the *Tro Breizh*, including the chapels.

■ **Les Chemins du Tro Breizh**: based in St-Pol-de-Léon. ☎ 02-98-69-16-53. This group organizes a pilgrimage between two of the towns on the *Tro Breizh* every year.

HEADGEAR AND COSTUMES

Traditional Breton costume is recorded only as far back as the 16th century. Records exist of nearly 70 different costumes and forms of headgear, each representing a different community, which can be anything from a parish to a whole region. These all contribute to a wider Breton identity.

A woman decked out in traditional Breton headgear is generally known as *une Bigoudène*. The name refers to the region known as the Pays Bigouden on the Penmarc'h peninsula in South Finistère, where the habit of wearing the traditional costume lasted longer than anywhere else in Brittany.

The everyday use of these costumes is now almost entirely a thing of the past, although a few women, particularly in the regions of Pont-Aven (South Finistère) and Plougastel-Daoulas (North Finistère), can still be seen wearing them. Traditional costume is still brought out for *pardons* and other processions and celebrations, and it is also sometimes worn by Celtic groups at traditional festivals. You may also catch sight of them at a *festnoz* ('festival of the night') or at the Lorient Celtic Festival.

BACKGROUND

FOOD AND DRINK

BRETON CUISINE

Long considered to be something rather rustic, staid and family-oriented, Breton cuisine is now rapidly catching up with *cordon bleu* standards and is experiencing a new lease of life. Skilled, dedicated Breton chefs – not to be confused with those in it merely for the money – are appearing or are even coming back to settle in the area. Foodies are now rediscovering the culinary heritage of the area, which offers a huge range of seafood, superb poultry, and excellent meats. The Bretons have also rediscovered sugar, and have invented some fabulous desserts.

Restaurant prices in Brittany are still affordable and everyone can make the most of their holiday by sampling some of the region's fresh and seasonal produce. Scallops are a speciality in winter, which is the only time they are caught, and langoustines come into season in the summer. Try to eat according to the seasons, to get the best of everything.

Fish: inevitably a speciality of a region that is bounded on two sides by the sea. Common species that are caught in Breton waters include sardine, tuna, red mullet, skate, mackerel, coley, monkfish, sea bass, sea bream and herring. The rivers and wetlands also provide a good number of salmon and trout, as well as frogs and eels. Fish is delicious eaten plain, with just a dab of butter, or it can be subjected to all kinds of flights of culinary fancy. The new cuisine that is now so popular in Brittany has produced a number of interesting treatments. Even fish soup, which may not sound exciting, has its own gourmet variations – the soup known as *cotriade* is a match for the much-vaunted *bouillabaisse* from the south of France. The principle is the same: add the fish of the day to a stock and add some wine.

Mussels and shellfish: oysters and mussels are two of Brittany's most important shellfish, with the produce from some areas having an especially high reputation – the mussels from Pénestin and from Vivier-sur-Mer in the Baie de St-Malo, for example, or the oysters from Belon, Cancale, the *abers* of Finistère and the Golfe du Morbihan These days, oysters are eaten every month of the year, even in months with an 'r' in them. Flat oysters (*huîtres plates*) are less rich than 'hollow' oysters (*huîtres creuses*), but it's a matter of taste, and both kinds are delicious.

Mussels can be found on just about every restaurant menu in the summer, and are eaten in a variety of ways, including *à la marinière* (in white wine sauce), *en éclade* and *en mouclade*. *Éclade* is a summer dish where the shells are placed face down on a slate plate, and covered with pine needles, which are then lit. Once the pine needles have burnt out, the ashes are blown away and the mussels underneath are ready to eat. Just be careful not to burn your fingers!

The recipe for *mouclade* is more complicated. The mussels are opened by heating them in a little white wine with a bouquet garni, then one half of the shell is removed. A white *roux* sauce is then prepared, using the juice in which the mussels were cooked, to which is added an egg yolk and (the magic ingredient) a small pinch of curry powder (not saffron).

It might be worth explaining that the recipe for *homard à l'armoricaine*, which recommends slicing a raw lobster before cooking it in olive oil and finally coating it in spicy tomato sauce, was invented in 1860 by a chef in Paris. It has absolutely nothing to do with the Bretons, although a lot of Bretons seem to think otherwise!

Seafood: a platter of seafood in Brittany is irresistible – and probably inevitable. In an ideal world, you would savour it in the open air, accompanied by a couple of glasses of decent Muscadet. To stimulate your taste buds visit the open-air market (*criée*), where you'll see a whole range of seafood on offer, including the different types of crab, prawns and, of course, lobsters. Breton lobsters are still thought of as 'the king of crustaceans and the crustaceans of kings'.

Crêpes and galettes: finding a really first-class '*crêperie*' is something of an art. What we call 'pancakes' are described in two different ways, depending on what part of Brittany you are in. In Northern Brittany, a pancake made with wheat is called a *crêpe* and one made with buckwheat, which is darker and heavier, is a *galette*.

The best way to identify a decent *crêperie* is to stand outside and breathe in. If there's an aroma of butter and fresh batter, go inside. If not – keep on looking. A *crêpe* may seem to be a simple enough thing to prepare, but getting it right demands high standards and precision. Fresh ingredients are essential, and every chef has his own recipe and must have a certain lightness of touch.

Breton *fars* and *bouillies*: the most common and most traditional cake in Brittany is called a *far*. It combines buckwheat flour (for the savoury version) or wheat flour (for the sweet version) with eggs and milk. Its originality lies in the addition of prunes (*prun ha farz*), bacon (*kig ha farz*), or pig's blood (the *farz gwad* of Ouessant). The many different versions of the Breton *fars* are considered by some to be the basis of traditional Breton cuisine. Eaten either natural or sprinkled with sugar, in slices or as breadcrumbs, the *far* was traditionally eaten as an accompaniment for meat.

Probably the best known type of *far* is the *kig ha farz* from the Léon region, which is served with vegetables and chunks of pork. This is often fat or bacon or smoked sausage meat, but better cuts are also used, depending on the circumstances. The *far* itself is cooked in broth in a muslin bag. This dish is often offered as a special on menus, usually one night each week. In Léon (north Finistère), they still make *pouloudig*, a big cake made of buckwheat flour, butter and milk flavoured with rum. The resulting dessert is very similar in quality and consistency to a traditional British fruit cake.

Cakes and pastries: the *kouign amann*, a cake made with butter, has been taken on board by local people and tourists alike. Originally from Douarnenez in South Finistère, these cakes can now be found all over Brittany. Made with a bread dough with added butter and sugar, the *kouign amann* is folded a number of times, which is how it acquires its lightness of texture. The ideal example is neither too fatty nor too sweet, but either way, it's a calorific experience.

The *far* (*see above*) also provides a sweet treat to die for. Just sink your teeth into a good *far aux pruneaux* (with prunes) and you are guaranteed an enjoyable experience!

DRINK

Cider: these days, cider has a lower alcohol content than it once had, and cooking with cider has come back into fashion, as the flavour of apples blends well with certain fish and meats. As a drinking experience, cider is widely available and is produced locally in many parts of Brittany, with each producer having his own recipe.

Beers: until recently, Brittany was the only Celtic country not to produce any of its own beer. Producers were never able to attain the same heights as the brewers of traditional British beer, and production stopped at the beginning of the 20th century. This changed about 15 years ago, and there are now 15 breweries in Brittany, all producing decent beer, which is not filtered, not pasteurized and high in alcohol content. The best known is Coreff, from Morlaix, which is amber-coloured and has a strong, hoppy flavour. Another heavyweight producer is Bernard Lancelot, who makes a number of specialist beers. Try the light and honey-flavoured *cervoise* (barley beer), a wheat beer (*bière blanche*) called *Blanche Hermine* or a buckwheat beer called *Telenn Du*.

Chouchen: this is the Breton word for mead, also known as *chamillard* in Gallo. Many a bad tale has been told about getting wrecked on this stuff, and years ago, it was thought that traces of bee venom were left behind in the honey from which the drink was made. The best you could expect from *chouchen* was a bad hangover, but at worst, your sense of balance could be affected. In fact, in some bars you can still see the hooks that were fixed at the counter for the old seamen to attach their belts to in order to keep upright! *Chouchen* has come back into fashion thanks to the efforts of a small group of beekeepers, and nowadays, good water, decent honey and natural yeasts are the only ingredients that go into the brew. Traditionally, the drink was sweet, as well as being 14 per cent alcohol, but drinkers are increasingly in favour of the less sweet, less potent varieties.

Excellent labels to try are *Chouchen du Pêcheur* and *Pétillant* by Pierre Dassonville, as well as *Yann Gamm* from Coray and *Lozachmeur* from Baye. Another good one is *Rucher Fleuri* from Rochefort-en-Terre, which seems to have caught the attention of chefs because of the interesting new flavours that it adds to their recipes, and there's a *chouchen* vinegar made by the same people – called *l'aigriade de miel*, it tastes of pure nectar.

SEAWEED AND SEAWEED FARMING

The role of a traditional seaweed farmer is somewhere between that of a farmer and that of a seaman. They do still exist, although there are fewer now than ever. However, a new generation of seaweed farms has appeared along the Léon coast, one of the most isolated, rocky parts of Brittany, which now supplies 80 per cent of the seaweed produced in France.

The industry has changed a great deal since the 1950s, and tractors and trucks have taken the place of horses and carts. The seaweed on the shore is still the same, though. *Fucus vesiculosus* forms the bulk of the harvest and is used as a fertilizer – this is the one with the bladders that children love to pop between their fingers. Other types of seaweed are also harvested, including *laminaria* – a giant of the Breton coast, which can reach an impressive 5 metres (16 feet) long. It is gathered from the sea using a *scoubidou*, which looks like a crane on board the boat and acts like a large set of hydraulic tongs.

Today, the factories burn the seaweed and take the soda from the ashes to extract the iodine from it. It takes 100 tonnes of soda to produce a single tonne of iodine, which is why such large harvests are required. A successful range of Breton fertilizers and seaweed bath products is now in production and research teams have begun to look at the feasibility of edible food products made from brown, green and red seaweed. The seaweed centre in Pleubian (Côtes d'Armor) is working to perfect recipes for bread, pâté, sausages and ready meals.

MUSIC

Like so many of the musical cultures around the world Breton folk music is closely tied to the history of its people. Originally an independent duchy, Brittany became part of France during the 16th century and has since survived many periods of political disunity to emerge with its regional identity intact. The Breton people have always strived to maintain a distinct cultural and linguistic heritage and nowhere is this more obvious than in the region's music. The traditional Breton pipe bands (*bagad, see* 'Instruments and Musicians'), originally used to accompany marches and festival processions, are still in evidence today, although the traditional line up has changed and the continued popularity of the *fest-noz* ('festival of the night') has provided the perfect medium for passing on songs and melodies from one generation to the next. The popularity of folksong collecting in the 19th century also contributed to the survival of the many laments and light-hearted songs of the Breton people which collectively provide a powerful insight into their troubled history.

After World War II, the formation of *Cercles celtiques* promoting local music and dancing, along with the *bagadou* (*see below*) helped to keep local musical traditions alive, but the turning point in the future of traditional Breton music came with the folk revival of the 1960s and 1970s. Amidst the climate of political agitation surrounding the Breton separatist movement, traditional music suddenly found itself on a new stage with a captive audience.

During this creative period, the Goadec sisters were rediscovered, new traditional-style 'bards' like Glenmor appeared, and young singers such as Gilles Servat, Gweltaz ar Fur and the harpist Kirjuhel also emerged on the scene. Leading the way, the Breton harpist Alan Stivell successfully introduced this ancient instrument to a new audience in 1971 with his album *Renaissance of the Celtic Harp*. In turn, he helped kickstart the renewal of interest in Breton and other Celtic folk music, going on to form one of the first folk-rock groups in Europe with the help of Dan Ar Braz and Gabriel Yacoub. In August 1972, the first Celtic pop festival took place in

Kertalg, where the line-up also included traditional Breton musicians such as the Goadec sisters.

For a long time Stivell was the only Breton to achieve international recognition, spreading Brittany's cultural message into France and beyond, but over the last few years the success of traditional music has seen a number of new talents emerging on the global music scene. Although Breton musicians tend to concentrate on the more traditional aspects of their art, they are now also forging links with their contemporaries in other cultures and with other musical styles, including rock. Pushing the music beyond its own traditional boundaries, bands such as Strobinell, Bleizi Ruz and Sonerien Du have combined electric guitar, bass, drum kit, flutes and accordion with the more traditional *bombarde*, *biniou* and *veuze* (*see below*) to take Breton music into the 21st century.

Music production in Brittany is largely split between two main labels, Keltia Musique and Coop Breizh. Whilst performers like Denez Prigent, Erik Marchand, Yann-Fanch Kemener, Ar Re Yaouank and Didier Squiban are at the forefront of the current music scene, performers like the Frères Morvan, who have been singing *kan ha diskan* (*see below*) for more than 50 years, still command a devoted following.

DISCOVERING BRITTANY'S REAL MUSICAL TRADITIONS

The revival of folk music during the mid-1970s gave rise to a tradition in which Breton music came together with music from other Celtic countries.

One of the best places to enjoy such music is at the **Festival Interceltique de Lorient** (the Lorient Celtic festival) in Morbihan, which takes place during the first two weeks of August.

Also worth investigating, although it is not specifically Breton, is the **Fête du Chant Marin** (festival of sea shanties), which also takes place during the first two weeks of August. For three days and three nights, a series of musical groups perform on different stages as well as on 'music boats' anchored in port. The majority of the musicians come from Brittany and Great Britain, although all of the world's coastal regions seem to be represented. Information is available from January in the *Chasse-Marée* newsletter in Douarnenez (South Finistère): ☎ 02-98-92-66-33.

Wherever you go to hear Breton music, don't hesitate to join in with the dancing as those who are more experienced will be only too happy to give you a few hints. Just make sure you have some sensible footwear.

Instruments and Musicians

Bagad (plural: *bagadou*): This is a group of musicians made up of *bombarde* players, *biniou-braz* players and percussionists. The *bagadou* are brought together under the umbrella of the BAS (Bodadeg Ar Sonerien) collective.

Biniou-braz: Larger than the *biniou-koz*, this instrument is very similar to the Scottish bagpipes, although its popularity in Brittany only dates back to the 1940s.

Biniou-koz: typically Breton, this set of bagpipes is more high-pitched than its cousin and only has a single drone. It consists of a pouch which the player inflates through one pipe, producing the notes on another small six-holed pipe.

Bombarde: the forerunner of the oboe, this instrument has six holes and one or more keys. To produce notes, the player has to hold the reed with his lips while blowing out at the same time.

Cercle celtique: a group of performers made up of instrumentalists, singers and dancers – an effective setting for learning Breton music.

Celtic harp: the traditional Breton harp virtually disappeared at the end of the Middle Ages along with Brittany's independence, but it was reintroduced with great success by the traditional musician Alan Stivell.

Clarinet (*treujenn-gaol* in Breton): A popular instrument in Brittany since the end of the 18th century.

Kan ha diskan: a type of song used to accompany dancing, particularly at the *fest-noz*. Two singers perform unaccompanied in a call and response pattern, coming together at the end of each verse.

Organ: this instrument is often played in Brittany accompanied by a *bombarde*.

Tambourines and bass drums: traditionally used for accompaniment in the *bagadou* (*see above*).

Veuze: a set of Breton bagpipes with a drone, similar to medieval bagpipes, originally from round the Nantes area.

DANCE AND THE *FEST-NOZ*

Dance and music in Brittany have always gone hand in hand and the *fest-noz* ('festival of the night' – the plural is *festou-noz*) has only served to continue this tradition, providing an excellent opportunity for people to dance, sing, drink and eat together, swap stories and learn new tunes. Traditionally a time for community celebration, a *fest-noz* would typically have taken place at harvest time.

Although there were local variations in style between the dances performed in the towns and those performed in the countryside during the 17th and 18th centuries, the classic Breton dances could generally be found everywhere. These were either circle dances, in closed or open chains, or line dances and included the *gavotte*, the *plinn* and the *fisel*, all originating from the mountains and the *an dro*, the *hanter dro* and the *laridé* from around Vannes. There was also the *kost er c'hoad*, a dance from the Léon region and the *rond de St Vincent*, from Loudéac.

During the 19th century, other dance forms were introduced into Brittany from abroad, these included popular dances for couples such as the waltz, the polka and Scottish dancing, but even with these outside influences Brittany managed to keep its traditional dances alive.

During the renewed general interest in folk music and the use of traditional instruments during the 1960s and 1970s, more professional groups were formed, and music and dance tuition became available. This meant that as well as a huge increase in the number of people wanting to listen to the music, there was an inevitable increase in the number of amateur and professional musicians able to handle the material.

Nowadays, the *fest-noz* has moved out of the rural villages and has become increasingly urbanized. This move has brought together dances from a number of different communities with the result that any proper *fest-noz* is likely to include as many as 30 different dances. What is most striking about attending a *fest-noz* is that it breeds community spirit and seems to appeal to every generation. People may not have the same techniques that they had a hundred years ago, but being able to dance without inhibition has brought a whole new community spirit to the event. Over the years, the *fest-noz* has changed its image: gone is the feel of the village fête and the traditional costumes are largely a thing of the past – clogs and long skirts are out and trainers and jeans are strictly *de rigueur*.

TRADITIONAL BRETON SPORTS

A few traditional sports can still be seen at festivals.

L'essieu de charrette ('the chariot axle'): the axle from a light chariot or a horse-drawn wagon, or a piece of wood with a square cross-section, weighing about 47 kilograms (103lb), is laid on top of two logs or two stones of the same size. The competitor stands between them and tries to lift the axle at arms' length above his head as many times as he can within two minutes. Between each lift, he has to rest the axle back down on the logs without letting go of it.

Lancer de la pierre lourde ('throwing the heavy stone'): the stone is actually a millstone with a metal ring on it, weighing 20 kilograms (45lb). The throwers have a run-up of 2.13m (7 feet) and can throw using one or two hands, but are not allowed to use the ring, or go over the line. Each competitor is allowed three attempts.

Bâton de bouillie ('pulp stick'): played between two opponents whose names are drawn out of a hat in advance. The *bâton* (stick) is a cylindrical piece of wood of between 50 and 60 centimetres (20 and 24 inches) in length. A board 2 metres (10 feet) long and 2 centimetres (1 inch) high is fixed to the ground on its edge. The players sit face-to-face on the ground on either side of the board, with their feet flat against it. The winner of each leg is the one who makes the other drop the stick. A game can consist of up to three legs, and the winner is the first person to win two legs. Practising seems to be pointless, as familiarity doesn't seem to help anyone understand the game any better!

Lever de la perche ('lifting the pole'): the cylindrical pole is made of hardened steel, and measures 6 metres (20 feet) in length with a slider at the 23-centimetre point (9 inches). The aim of the game is to lift the pole to the vertical and hold it in this position for at least three seconds.

Tug-of-war: the rope is 25–32m metres (80–105 feet) in length and 4.5 centimetres (2 inches) in diameter. There is one central marker – a yellow ribbon, 30 centimetres (12 inches) long – and two side markers positioned 3.5 metres (11.5 feet) either side of the central marker. Two teams of six men compete, plus a hoister and a substitute. A team member can be substituted during a match but not actually during a tug. The pullers are barefoot, and must remain standing throughout the tug; if anyone falls over, they must let go of the rope and get up before taking hold of it again. Digging out holes in the ground or marking them with the heels brings disqualification. The team member at the back is not allowed to wrap the rope around his body.

Relay with a 50-kilogram (110-pound) load: each team consists of six men, and no substitutes are allowed. Each competitor has to run 120 metres before passing the 50-kilogram sack on to the next team member. The load must be returned to behind the starting post, and if a runner drops a sack, he must lift it up again himself without any assistance. The competitors must clear an obstacle in their lane, and any throwing of the sack disqualifies the whole team.

TOWNS AND VILLAGES OF SPECIAL INTEREST

Historic Towns

Dinan (Côtes-d'Armor)

Fougères (Ille-et-Vilaine)

Rennes (Ille-et-Vilaine)

St-Malo (Ille-et-Vilaine)

Vitré (Ille-et-Vilaine)

Small Towns with Character

Bécherel (Ille-et-Vilaine)

Châteaugiron (Ille-et-Vilaine)

Châtelaudren (Côtes-d'Armor)

Combourg (Ille-et-Vilaine)

Guerlesquin (North Finistère)

Jugon-Les-Lacs (Côtes-d'Armor)

Moncontour-de-Bretagne (Côtes-d'Armor)

Pontrieux (Côtes-d'Armor)

Quintin (Côtes-d'Armor)

Roscoff (North Finistère)

Tréguier (Côtes-d'Armor)

TRADITIONAL RURAL VILLAGES

A number of little villages in Northern Brittany deserve a specific mention, either for the quality of their location, or the local way of life or the general liveliness of the place. They include: **Bulat-Pestivien, St-Juvat** and **Tréfunel** in Côtes-d'Armor, and **Commana**, **Lanildut**, **Plougonven** and **Plouvin-lès-Morlaix** in North Finistère.

Ille-et-Vilaine

The department of Ille-et-Vilaine may well be your first point of contact with Brittany. You won't find many of the *enclos paroissiaux* (walled parish closes) and calvaries that are so typical elsewhere in Brittany, particularly in Finistère, but Ille-et-Vilaine still has plenty to see and do. There's Rennes, the departmental capital, an attractive town steeped in art and history; fascinating St-Malo, the home of the infamous French *corsaires* – pirates exempt from punishment by royal charter; as well as a stunning coastline that stretches from Dinard to Mont-St-Michel. You can take unusual walks through lovely countryside scattered with magnificent churches and chapels, each full of treasures and wonderful stained-glass windows. There are even castles and ruins ranging from the romantic to the austere. It almost goes without saying that here, as everywhere in Brittany, there's the usual tempting range of Breton gastronomic delights.

USEFUL ADDRESSES

■ **Comité régional du tourisme breton** (Breton regional tourist office): 1 rue Raoul-Ponchon, 35069 Rennes Cedex. ☎ 02-99-28-44-30 or 02-99-36-15-15 to ask for publicity brochures. Fax: 02-99-28-44-40. Website: www.tourisme bretagne.com
■ **Comité départemental du tourisme** (departmental tourist office): 4 rue Jean-Jaurès, BP 60149, 35101 Rennes Cedex 03. ☎ 02-99-78-47-47. Fax: 02-99-78-33-24.

Website: www.bretagne35.com, for any kind of information about the region. Another office at **Point 35** (B3 on the map of Rennes): 1 quai Chateaubriand. ☎ 02-99-79-35-35. Open 8.30am–5.30pm Monday–Friday, 9am–noon Saturday. Closed Monday morning and Saturday in July and August. Free Internet access. Capable and friendly.
■ **Gîtes de France**: 8 rue Coëtquen, Rennes. ☎ 02-99-78-47-57. Fax: 02-99-78-47-53.

RENNES (*ROAZHON*) 35000   (Pop: 212,494)

Rennes is not much known to visitors, who often expect it to be a large, rather austere city. Large it is, with a population of almost 213,000, but there are no memorable landmarks in the way that Quimper has its cathedral. The town does, however, have some interesting architecture and a dynamic cultural scene. Rather surprisingly, it has become one of the liveliest towns in France, with an unusually high concentration of good bars. It also has a reputation for being the country's breeding ground for rock, and hosts a prestigious summer arts festival, the 'Tombées de la Nuit'.

Rennes in History

In the beginning, what is now Rennes was a little Gallic village called Condate. By the 11th century, people were already beginning to talk about it, largely because of its resistance to Norman invasion, and the town gradually emerged as the capital of the region. In 1337, Bertrand Du Guesclin, the legendary French knight of the Hundred Years War, made a name for himself by winning numerous chivalric tournaments here.

The city walls of Rennes were put to the test at the end of the 15th century, when French troops came to lay siege to the town, which was holding Anne of Brittany prisoner. A resolution came in 1491, when Anne was married to Charles VIII of France. The alliance was followed by the Traité d'Union (Act of Union) of 1532, which defined benefits and privileges for the region, but also marked the end of Breton independence.

The Breton parliament was created in 1561, and noblemen, administrators and artists began to arrive in Rennes, which became the official capital of Brittany. The construction of the parliament building began in 1618, and this was followed by the building of many prestigious private houses.

In 1720, a disastrous, week-long fire destroyed practically the whole of the town centre. The people of Rennes had to look for new building materials and techniques; timber-framed buildings were now banned from the streets, and all houses were built of stone. At the same time, strict regulations appeared to restrict the architects' imagination, and new, uniform residential areas were created. These rather severe-looking quarters contributed to the town's reputation for austerity, and also partially covered the River Vilaine, removing some of the charm from the urban landscape.

Rennes is actually far from austere, as you will discover during your stay. Wandering around the town centre, you come across a number of quaint little squares, tiny little streets and enclosed courtyards full of rustic charm. The former Breton parliament building, set on fire during fishermen's strikes in 1994, remains symbolic of the town, even as a burnt-out shell. It is currently the subject of a large-scale renovation project, which is set to last for a number of years.

Rennes has had a university since the 18th century, and it is now home to some 45,000 students. Over the years, it has also developed a significant industrial infrastructure, including the Citroën factories. Rennes is also the location of the publishers of *Ouest France*, the newspaper with the largest circulation in France.

Rennes is a dynamic, cultural town with a rich past – and you won't be disappointed.

USEFUL ADDRESSES

■ **Comité régional du tourisme breton** (Breton regional tourist office): 1 rue Raoul-Ponchon, 35069 Rennes Cedex. ☎ 02-99-28-44-30 or 02-99-36-15-15 to request publicity information. Fax: 02-99-28-44-40. Website: www.tourisme bretagne.com. Excellent publicity for the region, and information on everything.

🛈 **Office du tourisme**: 11 rue St-Yves (in the historic heart of the town), CS 26410, 35064 Rennes Cedex. ☎ 02-99-67-11-11. Fax: 02-99-67-11-10. Email: info@ tourisme-rennes.com. In season, open Monday–Saturday, 9am–7pm and 11am–6pm on Sunday. Closed at 6pm out of season. Located in the beautiful St-Yves chapel. Friendly

RENNES

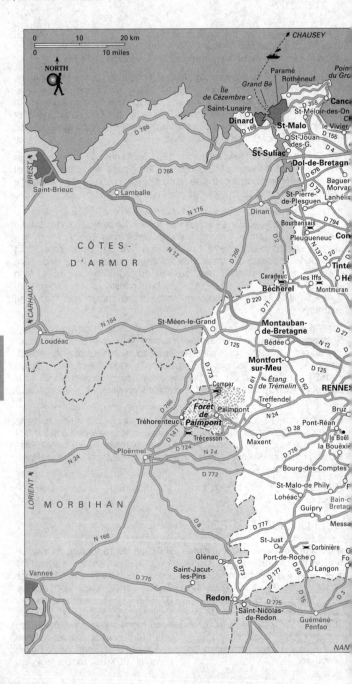

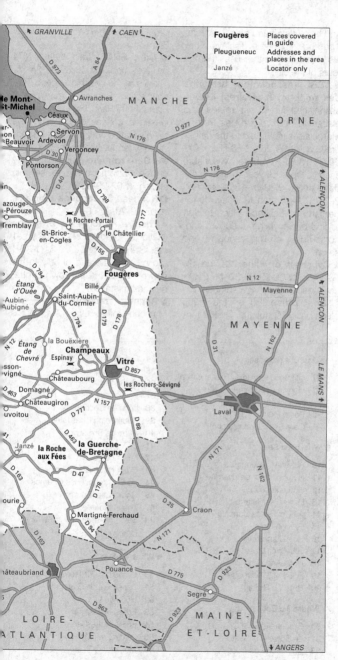

Fougères	Places covered in guide
Pleugueneuc	Addresses and places in the area
Janzé	Locator only

GRANVILLE   CAEN

D 973   A 84

MANCHE   ORNE

le Mont-
St-Michel   Avranches

Céaux   N 176   D 977

on   Servon
Beauvoir   Ardevon   Vergoncey   N 176
D 30

Pontorson   ALENÇON

D 40   ALENÇON

in   D 798

azouge-   le Rocher-Portail
-Pérouze   D 177

Tremblay   St-Brice-   le Châtellier
en-Cogles   D 155

D 794   A 84   N 12

Étang   Billé   Mayenne
d'Ouée   Fougères
-Aubin-   Saint-Aubin-
Aubigné   du-Cormier   D 179   D 178

D 794   MAYENNE

N 12   Étang   la Bouëxière   D 31
de   Champeaux
Chevré   Espinay   N 162
sson-   Vitré
vigné   D 857
Châteaubourg
Domagné   les Rochers-Sévigné
D 463   Laval
Châteaugiron   N 157
uvoitou   D 777   D 88

41   Janzé   la Guerche-
la Roche   de-Bretagne   N 171
aux Fées   N 162
D 163   D 47

D 178

ourie   D 25   Craon

Martigné-Ferchaud   N 171
D 34

D 163

hâteaubriand   Pouancé   D 775   D 923

Segré   D 923

D 963   MAINE-
LOIRE-   ET-LOIRE
ATLANTIQUE   ANGERS

RENNES

and helpful staff and plenty of literature and informative displays. They also run very interesting themed tours of the city.

■ **ABRI (Association bretonne des relais et itinéraires)** (Breton association for tourist routes and places to stay): 9 rue des Portes-Mordelaises (right next to the cathedral). ☎ 02-99-26-13-50. Fax: 02-99-26-13-54. Website: www.abri. asso.fr. Open all year round, Tuesday–Friday, 9.30am–12.30pm and 2–7pm; also open Monday, June–September. Essential place to visit to find out anything about walking, horse-riding, cycling, canoeing, and so on.

■ **Cybernet on Line**: 22 rue St-Georges. ☎ 02-99-36-37-41. Cyber café costing about 40F an hour.

✉ **Post office** (B3 on the map): place de la République. Open Monday–Friday 8am–7pm and Saturday 8am–noon.

🚄 **Gare SNCF** (train station) (B4 on the map): ☎ 08-36-35-35-35. Thanks to the new high-speed TGV connection, Rennes is now only 2 hours from Paris by train, with at least ten connections a day. The town's station was completely renovated when the line opened.

🚌 **Gare routière** (bus station) (B4 on the map): right next to the train station. ☎ 02-99-30-87-80.

✈ **Rennes St-Jacques Airport**: ☎ 02-99-29-60-00.

■ **Théâtre national de Bretagne** (National Theatre of Brittany): 1 rue St-Hélier. ☎ 02-99-31-12-31. Closed from the end of July to the end of August. In the town centre, next to the station.

■ **Rennes Musique**: rue du Maréchal-Joffre. One of France's

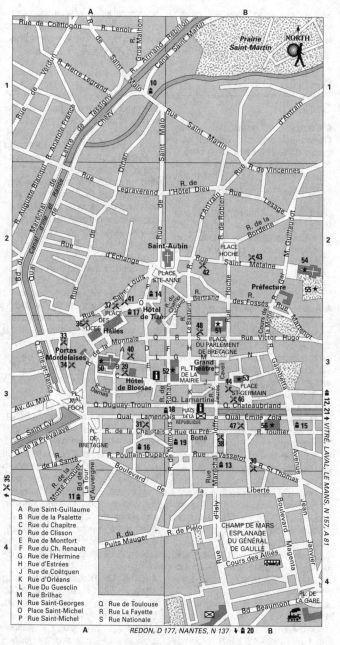

A Rue Saint-Guillaume
B Rue de la Psalette
C Rue du Chapitre
D Rue de Clisson
E Rue de Montfort
F Rue du Ch. Renault
G Rue de l'Hermine
H Rue d'Estrées
J Rue de Coëtquen
K Rue d'Orléans
L Rue Du Guesclin
M Rue Brilhac
N Rue Saint-Georges
O Place Saint-Michel
P Rue Saint-Michel

Q Rue de Toulouse
R Rue La Fayette
S Rue Nationale

REDON, D 177, NANTES, N 137

RENNES

few remaining independent music stores.

■ *La Griffe*: a free magazine, available from bars and venues that covers all kinds of cultural things: concerts, shows, gigs, cinema and exhibitions, in fact everything you need to enjoy a good night out.

WHERE TO STAY

Campsite

⌂ **Camping municipal des Gayeulles**: parc des Bois, 1 kilometre to the east of the town centre. ☎ 02-99-36-91-22. Open from 1 April to mid-October. To get there, take bus No. 3 from place de la Mairie towards St-Laurent. The campsite is in a terrific setting, and thoughtfully laid out. There are beautiful lawns, plenty of trees and a swimming pool close by. Allow about 40F for two.

⊠ Budget

⌂ **Auberge de jeunesse** (youth hostel) (A1, **10** on the map): 10–12 canal St-Martin. ☎ 02-99-33-22-33. Fax: 02-99-59-06-21. Open all year round, and all day from 7am–11pm. Located to the north of the town, within walking distance of the old town centre. From the station, take bus No. 2, 20 or 22 and get off at Coëtlogon; the hostel (or 'AJ', short for *auberge de jeunesse*) is at the intersection of rue St-Malo and the canal. The beautiful building is run by friendly staff, and has a nice cafeteria and kitchen facilities, and around 100 beds in rooms for one, two, three or four people. YHA cards required. It costs from 72F a night in a four-person room, with no sheets but with breakfast, to 135F a night for a single room with sheets and breakfast included. It's also a stop-off point for the boats passing along the canal.

⌂ **Hôtel La Tour d'Auvergne** (A4, **11** on the map): 20 boulevard de La Tour-d'Auvergne. ☎ 02-99-30-84-16. Fax: 02-23-42-10-01. Open all year round. Not far from the law courts, on the first floor of the lovely restaurant Le Serment de Vin. Rooms are simple but spotless and available with or without en suite bathroom. At 150–220F, it's the kind of traditional family-run bed and breakfast that those on a tight budget dream about. There's a telephone in every room, and the landlady is very friendly. Breakfast is served in the bedroom. Highly recommended.

⌂ **Hôtel de Léon** (off the map along B3, **12**): 15 rue de Léon. On a little island on the Vilaine, attached to the quai Richemont. ☎ 02-99-30-55-28. Open all year round. A quiet little hotel on the edge of town, where the furniture is good, old-fashioned – and definitely not bland. The rooms, from 123F (with washbasin) to 185F, are all very reasonable, and it's spotlessly clean.

⌂ **Hôtel d'Angleterre** (B3, **13** on the map): 19 rue du Maréchal-Joffre. ☎ 02-99-79-38-61. Fax: 02-99-79-43-85. Open all year round. Closed Sunday afternoon until 6pm. Located fairly centrally on the south bank, not far from the place de la République. This simple little hotel, situated in a tall building with an imposing staircase and lofty corridors, is very well run by its friendly owners. Traditional, spacious rooms are good value for money, at 165–225F.

⌂ **Hôtel Le Riaval** (off the map along B4, **20**): 9 rue Riaval. ☎ 02-99-50-65-58. Fax: 02-99-41-85-30. Closed Sunday afternoons. This unpretentious little place combines modest prices with a good position just behind the station. The area is not bad and the welcome is very good. The proprietors have taken lots of trouble doing the place up and it's all perfectly kept. There's a choice of rooms, some modern and colourful and others more rustic in feel. Noise is not a problem, whether the rooms are facing the road or the back. Get a room overlooking the garden and you'll have a lime tree outside the window and it's so quiet you can almost hear the grass growing! This hotel is very good for those on a tight budget, with rooms costing 140–205F.

☆☆ Moderate

⌂ Au Rocher de Cancale (A2, **14** on the map): 10 rue St-Michel. ☎ 02-99-79-20-83. Closed Saturday and Sunday and for two weeks in August. The location – on the famous medieval street nicknamed 'rue de la Soif' ('Thirst Street') – is one of the liveliest in town, and it goes without saying that this hotel is not one of the quietest. On the other hand, if you love nightlife, this place is within staggering distance from all the main bars. It has recently been renovated, and the four rooms are comfortable, pretty and cost only 220F a night – excellent value for money. There is also a good restaurant on the ground floor.

⌂ Garden Hotel (B3, **15** on the map): 3 rue Duhamel (corner of avenue Jean-Janvier). ☎ 02-99-65-45-06. Fax: 02-99-65-02-62. Open all year round, this is a charming, tasteful hotel, near the station and the old town, with a small, enclosed courtyard and a cafeteria. The landlady offers a friendly welcome. Lovely, individual rooms at 260–340F, decorated in fresh colours. The ones on the ground floor facing the garden are especially good. Try and take a look at the next-door building, which is decorated in pure

art nouveau style by one of the Odorico brothers, notable artists in mosaics at the turn of the century.

⌂ Hôtel Astrid (off B3 on the map): 32 avenue Louis-Barthou. ☎ 02-99-30-82-38. Fax: 02-99-31-88-55. Email: hotelastrid@wanadoo.fr. Open all year round except on New Year's Eve. This smart little hotel is ideally situated near the station but only 10 minutes' walk from the centre of town. It's more geared towards sales reps than backpackers, but having said that, the welcome is excellent. The rooms are modern, reasonably spacious and well equipped, and there's a certain tranquillity that makes it a pleasant place to stay. The breakfast room looks out over a pretty little garden. The whole place is spotlessly clean. Double rooms cost 265–350F, with a 20 per cent reduction at the weekend.

⌂ Hôtel Lanjuinais (A3, **16** on the map): 11 rue Lanjuinais. ☎ 02-99-79-02-03. Fax: 02-99-79-03-97. Open all year round. In a central position and looking out over the quai Lamennais, between place de la Bretagne and the post office, this is a quiet, well-kept hotel. The rooms are of a standard quality, and almost all face onto the street, although the ones overlooking the courtyard are a bit gloomy. Doubles cost 275–295F, with reduced rates out of season on weekends and public holidays

⌂ Hôtel des Lices (A2, **17** on the map): 7 place des Lices. ☎ 02-99-79-14-81. Fax: 02-99-79-35-44. Email: hotel.lices@wanadoo.fr. ♿ Open all year round. On one of the most beautiful squares in the old town, this hotel has been entirely renovated and feels fresh and modern. The rooms are very pleasant (with balconies) and the service and the welcome are just what you'd expect: young, dynamic and very efficient. The top floors have a lovely view over the rooftops of old Rennes. A double room costs 290–310F.

â **Hôtel Angelina** (A3, **18** on the map): 1 quai Lamennais. ☎ 02-99-79-29-66. Fax: 02-99-79-61-01. Email: angelinarennes@aol.com. Open all year round. Reception on the third floor. Don't be put off by the slightly melancholy appearance of this building: inside, it all feels like a very large apartment and you'll get a warm welcome from the family that runs it. The rooms are impeccable; they're also huge and fitted with all mod cons. The breakfast room is quiet and well lit – unlike some of the gloomy places tucked away behind reception that you find. Allow 260–300F for a double room.

☆☆☆ Chic

â **Hôtel M.S. Nemours** (B3, **19** on the map): 5 rue de Nemours. ☎ 02-99-78-26-26. Fax: 02-99-78-25-40. Open all year round. Central, close to the place de la République. The decor is fascinating: one wall in reception is completely decorated with leaves – and it looks superb! The other walls are kitted out with all kinds of old ships' fittings plus photographs, engravings and models in glass cases. The rooms are charming and spotlessly clean, and the ones on the courtyard side of the building are quieter – but they're not as light. There's a really friendly welcome, whether you're a backpacker, a sailor or just a landlubber. Double rooms from 265–345F.

WHERE TO STAY OR EAT NEARBY

â ✕ **Germinal**: 9 cours de la Vilaine, Cesson-Sévigné, just 5 kilometres (3 miles) from Rennes historic town centre. ☎ 02-99-83-11-01. Fax: 02-99-83-45-16. Email: info@le-germinal.com. ✤ Hotel and restaurant in a charming 19th-century mill on the banks of the River Vilaine. The village itself is as pretty as a chocolate box, so it's a pity that the rooms in this hotel (about 470F) are unremarkable and rather lacking in character. Still, they're comfortable and quiet. There's a comfortable restaurant (closed Sunday evening and Monday in season) with a terrace and a peaceful view. Their fish menu is particularly good, with some very unusual dishes. Set menus cost from 140–395F.

WHERE TO EAT

You'll be spoilt for choice for somewhere to eat in Rennes: somebody once counted more than 100 *crêperies* and getting on for 45 pizzerias in the town.

☆ Budget

✕ **Restaurant Le Bocal-P'ty Resto** (A3, **31** on the map): 6 rue d'Argentré, near the south end of the place de la République and very close to the quai Lamennais. ☎ 02-99-78-34-10. Closed Sunday and Monday and the first two weeks of January and August. Menus from 65F. This little restaurant has a bright, colourful decor, and there are bottles everywhere. The 'specials' on the slate are very enticing: you might see such things as a very generous pie filled with chicken, bacon and green pepper, a spiced fricassée of poultry or a smoked salmon *minute*. The desserts are also really good, with a great chocolate mousse. There's a decent selection of wines at sensible prices and all are available by the glass. Run by a friendly young couple, this is a relaxed place to eat.

✗ **Crêperie L'Épi d'Or** (B3, **30** on the map): 2 rue St-Thomas; near the Lycée Émile-Zola. ☎ 02-99-78-23-49. Closed Saturday lunchtime, Sunday and for one week in February and two weeks in May. Undoubtedly one of the best *crêperies* in town, and one of the cheapest, too: try the *brestoise*, with Breton sausage and potatoes fried in butter. There is a set menu at lunchtime, with three *crêpes* and a bowl of cider for just 40F.

✗ **Au Marché des Lices** (A3, **33** on the map): 3 place du Bas-des-Lices (market square). ☎ 02-99-30-42-95. ☖ Open noon–2pm and 7.30–11pm. Closed Sunday and the first two weeks in August. The rustic setting is pleasant and relaxed and the food is good value, always with a dish of the day, mixed salads, and *galettes*. Fixed-price meals cost 65F. The cider is good and there's an open fire in winter.

✗ **Café Breton** (A3, **34** on the map): 14 rue Nantaise. ☎ 02-99-30-74-95. Closed Saturday and Monday evening and all day Sunday. Closed for the first three weeks in August. Warm, stylish setting, somewhere between a teashop and an American-style coffee shop, with an air of ordered chaos. Choose from lots of delicacies, such as savoury tarts, *gratins*, or tasty main dishes such as pork in cider or rabbit in mustard. All the dishes come up to expectation. Book in advance.

✗ **Crêperie Le Boulingrain** (B2, **43** on the map): 25 rue St-Mélaine. Near the place Hoche. ☎ 02-99-38-75-11 or 02-99-79-64-62. Open every day except for Sunday lunch and a few days around New Year.

There's an 'Express' menu for 48F and fixed-price meals cost 70–140F. There's more than one good reason to cross the threshold of this particular *crêperie* – there's the excellent, friendly welcome given to absolutely everyone; there's the interior itself, which is warm and intimate, with lots of wood and stone and a huge chimney breast; and there's the menu – an excellent range of traditional *galettes* and *crêpes*. This place is specially recommended if you want to eat well and haven't much time.

☆☆ Moderate

✗ **Le Petit Sabayon** (off the map along A4, **35**): 16 rue des Trente. Looking out over the quai de la Prévalaye (near the law courts). ☎ 02-99-35-02-04. Closed Saturday lunchtime, Sunday evening and Monday. It's up there among the town's best restaurants, with diligent but friendly service. Specialities include crispy pie with feta cheese and dried fruit with basil (*croustillant de feta et fruits secs au basilic*), sardine tournedos in a port sauce (*tournedos de sardines au jus de porto*), rich chocolate mousse in coffee sauce (*marquise au chocolat sauce arabica*). All the prices are affordable, with a 78F weekday lunch menu or evening menus at 110F or 160F, and there is a good selection of reasonably priced wines.

✗ **La Biscorne** (B2, **42** on the map): 8 rue St-Mélaine. Parking on place Hoche. ☎ 02-99-38-79-77. ☖ Closed Sunday, Monday evening, and two weeks in August. This Rennes restaurant is a real winner with its warm welcome, first-class cuisine and decent prices. The setting is charmingly rustic, all pink and yellow, with wood everywhere and a huge fireplace on which the chef's trophies are on show. His awards are justly deserved, as everything on

RENNES

the menu is both conceived and executed extremely well. All the ingredients used are seasonal, so the dishes on offer vary from month to month, but there's a wide range of set menus including lunch at 60F and evening meals cost 75–195F. There's also a good wine list, which is also very reasonably priced.

✕ **Le Gange** (A3, **36** on the map): 34 place des Lices (opposite the covered market). ☎ 02-99-30-18-37. Closed Sunday. Towards the end of the week, booking is recommended. This is an Indian restaurant serving classic curry dishes in a wonderful setting, with friendly service. The 52F set menu (weekday lunchtimes) provides a pleasant taster of authentic, carefully produced food. In the evening you pay more, of course, but the warm welcome makes it all worthwhile.

✕ **Léon Le Cochon** (B3, **38** on the map): 1 rue du Maréchal-Joffre. ☎ 02-99-79-37-54. Open lunchtime and every day. Closed Sunday in July and August. The lunchtime menu costs 69F while the evening menu is 130F. A modern, sophisticated restaurant, offering simply prepared local specialities – a tasty chef's oxtail, steak in a curry sauce and a delicious homemade *foie gras*. The walls are the colour of red peppers and the understated decor consists of dried leaves and even trees. Unless you enjoy queueing, reserve a table in advance.

✕ **Le St-Germain-Des-Champs** (B3, **44** on the map): 12 rue Vau St-Germain (opposite the Église St-Germain). ☎ 02-99-79-25-52. Closed Sunday and Monday to Wednesday evening. Allow 70–100F for a meal. If you are worried about GM foods, mad cow disease and pesticides, then perhaps the time has come to go organic – in which case, this is *the* place to eat. With an array of appetising vegetarian dishes, this place is far from

dreary – quite the opposite, in fact. You'll discover all kinds of new textures and flavours in the cuisine they serve: it's colourful, tasty, the portions are generous – and it's good for you! The wine and fruit juice is organic, too, and there's a corner dedicated to information and publications. One dining room faces onto the street and there's another pleasant space in the garden at the back. They give a really warm welcome.

✕ **Le Khalifa** (A2, **37** on the map): 20 place des Lices (at the top end of the square). ☎ 02-99-30-87-30. Open until 11.30pm. Closed all day Monday, Tuesday and Saturday lunchtime. Just for a change, what about Breton artichokes prepared the Moroccan way, or some tasty, fragrant couscous, lamb or chicken *tajines* with lemon, all served in typically Moroccan surroundings? Here, the emphasis is on flavour, not on the size of the menu. At lunchtime, just one set menu, at 52F, or allow 100F if you're ordering from the à la carte menu. Very friendly service and some memorable liqueurs.

☆☆☆ Chic

✕ **Auberge St-Sauveur** (A3, **40** on the map): 6 rue St-Sauveur (behind the Cathédrale St-Pierre). ☎ 02-99-79-32-56. Fax: 02-99-78-27-93. Closed Saturday and Monday lunchtime and all day Sunday. This beautiful residence, originally home to canons in the 16th century, is now a warm, intimate and sophisticated restaurant. Menus for 78F (weekday lunchtime), and three evening menus (109–296F) give a taste of quality traditional food. Dishes of the day include grilled Breton lobster, and chef's special monkfish and the *foie gras* is excellent. There is an excellent lunch menu for 75F, which allows you to enjoy the ambiance without breaking the bank. If you can run to it, this is a good place for dinner with a special companion.

✗ **L'Auberge du Chat-Pitre** (A3, **39** on the map): 18 rue du Chapitre. ☎ 02-99-30-36-36. Open evenings only. Closed Sunday and all of the month of August. The cheapest set menu is 68F, with others between 124F and 164F depending on your appetite. This is a medieval inn within the cathedral quarter, where the dining experience is touristy but fun. You've barely got through the doors when you're greeted by a server in medieval garb who addresses you in something approaching medieval French (if you can tell the difference!). You're in for a feast. There's an aperitif to begin with – a pitcher of *hypocras*, which is a sort of medieval *sangria* with cinnamon and cloves instead of fruit. Main courses on the à la carte menu include spicy chicken liver stew or a rustic pâté made with prunes. To finish with, there might be an almond-flavoured blancmange-style dessert.

There's nothing delicate about this experience, and it certainly isn't 100 per cent authentic, but it's fun and the servings are copious. From time to time, the meal is interrupted by minstrels, jugglers and acrobats, which all adds to the jolly atmosphere. Everyone sits side-by-side at long tables, so it's fun to go with a group, or as a couple, but don't go looking for a quiet tête-à-tête. Booking is essential.

✗ **L'Ouvrée** (A2, **41** on the map): 18 place des Lices. ☎ 02-99-30-16-38. Closed Monday, Saturday lunchtime and Sunday evening, for the first week of Easter and the first two weeks in August. This is one of the poshest restaurants in town. The atmosphere is very muted and respectable, with an upmarket yet unostentatious decor. Very subtle cuisine and an excellent selection of wines. There are three set menus from 84F to 200F and you should allow 250F if eating from the à la carte menu. Specialities on the menu include langoustines, scallops and turbot dishes.

SALONS DE THÉ

– **Chocolatier Durand** (B3, **46** on the map): 5 quai Chateaubriand (opposite the Musée des Beaux-Arts). ☎ 02-99-78-10-00. Open 10am–8pm. Closed Sunday and for three weeks in July and August. You can get a dish of the day here for 60F, and cakes and pastries for 26F. Situated in a beautiful building with an ornate facade, this chic tearoom offers sweet and savoury treats and many different types of chocolate. Savoury tarts are available at any time of day: try one with fresh tuna, tomatoes and aubergines or the *brocciu* (a Corsican *fromage frais* made with ewe's milk and fresh herbs), or perhaps a plate

of smoked salmon served with a seaweed and lentil salad. If it's sweet things you fancy, the chocolate cake and the almond gâteau are both amazing. You can warm up with a hot chocolate or simply quench your thirst with a cup of tea. They also sell different varieties of chocolate, some made with spices and fruit, and some flavoured with herbs. Expect a warm welcome and excellent advice if you need it. There's a very pleasant mezzanine room overlooking a little garden. You can also buy goods to take away.

– **Thé au Fourneau** (B3, **47** on the map): 6 rue du Capitaine-Alfred-

Dreyfus. ☎ 02-99-78-25-36. Open daily except Sunday 10am–7pm. Closed Saturday and Sunday in summer, and the first two weeks of August. With coconut matting on the floor, bric-à-brac everywhere, and chairs that don't match, this eclectic little place offers the best cakes and pastries in town – chocolate or apple-and-lemon tarts, blackberry and blackcurrant crumbles, and so on. They're all so good that you just sit there imagining a whole brigade of well-meaning old dears beavering away in the kitchens.

It's certainly an all-female team, although they're not drawing their pensions yet. Their clientele seems to be mixed, but it's a good place to go for a tasty snack such as a savoury tart or a toasted sandwich. When it's hot, go there for iced tea and coffee. They also offer a take-away service.

– **Mrs Dalloway** (B3, **48** on the map): 5 rue Nationale. ☎ 02-99-79-27-27. Open Monday–Friday 11am–6pm, Saturday 1–6pm. Closed Sunday. Allow about 80F for a meal. This town-centre tearoom has what the French think of as typically English decor, and attracts a rather posh, nouveau-riche clientele (the kind with huge, flashy rings on their fingers). Picture a dark green carpet, English-style pine furniture and straw-yellow walls covered with mirrors and pictures; there are alcoves and shelves laden with crockery and old boxes and tins. There's a good list of teas and coffees and a choice of English desserts, as well as savoury dishes such as chicken pie, salads and vegetable dishes in cheese sauce. Portions here are very generous and everything is cooked on the premises using fresh ingredients.

WHERE TO GO FOR A DRINK

Before you hit the streets of Rennes, there are two things worth mentioning: first, there are around 45,000 students in Rennes among a total of 213,000 inhabitants, so the atmosphere is definitely young; second, the town has become something of a paradise for lovers of rock music (see 'Les Transmusicales'). The logical conclusion is that Rennes should be a paradise for lovers of nightlife – and, indeed, it has one of the largest concentrations of bars anywhere in Europe. Whatever sort of music you like, you will find it here, from mellow jazz through to heavy metal, via New Wave, underground, acid jazz, techno, funk, soul and reggae. If you were expecting a little provincial town with no character you'll be rather surprised. There are more people on rue St-Michel, rue St-Malo or place St-Michel at 1am than at noon . . . and Thursday night in particular is complete madness.

To get your bearings: basically, the best places are spread out across three streets (with a few notable exceptions). Popular **rue St-Georges** (B3 on the map) and **rue St-Michel** (B3 on the map) have a bar every few yards, and most of them are interesting in their own way – one challenge is to try to 'do' them all. Most of the bars listed below, and many that are not listed, hold regular gigs. Entrance is sometimes free, or may cost 30F or perhaps up to 50F. A little further away is the slightly rougher **rue de St-Malo** (A2 on the map), which tends more towards 'alternative rock', and opens its doors to the real party animals from midnight onwards.

❣ Head first for rue St-Michel, otherwise known as 'rue de la Soif', or 'Thirst Street'. On the left, **Sympatic Bar** (No. 11) is for hard-rock fans. On the right, **Barantic** (No. 4) is a safe bet for local drinking sessions and hosts really good Breton music jams every so often. A bit further on, also on the right-hand side, look out for **Taxi Brousse**, at the bottom of a little staircase. This bar, with its subdued atmosphere, is the meeting place for lovers of African or reggae music. A little further on is **Zèbre**, with its funky sounds, then **Autre Monde** (around 20 metres further on, on the left-hand side), a clean, quiet bar that is popular with well-behaved young people.

To avoid the crowds, head towards the end of rue St-Michel and turn left along rue St-Louis. **Bistrot de la Cité** (No. 5) is popular with local trendies; it may have an 'underground' atmosphere, but it's not as dodgy as it looks!

❣ Across place Ste-Anne from rue St-Michel is the legendary **rue de St-Malo**, a shrine to the 'Rennes sound', also described as 'anarcho-rock'. By day, this street is pretty much dead, but it comes alive after 10pm (except on Sunday and Monday nights). The street's atmosphere is reflected in the name of the bar at No. 40: the **Bernique Hurlante** (literally, the 'screaming limpet') ☎ 02-99-38-70-09; closed Sunday and Monday, which has become the in-place, with its eclectic decor. It's also the headquarters of a serious-minded political party Le Rut, which treats politics as art, the subject of creation, disruption and derision. There's also a lending library for gay literature.

Opposite are **Ozone** (at No. 9) and **Trinquette** (at No. 26), both also important places for anarcho-rock. A little further on is the **Déjazey Jazz Club** – don't miss it if you like Latin jazz (see 'Live Music and Theatre').

Most of these bars (above) close at 1am, when there is a mass exodus towards the following, which all have a licence to stay open later.

❣ **Le Chatham**: 5 rue de Montfort. Carry straight on after the end of the 'rue de la Soif'. ☎ 02-99-79-55-48. Open 6pm–3am. Closed Sunday. This place is a real institution, and you shouldn't miss it if you want to experience a typical Rennes atmosphere. It's a successful combination of an English pub and a French bar, and you almost feel like you've entered into the bowels of a smoky old ship. The maritime decor features highly varnished woodwork, old hulls, sea turtles and hoists from old sailing ships. The narrow central walkway gives customers the chance to have a good look around before getting to the second bar at the back. At the weekend, get there before 1am, otherwise you won't be able to make it through the crush of people. The music on offer is exclusively rock.

❣ **O'Connell's**: 6–7 place du Parlement-de-Bretagne. ☎ 02-99-79-38-76. Open every day 10am–1am. There's a great Irish atmosphere, and an excellent decor; there's a wooden floor, and you only need a bit of sawdust to imagine yourself in Ireland. You can eat here, and there's a good selection of dishes, often beer-based, such as Irish stew, duck, or beef cooked in Guinness. There's a good selection of beers and the Guinness is creamy, as it should be.

❣ **L'Aventure**: 5 allée Rallier-du-Baty (which leads into the rue Rallier-du-Baty). ☎ 02-99-79-37-44. Open 6pm–3am. Closed Sunday. Drinks cost 25–60F. Set in a courtyard at the end of a cul-de-sac (but still right next to all the other bars). The place itself is worth seeing – a large, warm nightclub decorated in an exotic baroque style, with casino lampshades, tall mirrors, hunting trophies, fabric wall coverings, plants, a piano and old American gadgets. The main bar is to the left, with a second bar in a room that is part hunting lodge, part smoking room. The music is a good blend of jazz and rock.

☛ **Le Nabuchodonosor**: 12 rue Hoche (behind the place du Palais). ☎ 02-99-27-07-58. Open from noon–1am. Closed Sunday and the first two weeks in August. A few steep steps up from the road, this wine bar with its ochre and grey tones is a favourite with art and architecture students. Allow about 75F for a meal. The wines are carefully chosen by the owner and sold at reasonable prices, with a few vintage wines sold by the bottle. The landlady serves roughly 8cl or 15cl – nothing more accurate – and also sells bottles to take away. The bar also serves snacks, with menus on slate boards; options might include grilled goats' cheese on toast (*chèvre grillé sur toast*) and a decent *pâté maison*. Desserts include apple crumble or chocolate gateau with

almonds. Two guitarists play live every Wednesday evening, but the music is nowhere near as loud as in other places in town.

☛ **Le Picca Bar**: place de la Mairie. ☎ 02-99-78-17-17. This is the ideal place if you want something to eat at any time of the day or night. It's the sort of place where bands hang out after the gig has finished. Everyone gets thrown out about 7am so that they can clean up. Since it's daylight by then, you can head for the market on place des Lices for more food or a glass of wine (if you can face it!).

☛ **Le Chantier**: 18 Carrefour Jouanst (at the bottom end of the place des Lices). ☎ 02-99-31-58-18. Open 11am–1am. Closed Sunday in winter. This techno bar has a DJ every night and special evenings every weekend, so it's a good place to go to find out about the local rave scene. The decor has 'building site' written all over it but there are also pictures by local artists on show.

☛ **Le Café des Beaux-Arts**: 3 rue Hoche (opposite the Nabuchodonosor). ☎ 02-99-36-28-75. Open Monday–Saturday 11am–1am (opens 3pm Saturday). Closed Sunday and public holidays. This place has a good atmosphere in typical Rennes rock tradition and is one of the 'top ten' for party animals. Don't miss it.

On the other side of the River Vilaine, things are much less frenetic but you'll find this is a really good little spot. It's not so much geared towards the under-25s and the music is less rock-centred.

☛ **Elsa Popping**: 19 rue du Poullain-Duparc. ☎ 02-99-78-31-71. Open 9am–1am (Saturday 5pm–1am). Closed Sunday and in August. This is a great little bar with a leftish sort of clientele of all ages from 17 upwards. It has a 'lived-in' feel and there's always someone at the bar to chat to. Local musicians and artists use it as a meeting place and there's live music on Wednesday evenings.

LIVE MUSIC AND THEATRE

– **Théâtre National de Bretagne** (National Theatre of Brittany): on the corner of avenue Jean-Janvier and rue St-Hélier. ☎ 02-99-31-55-33. Closed from the end of July to the end of August. A large complex that puts on a number of different shows throughout the year in its three theatres. All genres are represented, but the quality is consistently good.

– **Le Bacchus**: 23 rue de la Chalotais (behind the post office, in the direction of place de la Bretagne). ☎ 02-99-78-39-93. This café-theatre has a 'left-bank' ambiance and there are frequent performances from regional companies and from Paris. Telephone for details of the programme. Admission costs 70F, with the usual reductions.

– **Le Chat Qui Pêche**: 2 rue des Francs-Bourgeois. ☎ 02-99-79-63-64. There are two entrances: one on place St-Germain and one on quai Chateaubriand. Admission is free and yet the price of drinks is not too inflated – surprisingly. This is a great place for listening to good jazz in a relaxed atmosphere.

– **Le Déjazey Jazz Club**: 54 rue St-Malo. ☎ 02-99-38-70-72. Open 5pm–3am. Closed Sunday. Listen to the jazz or have a cocktail in a performance space that feels like a small club. They do two concerts a week, and some are free, but then the drinks cost more. The programme is on a par with the good jazz clubs in Paris.

– **L'Ubu**: 1 rue St-Hélier (attached to the Théâtre National de Bretagne). ☎ 02-99-30-31-68. This is the powerhouse of all rock activity in Rennes, run by the organizers of the 'Transmusicales' (*see below*). A top-quality, up-to-the-minute programme in a really great atmosphere.

– **Salle de la Cité**: 10 rue St-Louis. ☎ 02-99-79-10-66. Rock, jazz and other kinds of live music in a small auditorium.

WHAT TO SEE

The Old Town

Following a route around these sites makes for a very pleasant walk. Visiting on foot is much the best option – predictably, parking and getting around by car are very difficult these days – and some of the pedestrian streets still follow the medieval layout. The great fire of 1720 spared some of the buildings around the cathedral, and the contrast between this area and the surroundings of the Breton parliament building, which was rebuilt after the fire, is one of the more interesting aspects of the city centre.

★ **Cathédrale St-Pierre** (A3, **50** on the map): rue de la Monnaie. Open 9am–noon and 2–7pm. There is nothing left of the two buildings that were built on the site of a former Gallo-Roman temple prior to the 16th century. Work on the 'new' facade began in 1560, but was not completed until a century later. The sun at the top, representing Louis XIV, was put there to symbolize the dominant influence of France. The church largely collapsed during the 18th century and rebuilding was completed around 1850. All that remains of the classical period are the two balustrade towers. The result is a lack of unity, but the interior decoration provides some relief. The sober note of the neo-classical architecture is hidden behind the heavy gold-and-stucco ornamentation that was added in the second half of the 19th century. This was a typical example of the 'good taste' of Rennes' triumphant bourgeoisie. In the right-hand aisle is a splendid 16th-century altarpiece from the Anvers school; a series of beautiful scenes in medieval costumes retell the story of the Nativity.

RENNES

★ **Rue de la Psalette**: this little street running alongside the cathedral, and nearby rue St-Sauveur, have charming rows of old low buildings. One of the most attractive in the area is No. 3 rue St-Guillaume. At the corner of the rue de la Psalette and the rue du Chapitre there are some remarkable sculpted beams.

★ **Les Portes Mordelaises** (A3 on the map): these are the rare remains of the 15th-century town ramparts. The main gate into the town was located at the end of a little street off rue de la Monnaie. It was through this gate that the former dukes of Brittany entered the town for their coronation. Before being crowned, they had to take an oath that they would always fight for the independence of their country. The area around the Portes Mordelaises has recently been renovated.

★ **Place des Lices** (A3 on the map): this large square was the setting for tournaments in the Middle Ages, and the French hero Bertrand Du Guesclin would certainly have crossed a few swords here. During the 17th century, the square was lined with fine bourgeois residences and town-houses. The remarkable line of tall, half-timbered houses with their hull-shaped roofs (between the rue des Minimes and the rue des Innocents) is certainly worth seeing. It's a pity that one modern building now dominates the skyline – the architects and planners really deserve a booby prize for urban aesthetics.

On Saturday mornings, the square comes alive to the sounds and sights of one of the biggest markets in France. If you're in Rennes on a Saturday, be sure not to miss it.

★ Two quiet, pretty little streets, **rue des Dames** and **rue St-Yves,** follow exactly the line of the 14th-century city walls and are lined with townhouses and attractive bourgeois residences. On the corner of the rue Lebouteiller is the Chapelle St-Yves, built in 1494, which has just been restored and now houses the tourist office.

★ **Rue du Chapitre** (A3 on the map) has some fine examples of medieval architecture. At No. 22 is a sculpted facade dating back to 1580. At No. 6, the **Hôtel de Blossac** has a splendid gate, an interesting inner courtyard and, to the left (in the courtyard), a monumental staircase with an elegant wrought-iron banister. In rue de Clisson, **Basilique St-Sauveur** (St Saviour's Basilica) is one of the few buildings that survived the great fire of 1720. The composer Gabriel Fauré was organist here in the 1860s, before leaving for Paris. Strangely, Rennes seems to have ignored this famous resident and there is not so much as a plaque anywhere.

★ On the borderline between the old town of Rennes and the 'classical town' built after 1720, there is a lovely **townhouse** with a corner turret, on the corner of rue Le Bastard and rue Champ-Jacquet. About one hundred metres further on, the houses from Nos. 11–15 on place du Champ-Jacquet have wonderful facades that are completely lopsided. Nearby (at No. 5) is a townhouse, built in 1660, that demonstrates how the builders of Rennes began to use stone instead of wood.

★ On **rue St-Michel**, all the buildings are architecturally similar. The street has been very nicely renovated, and leads through to the place Ste-Anne, a quiet square that is home to the **Maison de Leperdit**, a beautiful house named after the mayor of Rennes at the time of the French Revolution, and to the **Église St-Aubin**.

The Classical Town

★ **Parlement de Bretagne** (Breton Parliament) (B3, **51** on the map): place du Parlement. ☎ 02-99-67-11-11 to book a tour. Admission costs 40F. This building, designed by Salomon de Brosse, is a major part of Rennes' architectural and civic heritage. Once the seat of the Breton parliament, and later used to house the law courts, the building was devastated by fire in 1994. Recently reopened after total restoration, it is now used by the Court of Appeal and is open to the public for guided tours.

★ **Hôtel de Ville** (B3, **52** on the map): place de la Mairie. Open Monday–Friday 8.30am–5pm, Saturday 8.30am–noon. Closed Sunday and public holidays. Admission is free. Rennes' town hall is the work of Jacques III Gabriel (father of Jacques IV, who designed the Petit Trianon at the Palace of Versailles and the layout for the place de la Concorde in Paris). This grand building has at its centre a lantern steeple bearing a clock, which sits above a sculpted pediment supported by four columns. Two curved pavilions join the centre to two large annexes.

Under the pediment there is a large empty alcove. For a long time, this held a sculpture that personified the union of Brittany and France. Brittany was depicted as a woman on her knees, holding the hands of the French king, who was seated. In 1932, on the anniversary of the Act of Union, this sculpture, seen as a humiliating symbol of oppression, was blown up by an organization seeking Breton autonomy. In Vannes, another sculpture, known as *La Cohue* or 'The Crowd', suffered the same fate at the same time.

Parts of the Hôtel de Ville are open to the public, including the old chapel, the large staircase, which is adorned with tapestries, and the room used for civil weddings.

Opposite the Hôtel de Ville is the neoclassical **Grand Théâtre**, built in 1831.

★ On the east side, the place de la Mairie leads into **rue St-Georges**, one of the few buildings to survive the great fire of 1720. It is a harmonious mixture of styles, with half-timbered houses standing alongside beautiful town-houses. Each building is worth special attention.

★ **Église St-Germain** (B3, **53** on the map): place St-Germain. Open 9am–noon and 2–6pm (Sunday 4–6pm). This former parish church for traders and haberdashers was built in the 15th century and has a fine west front in the Flamboyant Gothic style. Inside, there is a wonderful stained-glass window from the same period, depicting the story of the Virgin and the Passion.

At night, the streets surrounding the church glimmer in the pale light of the street lamps, before opening up onto the dazzling rue St-Georges. Rue Corbin leads into the old **Palais Abbatial St-Georges** (abbey palace), built in 1670 (on the corner with rue Gambetta).

★ **Église Notre-Dame** (B2, **54** on the map): place St-Mélaine. Open daily, 9am–noon and 3–7pm. This old abbey-church, originally dating back to the 11th century, was rebuilt in the 14th century. The elegant classical facade was added to the old Romanesque tower in 1672. Inside, all that remains of the Romanesque period is the transept crossing with its wide, sober arches.

★ **Jardins du Thabor** (Thabor gardens) (B2, **55** on the map): ever since the 18th century, the old abbey grounds, next to Notre-Dame, have provided a setting for pleasant walks through beautiful French-style gardens. Admission is free.

★ **La Cité Judiciaire**: boulevard de la Tour-d'Auvergne. Rennes' court-rooms are housed in an ultra-modern building that looks like a glass-and-steel mushroom. Unless you are keen on huge megalopolis-style complexes, the new Colombier district, next to the Champ-de-Mars, holds little interest. There is one modern sculpture of note – entitled 'Unity' – on the corner of boulevard de la Liberté and rue Tronjolly.

The South Bank

★ **Musée des Beaux-Arts** (museum of fine arts) (B3, **56** on the map): 20 quai Émile-Zola. ☎ 02-99-28-55-85. Open 10am–noon and 2–6pm. Closed Tuesday. This rich and rather eclectic collection includes Egyptian and Greek archaeology, Breton painters (with one room dedicated to the Pont-Aven artists), a few Italian Primitives and various 19th-century sculptures. Among the 19th-century paintings is Corot's *Passage du Gué* ('Crossing the Ford'), together with other academy works. The 18th century is represented by Chardin and Van Loo, while Le Brun *(Descente de la Croix*, or 'Descent from the Cross') and Philippe de Champaigne *(Madeleine Repentante*, or 'Mary Magdalene Penitent') carry the baton for the 17th century. The museum's masterpiece is *Le Nouveau-Né* ('The Newborn') by Georges de La Tour – a wonderful expression of light. The temporary exhibitions organized by the museum on a regular basis are also worth a look.

★ **Écomusée du Pays de Rennes (Ferme de la Bintinais)** (open-air museum of the Rennes area): on the road towards Châtillon-sur-Seiche, about 4 kilometres (2.5 miles) from the town centre. ☎ 02-99-51-38-15. ✗ Open April–September Tuesday–Friday 9am–6pm, Saturday 2–6pm, Sunday 2–7pm; October–March as before but closed daily noon–2pm. Closed on public holidays. Bus access from Rennes: route 14, stop at 'Le Gacet' (on Sunday, take route 1, stop at 'Tage'), or route 61, stopping at 'Le Hil-La Bintinais'.

The farm on this site was known as 'La Bintinais', and the name has now been adopted by this lovely open-air museum. A permanent exhibition has returned some of the land to its original use; the aim is to explain the relationship between man and his environment in the area around Rennes from the 16th century to the present day. The social and cultural changes are shown through architecture, costume, housing (including wonderful kitchen reconstructions), language and leisure, using excellent models and slide shows.

The centre depicts the history of farming techniques and production on an area of cultivated land covering 20 hectares (50 acres). The land also supports a number of regional livestock breeds, some of which were threatened with extinction until recently. These include the Rennes cuckoo-chicken (which you now find on sale at plenty of poultry counters as well as on the menu in some restaurants), the piebald Breton cow and the Breton *landes* sheep. The well-designed exhibition follows a marked route around the stables, the pig-sties, the sheep pens, and so on. There are temporary exhibitions and events covering a variety of topics. Allow a good 2 hours for a visit.

If you happen to be in Rennes on a Sunday at the end of November, try to go to the centre for **La Fête du Pommé**. They spend an entire day preparing apples, which are peeled, then cut up and cooked very slowly and gently in a huge cauldron in the fireplace. The result is an apple juice like a semi-liquid paste, full of delicate flavours, which is called *le pommé*. This is a day when, alongside the tastings, they organize talks, performances of traditional music and dancing.

★ **Industrial tourism**: the **Citroën** factory in La Janais, on the road to Lorient, was opened in 1961. Brittany is also the location for the print works of **Ouest France**, the newspaper for western France, which has a circulation of 790,000 (the largest circulation for any French daily paper). Both sites cater for visitors, primarily for pre-booked groups, but demand is high and there is a long waiting list. Citroën: ☎ 02-23-36-38-05. The 2-hour visit is free, but by appointment only. Ouest France: ☎ 02-99-32-60-00.

★ **Rue Vasselot**: a well-restored remnant in the old lower town. Look out for the excellent 17th-century external wooden staircase at No. 34, in the courtyard. Next door is the 17th-century **Église de Toussaints** (All Saints' Church).

★ **Lycée Émile-Zola**: avenue Janvier. Worth seeing not so much for its distinctive architecture, but more for what it symbolizes, as the scene of a major social and political event in France – the second trial of Captain Alfred Dreyfus in August 1899, which took place following the sensational '*J'accuse*' essay by Zola. At the time, the country was divided by opinion, with constant confrontation between the pro-Dreyfus intellectuals, left-wing militants, anti-militarists, humanists and liberals, and his opponents, many of whom were from the clergy, and anti-Semitic right-wingers.

★ **Les Mosaïques Odorico** (the Odorico mosaics): the end of the 19th century saw the arrival in Rennes of two Italian brothers who were skilled artists in mosaic. The Odorico brothers received commissions from a number of architects to provide the decorative finish for many kinds of buildings, including residences, commercial buildings, a swimming pool, a post office and various buildings on the university campus. If the work of Gaudí in Barcelona appeals to you, then you'll certainly like this – it's art deco at its most extravagant. The tourist office offers a tour of Rennes that takes in a lot of their work.

FESTIVALS AND HAPPENINGS

– The '**Tombées de la Nuit**', or 'Twilight' festival, takes place for a week in early July. The programme is specifically oriented towards local creativity – song, poetry, dance, theatre, café-theatre, mime, cinema, cartoon art – although it does have slots for the other regions of France, Europe and the world. The main aim is to give artistes from Brittany an opportunity to perform outside Paris, or perhaps be discovered.

The festival takes place in more than a hundred spaces all over Rennes and seems to take over the entire town. The old streets and squares provide a wonderful backdrop for performers and artists, who themselves, in a way, become part of the festival. The large squares host the major productions, while the little squares and courtyards are just right for the more intimate performances of poetry, puppetry and storytelling. The churches are used for some of the concerts, and out on the streets there are clowns, mime artists, jugglers and other street performers.

– **Les Transmusicales**: ☎ 02-99-31-12-10. The 'Transmusicales' is a major rock festival that brings together performers from all over France, and beyond, taking place annually for three days in the first week of December. It's a unique opportunity to get an overview of all the new developments and trends in music, and musical research. Many of the enthusiastic audiences come expecting to see previously unknown talents, and they are rarely disappointed.

The Transmusicales is a major event in the rock calendar, and perhaps because of it, Rennes has turned into a place where rock is everywhere. The city has seen the birth of lots of big names in the French rock world and there are plenty of bars where you can get to hear examples of every genre. There are also numerous rehearsal and recording studios, such as the 'Fun House' and the 'Balloon Farm Studio', which are used by all kinds of groups.

Purists claim that the 'Trans' is not the same as it used to be, and that it has become a showbiz festival, and a marketing machine for the major record labels. According to them, it has lost sight of its original aim, which was to give new bands a chance to be discovered. As a result, one group has set up the **Folies Rennaises**, a festival that tries to re-create the original intensity of the Transmusicales, during which the maddest groups perform in the hottest bars. However, it seems that severe financial difficulties may have got the better of the Folies. Watch this space.

– **Traveling**: this is a film festival on the theme of cities of the world (Berlin, Madrid, Quebec City, Cairo, imaginary cities . . . in 2001 it's Dublin). This festival takes place each year in the second week of March, and uses various cinemas and arts venues. There's a special programme for children.

– **Marché des Lices**: happens in the place des Lices every Saturday and it's the place to go if you want to meet the people of Rennes, who flock here in huge numbers, as well as students and people passing through. It's an entertaining experience, with street artists and many other distractions.

In the Rennes Area

CHÂTEAUGIRON

This characterful little town, about 15 kilometres (10 miles) to the southeast of Rennes in the direction of La Guerche and Angers, has so far remained relatively free of hordes of tourists. The medieval castle is stunning, with imposing ramparts and two beautiful towers framing the more traditional main building.

The tourist office (in the town hall in the castle) can provide all sorts of information and runs guided tours of the castle during summer weekends.

The main street, **rue de la Madeleine**, has a number of half-timbered houses dating from the 16th to the 19th century. Lower down is a picturesque lake, which is clean and makes a pleasant place for a swim.

🛏 ✖ **L'Auberge du Cheval Blanc**: 7 rue de la Madeleine (in the town centre). ☎ 02-99-37-40-27. Fax: 02-99-37-59-68. The hotel-restaurant, run by the Cottebrune family for four generations, is an old 17th-century post house, made entirely of wood. The traditional, simple rooms in the attic, with its exposed beams, are the most comfortable. A double room costs 280F and half board is available for 230F per person. The restaurant serves generous and well-prepared traditional meals, with set menus for 80F, 110F and 140F.

NOUVOITOU

★ **Nouvoitou** Until 1950, the people of this town, 3 kilometres (2 miles) to the west of Châteaugiron, relied on the production of sailcloth for their livelihood. The local farms produced the hemp and the flax and then carried out the actual production of the cloth. In winter, skeins would be spun by the women of the farm, then the cloth was woven on looms.

Nouvoitou's church has a wonderful late-15th-century altarpiece.

★ **Moulin à Farine du Tertron** (Le Tertron flour mill): near Nouvoitou (head in the direction of St-Armel, then aim for Épron; carry on as far as the hamlet, and take the steep road down, to the right of L'Ourmais). The mill is still in full working order, and there is also a pleasant walk along the banks of the Seiche here.

DOMAGNÉ

★ **Musée du Cidre Louis-Raison** (cider museum): in the village of Domagné, about 10 kilometres (6 miles) to the east of Châteaugiron on the D34. Well signposted from the centre of the village. ☎ 02-99-00-06-80. ♿ Open Monday–Friday 9am–noon and 2–6.30pm, Sunday and public holidays 2–6.30pm. Closed Saturday, and Monday morning out of season; also closed December–March. Price of admission (20F) includes a bowl of cider. This museum presents the entire history of the Raison family, which is behind one of the region's leading cider companies. On display are all the old tools and machinery that was once used in the production of cider – various stills, a press, a crushing tower, a bottle-washer and an apple-crusher – as well as reconstructions of old shops. Allow a good 2 hours.

THOURIÉ

★ **Musée de la Ferme d'autrefois: Le Grand-Beaumont** (museum of traditional farming): Le Grand-Beaumont, 35134 Thourié. ☎ 02-99-43-11-55. Located 35 kilometres (20 miles) south of Rennes on the D163; take the first turning on the right after you have passed through the town. Open mid-May to mid-October, 10am–noon and 3–6pm. Phone in advance to arrange a guided tour with M. Hunault, who used to be a farmer and is a collector of agricultural and craft equipment. He has put together an extraordinary collection of old tractors that he restores. The tours are very lively and he will even set the tractors going. Traditional threshing events are organized in the summer months.

NOYAL-SUR-VILAINE

★ **La Vallée des Canards** (duck valley): La Heurtelais, on the road to Châteaugiron at Noyal-sur-Vilaine. ☎ 02-99-00-65-66. From Rennes, take the N157 towards Vitré; from Châteaugiron, go to Noyal-sur-Vilaine on the CD92. Open during the season 9.30am–noon and 2–7pm; out of season 2–7pm only. There's an admission charge of about 32F. Here's where to come if you have an interest in ducks apart from on the dinner table. They have more than a hundred types of duck here and some pretty walks besides.

The Vilaine Valley

This route around the Vilaine valley may not be spectacular, but it is nice and gentle, with pretty little villages along the way, and picturesque spots. From Rennes to Redon, the Vilaine river meanders through rich agricultural land and massifs of sandstone and red schist (a crystalline rock commonly used in building in the area), which in places cuts deep into the hillsides. This route follows the river the whole time, crossing and re-crossing it, and provides pleasant views over its meanderings. Sometimes the road comes right up to the riverbank, running alongside a quiet towpath and surrounded by rolling countryside.

★ **Bruz**: 12 kilometres (7 miles) to the south of Rennes, and to the east of the Vilaine, is the **Parc Ornithologique de Bretagne**. ☎ 02-99-52-68-57. This bird sanctuary is open every day from 1 March to 15 November, 10am–noon and 2–7pm in July and August and more restricted hours the rest of the year. The sanctuary is home to more than 1,000 live exotic birds, including parrots, cockatoos and lories.

★ **Pont-Réan**: 3 kilometres (2 miles) to the south of Bruz, this town has a purplish appearance, because of the reddish-purple schist used in its buildings. There is a listed bridge dating back to the 18th century. The town makes a pretty base for anyone using the canoes, kayaks and pleasure boats that potter up and down the Vilaine.

★ **Le Moulin de Boël**: (mill, well signposted from Pont-Réan). The pretty, rolling countryside around this mill reminds you of the Dordogne region. This is one of the last mills built in the 17th century using a technique designed to cope with the current – it has a spur-shaped wall upstream. The roof is made in five sections. The mill is a favourite visitor attraction and it can get crowded at weekends in good weather. The surrounding area is very popular for hiking and horse-riding. Mountain bikers like it too and there are a few tracks that are rated as demanding great skill, according to the specialists.

★ **La Bouëxière**: on the road between Pont-Réan and Bourg-des-Comptes, as you come down towards the Vilaine, take a look at this hamlet, made up of three beautiful farms. Lower down is a pretty view over the river.

★ **Bourg-des-Comptes**: a village with character and a pretty main square. The church is surrounded by old houses all in a similar architectural style, built in granite with brick window surrounds. There are two medieval residences near the post office, one of which is flanked by a tall turret, while the other has a very elegant front door. The little **Port de la Courbe** (along rue de la Courbe) is a perfectly peaceful spot in green countryside and there's an old wooden pontoon. If you fancy a quiet drink, the perfect place is the terrace of the Rox-Bar.

If you walk down towards the river, you will see some pretty little stone houses amid all the greenery. Down the nearby rue du Moulin-de-la-Courbe, take a look at the mill. Twenty years ago it was still functioning as a mill, although it has now been transformed into a pretty house. This is a charming spot – although it gets invaded by picnickers at weekends.

✗ **Auberge du Relais de la Place**: 16 place de l'Église. ☎ 02-99-57-41-12. Fax: 02-99-57-41-57. Closed the first week in January. Booking is recommended. This inn, in a perfect country setting, offers traditional rustic cooking, with a selection of homemade pâtés, Rennes guinea fowl sautéed in cider, a filling local dish of rabbit with chestnuts, stewed in cider, and, to order, suckling pig (*cochon de lait*) with almonds. Game is also served (when it's in season). There's a set menu for 75F (except Saturday evening and public holidays) and others from 98F to 225F, and all the menus offer excellent value for money. Desserts are extra. The wine list is impressive and the service is extremely friendly. This place is definitely worth coming back to.

★ **Pléchâtel**: a little village on a hill overlooking the Vilaine, with lots of amazing old houses. In front of the post office is one of the most beautiful crosses in the area (dating back to the 14th century). To the left of the post office, take the one-way street, which will lead you along a pretty little road to a deliciously shady spot on the banks of the river.

While you're in the village, take a look behind the presbytery in the direction of La Levée, and you'll find some caves that have recently been opened up. There's also an ancient oak tree hidden away in the forest – ask for directions at the hairdressers in Pléchâtel. At St-Senoux, on the road towards Guichen, there's a lovely Byzantine church, also tucked away in the depths of the forest.

★ **St-Malo-de-Phily**: a peaceful village perched high up on a hill. About 500 metres away, in the middle of the countryside, is a lovely chapel (well signposted). There is also some wonderful rural architecture in the area. On the way to the chapel, there is an amazing farm with a facade beautifully decorated with schist and sandstone, with dovecotes set into it and topped with an elegant sculpted stone window. Keen walkers can pick up the route of the GR39 from the chapel, or one of many other superb footpaths in the surrounding area. At the lower end of the town, you can go for a little walk in front of the stylish and elegant Château de la Driennais.

★ The pretty **river port**, which separates **Messac** and **Guipry** (one on either side), is worth a detour. Messac is one of the most popular spots in Brittany for hiring a riverboat. Right in the middle of the river is the imposing silhouette of the former flour mill, which has now been converted into a *crêperie*.

ILLE-ET-VILAINE

â **Gîte d'étape municipal**: Information from Mme Guihard: ☎ 02-99-34-67-34. This municipal shelter (traditionally for long-distance walkers) is set in a typical mid-Vilaine-style house, beautifully maintained and with a lovely fireplace. It's open all year round and there are 40 beds, laid out in dormitories.

■ **Canoes/kayaks**: information on canoe/kayak rental from next door to the pretty ivy-clad tourist office in Messac, square de la Liberté. Open from 15 June to 15 September. ☎ 02-99-34-61-60.

■ **Riverboat hire** (including narrowboats that you can sleep on): operated by Crown Blue Line. ☎ 02-99-34-60-11. Fax: 02-99-34-25-27. Closed Sunday in season and weekends out of season. A pleasant way to discover the region.

★ **Les Corbinières**: follow the D77 then the D127, a gorgeous, narrow country road across one of the most beautiful valleys along the course of the Vilaine. The river narrows at the bottom of a gorge. A terrific spot for a walk or for mountain-biking.

– The bridge at **Port-de-Roche** provides another stunning view over the river and over the lovely manor house at La Chaussaie. It has elegant wrought ironwork, and, on the arch, the imperial seal of Napoleon III and Eugénie. The structure was one of the leading exhibits at the 1867 World Fair and was dismantled and rebuilt here the following year.

– 10 kilometres (6 miles) further east is the famous **Donjon du Grand-Fougeray**, Du Guesclin's keep, on the edge of a lake in a park full of splendid, ancient trees.

★ **Le Manoir de l'Automobile** (motor museum): at **Lohéac**, on the road to Lieuron, about 1 kilometre from the centre. ☎ 02-99-34-02-32. Open all year round, 10am–1pm and 2–7pm, every day except Monday (except in July and August). Also open on public holidays. There's an admission charge of 35F. This gigantic museum houses more than 200 cars – everything from an 1899 Dedion-Bouton to a Countach, via a superb 1961 Facel-Vega. The displays are informative and intelligently organized, and cover just about everything imaginable to do with cars. There are a number of cars that were popular before World War II, some amazing prototypes that took part in the Le Mans 24-hour rally, as well as dozens of Renault Alpines, including the first A106. There is also an Italian room, with 12 Lamborghini models – the ones with those breathtaking streamlines. The 'prestige' cars section is well stocked with Rolls-Royces, Packards, Cadillacs, and other convertibles (including some lovely Peugeot 304s, 504s and 403s). There's also a 'models' section and a 'garage' section to round off this impressive collection. It's worth knowing that every Saturday, visitors' names are drawn out of a hat and winners are taken for a drive in one of the cars in the collection.

★ At **St-Just**, if you take the D54 from Port-de-Roche, you come across an amazing megalithic site with rows of standing stones on the moorland at Cajoux and there's an incredible 'chaos' of rocks at Tréal (*see* 'What To Do in the Redon Area').

★ **Langon**: this is a little town built in terraces up the side of a hill. The **Église St-Pierre** has a very unusual steeple, surrounded by 12 mini-steeples, and features some Romanesque art, with one fresco dating back to the 12th century. One curiosity: the little Chapelle Sainte-Agathe has Gallo-Roman walls (alternating courses of brick and stone, in a style typical of the period), which makes it one of the oldest monuments in Brittany. Inside, in the apse, traces of a Roman fresco have been discovered beneath a later painting. You can clearly distinguish a little cupid astride a dolphin, surrounded by fish, and Venus emerging from the waves. Historians deduce that the chapel was originally a temple to the goddess of love.

Next to the town, on the Moulin moor, are about 30 menhirs (single standing stones), known locally as the *demoiselles* ('young ladies'). Legend has it that a group of young women preferred dancing on the moors to going to vespers, and that God turned them into stones as a punishment.

About 1 kilometre along the road from Langon to La Chapelle-de-Brain, a signpost marks a long section of Roman road. Located in the village of La Louzais, the road is still intact, and can be found under a tunnel of trees right next to the river. A little sign reminds the visitor that 'the Romans got their slaves, the Gauls, to build this road for them . . .'

🏠 **Local gîtes**: information is available at the town hall. ☎ 02-99-08-76-55.

★ Before arriving in Redon, the road from Brain-sur-Vilaine to Renac passes through lush green, peaceful countryside.

REDON 35600 (Pop: 10,545)

Situated at the confluence of the Vilaine, the Oust and the Nantes–Brest canal, Redon is Brittany's answer to Venice. There are bridges everywhere, so much so that you can end up forgetting which river you are actually crossing. The town is right on the edge of the departments of Ille-et-Vilaine, Morbihan and Loire-Atlantique, and is split between two administrative regions (Brittany and Pays de la Loire). Added to this, the town is an important hub of the rail network and this combination of factors makes it difficult to get to grips with the true identity of the place. The streets of the old town, however, bear witness to a time in the Middle Ages when Redon had influence across the whole of Brittany.

All around the town, you cannot miss the Vilaine and its tributaries:

– The **Oust**, whose valley alternates between wide, marshy depressions and steep-sided valleys. The best example is probably the Île aux Pies, at St-Vincent-sur-Oust.

– The **Isac**, whose size is doubled by the addition of the Nantes–Brest canal, cuts through beautiful forests (St-Gildas, Le Gâvre, Fresnay) and other pleasant spots including St-Clair and Pont-Miny.

– The **Don** winds its way from east to west alongside a ridge, finding its way out to the sea.

– The **Chère** and the **Semnon** to the north both meander tortuously across a landscape characterized by woodland, swamp and rolling hills.

– The **Aff**, a tributary of the Oust, is fed by the **Oyon**, whose source is in the Forêt de Paimpont. It's the prettiest valley in the Vilaine region, with several manor houses and mills with waterwheels. There are more than a thousand watermills in Brittany, and a watermill association has been set up to organize various events; it is based at the mill museum in Les Récollets at Pontivy.

Redon in History

Despite its position at the far end of an estuary, Redon is still classified as a maritime port of the Vilaine. The town grew up around a monastery that was founded in 832 by Konvoïon, a minister in the reign of King Nominoë. The ancient Abbaye St-Sauveur (St Saviour's Abbey, now the Église St-Sauveur) has been besieged, destroyed and rebuilt on a number of occasions over the centuries.

It is worth remembering that Redon, a regional administrative centre of Ille-et-Vilaine, has an important position as the meeting point of the waterways serving the west. Since so many rivers converge at Redon, it is the central docking point for all the horse-drawn barges that ply these rivers; information is available from the tourist office.

The town puts a lot of effort into its splendid floral decoration, and has won many awards in national competitions (including first prize in 1983).

Like many towns, Redon has had its share of economic difficulties. It was once the manufacturing base of Flaminaire cigarette lighters, and it was a centre for the development of mechanized agriculture. Fortunately, the Yves Rocher factory at nearby La Gacilly, in Morbihan, which produces a whole range of plant-based beauty products, is thriving.

USEFUL ADDRESSES

❿ Office du tourisme du Pays de Redon (tourist office for the Redon region): place de la République. ☎ 02-99-71-06-04. Fax: 02-99-71-01-59. Email: tourisme.redon@wanadoo.fr. In season, open Monday–Saturday 9am–7pm, Sunday 10am–noon and 4–7pm; the rest of the year, open Monday–Saturday 9am–noon and 2–6pm.

❿ Pays d'accueil de Vilaine: a welcome service for the area. ☎ 02-99-72-72-11. Fax: 02-99-72-36-68. Website: www.rivieres-oceanes.com

WHERE TO STAY

☆ Budget

⌂ Walkers' shelter: at the home of Mme Le Villoux, Le Lot, in Rieux, 10 kilometres (6 miles) to the south of Redon and 1.5 kilometres from Rieux. ☎ 02-99-91-90-25. Closed in December and January. Sleeping accommodation is in dormitories with 5–20 beds. The setting is rural, on an old farm, and there are kitchen facilities and an open fire in the lounge. One night costs 51F. Bring a sleeping bag. The owners are very nice and it is all very relaxed. There is also a camping area.

☆☆ Moderate

⌂ Hôtel Le France: 30 rue Du Guesclin. ☎ 02-99-71-06-11. Fax: 02-99-72-17-92. Closed from Christmas to 7 January. This is a rather unremarkable hotel, set in the pretty area around the port. It's essentially just somewhere to sleep, although some of the rooms are quite nice, with a balcony looking out over the quayside. Double rooms cost 180–290F.

⚐ ✗ **Asther Hotel**: 14 rue des Douves (facing place aux Marrons). ☎ 02-99-71-10-91. Fax: 02-99-72-11-92. The main selling point is that it's right in the centre of town. Open all year round, this hotel has comfortable, well-kept rooms for 250–260F. The welcome is good and overall the place offers good value for money. There's also a restaurant, offering set menus from 68F to 119F.

WHERE TO EAT

✗ **Crêperie L'Akène**: 10 rue du Jeu-de-Paume; near the old port. ☎ 02-99-71-25-15. Expect to pay about 85F for a complete meal. The setting is lovely and you can get good-quality food for reasonable prices. They serve a good range of *galettes* and salad dishes. After your meal, you could stroll a few yards along the road for a drink at the pleasant Bar du Port.

✗ **Auberge des Marais**: 80 avenue Jean-Burel. ☎ 02-99-71-02-48. Closed Sunday, Friday evening out of season, and for two weeks in July. This pretty little ivy-clad inn has a quiet, provincial atmosphere. It serves set menus from 68F to 115F, with the cheaper menus being very reasonable and the more expensive ones downright substantial. The service is friendly.

☆☆☆ Chic

✗ **L'Auberge du Poteau Vert**: 5 kilometres (3 miles) from St-Nico-las-de-Redon, on the Nantes road, on the right if you're coming from Redon. Outside, there's a green post – not surprising as the name translates as 'The Green Post Inn'. ☎ 02-99-71-13-12. ♿ Closed Sunday evening, Monday, Tuesday evening and public holiday evenings. This is *the* sophisticated and upmarket place to eat, although the atmosphere is still friendly and unpretentious. Set-price menus start at 95F (weekday lunchtime) and go up to 320F. For example, the 130F menu might start with fresh salmon carpaccio with lime (*carpaccio de saumon frais au citron vert*), or monkfish (*lotte*) bourguignon in Loire Valley wine, and finish with a selection of sorbets and a *coulis* of red fruits. It goes without saying that the more expensive menus are a real treat for the taste buds, although you might well end up paying more than you intended.

WHAT TO SEE

★ **Église St-Sauveur**: the former abbey-church of an 11th-century monastery. Its curious features include a wonderful 14th-century Gothic steeple, which is 57 metres (185 feet) high and stands strangely separate from the rest of the church. In 1780, the building was seriously damaged by a major fire. When it was rebuilt, the nave was made five rows shorter, probably for reasons of cost, and the tower ended up adrift. The roof was rebuilt in the shape of an inverted hull. The most interesting feature is the pretty multi-coloured Romanesque tower, built in an unusual mixture of red sandstone and grey granite, and the only example of this style anywhere in Brittany. The harmonious range of round-arched windows across three storeys,

ILLE-ET-VILAINE

which is also rare in France, creates a beautiful effect. Inside, the Romanesque nave is quite dark. The lowering of the roof ruled out the possibility of large stained-glass windows, although the windows in the Gothic chancel are quite high. There is a vast 17th-century altarpiece, and on the pillar to the right of the chancel is a delicate and highly decorated wooden Virgin dating from the 15th century. Before you leave, take a look at the cloisters.

★ **La Grand-Rue**: this is the town's main shopping street, and it has a few old houses, some of sandstone and some half-timbered.

★ **Quartier du port**: right at the bottom of the Grand-Rue, the port area of the town has a beautiful view over the series of floral locks. It is surrounded by the Vilaine and the docks, and has a distinctive style of architecture. An interesting combination of sandstone and granite was used to build the old salt stores, to be seen at 32–38 rue du Port (a continuation of the Grand-Rue). Right at the bottom there are two run-down townhouses, one of which has an elegant square corner tower (the 'Tour Richelieu'). To the left, there is a pleasant walk along the towpath next to the Vilaine.

★ **Musée de la Batellerie** (inland waterways museum): quai Jean-Bart. ☎ 02-99-72-30-95. From 15 June to 15 September, open every day 10am–noon and 3–6pm; out of season, open Monday, Wednesday, Saturday and Sunday 2–6pm. This is recommended for anyone who loves industrial tourism as well as fair-weather sailors. A small collection of photographs and models covers the golden era of Brittany's inland waterways. In summer, you can round off the visit by taking in the exhibition on the barge just in front of the museum.

WHAT TO DO

– **Les Nocturiales**: this festival of medieval, baroque and Celtic music is gradually developing into an enjoyable annual summer event. It lasts from the beginning of July to the end of August, with weekly meetings held in the interior of the Église St-Sauveur. Gregorian chants, baroque, romantic and contemporary music (generally in July) and Celtic music (in August) combine well with a great *fest-noz* (a traditional Breton 'festival of the night'), which is generally held around 15 August. Information is available from the tourist office: ☎ 02-99-71-06-04.

– **Beginners' lessons in Breton dance** are held every Friday at 9pm in July and August, in front of the Église St-Sauveur (you can find out more from the tourist office). There is always a good atmosphere at these lessons.

In the Redon Area

The region around Redon is densely wooded and so it's quite suitable for walking. The hills are dotted with windmills; one particularly fine example, in Queveneux, between St-Jacut and Peillac, houses a couple of weavers who are happy to show visitors round. The windmill at Brancheleux stands alone on a plain and you can climb up inside to admire the view.

The sites at St-Just and Glénac are good starting points for some lovely walks, which are all well signposted.

★ **St-Just**: 20 kilometres (12 miles) from Redon, on the road towards Rennes. Of the various megalithic sites, Lake du Val and the Tréal rocks are well worth a detour. Fragments of pottery have been found at St-Just, as well as a funerary urn, which was almost completely intact, dating back to 2000 BC. Shaped flints originating from outside the region, prove that this was an important site in the Mesolithic era. The covered alley at Tréal and a dolmen in the shape of a Lorraine cross are also worth seeing.

★ **Glénac**: between Redon and La Gacilly. This is marsh country, with a few scattered fishermen's houses. Typical of houses in the Vilaine basin, they were constructed with alternating courses of red schist and grey sandstone. The **Château de Sourdéac** has a 15th-century tower. The galleries of the old mines in Haut Sourdéac are home to four different species of bats.

★ **St-Jacut-les-Pins**: an exotic garden, the **Tropical Floral Parc**, covering 3 hectares (7 acres), is at Langarel, near Allaire. ☎ 02-99-71-91-98. Open every day 10am–7pm, in season; the rest of the year, open every day except Monday, 10am–noon and 2–7pm. Admission charge.

🛏 ✗ **Hôtel-restaurant des Pins**: place de l'Église. ☎ 02-99-91-23-65. ♿ Closed Wednesday. This is a country inn serving copious, simple meals, with set menus from 50F to 150F (Monday–Friday only). They have just three rooms, with shared bathroom facilities, costing 120F without breakfast. A good stopping-place for those into hunting or fishing.

FORÊT DE PAIMPONT

The Forêt de Paimpont is the old **Brocéliande Forest**, steeped in legend, and the backdrop for the stories of the Round Table, the exploits of King Arthur and his Knights, and the magic of Merlin the wizard. The forest is constantly changing – somewhere to lose yourself and be enchanted by its mysterious charm, magnificent pools and earthy smell.

Unfortunately, the forest is largely in private ownership, so visitors can only get to see a small part of it. Parts of it were devastated by fire in the summer of 1990. The ongoing re-forestation work has been generously financed by four benefactors, all industrialists with Breton origins – François Pinault, timber merchant and president of the huge retail group Printemps-Pinault-La Redoute, the perfumier Yves Rocher, Daniel Roullier, fertilizer distributor and Jean-Pierre Le Roch, the man behind the Intermarché supermarket chain.

In the forest, the Arbre d'Or (the 'Golden Tree') is a dead tree that has been covered in gold leaf; it is surrounded by spikes to deter thieves. If you want to go and see it, the tourist office at Paimpont will provide you with a map.

USEFUL ADDRESSES

🛈 **Pays d'accueil touristique de Brocéliande** (welcome service for the forest area): 37 avenue de la Libération (in the town hall), Plélan-le-Grand. ☎ 02-99-06-86-07. Fax: 02-99-06-86-39. Email: pays.

ILLE-ET-VILAINE

touristique.broceliande@wanadoo.fr. Open all year round, Monday–Friday 9am–noon and 1.30–5.30pm.

🖂 **Syndicat d'Initiative de Paimpont**: in front of the abbey. ☎ 02-99-07-84-23. In season, open daily, 9.30am–12.30pm and 1.30–6.30pm; out of season, open daily except Tuesday 10am–noon and 2–6pm. Closed January. The staff here are very helpful and will give you ideas for routes that are off the beaten track.

■ **Mountain bike hire**: bikes can be hired in Paimpont, at the friendly Brécilien bar, which is on the main road. ☎ 02-99-07-81-13.

WHERE TO STAY

🏠 **Camping municipal de Paimpont**: on the road to Gaël (the D773). ☎ 02-99-07-89-16. ♿ Open May–September. On the way out of the village, this campsite is a lovely green area next to the stadium – although there's not much shade. They charge 60F for two people, with a tent and a car. The facilities are impeccable and there's a relaxed and very friendly welcome.

🏠 **Walkers' shelter, chambres d'hôte**: in the tiny hamlet of Trudeau, on the D40 on the way out of Paimpont, on the St-Péran road. ☎ 02-99-07-81-40. This place is family-run, in a superb old ivy-clad farm that probably dates back to the 16th century. They have 30 places in two large dormitories, at 55–60F a night. There are also seven bed and breakfast rooms, camping facilities and a very nice restaurant (*see below* 'Ferme-auberge de Trudeau' under 'Where To Eat').

🏠 **La Corne de Cerf, chambres d'hôte**: in Le Cannée. ☎ 02-99-07-84-19. From Paimpont, take the D71 towards Beignon for 3 kilometres (2 miles), then it's signposted. Open all year, except January, by reservation. Very pretty house with exposed stonework, surrounded by a gorgeously romantic flower-filled garden. There are just three rooms, each stylishly decorated and furnished in an individual way. The hostess is like a fairy with a magic wand when it comes to anything from conjuring up your breakfast, or giving you advice on what to visit, to just decorating the place. Both she and her husband are artists and have breathed individual inspiration into their home, which is really charming. Allow 300F for a double room, including breakfast.

🏠 **Le Choucan-en-Brocéliande youth hostel**: 5 kilometres (3 miles) from Paimpont, in Le Choucan. ☎ 02-97-22-76-75. Open from mid-June to early September. From Paimpont, follow the D773, then take the forest road towards Concoret; take the first turning on the left as you arrive in the town of Concoret. This has to be one of the best settings in Brittany, on the edge of the Forêt de Paimpont, in a landscape of wild moors (the 'landes de Lambrun'). Surrounded by wonderful rolling countryside, scattered with splendid hamlets and old farms, this isolated youth hostel is in a pretty house made of the purplish schist so typical of the region. There are dormitories with seven to ten beds, costing 46F per night, and kitchen facilities are available. The surrounding countryside, the moors and the forest offer lots of good, romantic walks. The atmosphere here is very young. Camping is also possible.

🏠 **Local gîtes**: in Treffendel. These are well signposted from the village. ☎ and fax: 02-99-61-01-25. In a lovely, verdant setting, these little cottages are modern and functional, but lacking in any real character. They can be rented by the week or for a weekend.

♠ **Hôtel-restaurant Chez Maxime**: in Concoret, near Ploërmel (in Morbihan).

WHERE TO EAT

✗ **Ferme-auberge de Trudeau**: (*see above*: 'Walkers' Shelter' under 'Where To Stay'). Open lunchtime and evening by reservation only. Set menus at 100F except on Sunday and in the evening out of season, and à la carte prices start from 110F. There's a very warm atmosphere here, the meals are copious and are made with farm produce. They serve good home-made patés and chicken with potatoes cooked in a bread oven (*poulets et pommes de terre cuits dans le four à pain*). Their excellent cider is also sold by the bottle to take away.

✗ **L'Auberge du Presbytère**: 35380 Treffendel. Beside the N24, before you get to Plélan-le-Grand (coming from Mordelles). ☎ 02-99-61-00-76. Open lunchtime and evening until 9pm (reservations required for the evening). Closed Sunday evening and Monday. Set slightly outside the village, the inn is a lovely ivy-clad sandstone house that was a presbytery in the 19th century. When the weather is good, you can eat outside and soak up the peaceful atmosphere. The cuisine here has quite a reputation and the set menus start at 100F at lunchtime, with gourmet evening menus from 180F to 215F. A very seductive sort of place.

✗ **Hôtel-restaurant Chez Maxime**: in Concoret, near Ploërmel (Morbihan).

WHAT TO SEE

★ **Les Forges-de-Paimpont**: set between two lakes surrounded by ancient trees, this hamlet is made up of the buildings that housed the old forges that produced Brocéliande iron back in the Renaissance. Fortunately for the forest, the forges closed, but not before thousands of trees had been used for fuel.

★ **Paimpont**: 4 kilometres (2.5 miles) away, right in the middle of the forest, this is an ideal starting point for treks either on foot or on horseback. The village, entered via an archway, is on the site of an old abbey; one large 17th-century building remains, currently used as the town hall.

All along the main road, all the houses are made of granite and have a little garden in front. One of them has a plaque reminding visitors that it was here that Mme de Gaulle heard the broadcast by her son, General Charles de Gaulle, in 1940, when France fell to the Germans.

The old 13th-century **abbey-church** bears witness to the prosperity of the monastery, which had ample resources of wood, water and iron ore. The abbey buildings are no less impressive. In the church, you can see the **treasure-house** in the sacristy (visitors are admitted only in summer), religious gold-work and a beautiful ivory Christ. The panelling, the pulpit and the stalls all date back to the 17th century.

The ***pardon*** at Paimpont (*see* 'Tradition and Customs' under 'Background') takes place on Whit Sunday.

WHAT TO DO

The region is a real paradise for walkers. A particularly attractive walk starts from in front of the Château de Trécesson and follows the footpath for 10 kilometres (6 miles) across the moors of the Landes de Gurwant (GR37). Follow the red-and-white markers.

Another walk takes in the **Vallon de la Chambre au Loup** (Valley of the Wolf's Lair), to the northeast of the Forêt de Paimpont, right next to the village of Iffendic and takes you past some impressive 35-metre high cliffs (115 feet), known locally as the 'Little Canyon'.

IN THE AREA

★ **Étang and Château de Comper** (lake and castle of Comper): in Concoret. Open from 1 April to 1 October. In April, May and September, open every day except Tuesday and Thursday, 10am–7pm; in June, July and August, open every day except Tuesday, 10am–7pm. Admission is 30F. This beautiful castle has had a new lease of life since it became the Centre de l'Imaginaire Arthurien (Centre for Arthurian Legends) ☎ 02-97-22-79-96. Here, stories of Excalibur and the Holy Grail abound, and legend and history seem to be interwoven. The castle has also become a centre for research and meetings on Celtic culture.

Legend has it that this was the place where Merlin built a crystal castle for Viviane, 'the Lady of the Lake', who brought Lancelot up here. All that you see of it today are three towers linked by walls, built in the local purple-red schist. The main body of the castle dates back to the 14th and 15th centuries. It was partly destroyed by fire during the Revolution, before being rebuilt in the late 18th century in a Renaissance style.

The evidence suggests that this lake has inspired frenzied imaginations. If you go for a walk round the lake, soak up the mysterious atmosphere and listen to the gentle croaking of the toads . . . you might even find yourself beginning to believe all the stories.

Make sure you see the special exhibition in the Centre; it changes every year and is usually very well presented.

★ **Fontaine de Barenton** (Barenton fountain): from Comper, take the road to Concoret, and then head for Tréhorenteuc. Stop at the delightfully-named hamlet of La Folle-Pensée (literally, 'Crazy Thought'). From there, walk through the woods to reach the enchanted Fontaine de Barenton; a few drops of water from this fountain are believed to have cast many spells. Most commonly it would bring terrifying storms to the forest. This place is where all the legends converge; this is where Merlin met Viviane and where druids exercised their power over people with mental illnesses (the origin of the reference to 'crazy thoughts'). In the 19th century, the rector of Concoret would lead a procession here in times of drought, to dip the foot of his church's cross into the water.

★ **Tréhorenteuc**: 5 kilometres (3 miles) from Barenton, this village is famous for its **church**, which has a good mixture of Christian and pagan symbols. At the ninth station of the cross, you can see Morgan, the half-sister of King Arthur. At the back of the church is a mosaic depicting an episode from the legends of the Round Table.

B Office du tourisme: this is in the sacristy of the church at Tréhorenteuc. ☎ 02-97-93-05-12.

★ **Walk in the Val Sans-Retour** (the 'Valley of No Return'): 4 kilometres (2.5 miles). Allow one hour there and back, not including stops. This is an easy walk that follows a circular route starting from the church in Tréhorenteuc and flagged with yellow circles as well as the red-and-white markers of the GR37. After visiting the church in Tréhorenteuc, head towards Campénéac and follow the signs to Val Sans-Retour. The path climbs up a rocky spur giving a view over the Étang du Miroir aux Fées (the 'Fairy Mirror Lake'). It skirts round to the right of the lake before plunging down towards the bottom of the Val Sans-Retour. Don't go there if you are fickle in spirit – it is said that Morgan Le Fay will punish you. If you still dare, leave the GR footpath behind you and take the turning to the left: it follows the Gué de Mony stream, before coming to a fire-break. Soon you come to the high point of the valley, with its panoramic views from the ridges over the Lande de la Troche. Once you have surveyed the moors, the path takes you back to the lake and returns to Tréhorenteuc.

The Val Sans-Retour is the legendary hotspot of the Forêt de Brocéliande, and more than one horseman in history has quaked in his saddle here. The trees have strange silhouettes, every lake seems to hide a secret, and every rock looks as if it might be alive. This is a land of wizards and fairies, ruled over by Morgan Le Fay, half-sister of King Arthur. Using magic taught by Merlin, she shut her unfaithful lover Guyomart in this valley, imprisoning him with walls of air. The valley proved to be the last resting-place of Merlin, who came here to reveal his secrets to Viviane. They say that the wind still bears the lament of the great magician, who fell asleep at the bottom of the Val Sans-Retour, at the point where the Arbre d'Or now stands.

★ **Château de Trécesson**: from the Val Sans-Retour, head for Campénéac, then for Trécesson. The 14th-century castle is now in private hands and is not open to the public. Built of red schist, it's quite a sight, especially seen reflected in the waters of the surrounding lake.

★ **Church at Maxent**: 5 kilometres (3 miles) to the southeast of Plélan-le-Grand. Octagonal and full of light, with plenty of charm, this church was built in the same style as the Sacré-Coeur in Paris. The old church houses the tomb of Salomon III (ninth century), the last of the 14 kings of Brittany. Archaeological excavations are currently taking place.

★ **Lac du Barrage Jean-Descottes**: lake on the Chèze. This is a peaceful, colourful spot; the soil next to the water is of a reddish colour and the lake is surrounded by greenery. Lovely viewpoints.

★ **Le Parc de Treffendel**: leisure activities centre at Le Gué-Charret. ☎ 02-99-61-04-21. Open all year round, 10am–7pm. Closed Monday. Take the RN24, Rennes–Lorient road; come off at Treffendel and follow the signs. This is actually a circus, based out in the country and it's good for young and older audiences. Apart from performances, which take place on Wednesday and Sunday, and more often during school holidays, there's a museum, and you can visit the animals or play games. Circus skills workshops and courses are also on offer.

ILLE-ET-VILAINE

Western Ille-et-Vilaine

MONTFORT-SUR-MEU (*MONFORZH*) 35160
(Pop: 5,589)

The main income of this dynamic little town derives from food-processing services and industries. The old Abbaye St-Jacques, just 1 kilometre to the southeast of the town in the direction of Talensac, reveals how well the past and the present can live in perfect harmony. Many modern companies have made the most of the setting and have established themselves here. The remains of the famous arched gateway and of the 17th-century cloister are definitely worth a look.

Syndicat d'Initiative: in the Écomusée, or open-air museum (*see* 'What To See and Do', *below*). ☎ 02-99-09-31-81.

– **Market**: place des Douves, alongside the River Meu. Held on Friday morning.

WHERE TO STAY

Camping municipal: in the centre of town. This modest campsite is clean and quiet. The grass is well-maintained, with each site separated by little hedges.

WHAT TO SEE AND DO

★ **Tour de Papegaut**, **Écomusée du Pays de Montfort en Brocéliande**: 2 rue du Château. ☎ 02-99-09-31-81. Both the tower and the open-air museum are open all year round, 8.30am–noon and 2–6pm during the week, 10am–noon and 2–6pm on Saturday, and 2–6pm on Sunday and public holidays. Admission charge 20F. Very attractive with its greyish-green and red schist, the tower has a lovely sculpted chimney. There are various interesting permanent displays, on such subjects as traditional Breton costume, outdoor toys and life in a medieval town, as well as an exhibit on the legend of a young girl who was turned into a duck. There is also a temporary exhibition, which changes every year.

★ The **Forêt de Montfort** (Montfort forest) is superb. There is an interesting 'arboretum' route (information from the tourist office at the foot of the tower), which tells you how to recognize different types of trees. The tourist office also has details of a megalithic route.

★ **Étang de Trémelin**: at Ifferdic, 10 kilometres (6 miles) from Montfort, this lake, surrounded by woods and moors, is a popular base for sporting activities.

★ On the road towards Montauban, take a look at the little village of **Bédée**, where the church is surrounded by, of all things, palm trees.

MONTAUBAN-DE-BRETAGNE (*MENEZALBAN*) 35360   (Pop: 4,235)

This little town has a large, fortified castle, partly destroyed during the Franco-Breton war in 1487. Open from 14 July to the end of August. The building at the entrance has been well preserved and is a good example of 15th-century military architecture.

WHERE TO STAY AND EAT

⌂ ✗ **Relais de La Hucherais**: in the hamlet of La Hucherais, 2 kilometres (1.5 miles) from Montauban. ☎ 02-99-06-54-31. ✗ A roadside restaurant with a hotel but without a great deal of charm. The rooms are simple and clean and cost 250F. Set menus cost from 56F to 112F.

IN THE AREA

★ **Musée Louison-Bobet**: 5 rue de Gaël, in St-Méen-le-Grand, about 10 kilometres (6 miles) to the west of Montauban. ☎ 02-99-09-67-86. Open 2–5pm; every day in summer. Closed Tuesday out of season. Admission charge 15F. Born in this region in 1925, Louison Bobet was a world-class cyclist, winning the Tour de France three times in succession (1953, 1954 and 1955), the world championship in 1954, the Tour des Flandres in 1955, and the Bordeaux to Paris race in 1959. This little museum contains loads of great nostalgic photographs, documents, vests, cups, and articles about the champion and his friends.

BÉCHEREL (*BEGEREL*) 35190   (Pop: 673)

ILLE-ET-VILAINE

This little town, which was once fortified, is on the road to Dinan from Montfort. It was very prosperous in the 17th and 18th centuries, its wealth largely generated by trading in linen, but it went into a decline in the 19th century from which it never really recovered. Bécherel is therefore interesting on two levels: at a social level, it is a small town that is representative of the rural exodus in Brittany, and, at an architectural level, it has a collection of beautiful granite bourgeois residences. The place de l'Ancien-Marché is lovely, and the nearby street names reflect medieval occupations: rue de la Beurrerie and rue de la Chanvrerie ('buttery' street and 'hemp-making' street). Behind the church is a leather workshop, where traditional methods are still used. It's worth going for a quick stroll round the presbytery, and there's a decent *crêperie* next door. Down the 'Rocquet de la Couaille' path is the old wash-house, and from here, there's a lovely view of the town set amid the ruins of its ancient ramparts.

In more recent years, the town has reinvented itself and, since 1985, has officially been France's leading 'Town of Books' (*Cité du Livre*). Every year, it organizes all sorts of events to promote reading and books, especially second-hand volumes. It is amazing but true that there are now more bookshops per square metre in Bécherel than in the traditionally bookish Latin Quarter in Paris.

If you aren't turned on by the sight of so many books in one small place, don't worry. Bécherel is also home to an impressive number of artists and craftsmen, including a weaver, a cabinet-maker and . . . a bookbinder.

USEFUL ADDRESS

🛈 **Office du tourisme**: 9 place Alexandre-Jehanin. ☎ 02-99-66-75-23. From 15 June to 15 September, open every day except Monday, 10am–12.30pm and 2.30–6.30pm; out of season, open weekends and public holidays, same opening times.

WHERE TO STAY

🛏 **Chambres d'hôte with M. and Mme Demée** in La Croix-Calaudry. ☎ 02-99-66-76-48. Open all year round. The place is far from luxurious, but quiet and friendly, with four rooms costing 200F for two or 260F for three, including breakfast. It also acts as a shelter for walkers, with a dormitory with 15 beds costing 50F a night, plus two *gîtes* each accommodating five people.

🛏 **Campsite**: by the park.

WHAT TO SEE

★ **Parc du Château de Caradeuc**: on the road to Médréac. *See* 'Dinan – What To Do In The Area' under 'Côtes-d'Armor'.

WHAT TO DO

There is a major **Fête du Livre** ('book festival') at Bécherel over the Easter weekend. Each year, to open the season, discussions and talks take place around a chosen theme. The town becomes a meeting point for writers and their readers.

La Nuit du Livre ('literary evening'): happens on the second Saturday in August. The village is illuminated, and there's a programme of music and readings.

Le Marché du Livre ('book market'): on the first Sunday of each month. Booksellers and buyers of every description converge on the town.

Le Temps des Livres ('time for books'): a book bonanza on the second and third weekends in October.

IN THE AREA

★ **Les Iffs**: visit this tiny, pretty village to see one of the most fascinating churches in the region, and one of the least known. It was built in the 15th century in Flamboyant Gothic style. The porch is curiously squat and the steeple is also a bizarre shape. The spire was added in the 19th century, and is perhaps a little over-sculpted for such a modest village. The Bar du Village is the only bar in the village, on the little square.

On the way there, the little country road between Cardroc and St-Symphorien is worth the journey in itself.

★ **Château de Montmuran**: a stone's throw from Les Iffs, on the road to Tinténiac (another unspoiled country road). Open June to September 2–7pm; closed Saturday. Guided tours are available and there's an admission charge. You enter the superb castle along a triumphal alley. Two towers remain from the 12th century, while the elegant entrance tower, with its crenellated tower and drawbridge (which still works), dates back to the 14th century. The central part of the castle belongs to the 17th and 18th centuries. It was in the chapel of this castle that Du Guesclin was knighted in 1354.

≜ For anybody prepared to splash out, the castle has two sumptuous **bed & breakfast rooms**. ☎ 02-99-45-88-88. Fax: 02-99-45-84-90. Allow 400F a night for two people.

TINTÉNIAC (*TINTENIEG*) 35190   (Pop: 1,932)

Have a look at the **Musée de l'Outil et des Métiers** (tools and crafts museum) and the **Magasin à Grain** (grain store), 5 quai de la Donac, on the bank of the Ille-et-Rance canal. Open from the beginning of July to the end of September, every day except Sunday mornings, 10.30am–noon and 2–6.30pm. Here you can see re-creations of traditional workshops for blacksmiths, wheelwrights and saddlers, among others.

WHERE TO STAY AND EAT

≜ ✕ **Hôtel des Voyageurs**: 39 rue Nationale (the main road in Tinténiac). ☎ 02-99-68-02-21. Fax: 02-99-68-19-58. Closed Sunday evening and Monday except in July and August, and from mid-December to mid-January. A double room costs 185–275F and half board is available at about 225F. This nice little hotel is difficult to fault. It has traditionally decorated rooms, with en suite shower or bathroom, costing from 155F to 225F. They serve decent, well-made food, with Breton specialities, and there's a respectable menu for 69F at lunchtime during the week (except in August), with other menus from 98F to 195F.

HÉDÉ (*HAZHOÙ*) 35630   (Pop: 1,932)

The bridge on the D795 (the road from Combourg) provides a delightful view of the flight of locks. The canals are no longer used by working boats, but are still busy with little motor-powered pleasure boats. The locks are still all operated by hand. A gentle stroll along the banks is known as the *Balade des Onze Écluses* (the 'Eleven Locks Walk'). There is also a peaceful country

ILLE-ET-VILAINE

road along the hillside from Hédé to Les Iffs (via St-Symphorien and St-Brieuc-des-Iffs).

WHERE TO STAY AND EAT

🛆 **Camping Les Peupliers**: La Benelais, 35190 Tinténiac. ☎ 02-99-45-49-75. Fax: 02-00-45-52-98. Open from March to the end of October. Allow 90F a night for two people. This is a good, popular campsite, set back from the road. It has excellent facilities, including a swimming pool.

✕ **Restaurant Le Genty-Home**: at the lower end of Hédé, on the D795, 500 metres from the edge of the village. ☎ 02-99-45-46-07. Closed Tuesday evening and Wednesday; also closed for a month from 11 November and for two weeks in March. The lunchtime weekday menu costs 68F, with evening menus from 98F to 220F. This is a charming, pretty inn in a lovely floral setting, run by a talented young chef who attracts gourmet customers from miles around. The choice of set menus would satisfy even the most demanding of diners, with dishes such as an escalope of calves' sweetbreads and prawns in Meaux mustard, a fillet of John Dory with leeks or a fig purée in balsamic sauce. There's a warm welcome, too.

COMBOURG (*KOMBORN*) 35270   (Pop: 4,989)

This little town is not exactly steeped in history, but is the place where one of France's most famous writers and diplomats, Chateaubriand, spent part of his childhood. There is a pleasant atmosphere in the main square on market days, and the lovely castle is worth seeing, despite the fact that the writer detested it. There are several good restaurants in the area, too.

USEFUL ADDRESS

🖪 **Office du tourisme**: BP 1, place Albert-Parent. ☎ 02-99-73-13-93. Fax: 02-99-73-52-39. Website: www.combourg.org. Open all year round; in July and August, open Monday–Saturday 10am–7pm and Sunday 10am–12.30pm; out of season, open Tuesday–Saturday 10am–12.30pm and 2–6.30pm.

WHERE TO STAY AND EAT

🛆 **Camping Vieux Châtel**: ☎ 02-99-73-07-03. About 1 kilometre from the centre and well-signposted. This campsite is quiet, simple and rather pleasant.

🛆 ✕ **Hôtel du Lac**: 2 place Chateaubriand. ☎ 02-99-73-05-65. Fax: 02-99-73-23-34. Closed Friday and Sunday evening out of season, Friday lunchtime in season, and throughout February. A double room costs 220–360F. Once a dental hospital, this is now a pretty hotel with a slightly old-fashioned charm. On one side of the castle is the lake that Chateaubriand loved so much. The rooms, which are very reasonable (although the decor is unremarkable), cost from 200F to 358F, depending on the view. Try for a room with a view, which is worth the difference in price. The restaurant has set menus from 70F (not on Sunday) to 180F, which might include such delicacies as warm oysters with fennel or leg of veal stuffed with mushrooms.

♠ ✕ Hôtel du Château: 1 place Chateaubriand. ☎ 02-99-73-00-38. Fax: 02-99-73-25-79. Restaurant closed Sunday evening and Monday, and from mid-December to mid-January. Allow 300–600F for a double room, depending on the comfort and the view. This is a charming hotel where all the rooms have recently been refurbished. Some of them are very large and have a view over the garden. The restaurant is a good one, with mouthwatering set menus priced from 98F to 295F. Dishes are carefully prepared and might include such Breton specialities as boned pig's trotter stuffed with vegetables. If you're prepaped to eat from the à la carte menu, you could taste a real steak Chateaubriand, which is a piece of fillet of beef grilled between two other thin slices of beef – but of course, it will cost you more.

✕ Chez Moustache: 11 place Albert-Parent (the main square). ☎ 02-99-73-06-54. Closed Tues-day evening and Wednesday out of season, and on Wednesday in July and August, as well as for the first two weeks in March and September. Coming here is something of a pilgrimage for those in the know, and the *crêpes* are really special. The prices are very reasonable, and the ice-creams are delicious. It's worth booking at the weekend, as the place is full of locals who come to soak up the atmosphere and generally have a good time.

✕ Restaurant L'Écrivain: place St-Gilduin, opposite the church. ☎ 02-99-73-01-61. ♿ Closed Wednesday and Sunday evening, all day Thursday, as well as February and two weeks in October. This restaurant is one of the important ones in the region, and it has built a solid reputation, over the years, without either becoming full of itself or putting its prices through the roof. In fact, the prices are amazingly good, considering the inventiveness and the flavour of the food. Specialities include their own smoked fish, or, for example, an excellent *foie gras* with artichokes in *millefeuille* pastry. There's a set menu for 85F (except at weekends) and other menus for 120F and 160F, so the place really is excellent when it comes to value for money. They also sell second-hand illustrated books.

Further afield, there are some lovely farms with guest rooms, as well as bed and breakfast places, in the area around Combourg.

♠ ✕ Chambres et table d'hôte: (bed and breakfast, and dinner) Le Petit-Plessix, 35560 Marcillé-Raoul; 11 kilometres (7 miles) to the east of Combourg. The farm is on the left-hand side, about 1 kilometre before Marcillé. ☎ and fax: 02-99-73-60-62. Open all year round by reservation. There are five rooms with en suite bathrooms (two of which are family rooms) in a large farm building. The better rooms go by the names of *Écurie* ('stable'), which is huge, and *Fournil* ('bakehouse'), which has a pretty bread oven. Allow 225F for two, including breakfast. Dinner starts at 65F, including a homemade aperitif, wine and cider. Meals are taken with the family, using farm produce. Authenticity is definitely the order of the day, and the welcome is warm.

♠ Chambres d'hôte du Petit Moulin du Rouvre: 35720 St-

ILLE-ET-VILAINE

Pierre-de-Plesguen; on the edge of the Étang du Rouvre, to the west of Combourg. ☎ 02-99-73-85-84. Fax: 02-99-73-71-06. Open all year round by reservation. Allow about 380F for a double room, including breakfast. There are four top-of-the-range rooms in an old 17th-century watermill in an absolutely stunning setting, which is peaceful, although it is becoming increasingly popular. They also serve meals, by reservation, so allow about 100F for local dishes. There is a pretty private fishing lake in front of the house. Excellent welcome.

🛏 **Chambres d'hôte Le Lézard Tranquille**: 2 rue de Lorgeril, les Cours-Verdiers, Pleugueneuc. ☎ 02-99-69-40-36. ✗ Open all year round. A double room costs 290F including breakfast. Situated on the edge of the grounds that surround the Château de la Bourbansais (*see* 'In the Area', *below*) on which it once depended, the house (its name means 'The Peaceful Lizard') was originally built by the present owner's ancestors as a school. There are five spacious, comfortable rooms set apart from the house, and a sunny terrace. The rooms that look out over the back have a view to the meadows and the woods in the distance. The owner will do her best to ensure that you enjoy your stay. If you enjoy riding, she might even lend you her horse. You're sure to love this place.

🛏 **Chambres d'hôte et gîtes Les Bruyères**: in Pleugueneuc; on the D794, to the west of Combourg. ☎ and fax: 02-99-69-47-75. Open all year round. The accommodation consists of a few rooms in an old house – all small and pretty, in a floral style. The cost is about 380F for two, including breakfast. There are also two *gîtes* sleeping six to eight.

☆☆☆ Chic

🛏 **Chambres d'hôte at Château de la Ballue**: 35560 Bazouges-la-Pérouse; 15 kilometres (9 miles) to the east of Combourg, on the D796; well signposted from the centre of Bazouges. ☎ 02-99-97-47-86. Fax: 02-99-97-47-70. Website: la-ballue.com. Closed in January. This wonderful 17th-century chateau opens up its gardens to the public and also arranges temporary exhibitions. It also has five luxury rooms, which are superbly decorated, with four-poster beds, fabric wall-coverings and antique furniture, so you're getting real class at royal prices: 650–850F for a double room. Breakfast is substantial. There's a terrace with an excellent view, and amid all the greenery at the bottom of the garden (which is listed as a historic monument) is an old, restored swimming pool. Guests are offered a free guided tour on arrival.

WHAT TO SEE

★ **Château de Combourg**: the main attraction in the town, right in the centre. ☎ 02-99-73-22-95. In April, May, June and September, open 10am–12.30pm and 2–6pm for the grounds, 2–5.30pm (except Tuesday) for the interior; in July and August, open every day 10am–12.30pm, and 1.30–6pm (1.30–5.30pm for the interior); in October, open 10am–noon and 2–4.30pm for the grounds, 2–4.30pm only for the interior. You can either visit everything, or just the grounds, but the castle is really worth a visit, and the guided tour is very interesting.

The austere appearance of this medieval fortress gives some idea of what Chateaubriand's youth must have been like. The writer's mood seems to have alternated between despair and exaltation and he was later to remember Combourg in the pages of his *Mémoires d'Outre-Tombe* or 'Memoirs from beyond the grave'. Madame la Comtesse de La Tour du Pin, a descendant of Chateaubriand's elder brother, still lives in the castle today.

Chateaubriand described the place thus:

'*Des cachots et des donjons, un labyrinthe de galeries . . . partout silence, obscurité et visage de pierre, voilà le château de Combourg.*' In other words: 'Priests' holes and dungeons, a labyrinth of galleries . . . silence everywhere, darkness and a stony face, that is the Château of Combourg.'

The facade represents the feudal part of the castle, which was built in the 13th and 15th centuries. The steps were modified in the 19th century. Inside, there is some beautiful 16th- and 19th-century furniture. The decor was completely redone in the 19th century, so what you see is not what the writer would have known. You can visit the church and the chapel where Chateaubriand's mother used to go and pray. There is also a well-furnished guardroom, with interesting paintings of the Flemish school. The canvases that cover the walls have been acquired over the centuries by different members of the family.

In the archive room, there is a collection of souvenirs and items relating to the famous writer: IOUs, decorations, his marriage licence, his desk, his armchair, his deathbed, and so on. Ask about the legend of the black cat, and don't miss the view from the ramparts. The writer's bedroom was thought to be in what is called the *Tour du Chat* (the 'cat's tower'), where a cat was found between the walls. At night, the subtly lit castle is a superb sight.

IN THE AREA

★ **Zoo-Château de la Bourbansais**: this is a park, a little zoo and a castle all in one, and you can visit the different parts together, or separately. From April to September, open every day 10am–7pm; from October to March open 2–6pm. For the castle itself, there are one-hour guided tours at 11.15am, 1.30pm, 3.30pm, 4.30pm and 5.30pm; in winter, ring for times. There's an admission charge of 58F for the zoo and the park, or a combination ticket costs 70F.

This superb granite castle, which stands majestically at the centre of its park, dates from the 16th and 18th centuries. Its architecture displays all the traditional features of the centuries of its construction, although it essentially marks the end of military architecture in Brittany. It is in perfect condition, as it has not changed hands since the day it was built. The attractions include wonderful views and French-style gardens.

The guided tour takes you no further than the ground floor, but you do get to see the wonderful wooden panels in the Blue Room, which is a masterpiece. There are also leather chairs from Cordoba, and Aubusson tapestries, one of which shows the castle as it would have been in the 16th century. The 19th-century courtyard houses a sort of miniature museum of all the objects acquired by the family over a number of centuries. It is an amazing collection full of interesting items, from whalebones and shells to all kinds of weapons.

The zoo and the gardens round off the visit. There are more than 400 animals from all five continents, from giraffes and monkeys to tigers. Aside from entertainment, the zoo's main priorities are education and the protection of endangered species. The park is also open to the public.

★ **Château de la Ballue**: (*see* 'Where To Stay or Eat'). Just outside Bazouges-la-Pérouse. Admission charge. This wonderful 17th-century castle has an amazing garden that is actually rather small, but is nonetheless a treat for enthusiasts. The style is French at the front and mannerist to the side. Inside, the rooms usually house an art exhibition.

★ **Cobac Parc**: in Lanhelin. This is a leisure park specially designed for children, with a miniature train, model village, an aviary and all sorts of rides.

La Côte d'Émeraude (The Emerald Coast)

ST-MALO (*SANT-MALOÙ*) 35400   (Pop: 52,737)

'*Couronne de pierre posée sur les flots*' ('a crown of stone sitting on the waves') is how the 19th-century writer Gustave Flaubert described St-Malo.

St-Malo is one of the most frequently visited towns in Brittany – and with good reason. Enclosed within tall ramparts, surrounded by the sea and steeped in so much history, the town has a very special place in the hearts of all Bretons, and it is an inevitable stop on any trip to the area.

Tourists flood into the town pretty much all year round, and the cross-Channel ferries disgorge daily boatloads of British visitors. Unfortunately, as it gets increasingly busy in peak season, the chips get greasier, coaches become a blot on the landscape, and some of the shopkeepers' eyes light up at the thought of all that money.

What with the tourist invasion, and the fact that St-Malo's inhabitants have a reputation for being rather withdrawn, you will have worked out for yourself that this is not the place to come for a relaxed, friendly atmosphere. Come here instead for the architecture and history, or to enjoy the uncommonly beautiful bay, which, with its rocky little islands, its tricky currents and extraordinary quality of light, often seems quite magical.

This centre of the Côte d'Émeraude (the 'Emerald Coast') was very fashionable from the end of the 19th century onwards. Outside its ramparts, St-Malo looks like a charming, middle-class seaside resort, with lovely early 20th-century houses stretching out along the coast from Paramé to Rothéneuf.

History

It was a Welshman, MacLow ('Maclou'), who came to convert the lawless folk of St-Malo in the sixth century. The site was well chosen from a defensive point of view as the Norman invasions had forced the people to take refuge on an island, which they then fortified. The community gained its own bishop in the 12th century, and this was when St-Malo really began to exist as a town, continuing to grow in importance over the centuries.

The town's somewhat haughty isolation meant that a number of major conflicts and other wars among the Bretons simply passed it by, and it was able to resist submitting to a number of different ruling powers. In the early 14th century, the town got its first taste of government support when the king of France granted it a port charter. In 1590, the town stood up to Henri IV and even declared itself a republic. This spirit of independence is quite probably one of the reasons why St-Malo has produced so many adventurers, famous navigators and other great men.

During the 15th century, the town was already developing strong merchant and maritime links. Cod fishing, conquests of distant lands and textiles all contributed to the wealth of the town, its development and the position of respect in which it was held by the ruling powers. By the end of the 17th century, St-Malo was France's leading port and also the base for a number of major shipping companies. Beautiful townhouses reflect this period of prosperity. Vauban built the last of the fortifications and St-Malo took on the look it still has today.

Throughout the 18th century and on until 1815, the port was the capital of the privateering war. This was the legendary era of the infamous *corsair* pirates, who enjoyed immunity from the law. Every French child is brought up on the legends surrounding this glamorous band of adventurers.

St-Malo experienced its first defeat in August 1944. German forces had retrenched there and 80 per cent of the town was destroyed by Allied raids using incendiary bombs, when the Americans, believing the town to be full of Germans, decided to smoke them out. Curiously, the house where Chateaubriand was born remained intact, and his tomb was not damaged, despite the number of bombs that were dropped on the port.

What visitors actually see today is a city that was rebuilt after the war. Such was the prestige of St-Malo, a town held in great esteem by the French nation, that plans were quickly set in motion to re-create it exactly as it had been. Local people became involved, with stones from damaged buildings being meticulously numbered, and photographs and documents were used as a model for the restoration.

Although some of the finest townhouses were faithfully re-created, the scale of the project was so enormous that many of the streets and the facades had to be redone only in the general spirit of the original. The main priority was to give the town back its traditional atmosphere, and in this they succeeded totally. A display in the castle museum shows the many stages of the resurrection of St-Malo.

The People

Locals of St-Malo are known as *Malouins*, and few other towns in France can claim so many great entrepreneurs and adventurers as their own. **Jacques Cartier** discovered Canada in 1534, and went back there on a number of occasions. **Duguay-Trouin** (1673–1736) and **Surcouf** (1773–1827) were legendary *corsairs*. Having worn out the Dutch and the English under Napoleon Bonaparte, Surcouf became so rich that he retired at the age of 35 and ended up as a merchant, ship-owner and well-known figure-about-town. **Mahé de La Bourdonnais** (1699–1753) is less well known, but was a great adventurer who discovered distant lands before becoming governor of the French colonies of Mauritius and Réunion. **Pierre Maupertuis** (1698–1759) was a scientist, mathematician and geographer who made a number of discoveries. **Broussais** (1772–1838) started off as a navy doctor before moving on to practise in Paris, where a hospital is named after him. **Lamennais** (1782–1854), a former priest, writer and great humanist, was elected as a deputy to the Assembly in 1848. Finally, **Chateaubriand** (1768–1848), the great voyager and pre-eminent figure in French literature, is perhaps the person most frequently associated with this vibrant port.

USEFUL ADDRESSES

🚹 **Office du tourisme** (B1 on the map): esplanade St-Vincent, in front of the entrance to the walled town. ☎ 02-99-56-64-48. In summer, open 8.30am–8pm (Sunday, 10am–7pm); from Easter to the end of June, open 9am–noon and 1.30–7pm (Sunday, 10am–12.30pm and 2.30–6pm); the rest of the year, open 9am–12.30pm and 1.30–6pm. The tourist office keeps a good selection of material, including brochures and a street map, and the staff are capable and helpful. St-Malo, with its marina, sailing resort and aquarium, has a strong bias towards things to do with the sea. A *station-voile* ('sailing station') kiosk in the office gives all sorts of information on watersports in and around the town (*see also* 'Watersports').

🚃 **Gare SNCF** (train station): Paris via Rennes, reservations: ☎ 08-36-35-35-35. There are connections to Rennes leaving almost every hour.

🚌 **Gare routière** (bus station) (B1 on the map): opposite Porte St-Vincent, in front of the main gate of the ramparts. There are two companies operating. **Tourisme Verney** primarily serves Rennes and Dinard (departures throughout the day for the latter). ☎ 02-99-40-82-67. **Les Courriers Bretons** serves Cancale, Rennes, Dol-de-Bretagne, Fougères and Mont-St-Michel, with five return-trips a day in summer. ☎ 02-99-56-20-44. Another company, **CAT**, operates a service to Dinan throughout the day. ☎ 02-96-39-21-05. Departures are from esplanade St-Vincent. There is also a service to Cap Fréhel in season.

⚓ **Gare Maritime du Naye** (harbour station exclusively for ferries): **Brittany Ferries** ☎ 02-99-40-64-41. **Emeraude Line** ☎ 02-23-18-01-80. Fax: 02-23-18-15-00. Car ferries travelling to and from England (and Ireland, with Brittany Ferries).

⚓ **Gare Maritime de la Bourse** (harbour station exclusively for foot-passengers): **Emeraude Line** ☎ 02-23-18-01-80, or **Condor** ☎ 02-99-20-03-00. For services to the Channel Islands.

⚓ **St-Malo–Dinard shuttle service** (A2, **1** on the map): with **Emeraude Line**. Departures every 40 minutes (in season) from the Dinan

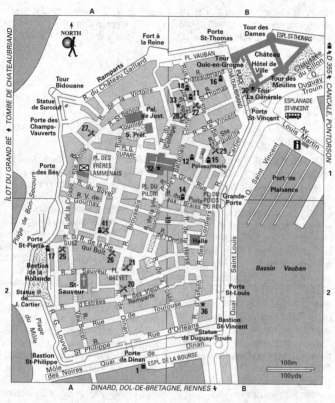

ST-MALO

■ Useful Addresses

🛈 Office du tourisme

🚌 Gare routière (bus station)

1 St-Malo–Dinard shuttle service

▤ Where To Stay

11 Hôtel du Commerce

12 Hôtel Le Croiseur

14 Hôtel du Louvre

15 Hôtel Bristol-Union

16 Hôtel de l'Univers

17 Hôtel-Restaurant Les Chiens du Guet

18 Hôtel Le Nautilus

19 Hôtel Brocéliande

41 Auberge Les Vieilles Pierres

✕ Where To Eat

20 Crêperie La Brigantine

21 Crêperie Le Gallo

25 Restaurant de la Porte-St-Pierre

26 Chez Gilles

27 Le Chasse-Marée

28 Le Chalut

29 Le P'tit Crêpier

41 Auberge Les Vieilles Pierres

★ What To See

30 Musée d'Histoire de St-Malo and Musée du Pays Malouin

32 Cathédrale St-Vincent

33 Maison Internationale des Poètes et des Écrivains

36 L'Hôtel d'Asfeld

ST-MALO

slipway (*Cale de Dinan*). ☎ 02-23-18-15-15. In Dinard, ☎ 02-99-46-10-45.
■ **Bicycle hire**: **Cycles Nicole**: 11 rue Robert-Schuman. ☎ 02-99-56-11-06. **Cycles Diazo**: 47 quai Duguay-Trouin. ☎ 02-99-40-31-63.

WHERE TO STAY

During the peak season, you will definitely need to reserve your accommodation if you want to sleep inside the ramparts.

☆ Budget

⌂ **Centre Patrick Varangot** (youth hostel and international centre): 37 avenue du Père-Umbricht. ☎ 02-99-40-29-80. Fax: 02-99-40-29-02. Email: fjt.ajcri.patrickvarangot@wanadoo.fr. ♿ Open all year round, 24 hours a day. Situated in Paramé, on the west side of the walled town and very close (a 5-minute walk) to the beach at Rochebonne, this hostel is a 30-minute walk from the station, or you can take bus No. 2 or 5. There are 250 beds in small dormitories for two to six people. The atmosphere is great and there's no shortage of extras. Prices range from 59F to 111F per person, excluding breakfast, depending on whether you take a dormitory place or a double room. YHA cards are required. There's a car park, launderette, table tennis, tennis (which is free), and kitchen facilities are available. You can eat in the cafeteria, which serves four good-quality set menus for between 36F and 68F. There's no curfew, the place is very friendly and it's well run.

⌂ **Camping de la Cité d'Aleth**: Cité d'Aleth, St-Servan. ☎ 02-99-81-60-91. Open all year round. This is the closest campsite to the walled town of St-Malo, being actually situated within the walls. It's very peaceful, with a breathtaking view over the walled town from the edge of the campsite.

☆☆ Moderate

⌂ **Hôtel-Restaurant Les Chiens du Guet** (A2, **17** on the map): 4 place du Guet (inside the ramparts). ☎ 02-99-40-87-29. Fax: 02-99-56-08-75. Closed Sunday evening and Monday in February, March and October, and from mid-November to end January. Double rooms vary in price according to the season and the level of comfort, ranging from 160F to 290F. The restaurant offers several set menus from 78F to 175F. Tucked away below the town walls, this traditional little place is quite economical. The rooms are simple, furnished in the old style, but there's plenty of room to park a rucksack. The terrace is a pleasant place to sit, and in the delightfully old-fashioned restaurant, you could just picture Inspector Maigret sitting there coolly ordering his usual brandy and water. Tradition continues on the menu, with seafood platter and fish and lobsters from the tank. The welcome and the service are exactly what you'd expect from such a place – as is the clientele.

⌂ **Hôtel Le Nautilus** (B1, **18** on the map): 9 rue de la Corne-de-Cerf (inside the ramparts). ☎ 02-99-40-42-27. Fax: 02-99-56-75-43. Email: nautilus-saint-malo@wanadoo.fr
Open all year round. Double rooms cost from 250F to 350F. Just 5 minutes' walk from the beach, this is a really excellent little hotel. Everything is new and sparkling clean, and the decor is lively – youthful, even – and you could say the same

for the service and the welcome. The rooms are not large, but they are well equipped and attractive – some are attic-style. There's a busy pub on the ground floor, where the walls are decorated in a psychedelic colour scheme that reminds you more of the *Yellow Submarine* than Jules Verne's *Nautilus*. Try to avoid the first-floor rooms at weekends unless you're up for some serious partying, because it will be heaving on the floor below.

🛏 **Hôtel du Commerce** (B1, **11** on the map): 11 rue St-Thomas (inside the ramparts). ☎ 02-99-56-18-00. Fax: 02-99-56-04-68. This is a modest, quiet little hotel within the walls, offering the minimum, for a minimum price. Perfect for very tight budgets, with simple rooms with en suite toilet, shower or bath, costing from 180F to 360F. There's also a restaurant that offers the same value for money.

🛏 **Hôtel Le Croiseur** (B1, **12** on the map): 2 place de la Poissonnerie (inside the ramparts). ☎ 02-99-40-80-40. Fax: 02-99-56-83-76. Closed mid-November to mid-December. This hotel has no particular charm and doesn't offer a ridiculously low tariff, but it's a reasonable place charging honest prices, especially as it's located within the walled town. The rooms are small and functional, but they are well kept and the bedding is good. Double room prices range from 220F to 300F.

🛏 **Les Charmettes**: 64 boulevard Hébert, at Paramé. ☎ 02-99-56-07-31. Fax: 02-99-56-85-96. Closed in January. Facing the sea and just a few yards from the beach, this hotel has rooms ranging from 150F to 320F. The hotel is actually made up of two little houses, one behind the other, and only the second building has rooms with a sea view. Some of the other rooms seem over-priced for what

they are. You can take breakfast on a pleasant terrace that looks out over the beach. The area is quiet at night.

☆☆☆ Chic

It goes almost without saying that rooms in the hotels inside the walls are more expensive than those outside.

🛏 **Hôtel du Louvre** (B1, **14** on the map): 2 rue des Marins (inside the ramparts), close to the place de la Poissonnerie. ☎ 02-99-40-86-62. Fax: 02-99-40-86-93. Email: lelouvre@aol.com. Open all year round. This has a certain charm and still keeps the feel of a family-run hotel despite having 44 rooms. It's comfortable and the service is friendly. Double rooms cost from 230F to 370F, and there are some triple rooms, and even one room that sleeps seven.

🛏 **Hôtel Bristol-Union** (B1, **15** on the map): 4 place de la Poissonnerie (inside the ramparts). ☎ 02-99-40-83-36. Fax: 02-99-40-35-51. Email: hotel-bristol-union.com. Closed from mid-November to mid-December and in January. The place feels a tiny bit formal, but it has a pleasant, hushed atmosphere and a wonderful location (between the portes St-Vincent and the place du Poids-du-Roi). Some of the rooms are unremarkable, and a bit on the small side, but they're all very well kept. Allow 235–315F for a double. The breakfast is good.

🛏 **Hôtel de l'Univers** (B1, **16** on the map): place Chateaubriand (inside the ramparts). ☎ 02-99-40-89-52. Fax: 02-99-40-07-27. Open all year round. Restaurant closed Wednesday. The hotel has a good atmosphere and comfortable, if slightly old-fashioned rooms, from 300F to 340F. Rooms for three or four people are also available. In the same building as the legendary **Bar de** l'Univers, this hotel has witnessed the splendours of a bygone age and is one of the few St-Malo buildings of a certain style, with a certain period charm. In fact, it feels positively 'English'. There's a huge reception lobby and vast sitting rooms and long corridors, all of which add to the feeling that this is a place unlike any other. Unfortunately, the welcome does not always match up. The restaurant serves set menus ranging from 85F to 210F.

⚓ Hôtel La Rance: 15 quai Sébastopol, Port Solidor, in St-Servan, near the Solidor tower and the cité d'Aleth. ☎ 02-99-81-78-63. Fax: 02-99-81-44-80. Open all year round. This is a small establishment with only 11 rooms, the most expensive of which have a good view over the port and the Baie de la Rance. The hotel is family-run, making it chic but friendly; the decor is very tasteful, from the front doors right through to the spacious bedrooms, including some attic rooms, which are fitted out in an individual style. Prices vary from 340F to 525F, according to the season. The breakfast is very substantial. Highly recommended.

☆☆☆☆ Très Chic

⚓ Hôtel Le Valmarin: 7 rue Jean-XXIII, in St-Servan. ☎ 02-99-81-94-76. Fax: 02-99-81-30-03. Closed from mid-November to 24 December and from 4 January to February half-term. Set in an elegant typical St-Malo-style 18th-century building, the hotel has a *grand bourgeois* air. The rooms are sumptuous and cost from 550F to 750F. The park is beautifully maintained and it's possible to take your breakfast out of doors. The rooms overlooking the park are splendid, but ask when reserving or you're unlikely to get one. The service is extremely friendly.

⚓ La Korrigane Hôtel: 39 rue Le Pomellec, in St-Servan. ☎ 02-99-81-65-85. Fax: 02-99-82-23-89. Email: la.korrigane.st.malo@wanadoo.fr. Situated in an old townhouse that has undeniable charm and elegance, and a lush green garden. The rooms are named after great couturiers (Dior, Lanvin, etc.) and everything has a feel of real class: luxurious carpets, elegant tables, screens and so on. It feels like much more than a hotel – everything is refined, and the lounge is decorated in the same good taste, using a perfect combination of the old and the new. Rooms from 600F to 950F, with en suite shower or bath and toilet.

⚓ Hôtel Brocéliande (off B1, 19 on the map): 43 chaussée du Sillon. ☎ 02-99-20-62-62. Fax: 02-99-40-42-47. Email: hotelbroceliande@wanadoo.fr. Closed in December. Double rooms cost from 360F to 580F. This little hotel has a bijou English feel to it and every room (except two overlooking the courtyard) has a view of the ocean. The decor is sweet, pretty and very tasteful, with the accent on flowers, but the rooms are named after the characters of Arthurian legend – Merlin, Viviane, Lancelot and so on. The best of the first-floor rooms have a balcony or terrace. There's also a pleasant sitting room with a large bay window that looks out over the beach. Overall, this hotel has a good, intimate atmosphere and a friendly management. Excellent breakfast.

ST-MALO

WHERE TO EAT

☆ – ☆☆ Budget to Moderate

Rue Jacques-Cartier, which stretches along the length of the ramparts, is dedicated entirely to food. It is the sort of street where the very good and the very mediocre exist side by side. Be wary of extremely busy terraces where you may be served rubbish from which both your stomach and your wallet will suffer.

✖ **Le P'tit Crêpier** (B1, **29** on the map): 6 rue Ste-Barbe (inside the ramparts). ☎ 02-99-40-93-19. Open every day July–September. Closed Wednesday out of season. Allow 85F for a complete meal. Be warned – this is no ordinary *crêperie*, but let's just stick to the selection of *crêpes* and *galettes*, which are as good as they are unusual. Some pancake-houses seem to forget that they're serving real food, but this chef is first-class, using good-quality produce that is given a subtle flavour by daring juxtapositioning of ingredients. Imagine a 'Turk's head' mussel flan, *galette* with fish fresh from the market and heavily laced with garlic, or a jam made with onions. Or how about a seafood *foie gras*, made with monkfish (*lotte*) and prawns on a bed of salad? The desserts almost defy description: if you can move beyond the sugared *crêpes*, which are heavenly, you could try pears poached in orange caramel or a pancake '*chaud-froid*', which is a plain butter pancake confected with hot caramel sauce, caramel ice-cream and topped with crunchy peanuts. The seaweed marmalade, baked in the oven, just about makes your eyes pop! It's all so good that you're tempted to keep on eating in order to try more of these daring tastes. Beer and Breton cider are also served. There are two little dining rooms here, with a maritime decor.

✖ **Crêperie La Brigantine** (A2, **20** on the map): 13 rue de Dinan (inside

the ramparts, near the Porte de Dinan). ☎ 02-99-56-82-82. Closed Tuesday evening and Wednesday during school term-time; also closed for the last two weeks in November and the first week in December, and the last two weeks in January. This is a charming *crêperie* with a friendly atmosphere. The decor is pleasant – all light-coloured wood, check tablecloths and straw-bottomed chairs. The walls are covered with some lovely pictures of old sailing boats, including some by the English photographer Beken of Cowes, who was a master of the genre. They serve excellent, classic *crêpes* at reasonable prices. Set menus start at 60F. Friendly welcome.

✖ **Crêperie Le Gallo** (A2, **21** on the map): 21 rue de Dinan (inside the ramparts). ☎ 02-99-40-84-17. Closed Monday out of season, for three weeks in December and two weeks in March. Allow 95F for a complete meal. This *crêperie* is distinctly unexciting, and does not really look that great, but it attracts numerous regulars, who come here for good, consistent-quality classical *galettes* served in a simple, unassuming atmosphere.

✖ **Crêperie-snack Sainte-Barbe**: 14 rue Sainte-Barbe. ☎ 02-99-40-98-11. Closed the first two weeks in December and the last two weeks in March. The set menu costs 75F; allow 95F if eating à la carte. A lovely terrace on which you can eat excellent, fresh food. In season, they serve generous portions of tasty mussels as well as fish dishes and salads.

✕ **Le Teddy Bear** (A2, off the map): Gare Maritime de la Bourse. ☎ 02-99-56-03-80. Open lunchtime and evening throughout the year. The restaurant is well known among the locals and relatively unknown by tourists, as it's a little way away from the centre. The decor is very British and, as you might expect, the company emblem is a teddy bear (you see it all over the place). The food is generous, well-prepared, delicious, and very affordable, with menus from 59F to 79F. Allow 100F if ordering à la carte. On top of all that, there's a spectacular view of the sunset over the town from the restaurant's wide bay windows. Not to be missed.

☆☆–☆☆☆ Moderate to Chic

✕ **La Corderie** (B2, off the map): Cité d'Alet, chemin de la Corderie, at St-Servan. ☎ 02-99-81-62-38. Open from mid-March to mid-October. The set menu costs 98F; main menu prices start from 150F. Next to the campsite at the Cité d'Alet, this old rope factory is a little off the usual tourist track and is in a rather good location. The noise of traffic doesn't reach this far, making it a comfortable place where you can feel at ease. As well as this, you get the feeling of being in a family house, with antique furniture, books and pictures. From the dining room and the terrace, there are excellent views of the sea, the Solidor tower, the Baie de La Rance and across to Dinard. The menu here is short in comparison with other restaurants, but it changes almost every day and the food is always well presented whether the dish is modest or exotic. Prices are very reasonable, and the service and the welcome are charming. It's the sort of place you'd come back to.

✕ ♠ **Auberge Les Vieilles Pierres** (A2, **25** on the map): 9 rue Thévenard (inside the ramparts). ☎ 02-99-56-46-80. In season, open every evening and lunchtime at weekends. Out of season, open every evening and Sunday lunchtime. Double rooms cost 150–250F. Set menus are priced from 92F to 170F and eating à la carte will set you back 200F. This inn, built in the 17th century, is very atmospheric, with old stone walls and exposed beams, and there's an imposing open fireplace, where meat and fish are grilled. Added to all this are a roomful of attractively laid tables and a warm and friendly welcome. All the products used in the kitchen are fresh, whether you choose a grilled dish, a seafood platter or calf's sweetbreads with mushrooms. On the first floor, up a narrow set of stairs, several bedrooms have been fitted out. They are not over-elaborate, but the young owners are increasing the level of comfort bit by bit. For jazz enthusiasts, there's live music on the second Saturday of the month.

✕ ♠ **Restaurant de la Porte-St-Pierre** (A2, **25** on the map): 2 place du Guet; in front of Porte St-Pierre (inside the ramparts). ☎ 02-99-40-91-27. Restaurant closed all day Tuesday and Thursday lunchtime. Hotel and restaurant closed from the end of November to the end of January. The restaurant is an institution in St-Malo, famed for its seafood, and you can get a wonderful seafood platter for 100F, and good set menus at prices ranging from 100F to 300F. It's also a hotel, with simple, reasonably well-kept double rooms for 300F to 400F, with a 10 per cent discount out of season, in school holidays and on holiday weekends.

✕ **L'Âtre**: 7 esplanade du Commandant-Menguy, in St-Servan. ☎ 02-99-81-68-39. ✕ Out of season, closed Tuesday evening, all day Wednesday and Sunday evening, and from mid-December to mid-January. Set menus cost from 95F to 195F. The charms of this restaurant lie in a combination of its view of the sea, its waitresses, dressed in black skirts and white blouses, and its chef, who knows just what to do with fish. This is the sort of place where the quality is reliable, and it won't break the bank.

✗ **Chez Gilles** (A2, **26** on the map): 2 rue de la Pie-Qui-Boit (inside the ramparts). ☎ 02-99-40-97-25. Closed all day Wednesday out of season, Wednesday lunchtime in July and August, from the end of November to mid-December and for the February holidays. Freshly caught fish is the house speciality; it's prepared with imagination and served in a cosy, up-market setting. Dishes such as *aiguillettes de St-Pierre aux huîtres chaudes et lardons frits* (John Dory fillet with warm oysters and bacon) are cooked to perfection, with beautiful, flavoursome sauces. On weekday lunchtimes, there's a set menu for 78F. In the evening, there are other set menus from 94F to 182F, and the quality of the chef is obvious in even the cheapest menu.

✗ **Le Chasse-Marée** (A1, **27** on the map): 4 rue du Grout-St-Georges (behind the Hôtel des Finances, inside the ramparts). ☎ 02-99-40-85-10. Fax: 02-99-56-49-52. ✗ Closed Saturday lunchtime and Sunday (except public holidays) out of season. This is a charming little place, somewhat off the tourist track, serving mainly seafood. The cheapest menu (87F) is available every day until 9pm, and is not unsophisticated, while the menu for 145F is a real gourmet option. Be careful about going for the à la carte option, when the bill can really mount up.

▣▣▣▣ Très Chic

✗ **Le Chalut** (B1, **28** on the map): 8 rue de la Corne-de-Cerf (inside the ramparts). ☎ 02-99-56-71-58. Closed Monday and Tuesday. There's a menu for 100F (except Sunday and public holidays) and others from 190F to 270F. There's no doubt that this is one of the best fish restaurants in town. The setting is spruce and tidy although it's a bit cramped, but you get the impression that what matters is what goes on the plates. The staff get full marks for professional service and the food is first-class.

WHERE TO STAY AND EAT IN THE AREA

✗ **Ferme-auberge de La Porte, chambres d'hôte and gîtes**: with Jocelyne and Laurent Harzic, 35430 St-Jouan-des-Guérets. ☎ 02-99-81-10-76. ✗ Just 3 kilometres (2 miles) to the south of St-Malo on the N137, take the exit for St-Jouan and head for the town centre, then there are sign-posts to 'Ferme-auberge de La Porte' or just 'La Porte'. On the way, you will be following the walls of a castle before turning onto a shady little road. This large farm is in a wonderful setting between the river Rance and the village of St-Jouan-des-Guérets. Closed Wednesday out of season and at Christmas. The dining room is beautiful, and all the meat – leg of lamb, chicken, duck or even suckling pig – is cooked in the room, on a spit over an open fire. Set menus cost from 89F to 155F. Booking is essential out of season. There are also two comfortable bedrooms costing 320F for a double. The farm also has *gîtes*, which you can use as a base to discover the countryside on foot. You could even go for a swim (in the Rance) at the Plage du Vallion, which is just 500 metres from the farm.

WHERE TO GO FOR A DRINK

Nightlife in St-Malo is gradually moving away from the 'rue de la Soif' towards rue Sainte-Barbe, where most of the old sailors' bars have now been converted into restaurants.

☞ **Bar de l'Univers**: place Chateaubriand (inside the ramparts). ☎ 02-99-40-83-62. Open every day until 2am. Don't miss this place. It looks as though it's been decorated using the contents of a pirate's treasure chest, and the atmosphere is charmingly historic. The walls are covered with literally hundreds of fascinating photographs. The bar still has a certain chic, having been home to the St-Malo yacht club for some time.

☞ **Pub l'Equinoxial**: 3 rue du Puits-aux-Braies (inside the ramparts). A stone's throw from the Porte de la Vierge. ☎ 02-99-40-82-89. Open until 1am (2am May–September). Closed Sunday (except in summer) and in early October. This is one of the nicest bars in St-Malo. They pull a wonderful pint of Guinness and there's a really friendly 'Irish pub' atmosphere. They also serve a good range of whiskies and bourbons. Down in the basement is a cellar bar where jam sessions take place from time to time. The place is very lively and the owners never seem to need an excuse for a party.

☞ **Cunningham's Bar**: 2 rue des Hauts-Sablons, opposite the Port des Bas-Sablons, in St-Servan. ☎ 02-99-81-48-08. Open every day 4pm–3am. One of St-Malo's best-looking bars, this place has been done out in mahogany and chestnut by a ship's carpenter, and it looks great. At weekends there's a lively atmosphere and it's *the* place for the youth of St-Malo to hang out and, even better, it's away from all the crowds in the walled town. Superb views over the port.

☞ **L'Aviso**: 12 rue du Point-du-Jour. ☎ 02-99-40-99-08. Open 6pm–3am. Closed in January. Here there's a great atmosphere and a superb selection of more than 300 kinds of beer. The landlord has put up a 'doctor's surgery'-type sign that reads, 'Jean-François Fiévet, Beer Therapist, Consultations from 6pm–1am'. Only the opening hours have changed.

☞ **Le Saint Patrick** (B1 on the map): 24 rue Sainte-Barbe. ☎ 02-99-56-66-90. Open 2pm–2am. This pub made a wise decision when it preserved the original architecture of the building, which was probably an abbey. There are stone walls and vaulted ceilings, and the various rooms are connected by little wooden staircases. The top room has stained-glass windows, old church pews, and a highly original central feature (go and find out for yourself what it is). Prices are reasonable, there's a warm atmosphere and the service is very friendly.

WHAT TO SEE AND DO

★ **A walk along the ramparts**: this is definitely the first thing to do in St-Malo. The ramparts were the work of the military architect Vauban, whose fortifications were almost indestructible. As proof of this, they survived the Allied bombing raids in 1944.

The main entrance into the town, the **Porte St-Vincent**, dates back to 1709. Walking south in order to go round the ramparts in an anti-clockwise direction, you first reach the 15th-century **Grande-Porte**, consisting of two large machicolated towers at the southern end of rue Jacques-Cartier. Near the **Porte de Dinan** there remain 14 ship-owners' houses, all with plain, rather severe facades. Only the first two escaped destruction in the bombing raids, and the others were painstakingly rebuilt after the war. One of these houses, lived in by the *corsair* pirate Surcouf for the last 30 years of his life, can be found to the left of the Porte de Dinan.

There is an interesting view from the **Bastion St-Philippe**, but an even more stunning vista opens up from the **Bastion de la Hollande** (the one with the statue of Jacques Cartier). The **Porte St-Pierre** gives access to the beach at Plage de Bon-Secours. Offshore is the **Îlot du Grand-Bé**, where Chateaubriand was buried. As you carry on, you get to the **Porte des Champs-Vauverts,** where there is a statue of Surcouf. Here, there is a lovely corner watch-tower, built in 1654. The **Tour Bidouane**, once a powder-tower, dates back to the 15th century. As you arrive at the chateau, the **Porte St-Thomas** leads to Éventail beach.

★ **The chateau** (B1 on the map): built by the dukes of Brittany in the 15th and 16th centuries, the castle is currently used as the town hall. Although it is not open to the public, you can go into the inside courtyard, which is possibly the prettiest picture-postcard sight in the town. The large keep houses the history museum (*see below*) and in the courtyard are the old barracks. The **Tour Quic-en-Groigne** was added by Anne of Brittany. Its name is a reminder of Anne's famous words of warning, issued to the overly independent people of St-Malo: '*Qui qu'en groigne, ainsi sera, car tel est mon bon plaisir*!' ('That's how things will be, whoever may complain, because that's how I want it!').

★ **Musée d'Histoire de St-Malo** (museum of the history of St-Malo) (B1, **30** on the map): the history museum can be found in the large keep. ☎ 02-99-40-71-57. From 1 April to 30 September (except 1 May), open every day 10am–noon and 2–6pm; the rest of the year, closed Monday and public holidays. It's a wonderful setting for a museum, with granite-walled rooms and lofty fireplaces, and it contains a mine of information on the history of the *corsairs* and on the other celebrities upon which the town's reputation was built.

The first room houses two scale models of the town in the 16th century and the tidal port around 1700.

On the first floor is a room dedicated to the town's maritime history, containing a superb ship's figurehead representing a *corsair* (thought to have been modelled on Duguay-Trouin).

Located in what was the castle's chapel is a splendid painting, *La pitié du Seigneur* ('the Lord's mercy') by Jean-Baptiste Santerre, as well as documents written by Chateaubriand in 1848 about the Îlot du Grand-Bé, and the last will and testament of Lammenais, one of the founders of social Catholicism and a member of parliament in the Second Republic (1848–52) with Proudhon, Barbès, Louis Blanc and Ledru-Rollin.

On the second floor there are also memorabilia of the lives of Chateaubriand and of Surcouf, as well as paintings and models. There is a portrait of

Surcouf and an amazing little picture of the room in which Chateaubriand was born, bizarrely made from the writer's hair by his hairdresser.

On the third floor is a record of Duguay-Trouin's exploits, and stories about the geographer Maupertuis (who discovered that the Earth was not round but slightly flattened at the two poles). One curiosity here is a horrible 'restraint collar', which would have been used on prisoners.

Finally, you can go up into the lookout towers, from where there's a unique panoramic view over St-Malo and the surrounding area.

★ **Musée du Pays Malouin** (museum of St-Malo life) (B1, **30** on the map): in the Tour La Générale. This museum makes an excellent partner to the history museum (despite being a little under-developed), with entrance (on the same ticket) from the second floor of the keep, down the corridor that goes off from the castle chapel. The museum houses socio-cultural collections relating to deep-sea fishing and the everyday life of the trawler-men, as well as model boats, ships' documents and equipment, ship-building tools, furniture, headgear, costumes and pictures, all bringing to life the St-Malo of another age. There are some evocative images of the first intrepid holidaymakers to bathe in the sea, and of St-Malo just after the war.

★ **Cathédrale St-Vincent** (A1, **32** on the map): restoration work on the cathedral, severely damaged in 1944, was completed in 1971. It was originally built in the 12th century, with the eastern end constructed in the following century. There is a fine, elegant chancel complete with Gothic arches, and a nave that is curiously short in relation to the chancel's depth. Twenty years ago, the large rose window was fitted with a series of modern stained-glass pieces, and the colours are breathtaking. There are still visible remains of Romanesque cornices, animals and tracery, especially above the pulpit. On the floor in the nave is a mosaic depicting Jacques Cartier's visit here before he set sail for Canada in May 1535. His tomb is in the north chapel: when the tomb was opened up in 1949, only his head was found. The tomb of Duguay-Trouin is also here. The great door dates back to the 18th century.

★ **Old St-Malo**: a signposted circular walk leaves from place Chateau-briand and follows a route that takes in all of St-Malo's old buildings – both the original ones and those that have been rebuilt – taking you past townhouses, pretty courtyards, alleyways and various historical relics. A brochure from the tourist office or the castle museum describes nearly all of these.

At 3 **rue Chateaubriand** is the 17th-century Hôtel de la Gicquelais, where the writer Chateaubriand was born. No. 11 is an interesting house, with a courtyard, a wooden balcony and a staircase with balustrades. **Rue du Pélicot** is one of the most typical of the town's streets, and Nos. 3, 5 and 11 stand out. There is a reconstructed interior courtyard at 23 **passage de la Lancette**.

Rue Vincent-de-Gournay is full of 17th-century residences. At 4 **rue de la Fosse** is the Hôtel de 1620, complete with a turret. At 5 **rue d'Asfeld**, you can visit the courtyard and the staircase of the Hôtel Magon de La Lande.

Organized tours with specialist guides are also offered, during July and August.

★ **Maison Internationale des Poètes et des Écrivains** (international centre for poets and writers) (B1, **33** on the map): 5 rue du Pélicot (inside the ramparts). ☎ 02-99-40-28-77. Generally open Tuesday–Saturday 2.30–6pm. Closed for two weeks at the end of January and beginning of February. Admission free. Set up in 1990 in one of the few houses to have survived the 'great fire' of 1661 and the bombs of 1944, this writers' centre is a welcoming place. The project was brought into being by Federico Mayor (Director-General of UNESCO) and Camilo José Cela (winner of the Nobel Prize for Literature) in order to promote poetry, which tends to be rather neglected in France.

The centre is a venue for literary conferences, author appearances, exhibitions of photographs, painting, sculpture, and so on. It also houses an ever-expanding library of international poetic literature. Some evenings in summer, they organize walks with storytellers through St-Malo and the surrounding countryside. There are also literary walks through the town.

★ **Hôtel d'Asfeld** (B2, **36** on the map): 5 rue d'Asfeld. Open every day from 1 March to 15 November, 10am–noon and 2–6pm (2.30–6.30pm in July and August). Guided tours last about half an hour. Dating back to the 18th century, this residence is the only *corsair*'s home to survive the 1944 Allied bombing raids. A voluntary organization has restored many of the rooms to their former glory. The visit is an opportunity to go back 200 years, to the time when the owner, François Auguste Magon de La Lande, abandoned his life as a *corsair* to adopt the more lucrative and less dangerous lifestyle of a merchant.

The furniture is not in period, but the structure of the building has not changed since it was built. You can see the rooms where the ship-owners would have been received, and those where goods would have been stored, the staff quarters upstairs, and the amazing vaulted cellars, now used as a wine store.

★ **Le Fort National** (national fort): opposite Porte St-Thomas. Open from Easter to September. Accessible by foot at low tide. This fort is a fitting monument to Vauban, the military architect who built the St-Malo fortifications in 1689. More recently, several hundred people were held hostage in the fort in August 1944. A guided tour of the outer walls and the underground passages lasts about half an hour. Opening hours depend on the tides and you can tell from a distance when the fort is open as it then flies the French flag.

★ **Beaches**: St-Malo has a number of beaches. The **Grande Plage**, to the east of the ramparts, is safe and superb; the **Bon-Secours** and **Môle** beaches are a lot smaller, but much quieter. The Plage du Môle is the most sheltered.

★ **L'Escalier**: in La Buzardière, near Petit-Paramé. ☎ 02-99-81-65-56. This nightclub is very popular among the local late-night revellers and has a wonderful decor that will bowl you over.

ST-MALO

FESTIVALS

– **Étonnants Voyageurs**: this famous annual international festival of travel writing takes place for three or four days in May, in the Palais du Grand Large. Behind the festival is the well-known writer and editor Michel Le Bris, who set it up in the late 1980s. Since then, a number of top-notch English and French travel writers have appeared, including Bruce Chatwin, Hugo Pratt, Nicolas Bouvier and Jacques Lacarrière. The programme of events includes talks by writers, discussions and photographic exhibitions; a vast bookshop is set up in a marquee and, as you would expect, there's a literary café. Each year a different topic is taken as the festival's theme. For information: ☎ 02-23-21-06-21.

– **Solidor en Peinture**: held each year on the last weekend in June. This weekend focuses on the challenge of painting the Tour Solidor. On the Saturday, the required subject is the tower and the port; on the Sunday, artists can paint the subject of their choice and the works are then offered for sale. This event attracts both professional and amateur artists. For information: ☎ 02-99-81-60-89.

– **Folklore du Monde**: this week-long international folklore festival takes place each year at the beginning of July and features folk music and dance from many parts of the world. A worldwide audience seems to come to this event, making it a good place not only to find out about other cultures through their music, costume and dance but also by meeting people of other nationalities. The programme consists of music and dance competitions interspersed with processions. Some tuition is also available. For information: ☎ 02-99-40-42-50.

– **Festival de Musique Sacrée**: established almost 30 years ago, this festival of sacred music, held in the cathedral, happens every year from July to mid-August. It attracts some of Europe's best musical ensembles.

– **La Route du Rock**: three days in mid-August. This long-established rock festival, along with the 'Transmusicales' at Rennes, has become Brittany's most important rock event. Gigs take place every afternoon and evening, at Fort Saint-Père and there's usually a great line-up, with British, American and French bands of the moment. Information from Rock Tympans: ☎ 02-99-53-50-30.

– **Quai des Bulles**: takes place on the last weekend in October at the Palais du Grand Large. This is a cartoon-strip festival where it's possible to meet the nation's favourite cartoonists and perhaps pick up an illustrated autograph or two.

WATERSPORTS

Sailing

For centuries, St-Malo has looked to the sea for its culture and, inevitably, it is one of France's main sailing centres. At the recently established **station voile** ('sailing station'), experts give information to visitors on the wide range of sailing options in the city, from dinghies and windsurfers to ocean-going cruisers and old-fashioned rigs. Everyone, from beginner to confirmed watersports fanatic, should find something suitable.

Information: ☎ 02-99-56-18-88 or 02-99-40-34-04. The sailing station's office is open at the tourist office, from April to September.

■ **Société Nautique de la Baie de St-Malo** (nautical society of the bay of St-Malo): quai du Bajoyer. ☎ 02-99-20-22-95. Open Monday–Friday 2–7pm, Saturday 9am–noon. Here you can buy quality equipment and also get tuition, if your interest is in dinghies or sports catamarans. These are the people who organize the technical side of the departure of the Rum Route Race, which takes place every four years with St-Malo as its point of departure.

■ **Association du Cotre Corsaire** (corsair cutter association): at the west tower (*tour ouest*), Grande-Porte. ☎ 02-99-40-53-10. Here's an opportunity to go aboard the *Renard*, the boat skippered by Sur-couf, which was rebuilt for the festival of old sailing ships in Brest in 1992. The trips are quite memorable and last either a half-day, a full day or several days, between March and October.

■ **Étoile Marine**: 6 avenue Louis-Martin. ☎ 02-99-40-48-72. They offer days at sea aboard the *Étoile Molène* or the *Popoff*, a wonderful old ketch, and also rent out modern yachts, with or without a skipper.

■ **Chartering cruise yachts** (for trips of 6–15 nautical miles): **ALET**: 44 rue Dauphine: ☎ 02-99-82-07-48; **Naviloc**: ☎ 02-99-82-12-72; **St-Malo Nautique**: ☎ 02-99-81-84-55; or **Yachting Passion Chartering**: ☎ 02-99-81-47-52.

Surfing and Boarding

St-Malo and Dinard have a wide range of spots suitable for surfing and boarding (depending on the direction of the wind and the surf). These sites are *not* for beginners, so don't overestimate your ability. On days of very high wind, the wide **Plage du Sillon** at Paramé is a major spot for wave-jumping, and its east end, **La Hoguette**, has the reputation of being one of the most dynamic surfing spots in Brittany. If you fancy just watching, it's a good idea to get down there as soon as rough weather is forecast, as it's quite a sight.

■ **Surf-school St-Malo**: 2 avenue de la Hoguette. ☎ 02-99-40-07-47. Email: surfschool.saintmalo@wanadoo.fr. Open all year round, this is an excellent school for windsurfing, fun-boarding, surfing, sand-yachting and speed sailing.

Sea Canoeing

■ **Les Corsaires Malouins** (canoeing section): 28 rue de Toulouse. ☎ 02-99-40-92-04.

Diving

The first time you go underwater, you can't fail to see the magnificent emerald colour that gives this coast its name. Don't underestimate the heavy swell.

■ **St-Malo Plongée Émeraude**: salle Omnisports, terre-plein du Naye 35400 St-Malo. ☎ 02-99-19-90-36. Website: www.perso.wanadoo.fr/smpe. Open April–November. Allow 110F for a dive. Diving expeditions are offered, as well as training up to Level III, by fully qualified and registered

ST-MALO

coaches. Beginners are welcome, including children aged eight plus. On board the *Mercière* they run courses, including wreck exploration. It's essential to make a reservation.

The best places to dive

Le Laplace: if you're brave but not foolhardy, you can dive down to the wreck of this frigate, which sank in 1950 in the Baie de la Fresnaye. It lies at a depth of 20 metres (65 feet) and you can swim among shoals of little orange-and-blue fish, to see lobsters and huge conger eels at close quarters. It's best to avoid exploring the hull, which is split in two and is dangerous. Level I ability.

Le Catis: to the northeast of Cap Fréhel, this is the most outstanding dive in the region. This rock is 40 metres (130 feet) down, and as you swim around it, you'll be able to see colonies of sea anemones, sponges and lurking whiting and dogfish. You might even glimpse a few sea bass or coley, and there are sea urchins and a few surprises down in the chasms. Level II ability.

Le Fetiar: this large English steamer went down in 1919. It's in a good state of preservation and is resting on sand at a depth of 25 metres (82 feet). Around the wreck you might meet copper-coloured coley or frisky young whiting, and there are lobsters and conger eels hiding in the shadows, so take a flashlight. Level II ability.

La Grande Hupée: a little way north of the previous wreck, this jewel of a rock takes its name from its crest-like shape. At a depth of 20 metres (65 feet), the rock is draped with rich fronds of laminaria (a long, brown seaweed) and feathery gorgonia (sea-fans). These provide a good screen for the conger eels, common crabs and spider crabs that tuck themselves away in fissures in the rock. You're also likely to see mullet and bass chasing around. You can only dive here at low tide, because the access channel to the port is right alongside. Level I ability.

Le Bizeux: at the mouth of the river Rance, this rock seems to be the meeting-place for all the species that live in the Bay of St-Malo. The maximum depth here is 20 metres (65 feet), and this impressive rock is positively carpeted with orange-tinted sponges, sea roses and large hydras, all swirling about in the current. At the base of the rock, you can see a massive anchor, dropped by an unknown boat. Diving here is only possible as the tide is going out, because of the rock's proximity to the tidal power station. Level I ability.

SHOPPING

Céramiques de Dodik: 4 rue Chateaubriand (inside the ramparts). ☎ 02-99-56-68-82. Dodik makes panels in vivid colours, often on medieval themes, inspired by the stories and legends of Brittany. Opening hours are available from the tourist office: ☎ 02-99-56-64-48. The work can also be seen at the Galerie Gwen et Dodik, 5 rue Boyer (near the post office), which is open from 11am to noon and 3–6pm.

Le Comptoir des Épices: 5 rue des Merciers. ☎ 02-99-40-98-25. Here they sell all sorts of exotic spices for conjuring up explosive culinary mixtures.

ST-MALO

AROUND ST-MALO

★ **Île du Grand-Bé**: accessible by foot at low tide. Opposite the Porte des Bés and the Porte des Champs-Vauverts, this is the final resting-place of the legendary writer Chateaubriand, who was buried facing out to sea. His grave is marked by a very simple stone with a cross on top. From the summit of the island, there is a wonderful view of the coast.

★ **Île de Cézembre** (35800 Dinard): this tiny island is accessible from 1 July to the beginning of September from St-Malo and Dinard on the Emeraude Line shuttles, with three departures a day from the Dinan slipway (*cale*). A few nautical miles from the ramparts, the island was home to the small-time pirates who were not allowed into St-Malo. In 1940, the German navy turned it into an impregnable fortress that was bombed as many times between 13 August and 2 September 1944 as Stalingrad. Apart from a marked-off area around the restaurant, you cannot walk around on the island because of the risk of unexploded bombs.

✗ Behind the beach is a little restaurant, **Le Repaire des Corsaires**: ☎ 02-99-56-78-22. Open from the end of March to the end of October. The restaurant is often supplied with seafood by the fishermen, who come here for a quick drink at the bar before going back to port. It's a good place to go for a slap-up meal, preferably out of season. Dishes cost around 70F.

★ **Musée International du Long Cours Cap-Hornier** (international museum of the Cape Horn sailing races): in St-Servan (an old suburb of St-Malo, to the south), in the Tour Solidor. ☎ 02-99-40-71-58. Open every day from Easter to September, 10am–noon and 2–6pm. Closed Monday out of season. The 14th-century castle is almost 30 metres (100 feet) high, with three turrets. The museum is dedicated to the sailing races round Cape Horn, which took place at the end of the 19th century. The story is told through wonderful artefacts, superb paintings and thousands of souvenirs, model ships, on-board instruments, decorated paddles from New Caledonia, rolling pins, polished whale's teeth, charts, ships in bottles and even a huge albatross with a 3-metre wingspan. There is an interesting view over the estuary and the surrounding area, from the circular path.

★ **Le Grand Aquarium**: avenue du Général-Patton, La Ville-Jouan. ☎ 02-99-21-19-00. About 4 kilometres (2.5 miles) from the town centre. Reached by going through St-Servan. In July and August, open every day 9am–9pm (doors close an hour earlier); from September to June, open every day 10am–7.30pm or 8pm (doors close an hour earlier). Admission charge (75F). There's a shop and cafeteria. This enormous, ultra-modern aquarium is an in-depth, fun way to find out about all the inhabitants of the seas and oceans of the world.

First, you enter the icy waters where Japanese crabs and Norwegian sea bass await you. To experience the Atlantic, you go into a platform constructed like the bottom of an oil rig, while the Mediterranean species appear in a shipwreck setting. The 'touch pool' allows visitors to handle fish, including sharks, if they dare. Most impressive is the gigantic circular aquarium, where sea bream and six large sharks (of four different species) dance in an endless ballet. The sunken ship is home to some beautiful turtles of various exotic species, a number of which are more than 30 years old. A recent addition to the aquarium is a superb trip below the water in a submarine. There's also a 3D cinema to round off the visit. All in all, it's an unmissable attraction.

★ **Paramé and surrounding area**: St-Malo's seaside resort, which specializes in thalassotherapy – the use of sea water for health and beauty treatments. It has beautiful beaches, which can get very busy in summer. A little further on is **Rothéneuf**, which is great for lovers of naïve art, where there are almost 300 figures sculpted from the rocks. This was the work of a 19th-century priest, Father Fouré, who was severely handicapped. His fantasies include monstrous faces, a household scene where a husband is beating his wife, huge lizards, and so on. All the figures were sculpted between 1870 and 1895, and have their origin in the legends of the Rothéneuf *corsairs*. It's an interesting place to go for a walk, although you do have to pay to get in. There is a little terrace in front of the site, where you can go for a drink.

Paramé was also the home of Théophile Briant (1891–1956), poet, humanist and adopted son of St-Malo, who wrote historic novels but is little known in France. He carried out extensive work to increase the popularity of poetry in the area around St-Malo, and in Brittany as a whole. He was a friend of Max Jacob, Colette and St-Pol-Roux, and ran a literary review, *Le Goéland*, which he made accessible to all young poets. An association, the *Amis de la tour du Vent*, has been set up to publicize his work.

The area around St-Coulomb is the setting for Colette's novel *Le Blé en herbe* (translated as *Ripening Seed*).

★ **The 'Malouinières'**: this is the name given to the wonderful countryside residences built around St-Malo in the 17th and 18th centuries by the bourgeoisie and by merchants and ship-owners when they had had enough of living within the walled town. The architects of these houses were frequently the same people who worked on building or extending the ramparts, which goes some way towards explaining why these luxury country houses often look a little severe.

★ **Manoir Jacques-Cartier**: rue David-MacDonald-Stewart, in **Limoëlou-Rothéneuf**. ☎ 02-99-40-97-73. From June to September, guided tours 10am–11.30am and 2.30–6pm; from October to May, guided tours at 10am and 3pm. Closed weekends and on public holidays except in July and August. Admission charge. This is the oldest and most famous of the *malouinières*. From the outside, the house looks rather like a large farm. It has been fantastically restored, and the house brings to mind the life and travels of Jacques Cartier, who discovered Canada. He lived there from 1541 to 1557, after his three journeys to the New World.

You can see how Cartier extended the house. The tour takes you into the hall, the kitchen and upstairs to his bedroom. The manor belongs to a foundation based in Montreal and the guided tour is often conducted by people from Quebec, who are keen to emphasize Jacques Cartier's importance in Canadian history.

★ The furnished **malouinière du Bos** at St-Servan (guided tour daily at 3.30pm in July and August) is lovely, as is the house called **La Chipaudière** in Paramé. Although some of the *malouinières* are not open to the public, the architecture is always worth admiring from outside.

DINARD (*DINARZH*) 35800   (Pop: 10,988)

One of the oldest seaside resorts in France, Dinard is sometimes known as the 'Nice of the North'. In the second half of the 19th century, the British aristocracy fell in love with the place and its gentle climate. They contributed a great deal to the development of the resort, setting up the first tennis club in France in 1879, and the second golf course in France, in 1888. Dinard was visited in quick succession by Charles of Austria, Kaiser Wilhelm of Germany, Oscar II of Sweden, Edward VII and T.E Lawrence (of Arabia). A number of individual and highly idiosyncratic villas (over 400 of them in all) in all sorts of different architectural styles sprang up around the town.

Dinard is still a classy holiday resort, and there is definitely a marked contrast between tough, austere St-Malo and its extravagant, almost exotic neighbour. The two towns represent a curious mixture of granite and palm trees, despite the short distance between them. Don't miss the 'moonlight' walk ('*Promenade du Clair-de-Lune*'), which takes place at night and is enhanced by classical music. If you get the chance, see the film *Conte d'Été* (*A Summer's Tale*), by the legendary French film-maker Éric Rohmer, which really succeeds in capturing the quality of the light in this beautiful part of Brittany.

USEFUL ADDRESSES

🅱 **Office du tourisme** (C2 on the map): 2 boulevard Féart. ☎ 02-99-46-94-12. Fax: 02-99-88-21-07. In July and August, open 9.30am–7.30pm; the rest of the year, open 9am–12.15pm and 2–7pm (6pm in winter).

🚄 **Gare SNCF** (train station): ☎ 08-36-35-35-35.

🚌 **Bus companies**: the bus operator's name is TIV. ☎ 02-99-82-26-26. Connections to St-Servan, St-Malo, St-Briac, Ploubalay and Mont-St-Michel.

➌ **Dinard-Pleurtuit airport**: ☎ 02-99-46-18-46 (reception). Flights to the Channel Islands: ☎ 02-99-46-70-28.

■ **Shuttle boat services** (D2, **1** on the map): runs between Dinard and St-Malo, with connections every hour.

■ **Useful Addresses**

   🅱   Office du tourisme
   1   Shuttle boat services Dinard–St-Malo

⚓ **Where To Stay**

  11   Hôtel du Parc
  12   Hôtel Les Mouettes
  13   Hôtel Les Bains
  15   Hôtel Printania
  16   Hôtel La Vallée

✕ **Where To Eat**

  20   Snack Full Time
  21   Le Cancaven
  22   Castor-Bellux
  23   Bar-restaurant Le Macao
  24   Restaurant L'Escale à Corto
  26   Hôtel-restaurant Le Prieuré
  27   Restaurant Altaïr

★ **What To See and Do**

  30   Musée du Site balnéaire
  31   Petit Musée de la Mer et l'Aquarium

LA CÔTE D'ÉMERAUDE

Map labels (A–B, 1–4):

ST-BRIAC-SUR-MER, D 786

SAINT-LUNAIRE

Plage de Saint Enogat

Port R

Port

Av. de Menez Bleu

Château Hébert

R. des Métairies

Rue Roger Vercel

R. de la Vistule

Boulevard

R. du

PORT BLANC

Rue du Port Blanc

Sentier

Rue du Boulanger

Rue de

Starnberg

Avenue

R. Abbé Langevin

Saint Lunaire

PL. DU
CALVAIRE

Boulevard

SAINT ENOGAT

Rue

Rue

Legard

Minéas

des

Edouard

R. du Petit Manoir

L'Hôt

Boulevard

Rue

Alain

Rue

Henri

Dunant

VII

Gardner

R.

Rue

Botrel

des

Rue

du

Rue

Renan

Rue

de

la

LE VILLOU

Rue

Alexandre

PLACE DE
NEWQUAY

Rue

Rue

Bd Alexis Carel

Rue

Rue

des

Salm

P

R. des

R. Faraday

R. des
Trois F. Julien

Rue de

Rue de

LES QUATRE
CHEMINS

Boulevard

du

Villou

Villa Mauny

R. des Glycines

des

Brossardières

R. Branly

Rue Gramme

R. Edison

R. Ampère

Cro

Villou

Rue

R. M. Nogues

Rue

André

Chapron

R. des Trois Frères Julien

R. du Docteur Darren

Rue du Champ Picou

Verger

Bd Jules

Rue du Clos B. Tais

PICOU

Rue

Gouyon

Matigno

200 m
200 yds

NORTH

Pointe de
la Malouine

LA MALOUINE

Pointe du
Moulinet

Avenue du Vallon

Av. Boussineau

la Maloutre

Mai

Grande Plage de l'Écluse

roix

Corbières

Bd. Albert Ier

Pionnière

20

Casino

Palais
des Congrès

PL. DU
MAL JOFFRE

Bd Pr. Wilson

Promenade Robert Surcouf

Coppiger

PL. J.
BOUTIN

24 15 16

Rue R. G.

la

Rue

Sadi Carnot

Clemenceau

22

de la Paix

R. R. Leclerc

R. W. Churchill

Énogat

PL. DE LA
RÉPUBLIQUE

Rue

R. Kléffer

13 31

Levavasseur

Édouard VII

21

Rue Levavasseur

1

erle

aine

PLACE
CROLARD
ROCHAID

27

Boulevard

Veil

Rue de

R.
F. Hénon

Jacques

Cartier

Promenade du Clair de Lune

George

P

12

Rue

Émile

Féart

Avenue

Bara

Rue

R.

Caillibotais

Baie

du Prieuré

R. de la Salle

R. des
Français
Libres

30

Boulevard

Bd Général Giraud

PL. DU
GÉN. DE
GAULLE

fre-
me

egraverend

26

Plage du Prieuré

Boulevard des Maréchaux

D 114

LA BELLE ISSUE

SAINT-MALO, D 168

DINARD

WHERE TO STAY

☆ Budget

⚓ **Camping municipal de Port-Blanc**: by the sea. ☎ 02-99-46-10-74. ♿ Open April–September. This campsite is in a lovely, leafy setting, full of trees and with well-tended grass. It's very busy in summer.

☆☆ Moderate

Despite the town's reputation as being expensive, there are a few reasonably priced hotels.

⚓ **Hôtel du Parc** (C2, **11** on the map): 20 avenue Édouard-VII. ☎ 02-99-46-11-39. Fax: 02-99-88-10-58. Closed in winter, except during school holidays. Very near the centre and only a 5-minute walk from the sea, this little family-run hotel is in typically 'Dinard' style. A double room costs from 160F to 300F (cheaper out of season). It's excellent value for money and the rooms are very quiet. Despite its name, you won't find a park, but there is a decent, pleasant restaurant, with set menus from 60F to 115F.

⚓ **Hôtel Les Mouettes** (C3, **12** on the map): 64 avenue George-V. ☎ 02-99-46-10-64. Fax: 02-99-16-02-49. Closed in January. Just a stone's throw from the yacht club and the port, this family-run hotel offers very friendly service and ten nice, simple, little rooms, all recently renovated, for 190F to 230F. These prices are low for what you can expect to pay in Dinard. Ask at reception about parking.

⚓ **Hôtel Les Bains** (D2, **13** on the map): 38 avenue George-V. ☎ 02-99-46-13-71. Fax: 02-99-46-97-61. Closed from mid-November until Easter. Just 5 minutes' walk from the Écluse beach. This is a pleasant, family-run hotel, with double rooms costing 280–380F. Set menus cost 85–165F. They give excellent service and a good welcome.

☆☆☆ Chic

⚓ **Hôtel Printania** (D2, **15** on the map): 5 avenue George-V. ☎ 02-99-46-13-07. Fax: 02-99-46-26-32. Email: printania.dinard@wanadoo.fr. Open from 20 March to 15 November. The atmosphere is Breton kitsch on a grand scale, with beautiful furniture that seems to exude the smell of the sea. There are traditional box beds in two of the rooms, and one of the loveliest views over the bay of Dinard. Rooms from 340F to 480F, depending on the view and the time of year.

⚓ **Hôtel La Vallée** (D2, **16** on the map): 6 avenue George-V. ☎ 02-99-46-94-00. Fax: 02-99-88-22-47. Closed mid-November to mid-December and the last week of January. Restaurant closed Tuesday and Sunday evening, out of season. Rooms cost from 300F to 500F. The main attraction of this hotel is its superb location, in a quiet spot overlooking the sea – providing you get a room with a view. The rooms have all mod cons, but the place is rather characterless and the cleanliness is variable. There's a pleasant terrace that's very close to the sea. The welcome is professional. The restaurant is reasonably priced and serves traditional cuisine with an emphasis on fish dishes.

WHERE TO EAT

☆ Budget

✕ **Snack Le Glacier**: Plage de l'Écluse, on the sea wall. ☎ 02-99-46-54-39. ♿ Open every day February–November. Allow 50–100F for a complete meal. This is a large bar in a great spot, with a sunny terrace facing the beach. It commands a typical view of Dinard that encompasses a string of smart, striped beach huts, outlandish villas and the Île Cézembre out at sea, so it's an ideal spot for a coffee or a light summer meal in between swimming and sunbathing. Apart from salads, they serve very good mussels and seafood platters, with freshness guaranteed. Allow about 50F to 100F for a meal. They also do some wonderful hot-dogs in tasty sauces; make the most of these, as in other parts of France, the sausages can be dry or overcooked. There is also a wide range of ice-creams.

✕ **Snack Full Time** (C2, **20** on the map): at the entrance to the Plage de l'Écluse. ☎ 02-99-46-18-72. ♿ Closed from mid-October to April outside school holidays. Meals cost from 60F. In the summer, this is a popular meeting place for the young people of Dinard, for a quick snack between tennis and windsurfing. In fact, this is the other establishment run by the proprietor of the **Castor-Bellux**, so you can expect salads, sandwiches and pasta that's cheap and good.

✕ **Le Cancaven** (C2, **21** on the map): 3 place de la République. ☎ 02-99-46-15-45. Open all year round. A brasserie and bookmakers right in the centre of town, so it's the ideal place to soak up the local atmosphere. The walls are lined with fabric that reminds you of a Burberry raincoat. There's mainly fish and seafood on the menu, with excellent mussels. Good value for

money. Set menu for 68F (except on Sunday) and other menus from 69F to 112F.

✕ **Castor-Bellux** (C2–D2, **22** on the map): 5 rue Winston-Churchill. ☎ 02-99-46-25-72. Closed Monday lunchtime and from mid-September to the end of March. Booking a table is recommended. This is *the* cult restaurant and pizzeria for the young people of Dinard. There's a warm atmosphere and the prices are very reasonable for their pizza, fresh pasta and excellent mixed salads. Set menus cost from 60F. It's not unusual for customers to keep coming until past midnight, and the place is often full to overflowing.

☆☆ Moderate

✕ **Bar-restaurant Le Macao** (off A2, **23** on the map): 39 rue de Starnberg. ☎ 02-99-46-19-01. About 1 kilometre from the centre on the road to St-Lunaire, just opposite the Port-Blanc campsite. Open every day in season. Closed Monday–Wednesday in winter and mid-September to mid-October. They serve the best paella in Dinard – hardly surprising, as they do almost nothing else, and the chef learned his trade in Spain. There's a very good welcome. Eating in costs 80F and it's about 60F to take away. Telephone half an hour in advance for take-away orders. You can also get a piece of *far breton* (traditional Breton cake) for dessert.

☆☆☆☆ Très Chic

✕ **Restaurant L'Escale à Corto** (D2, **24** on the map): 12 avenue George-V. ☎ 02-99-46-78-57. Open evenings only. Closed Monday evening except during school holidays. Allow about 150F for a meal. Opposite the Hôtel Printania, and close to the sea, this fashionable little restaurant, also known as the Restaurant des Marins, has real character. Here you can get a good, invigorating meal such as fisherman's salad (*salade des marins*), oysters, salmon tartare and lots of fish dishes. There are no set menus.

✕ **Restaurant Altaïr** (C2, **27** on the map): 18 boulevard Fréart. ☎ 02-99-46-13-58. Fax: 02-99-88-20-49. Closed Sunday evening, and Monday out of season. This is the restaurant of the hotel with the same name. The dining area has a pleasing, slightly old-fashioned charm, and has the advantage of opening out onto the garden. The food has a good reputation; it can be quite expensive if you go à la carte, but there are five set menus ranging from 78F to 200F. Keep to the cheaper menus and you'll be OK. When it comes to the rooms, there's the same old-fashioned feel and without the charm of the restaurant. Some of the rooms are quite nice, with antique furniture and views out over the garden, but overall it's a long way from your first choice.

✕ **Hôtel-restaurant Le Prieuré** (C3, **26** on the map): 1 place du Général-de-Gaulle. ☎ 02-99-46-13-74. Closed Monday, Tuesday out of season, as well as two weeks in December and throughout January. Situated opposite the church, on the Prieuré beach. This is one of the best restaurants in town, serving seafood and fish specialities in a pleasant dining room overlooking the sea. Set menus for 98F (not Sunday), 150F and 200F. Some of the hotel rooms also have sea views.

WHERE TO GO FOR A DRINK

🍸 Along the rue Yves-Verney (C2 on the map), between the beach and the place de la République, you will find a string of bars frequented by young locals. Slaves to fashion should know that the only ones to be seen in are **Le Newport**, **La Croisette** and **Le Petit Casino**.

🍸 **Bar du resto L'Escale à Corto** (*see* 'Where To Eat'): great atmosphere. Less popular with young people than the bars in rue Yves-Verney, but worth a visit.

🍸 **Le Dériveur**: in St-Briac, at the end of Boulevard de la Houle. An excellent bar that is perfect for rainy days, with leather used in the interior decor and lovely prints of the Americas Cup. Pool table at the back.

WHAT TO SEE AND DO

– Dinard is home to the best **market** in the region, which takes place every Saturday morning. The whole of Dinard goes, creating a great atmosphere.

– **Guided tours** of the town are run by Le Gacem: ☎ 02-99-46-94-12. Departure from the tourist office. In season, Monday and Wednesday–Saturday at 2.30pm and 4.30pm; out of season, by reservation.

★ **Grande Plage de l'Écluse** (C2–D2 on the map): this is the main beach and it's the focal point of the town. There are still reminders of the 'British Golden Age', and even a plaque, attached to a rock, bearing the inscription '1836–1936. From the town of Dinard to its British friends, in commemoration of the centenary of the arrival of the first British residents.' Today's beautiful people still display Anglophile characteristics, which may make them seem a bit snobbish. Gourmets queue up at the Pâtisserie Nuillet, on rue Levavasseur. For people-watching, head for the terrace of the Petit Casino.

★ This smart seaside resort also offers some lovely **walks**. The shady 45-minute walk to the Pointe de la Vicomté, from the dam over the Rance as far as the Prieuré beach (C4–D4 on the map), is just one example.

If you are in reasonably good shape, the walk from the Prieuré beach to the next beach, the Port-Blanc, along the coast, will take just under 2 hours. The first part of the walk is accompanied by the tones of classical or jazz music. The walk takes you along the famous Promenade du Clair-de-Lune, past houses, hotels and villas that seem to be all piled up on top of one another. It passes the Pointe du Moulinet (with its unique view and a collection of fascinating and rather strange villas), the wide Plage de l'Écluse, the Pointe de la Malouine and the pretty Plage de St-Énogat. Finally, there is a fairly steep coastal path that leads down to the Plage de Port-Blanc.

★ **Musée du Site Balnéaire** (seaside resort museum) (C3, **30** on the map): 12 rue des Français-Libres. ☎ 02-99-46-81-05. The museum is housed in a villa built for Empress Eugénie, who was due to arrive in 1868 . . . but never came. There are modest collections of archaeological, prehistoric and traditional artefacts, as well as a small art collection. The most interesting bit is upstairs, where you can find souvenirs of Dinard at the beginning of the 20th century, when the town was swarming with English visitors. As well as photographs, there are swimming costumes, a model of the casino, sculptures by local artist Armel Beaufils, and lots of other little souvenirs of the Belle Époque.

★ **Petit Musée de la Mer et l'Aquarium** (little museum of the sea, and aquarium) (D2, **31** on the map): 17 avenue George-V; at the end of the Promenade du Clair-de-Lune (Pointe du Moulinet). ☎ 02-99-46-13-90. Open daily from Ascension Day to 15 September, 10.30am–12.30pm and 3–7pm (Sunday 2–7pm). Admission charge. This charming little aquarium has been here since 1935. It is quite modest, but presents a good cross-section of local fauna and also acts as a research centre.

★ **Usine Marémotrice de la Rance**: the tidal power station is on the bridge over the Rance estuary, on the Dinard side. ☎ 02-99-16-37-14. It was the first of its type to be built anywhere in the world, and is open every day from 10am–5.30pm, although visits are by appointment only. It was built using the same principle as the old tidal mills and can supply enough electricity for 250,000 people. However, very few power stations have been built following this model, as the energy produced proved very expensive. The tour itself is limited to photographs and short audio explanations, and you don't get to see anything of the power station itself.

★ **Hôtel de Ville**: the town hall is housed in the Villa Montplaisir, a fine example of 1930s architecture, and the former residence of the 'Queen' of Dinard, Mme Hugues Halett.

– **Dinard golf course**: actually in St-Briac. ☎ 02-99-88-32-07. Website: www.dinardgolf.com. A real treat for golf enthusiasts, with a wonderfully maintained links course right next to the sea. Not surprisingly, the atmosphere can be a little snooty and it isn't cheap, but if you love your golf enough, then money is probably no object.

LA CÔTE D'ÉMERAUDE

WATERSPORTS

Sailing

■ **Yacht-Club de Dinard**: promenade du Clair-de-Lune. ☎ 02-99-46-14-32. This is the hub for anything to do with sailing. It's a traditional place, with a wonderful English-style bar looking out over the bay, where anyone who's sentimental about the era of 'real sailing' comes for a drink. It is also a real, active sailing club, with all sorts of different options, from dinghies to sports catamarans. There are other excellent catamaran clubs in St-Lunaire and Lancieux.

Windsurfing

Dinard has a wide variety of windsurfing spots, from beaches suitable for beginners to the wildness of the Plage de Longchamp, where you can watch top windsurfers use all their skills on stormy days.

■ **Wishbone Club**: at the end of the Promenade des Alliés, on the far right of the Plage de l'Écluse. ☎ and fax: 02-99-88-15-20. Closed in January and February. Super windsurfing club suitable for all levels from beginners to professionals. They hire out good-quality windsurfing equipment, as well as dinghies, catamarans and canoes.

Surfing

Surfing headquarters is the Plage de Longchamp in St-Briac. On the edge of the beach is a wooden cabin that houses the bar Le Moustique, which is a gathering-place for surf addicts.

NEAR DINARD

Saint-Lunaire, near Dinard, has four family beaches, all blessed with plenty of fine sand. The place has kept all the charm of an old-style seaside resort, even down to the old colour schemes, and the Grand Hotel, around which the rest of the settlement grew up at the end of the 19th century, has recently been renovated using the original pink-and-red paint colours. If you take a walk out to the Pointe du Décollé, where there's a terrific panoramic view from Cap Fréhel across to St-Malo, you will see along the route a good number of turn-of-the-century villas. In the village itself, there's an attractive art deco post office with a mosaic by the Odorico brothers, and an unusual Romanesque church, which gave shelter to an Irish monk who crossed the sea in ancient times to convert the Bretons.

WHERE TO STAY AND EAT

✕ **La Pensée Gourmande**: 35 rue de la Grève, 50 metres from the Grande Plage in the direction of the post office. ☎ : 02-99-46-03-82. Open 10am–1pm. Closed Sunday in summer and at weekends out of season. Set menus for 68F and 108F. You can sit out on a flower-filled verandah or a sunny terrace that overlook a charmingly wild garden. Here you'll find a good choice of cakes (both Breton and English-style). It's a peaceful environment for having breakfast, brunch or supper. The cuisine is family-style, with savoury pies, fish specialities, and desserts such as apple charlotte, crumble and seasonal fruit pies, all made with fresh ingredients.

♠ **La Pensée** offers rooms by the week in summer. Out of season, they offer charming studio rooms with kitchenette. The place has been renovated with a homely feel, using wood panelling and old mosaics. Allow 290F a night for two people, including breakfast. ☎ : 02-99-46-03-82.

ST-SULIAC (*SANT-SULIAV*) 35430   (Pop: 875)

This little port on the Rance is a really lovely spot, and quite remote. To get there, take the N137 towards Châteauneuf-d'Ille-et-Vilaine, then the D117. It's a town that has retained the natural charm so many others seem to have lost.

The narrow main street, lined with very old houses, leads down towards the port. There's a 13th-century church with a 17th-century facade and various interesting sculptures and statues. Inside is the tomb of St Suliac, the founder of the village. There is a pretty rose window in the south transept.

The port is a lovely place for a walk at dusk or, alternatively, there are some great walks to the Pointe de Grain-Folet and Mont Garrot.

WHERE TO STAY AND EAT

♠ **Camping Les Cours**: about 500 metres from the village, on the right-hand side as you come in. ☎ 02-99-58-47-45. Open from 15 March to 30 September. This lovely municipal campsite is green and pleasant. It's very quiet and is well run.

♠ **Les Mouettes, chambres d'-hôte**: 17 Grande-Rue; in the centre of St-Suliac. ☎ 02-99-58-30-41. Fax: 02-99-58-39-41. ♿ Rooms cost 250–290F including breakfast. There are five airy rooms tastefully decorated in fresh spring colours, with wooden beds and floors. You won't find the rooms very quiet as it's right in the centre of town. At the back is a very pretty little garden. Overall, it's a good place to stop if you're after a couple of nights in a quaint little village. It's run by young people, who offer a warm welcome.

✕ **Restaurant La Grève**: on the port. ☎ 02-99-58-33-83. Closed Sunday evening and Monday out of season, and from mid-November to the end of March. The dining room is very pleasant and is tastefully decorated in a rustic style. The à la carte menu includes such things as a warm cockle salad in raspberry vinegar or stewed rabbit with *foie gras*. Set menus cost from 125F to 195F. The restaurant has a lovely terrace facing the Rance, but it seems a bit mean not to serve the set menus outside.

✕ **Crêperie Le Grainfolet**: 10 rue du Pavé (the main road). ☎ 02-99-58-40-16. ♿ Open all year round. Closed Tuesday out of season. Allow about 85F for a meal. Pleasant setting.

✕ There is another crêperie, **La Guinguette**, on the seafront.

CANCALE (*KANKAVEN*) 35260   (Pop: 5,351)

Once famous for its *terre-neuvas* (sailors who went fishing for cod off Newfoundland), its fantastic fleets of sailing ships and its matriarchs, Cancale is also the 'oyster capital'. In the 17th and 18th centuries, its celebrated oysters were delivered to the king and his nobles twice a week by special courier. The oysters here are flat, sometimes as big as a small tea-plate, and have to be eaten with a knife and fork. At the port at low tide, you can admire the formal layout of the oyster beds at the end of the promenade.

If you are approaching from the south, take the coastal road, which will give you a stunning view as you drive down into the Port de la Houle. The houses that you see huddled together along the length of the quay belonged to the *terre-neuvas*, the fishing families, while those further up into the town were the residences of ship-owners, merchants and other town notables. The long quayside in the Port de la Houle is always lively, with numerous seafood restaurants and a good mixture of fishermen (although these are less common of late), oyster-farmers, tourists and holidaymakers. The atmosphere is great.

There is a wonderful walk along a section of the long-distance GR34 path that will give you a first sight of the famous Rocher de Cancale as it rises out of the sea, then reaches the wild Pointe du Grouin before coming to the Plage du Verger. The four-hour walk covers about 12 kilometres (7.5 miles) – allow the same again for the return trip. The route takes in towering cliffs, steep paths, oyster-beds, and pretty fishing ports and beaches. There's a spectacular view from the Pointe du Grouin across to the bird sanctuary on the Île des Landes. On a clear day, you can see the island of Chausey and its surrounding islets, Mont-St-Michel and Cap Fréhel.

History

The parish was created in the sixth century by St Méen (another British monk). The sailors of Cancale had begun to acquire their reputation as early as the 15th century. Cancale was evidently a *corsair* port in the same tradition as St-Malo, which is why it was extensively raided and pillaged by the English in 1758 and 1779 – there is still an English cannonball embedded in one of the walls of the presbytery in rue de la Vallée-Porcon.

However, Cancale's history is primarily associated with the story of the *terre-neuvas*, the intrepid sailors who braved real dangers to fish cod off the shores of Newfoundland on board the famous *bisquines*, elegant fishing boats with powerful sails. The impressive Cancale fleet had a strength of more than 300 vessels and employed most of the men in the town when it set sail to confront the storms of the North Atlantic. The men were away for months at a time, and an important matriarchal society flourished in their absence. As a result, the French have stereotyped the women of Cancale as being very determined, with a bit of an attitude.

USEFUL ADDRESSES

Office du tourisme: 44 rue du Port. On the main square in the upper part of town. ☎ 02-99-89-63-72. Fax: 02-99-89-75-08. Open 9am–12.30pm and 2–6pm (7pm during school holidays and mid-season); in July and August open 9am–8pm.

There is also an information point for the port at the Halle à Marée: ☎ 02-99-89-74-80. Open in season 10am–1pm and 5–9pm; in winter, only open during the school holidays, and Friday–Sunday, open afternoons only.

WHERE TO STAY

☆–☆☆ Budget to Moderate

There are four **campsites**, including one at the Pointe du Grouin (☎ 02-99-89-63-79) in a lovely setting right next to the sea. There's not much shade, but it's clean and quiet.

✕ **Hôtel-brasserie Le Quérrien**: 7 quai Duguay-Trouin. ☎ 02-99-89-64-56. Fax: 02-99-89-79-35. Open all year round. Double rooms cost 350–520F according to facilities and view. The brasserie serves menus costing from 89F to 189F. These are probably the best rooms in Cancale, with everything gleaming and new. Each room is spacious, well-lit and has lovely bathroom fittings. There's a slight nautical flavour to the place. The welcome is warm and thoroughly professional – in fact, they take the whole thing rather seriously. The brasserie decor is very smart, with plenty of woodwork, brass fittings and a fish-tank for you to choose from. Cuisine and service are both excellent.

Hôtel-restaurant Chez Louisette: 39 *bis* rue du Port (on the hill, on the left as you drive down to the Port de la Houle). ☎ 02-99-89-61-98. Fax: 02-99-89-60-10. Closed Monday and Tuesday evening, one week in February and two weeks in October. Double rooms cost 180F. This is an excellent and typical Cancale address and is not terribly touristy. They have three simple rooms – they're not totally spotless, but OK for spending a night in Cancale without damaging either your back or your bank balance. There's a warm welcome. It's a good place to go if you like *couscous* or calf's head and they also do fish dishes. Otherwise, there's a set menu for 60F (weekday lunchtime); evening menus from 78F to 142F.

Le Grand Large: 4 quai Jacques-Cartier (just before the Port de la Houle if you are coming from the south, along the coast). ☎ 02-99-89-82-90. Fax: 02-99-89-79-03. Email: rietz.alain@wanadoo.fr. Double rooms cost 250–380F. Open all year round. Set in an attractive, old, ivy-clad house with the sea just over the road, the hotel has a number of cosy, light rooms, fitted with all mod cons. Many of the rooms can accommodate three, four or five people. The restaurant is not wonderful, but they do a set menu for 78F during the week, or you can eat à la carte for about 170F.

Hôtel La Houle: 18 quai Gambetta. ☎ 02-99-89-62-38. Fax: 02-99-89-95-37. Closed in January. Double rooms with a variety of facilities cost 220–320F. A nice, unpretentious, family-run little place with friendly service and clean, simple rooms. The best rooms are those higher up, as the views are very good, but the lower rooms are pleasant, and quieter, looking out onto the side-streets. There's a nice, homely atmosphere.

â **Hôtel La Voilerie**: le Chemin Neuf. ☎ 02-99-89-88-00. Fax: 02-99-89-74-00. Double rooms from 230F to 310F according to the season. This is a pleasant little hotel at the far end of the quai Gambetta and slightly raised up. It's modern, without too many frills, and while the rooms aren't huge, they are quite nice, well-kept, and have decent bedding. What's more, it's very quiet. The breakfast room is attractive and the welcome is refreshingly youthful. In the low season, guests may be offered a visit to the family oyster-farm.

WHERE TO EAT

☆ Budget

✕ **Crêperie La Cancalaise**: 3 rue de la Vallée-Porcon. ☎ 02-99-89-71-22. Open every day in July and August. In low season, closed Monday–Thursday. Allow about 80F for a complete meal. Just 2 minutes' walk from the Musée des Arts et Traditions Populaires. This restaurant has a pretty little dining room, with stone walls decorated with photographs of life in the old days, and it attracts plenty of regulars as well as visitors to the town. At the back, there's a long row of hotplates where cooking is seen to be done to order. They serve a good, crispy *galette* with a choice of fillings ranging from sausage to jam, so there's nothing unusual here, but everything is made with excellent local produce and cooked with just the right touch. Prices are very reasonable. There's a good choice of Breton ciders and they offer a take-away service.

✕ **Le Herpin**: 5 quai Gambetta. ☎ 02-99-89-86-42. Closed Wednesday evening and Thursday out of season; also closed from mid-November to Easter. This is a good place to come for seafood, a platter of stuffed mussels, spider crab or a dozen oysters, served raw or cooked and delicious either way. You can sit on the terrace, which is quiet and informal. Perfect when you fancy a snack.

☆☆ – ☆☆☆ Moderate to Chic

The following are the best places for seafood and other good food in Cancale.

✕ **Au Pied d'Cheval**: 10 quai Gambetta. ☎ 02-99-89-76-95. Open daily, 9am–10pm. Out of season, open weekends only, 10am–7pm. Allow between 80F and 130F depending on how hungry you are. The place is famed for its excellent oysters, which is hardly surprising as it's run by a family whose mussel- and oyster-farming business is run from the Port de la Houle. In fact, they serve many other dishes that are equally excellent and you can eat seafood and delicious hot dishes that are extremely fresh. You could try their succulent *écuelle du père Dédé*, which is concocted from shellfish in a creamy lemon sauce, or their whelks (*bulots à la sauce armoricaine*). On the ground floor they have rustic-style tables with stools; up at the next level it's a little more comfortable. The service is very spirited, by ladies with true Cancale spirit (*see* 'History'). Good wine, served by the jug.

✕ **Le Narval**: 20 quai Gambetta. ☎ 02-99-89-63-12. Closed Wednesday evening and Thursday (out of season). This place is always a safe bet. There's a small dining room decorated with a maritime theme. Set menus for 78F (except Sunday) and from 98F to 198F.

✖ **Restaurant Le Saint-Cast**: route de la Corniche. ☎ 02-99-89-66-08. Closed Wednesday in season and Tuesday evening, Wednesday, and Sunday evening out of season; also closed from mid-November to mid-December and for the February school holidays. The restaurant is delicious in every sense of the word, and manages to serve a remarkable set menu for only 115F. It is slightly outside the centre, in an elegant residence overlooking the ocean, and is the perfect spot to spend a lovely evening savouring extremely fresh seafood prepared with skill but without pretension. They serve other set menus in the same vein for up to 200F.

☆☆☆☆ Très Chic

✖ **La Maison de Bricourt**: 1 rue Du-Guesclin. ☎ 02-99-89-64-76. Fax: 02-99-89-88-47. ♿ Booking is essential, usually some way ahead. Closed Tuesday and Wednesday (open Wednesday evening in July and August), and from mid-December to mid-March. Prices at lunchtime go from 250F (weekdays) to 650F and evening menus range from 420F to 660F. This is the brainchild of Olivier Roellinger, a local man who has become one of the new stars of French cuisine and now has an international reputation. The clientele includes people from all over Europe as well as Japanese and Americans – all on a pilgrimage to Cancale for what is held to be the best food you can get anywhere. The setting is a beautiful, peaceful old residence in the St-Malo style and a meal here is a real ceremony. The kitchens serve up the very best produce from the sea and the surrounding area, and what is always noticeable is the aroma that comes from this chef's own special treatment. His reputation has been made on his imaginative use of spices and herbs. You can choose according to your means, such dishes as John Dory (*St-Pierre*) in a tartare sauce made with sesame seeds and a nut oil, or winkles (*bigorneaux*) with cured ham, followed, perhaps, by pineapple in *millefeuille* pastry laced with rum. The wine list is reasonable, with a good selection of half-bottles.

WHERE TO STAY AND EAT IN THE AREA

🛌 **Auberge de jeunesse** (youth hostel): Port Picain. ☎ 02-99-89-62-62. Fax: 02-99-89-78-79. Email: cancale@fuaj.org. From Cancale, drive towards the Pointe du Grouin and then follow the signs. Accommodation costs 51F per night for YHA members, and another 19F for breakfast. Lunch and evening meals are also served, if you book them, for 50F. This modern youth hostel is right at the water's edge and you can get to it if you're walking along the GR34. Recently revamped, it offers 80 beds in rooms sleeping from two to eight. There's a feeling of space, plenty of natural light and the place is decorated in a nautical style, all of which makes for a really pleasant stay. There are kitchen facilities and even a campsite. You can also get access to tuition at the Port-Mer sailing school. Excellent welcome.

🛌 **Hôtel Le Chatellier**: route de Saint-Malo (D355), just outside Cancale. ☎ 02-99-89-81-84. Fax: 02-99-89-61-69. ♿ Open all year round. Double rooms cost 300–330F. This pretty little hotel occupies an old house, where the rooms are decorated in what the French call *style anglais*, with flowery wallpaper. They serve a very generous breakfast; try to get into conversation with the lady proprietor, who is full of information about the area.

⬥ **Chambres d'hôte (Martine Monsimet)**: La Rimbaudais, 35350 St-Méloir-des-Ondes; 4 kilometres (2.5 miles) to the southwest of Cancale. In the township of St-Méloir, take the D2 for 1.5 kilometres. ☎ 02-99-89-19-75. Open all year round. This is a simple yet comfortable stone-built house, set in the middle of the countryside. A double room costs 225F including a generous breakfast. Friendly welcome.

⬥ ✗ **Hôtel-restaurant Tirel-Guérin**: Gare de la Gouesnière, 35350 St-Méloir-des-Ondes. A little way south of Cancale on the D76. ☎ 02-99-89-10-46. Fax: 02-99-89-12-62. ✗ Closed from mid-December to mid-January. Restaurant closed Sunday evening out of season. This place, by the roadside, doesn't look exciting from the outside, but inside it's almost faultless. A selection of quiet rooms, some with a view over the large garden and none facing onto the road, cost from 380F up to 640F. There's a wide range of facilities, including tennis (for a fee), a covered, heated swimming pool, and a weights room. The dining room is warm and lavish in feel, with excellent service. Don't forget to ask for a table next to the garden (reserve it – it's definitely worth it). The food is tasty, generous and imaginative. Set menus start at 128F, with four additional menus going up to 450F. The cheapest menu changes every day, but you might find, for example, lobster, pigeon and smoked salmon dishes. Whatever your budget, it's tremendous value for money.

⬥ **Chambres d'hôte: Le Mur Blanc (Brigitte Herteau)**: 35350 St-Méloir-des-Ondes. ☎ 02-99-82-00-60. Coming from St-Malo, follow signs for Cancale until you reach the roundabout where you fork off to Mont St-Michel (the D155). The house is on the right, about 2.5 kilometres (1.5 miles) after the St-Malo junction and 6 kilometres (3.5 miles) southwest of Cancale. Closed mid-December to mid-February. A double room costs 325F including breakfast. Despite its name, the walls are not so much white as pinkish. Set back from the road and therefore very peaceful, this superb large house is a listed building. Saved from being used as a store for a local market garden, it has been brought back to life after a massive restoration programme. An elegant staircase leads up to the three available bedrooms, which are pleasantly decorated, with oak floors, and mahogany finishes in the bathrooms. The sitting room has wood panelling and lofty ceilings. The proprietress is a fishing fanatic and will happily take her guests on expeditions at high tide. Altogether charming, this house makes an excellent base for exploring the region, and the nearest beach is only four miles away.

✗ **Le Coquillage**, **Bistrot marin**: Maison Richeux, 35350 St-Méloir-des-Ondes. ☎ 02-99-89-25-25. Closed on Monday and Tuesday lunchtime. This restaurant is the most affordable branch of **La Maison de Bricourt** (*see* 'Très Chic'), set in a lovely little chateau overlooking the Baie du Mont-St-Michel. Olivier Roellinger, the new star of French cuisine, always prepares the best food the sea can offer: Cancale oysters, gilt-head bream tartare or miniature sole in butter, as well as a selection of shellfish and crustaceans. There is a tapas-style formula, with three cold starters and three hot dishes for 370F for two. Allow 250F if you're eating à la carte. Set menus for 115F and 230F.

⬥ **Hôtel de la Pointe du Grouin**: 3 kilometres (2 miles) from Cancale. ☎ 02-99-89-60-55. Fax: 02-99-89-92-22. Restaurant closed Tuesday and Thursday lunchtime out of season. Right on the Pointe du Grouin, facing out towards the open sea, this hotel is a good starting point for some long walks around this wild part of the coastline. Double rooms cost between 420F and 520F, and three have a terrace. The decor is cosy but perhaps a little dated now, and a fresh lick of paint in the corridors, and elsewhere, would not go amiss. The rooms are relatively simple, and a little disappointing, making the place feel rather functional. What you really pay for is the view, and there's a panoramic view from the dining room, too, where they serve traditional cuisine, with set menus costing from 118F to 295F.

WHERE TO HAVE A DRINK

♈ Le Café du Port: 2 place du Calvaire, La Houle. ☎ 02-99-89-62-85. Closed Tuesday out of season and the last two weeks in November. This is not only a good sailors' café (where you can get decent sandwiches, a *croque-monsieur* or a very generous breakfast), it's definitely the headquarters for the infamous local 'attitude', which was, and still is, embodied in the local sea-faring people. This place is both the registered address of and the main meeting place for the organizers of Cancale's amazing sailing spectacular, the famous 'Voile-Aviron' (*see* 'What To Do'). It's worth asking if you can go out sailing with the fishermen for a day. Occasionally you might be able to hear traditional Breton music and singing.

♈ Le Tapecul: 10 place du Calvaire. ☎ 02-99-89-80-83. Open daily, from April to the beginning of November, 11am–2am. Out of season, open only at weekends. Right on the Port de la Houle. The counter of this bar is like a small boat. It's a relaxed sort of place with a good atmosphere whenever you go. They also serve decent snacks.

WHAT TO SEE

★ **Pointe du Grouin**: wild flowers in a mass of violet, white and gold cling to the rocks, which plunge down into an azure blue sea. Opposite the point, above the Île des Landes, the seagulls swoop endlessly. In July and August, however, you're no longer alone with the gulls. Each day guides are available to tell visitors about the bird species that live here, including cormorants, shelducks and oyster catchers. Sessions start out from the meeting point opposite the Île des Landes, between 1pm and 6pm Tuesday to Sunday. It's a terrific experience. Further details from the **Société pour l'Étude et la Protection de la Nature en Bretagne** in Rennes: ☎ 02-99-30-64-64. Website: www.bretagne-vivante.asso.fr

★ **Musée des Arts et Traditions Populaires de Cancale et sa Région** (museum of popular arts and culture in and around Cancale): ☎ 02-99-89-71-26. Open in June and September, Thursday–Sunday 2.30–8.30pm; in July and August, open every day (except Monday morning) 10am–noon and 2.30–6.30pm. Admission charge. Housed in a restored church, this museum of popular arts and culture tackles all the subjects associated with the Cancale region (history, geography, local personalities, etc.), and stages a different exhibition every year.

★ **La Ferme Marine**, **Musée de l'Huître**, **du Coquillage et de la Mer** (oyster, shellfish and sea museum): les parcs St-Kerber, L'Aurore, on the coast road. ☎ 02-99-89-69-99. Closed for three weeks in late December and early January. Guided tours from mid-June to mid-September at 11am, 3pm and 5pm; the rest of the year, tours only at 3pm Monday–Friday. Admission charge (38F). The guided tour is excellent, with interesting explanations about oysters in general and Cancale ones in particular. You can follow the development of these little creatures all the way from the oyster beds to the back of someone's throat. There are slide shows and information on the deceptive nature of the tides in the Baie de Cancale. After that, you get free entry to the shellfish museum, which houses a collection of several hundred different specimens from all around the world.

WHAT TO DO

– **Market**: every Sunday morning behind the church, the Cancale market sells food and other general market-type goods.

– **Boat trip**: ☎ 02-99-89-77-87. A *bisquine* (a type of fishing boat typical to Cancale and Granville) has been built in the interests of preserving local marine heritage. With 350 square metres (3,766 square feet) of sails, *La Cancalaise* is now the fishing boat with the largest sails in France. You can take it out for a trip or a fishing expedition. The boat sails every day, March–October. A half-day costs 150F and a full day 270F.

– **Le Voile-Aviron**: a sailing and rowing festival held in June. The event is an excuse to gather together a huge number of traditional undecked fishing boats, driven by either sails (*voiles*) or oars (*avirons*), or both. It is organized by a group of volunteers from Cancale, with the support of the magazine *Le Chasse-Marée*, and is attended by enthusiasts and sailors from all over the world. It is a unique opportunity to see boats that have now become very rare, and to take part in friendly regattas attended by skiffs from the Shetlands, curraghs from Ireland, whaleboats from the Faroes, skiffs from Bantry, dories from Cancale and fishing smacks from Arcachon. The festival stretches late into the nights over a long weekend, to the accompaniment of good beer and fantastic sailors' shanties. Information from Vincent Locqen: ☎ 02-99-89-69-57.

FESTIVALS AND PROCESSIONS

– **Fête des Reposoirs**: each year on 15 August (Assumption Day). The sailors return to rejoin their families and their community for this procession to the altars of repose (*reposoirs*), which are bedecked with flowers for the occasion.

– **Fête des Hites**: takes place on the third Saturday in September. In Cancale dialect, the word *hite* means 'brotherhood'. This festival celebrates the brotherhood of oyster-farmers, with a procession, and a white wine and oyster feast.

IN THE AREA

★ **Chausey**: the only part of the Channel Islands to remain under French rule after the Treaty of Brétigny in 1360 – the largest island is surrounded by 52 islets. During the 19th century, there were sometimes 500 workers extracting the granite from these islands; it was used to build Mont-St-Michel, the London docks and the ramparts of St-Malo. The main island currently has 10 inhabitants over the winter, who are overwhelmed by a tidal wave of tourists in the summer. Departures to the island are from St-Malo and Granville.

🛏 ✕ **Hôtel du Fort et des Îles**: Chausey. ☎ 02-33-50-25-02. Open from March to the end of October. Closed Monday (restaurant only). This is the one-and-only hotel and restaurant on the island, so it's almost a must. If you stay in the hotel, half board is obligatory and costs 315F per person on the basis of two people sharing. Set menus are between 105F and 330F, and specialities include grilled sea bass and lobster. It goes without saying that booking is essential.

DOL-DE-BRETAGNE (*DOL*) 35120 (Pop: 5,019)

If you are coming from Normandy, Dol-de-Bretagne is the first reasonable-sized town you hit as you come into Brittany. It is a quiet little town, and a pleasant place to stop before exploring the marshes, farmland, forests and historic towns all around. It is very proud of its cathedral, one of the most beautiful Gothic churches in the area. The surrounding countryside is wonderful.

USEFUL ADDRESS

🛈 **Office du tourisme**: 3 Grande-Rue. ☎ 02-99-48-15-37. In July and August, open 10am–7.30pm; out of season, open Monday 2.30–6.30pm, Tuesday–Saturday 10am–12.30pm and 2.30–6.30pm. The staff are friendly and capable.

WHERE TO STAY IN AND AROUND DOL-DE-BRETAGNE

Chambres d'Hôte

Probably because of the town's proximity to St-Malo and Mont-St-Michel, Dol-de-Bretagne is a paradise for anyone wanting bed and breakfast, with a wide selection of good-quality rooms in the town and the surrounding area. They are located in a variety of buildings, from farms to sumptuous manor houses. The following is just a small selection, giving you what are considered to be the best three plus a few outsiders. You could spend quite a few days in and around Dol, going from one chambres d'hôte establishment to another . . .

🛏 **Chambres d'hôte with Mme Roussel**: 24 rue de Rennes. ☎ 02-99-48-14-78. Four rooms in a pretty house in the town centre, one en suite and the others with shared facilities. Allow 200F for a double room, including a generous breakfast, often supplemented with delicious pastries.

♠ **Chambres d'hôte, Ferme-manoir d'Halouze**: in Baguer-Morvan, in the middle of the countryside, 3 kilometres (2 miles) from Dol. ☎ 02-99-48-07-46. Closed Wednesday, Thursday and Sunday. This is a large residence with a beautiful corner tower, and there are five rooms (all with en suite) for between two and five people. Allow 250F for a double room, including breakfast. Dinner is served for 100F, including aperitif, wine and coffee. If you're a keen fisherman, there's a private lake, and you can borrow bikes, books and comics, and board games.

♠ **Chambres d'hôte at the Manoir de Launay-Blot**: in Baguer-Morvan, 4 kilometres (2.5 miles) from Dol in the direction of Dinan. ☎ 02-99-48-07-48. Fax: 02-99-80-94-47. Website: www.pays-de-dol.com. Open all year round. Right in the countryside, this is a huge, 17th-century manor house that was home to Chateaubriand's aunt before the Revolution. The property is slightly down-at-heel and covers 50 hectares (125 acres). The three tastefully decorated rooms each have en suite bathrooms. Allow 300–400F for a double room, including breakfast – which seems a bit expensive, considering it is a little on the scruffy side. Dinner is served (except Sunday) if you reserve the night before, and costs 100F including an aperitif and wine. You can hire a bike, or fish in the lake or the moat (you can borrow the tackle).

♠ **Chambres d'hôte with Mme Roncier**: in a lovely farm in L'Aunay-Bégasse. ☎ 02-99-48-16-93. Comfortable double rooms for 230F, including a delicious breakfast with *crêpes* and home-made jam. The welcome is charming.

♠ **Chambres d'hôte with Mme Robidou**: La Petite Rivière. ☎ 02-

99-48-15-64. 1 kilometre from the village of Roz-Landrieux. Take the D78 towards Le Vivier-sur-Mer, then follow the signposts. Closed December to end of March. They offer three simple rooms with en suite facilities. Allow 200F for two and 270F for three, including breakfast. Children will love Ysatis, the family's charming donkey, who offers rides in her cart. The service is extremely friendly.

♠ **Hôtel de Bretagne**: 17 place Chateaubriand. ☎ 02-99-48-02-03. Fax: 02-99-48-25-75. The whole place is closed in October, and the restaurant is closed on Saturday from mid-November to the end of March. Double rooms cost from 214F to 320F and half board from 153F to 234F, depending on the time of year. Right in the town centre, this well-run hotel has very light rooms and offers good service, added to a family atmosphere that is especially warm in the low season. The inexpensive restaurant serves good, no-frills food, with set menus from 63F to 165F.

♠ **Grand Hôtel de la Gare**: 21 avenue Aristide-Briand. ☎ 02-99-48-00-44. Fax: 02-99-48-13-10. Open all year round. This is a simple, unpretentious little hotel in an unremarkable setting. Double rooms cost 215F and are not the freshest in the world but they do have the advantage of size. There's also a café and bookmakers (PMU), which livens things up a little; the place has a car park as well as a locked garage.

Campsites

♠ **Camping des Tendières**: in the town, on the road to Dinan. ☎ 02-99-48-14-68. Fax: 02-99-48-19-63. Open from mid-May to mid-September. This small, family-run campsite is situated under poplars and weeping willows next to a little pond, so it's quiet and shady.

🏕 **Camping Le Vieux Chêne**: in Baguer-Pican, 3 kilometres (2 miles) to the east of Dol-de-Bretagne. ☎ 02-99-48-09-55. Fax: 02-99-48-13-37. ♿ Closed in December. Here is a four-star campsite with excellent facilities and in a quiet setting – the pitches are separated by tall hedges. Despite its size, there's a good family atmosphere and the team in charge are very friendly. Facilities include a swimming pool, waterslide, fishing in the lake, and other organized activities.

🏕 **Castel-camping des Ormes**: 6 kilometres (4 miles) to the south of Dol, towards Combourg (D795). ☎ 02-99-73-49-59. Fax: 02-99-73-49-55. Open from May to mid-September. This is probably the most luxurious campsite in Brittany, set in a huge park around a magnificent 16th-century castle. It has all the facilities you could ever want, as well as countless sports and activities, including fishing in the lake, free swimming pools, golf lessons, horse-riding (for beginners or hardy trekkers), tennis, boating, pedaloes, restaurant, bar and disco. There's a huge amount of space to pitch a tent, and it's very popular with foreigners.

WHERE TO EAT

✕ **Auberge de la Cour Verte**: route de Rennes. ☎ 02-99-48-41-41. Out of season, closed Monday and Tuesday plus over Christmas and New Year. A low-season set menu costs just 50F, but allow 120F to eat à la carte. The building is an old farmhouse that is typical of many in the region, and has been painstakingly restored to a high standard. Situated in a pretty, green spot, it also has a children's play area. The big fireplace in the rustic dining room is the main focus of attention, as the chef, who is also the owner, struts his stuff over a hot grill. All the meat is cut on a wooden butcher's block and he never fails to produce exactly what was ordered, whether it's a piece of rare steak or a succulent lamb chop. Also partly open to view are the kitchens, where they put together a good selection of salads, *crêpes* and desserts. Originally from Belgium, the chef has included some of his own native recipes, with a delicious way of doing mussels. There's also Stoemp beer to accompany the main course, or a refreshing cordial from Liège. The wine is served in measured jugs, so you pay by the centimetre according to what you have drunk. The serving staff are all very young, giving the place a warm and friendly atmosphere.

✕ **Grill-crêperie Le Plédran**: 30 Grand-rue-de-Stuarts. ☎ 02-99-48-40-80. Closed Monday except in July and August; also closed from mid-November to mid-December. Allow 80–110F for a complete meal. Right in the town centre, in a beautiful old house. A huge open fire gives the place atmosphere and grills the meat to perfection. The *galettes* are also delicious. You can also eat on the terrace. Unfortunately, the service can be a little erratic.

✕ **Le Saint-Samson**: 21 rue Ceinte. On the street that leads off just behind the cathedral. ☎ 02-99-48-40-55. Closed Monday evening and Wednesday out of season. Set menus here cost from 59F to 160F. This restaurant is located in a pretty room tucked away at the far end of a little courtyard amid wonderful stone houses and a cascade of sloping slate roofs. A good variety of *gal-*

LA CÔTE
D'ÉMERAUDE

ettes is on offer, as well as grilled meat dishes, and so on – all simple and well done. It's an unpretentious place, and is perfect for lunch.

☆☆☆ Chic

♠ ✕ **Restaurant La Bresche Arthur**: 36 boulevard Deminiac. On the edge of town, heading in the direction of Pontorson. ☎ 02-99-48-01-44. Fax: 02-99-48-16-32. Email: labresche.arthur@wanadoo.fr. ✕ Double rooms with shower or bath cost from 180F to 280F. Closed Sunday evening and Monday out of season; also closed for the February school holidays. This is an excellent restaurant and one of the best in the region, despite being rather sober in feel. The set menus cost from 78F to 195F, and all of them offer amazing value for money. The dining room is beautiful and there's an air-conditioned verandah. The chef is fantastic; he makes excellent sauces and really knows how to bring out the natural flavour of the ingredients. Specialities include grilled pink bream in smoked bacon sauce (*daurade rose grillée à la crème de bacon*) or eight-hour leg of lamb terrine with herbs (*terrine de gigot de 8 heures aux herbes*). Definitely worth a detour.

WHAT TO SEE

★ **Cathédrale St-Samson**: generally open 9am–noon and 2–7pm. The cathedral dates back to the 13th century, with numerous additions over a period of 300 years. The richness of the building reflects the importance of the bishopric of Dol up to the end of the 18th century. The exterior is surprisingly hybrid in character: the west facade, with its two towers and gabled pediment, bears very little decoration, while a few vestiges of the Romanesque church that stood on the site are still visible. The left (or north) tower was never actually completed because of a lack of funds, while the north side (facing towards the countryside) has an austere and strongly fortified appearance. The south side, by contrast, is different again. Its porch is dazzling, with a display of pinnacles, balustrades, Flamboyant Gothic bays and low-reliefs. There is a smaller porch to the side, with double diagonal rib vaults.

Inside, the architecture is entirely uniform. The nave seems to stretch away into the distance: it is 100 metres (330 feet) long and is constructed on three levels. Its huge arches, triforium and high windows give a real soaring feeling. The diagonal rib vaults are pure and simple. The style of the vaults is quite rare in that the springings are held by columns that are separate from the pillars. The furniture and statues are of interest, too. In the right-hand aisle is a highly expressive '*Christ aux outrages*' ('Christ affronted').

The chapels of St-Michel, Notre-Dame-de-Pitié and the chapel of the Crucifix have beautiful stained-glass windows, some of which date back to the 14th and 15th centuries. The carved tomb of a 15th-century bishop was the first Renaissance work created in Brittany. Although it suffered some hammer blows during the Revolution, it is still possible to make out this remarkable piece of sculpture, inspired by ancient art forms. The large **stained-glass window** in the chancel is the oldest in Brittany, dating from the late 13th century. There is also a wonderful 16th-century organ, some superb 14th-century oak choir stalls, and a finely sculpted episcopal **throne** (16th century).

★ **La Cathédraloscope** (cathedral discovery centre): place de la Cathédrale. ☎ 02-99-48-35-30. Fax: 02-99-48-13-53. ☧ Open May–September 9.30am–7.30pm; October–April 10am–6pm. In July and August, open on Thursday evening until 11pm. Admission charge. Ticket counter closes one hour before closing time. Cathédraloscope is the brainchild of one man, an architect and lecturer in architecture called Olivier Delépine, who turned his dream into reality after years of preparation. This is a voyage of initiation, and in no time at all you forget where you are, transported into ten different cathedrals almost simultaneously. Each cathedral in turn reveals its inner secrets, from the details of its construction to the religious symbolism that it contains. A wealth of information is offered, about everything from the masonry to the stained glass and there are insights into the tools and equipment used by the stonemasons as well as into what kind of people they would have been and the lives they lived. The visit is something of an eye-opener, and you're sure to see cathedrals in a different light as a result.

★ **Musée historique (La Trésorerie)** (history museum, in the Treasury): place de la Cathédrale (on the corner of rue des Écoles). ☎ 02-99-48-33-46 or 02-99-48-09-38. Open from Easter to September, although the hours are rather irregular (try between 2.30pm and 6pm); in July and August open 9.30am–6.30pm; the rest of the year, open by appointment only. This 15th-century chapter house has collections of popular art, history, sculpted polychrome wood, earthenware, and so on, as well as displays on prehistory.

★ **La Grande-Rue** and **rue Lejamptel**: the main shopping streets in the town retain a few fine examples of medieval architecture, especially the 12th-century **Maison des Palets** at No. 17 (with finely wrought Romanesque arches), the **Cour Chartier** at No. 32 (has a pretty door and sculpted granite pillars), and half-timbered houses supported by solid pillars, similar to those seen in Dinan.

★ From the place Chateaubriand, you can set off on the 15-minute **Promenade des Douves** ('Ditches Walk'), which offers a wonderful view over the Dol marshes.

IN THE AREA

★ **Le Mont-Dol**: on the road to Le Vivier-sur-Mer. This strange granite dome stands 65 metres (215 feet) high and dominates the marshes like a lonely giant. Once it would have been surrounded by water, but a freak of geological nature left it stranded on dry land. For a long time, the Mont-Dol was held sacred by the druids. From the top (accessible by car), you have a spectacular view over the plain. There is a little chapel and the remains of a windmill, as well as a bar, a *crêperie* and a picnic area.

★ **Musée des Noces d'Antan** (museum of weddings of yesteryear): as you come into Dol from the direction of Le Vivier-sur-Mer; it's well signposted. ☎ 02-99-48-26-31. Open from 1 June to 11 November, daily 10am–7pm; in April and May, open daily noon–6pm; the rest of the year, open Sunday only, at the same times. Admission charge. Everything you always wanted to know about marriage but were afraid to ask. . . . This museum has more

LA CÔTE
D'ÉMERAUDE

than a thousand objects on display, as well as wedding dresses from the late 19th and early 20th centuries.

A series of showcases takes visitors through a traditional wedding day, all the way from the preparations of the bride getting dressed in the morning to the moment when she gets undressed again, in the conjugal bed. You see the sumptuous embroidered outfits, the making of the bouquets, china inscribed 'to the bride', the presentation at the civil ceremony in front of the mayor. Hundreds of bridal globes are on display. These glass cases were used to preserve and display the bridal bouquet, and the richness and style of the globe was an indication of the social status of the couple. Other exhibits connected to romance and marriage include dance cards, young ladies' accessories, embroidered tights, and presents exchanged between lovers, including exotic stuffed birds. Finally, a series of black-and-white photographs show what a wedding in the old days would have been like.

★ **Menhir du Champ-Dolent**: 2 kilometres (1.5 miles) away, on the road to Combourg (D795); well signposted. This impressive menhir stands 9.3 metres (30 feet) high, rising up in the middle of the open fields.

★ **Musée de la Paysannerie** (museum of country life): Les Cours-Paris, in Baguer-Morvan. A few kilometres south of Dol, on the road to Combourg. ☎ 02-99-48-04-04. Open every day from May to September, 9.30am–7pm. Admission charge. This interesting exhibition of old agricultural machinery and tools is displayed in a number of barns at an old farm. There are reconstructions of workshops belonging to cobblers and wheelwrights, and of an old classroom. There's an amazing collection of tractors dating back a hundred years or more. Spread out over one of the lawns, they look more like a collection of sculptures from a bygone era.

★ **Église de Broualan**: take a quick look at this lovely 15th-century church, built in granite. Inside, there are 16th-century altarpieces, also in granite, and, in one of the recesses, a *pietà* decorated in the Flamboyant style. In the square, there is a very old calvary with a Gothic inscription.

Meandering towards Mont-St-Michel

LE VIVIER-SUR-MER

An old fishing port that has reinvented itself as a centre for mussel farming. The village, which stretches out alongside the water, is quite pretty, although not vastly so.

WHERE TO STAY AND EAT

⌂ **Camping municipal**: ☎ 02-99-48-91-57. Open from Easter to the end of September. On the main street of the village. Slightly cramped site on what used to be a football pitch behind the mussel sheds.

⌂ ✕ **Hôtel-restaurant de la Mer**: 23 rue de la Mairie. ☎ 02-99-48-91-67. Closed Tuesday out of season and at the end of October. This is a modest roadside establishment that offers decent, inexpensive rooms. A double costs from 140F to 220F depending on facilities. Restaurant menus cost from 79F to 149F; they serve honest traditional food, although it's not very adventurous.

🛏 ✕ **Hôtel-restaurant Beau Rivage**: 21 rue de la Mairie. ☎ 02-99-48-90-65. Fax: 02-99-48-85-40. 🦌 Open lunchtime and evening. Closed Friday from September to April and from mid-November to mid-December. Double rooms cost from 250F to 290F; set restaurant menus range from 78F to 220F. Pleasant welcome. They offer clean, modern rooms that are functional and comfortable, although rather lacking in character. Good basic restaurant.

WHAT TO DO

– **Centre d'Animation de la Baie du Mont-St-Michel**: activities centre on the east side of the Bay of Mont-St-Michel, educating visitors about mussel and oyster farming, and much more. ☎ 02-99-48-84-38. Fascinating guided visits of the centre are on offer, as well as commentated walks out into the bay at low tide. Go either on foot or by tractor, to discover the local flora and fauna and learn about the trades connected with the shoreline such as mussel and oyster farming. Admission fee charged for both. The excursion takes 4–5 hours and departure times depend on the tides, obviously. Telephone in advance for times. There is also a permanent exhibition on mussel farming and local flora and fauna.

CHERRUEIX

This pretty village full of low houses stretching along the seafront is the European capital of sand-yachting. If you head towards Le Vivier-sur-Mer, you will see a number of old windmills. It is also worth going to the lovely, 17th-century **Chapelle Ste-Anne**, which sits on raised ground in a completely wild corner of the countryside. Opening hours are very variable. In the distance, you can just make out the tiny outline of Mont-St-Michel.

WHERE TO STAY AND EAT

🛏 **Camping municipal**: a five-minute walk from the centre. ☎ 02-99-48-14-68. Open from 15 May to 15 September. Modest and very small.

🛏 **Chambres d'hôte with Mme Taillebois**: in La Croix-Galliot, 2 kilometres (1.5 miles) south of Cherrueix. ☎ 02-99-48-90-44. A double room costs 250F, with breakfast included. This is a pretty farm, recently restored, offering clean and functional rooms with en suite bathrooms.

🛏 **Walkers' shelter and camping du Manoir de l'Aumône**: 300 metres from the centre of Cherrueix and well signposted. ☎ 02-99-48-97-28 or 02-99-48-95-11. Open all year round. The restaurant (open by reservation), has a 65F menu. This 15th-century manor house offers shelter for walkers (55F a night) in large communal dormitories under the eaves. Large kitchen-cum-dining room. There is also a quiet campsite (closed in the winter) with 70 pitches; it's in a nice, green setting, although there is not much shade. Tokens required for the showers. You can hire a *gîte* for four to six people, costing 1,500– 1,800F per week, depending on the season, and there are also caravans and mobile homes. There are opportunities for boat trips, and centres for horse-riding, sand-yachting and archery are located nearby.

WHERE TO STAY IN THE AREA

â La Bergerie, chambres d'hôte: in La Poultière, on the D797, a hamlet near Roz-sur-Couesnon (35610), on the right of the road as you come from Mont-St-Michel, and about 8 kilometres (5 miles) from Cherrueix. ☎ and fax: 02-99-80-29-68. Open all year round. Double rooms cost from 230F to 280F, with breakfast included. Rooms also available for three or four people. About 200 metres from the road, this place is nice and quiet. It's a beautiful old sheepfold that has been completely modernized, and is kept by a friendly couple.

Guests can use the large lounge and there's a lawned garden with deckchairs.

â Le Logis de Colombel, chambres d'hôte: on the D797, level with St-Marcan, on the left as you come from Mont-St-Michel and 8 kilometres (5 miles) to the east of Cherrueix. ☎ 02-99-80-22-78. A double room costs 220F. It's a pleasant and rather attractive building, but its proximity to the road means that it's not the quietest place. It's nice, nevertheless, with well-equipped rooms and courteous service.

WHAT TO DO

■ **Noroît-Club**: lessons and courses in sand-yachting. Beginners welcome. Expect to pay 90F per hour. Information: ☎ 02-99-48-83-01.

★ **Walking on the Polders**: The *polders* are the fertile lands recovered from the sea over the centuries, and protected where necessary by long earthen dykes planted with lines of trees. There is a lovely walk from Cherrueix that follows a variant of the long-distance GR34 footpath along a vast stretch of grassland next to the sea. This is where the famous *pré-salé* ('salt meadow') lambs come from, and the salt content of their grazing land gives their meat a distinctive flavour. Off Cherrueix are living reef platforms, known as *hermelles*. They are the largest in Europe, due to the strength of the currents in the bay. Walking on the polders is a completely new experience that brings you face to face with untamed nature. On less busy days, there is a feeling of intense solitude.

If you're travelling by car, when you reach Roz-sur-Couesnon, there is a little road (passing through Les Quatre-Salines) leading to the bay.

LE MONT-ST-MICHEL
(*MENEZ-MIKAEL-AR-MOR*) 50116 (Pop: 50)

Like all good legends, the story of Brittany's St Michael's Mount began with an apparition. The Archangel Michael appeared to Aubert, Bishop of Avranches, and ordered him to build an oratory on top of Mont Tombe, which at the time rose up in the middle of a forest. The legend says that at first, Aubert did not believe he had seen an apparition. St Michael reappeared to the bishop, this time in his sleep, and ordered him a second time to build the oratory, wagging his finger at the bishop to make sure he got the message (wagging it fairly roughly, too, if the scene depicted in one of the treasures at the Église St-Gervais in Avranches is anything to go by). The archangel also pointed out a spring, which would give the first monks a supply of water and enable them to live on the site. The site was first officially recognized when King Childebert came to put down his crown at the foot of the oratory in 710. In 713, several relics were donated by the Pope. Aubert died peacefully in 725, his mission accomplished.

As the result of a geological phenomenon (perhaps a tidal wave), the land around the mount collapsed, leaving it rising up out of the sea. Pilgrims continued to flock to the site, and what started out as a modest chapel was constantly extended. By the end of the Hundred Years War, it had become the magnificent abbey that it is today. The construction work was completed thanks to a handful of Benedictine monks who came from St-Wandrille in Normandy. They proved to be remarkable builders as well as skilled engineers. Huge blocks of granite were transported by boat from the Îles de Chausey, 40 kilometres (25 miles) away, before being cut to size and hoisted to the summit of the mount.

This wonderful building might have disappeared completely during the 19th century without the intervention of the brilliant architect Viollet-le-Duc (one of the restorers of Notre-Dame in Paris), who successfully carried out at Mont-St-Michel his most impressive restoration project ever.

The mount receives more than two million visitors every year, making it one of the most popular tourist attractions in France. There are still disputes between the Bretons and the Normans as to which department it belongs in. The *commune* of Mont-St-Michel is officially in the department of Manche, and is therefore administered as part of Normandy, although the mount originally belonged to Brittany and was only ceded to the Normans in the year 933. The border between the two departments, and thus between Brittany and Normandy, is actually the Couesnon, an irregular river that has now been channelled and flows past the base of the rock.

The bay encroaches as much as 23 kilometres (14.5 miles) into the land. It is said that the tide rises at the speed of a galloping horse, although to be precise, it's more like the speed of a running man, and this only happens during the highest tides of the year. *Never* go out into the bay on foot without first consulting a tide-table. You need to plan to get to the mount two hours before high tide, and be aware, too, that there are dangerous quicksands. The mist can also come down over the bay alarmingly fast.

Nowadays, the mount is in less danger from the sea than from the bay itself, which is in real danger of silting up. To recover cultivable land from the sea, dykes have been built further and further out into the sea. The River Couesnon has been run into a channel and is controlled with a dam. As a result, the power of the water has been reduced, and sediment is now deposited around the mount rather than being taken out to sea.

Scientists and politicians have been looking for remedies to the situation since 1972. One radical solution under consideration is to give the mount back to the sea. This would restore the cross-currents between the island and the mainland, and a bridge would then provide access to what would revert to being an island once the causeway is removed. The Couesnon would be left to run its own course, unrestricted by artificial channels. It would cost a fantastic 550 million francs just to let Mother Nature do her job, and it seems ironic that engineers can have devoted so many years to technical advancement, only to reach the final conclusion that nature knows best. UNESCO may contribute to financing the scheme, as Mont-St-Michel has been listed as a World Heritage Site since 1984.

The other danger to the mount is, of course, the tide of tourists – a flood that increases in volume every year.

Astonishingly, a small community of Benedictine monks still lives right at the heart of all this consumerism, and there is a strong contrast between the monks' quest for silence and spirituality and the noise from the tourist masses. Although the monks fled from the mount during the French Revolution, they returned to the abbey in 1966. The prior was quoted not long ago as having said: 'The rules of St Benedict prescribe silence. You can already see the paradox, when there are two-and-a-half million people whom we must not only accept, but also love . . .'

The Tides

The bay of Mont-St-Michel has some of the strongest tides in Europe, rising around 15 metres (50 feet) during the spring and neap tides. The strongest tides in the world are in the Bay of Fundy in New Brunswick on the east coast of Canada, where the water is known to rise 18 metres (60 feet). When the sea recedes from the mount, it leaves exposed 25,000 hectares (over 60,000 acres) of seaweed and grassy sand, streaked by small rivers. Dutch engineers were so impressed by this in 1609 that they suggested to the French statesman Sully that a dyke should be constructed that would reach across the bay from Cancale in the west across to Carolles on the eastern side.

During the strongest tides of the year, the sea can go out as far as 18 kilometres (11 miles) from the innermost point of the bay. Before the scientific advances of the 18th century, a variety of explanations was put forward for these enormous tides – anything from 'fits of fever' and 'the sea's breathing patterns' to 'divine intervention'. Whenever the boats came safely into harbour, the explanation was down to 'providence'. The Roman poet Pliny had, however, already observed that the seas 'drained themselves' during a full moon.

It was Newton and his theory of gravity that provided the scientific explanation for the phenomenon: the masses of water in the oceans rose up as a result of the combined attraction of the sun and the moon, and ebbed again when the attraction abated. The time of the new moon (when the mount, the earth, the moon and the sun are all in the same axis) is the period for spring tides. At full moon, when the sun, the earth, the mount and the moon are in the same axis (but this time, the earth is between the sun and the moon), there are also spring tides, this time with the famous 15-metre (50-foot) difference. In March and September, the sun and the moon are the closest to the earth, and this results in the equinoctial tides, which are the strongest of the whole year. By contrast, the tides in June and December are the solstice tides, which are the weakest, at which time the difference between high tide and low tide can be as little as 5 metres (16 feet).

To complicate things even more, in the bay, as on the other coastlines along the English Channel, the sea rises and ebbs twice a day (6 hours rising, 6 hours 30 minutes ebbing). Because the position of the moon changes and the earth rotates about its own axis, the times of the tides differ by 50 minutes between one day and the next. As the distance from the earth to the moon is not constant, varying from 356,000 kilometres to 407,000 kilometres (222,500 miles and 255,000 miles), the strength of the tides varies according to the month of the year. Added to this is the fact that the English Channel is a special case, where the tides are also affected by the whims of the Atlantic tide in the form of a wave that travels from Brest to Dunkirk. As this wave hits the Cotentin coastline perpendicularly, it increases in size in the Baie du Mont-St-Michel.

The question of the speed with which the tide rises is interesting. In fact, as the tidal wave enters the very flat bay (at the time of the spring tide), the series of waves quickly becomes a single wave as it approaches the Rocher de Tombelaine, by now travelling at a speed of 10kph (6.25mph).

Interestingly, Auckland in New Zealand, which is on exactly the same spot on the other side of the world from Mont-St-Michel, has identical powerful tides at exactly the same time.

Ask for a tidetable at the tourist office at Mont-St-Michel. This will come in useful if you want to join the throng of other tourists to see the famous onrush of the waters at the equinoctial tides.

GETTING THERE FROM PARIS

By train, departures are from the Gare Montparnasse. There are two alternative routes: either, take the line for Granville, get off at Folligny, and pick up a connection for Pontorson (9 kilometres/5.5 miles); or, go to Rennes on the TGV (high-speed train) (2 hours), and then take the bus to Mont-St-Michel. The journey takes 1.5 hours. (Courriers Bretons: ☎ 02-99-56-20-44). Or take the train to Pontorson. At Pontorson station, there is a shuttle bus to Mont-St-Michel (STN: ☎ 02-33-58-03-07), or you can hire a bike (☎ 02-33-60-00-35).

USEFUL ADDRESSES

🏠 Office du tourisme: the tourist office is in the Bourgeois guard-room, at the entrance to the mount, on the left after the first gate. ☎ 02-33-60-14-30. In summer, open every day 9am–7pm; in low season, open 9am–12.30pm and 2–6pm. Leaflets are available in a wide variety of languages.

🚆 SNCF (train station) **in Pontorson**: ☎ 08-36-35-35-35 (premium rate).

■ Flight over the mount in a microlight: contact M. Hulin. ☎ 02-33-48-67-48. An original, if expensive and noisy, way of discovering the bay. Available all year round, on request. A 20-minute flight costs 130F and takes you up to a height of 100 metres (330 feet).

■ Bicycle hire: go to Cyclo'vert (on the causeway). ☎ 02-33-60-09-33.

WHERE TO STAY AND EAT

There are two options: staying on the mount or off it, either at the entrance to the causeway or, better still, in the surrounding area. The first solution is the most appealing, but the hotels and restaurants on the rock itself are often full, the rooms aren't great and the prices can be on the steep side. Off the mount, there is a wider choice, the quality and service are markedly better and the prices will be lower. What's more, the view of the mount set against the beautiful bay on a fine morning is priceless.

On the mount

There are about ten hotels with a total of 130 rooms along the length of Grande-Rue.

☆☆ Moderate

🛏 ✕ **La Vieille Auberge**: ☎ 02-33-60-14-34. Fax: 02-33-70-87-04. Very simple rooms spread across a number of houses, for between 380 and 600F, which seems expensive considering just how plain they are. As far as the service is concerned, an occasional smile wouldn't go amiss. They also have a restaurant.

🛏 ✕ **Hôtel Du Guesclin**: ☎ 02-33-60-14-10. Fax: 02-33-60-45-81. Closed Tuesday evening and Wednesday, and from 5 November to the end of March. The double rooms are comfortable and well kept, and are pretty good value for between 320F and 450F. There is a two-speed restaurant, with good-value fast food downstairs and more traditional menus from 90F to 200F upstairs, in a very refreshing setting with a stunning view overlooking the bay. The service is efficient and not unfriendly.

✕ **Crêperie La Sirène**: on the first floor of a souvenir shop. ☎ 02-33-60-08-60. Closed Thursday and Friday. Meals here start from 62F. A charming spiral staircase takes you up to an excellent, friendly crêperie with sensible prices that do not rip tourists off.

🛏 ✕ **Hôtel-restaurant Le Saint-Michel**: in front of the Hôtel du Mouton Blanc. ☎ and fax: 02-33-60-14-37. Closed Friday and mid-November to the end of December. Set menus start at 80F. This is a nice little restaurant; although it doesn't look special, it produces very simple, excellent food. They offer a few reasonable double rooms for 250F.

☆☆☆ Chic

🛏 ✕ **Hôtel de la Croix Blanche**: ☎ 02-33-60-14-04. Fax: 02-33-48-59-82. Closed Thursday, and from mid-November to mid-December. Double rooms with all mod cons cost about 520F depending on the view and the season. Breakfast is 50F. The recently renovated dining room has a spectacular view over the sea. Set menus cost from 98F to 240F. Specialities include poached salmon with sorrel (*saumon poché à l'oseille*) and Mont-St-Michel-style leg of lamb (*gigot d'agneau montoise*). The place is well kept and there's a good welcome, although they seem a bit overstretched, like everywhere else on the mount.

☆☆☆☆ Très Chic

🛏 ✕ **Terrasses Poulard**: ☎ 02-33-60-14-09. Fax: 02-33-60-37-31. Open all year round. Pleasant service. The decor of the rooms and their level of comfort make this the best hotel on the mount. If you can afford it (double rooms start at 550F with a view of the bay), you can choose from rooms named after Victor Hugo, Terence Stamp or the Duke of Bedford. Two rooms are more affordable: – the Guy de Maupassant (No. 108) and Du Guesclin (No. 101) – but they are minuscule. Don't go for half board; the restaurant, a little further on than the hotel, is classic brasserie stuff, despite the signs announcing that the food is 'acclaimed'.

La Mère Poulard: ☎ 02-33-60-14-01. In the same building as Terrasses Poulard (*see above*). The rooms are very comfortable, but you should allow between 500F and 1,000F for a double room.

La Table de La Mère Poulard is an institution. Gourmets flock to this home of the famous 'golden omelette'. It is worth going along just to watch from outside as the eggs are whisked and cooked with all the efficiency of a metronome. Pyramids of eggs and slabs of butter are arranged on a big oak table. Much has been written about the famous omelettes of Annette Poulard (1851–1931), which have been savoured by politicians and film-stars from all over the world. The visitors' books contain hundreds of famous signatures. To celebrate the centenary of La Mère Poulard, all these famous autographs were framed and mounted along with photographs, and these now line the walls in both establishments. Reading the walls takes you on a trip back through time.

Following a recent change of management, the restaurant has received a number of enthusiastic reviews, but be warned – the successful formula is ruthlessly exploited for the tourists. The prices are unjustifiably high, the quality of the food is not what you would expect for the price and the wine and the cider are expensive. If you want to experience what's good about the place, just remember to keep control of your wallet and don't say 'yes' when you're offered an aperitif, a mineral water, some wine and then some coffee – and then a digestif. It will all add up very quickly.

Between the Entrance to the Causeway and Beauvoir (2 kilometres from the Mount)

This is the closest mainland option to the mount. The entrance to the causeway is nothing more than an enclave of hotels built to absorb the tourist excess. Beauvoir is a peaceful village a little further away. In season, it is worth reserving in either place.

✰ – ✰✰ Budget to Moderate

Camping du Mont: ☎ 02-33-60-09-33. Fax: 02-33-60-20-02. The closest campsite to Mont-St-Michel. Open from 10 February to 11 November. There are 300 pitches and all the usual facilities.

Camping du Gué de Beauvoir: at Beauvoir. ☎ 02-33-60-09-23. Open from Easter to the end of September. A 30-pitch campsite in the pleasant grounds of the hotel of the same name (*see below*). Breakfast is available, for 30F.

Camping Sous les Pommiers: at Beauvoir. ☎ and fax: 02-33-60-11-36. Email: pommiers@aol.com. Open from mid-March to the beginning of October. If you're coming from Pontorson, it's the first campsite on the right as you come into Beauvoir. A pitch will cost from 50F to 55F for two people, a tent and a car. There are about 100 pitches as well as lovely little wooden chalets for four people. These have newly done rooms (with shower and WC), and cost about 180F per person per night; mobile homes too. All sorts of facilities, including a swimming pool.

â **Chambres d'hôte La Bourdatière (with Monique Hennecart)**: at Beauvoir. As you get to the crossroads by the town hall, take the first turning on the right. ☎ and fax: 02-33-68-11-17. A double room costs 200F for two, including breakfast. Monique will give you the warmest welcome to her charming house. Her rooms are spacious and comfortable and the prices are very sensible. A table d'hôte dinner (80F), using local produce, is available to order (before 10am).

â **Hôtel Le Gué de Beauvoir**: at Beauvoir. ☎ 02-33-60-09-23. Closed from 1 October to Easter. A double room costs from 170F to 270F. This lovely house is set in pretty grounds, next to the campsite of the same name, and it's a real antidote to the blandness of most of the hotels in the area. There's a good welcome and the rooms are simple, but full of character. Breakfast is served on a pleasant verandah.

â ✕ **Motel Vert**: ☎ 02-33-60-09-33. Fax: 02-33-68-22-09. ♨ Closed from mid-November to the beginning of February. A double room costs from 200F to 310F. The rooms (some are in little bungalows amid the greenery) don't necessarily have all the mod cons, but they are pleasant enough. Right next door is a grill-restaurant with menus from 68F to 130F (open non-stop from 11.30am to 10.30pm).

â **Hôtel Saint-Aubert**: ☎ 02-33-60-08-74. Fax: 02-33-60-35-67. Open all year round. This modern hotel has 27 comfortable and well kept rooms, with prices starting at 250F according to the season. It's

nice and quiet, with views over the garden. A warm welcome is offered.

✕ **Restaurant-crêperie Les Mouettes**: as you come into Beauvoir from the direction of Pontorson. Closed Wednesday evening and Thursday out of season. ☎ 02-33-60-58-12. It has a pleasant little bar and restaurant that is also a *crêperie*. A respectable little menu at a very reasonable price. Allow 120F to eat à la carte.

☆☆☆ Chic

â ✕ **Hôtel de la Digue**: ☎ 02-33-60-14-02. Fax: 02-33-60-37-59. E-mail: hotel-de-la-digue@wanadoo.fr. Closed from mid-November to the end of March. Rooms with all mod cons from 365F to 470F; breakfast buffet for 54F. View of the mount from the dining room. Also has a restaurant.

â ✕ **Relais du Roy**: ☎ 02-33-60-14-25. Fax: 02-33-60-37-69. Email: le.relais.du.roy@wanadoo.fr. ♨ Closed from 1 December to 20 March. Rooms from 370F to 460F. The old part has a warm, rustic style. The restaurant has a good reputation and even the cheapest set menu is quite interesting. Half board is obligatory in July and August.

â ✕ **Hôtel Mercure**: route de St-Michel. ☎ 02-33-60-14-18. Fax: 02-33-60-39-28. Closed from the beginning of November to mid-February. Comfortable, although unremarkable rooms (typical 'Mercure') from 390F to 610F depending on the season. The set menus start at 160F and are fairly predictable, although you can get local salt meadow lamb (*agneau de pré salé*), which is quite delicious simply grilled.

☆☆☆☆ Très Chic

✕ **Bar-restaurant Relais St-Michel**: on the causeway, among the first houses in front of the mount;

run by the Poulard group (see 'Where To Stay and Eat, On the Mount', under 'Très Chic'). ☎ 02-33-89-32-00. ☓ Various set menus from 140F to 290F. The view is spectacular, and the atmosphere is elegant and tasteful, without being too formal. A drink at the bar at the end of the day, at the time when the setting sun puts the mount into silhouette, is certainly a memorable experience. The restaurant shows promise, and its prices are not (yet) inflated. Options if you eat à la carte include rack of lamb (carré d'agneau), roast chicken from the Auge valley (poulet rôti de la vallée d'Auge), gourmet salad with Normandy foie gras (salade gourmande au foie gras de Normandie) or savoury vegetable pasty with basil (feuilleté de légumes au basilic).

🛏 At the hotel next door, the **Relais Saint-Michel**, the prices are sky high (from 750F for two) but the rooms are absolutely gorgeous, and all have a view of the mount.

In the Surrounding Countryside

This is the 'pastoral' option, which is possibly the best. It allows you to spend the day unwinding in some of the loveliest countryside in France, either in the salt meadows or on farmland dotted with trees.

☆–☆☆ Budget to Moderate

🛏 **Walkers' shelter with Élie and Marie-Joseph Lemoine**: at La Guintre. On the route de la Baie (the D75), it's before you arrive in Courtils coming from Mont-St-Michel. ☎ 02-33-60-13-16. The shelter has three rooms and a dormitory that sleeps ten people. It costs 50F a night, and breakfast is extra. Open all year round. This is on a farm typical of the salt meadow region.

🛏 **Chambres d'hôte with Damien and Sylvie Lemoine**: opposite the walkers' shelter (see previous entry above). ☎ 02-33-60-06-02. Fax: 02-33-60-66-92. ☓ A room costs 200F a night for two (breakfast included). This young couple – the son and daughter-in-law of the owners of the shelter – raise sheep on the salt meadows. Their well-kept rooms have a wonderful view over the meadows (and the sheep), and over Mont-St-Michel. Kitchen facilities are available.

🛏 **La Ferme de la Rive**, **Chambres d'hôte**: 50170 Ardevon. ☎ 02-33-60-23-56. Open all year round. 2 kilometres from the causeway, heading towards Caen on the D275. It costs 200F for two, with breakfast included. Five comfortable rooms are offered; they have a magnificent view over the mount (especially the rooms on the first floor) and the salt meadows. Farm produce and friendly service.

🛏 **Chambres d'hôte Les Forges, with M. and Mme Jean Perrier**: on the route de St-Michel, 50220 Céaux. ☎ 02-33-70-90-54. On the road from Mont-St-Michel around the bay (D43). It costs only 220F for two (breakfast included), which is very reasonable. A pretty house, a warm welcome, and lovely, separate rooms, which are slightly old-fashioned. Jean Perrier used to be a teacher in Céaux. He's a real enthusiast about the bay and its history, and organizes 'discovery' walks in the area.

🛏 ☓ **Chambres d'hôte La Ferme de l'Étang, with Brigitte and Jean-Paul Gavard**: at Boucéel, 50240 Vergoncey. A dozen or so kilometres from the mount. At La

Croix-Avranchin, head towards Vergoncey on the D40 for about 2 kilometres, then turn right on the D308. Then it's well signposted. ☎ 02-33-48-34-68. Fax: 02-33-48-48-53. A double room costs 225F, with breakfast included. Table d'hôte meals with an ambitious menu made with farm produce are available, evenings only, by reservation. This is a lovely old ivy-clad house in the middle of the countryside, by a pond. Excellent service and beautiful rooms with en suite. There is also table-tennis and billiards.

≜ Chambres d'hôte La Ferme du Petit Manoir, with Annick and Jean Gédoin: 21 rue de la Pierre-du-Tertre, 50170 Servon. About 10 kilometres (6 miles) from the mount, between Pontaubault and Pontorson, on the D113. ☎ 02-33-60-03-44. Fax: 02-33-60-17-79. Two double rooms for 220F, including breakfast.This lovely farm is on the way out of the village. It also has a swimming pool.

≜ ✕ Hôtel-restaurant Au P'tit Quinquin: Les Forges, route de Courtils, 50220 Céaux. ☎ 02-33-70-97-42. From Mont-St-Michel, head towards Avranches on the D275, then take the D43; the hotel is at the crossroads, 2 kilometres after the village of Courtils. Closed Sunday evening, Monday (except in season) and from 5 January to 15 February. The cheapest double room is 150F, with others going up to 240F. This is a small establishment that offers a choice of rooms at a number of different prices. Avoid the rooms on the road side, which are noisy. Good-value, very generous menus from 72F to 180F, with such specialities as breast of goose in cider (magret d'oie au cidre) and scallops au gratin flavoured with vanilla (gratin de Saint-Jacques à la vanille).

≜ ✕ Auberge du Terroir: Le Bourg, Servon. ☎ 02-33-60-17-92. Fax: 02-33-60-35-26. ✕ Closed mid-November to the beginning of December and during the February school holidays. On the road from Pontaubault to Pontorson, turn right on the D107. Car park. This is a charming, completely renovated little hotel in what used to be a school and a presbytery, in a quiet village, and is run by a welcoming young couple. The atmosphere is peaceful. All the tastefully decorated rooms are named after famous musicians or composers. Double rooms cost 290F to 340F, with breakfast extra. There's a tennis court and pretty grounds, and they also serve delicious food in a lovely dining room. The chef cheerfully prepares specialities from the Perigord region, such as duck breast in honey sauce (magret au miel), as well as many choices of fish: fisherman's casserole (la marmite du pêcheur) or salmon in green cabbage (saumon au chou vert). Menus from 92F to 240F.

In Pontorson (9 kilometres/5 miles from the mount)

A quiet little town right on the border between Brittany and Normandy, Pontorson is perfect for those who prefer to stay a little further away before tackling the mount early in the morning.

☆–☆☆ Budget to Moderate

≜ Camping municipal: on the edge of the Couesnon. This campsite has about a hundred pitches and is comfortable and reasonably priced.

≜ Auberge de jeunesse: the youth hostel is at the Centre Du-Guesclin, boulevard Patton. ☎ and fax: 02-33-60-18-65. Email: aj@ville-pontorson.fr. Double rooms cost 48F in the hostel and 55F in the *gîte*. Open from May to the end of September. Housed in a large building dating back to the early 1900s, the hostel is not very lively (it feels a bit like a disused hospital), but is well run and friendly. Cooking facilities are available.

⌂ **Hôtel de l'Arrivée**: 14 rue du Docteur-Tizon. ☎ and fax: 02-33-60-01-57. Closed for the last two weeks of November, and Monday out of season. Rooms cost from 99F up to 160F (130F out of season). This hotel is close to the station. It's small and very simple and is ideal for those on tight budgets. There's also a local bar that serves snacks.

✗ **Le Relais gourmand**: 15 rue du Tanis. ☎ 02-33-58-20-96. Open every day in season. An excellent family restaurant in the hands of real professionals, right on the tourist route, serving typical Norman cuisine such as veal in cream and a variety of fish dishes. The chef hasn't forgotten his southern origins either, and dishes such as preserved duck (*confit de canard*) are usually on offer, with menus starting at 70F. Recommended.

⌂ ♔ **Pub (and rooms) Le Relax**: 20 rue du Docteur-Tizon. ☎ 02-33-68-32-10. Open all year round. Next door to the Hôtel de l'Arrivée. Double rooms cost from 130F to 170F according to the facilities and the season. It's a place that really lives up to its name. The young landlord is an animated, energetic man, and his pub is the meeting place for the local youth, with its pool table and wonderful weights room next to the bar. He also rents out five simple, but well-kept double rooms. After trying out the instruments of torture, head for the sauna (60F).

⌂ ✗ **Hôtel-restaurant La Cave**: 37 rue de la Libération. ☎ and fax: 02-33-60-11-35. ♿ to the restaurant. Closed from mid-November to the beginning of December, and Friday out of season. Double rooms from 220F to 270F. The charming restaurant has a pretty facade and a warm atmosphere, and the food is excellent value for money, with set menus from 65F to 195F, as well as *crêpes*. The private car park is locked at night.

☆☆☆ Chic

⌂ ✗ **Hôtel Montgomery**: 13 rue Couesnon (the main road in Pontorson). ☎ 02-33-60-00-09. Fax: 02-33-60-37-66. Email: hotel-montgomery@wanadoo.fr. Open all year round. Double rooms with all mod cons cost 350F to 550F according to the room and the season. Residents-only restaurant (open evenings only and by reservation) offering a menu for about 100F. This is a splendid hotel, set in what was once the home of the counts of Montgomery. Right on the main road in Pontorson, the building has a stone facade covered with ivy. Inside, there are luxurious carpets and parquet floors, which combine with the fireplaces and the wood panelling, which has a real patina of age, to create a remarkable atmosphere. There are 30 rooms, all with mod cons, of a high standard, and some even have four-star bathrooms with spa bath or thalassotherapy shower. Some of the rooms have period furniture and four-poster beds, which is the height of luxury. Staying here might seem like madness, but actually it's very good value for money and the service and the welcome come well up to expectation.

⌂ ✗ **Hôtel-restaurant Le Bretagne**: 59 rue Couesnon (the main road in Pontorson). ☎ 02-33-60-10-55. Fax: 02-33-58-20-54. Closed Monday out of season, and from

January to mid-February. Comfortable double rooms for 280F to 300F. Set menus for 90F to 260F. This hotel-restaurant is in what was an old post house. It has fine reception rooms with wood panelling and pleasant, well-furnished, very spacious bedrooms. The service is excellent. Largely made up of local regulars, the clientele enjoys excellent food, and the place deserves its good reputation. The menus offer such specialities as: oysters in Camembert (*huîtres gratinées au camembert*), warmed goat's cheese in honey (*chèvre chaud au miel*) or chitterling sausage with apple, wrapped in flaky pastry (*mille-feuille d'andouille aux pommes*). The lady proprietor (Mme Carnet) has been in charge of the kitchen for 35 years or so and only uses the best fresh local produce. Overall, the place offers extremely good value for money.

VISITING THE MOUNT

★ The causeway is 2 kilometres (1.5 miles) in length and has linked the mount to the mainland since 1877. It leads to the Porte du Roi ('King's Gateway'), which is now sealed up. A wooden gangway leads to the **Porte de l'Avancée**, the only opening in the ramparts.

★ **La Grande-Rue**, once used mainly by the pilgrims, this main street makes its way up the rock, flanked on both sides by two lines of souvenir shops. It takes a little imagination to ignore the knick-knacks and foreign rubbish and go back in time, but there are a few old houses with typical medieval architecture to help you build up your picture.

The **Maison de l'Artichaut**, straddling the road, is remarkable for its wooden cladding. Further on are the **Maison de la Sirène** and the **Maison du Mouton Blanc**, which now houses a restaurant.

★ **Église Paroissiale St-Pierre**: the parish church is flanked by the cemetery that is the burial place of St Aubert, the founder of the mount. It is worth stopping here before braving the steps that lead up to the barbican and mark the entrance to the abbey.

★ On the mount, there are no end of **steps**. The staircase known as **Le Gouffre** ('the abyss') takes you to the guardroom, where the ticket office is located.

★ You need to climb still more, up between the abbatial residence and the retaining walls, in order to get to the **Terrasse de l'Ouest** (there's an admission charge). On a clear day, you can see the Chausey islands, 40 kilometres (25 miles) away.

THE *ABBATIALE* (ABBEY-CHURCH)

During the day

There are three different sorts of tour around the abbey-church:

– **Unguided visit**: access to a limited area, and a guidebook (42F).

– **Detailed guided tour**: an interesting, enthusiastic guide will take you on a two-hour voyage of discovery of every forgotten corner of the abbey. There's an admission charge of 67F. On weekdays out of season, you need to book in advance (☎ 02-33-89-80-00). The tour is an absolute must if you have the time.

– **Audio-guide**: the third option offers you a headset (an extra 25F on top of the entrance fee), and the chance to wander about at your own pace, listening to an interactive commentary. It's the best possible way of avoiding the sort of people who talk through normal guided tours!

Worth Knowing . . .

– **Opening times**: from 2 May to 30 September, 9am–6.30pm; from 1 October to 30 April, 9.30am–5.30pm (9.30am–6pm during school holidays). Closed on 25 December, 1 January, 1 May, 1 and 11 November.

– **Guided tours**: the tours are lively and interesting, and are indispensable for a better understanding of the mount and its history.

– For those for whom the religious nature of the mount is important, **Mass** is held every day at 12.15pm.

– **For purists**: it is worth knowing that the mount is also open during the winter, when it is very different from the island that teems with tourists in the summer. The guides will pamper you, and you will have all the time in the world to discover the real magic and the asceticism of the place. The granite and the winter weather make a wonderful combination, as long as you remember to take a warm sweater!

Inside the *Abbatiale*

Most visitors feel a certain *frisson* when they look up from the huge nave at the stone arches, bathed in light as they soar towards the roof. The chancel is one of the finest examples of Flamboyant Gothic architecture in Europe. After centuries of trying, the craftsmen who built the abbey-church had worked out how to pierce the vaulting with openings that would let the sun shine through.

The original Romanesque chapel collapsed in 1421, and each of the Gothic columns rests on top of what remains of a Romanesque column. The whole construction of the place borders on technical genius, as it is largely supported on an artificial platform balanced on the top of the rock. For both aesthetic and symbolic reasons, the church was designed so that its length was the same as the height of the island – a distance of 80 metres (260 feet). This 'perfect square' was intended to symbolize the centre of the world. The plan meant that they had to build a series of highly complex structures, within which is enshrined the pre-Romanesque 10th-century church.

– As you go into the cloister, you enter the **Merveille** (the 'Wonder'). This collection of six rooms spread over three storeys was started in 1211 and took only 17 years to complete. Suspended between the sky and the sea, the **cloister** seems to be open to infinity. As all the walls are cantilevered, the construction absolutely had to be light, which explains the presence of the 227 small columns made of Caen stone, arranged in staggered rows. The cloister was a place for meditation and prayer, and the box-tree garden and Cherbourg schist roof have now been restored. Here, unlike the other parts of the monastery, everything is on a human scale.

– The most surprising thing about the **refectory** is its immense size. It looks more like a church, with its barrel vault. This is where the monks took their frugal meals in silence, and listened to the reading of sacred texts. The architect used extraordinary techniques to capture as much light as possible without compromising the strength of the walls. The clever optical trick also works at a symbolic level – you shut yourself in, but you still let the light enter. The space is superbly controlled, and the room epitomizes all the spirituality of the Mont-St-Michel community.

– **La Salle des Hôtes** ('Guests' Hall') was reserved for the pilgrims of noble blood. Although it has lost its brightly coloured decoration, the room retains its majestic, elegant architecture, which was highly suited to the function of the room. The weight of the room is supported by internal buttresses – this was a revolutionary idea, seen also at the Cistercian abbey at Royaumont to the north of Paris and at the Sainte-Chapelle in Paris itself. There are two gigantic fireplaces in which several lambs could be roasted at the same time. It must have been a noisy place on occasions.

– There is an impressive – even slightly oppressive – **crypt** with wide pillars, which are the original Romanesque pillars reinforced.

– **Crypte St-Martin**: this crypt is under the south wing of the transept. It has a beautiful barrel vault, which, at 8 metres (26 feet) wide, is a real feat of technical engineering, supporting the weight of the whole church above.

– **The goods lift**, which would have been powered by prisoners – the mount was also a prison at times – is certainly original, with a huge wheel that could hold up to six men. They say that Louis XI came on pilgrimage here three times, and had an iron cage that is still talked about today. In the 18th century, the mount housed political prisoners, incarcerated on the basis of letters of authorization signed by the king.

Then it was transformed into an institution for young offenders and accommodated up to 500 non-political prisoners. After the 1848 revolution, a number of political activists, including Blanqui, Barbès and Raspail were interned in the monastery-cum-prison, to the outrage of many, including Victor Hugo. Its use as a prison stopped in 1863, under Napoleon III.

– The **oldest chapel** in the abbey-church is in Carolingian style, and has brick arches joined by mortar of the same thickness. It has a double nave, two side chancels and a gallery for displaying relics. In 1960, the original wall of the sanctuary was discovered in the right-hand chancel and the chapel was then enshrined within the structure of the abbey (the bays are now blocked).

– The **hospital** was the only place where the monks could eat red meat (although this was only to bring them back to good health) and they were also allowed to get up when they liked. It must have been tempting to pretend to be ill every so often! Less appealing is the ditch filled with lime (used for its disinfectant properties), into which the bodies of dead monks were thrown, in order to avoid the spread of disease.

– **Le promenoir des moines** ('the monks' walkway'): below was the pilgrims' room, above was the **dormitory**. In the 11th and 12th centuries, this was a primitive refectory with thick Romanesque walls. In 1103, the vaulting was redone as rib vaulting, and this was the first time that the technique had been used. Mortar joints had mistakenly been used during the more primitive Gothic period.

– Peace would have reigned in the **scriptorium**, known as the Salle des Chevaliers, where the monks worked on copying and on illuminating manuscripts. It is the same height as the nearby **Salle des Hôtes**, but it feels considerably lower. The two huge fireplaces conceal external latrines.

– The final point of the tour ends in the **cellar** and the **chaplaincy**. The latter was for the use of pilgrims with more modest backgrounds. Today, it houses the library benches.

– Finally, it's a good idea to make the time for a stroll around the gardens. From here, you can see out over the polders and all the way across the bay to the west, as far as Cancale.

Tour of the Ramparts

Walking round the ramparts is something you must do, especially as you get a view over the bay and of the Rocher de Tombelaine. Just 3 kilometres (2 miles) away, this twin island was occupied by the English during the Hundred Years War. It is believed that the mount has always remained in French hands thanks to the protection of the Archangel Michael. In an effort to save the kingdom, he went to Domrémy to find a little peasant girl who became known as Joan of Arc. As we all know, her story would come to an end on a stake in the place du Marché, in Rouen.

As part of your visit to the mount, try to walk round in the evening, when the ramparts are deserted and the shopkeepers have drawn the iron curtains down over their wares. The walls of the abbey-church are floodlit, and the building seems almost to surge from the rock as you watch. The golden-winged archangel at its very top, which was restored and replaced (using a helicopter) in November 1987, stands out amid the stars. Seen in this light, the place really is magical.

Let yourself be carried away by the night-time experience, which will give you an entirely different perspective on the place. Tours cost 60F.

FESTIVALS

– **Fêtes de la St-Michel**: two festivals: the spring festival is in May and the autumn festival takes place in September, on the Sunday closest to St Michael's day.

– **Musique sous les ailes de l'archange** ('music under the wings of the archangel'): also held on the Sunday closest to St Michael's Day. Classical music concerts take place in the abbey-church.

– **Pilgrimage across the shores**: in July.

AROUND MONT-ST-MICHEL

★ **La Baie du Mont-St-Michel en calèche** (carriage trips around the bay): place de l'Hôtel-de-Ville in Pontorson (opposite the post office). ☎ 02-33-60-68-00. Fax: 02-33-60-85-66. Pleasant rides in a little horse-drawn carriage at a gentle trot, for one, two or three hours, with or without lunch, or for a half-day. They also organize boat trips on the Couesnon and mountain bike hire. Accommodation is possible.

★ **La Maison de la Baie** (visitors' centre): at Relais de Courtils, route de Roche-Torin, Courtils. ☎ 02-33-89-66-00. Fax: 02-33-89-66-09. Here you can see lovely exhibitions of photographs or paintings, all related to the bay in one way or another. There's an interesting presentation on the formation and development of Mont-St-Michel over 20,000 years, with an audio guide system, and they have an observatory in the grounds. 'Discovery' walks are offered on a range of subjects, from the tides and local flora and fauna, to the literature of the region.

★ **Église St-Georges de Gréhaigne**: 3.5 kilometres (2 miles) to the northwest of Pontorson, this charming little 15th-century Benedictine church is a touching sign of popular and traditional faith. The statuary is impressive and the names of each are painted in bold characters on the smooth walls. Examples include St Samson on his horse and the Madonna as a Breton peasant. The oak vault is very fine.

In the direction of Fougères (along the D155)

★ **Église de Tremblay**: an 11th-century primitive Romanesque-style church that is gracious yet sober. There are examples of ornately sculpted fonts. The thick walls have little openings. The north and west facades must have been part of the outer wall.

★ **Le Rocher-Portail**: set by the waterside, this prestigious 17th-century residence has a superb roof and two matching courtyards. Although the place is not open to the public, it's certainly worth a look. The owners allow the route of the GR footpath to pass through their land, which makes a wonderful walk.

â **Chambres d'hôte with M. Harlais**: Le Guéret, in St-Brice-en-Coglès. ☎ 02-99-97-76-49. They offer a few rooms (with shared bathrooms) from 199F including breakfast. The place is run by a former clog-maker, who will show you round his workshop if you're interested. It's a real treasure trove, with piles of unusual tools.

Eastern Ille-et-Vilaine

FOUGÈRES (*FELGER*) 35300   (Pop: 22,819)

On Brittany's eastern frontier, perched atop a promontory overlooking a lush green valley, Fougères is one of the fortified towns that was built in order to keep a lookout for the enemy. Its imposing castle is still standing today. Many writers have appreciated the slightly doleful charm of the place, including Flaubert, Chateaubriand, Alfred de Musset, Julien Gracq, Victor Hugo and Balzac. The latter used it as their inspiration for their books *Quatre-vingt-treize* and *Les Chouans*, and Juliette Drouet, Hugo's muse, was born in the town. The '*chouans*' were members of a counter-revolutionary movement in northwest France in the 18th century, and had a strong base in Fougères.

The name Fougères was synonymous with the footwear industry for a long time. In the first half of the 20th century, the industry employed up to ten thousand people in Fougères, although now it provides work for barely one thousand.

USEFUL ADDRESSES

🛈 Office du tourisme (B1 on the map): 1 place Aristide-Briand. ☎ 02-99-94-12-20. Fax: 02-99-94-77-30. Open every day, all year round. In summer, open Monday–Saturday 9am–7pm and Sunday 10am–noon and 2–4pm; out of season, open Monday–Saturday 9.30am–12.30pm and 2–6pm; Sunday 10am–noon and 1.30–5.30pm. Wonderful premises. Good documentation and friendly, efficient service.

🛈 In summer, there's an **info-point** (called the '*Passage Mélusine*') at the castle ticket office. Open every day.

🚌 Coach station (B2 on the map). ☎ 02-99-99-08-77. Information from 11am–12.30pm and 4–6.30pm. Provides connecting services to local train stations.

WHERE TO STAY

⛺ Camping municipal: at Paron. Out of the town centre. ☎ 02-99-99-40-81. ♿ Closed from December to February. A small and pleasant campsite, with pitches separated by large hedges and set on decent grass. It's located next door to an excellent sports complex.

🏠 Hôtel de Bretagne (B1–B2, **10** on the map): 7 place de la République. ☎ and fax: 02-99-99-31-68. Open all year round. A double room costs from 115F to 170F. The place has no real charm but the prices are low, the service is friendly and the rooms are clean. There's also a family room with two double beds. This place is a reasonable bet in its price bracket.

🏠 Grand Hôtel des Voyageurs (B1, **12** on the map): 10 place Gambetta. ☎ 02-99-99-08-20. Fax: 02-99-99-99-04. Website: www.groupatotel.com/hotels/voyageurs.html. Closed over Christmas and New Year. Good service. Reasonable double rooms for 255F to 295F. This is a rather ordinary sort of hotel

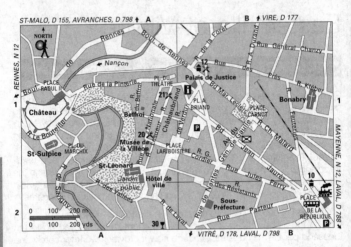

FOUGÈRES

■ Useful Addresses	✕ Where To Eat

🛈 Office du tourisme
🚌 Coach station

🏠 Where To Stay
10 Hôtel de Bretagne
12 Grand Hôtel des Voyageurs

✕ Where To Eat
20 Le Buffet
21 Le P'tit Bouchon

🍷 Where To Go for a Drink
30 Le Coquelicot

that is useful for a single night. Some of the rooms have been done up but others are rather old-fashioned.

Good welcome, though. The restaurant is thought of as the best in town (*see below* 'Where To Eat').

WHERE TO EAT

☆ Budget

✕ Le P'tit Bouchon (A1, **21** on the map): 13 rue Chateaubriand. ☎ 02-99-99-75-98. Closed on Sunday. They offer a cheap menu comprising a dish of the day and dessert for 40F and other menus for 62F and 92F. Right in the centre of Fougères, you'll feel at home in this little bistrot run by a pleasant young couple. You can eat a delicious family-type meal at incredibly low prices, either in the bar or out at the back. The 40F menu is particularly good news when you're on a low budget and are short of time. For example, they do a succulent rib of beef with a huge portion of chips, or a *boeuf bourguignon*, followed by a home-made apple tart, and they're all pretty extraordinary. Some of the dishes are quite simple, but others, such as the mullet with capers (*mulet aux câpres*) and the warm Camembert on a bed of lettuce (*camembert chaud sur un lit de salade*), are quite ambitious. When the weather is up to it, the chef takes his barbecue out onto the pavement. Recommended.

✗ **Le Buffet** (A1, **20** on the map): 53 *bis*, rue Nationale. ☎ 02-99-94-35-76. Open lunchtime and evening until 10pm. Closed Wednesday evening and Sunday; also closed for the last week in July and first two weeks in August, plus the last week in December. The set menus offer excellent value for money, at prices from 62F to 130F. The dining room has a fresh, clean decor, with exhibitions of photographs and paintings.

☆☆☆ Chic

✗ **Les Voyageurs** (B1, **12** on the map): 10 place Gambetta. ☎ 02-99-99-08-20. Closed Saturday lunchtime and Sunday evening. There are four set menus from 95F to 210F. Reservation is strongly recommended here, as this restaurant is an institution in Fougères. First, here's what sort of decor to expect:

the place is a bit like a 1970s night-club, with columns covered in mosaic, and gilded mirrors. The windows are festooned with bold curtains and the wallpaper is busy with medallion shapes. It's amazing that there isn't a mirror-ball to top it all off. All this is rather unexpected for a restaurant pitched as a gastro-nomic experience, which it certainly is. The dishes on offer really are something else – timeless, in the hands of a chef who knows how to respect tradition. The menu includes copious portions of succulent *foie gras*, tender escalope of calf's sweetbread in Madeira (*fondante escalope de ris de veau au madère*), and much more, served on dishes with silver lids. The staff is very attentive and, refreshingly, they don't badger you to drink too much. The place is excellent in every respect, and however much or little you spend here, you won't be disappointed.

WHERE TO STAY AND EAT IN THE AREA

🛏 ✗ **Chambres d'hôte and Ferme-auberge de Mésauboin**: in Billé, 8 kilometres (5 miles) south of Fougères on the D179. ☎ 02-99-97-61-57. Fax: 02-99-97-50-76. A double room costs 235F and set menus start at 95F. In the village, take the D23 towards St-Georges-de-Chesné, then it's sign-posted. Rooms are available by reservation only. Out in the heart of the countryside, this is a pretty, characterful farm (complete with turret) that was once a manor house. The bedrooms are pleasant. The set menus allow you to try some of the specialities, including chicken in cider (*coq au cidre*), duckling roasted with apples (*canette rôtie aux pommes*), and a selection of delicious tarts, all washed down with a lovely fruity cider. The most expensive of the set menus is in fact a 'food and drink' menu. They have six bedrooms that can sleep 2, 3, or 4 people, all with en suite facilities. Friendly service.

WHERE TO GO FOR A DRINK

🍷 **Le Coquelicot** (A2, **30** on the map): 18 rue de Vitré; just 600 metres from the centre. ☎ 02-99-99-82-11. Open from 4pm to 3am. Closed Sunday, and from mid-July to mid-August. Nicknamed 'Le Coq', this place is a good live music pub (*see also* 'What To Do'), with a friendly atmosphere. There are nearly 70 good beers to choose from, and you'll soon feel at home here. The music ranges from jazz and blues to folk, rock and '*chansons*', with the occasional bit of café-theatre. Music always takes place on Thursday and Saturday evenings, starting at 9pm. Make a note that once a year, on 22 September, they hold a festival to celebrate their anniversary. It's worth going to.

Ÿ Le Café de Paris: 9 place Aristide-Briand. ☎ 02-99-94-39-38. Right opposite the tourist office. At first glance this seems much like all the other bistrots, but it's good to know that, during the season, they hold excellent musical evenings under the title of 'Les Estivales du Café de Paris'.

WHAT TO SEE

★ From place Aristide-Briand (where the tourist office is), climb up the **rue Nationale** (A1 on the map), an elegant pedestrianized street lined with noble 18th-century buildings. As you go along, look out for a beautiful 14th-century belfry emerging over the rooftops. The little **Musée Emmanuel-de-La-Villéon** (51 rue Nationale) is located in the last house in the town with a porch. Open from mid-June to mid-September, every day 10am–12.30pm and 2–5.30pm; out of season, open Wednesday–Sunday. Closed in January. Admission is free. The museum contains various collections of paintings, including about a hundred by La Villéon, one of the last Impressionist painters, who was born in Fougères. This was an artist who really knew how to capture the charm of the beautiful Breton countryside, and the exhibition is recommended.

★ Right at the top is the 16th-century Hôtel de Ville, and the **Église St-Léonard** (A1 on the map), which was extensively renovated in the 19th century. It is definitely worth climbing up the steeple, as the view from the top is spectacular. Inside are some beautiful, brightly coloured modern stained-glass windows. Outside, note the cannons pointing out at the corner of the belfry. The **public garden** around St-Léonard is definitely the place to watch the sun rise over the valley and the castle. The breathtaking view has now, unfortunately, been rather marred by new housing.

★ From the public garden, head down the valley to get to the **old quarter** huddled around the River Nançon. This was the home of craftsmen (mainly tanners and dyers), who used the waters of the river. On place du Marchix you can see a number of pretty, wood-panelled houses, and on the corner of the rues de Lusignan and Providence, there is one of the most beautiful butcher's shops in Brittany. At 6 rue de Lusignan, there is a medieval shop with a carved wood frontage.

★ **Église St-Sulpice** (A1 on the map): this church was built in the 15th century. Its front bears typically rich Flamboyant Gothic ornamentation. Inside is a decorated wooden ceiling in the shape of an upturned hull, and a large baroque altarpiece. The nave features two interesting stone altarpieces, one of which has a lovely polychrome *pietà*. The one on the right-hand side was donated by the tanners' association. The statue of Notre-Dame-des-Marais is quite ancient.

★ **Château de Fougères** (A1 on the map): place Pierre-Symon. ☎ 02-99-99-79-59. From mid-June to mid-September, open every day 9am–7pm; from April to mid-June and the last two weeks in September, 9.30am–noon and 2–6pm; the rest of the year, 10am–noon and 2–5pm. Closed in January.

Admission charge. The inside is open to the public (for guided tours), although the furniture is contemporary. This charming and atmospheric castle is one of the best-preserved medieval castles in France. Built between the 12th and the 15th centuries, it has a dozen towers, which are beautifully reflected in the water of the moat when the sun shines, as well as numerous passageways, turrets, crenellations and much more. The oldest part of the castle is the keep, which is 5 metres (16.5 feet) thick at the base. The **Porte Notre-Dame** (in the direction of the church of St-Sulpice) is also impressive. Some sections of the path round the battlements are open to the public.

★ Rather than having to climb back up to the upper town along the rue de la Pinterie (which, incidentally, was completely rebuilt after bombing in 1944), you could try the gentler walk along the **ruelle des Vaux**. This runs along the outside of the old town ramparts, which is signposted as the 'Promenade du Nançon' on the left as you climb up.

WHAT TO DO

– **Marché aux Bovins de l'Aumaillerie** (cattle market): route d'Alençon. This is one of the largest cattle markets in France, and can accommodate up to 10,000 head of cattle. Free access on Friday mornings, so go there if you are an early riser (open 5–9am).

★ **Forêt de Fougères**: there are lovely walks along a number of well-marked routes in and around this forest dotted with megaliths. **La Pierre-Courcoulée** (with yellow markings) is a varied walk running 4.5 kilometres (3 miles) along a narrow path under the trees and beside the river. It starts at the Moulin d'Avion, before turning immediately left into the forest. **Les Vieux-Châteaux** (with blue markings) takes a pretty route for about 4 kilometres (3 miles) along the banks of the St-François lake. There is a man-made lake suitable for swimming at Chênedet-Landéan.

■ **Open-air centre**, **walkers' shelter** and **campsite**: 6 kilometres (4 miles) from Fougères. ☎ 02-99-97-35-46. Fax: 02-99-97-34-13. There is also a riding centre, a fitness trail and a mountain-bike circuit out in the forest.

FESTIVALS AND EVENTS

– **Voix des Pays**: an excellent weekend's entertainment that takes place in the chateau in early July. Things kick off with a Breton evening, followed by a whole range of different events, with music in all the bars as well as out on the streets.

IN THE AREA

★ **Parc Floral de Haute Bretagne** (botanic gardens of North Brittany): at La Foltière, 35133 Le Châtellier. From Fougères, take the D798/A84 north, leave at exit 30, pick up the signs for St-Germain and head north, following the signs, then turn left onto the D19. ☎ 02-99-95-48-32. From 20 March to 11 November, open during the week 2–6pm, on Saturday, Sunday, public holidays, and from 10 July to 21 August 10.30am–6pm; the rest of the year, open Saturday only, 2–5pm. Admission charge. At this superb park, which dates back to the 19th century, they have reconstructed a number of wonderful, elegant gardens, including Persian and Mediterranean gardens, and the 'city of Knossos', with its camellias. Perhaps the most successful of the gardens is the 'poets' dale', with its ornamental lake, its little bridges and its clumps of wild flowers. There is a tea room in the beautiful house at the bottom of the garden, where they also sell young shrubs.

On the road from Rennes

★ **Valley of the Couesnon**: from La Ville-Olivier, the Couesnon river plunges magnificently into the greenery, sweeping its way through a gorge. There is a fantastic 10-kilometre walk (6 miles) along part of the GR as far as Minette. You can only cross the Couesnon 3 kilometres (2 miles) into the walk. It's also possible to go climbing at the Roche du Moulin, go on a cycle tour, or take out a canoe (all the way to the Mont-St-Michel, if you have the energy!).

■ **Open-air club at the Lande-d'Ouée lake**: ☎ 02-99-66-34-14. Canoe lessons and trips on the lake. Mountain-bike hire.

★ **St-Aubin-du-Cormier**: these ruins of the fortress on the edge of the duchy serve as a reminder of the last great battle between the Bretons and the French. In 1488, the French army invaded Brittany and laid siege to Fougères. The Breton troops lacked unity and were soon beaten and dispersed. Six thousand of them were massacred in the Bois d'Usel, where they had taken refuge. This defeat marked the beginning of a gradual victory for France over the whole duchy, with Anne of Brittany eventually being forced to marry King Charles VIII (in 1491). There is also an original neo-Byzantine church dating from the beginning of the 15th century.

★ **Étang de Chevré**: lake in La Bouëxière. A charming valley set among lush green hills offers the gentle pleasure of a walk among the anglers. There is an unusual medieval bridge built on top of Gallo-Roman remains. All around, the valleys break up the hedged farmland nicely.

CHAMPEAUX (*KAMPAL*) 35500   (Pop: 15,908)

Don't pass by without visiting this tiny village, which is lost in the countryside about 8 kilometres (5 miles) to the west of Vitré. Its church is one of the most fascinating in the Rennes area.

WHAT TO SEE

★ **The church**: originally built in the 15th century, with a steeple dating back to the 18th century, this church has a splendour that is disproportionate to the size of the village. This is because the d'Espinay family, who lived in the region in the 16th century, was powerful enough to bring a whole chapter of canons along with it. They were responsible for the harmonious architecture around the square, and the pinnacled well, dating from 1601.

The church furniture inside is breathtaking, with about 50 superb sculpted Renaissance stalls, complete with carved canopies. To the left of the altar is the outrageously opulent tomb of Guy III d'Espinay. The tomb of his daughter, by his side, is more delicate. The pulpit dates back to the early 18th century. It is worth lingering a little while in the south chapel to see the wonderful altarpiece made of five polychrome panels depicting the Passion.

The real show-stoppers at Champeaux are the 16th-century **stained-glass** windows, which must be among the best in Brittany (along with those in Moncontour, Les Iffs, and a few others). The blue glass has an extraordinary quality and luminosity, especially in the *Verrière de la Crucifixion* and the one depicting the *Martyre de Sainte Barbe* (the martyrdom of St Barbara). The *Sacrifice d'Abraham* is also remarkable, as is the stained-glass window entitled the *Vitrail de la Pentecôte* (with a deluge of fire pouring down from the heavens), in the first chapel on the right.

IN THE AREA

★ It would also be a mistake to miss the **Château de l'Espinay**, just 2 kilometres (1.5 miles) to the south. Unfortunately, you can only admire the exterior of this lovely Renaissance building, as it is not open to the public, but it is worth a look.

VITRÉ (*GWITREG*) 35500   (Pop: 15,908)

The economy of this major medieval town relied on cotton and textiles until the end of the 17th century. It was also one of the great frontier towns charged with protecting the independence of Brittany. Dating from this period are a splendid castle and medieval streets that are among the most harmonious and prettiest in Brittany (on a par with Dinan, and even better than Quimper perhaps). In this little town, even the train station is charming!

USEFUL ADDRESSES

🛈 **Office du tourisme**: place St-Yves; just 2 minutes from the station. ☎ 02-99-75-04-46. Fax: 02-99-74-02-01. Email: infos@tourisme-rennes.com. In July and August, open every day 9am–7pm; the rest of the year, open 9am–6pm, Sundays and public holidays 11am–6pm. In summer, there are guided tours of the town, and some include access to the museums. Night tours are also organized, on request.

🚃 **Gare SNCF** (train station): the line from Paris to Brest stops at Vitré, where there are connections to Rennes twice a day.

WHERE TO STAY

🛏 **Hôtel Le Petit Billot**: 5 place du Général-Leclerc. ☎ 02-99-75-02-10. Fax: 02-99-74-72-96. A double room costs 280F to 300F and you get free secure parking in a garage. They give a warm welcome here, and this is a hotel where they take pride in what they do. The rooms are very spacious as well as being quiet and pleasant.

🛏 **Walkers' shelter**: 13 rue Pasteur; not far from the town centre. ☎ 02-99-74-61-73. Fax: 02-99-74-18-60. Just 50F per person per night. Open all year round, this shelter is pretty nearly new. It's small, with only 12 beds, in rooms for 2, 4 or 6. Kitchen facilities are available.

Hôtel du Château: 5 rue Rallon. ☎ 02-99-74-58-59. Fax: 02-99-75-35-47. Double rooms cost 235F to 260F. Open all year round. Set below the castle outside the walls, in a little street that's not wonderful but at least it's quiet. On the second floor and above, the rooms have a view of the castle. They are well kept, and provincial in style, although some are a bit old-fashioned. The service is friendly.

Hôtel Du Guesclin: 27 rue Du-Guesclin. ☎ 02-99-75-02-96. Fax: 02-99-74-49-17. Open all year round. A double room costs from 115F to 195F, making this place the best value for money in town. The rooms are simple, and quite small, but they're well looked after. Look at the room before deciding, as some are better than others. There's a hotel bar. Nice welcome.

Chambres d'hôte with Mme Faucher: 2 chemin des Tertres-Noirs. ☎ and fax: 02-99-75-08-69. Rooms cost 250F for two, including a copious breakfast. Just a stone's throw from the centre of town, this townhouse offers a warm welcome and very good service. The rooms have all been individually decorated, and the house is lively and full of good vibrations – it takes no time to feel at home. The attic room has been particularly well done, with wonderful exposed beams and decorated in bright, fresh blues and yellows.

Hôtel Le Minotel: 47 rue Poterie. ☎ 02-99-75-11-11. Fax: 02-99-75-81-26. Website: www.ot-vitre.fr. Double rooms cost 295F, or a 'family' room (4 people) for 420F. Open all year round. This house in the old town has been rebuilt, respecting traditional style while still offering all mod cons. Perhaps it's all a bit too homogenous for some tastes. The atmosphere is green and almost Scottish, in the style of a golf clubhouse. If you're keen on golf, the hotel offers a special rate combined with the golf course at Rochers-Sévigné (18 holes). Good service.

WHERE TO EAT

✕ **Crêperie La Gavotte**: 7 rue des Augustins. ☎ 02-99-74-47-74. Closed Monday and Tuesday (except during school holidays) as well as for two weeks at the end of September and at the beginning of March. Two menus are on offer: 53F at lunchtime and 69F in the evening; allow 100F for a meal if you eat à la carte. Vitré is a lovely little village and this eating place fits into the landscape very well. It's a *crêperie* that uses local ingredients, often unusual ones, in a way that makes the *galettes* really come alive! For example, think of a *galette* made with local Darley cheese (it tastes a bit like Reblochon cheese), with an-

douille sausage and some nice homemade charcuterie. They also serve what they call *pommé*, which is creamed pear (a cross between a jam and a chutney), and a whole host of other local products. You can wash it all down with either cider, *chouchen* or barley beer (*cervoise*). The proprietor is a friendly, smiling sort, too.

✕ **Auberge St-Louis**: 31 rue Notre-Dame. ☎ 02-99-75-28-28. ♿ Closed Sunday evening and Monday throughout the year, and for two weeks in February. Set menus from 75F up to 142F. Set in an elegant 15th-century inn, the restaurant has built up a solid reputation. The wood panelling in the dining room creates a warm and sophisticated atmosphere. The young landlady provides a plate of nibbles to go with all the set menus. Afterwards, the serious business of eating begins with a good choice of grilled meats and superb fish, accompanied by excellent sauces. The linen napkins and table-cloths add to the class of the place.

WHERE TO STAY AND EAT IN THE AREA

♠ ✕ **Ar Milin** (Breton for 'the Mill'): 30 rue de Paris, Châteaubourg. Between Vitré and Rennes. ☎ 02-99-00-30-91. Fax: 02-99-00-37-56. Email: armilin@wanado.fr. ♻ Closed for Christmas and the New Year; restaurant closed Sunday evening from November to March. A double room costs from 490F to 650F. Weekday set menus cost from 120F to 220F. This is an inn in a lovely country setting, in 5 hectares (12 acres) of grounds, within an old watermill on the Vilaine, which used to provide the electricity for the town at the beginning of the 20th century. There is a good-quality restaurant, with views over the park, serving decent cuisine using local fresh produce in menus that offer good value for money. The country setting is lovely. The mill is also a hotel, with rooms in a separate modern building that is nicely located in the middle of the well-kept grounds. There are slightly smarter rooms in the mill itself, although they are more expensive. Superb breakfast buffet. Everything here is done in 'grand hotel' manner, and it's very pleasing.

WHAT TO SEE

The ticket for the castle also gets you into all the other museums in town, and the Château de Sévigné.

★ **Château and Musée du Château**: ☎ 02-99-75-04-54. Castle museum and castle itself open every day from 1 July to 30 September, 10am–6pm; from 1 April to 30 June, 10am–noon and 2–5.30pm; same opening times from 1 October to 31 March, but closed Tuesday, and on Saturday, Sunday and Monday mornings. Admission charge. Guided tours of the castle are available, in season, at 10.30am, 11.30am, 12.30pm and 1.45pm, 2.45pm, 3.45pm and 4.45pm. The castle was rebuilt from the 13th to the 15th centuries on the basis of an older structure. It is triangular in shape, like the rock on which it sits, and has the powerful lines typical of military architecture. There is an amazing display of pepperpot towers and machicolations at all different heights. A magnificent esplanade leads up to the castle itself.

There is a very interesting **museum** in one of the towers. In the first room, there are some delicate woodcarvings that date back to the 16th century (including pieces of Gothic staircases and a door). On the second floor is a stunning Renaissance chimney, a Flanders tapestry and some tomb ornamentations. On the next floor is a number of Aubusson tapestries. On the top floor, under the roof, are plans and photographs detailing the architectural history of the town, including excellent prints of the castle. Finally, don't miss the little staircase leading to the path round the battlements, and the **oratory**, where you can admire some amazing 16th-century Limoges enamel plates that depict the life of the Virgin Mary and Christ.

On the other side of the courtyard, the temporary exhibitions are also worth a look.

★ **Chapelle-Musée St-Nicolas**: go back down rue de Brest, then take rue Pasteur to get to this little 15th-century hospital chapel, which has now been transformed into a museum of religious art. A ticket to the castle museum gives admission here, and the opening hours are the same.

Inside, you will find a Gothic tomb, a wonderful high altar, and an 18th-century wooden tabernacle, as well as some superb frescoes that are concealed behind the layers of paintings. There is now a permanent exhibition of French ecclesiastical goldware from the late 19th and early 20th centuries.

★ **Église Notre-Dame**: built in the 15th century in Flamboyant Gothic style, the church has a most interesting exterior, especially on the side facing the road, where the facade has a series of gables that rise up like the teeth of a saw. There is an unusual outdoor pulpit on the south facade. On the side facing place Notre-Dame, there is a fine door dated to 1586. The interior is largely unremarkable, with thick, octagonal pillars, and a Gothic pulpit decorated with flowers. There is a wonderful 16th-century stained-glass window, L'Entrée du Christ à Jérusalem ('Christ's entry into Jerusalem') in the third chapel on the right (coming from the entrance on place Notre-Dame), and a fine Gothic confessional.

★ **Vitré old town**: it is a miracle that the precious architectural heritage of this town has survived so well across the centuries. If you wander through the rues d'Embas, Baudrairie, St-Louis and Notre-Dame, you will see any number of wonderful buildings from every different era of history, each with a character all its own. In **rue d'Embas**, look out for No. 30, with its staircase into the courtyard and its galleries. At No. 20, there is a superb slate-covered gable by two corniced towers sculpted into something that seems to be halfway between a man and a monkey. The house at No. 10 is the one that attracts all the painters and photographers.

In **rue Baudrairie**, No. 30 is a beautiful Gothic hotel, while next door is a good example of a recent construction in keeping with the rest of the street. At No. 25 is a sculpted Renaissance wooden panel. No. 18 is the only 18th-century building, with iron balconies that are typical of the period. It is worth hunting down the carved heads that can be seen decorating the pilasters. On **rue Notre-Dame**, opposite the church, is the **Hôtel Ringues**, a wonderful 16th-century building, which must be one of the most beautiful community centres in Brittany today.

FESTIVALS AND EVENTS

– **Les fêtes du Bocage vitréen**: the Vitré countryside festival happens in the first two weeks in July. This is a local village festival where the countryside comes alive with dancing, folk music and songs of the sea. All kinds of different free events happen all over the place.

– **Grand Marché**: the local market takes place on Monday, on place Notre-Dame, place du Marché and place de la République.

– On **rue de la Poterie** every Saturday morning, there's an excellent little **market** called 'le panier du samedi' or 'the Saturday basket'. Local producers of uncooked foods sell their wares here, with stalls set out in the arcades.

IN THE AREA

★ **Château des Rochers-Sévigné**: 6 kilometres (4 miles) to the southeast of Vitré, on the D88. Same opening times as the Château de Vitré (*see* 'What To See'), and the ticket for there is also valid for entry to part of this castle. The castle may be small, but its architecture is elegant and sophisticated, and its pretty rooftops are a real sight to behold. The castle is haunted by the memory of Marie de Rabutin-Chantal, the wife of Sévigné, who was famous as a writer of letters. She came to stay at the castle on a number of occasions to take a break from the Royal Court and found the place a source of inspiration. As a result, she wrote 267 letters to her daughter, the Comtesse de Grignan. (In one of them, she observed that there was 'as much wine in the bloodstream of a Breton as there is water passing under the bridges'.)

There is an interesting guided tour around the castle. The decoration and the furniture date from the 17th to 19th centuries. One item on show is a *bourdalou*, named after the priest whose sermons were so long that women would use this receptacle to relieve themselves under their dresses during the service! In the tower, there are some interesting portraits of Mme de Sévigné and her son Charles. The French-style garden has been painstakingly restored to how it would have been when Charles designed it. It is also worth seeing the strange octagonal chapel, built in 1671, which very much resembles the upturned hull of a boat, but with a little steeple on top. Note the wallpaper designed to look like stone.

★ **Musée de la Faucillonnaie**: ☎ 02-99-75-04-54. 5 kilometres (3 miles) to the north of Vitré in Pérouse, on the D179. Same opening times as the other museums in the area: *see above*. This is a modest museum of rural life, with furniture, a little crockery, clothing, paintings and ceramics, as well as the front of a chest, and some lovely Aubusson tapestries in shades of green.

★ **Château du Plessis**: at Argentré-du-Plessis, 35370. ☎ 02-99-96-70-46. Take the D88 out of Vitré and then follow the signs. Open all year round; open every day from 1 June to 30 September and weekends only out of season (when it's best to telephone). Admission charge. This is a superb house, built in the 13th century for the Du Plessis family and constantly modified up until the 19th century. There's an interesting guided tour that lasts about an hour and you shouldn't miss the chance to take a walk through the park, which is tremendous.

LA GUERCHE-DE-BRETAGNE (*GWERC'H-BREIZH*) 35130   (Pop: 4,090)

A dynamic little town that relies on commerce and services. The main square is lined with 17th-century timbered houses and is home to the Collégiale Notre-Dame (*see* 'What To See'). The name 'Guerche' comes from Frankish (the language spoken by the Franks) and means 'fortified place'.

USEFUL ADDRESS

🚹 **Office du tourisme**: place Charles-de-Gaulle. ☎ 02-99-96-30-78.

WHERE TO STAY AND EAT

🛏 ✖ **La Calèche**: 16 avenue du Général-Leclerc. ☎ 02-99-96-21-63. Fax: 02-99-96-49-52. ☕ Restaurant closed Sunday evening and Monday. All closed for the first three weeks in August. Double rooms cost 290F to 315F. Half board is available for 315F per person. This big, quiet hotel has been renovated fairly recently and has a comfortable atmosphere. The decor, in muted green, blends well with the lush setting. The rooms are spacious and comfortable. The dining room is set under a large verandah, and the food is imaginative and well prepared.

🛏 ✖ **Bar-hôtel-restaurant 'Les Routiers'**: 11 faubourg d'Anjou. ☎ 02-99-96-23-10. ☕ Closed Friday evening and Sunday evening.

Double rooms cost 140F to 180F. This is a nice little roadside hotel offering very simple rooms. The food is nothing fancy but is copious, with set menus from 50F to 135F.

✖ **Restaurant Les Marchands**: 2 rue d'Anjou. ☎ 02-99-96-45-03. Open Monday–Saturday at lunchtime and Thursday, Friday and Saturday evening. Closed on Sunday and for the first two weeks in August. Lunchtime set menu for 59F and evening menu for 98F. The restaurant is in one of the oldest houses in town on La Guerche's lovely main square. The decor is slightly old-fashioned, but pleasant. Specialities include home-smoked salmon (*saumon fumé maison*) and meat grilled over vine stems (*grillades sur ceps de vigne*).

WHAT TO SEE

★ **Collégiale Notre-Dame**: this collegiate church is a real architectural gem. Pick up the leaflet as you go in, as it is very well done. The midnight-blue barrel vault dates back to the 16th century. The south side is fantastic, with bright stained-glass windows, majestic finely-ribbed vaults and carvings. The stalls are made up entirely of fine and original foliage and figures. The tourist office offers guided tours on request.

EVENTS

– Every Tuesday since the 12th century, a huge country **market** has been held in town. It may not be quite up to competing with the agriculture halls of Paris, but it's still a pretty impressive sight and one that you should try hard to get to see. A vast array of goods is on sale, from textiles to food, from animals and poultry to agricultural machinery and cars. At the very least it makes for a colourful stroll, and you can do as the locals do and walk around eating a *galette-saucisse*, or sausage in a *galette*, which is eaten like a hot-dog. The tourist office gives guided tours of the market on request.

IN THE AREA

★ If you're in need of a little exercise or relaxation, the **Étang de la Forge** (lake) in Martigné-Ferchaud, 15 kilometres (10 miles) to the southwest of La Guerche, has all the right facilities. It's open at the weekend between June and September and every day in July and August, and there are pedaloes, boats, ponies, and so on.

LA ROCHE-AUX-FÉES

La Roche-aux-Fées (the 'fairies' rock') is one of the most impressive megalithic monuments in France. The closest town is Retiers; from there, follow the signposts; the site is about 5 kilometres (3 miles) to the north of Retiers, near the village of Essé.

The monument dates back to about 3000 BC. It consists of a porticoed dolmen, like a covered walkway, measuring 11 metres (36 feet) long and 2 metres (6.5 feet) wide. Schist slabs weighing more than 40 tonnes each form the cover to the walkway.

According to legend, the fairies summoned up a strength not usually associated with fairies to move the stones here, carrying them in their veils. Tradition has it that, at the time of the full moon, you should come out and count the stones with your betrothed. It's a bad sign if you don't both come up with the same result.

Next to the site is a cabin with some interesting displays.

Côtes-d'Armor

Without any substantial urban settlements – the town of St-Brieuc numbers scarcely more than 44,000 inhabitants and the next largest towns have fewer than 20,000 – and with a relatively modest economy, the *département* of Côtes-d'Armor could be considered the poor relation of Brittany. It can boast no important regional capital such as Nantes or Rennes, nor any arsenals or shipyards. Its seaside resorts are less developed than on the region's southern coast, and its agriculture is not extensive (although it is the region's leader in pig farming).

Yet it is these very aspects of the Côtes-d'Armor that give the area its special appeal and particular charm. Here you'll find nature still largely untouched: the green and peaceful interior (the *Argoat* or 'country of the wood') is still covered with copses which encroach on the heights of the Armorican Massif, while the coast (the *Armor* or 'country of the sea') boasts some of the most beautiful bays and beaches in France, from the wild, unspoiled cliffs of the Cap Fréhel, to picturesque little ports, the Île de Bréhat, and the strange mineral world of the Côte de Granit Rose (the Pink Granite Coast), set like a jewel in the sea.

The towns of the Côtes-d'Armor, with the possible exception of St-Brieuc, have also managed to preserve some noteworthy architectural heritage. Dinan, Guingamp and Lannion rival one another with their centuries-old cobblestone alleyways and squares, and their well-preserved medieval and Renaissance houses. Castles and manor houses are scattered about the countryside, and many basilicas and chapels seem also to have escaped the ravages of time.

The border between upper and lower Brittany – between Breton-speaking country and Gallo-speaking country – passes through the *département*. Indeed, for many visitors, the Côtes-d'Armor seems to represent the whole of Brittany in miniature, combining all of the region's charms in one area.

The journey begins at the town of Dinan, goes along the Côte d'Éméraude (the Emerald Coast) and reveals the mysteries of the interior, before coming to an end at the Trégor region and the Côte de Granit Rose, the grand finale before setting off for Finistère.

USEFUL ADDRESSES

🏛 **Comité Départemental du Tourisme** (departmental tourist board): 7 rue St-Benoît, BP 4620, 22046 St-Brieuc Cedex 2. ☎ 02-96-62-72-00. Website: www.cotes darmor.com. Central booking office: ☎ 02-96-62-72-15. Write for information on all aspects of tourism in the Côtes-d'Armor. Plenty of literature available.

■ **Côtes-d'Armor Tourisme**: 7 rue St-Benoît, 22000 St-Brieuc. ☎ 02-96-62-72-15. Reservation service offering two types of assistance: hotel reservations, seasonal letting, campsites and holiday villages, as well as 'activity holiday' packages, including sea fishing, golf, horse-riding, hiking and watersports.

■ **Relais Départemental des Gîtes de France** (departmental office for Gîtes de France): 7 rue Benoît, 22045 St-Brieuc Cedex 2. ☎ 02-96-62-72-00.

■ **Boat rental – Messac: Crown Blue Line** ☎ 02-99-34-60-11.

– Lézardrieux: Ateliers du Trieux ☎ 02-96-20-17-76.

DINAN (*DINAN*) 22100 (Pop: 11,833)

One of the most beautiful Breton towns, Dinan is a place of art and history that every visitor to Brittany should take time to explore. The hero of this once-powerful medieval trading city is Bertrand Du Guesclin. In 1357 he fought a famous duel against an Englishman on what is now called place du Champ, before going on to win the heart of his fair maiden.

Dinan is a town that should be explored on foot. It casts a never-ending spell, for which it pays the inevitable price of an enormous influx of tourists in summer and is a particularly popular spot with British visitors, who even have their own Anglican church in the town.

USEFUL ADDRESSES AND INFORMATION

🛈 **Office du tourisme du District de Dinan** (tourist office for the Dinan district) (B2 on the map): Hôtel Kératry, 6 rue de l'Horloge, BP 261, 22105 Dinan Cedex. ☎ 02-96-87-69-76. Open daily in summer, 9am–7.30pm (Sunday 10am–12.30pm and 2.30–6.30pm); in winter, open Monday–Saturday 8.30am–12.30pm and 2–6pm, closed Sunday. Brochure and map (15F). Guided tours of the town: in summer, tours at 10am and 3pm from the tourist information office, tours with a special theme in the morning, general tours in the afternoon; the rest of the year, by appointment. Telephone or ask for the address of the office, as a move was anticipated at the time of writing.

– '**Les Clefs de Dinan**': this is a special ticket, for families or individuals, available from the tourist office and at the venues concerned. It gives reduced-price admission to several of Dinan's monuments: the chateau, the Tour de l'Horloge, the Maison d'Artiste de la Grande Vigne and the Maison du gouverneur (governor's house), as well as the major summer exhibitions.

🛈 **Pays d'Accueil de Dinan** (Dinan information centre): Le Grand-Clos, in Quévert, west of Dinan. ☎ 02-96-39-62-64.

– **La Ronde de Nuit** (night tours of Dinan): in July and August, every night (except Sunday), starting at 10pm; the rest of the year, by appointment, for organized groups (minimum 12 people). Telephone reservations compulsory (several days in advance in high season): ☎ 02-96-85-37-74. Email: pmea zey@aol.com. Departure from the Tour de l'Horloge. Peter, a storyteller in medieval costume, organizes lively and original nocturnal tours around the dark alleyways, cemeteries, ramparts and dungeons of the town, all by candlelight. This is a terrific idea that works really well.

🚂 **Gare SNCF** (train station) (A1 on the map): services for St-Brieuc, Rennes and Caen. ☎ 08-36-35-35-35.

🚌 **Gare routière** (bus station): ☎ 02-96-39-21-05.

■ **Free car parks**: open in summer, in the Cour de l'Inspection Départe-

CÔTES-D'ARMOR

CÔTES-D'ARMOR

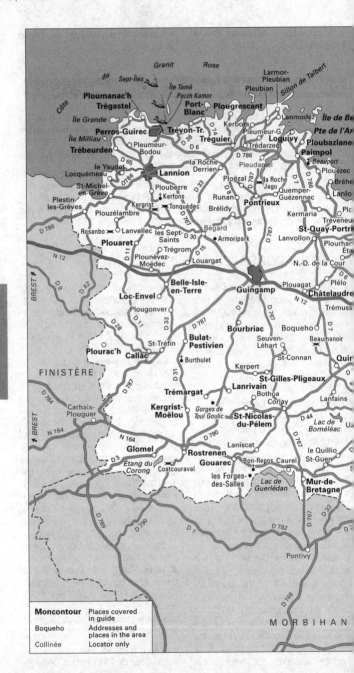

Granit Rose

Larmor-Pleubian

Pleubian

Sillon de Talbert

Côte de Sept-Îles

Île Tomé

Porzh Kamor

Ploumanac'h

Trégastel

Île Grande

Perros-Guirec

Île Milliau

Trébeurden

Port-Blanc

Plougrescant

Lanmodez

Île de B

Pte de l'Ar

Kerbors

Pleumeur-G.

Loguivy

Ploubazlane

Trévon-Tr.

Tréguier

Trédarzec

Paimpol

Beauport

Pleumeur-Bodou

D 6

D 38

Plouézec

Bréhe

D 786

Pleudaniel

Quemper-Guézennec

Lanlo

le Yaudet

Lannion

la Roche-Derrien

Ploëzal

la Roche Jagu

Plc

Locquémeau

D 186

D 33

Pontrieux

Treveneu

St-Michel-en-Grève

Ploubezre

Runan

St-Quay-Portri

Kerfons

Brélidy

Kermaria

Plestin-les-Grèves

Kergrist

Tonquédec

Bégard

D 7

D 786

Lanvollon

Plourhar Éta

Plouzélambre

D 767

Armoripark

D 8

D 787

N.-D. de la Cour

Rosanbo

Lanvellec les Sept-Saints

D 30

D 15

D 6

Plélo

Plouaret

Trégrom

Plouagat

Châtelaudre

D 11

Plounévez-Moëdec

Louargat

Guingamp

N 12

Trémuss

BREST

N 12

D 9

D 42

Belle-Isle-en-Terre

D 8

D 767

Boqueho

D 7

Loc-Envel

Plougonver

Bourbriac

Beaumanoir

D 28

D 11

D 33

D 787

St-Tréfin

Bulat-Pestivien

Seuven-Léhart

St-Connan

Quir

Plourac'h

Callac

Burthulet

Kerpert

St-Gilles-Pligeaux

FINISTÈRE

D 31

Lanrivain

Bothoa

Corlay

Lanfains

D 764

Trémargat

D 787

D 790

Kergrist-Moëlou

Gorges de Toul Goulic

St-Nicolas-du-Pélem

D 44

Lac de Boméléac

U

BREST

N 164

Carhaix-Plouguer

N 164

Laniscat

le Quillio

St-Guen

Glomel

Rostrenen

D 3

Étang du Corong

Coatcouraval

Gouarec

Bon-Repos

Caurel

Mur-de-Bretagne

D 790

D 1

les Forges-des-Salles

Lac de Guerlédan

D 767

D 32

D 769

Pontivy

D 782

D 768

MORBIHAN

Moncontour	Places covered in guide
Boqueho	Addresses and places in the area
Collinée	Locator only

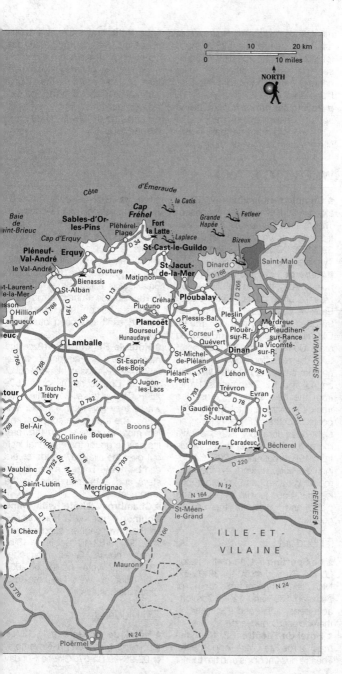

0   10   20 km
0   10 miles

NORTH

CÔTES-D'ARMOR

Côte   d'Émeraude
                              la Catis
                    Cap
                   Fréhel   Grande   Fetleer
Sables-d'Or-   Hapée
les-Pins   Pléhérel-   Fort
              Plage   la Latte   Laplace   Bizeux
Cap d'Erquy   St-Cast-le-Guildo
Baie
de   AVRANCHES
aint-Brieuc
Pléneuf-   Erquy   St-Jacut-
Val-André   de-la-Mer
le Val-André   Dinard
                    la Couture   Saint-Malo
t-Laurent-   Bienassis   Matignon
e-la-Mer   St-Alban   D 168
esson OHillion   Créhan   Ploubalay
Langueux   Pluduno
euc   Plessis-Bal. Pleslin
             D 13   Plancoët   Mordreuc
                      Bourseul   Corseul Plouër- Pleudihen-
       Lamballe   Hunaudaye   sur-R. sur-Rance
                                     Quévert   la Vicomté-
                      St-Esprit- St-Michel-   Dinan   sur-Rance
                      des-Bois   de-Plélan
                              Plélan-   Léhon
tour   Jugon-   le-Petit
       la Touche-   les-Lacs   N 176   Trévron   Evran
       Trébry   D 78
                                 la Gaudière
       Bel-Air   St-Juvat
          Collinée Boquen Broons   Tréfumel
                                 Caulnes Caradeuc Bécherel
e Vaublanc
   Saint-Lubin   D 220
c   Merdrignac   N 12
   la Chèze   St-Méen-
                                 le-Grand   ILLE-ET-
                                          VILAINE
                    Mauron
                                              N 24
             Ploërmel   N 24

RENNES

THE CÔTES-D'ARMOR

mentale de l'Éducation Nationale, in the town centre rue Victor-Basch (parallel with the rue R.-W.-Rousseau). There's another car park nearby, in the courtyard of the Collège Roger-Vercel.

■ **Paying car parks**: numerous and not too expensive. Particularly useful is the underground car park opposite the town hall (A1 on the map).

– **Le Petit Train**: this is a tourist train that tours the town every day, 10am–6pm. There's an accompanying, rather lightweight commentary. It starts from the tourist information office at the place Duclos or from the harbour every 40 minutes. ☎ 06-08-55-08-30 and 06-08-55-08-43.

WHERE TO STAY

⌂ **Camping municipal** (A2, **10** on the map): 103 rue Chateaubriand. The nearest campsite, 300 metres from the town centre. ☎ 02-96-39-11-96. Open June–September. Two-star. About 50 spaces.

⌂ **Auberge de jeunesse** (youth hostel) (A1, off the map): Moulin du Méen, Vallée de la Fontaine-des-Eaux. ☎ 02-96-39-10-83. Fax: 02-96-39-10-62. Open all year round. Old mill in a very pleasant wooded area. Coming from Dinan harbour, take the road for Plouer and then another small road, on the left, with an 'AJ' sign. It is 2 kilometres (1 mile) from the train station – cross the track, turn right, and follow the signposts. It costs 50F per night in an eight-bed dormitory or a double room for the same price. Meals from 49F, breakfast for 20F. Camping possible. Hiking in the surrounding area and photography lessons. Lounge with fireplace, and piano and guitar for the use of guests.

⌂ Budget

⌂ **Le Sporting** (A1, **11** on the map): 20 rue Carnot. ☎ 02-96-39-03-67. Nine plain but acceptable rooms for between 130F and 190F. Comfortable beds, a TV, and a car park in the enclosed courtyard.

⌂ **Hôtel du Théâtre** (B2, **12** on the map): 2 rue Ste-Claire, opposite the Théâtre des Jacobins and the tourist

office. ☎ 02-96-39-06-91. Closed Sunday evening and Monday in winter, and for the month of January. A simple little hotel with clean rooms: a double costs 160–220F, and there's one very simple room for 85F, if you're on a tight budget. Breakfast is a bargain at 25F and the homemade rhubarb jam is good. There is a bar on the ground floor, but it doesn't stay open late so it's not noisy.

⌂ **Hôtel le Régent** (A2, **19** on the map): 9 rue de la Ferronnerie. ☎ 02-96-39-22-23. Closed Monday out of season. Double rooms cost 160–250F. This is a well-kept little hotel where they give you a good welcome. The rooms are spacious and feel more expensive than they are. It's best to go for the ones that look out over the alleyway as the others can be noisy. There's a bar downstairs and a billiards room in the basement.

⌂ **Chambres d'hôte with Mme Dodinot**: 7 rue de la Poissonnerie (in the town centre), second floor. ☎ 02-96-39-82-40. Set in an 18th-century house. Guest rooms for 180F with private shower, or 200F with toilet as well. No breakfast. Charming hostess.

⌂⌂ Moderate

⌂ **Hôtel de la Gare** (A1, **13** on the map): place du 11-Novembre. ☎ 02-96-39-04-57. Closed Sunday

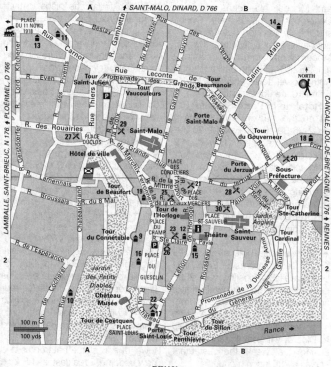

DINAN

■ Useful Addresses

🛈 Office du tourisme

🚄 Gare SNCF (train station)

✉ Poste (post office)

🏠 Where to Stay

9 Hôtel d'Avaugour

10 Camping municipal (campsite)

11 Le Sporting

12 Hôtel du Théâtre

13 Hôtel de la Gare

14 Hôtel de la Porte St-Malo

15 Hôtel d'Arvor

16 Hôtel Le Challonge

17 Hôtel Les Grandes Tours

18 Le Logis du Jerzual

19 Hôtel du Régent

✗ Where To Eat

20 Crêperie des Artisans

21 Crêperie Ahna and L'Albatros

22 Le St-Louis

23 Le Cantorbery

25 Chez la Mère Pourcel

26 La Fleur de Sel

27 La Léonie

28 Chez Flocon

29 La Courtine

30 Le Bistrot d'en Bas and
   Clafoutis

and Monday afternoon, and mid-December to mid-January. Opposite the station, the hotel is distinguishable by its dark red awning. Modern rooms, bright and comfortable, from 140F (with basin) to 265F (with shower, toilet. and TV). Nos. 1, 5 and 10 are double-glazed.

♠ **Hôtel de la Porte St-Malo** (B1, **14** on the map): 35 rue St-Malo. ☎ 02-96-39-19-76. Fax: 02-96-39-50-67. ♿ Outside the city walls, in a quiet district next to the Porte St-Malo (city gate) and five minutes from the town centre. Simple but charming small hotel with double rooms from 180F to 320F.

♠ **Hôtel Les Alleux** (off A1 on the map): on the road to Ploubalay. ☎ 02-96-85-16-10. Fax: 02-96-85-11-40. Email: hotel.alleux@wanadoo.fr. Double rooms for 280F. Half board available, costing from 250F per person. A modern hotel without any great charm but benefits from being in the countryside. A good stopover on the way from St-Malo to Dinard, with comfortable rooms. During the week the restaurant serves a 78F lunch menu.

♠ **Chambres d'hôte** (off A2 on the map): 53–55 rue de Coëtquenm; coming from the place St-Louis, heading down towards the River Rance. ☎ 02-96-85-23-49. Fax: 02-96-87-51-44. Open from March to November. Rhona Lockwood, one of the many English people settled in the area, offers a couple of cosy little double rooms for 300F including breakfast.

♠ **Hôtel Les Grandes Tours** (A2, **17** on the map): 6 rue du Château. ☎ 02-96-85-16-20. Fax: 02-96-85-16-04. Email: carregi@wanadoo.fr. Closed for two weeks in December, January and February. In the town centre, opposite the Château de Dinan. Victor Hugo and Juliette Drouet stayed here on 25 June 1836, during a five-week trip. Apparently 'they ate their dinner, spent the night, found the place to their liking and had lunch there the following day'. The rooms have been completely renovated since those days and equipped with all mod cons (bath, telephone and TV). The hotel also has a half board arrangement with the restaurant next door. Car park in the courtyard (free in low season). Offers 36 rooms (five on the street side) from 200–295F (family rooms for 400F and 450F).

♠ **Hôtel Le Challonge** (A2, **16** on the map): 29 place Du-Guesclin. ☎ 02-96-87-16-30. Fax: 02-96-87-16-31. Open all year round. In the heart of the town, with 18 rooms (refurbished in 1996), including two suites and three family rooms. Eleven rooms overlook the square, but the double-glazing is effective. Prices vary from 290F to 420F for double rooms according to size. The family rooms are suitable for four (with twin beds in an adjoining room), with TV, desk and large wardrobes. One room has disabled access. Suites for 590F. Heated towel rails in all the bathrooms and new bedding. Breakfast is 40F for a basket of pastries. All in all, excellent value for money.

♠ **Chambres d'hôte Le Moulin de la Fontaine-des-Eaux**: in the Fontaine-des-Eaux Valley, not far from the port and about 2 kilometres (1 mile) by car from Dinan, or 20 minutes' walk (but it's all uphill). To get there, take the same route given above for the youth hostel (*Auberge de jeunesse*) and it's 200 metres further on. ☎ and fax: 02-96-87-92-09. Double rooms cost 300–350F including breakfast. The accommodation here is set in an old mill in a pretty countryside location, run by a pleasant British couple. There's a lovely garden with a pond. There are five rooms on offer, all decorated with flowers in a rather kitsch way. The dearest rooms seem a little over-priced.

☆☆ Moderate

🛏 **Chambres d'hôte Le Logis de Jerzual** (B1, **18** on the map): 25–27 rue du Petit-Fort. ☎ 02-96-85-46-54. Fax: 02-96-39-46-94. Comfortable rooms from 300F to 430F including breakfast. This is a very pleasant location not far from the port in Jerzual, on one of the town's oldest streets. The rooms here are extremely cosy and there's a lovely large sloping garden where you can eat breakfast when the weather's fine. The proprietors are very friendly and offer a warm welcome. An excellent place to stay.

☆☆☆ Chic

🛏 **Hôtel Arvor** (B2, **15** on the map): 5 rue A.-Pavie (right in the centre, opposite the tourist office). ☎ 02-96-39-21-22. Fax: 02-96-39-83-09. Email: arvor@destination-bretagne.com. ♿ Open all year round. An elegant hotel recently installed in an 18th-century building, which retains a superb Renaissance portal in sculpted stone. The whole building is on the site of a former Jacobin monastery. Newly painted rooms with all mod cons (bath or shower, toilet, TV, telephone), at affordable prices for the area: from 290F to 390F according to the degree of comfort. A great advantage is the free car park (parking is expensive round here). Excellent welcome.

☆☆☆☆ Très Chic

🛏 **Hôtel d'Avaugour** (A2, **9** on the map): 1 place du Champ. ☎ 02-96-39-07-49. Fax: 02-96-85-43-04. Email: avaugour.hotel@wanadoo.fr. Closed in January and February. A double room costs 400–800F, with suites starting at 800F. This plush hotel right in the centre of Dinan has extremely comfortable rooms, some overlooking the hotel's gardens and some with a view over the ramparts.

WHERE TO EAT

☆ Budget

✗ **Chez Flochon** (B2, **28** on the map): 24 rue du Jerzual. ☎ 02-96-87-91-57. Open daily except Sunday lunchtime. Closed November–January. A typical bill here comes to 55–60F. Set in a 17th-century house, this restaurant offers a warm atmosphere. The decor is colourful and rather eclectic, taking as its theme the legendary seafarers of Brittany. They take care to stimulate the tastebuds too, offering superb tarts (*galettes*) with a large choice of original fillings and beautifully presented *crêpes*. The menu is not kept purely local, though, and features a number of cheese-based dishes from the mountainous regions, such as *raclette*, often combined with fruit. You might try the Roquefort purée with celery, grapes and olives, or the Camembert and pear *fondue* with onions, cooked in cider. An excellent place.

✗ **Crêperie Ahna** (B2, **21** on the map): 7 rue de la Poissonnerie. ☎ 02-96-39-09-13. Closed Sunday, and for three weeks in March and the last two weeks of November. Allow about 60F for a meal. Inexpensive, with delicious and unusual *crêpes*. Try the savoury *crêpe* with sliced potatoes and sausages simmered in Muscadet (*galette de Langueux*). They also serve a range of grilled meat dishes. The owners are charming and the setting is pleasant.

✗ **Crêperie des Artisans** (B1, **20** on the map): 6 rue du Petit-Fort. ☎ 02-96-39-44-10. Closed Monday

DINAN

(except in July and August) and from mid-October to the end of March. Three *crêpe* and *galette* menus are offered: two at 44F and 55F, with an evening menu using local produce (69F) and another at 72F. There's an amusing kids' menu, with a *crêpe*, a *galette* and a cocktail! This is a beautiful old rustic dwelling, in one of the most charming streets of the Old Town (full of tourists and restaurants). Relaxed atmosphere. Run by a group of friendly young people. Excellent traditional *crêpes*, as well as cider from the barrel, and quantities of *lait ribot* (a drink made from whey). Pleasant music adds to the atmosphere, and in summer you can sit outside on the street terrace.

✗ **Le Bistrot d'en Bas** (B2, **30** on the map): 20 rue Haute-Voie. ☎ 02-96-85-44-00. Open 11am–3pm and 5pm–1am. Closed Monday, Sunday lunchtime and during the October and February school holidays. This welcoming little bistrot is tucked away in a pretty street that's slightly off the tourist track. It's a convivial place, decorated in bright colours with some art-nouveau touches, with added character from a strong jazz presence with some French *chansons* thrown in for good measure. You can eat cheap hot or cold snacks here in the shape of open sandwiches (*tartines*) served with salad, with such fillings as sausage and onion or duck with Reblochon cheese and potatoes. On the slate you'll find a number of wines by the glass and there are two decent beers on draught. There's a lovely street terrace in summer.

✗ **Clafoutis** (B2, **30** on the map): 14 rue Haute-Voie. ☎ 02-96-85-10-78. Open noon–7pm. Closed Monday all year round and Sunday from April to the beginning of June. This is a tasteful little place that you shouldn't miss. The proprietor is also the chef and she has mastered the art of sweet and savoury pies

to perfection. All the pastries are delicious, as are the fillings, and only fresh, seasonal fruit and vegetables are used. Savoury tarts cost from 29F and sweet ones from 20F. The cakes are excellent too. A take-away service is available.

☆☆ Moderate

✗ **Le Saint-Louis** (A2, **22** on the map): 9 and 11 rue de Léhon. ☎ 02-96-39-89-50. Closed Sunday evening, Monday lunchtime and Wednesday (except in July), plus one week in November, one week in January and two weeks in February. Beautiful display of flowers on the facade, and three large dining rooms and a patio. Offering good value for money, this restaurant owes its popularity to its range of set menus with a choice of starters, cheeses and desserts from the buffet (from 58F on weekday lunchtimes). Other set menus for 72F, 80F and 155F. Specialities include such dishes as goat's cheese and potato with honey and cider in a *millefeuille* pastry, duck in a Muscadet marinade or salmon smoked over an open fire. Expect medieval-style aperitifs and a homely dessert such as apple pie.

✗ **Le Cantorbery** (B2, **23** on the map): 6 rue Ste-Claire. ☎ 02-96-39-02-52. Closed Monday. Set menu of the week for 75F, other menus from 125F to 190F. The restaurant occupies a late 17th-century house with old stone walls and beamed ceilings. There are wooden tables with pretty salmon-pink tablecloths and a fireplace for grilling meat. The first-floor dining room is most attractive, with wood panelling and a grand fireplace. The whole place has a pleasant setting, where eating is a delight. The menu is changed regularly, according to seasonal availability.

DINAN

✕ **L'Albatros** (B2, **21** on the map): 11 rue de la Poissonnerie, next to the Crêperie Ahna, in the heart of old Dinan. ☎ 02-96-85-06-50. Closed on Thursday except in July and August, for three weeks in October and the last two weeks in January. Expect to pay about 75F à la carte. The young owners offer Italian dishes and excellent pizza, as well as local specialities, in a tastefully decorated, flower-filled room. A relaxed atmosphere, with discreet background music and oil lamps in the evening. Reasonable prices and a charming welcome.

✕ **Restaurant La Courtine** (A1, **29** on the map): 6 rue de la Croix. ☎ 02-96-39-74-41. Closed Wednesday and Saturday lunchtimes in summer, all day Wednesday and Sunday evening out of season, two weeks at the end of November and one week in January. Set menus for 70F (weekday lunchtime), and evening menus from 98F to 195F. The welcome is warm and the decor is cosy. The chef is obviously someone of talent and is well-travelled, offering exquisite seafood and fish dishes that often have a touch of the exotic. Excellent meat dishes too, especially the saddle of lamb in cream with garlic. An unusual and welcome feature is the choice of eight different types of coffee. It's a good idea to make a reservation in the evening. On alternate Fridays in winter, there's a themed evening.

✕ **Le Léonie** (A1, **27** on the map): 19 rue Rolland. ☎ 02-96-85-47-47. Closed Monday, Sunday evening out of season and for three weeks in September. There's a lunchtime special (Tuesday–Saturday only) of a dish of the day, dessert and coffee for 48F, with other set menus at 75F and 95F. This modest little restaurant is in the centre but off the main tourist track – just a few tables in quite a pleasant setting – and it's a

first venture by a young couple who certainly know how to hold onto their regular local clientele. They deserve their success: the husband is the chef, preparing only the freshest of produce; his wife, who is charmingly attentive, looks after the customers. The menu changes regularly and everything is well cooked and unpretentious.

✕ **La Fleur de Sel** (A2–B2, **26** on the map): 7 rue Ste-Claire, near the tourist office. ☎ 02-96-85-15-14. Fax: 02-96-85-16-66. Closed Tuesday and Wednesday. Chef Nicolas Boyère, having gained a strong reputation elsewhere, has returned to the region to offer genuine good cooking using fresh produce. His speciality is to offer a *menu-carte*, which allows you to benefit from set-menu prices while still choosing one dish from the à la carte menu; these menus are offered at 120F and 220F. There is also a children's menu at 90F, comprising a main course and a dessert. Agnès Boyère oversees the two dining rooms (one with a predominantly blue decor, the other rust-coloured) and looks after the bar. Beautifully laid tables with elegant cutlery and tableware makes eating here even more enjoyable. Very good service. Reasonably priced house wines and wine of the month, also available by the glass.

☆☆☆ Chic

✕ **Chez la Mère Pourcel** (B2, **25** on the map): 3 place des Merciers. ☎ 02-96-39-03-80. Closed Sunday evening and Monday out of season, and in February. This restaurant offers a classic à la carte menu and set-price menus for 97F and 168F, with other more sumptuous menus at 230F and 395F. Tucked away in a splendid 15th-century house in Dinan's most beautiful square. Impressive dining room with huge beams and a massive old spiral staircase in dark wood. Cooking is done exclusively using fresh products from the market and small local suppliers, and specialities might include baby lamb from the Bay of Mont-St-Michel and pigeon stuffed with *foie gras* and prunes. Very nice terrace outside.

✕ **Le Bistrot du Viaduc**: 22 rue du Lion-d'Or. ☎ 02-96-85-95-00. Fax: 02-96-85-95-01. ✕ Closed Monday, Saturday lunchtime and Sunday evening; also closed from mid-December to mid-January and the last two weeks in June. Limited lunchtime set menu for 90F during the week. Other menus for 165F and 190F. Also à la carte (expect to pay about 280F without wine). Reservations essential. On the left at a bend just after the viaduct (on the road to Rennes), this fantastic location offers one of the best views over the Rance Valley. Inside is a pleasant setting of flowers and pastel shades, an open stove in the dining room and delicious regional cooking. The menu includes pigs' trotters, Breton salted cod, or a good, old-fashioned marrrowbone (*os à moelle*). Good selection of affordable wines.

SWEET TREATS

– **Pâtisserie Loyer**: 2 rue des Rouairies. ☎ 02-96-39-21-32. Closed Sunday afternoon and Monday. This is a long-established business, having supplied the people of Dinan with sweet goodies for many years.

– **Pâtissier Patrick Mazoyer** (B1 on the map): 4 rue de l'École (on the corner of the rue du Jerzual). ☎ 02-96-39-03-55. Closed Monday. A good place to try a *flor'ig*, a sweet butter pastry with a choice of three fillings. Other local specialities are sold, including some made in the shop, such as *corbelets*.

– Also for those with a sweet tooth, the famous *gavottes bretonnes* (paper-thin *crêpes* often served as a dessert) are available in the shops, or directly from the factory, on the road to Dinard (after the youth hostel coming from the harbour).

WHERE TO STAY AND EAT IN THE AREA

North of Dinan

🛏 ✕ **La Renardais**: coming from the direction of Dinan, 1 kilometre before Plouër-sur-Rance. ☎ 02-96-86-89-81. Fax: 02-96-86-99-22. Closed February. Four comfortable rooms from 320F to 350F including breakfast. Meals also served, at 99F and 119F, and they can offer a restaurant-style wine list. This is a sturdy house, built in local stone and run by a charming British couple. The sitting room has a large fireplace, and there's a terrace and a large, rather beautiful garden out back. Courteous welcome.

🛏 **Manoir de Rigourdaine**: at Plouër-sur-Rance, on the road towards Langrolay. ☎ 02-96-86-89-96. Fax: 02-96-86-92-46. Website: www.hotel-rigourdaine.fr. ✕ Open from April to mid-November. Double rooms from 300F to 450F. A hotel of assured quality has been created from a large, old farmhouse. It's comfortable and very pleasant.

🛏 **Manoir de la Pépinière**: in Pont de Cieux, 1 kilometre past Pleudihen-sur-Rance, on the D29 heading towards St-Malo. ☎ 02-96-83-36-61. Fax: 02-96-83-26-26. Open all year round. Beautiful 18th-century stone-built house. The owners offer five guest rooms, each with a different and original decor, and all overlooking the garden. The theme of each room is a famous person of the region and all have brand-new private bath-rooms. Expect to pay 320F for two people, with a copious breakfast included. Billiards room available. A *gîte* for five people is situated in the old stables. First-rate welcome.

South and West of Dinan

🛏 ✗ **Chambres d'hôte La Corbinais**: 22980 St-Michel-de-Plélan. ☎ 02-96-27-64-81. Fax: 02-96-27-68-45. Email: corbinais@corbinais.com. Signposted on the road between Dinan and Plancoët (D794), in Corseul. Guest rooms with shower for 290F for two people; breakfast for 25F. Evening meal for 90F (perhaps a farmhouse supper of stew cooked on the hearth). Children's menu for 40F. A cheerful couple welcome you to a lovely and tastefully decorated Breton farm. Here you can enjoy nature, and activities such as horse-riding, mountain biking and golf on a nine-hole course. An excellent place to stay.

✗ **Relais de la Blanche Hermine**: Lourmel, 22980 Plélan-le-Petit. ☎ 02-96-27-62-19. Fax: 02-96-27-05-93. Closed Tuesday except in July and August. About 15 kilometres (10 miles) from Dinan, heading towards Jugon-les-Lacs. Come off at the Plélan-le-Petit roundabout and take the old road heading for the *zone artisanale* (industrial estate); the restaurant, a long stone house at the edge of the road, is 800 metres further along on the left. Large, pleasant and lively dining room. The restaurant has a good reputation among the locals. Set menus for 75F (except Sunday lunchtime), 98 and 158F, with mixed salad (*salade folle*), grilled fillet of beef (*filet de boeuf grillé*), cheese and dessert. Seafood by prior request only. Suckling pig roasted on the spit (*cochon de lait à la broche*) is offered twice a month.

🛏 ✗ **Chambres d'hôte Malik**: chemin de l'Étoupe, Plélan-le-Petit. ☎ 02-96-27-62-71. Closed December–March. Reservations essential. Twelve kilometres (7.5 miles) from Dinan via the N176. Fifty metres past the town hall, head towards St-Maudez, then take the second street on the right, and look for a surprisingly modern house made completely of wood, with huge bay windows overlooking the countryside. This very sophisticated establishment has one small suite for two people, with a living room, for 320F including breakfast, and one suite with two bedrooms for four people, which costs 500F. The decor is very elegant in its choice of colours, materials and objects. Wonderful brunch-type breakfast with cheese, scrambled eggs with chives (*oeufs brouillés à la ciboulette*) and home-made bread, served on the terrace or in a room on the ground floor. Martine and Hubert Viannay give their guests a reserved but warm welcome. A wealth of small details make this house an exceptionally charming stopover.

🛏 ✗ **Ferme-auberge La Priquetais**: Trévron, 1 kilometre from the town. ☎ 02-96-83-56-89. Fax: 02-96-83-65-56. A lovely farm right out in the country. Very reasonably priced: double room for 180F with basin. Half board 190F. Let the hostess know in advance if you would like a simple evening meal – stuffed poultry (*volaille farcie*), duck with turnips (*canard aux navets*) or rabbit stew with cider (*civet de lapin* *au cidre*) – from 88F, with garden vegetables, cakes, and so on. Camping allowed for 25F per person. There is also a short-stay *gîte*.

☎ **Chambres d'hôte at Le Manoir**: at La Gaudière, a hamlet about 2 kilometres (1 mile) to the west of Saint-Juvat. ☎ 02-96-83-49-48. Fax: 02-96-83-49-51. Double rooms cost 280F and 300F including breakfast, with table d'hôte meals for 100F.

No smoking and no animals. You get a smiling welcome from the proprietress of this large, turreted house. The bedrooms are very spacious, impeccably clean and decorated in pastel colours. The meals served here are all prepared using local produce. Prices are very reasonable and the best thing of all is the peace and quiet. It's not surprising that people come back again and again.

WHERE TO GO FOR A DRINK

♈ The rue de la Cordonnerie, an alleyway leading to the place des Merciers, is commonly known as the 'rue de la Soif' ('thirst street'). There is a string of six or seven bars here, which are always full. Among them is **À la Truye qui File**, a listed 15th-century house, where Alain livens up the atmosphere every evening (at about 9pm) during high season with his guitar playing. A youthful clientele and a sociable atmosphere.

♈ Just opposite the previous entry is another bar, the **Saut de la Puce**, which is popular and seems to attract a decent crowd.

♈ If, around 2 or 3am, you haven't had enough, you can finish the job or just collapse at **Chez Maryvonne (Les Templiers)** at 7 rue de la Cordonnerie, an utterly tacky little dance hall and bar with red pouffes and leatherette armchairs. It is the last place to close (around 5am).

WHERE TO GO FOR A DRINK AND MUSIC IN THE AREA

♈ **Café de la Gare**: 1 route de Langrolay, at Pleslin. ☎ 02-96-27-80-04. Open Tuesday–Sunday (daily in July and August) noon–2am. Closed from January until mid-February. About 12 kilometres (7.5 miles) north of Dinan, on the road to Dinard. Concerts on the second Saturday of each month. Very friendly atmosphere, 1930s decor. Lunchtime and evening meals are available, with set menus from 89F.

WHAT TO SEE

★ **Basilique St-Sauveur**: place St-Sauveur. One of Brittany's best Romanesque works of art, this church was built in the 12th century for a knight who had vowed to construct a basilica after returning safely from a crusade, and who was influenced by the eastern and Byzantine architecture he had seen. It has an admirable facade in a pure style. The statues have lost their heads, but there are superb capitals with many unusual details. Above are a bull and a winged lion (symbols of St Luke and St Mark). Only the rather plain 19th-century tympanum seems out of place.

Inside the building, one part Romanesque and one part Gothic, there are interesting 18th-century furnishings, including altars, altarpieces, and a baptismal font. On the left is what is called the 'cenotaph', containing Du Guesclin's heart. The term is a misnomer since true cenotaphs contain neither all nor part of the body of the deceased, yet to call it a 'coffin' would be inappropriate, as would the term 'reliquary', since Du Guesclin was neither a martyr nor a saint. In reality, it's little more than a box. In the fourth chapel of the left aisle, a beautiful 15th-century stained-glass window shows Evangelists and angelic musicians, some of whom are playing the hand organ – a rare sight. There are also some pretty, modern stained-glass windows.

★ **Place des Merciers and Place des Cordeliers**: with a fascinating and completely harmonious blend of medieval and Renaissance styles, all the alleyways and lanes in the area around these squares contain beautiful architectural detail and are worth exploring. At No. 1 rue Haute-Voie is the attractive 16th-century Hôtel Beaumanoir, with its Portail aux Dauphins (portal). On the rue de l'Horloge is a 15th-century belfry, whose bell was a gift from Duchess Anne (open to visitors in summer). From the top of this street, there is an interesting panorama of the town. In rue de Léhon is the school where Chateaubriand and Broussais once studied. The Grand Rue is lined with mansions. The **Église St-Malo** has a Renaissance portal and an elegant 19th-century English organ with its pipes painted in many colours. The former Couvent des Cordeliers (monastery), founded in 1241, is now a private school (visits possible during the school holidays).

★ **Rue du Jerzual**: probably the most medieval of all Breton streets. A solitary stroll down the rue du Jerzual, early in the morning or out of season, is something to be savoured. Craftsmen and artists have taken the place of the shopkeepers of bygone days in pretty 15th- and 16th-century half-timbered houses. Go through the Gothic Jerzual gateway via the rue du Petit-Fort. At No. 24 is the beautifully restored **Maison du Gouverneur** (governor's house). A bit further along, and in sharp contrast, there has been a somewhat misguided attempt at ultra-modern reconstruction, which is supposed to be neo-medieval.

At the end of the street lies the little harbour on the River Rance, with its old Gothic bridge. Retrace your steps back to the Jerzual gate, and take the lane on the left to visit the *Jardin Anglais* (English Garden). The large terrace (formerly the town cemetery) offers a lovely view over the Rance Valley. Continue along the promenade de la Duchesse-Anne (Duchess Anne's Walk) to reach the castle.

★ **Château-musée** (castle and museum): ☎ 02-96-39-45-20. Open from 1 June to 15 October, daily, 10am–6.30pm; from 16 November to 31 December and from 7 February to 15 March, daily except Tuesday, 1.30–5.30pm; from 16 March to 31 May and from 16 October to 15 November, daily except Tuesday, 10am–noon and 2–6pm. Closed in January. Last tour begins 45 minutes before closing. Admission charge 25F. Built in the 14th century, the castle has an elegant and well-proportioned grouping of sturdy towers. Its keep, 34 metres (110 feet) high, is decorated with notable machicolations. Today, it houses an unpretentious museum tracing the history of the Dinan area with a mixed bag of religious art, portraits of notable local figures and archaeological artifacts, not all of which are of equal interest. There's an exhibition of recumbent figures on tombstones in a room of the Tour de Coëtquen. To round it all off, there is also a display of furniture, head-dresses from the area and religious objects in gold and silver plate. Another beautiful view of the town can be enjoyed from the terrace.

DINAN

The pleasant **promenade des Petits-Fossés** (Little Ditches Walk) skirts the outside of the castle ramparts.

★ **La Maison d'Artiste de la Grande Vigne**: 103 rue du Quai, the last house at the far end of the Dinan quayside. ☎ 02-96-87-90-80 or 02-96-39-22-43. Open July–September, 10am–6.30pm. Admission charge 16F (10F for children and students; under-12s go free). This pretty little house overlooking the River Rance was home to a lady called Yvonne Jean-Haffen, friend and pupil of Mathurin Méheut, a well-known Breton painter. During her lifetime she held regular artistic gatherings here, and on her death in 1993, the house, together with 4,000 works of art, was bequeathed to the town. Some of these works are now on display inside, and themed temporary exhibitions are arranged. Another positive initiative of the house is a small cottage in the grounds which is given over for use by artists for one month each. The only cost to the artist is the donation of one work of art.

★ **The ramparts**: built between the 13th and 15 th centuries, the ramparts are 3 kilometres (2 miles) long and still retain 15 towers and 4 gates. Every two years at the end of August or beginning of September, they provide the backdrop for a spectacular festival of fireworks and music (*see below*).

★ **Musée du Rail** (railway museum): in the train station. ☎ 02-96-39-81-33. Open from June to 15 September, 2–6pm. Admission charge 20F. Here you can see scale models of trains, miniature trains, posters and other railway memorabilia.

WHAT TO DO

– **La Fête des Remparts**: every two years (the next being in 2002), for a weekend during the summer. For information: ☎ 02-96-87-94-94. Admission free on Saturday, 70F on Sunday. A fireworks and musical display with a cast of 600 local actors in medieval costumes, which attracts 80,000 visitors per day. The show lasts all weekend and continues virtually day and night without interruption, with all the bawdy humour of the good old days – free-flowing wine, meat roasted on spits, ribald monks and wenches of every type. It's an experience not to be missed.

– **Le Festival harpe celtique**: lasts for one week, around 14 July. This harp festival consists of concerts, workshops and demonstrations in the presence of a number of harp experts from Brittany.

– **Boat trips**: regular boat service on the River Rance to St-Malo and Dinard from mid-April to mid-September. A pleasant excursion lasting about 2 hours 30 minutes, which reveals how surprisingly unspoiled the Rance estuary has remained. About 120 species of migrating birds nest here, including mallards, Brent geese, white egrets and herons. A one-way ticket costs 95F and the return is 135F. Return is by coach.

– For information in Dinan, contact **Emeraude Line**: ☎ 02-96-39-18-04.

WHAT TO SEE IN THE AREA

South of Dinan

See also 'Where To Stay and Eat in the Area'

★ **Léhon**: positioned in a pretty location on the banks of the River Rance, about 1 kilometre upriver from Dinan, this ancient township is worth a detour just to take in its architectural harmony. There are houses built in the 17th and 18th centuries, as well as the ruins of its 12th-century castle. In addition, there's the Abbaye de Saint-Magloire.

★ **Abbaye de Saint-Magloire**: open July and August, 10am–noon and 3–6pm. During the rest of the year, open for group visits, by appointment. ☎ 02-96-39-07-19 (the number of the town hall in Léhon). Founded in AD 850 by Nominoë, king of Brittany, and six monks with building skills, the first church was destroyed by fire by the Normans in 930. It was rebuilt in the 11th century by the Benedictines, then enlarged by Geoffroy de Corseul at the end of the 12th century, blending together the Gothic and Romanesque styles. Few alterations were made after that and the abbey was completely abandoned by 1767. A programme of restoration did not begin until the end of the 19th century.

A complete tour of the abbey is available, taking in the church, with its splendid 13th-century baptismal fonts, the cloisters, the gardens, the monastic buildings, the monks' refectory and even the attics.

★ **St-Juvat**: 3 kilometres (2 miles) from Trévron. Coming directly from Dinan, take the D2 and then the D39 via Évran. One of the most flower-bedecked villages in France, with houses weighed down under a mass of petals and road signs practically disappearing behind them. Always a favourite with photographers.

There is also a half-Romanesque and half-Gothic church to visit, along with a recorded commentary, and descriptions pinned up on the pillars.

A **marché gourmand** (food market) takes place every Friday from 4–8pm, mid-May to mid-September. ☎ 02-96-83-44-11. It is held in a place called Le Bas Mottais, which is about 3 kilometres (2 miles) west of Saint-Juvat, near the *Ferme fleurie*. Up to 15 local farmers and craftsmen work and sell their produce here, sometimes offering tastings, and there's a lovely atmosphere.

In the same place, all year round, foodies might care to visit **Les Délices de Tantine** where you can watch a very pleasant lady preparing jams before a fascinated audience. She sells these conserves, as well as various other local products. She can also be tracked down at the Marché des Lices in Rennes every Saturday.

★ **Quevert**: a small neighbouring village whose mayor has converted the football pitch into a botanical garden with 2,600 flowering plants. Every year, there is the Fête des Senteurs (festival of fragrances) and in the autumn yet another called the Fête de la Pomme et du Cidre (apple and cider festival), with numerous varieties of apples and farmhouse cider from the barrel.

DINAN

★ **Tréfumel**: a charming little 12th-century church and one of the oldest in the vicinity, with a yew tree that is at least a thousand years old. There are numerous 17th-century dwellings around.

★ **Base de loisirs de Bétineuc** (watersports lake): a large lake beside Évran offering the widest possible range of watersports, including sailing, windsurfing and canoeing.

★ **Caulnes**: two beautiful country chateaux are worth a visit. One, reconstructed in the 17th and 18th centuries, is in Couëllan, and the other is in La Perchais.

★ **Château de Caradeuc**: near Becherel, 22 kilometres (13 miles) from Dinan on the D68 and then the D20. ☎ 02-99-66-77-16. Grounds open from June to mid-September daily, noon–6pm. The castle itself is not open to the public. Nicknamed the 'Breton Versailles', partly because of the building's dignified facade, which is in the 18th-century Regency style, but above all for its grounds, which are a listed site and among the finest in Brittany. Beautiful panoramic view from the terraces. The 5-metre (16-foot) high statue of Louis XVI is one of very few in France to have survived the Revolution.

North of Dinan

On the right bank of the Rance

★ **La Vicomté-sur-Rance**: a good stopping-off place at the port of Lyvet. This is where the lock that controls the tidal flow (the Écluse du Châtelier) straddles the Rance. To the right of the bridge you will see what remains of the old, square fishing nets, now abandoned by fishermen due to the riverbed having silted up. To the left of the bridge, a number of pleasure craft have their moorings, which makes a pretty sight. If you fancy a drink or something to eat, try **Ty Corentin**, facing the port, or the **Bar-restaurant la Rance**, at the entrance to the bridge.

★ **Mordreuc**: just beyond La Vicomté, Mordreuc is a pretty little mooring place. From here, there's a fine view of the Rance as it begins to widen.

★ **Musée de la Pomme et du Cidre** (apple and cider museum): in Pleudihen-sur-Rance, 10 kilometres (6 miles) from Dinan on the road to St-Malo. ☎ 02-96-83-20-78. ⚒ Open April, May and September, Monday to Saturday, 2–7pm; from June to August daily, 10am–7pm. Admission charge 20F. All anyone could wish to know about cider (its history and how it is made) is explained on this restored farm. There is a tour of the cooper's workshop to see how barrels are made and ringed, displays of traditional apple-pressing equipment, audio-visual presentation and tastings of the famous local cider (on sale afterwards if you want to fill up the boot of your car).

On the left bank of the Rance

★ **Plouër-sur-Rance**: this is a traditional village centred on its church. Just below it is La Cale, one of the main ports on the Rance and very popular with the British. Here, there's a good bar-restaurant in an old house.

★ **Pont Chateaubriand**: this bridge spanning the Rance is a remarkable sight, with a modern and aesthetically pleasing design. Not a single pillar or vault connects the bridge to the riverbed. The roadway, which is from 424 metres (1,378 feet) to 30 metres (97 feet) above the ground, is suspended from a single arch 265 metres (860 feet) in length.

PLOUBALAY (*PLOUVALAE*) 22650 (POP: 2,452)

This large village is in a fantastic location, close to the sea but nestling in a wood, at the crossroads of the beaches of the Côte d'Émeraude. The land around Ploubalay and Lancieux was once part of a peninsula but the sea receded, leaving behind the marshes. The village is a good starting point for exploring a region criss-crossed by ramblers' paths. Although Ploubalay has no monuments of note, it does offer some handy places to stay, which are just a short distance from St-Malo, Dinard and Dinan, making it an ideal stopover point.

USEFUL ADDRESS

🛈 **Syndicat d'initiative** (tourist office): just behind square Edouard-Durst. ☎ 02-96-82-64-90. Open in high season only, Monday–Saturday 10am–12.30pm and 4.30–7.30pm, Sunday 10am–noon.

WHERE TO STAY IN THE AREA

🛏 **Le Clos St-Cadreuc**: from Ploubalay, take the D768 heading towards St-Brieuc and then the D26, on the left, towards Plessix-Balisson, which is about 1 kilometre further on. ☎ and fax: 02-96-27-32-43. Open from Easter to the end of October. Yet another charming place in an exceptionally nice setting. M. and Mme Rey du Boissieu meticulously renovated the two buildings in 1995. The four self-contained rooms are in an extension separated from the main building by a rockery with deckchairs where guests can relax. Expect to pay 3255F for two people, which includes a copious breakfast with sweet pastries and homemade jam. There is a family room for four people, for an additional charge. Excellent value for money. The owners, who know the region like the back of their hand, will show you all the good places to go (walks, quiet beaches, old stone buildings). An lovely, peaceful place to stay. Credit cards not accepted.

WHERE TO EAT IN PLOUBALAY

✕ **Restaurant des Sports**: rue du Colonel-Pleven. ☎ 02-96-27-20-07. Closed Monday. Seafood specialities served in three dining rooms, which are never empty in high season. On one wall there is a copy of a 1996 *Le Monde* newspaper article about the restaurant: 'The restaurant is known far and wide for the generous portions it serves. Plates piled high with crabs, lobsters, oysters, and spider crabs. Roomfuls of people busy munching, breaking open, sucking, and shelling. It's a culinary celebration at a reasonable price.' The cheapest set menu costs 80F, with four other menus going up to 188F, and you can see why making a reservation is necessary. Children's menu at 40F.

CÔTES-D'ARMOR

✘ **Restaurant de la Gare**: 4 rue des Ormelets. ☎ 02-96-27-25-16. Closed Tuesday evening and Wednesday. Don't bother to look for the station that the name suggests; it's been a long time since the last train passed through. Set menus cost from 80F to 220F. The former simple bar-café was transformed 10 years ago by the owners and the successful design of the three dining rooms perfectly complements the excellent cuisine. Xavier Termet's set menu for 105F might include his grandmother's old-fashioned recipe for black pudding (*boudin*) and a choice of dessert from the trolley. For 160F and 210F, the chef displays all his talent in seafood dishes and mouthwatering desserts, such as dark chocolate cake (*pavé de dame Ferière au chocolat noir*) and fresh pears on puff pastry, with chocolate-flavoured caramel sauce (*griottes du 'Douceur de Lucie'*). The fine wine list includes a Muscadet-sur-lie du Clos du Bois Gautier for 106F, a red Anjou for 125F and a grand cru classé de Graves (vintage Graves), the 1994 Château Bouscaut, for 264F. Reservations are essential in the evening, since the place is known all over the region and has been praised in numerous guides.

WHERE TO EAT OR GO FOR A DRINK IN THE AREA

✘ **La Maison des Cavaliers**: in Plessix-Balisson, 5 kilometres (3 miles) from Ploubalay on the D26, in the heart of one of the smallest and most charming *communes* in France, with many old houses. The café-restaurant is opposite the church. ☎ 02-96-27-24-62. Open lunchtime only (don't arrive after 1pm). Closed Saturday and Sunday. Just one menu for 70F (children's menu at 45F): home cooking, with soup (even in summer), a starter, such as terrine, fish or mussels, and a main course. Depending on the proprietor's mood or inspiration, this might be veal (*blanquette de veau*), lamb (*sauté d'agneau*), pork casserole (*rouelle de porc à la cocotte*) or beef and vegetable stew (*pot-au-feu*). The desserts are also homemade, except for the ice cream. Try the famous *tarte*, rice pudding (*gâteau de riz*) or the cream puddings. House wine for less than 40F a bottle and a Bordeaux Côtes de Castillon for 85F. One quiet and pleasant dining room overlooks the back garden, while the larger one has a bar and fireplace. Credit cards accepted.

✘ **Café de la Gare**: at Pleslin (*see* 'Dinan', 'Where To Go for a Drink and Music in the Area').

La Côte d'Émeraude (The Emerald Coast)

Brittany's 'Emerald Coast' is a beautiful coastline, with wonderful walks along the hilly areas of Cap Fréhel or Cap Erquy, and wide, sandy beaches. For decades it has been traditional for French middle-class families to spend their holidays in the seaside resorts along this coastline, which have a distinctive early 20th-century charm. You will not experience the 'real Brittany' here, but it is still possible to escape from large-scale tourism.

CÔTES-D'ARMOR

ST-JACUT-DE-LA-MER
(*SANT-YAGU-AN-ENEZ*) 22750   (Pop: 893)

St-Jacut possesses, in addition to 11 beautiful beaches, a certain indefinable quality, which sets it apart from other places in North Brittany.

Rabelais's Gargantua was one of the first tourists to visit, if only in fiction, this long peninsula between the Baie de l'Arguenon and the Baie de Lancieux. At low tide, it is lined with huge strands where there is particularly good shoreline angling. The village of St-Jacut-de-la-Mer occupies the largest part of the peninsula. Still called St-Jégu by local old-timers, it was founded by an Irish monk in the 10th century. Today, it looks almost exactly as it would have done in the 19th century. Small groups of five or six houses crowded together for protection from the north wind, with gable side to the street and beautiful stone facades, make the architecture unique; they are known locally as *rangées*. In the winter the village has just 600 inhabitants, but its population swells to 20 times that number in the summer.

The 'Jaguens', as the people of St-Jacut-de-la-Mer are called, consider themselves to be almost a race apart from other Bretons. They describe themselves as stubborn and a bit quarrelsome. Above all, they have their own language, known as Jégui, which is a variant of the Gallo language spoken in the eastern part of Brittany. Neither a degenerate language nor a peasant dialect, Jégui is clearly the descendant of the French spoken before the centralization of the country carried out under the monarchy, and still contains some echoes of the pure forms of French that have disappeared from today's standard language. Of course, it is practically impossible to find a young person who speaks Jégui, but the 'Friends of Old St-Jacut' continue to strive to preserve it.

For centuries, there was so much inter-marrying among the people of the village that many families ended up with the same name. Ultimately, it became necessary to create new surnames. The tax collector from Ploubalay was obliged to mention these new names on his roll of taxpayers in order to distinguish between families. For a long time, the villagers earned their living exclusively from fishing, especially mackerel fishing.

At low tide, small private islands called the Ébihens can be reached via an offshore sandbar, known as a *tombolo*. However, the maximum stay is three hours and care must be taken not to become trapped by the incoming tide.

– **Buses to St-Malo**: only run in July and August, three departures daily by C.A.T. ☎ 02-96-39-21-05.

USEFUL ADDRESS

🄷 **Syndicat d'initiative** (tourist office): in the village, beside the post office. ☎ 02-96-27-71-91. Open July to August, Monday to Saturday 10am–1pm and 2–7pm and Sunday 10am–noon; June and September, Monday to Friday 10am–noon and 2–5.30pm and Saturday 9am–noon; October to May, daily except Tuesday 10am–noon and 2–5.30pm (Saturday 9am–

CÔTES-D'ARMOR

noon). Welcoming staff and some very useful brochures. They also organize free walking tours of the village in the summer season.

WHERE TO STAY OR EAT

⚓ **Camping municipal**: nice location on the edge of the Plage de la Manchette. ☎ 02-96-27-70-33. Open from April to September. Costs 37F per day for one person and 58F for two.

⚓ ✕ **Hôtel-restaurant Le Vieux Moulin**: ☎ 02-96-27-71-02. Fax: 02-96-27-77-41. Open April to September. In a quiet area in the centre of the peninsula, near the beaches and harbour. Set in a large, U-shaped house, built in the 1930s and embellished with a beautiful garden, about 20 rooms from 220F to 300F, including two very quaint ones in the tower of a 15th-century mill. Comfortable and friendly. Delightful owners. Half board compulsory from mid-June to mid-September, from 320F to 340F. Restaurant with traditional cooking

('a first-class meal and no frozen food!') with menus for 100F and 150F.

✕ **Restaurant La Presqu'île**: 164 Grande-Rue. ☎ 02-96-27-76-47. Open lunchtime and evening. Closed Monday out of season, and in February. Jacky, the owner, has sailed all over the world and knows how to cook excellent fish dishes, such as turbot in lime juice (*turbot au citron vert*), squid in prawn sauce (*aiguillette de calmar au coulis de langoustines*) and grilled bass in fennel cream sauce (*bar grillé à la crème de fenouil*). There are also delicious meat dishes. Set menus for 110F and 145F, and a children's menu for 40F. In winter, reservations must be made 48 hours in advance because Jacky only 'works' with fresh fish.

WHAT TO SEE AND DO

★ A walk out to the picturesque **Pointe du Chevet**, a verdant headland facing the open sea and the Île des Ébihens (dominated by a tower designed by Vauban). Lovely view of St-Briac and St-Cast. Nearby is the superb Plage du Rougeret, which is protected by the rocky expanse of La Houle-Causseule (which shelters a fishing port as well).

★ There are plenty of places in which to swim around St-Jacut. There is another beautiful beach at the seaside resort and fishing port of **Châtelet**, which merges into the Plage de la Pissotte, before becoming the beach of the municipal campsite.

★ Guided tours of St-Jacut in July and August every Monday at 2pm, organized by the tourist office.

PLANCOËT (*PLANGOED*) 22130 (Pop: 2,645)

'A little bit of town out in the country with the added bonus of the sea on its doorstep.' This is how the Plancoët tourist office describes this place which lies on the main road between Dinan and the coast. The 'pretty village' recalled by Chateaubriand has seen many changes since the writer spent his 'first exile' here with his grandmother, Madame de Bédée. Plancoët owes its current reputation to the fact that mineral water is available on the spot, free of charge – the only source of mineral water in all of Brittany. The quality is excellent, thanks to the low nitrate content. The town is also known for its production of traditional tiles and for its two leather workrooms, which produce items for the main fashion houses. One of Brittany's most famous restaurateurs lives here, and the surrounding area has some interesting places to see off the beaten track.

USEFUL ADDRESSES

🛈 Syndicat d'initiative (tourist office): 1 rue des Venelles; right in the heart of town, in a beautiful old house. ☎ 02-96-84-00-57. Fax: 02-96-84-18-01. Website: www. ot-plancoet.fr. Open July and August, Monday–Saturday 9.30am–12.30pm and 2.30–6.30pm plus Sunday 10am–noon; out of season, Monday–Saturday 10am–12.30pm and Wednesday and Friday 2.30–5.30pm. Closed Sunday. Helpful staff.

🚂 Gare SNCF (train station): ☎ 02-96-50-90-28. Office open from 30 June to 10 September, Tuesday–Saturday 9am–noon and 2–5.30pm.

■ Canoë-kayak (canoeing): near the campsite. ☎ 02-96-84-16-12. Open Monday–Saturday 9.30am–noon and 2–6pm. Closed Sunday. Lessons for beginners and experienced canoeists, and canoe rental.

■ Purchase of leather goods: C. de Swan and Renouard, two designers of fine leather goods, are located in Plancoët, where each has a showroom and salesroom. Their creations represent excellent quality at very affordable prices. Plancoët has a long-standing tradition of working with leather, and in the 19th century tanneries were built all along the River Arguenon.

WHERE TO STAY AND EAT

🛏 Camping: ☎ 02-96-84-03-42. Open 1 June to 15 September. In a pleasant setting on the banks of the River Arguenon, beside the Jardin du Pré Rolland.

🛏 ✕ Le Relais de la Source: 67 rue de l'Abbaye. ☎ 02-96-84-10-11. At the lower end of the town, by the roundabout near the quays, head for Dinan. Offers eight rooms for less than 200F and five set menus from 75 to 160F.

✕ Le Chateaubriand: 12 rue de l'Abbaye. ☎ 02-96-84-29-57. Open noon–11pm. Closed Sunday evening and Sunday lunchtime out of season. Also closed mid-February to mid-March. Car park. Lunchtime menu for 60F, except Sunday and public holidays. Allow about 150F if you eat à la carte. Copious portions

of good-quality, low-priced homemade food. More expensive on Sunday, when the food is even better. The menu includes some interesting dishes as well as 12 sorts of pizza, available to take away. The white-and-blue decor is functional, with a hint of a marine theme. Credit cards accepted.

▱▱▱▱ Très Chic

🛏 ✕ Restaurant de Jean-Pierre Crouzil: 20 les Quais. ☎ 02-96-84-10-24. Closed Monday, Sunday evening out of season and in January. Foodies in the know come from far and wide to eat at this famous place. This is very high-class cooking, with prices to match. Set menus from 250F to 550F. The culinary marvels include

CÔTES-D'ARMOR

such dishes as hot-and-cold oysters in a Vouvray sauce (*huîtres chaudes et glacées au sabayon de Vouvray*), baked turbot with spider crab (*blanc de turbot fourré à l'araignée de mer*), and Breton roast lobster (*homard breton rôti*). Accommodation is also offered here, with double rooms costing from 650F to 980F.

WHERE TO STAY AND EAT IN THE AREA

♙ ✕ Auberge du Petit Bignon: in Pluduno, 1 kilometre along the road to Cap Fréhel. ☎ and fax: 02-96-84-15-37. ✗ Hotel closed Sunday out of season. Restaurant open daily in summer, lunchtime and evening. In an old renovated farmhouse, seven rooms with shower or bath for 195F, with breakfast extra. Large room for the use of customers, where cooking and eating are permitted. In the restaurant, Isabelle Maitralain offers specialities of locally grown mussels (*bouchots*), delicious pizzas, and *crêpes* made to order, perhaps with scallops and buttered leeks (*galette 'Petit Bignon' garnie de noix de St-Jacques au fondu de poireaux*). Lunchtime menu for 55F from Monday to Friday, with an 'all you can eat' buffet of starters.

♙ ✕ Chambres et table d'hôte St-Maleu: in Bourseul, 6 kilometres (4 miles) from Plancoët. Head for Bourseul and then Jugon-les-Lacs. Open all year round. ☎ and fax: 02-96-83-01-34. On a working pig farm, Isabelle and Éric Tranchant offer six guest rooms with private shower room located in a beautiful building covered with flowers. Expect to pay 200F for two people, including breakfast, and 280F for a room for four people. Table d'hôte in the evening for an all-inclusive price of 75F. Meals are eaten with the owners at a large family table in a beautiful rustic dining room with a fireplace. The menu includes an aperitif, a starter, a choice of meat dish, local cheese, and a homemade dessert followed by coffee and homemade liqueur (*toupinette*).

The sea is just 15 kilometres (10 miles) away, but they also have private ponds 500 metres away, where you can fish and picnic beside a small animal enclosure. *Gîte* for four to five people available for rental on a weekly basis.

♙ Manoir de la Pichardais: in Créhen, 6 kilometres (4 miles) from Plancoët. ☎ 02-96-41-09-96. Open from Easter to 1 November. Take the D768 heading towards St-Malo and in Créhen, in front of the church, head for Guildo; it's 2.5 kilometres (1.5 miles) from there. You are guaranteed peace and quiet in this beautiful 16th- and 18th-century manor house, owned by their antecedents for four centuries, the Courville family have two rooms for guests – the 'Bleue' and the 'Renaissance' (named after the colossal fireplace of the same period) – with modern bathrooms. Expect to pay 400F for a double room, including breakfast served in the dining room of the house. You can also ask to have it in the kitchen, which still looks as it would have done when the house was first built. The sea is 800 metres away and the beach is just 2 kilometres (1 mile) away. Credit cards not accepted.

✕ Les Deux Moulins: in Créhen, 3 kilometres (2 miles) further along the D768 heading for Ploubalay. ☎ 02-96-84-15-40. Fax: 02-96-84-24-62. Closed Sunday evening out of season and for the first three weeks in January. They offer seven set menus ranging in price from 55F to 230F. No sophisticated gastronomic delights but healthy good cooking, with such dishes as scallop kebabs (*coquilles Saint-Jacques*), turbot in Hollandaise sauce and a very generous seafood platter. Accommodation is also available, with a double room costing 180–250F.

✕ **Chambres d'hôte La Rompardais**: at Pléven, 14 kilometres (9 miles) southwest of Plancoët. ☎ 02-96-84-43-08. Double rooms cost 235F including breakfast, with family table d'hôte meals at 85F. This is a large farmstead a little way from the village. The proprietor, Madame Blanchard, offers a friendly welcome and is a mine of information about the area. Try to get one of the rooms on the upper floors, which are the best and have attic ceilings. There's a pleasant garden with a terrace behind the house. Guests can make use of the good collection of magazines and books and there is plenty of literature about Brittany (in French).

WHAT TO SEE AND DO IN THE AREA

★ **Château de la Hunaudaye**: southwest of Plancoët, beside the D28. ☎ 02-96-34-82-10. Open April, May and September, guided tours on Sunday and public holidays 2.30–6pm; in June, tours with presentations on Sunday and public holidays 2.30–6pm; in July and August, tours with presentations daily except Saturday, 11am–noon and 2.30–6pm. Closed Sunday morning. Out of season, group visits are available if you book in advance. There's an admission charge (30F for adults; 16F for those aged 6–16), which is cheaper out of season. This impressive ruined castle, with its five large towers still standing and reflected in the moat, has a wild, rustic setting. Tours feature costumed actors, who stage a battle just for you – ideal for making childhood dreams of jousting knights come true. Theme night every Wednesday at 9pm in July and August. Inside the castle there is a fine Renaissance staircase.

★ **La Ferme d'Antan** (historic farm): in **St-Esprit-des-Bois**, 2 kilometres (1 mile) from the Château de la Hunaudaye (well signposted as you leave the latter). ☎ 02-96-34-14-67. Open daily in season 10am–7pm; in winter, open to groups by appointment. Admission charge 25F. Well laid-out open-air museum showing the history of rural life through a collection of old tools and a variety of mementoes. An educational and moving 30-minute film describes the existence of a rural family in 1924.

If you continue on towards Lamballe, don't miss the Abbaye de Boquen (*see* 'Lamballe', 'In the Area').

★ **Brasserie des Diaouligs**: to the west of Plancoët, on the D794 between Pluduno and Saint-Pôtan. ☎ 02-96-83-74-61. Open mid-June to August, daily 10am–noon and 2–6pm. Out of season, open Saturday afternoon only. This is a traditional brewery which produces three beers – a brown ale, called '*Olde Breizh*', a barley beer called '*La Diaoul*' and a lager, '*La Gwilh*'.

CÔTES-D'ARMOR

ST-CAST-LE-GUILDO
(*SANT-KAST-AR GWILDOU*) 22380 (Pop: 3,291)

This well-known seaside resort has seven beaches, the largest of which stretches for 2 kilometres (1 mile) and is protected by the Pointe de St-Cast (pronounced 'San-ka') and the Pointe de la Garde. Bathers have been walking on its fine, white sand since 1900, and artists such as Bernard Buffet, Brel and Albert Simon made the resort fashionable. Today it is a good, middle-class family resort and has even been nicknamed 'Neuilly-sur-Mer', after the highly respectable suburb of Paris. The three main meeting places are a cake shop called *La Belle Meu* (short for 'Meunière'), the sailing school and the town church at the end of Mass.

Don't miss climbing the hill at the end of the beach to reach the fishermen's quarter and the viewpoint indicator. There is a superb panoramic view of the Baie de la Fresnaye, Fort La Latte and Cap Fréhel. This is a magnificent spot from which to view the sunset.

There is a beautiful coastal walk of about 6 kilometres (4 miles) from the Pointe de St-Cast to Port-St-Jean, with pretty jagged cliffs cut by valleys. Also unmissable is the walk on the Pointe de la Garde, which provides beautiful views all along the way.

USEFUL ADDRESSES

Office du tourisme: place Charles-de-Gaulle. ☎ 02-96-41-81-52. Fax: 02-96-41-76-19. Website: www.ot-st-cast-le-guildo.fr. Open July and August, Monday to Saturday 9am–8pm, Sunday 10am–12.30pm and 3–6.30pm.The rest of the year, open Monday to Saturday 9am–noon and 2–6pm.

■ **Boat trips**: trips can be taken on the old sailing ship *Le Dragous*. ☎ 02-96-41-86-42.

■ **Centre nautique**, **école de voile** (watersports centre, sailing school): at the harbour. ☎ 02-96-41-86-42.

■ **Station de gonflage** (where divers can refill air tanks), (underwater diving): ☎ 02-96-41-81-40. Open in season 9am–7pm.

■ **Piscine municipale** (swimming pool): boulevard de la Mer. ☎ 02-96-41-87-05. Covered, heated, saltwater pool. Ideal when the weather is bad.

■ **Golf**: Plage de Pen Guen. ☎ 02-96-41-91-20. An 18-hole course.

■ **Tennis**: boulevard des Tennis. ☎ 02-96-41-80-18 (town hall) or rue du Chêne-Vert. ☎ 02-96-41-83-04.

■ **Horse-riding**: l'Écurie du Gallais – a school run by Jean-Yves Merdrignac, an accredited instructor. On the D786 between St-Cast and Notre-Dame-du-Guildo and clearly signposted. ☎ 02-96-41-04-90 or 06-86-23-75-44. Open all year round. Rides are offered on various routes: around the bay, by the sea, on the banks of the River Arguenon or through the woods. Jean-Yves knows the territory very well and loves to talk about it. During the course of the ride around the bay, he gives a detailed explanation about mussel farming. There are also pony rides for children around the farm itself. The prices are very reasonable.

■ **Marché fermier** (farmers' market): every year the **Ferme des Landes** holds a farmers' market. *See below* 'Where To Find Good Farmhouse Cider'.

WHERE TO STAY AND EAT

⛺ Nine **campsites**, one of which is **Le Châtelet** on rue des Novettes. ☎ 02-96-41-96-33. Fax: 02-96-41-97-99. Website: www.lechatelet.com. ♿ Open 1 May to 10 September. Allow about 150F for two. The most comfortable campsite (four-star) and also the most expensive. Overlooks the Baie de la Fresnaye. Beach 150 metres away. Also has a *crêperie*, TV room, games room, kids' playground, swimming pool, tennis court, volleyball court and lake for canoeing.

✩–✩✩ Budget to Moderate

⛺ ✗ **Hôtel Ker-Louis**: 15 rue Du Guesclin. ☎ and fax: 02-96-41-80-77. In a quiet spot about 200 metres from the beach. Double rooms cost 195–320F in summer and 170–280F the rest of the year. Some of the large family rooms can sleep up to eight people (expect to pay 250F for four and 570F for eight). There's a pleasant, old-fashioned charm about this modest little hotel and the welcome is excellent. The prettiest rooms are the ones with the bay windows and there's a terrace and bar, plus indoor games such as table football, billiards and table tennis. The restaurant offers a variety of seafood and fish dishes, with menus from 75F to 158F. Allow about 250F to eat à la carte.

⛺ ✗ **Hôtel Les Mielles**: in the pedestrian precinct, just 30 metres from the beach. ☎ 02-96-41-80-95. Fax: 02-96-41-77-34. Open May to mid-September only. Youthful and friendly welcome. Set in a large grey stone building, the rooms are modern, comfortable and very well looked after. Courtyard garden with an annex of two or three quiet rooms. From 365F to 450F including breakfast, in high season. Half board from 295F to 335F per person. They

also have a restaurant, Le Surnoit, with set menus from 79F to 118F.

⛺ ✗ **Hôtel des Arcades**: in the pedestrian precinct. ☎ 02-96-41-80-50. Fax: 02-96-41-77-34. Open April to September. Special weekly rates. Rooms from 415F to 620F per person, including breakfast; half board from 320F to 425F per person. The restaurant specializes in fish and seafood, and is open all day from noon to 11pm. Set menu for 84F.

✗ **Crêperie Le Bretan'or**: 8 place Anatole-Le-Braz. ☎ 02-96-41-92-45. Closed Wednesday out of season; also closed in December and January except school holidays. This is an excellent *crêperie* for holiday-makers. The owner is a nice lady who takes good care of her customers, and serves fine *crêpes* at a reasonable price.

✗ **Les Halles**: 21 rue du Duc-d'Aiguillon. Open April to September. Closed Tuesday lunchtime and Wednesday except in July and August. This is a friendly little brasserie where the dishes are advertised on a large board outside. They specialize in seafood and fish dishes; mussels and oysters are available at any time of day. Set menus start at 72F.

✩✩✩ Chic

⛺ ✗ **Hôtel-restaurant Les Dunes**: rue Primauguet, in the town centre, 200 metres from the beach. ☎ 02-96-41-80-31. Fax: 02-96-41-85-34. Open April to October. Warm, refined and very well run, this is a typical Logis de France of the 1930s. Rooms from 370F to 390F, all with shower, toilet and TV. Compulsory half board during school holidays and holiday weekends. Expect to pay from 350F to 400F per person, with breakfast extra. The

CÔTES-D'ARMOR

restaurant is renowned for its cuisine, with set menus from 110F to 380F and offers such fish and seafood specialities as prawn fritters with citrus fruits (*beignets de langoustines aux agrumes*), warm lobster salad (*salade de homard tiède*), or escalope of duck's liver in Sauternes (*escalope de foie de canard au sauternes*). Complimentary house aperitif. Tennis court for hotel guests only.

WHERE TO STAY AND EAT IN THE AREA

🛏 ✕ **Hôtel-restaurant de la Poste**: 11 place Gouyon, 22550 Matignon; 6 kilometres (4 miles) from St-Cast on the D13. ☎ 02-96-41-02-20. Fax: 02-96-41-18-21. ⚒ Closed Sunday evening and Monday out of season; also closed for two weeks in October and three weeks in January. Good location as a base for touring around the whole region and returning in the evening to a bit of peace and quiet, comfort and fine food. Rooms are pleasant and Marcel Girard's cooking is good and varied, using home-grown products. Expect to pay from 170F to 270F for a double room, according to the degree of comfort. Attractive prices for single nights and half board. Cheapest set menu for 75F; expect to pay around 115F for à la carte. Excellent smoked salmon and homemade *foie gras*. A very good choice for a peaceful stopover.

🛏 **Château du Val d'Arguenon**: with M. and Mme de la Blanchardière, 22380 Notre-Dame-du-Guildo. ☎ 02-96-41-07-03. Fax: 02-96-41-02-67. Located 9 kilometres (5.5 miles) to the south on the road to St-Jacut-de-la-Mer. Closed from October to March. A 16th-century private home, set back around 200 metres from the road, where Chateaubriand came several times to relax. Five spacious guest rooms with antique furnishings, costing from 460F to 610F including breakfast. Tennis court on site, and a wide choice of activities close by. Three substantial houses, very roomy and well equipped, for four to six people, are available for rental in the grounds for 1,400F to 4000F per week according to the season.

🛏 **Chambres d'hôte at the Logis du Gallais farmhouse**: on the D786 between St-Cast and Notre-Dame-du-Guildo and well signposted. ☎ 02-96-41-04-90 or 06-86-23-75-44 (mobile). Open from Easter to the beginning of September. A double room costs 220F including breakfast. This pretty little stone-built house is tucked away in a quiet country spot not far from the sea and is run by two very likeable farmers, Pascale and Jean-Yves Merdrignac. The rooms are attractive, with everything that you need, and there's a relaxed, family atmosphere about the place. Jean-Yves has another string to his bow as he offers excellent horse-riding sessions by the sea and around the nearby bays. *See* 'Useful Addresses'.

✕ **La Crêperie de Saint-Germain**: from Matignon, 6 kilometres (4 miles) from St-Cast on the D13, take the D786 towards Fréhel and drive for about 1 kilometre. Then turn right towards Saint-Germain, which is about 2 kilometres (1 mile) further on. The *crêperie* is on the village square. ☎ 02-96-41-08-33. Allow 40–50F to really fill yourself up. Open every day from noon, during the Easter holidays and during July and August. A visit to this quiet little village overlooking the Bay of Fresnay is worthwhile just to get a taste of some excellent *crêpes* and *galettes*. The proprietor, Madame

Eudes, knows exactly what she's doing when it comes to batter and pastry, making traditional specialities in the time-honoured way and with quality ingredients. The ham used in the *galettes* is the real thing and not from a vacuum-pack – which is quite rare. Everything is excellent, including the ancient building itself, and it's not expensive. In summer you can eat on the terrace.

✗ **Le Gilles de Bretagne**: by the harbour in Notre-Dame-du-Guildo, 9 kilometres (5.5 miles) from St-Cast. ☎ 02-96-41-07-08. Closed Monday and Tuesday except in summer; also closed in January. Reservations recommended for the evening meal in summer and at weekends. Fish and seafood specialities. Menus from 78F to 176F. The seafood menu for two people for 570F includes a huge platter of seafood, a *trou normand* ('Norman hole' – a break between courses for a glass of Calvados), 700g (24oz) of grilled Brittany lobster brought live to the table, and then cheese and

dessert. From the picture windows of the first-floor dining room, there is a view of the River Arguenon. This restaurant is well known in the area thanks to the consistently high quality of its cuisine and the personality of the lady who owns it.

✗ ♠ **Le Vieux Château**: 10 kilometres (6 miles) to the south, on the road to St-Jacut-de-la-Mer; on the left after the bridge if you are coming from St-Cast. ☎ 02-96-41-07-28. Fax: 02-96-41-14-36. Closed Wednesday in winter; also closed in February. A hotel-restaurant recommended above all for the cuisine. The fresh produce, pleasant setting and cheerful service cannot be faulted. The set menu for 79F, for example, might include six excellent oysters, calf's head (*tête de veau*), and crispy pig's trotter (*croustillant de pied de porc*), which will delight connoisseurs of good food, as well as beautifully prepared homemade desserts. The other set menus cost 98F and 145F. Rooms for 250F unfortunately all overlook the street, but they are double-glazed.

SWEET TREATS

– **La Belle Meunière**: 18 rue du Duc-d'Aiguillon (a shopping street near the beach). ☎ 02-96-41-82-22. Open during school holidays and daily from Easter to mid-September. Known as '*La Belle Meu*', this is a favourite port-of-call for regular visitors, who come to take a break from sunbathing and enjoy a drink and some cake. Try the *castin*, a speciality from St-Cast, the *Coupe Windsurf* or the *kouign aman tatin* (with apples).

WHAT TO SEE IN THE AREA

★ **Port du Guildo**: on the road from Matignon to Ploubalay. One of the most beautiful scenic spots in the area. On the left as you come from Matignon, after crossing the large bridge, lie a delightful group of granite fishermen's houses and the ruins of the 14th-century Château du Guildo. At low tide, the estuary shimmers with fascinating plays of light. Located on the hill, as you enter the village of Notre-Dame-du-Guildo, the Miriel bakery makes delicious cakes and pastries, and a famous bread baked in a wood-fired oven.

★ **Plage des Quatre-Vaux**: beach between St-Cast and Notre-Dame-du-Guildo. Just about the nicest little place you could ever wish to find.

CÔTES-D'ARMOR

WHERE TO FIND GOOD FARMHOUSE CIDER

– **La Ferme des Landes**: on the D786 just before Notre-Dame-du-Guildo as you come from Matignon or St-Cast. ☎ 02-96-41-12-48. Open April, May and September, daily except Sunday 2–9pm; in June, July and August, daily 10am–8pm; October to March, Friday and Saturday 9am–noon and 2–6pm. It's possible to book in advance. For a number of years now Jehan Lefèvre has been making his delicious farmhouse cider using local fruit, producing a drink that has just the right balance of tang and sweetness. The more elderly people of the area say that his cider tastes just like the cider of old. Jehan also produces an excellent prize-winning apple juice and a cider vinegar. You can come here to sample the goods and buy, of course, but there's also a very interesting little exhibition on apples and traditional methods of making cider. It's worth noting that there's an excellent **farmers' market** held on the farm every Friday in July and August (5–8.30pm). About 15 local producers come to sell their crops and craft products. There are demonstrations of traditional methods, musical entertainment, and the inevitable bar selling cider, *galettes* and *crêpes*.

CAP FRÉHEL AND FORT LA LATTE

Often buffeted by strong winds blowing off the open sea, Cap Fréhel is one of the most impressive places on the Côte d'Émeraude. When visibility is good, the Normandy peninsula (known as Le Cotentin), the Channel Island of Jersey and the Île de Bréhat can be seen from here. A lighthouse stands atop a cliff with a sheer 70-metre (227-foot) drop. Vegetation is sparse and there are large expanses of heathland. In **Pléhérel**, 6 kilometres (4 miles) before the point, there is a splendid dune-lined beach. Here, on certain days, the emerald green appearance of the sea explains the name given to this stretch of coastline. Halfway between Fréhel and the Plages de la Guette, there is the naturist beach of Port-du-Sud-Est.

The district maintains 70 kilometres (40 miles) of paths; one of the best is the superb circuit from the point to the Fort La Latte. The coastal path runs alongside high cliffs with constantly changing colours, actually following the GR34 hiking path, which goes as far as Port-à-la-Duc at the bottom of the bay. There is a bird sanctuary (*réserve d'oiseaux*), where certain species remain rare in spite of everything being done to protect them. A modest charge for admission to the point is more than justified by the efforts being made to protect and re-establish endangered species.

WHERE TO STAY AND EAT IN THE AREA

⌂ **Camping du Pont de l'Étang**: Pléhérel-Plage, among the dunes. ☎ 02-96-41-40-45. Open from May to September.

⌂ **Auberge de jeunesse du Cap Fréhel** (youth hostel): in La Ville-Hardrieux, Kérivet-en-Fréhel (signposted from the road). ☎ and fax: 02-96-41-48-98. ☖ Open April to September. 45F per night per person and breakfast for 20F. Half board for 114F per person. Rooms accommodate between two and eight people. Camping allowed. Meals served. Bicycle and mountain bike rental.

🏠 **Le Fanal**: go as far as Cap Fréhel, then head back towards Plévenon. ☎ 02-96-41-43-19. Open May to September. Tall, impeccable chalet in a surprisingly modern and quite successful architectural style reminiscent of Scandinavia, which fits in perfectly with the landscape of barren moorland stretching as far as the ocean. Comfortable rooms from 250F to 340F. Nos. 6 to 9 are roomier than the others. Private car park and large, peaceful garden. Excellent welcome.

🏠 **Le Relais de Fréhel, gîtes and chambres d'hôte**: 1.5 kilometres from Plévenon on the Cap Fréhel road. ☎ 02-96-41-43-02. Fax: 02-96-41-30-09. Open from Easter to 1 November. A double room costs 300F including breakfast. An old farmhouse beautifully restored by the granddaughter of the former owners, set in 2 hectares (5 acres) of peaceful wooded grounds, right at the heart of the rather intriguing moorland landscape that sweeps across to Cap Fréhel. The five guest rooms and the dining room are all very elegant, and the whole place

has a tasteful simplicity. They also have *gîtes* to rent by the week, with prices varying according to the season. Myriam Fournel gives a warm welcome and advice about activities available, such as walks, beaches, mountain biking, horse-riding, the 18-hole golf course and the on-site tennis court. A high-quality stopover point that is ideal for discovering the genuine and unspoiled Brittany. Highly recommended.

✕ **Crêperie La Clepsydre**: in the old town at Pléherel-Plage, about 5 kilometres (3 miles) from Cap Fréhel in the direction of Sables d'Or. ☎ 02-96-41-41-21. Open daily lunchtime and evening from April to September. Closed January to March. Allow 70–100F for a really big meal. This restaurant is in a little white house with a terrace. The charming village location is popular with local people and its fame is justified. Everything is prepared to order using fresh produce, and the menu specializes in *galettes* and *crêpes* that have unusual and very tasty fillings. They also sell decent cider and Breton beers.

SWEET TREATS

– **Pâtissier-Chocolatier R. Jouault**: at Fréhel. ☎ 02-96-41-41-31. Open daily in summer 7.30am–8pm; shorter opening hours out of season. Don't leave Fréhel without tasting the specialities they make in this excellent place. Their *kouign amann* cakes are also delicious.

WHAT TO SEE

★ **Le phare** (lighthouse): can be visited daily in summer, 2–6pm, and the friendly keeper explains its workings. One of the most important lighthouses in Brittany, its beacons are visible for almost 120 kilometres (75 miles) in fine weather. Beautiful granite architecture dating from the 1950s. Those who are brave enough to climb the 145 steps to the top are rewarded by an amazing panoramic view of the Côte d'Émeraude and fields of heather. Weather permitting, it is even possible to catch a glimpse of Jersey. There's a strong wind up there, so take a sweater.

★ **Fort La Latte**: open all year round, on Sunday and during the school holidays, 2.30–5.30pm; during the Easter holidays and from June to

September, 10am–7.30pm. ☎ 02-96-41-40-31. Guided 45-minute tour. Admission charge 20F. Renovated in the 17th century, the fort was originally built in the 13th century on the site of a fortified town protecting the entrance to the Baie de la Fresnaye. Du Guesclin laid siege to it in 1379. *The Vikings*, a film starring Kirk Douglas and Tony Curtis, was made here in the 1950s. Perched high up on a very picturesque, steep slope, it towers above one of the most beautiful bays in Brittany. There is not a great deal worth seeing inside the fort but the journey on foot to get there is pleasant enough. It is also interesting to visit the foundry, which made it possible to fire red-hot cannonballs and set fire to enemy ships. Only a few examples of this type of furnace are left in Europe.

SABLES-D'OR-LES-PINS 22240

A seaside resort created from scratch in the 1920s to compete with Normandy's Deauville, further along France's northern coast. Due to financial problems, Word War II and perhaps over-ambition, Sables-d'Or-les-Pins was never actually completed. As a result, there is a handful of hotels with Normandy-style facades and a few large villas lining wide avenues leading to nowhere. It is nothing spectacular in itself and in low season there is something rather surreal about the place. However, it's easy to feel a fondness for it, if for no other reason than the fact that it has a magnificent beach with 3 kilometres (2 miles) of fine sand.

USEFUL ADDRESSES

◻ Syndicat d'initiative (tourist office): on the beach. ☎ 02-96-41-51-97. Open from 15 June to 15 September. Out of season: ☎ 02-96-41-53-81 (in Fréhel).

◻ Office du Tourisme: in the village of Plurien, 2 kilometres (1 mile) from Sables d'Or. ☎ 02-96-72-18-52. Email: otplurien@aol.com. Open in summer, Monday–Saturday 9.30am–12.30pm and 2–7pm, Sunday 10am–noon. Out of season, open 2.30–5pm (10am–noon in January).

■ Casino: facing the beach. Very small, and full of slot machines.

■ Pony and horse-riding on the beach: run by the 'Les Cognets' riding school at Plurien. ☎ 02-97-72-47-00 or 06-10-75-86-64. Lessons and rides in the countryside and by the sea, for all ages and all abilities.

WHERE TO STAY AND EAT

⌂ Camping municipal: coming from Erquy, as you come into the town, on the left. ☎ 02-96-72-17-40. Allow about 75F for two people with one car, including parking space and electricity. In terraced rows on the hillside. Pleasant location. Beach about 500 metres away.

⌂ ✕ Hôtel-Restaurant-Bar Le Commerce: rue Montaque, in the village of Plurien. ☎ 02-96-72-46-50. Double rooms for 170F (230F with a third person). Shared shower and toilet. This little hotel is good to know if you're on a tight budget. It's a modest place, recently renovated and well kept. You can eat in the restaurant for 55F.

⌂ ✕ Hôtel des Pins: not far from the beach. ☎ 02-96-41-42-20. Fax:

02-96-41-59-02. Closed from 1 October to 1 April. Rooms for 220F (shower) and 300F (shower and toilet). Half board compulsory in July and August, from 220F to 310F per person. Cheapest set menu for 78F. A charming, old-fashioned little hotel, and very clean. Mini-golf and garden.

🛏 **Chambres d'hôte Les Cognets**: in Plurien. ☎ 02-96-72-47-00. Open all year round. Beautifully restored 16th-century farmhouse, with four rooms and a two-room apartment with a view of the sea, which can sleep up to six. There's also a pretty little cottage. The double rooms cost 220F (300F for four), the apartment costs 600F and the little house is available for 300F per day or 2,000F for a week. Breakfast is extra (30F). The modern, brightly coloured furniture goes well with the pointed arches of the doorways, and it doesn't take long to feel at home in the warm and friendly atmosphere of the place. There are two very nice living rooms for guests as well as a huge garden. Riding school with ponies. Lessons with a qualified instructor, for children from the age of four.

🛏 **Manoir de la Salle**: rue du Lac, 22240 Plurien; 2 kilometres (1 mile) from Sables-d'Or-les-Pins, out in the countryside and just before you reach Fréhel. ☎ 02-96-72-38-29. Fax: 02-96-72-00-57. Website: www.manoir-de-la-salle.com. ♿ Open from the beginning of April to the beginning of October. This is a large and dignified 16th-century stone building, which seems to be quite the fashion around these parts. You enter through a 15th-century Gothic portal. The rooms are bright and comfortable, with modern furniture, and cost 250–400F for a double room (reduction for bookings of a week or more); in low season, they cost 200–300F. There are also two *gîtes* that sleep four to six people, costing 500–650F depending on the season. There's a billiards table, table tennis and a solarium on site, plus a golf course close by. A very good place, run by a relaxed and friendly young couple.

✕ **La Potinière Mady**: facing the beach. ☎ 02-96-41-54-69. Open from Easter to the end of September, 9.30am–midnight. Outside normal mealtimes, this is a bar and tearoom. Pleasant and reasonably priced (dishes cost 26–50F); just the place in summer to indulge in seafood, mussels and chips (*moules-frites*), scallops or a salad – all quick and inexpensive dishes.

☆☆☆ Chic

🛏 ✕ **La Voile d'Or**: as you come into the resort, opposite the lagoon. ☎ 02-96-41-42-49. Fax: 02-96-41-55-45. Set menus are offered for 160F up to 400F. The very comfortable rooms have all been renovated, and cost 400–700F. This establishment has been taken over by a chef with a good local reputation, who serves excellent cuisine in a very elegant dining room.

FESTIVAL

– **Fête mediévale de Plurien**: held the penultimate week of July. This enjoyable medieval festival includes people in costume, demonstrations of old skills, plus plenty of good food and drink, and live music and performances.

CÔTES-D'ARMOR

WHAT TO SEE

★ **Atelier Orfeu**: place de l'Église, Plurien. ☎ 02-96-72-04-07. Open in July and August daily, 11am–12.30pm and 4–7.30pm; also open at weekends at Easter, in May and at Christmas, and by appointment for the rest of the year. This workshop has a marvellous range of goods, from ceramics, sculpture and jewellery to photographs and drawings.

ERQUY (*ERGE-AR-MOR*) 22430 (Pop: 3,841)

This busy fishing port is also the capital of the *coquille St-Jacques* (scallop). Although popular with tourists in summer, the town has managed to avoid becoming filled with ugly hotels and has retained its charm. It is largely given over to sports and leisure activities such as kayaking, mountain-biking and rock-climbing.

The Cap d'Erquy is famous for hang-gliding and shoreline fishing, as described in Colette's novel *Le Blé en Herbe*.

USEFUL ADDRESSES

🅸 **Office du tourisme**: boulevard de la Mer; in the same building as the sailing school, the Immeuble de l'Escurial. ☎ 02-96-72-30-12. Fax: 02-96-72-02-88. Website: www.erquy-tourisme.com. In high season, open daily, 9.30am–12.30pm and 2–7pm; out of season, open daily, 9.30am–noon and 2–5pm. Friendly staff.

■ **École de voile** (sailing school): on the harbour, at the 'Maison de la Mer'. ☎ 02-96-72-32-62.

■ **École de plongée** (diving school): at the same address as the sailing school. ☎ and fax, 02-96-72-49-67. Offers diving at the Cap d'Erquy, which is a beautiful site.

■ **École de pêche du bord** (fishing school): in summer, twice a week, local fishermen offer lessons in line fishing. All equipment is provided. Ask at the tourist office for details.

■ **Char à voile** (sand-yachting): on the Plage de St-Pabu and the Plage de la Ville-Berneuf. ☎ 02-96-72-95-28. Lessons and courses are offered by this sand-yachting club.

■ **Quincaillerie Morgand**: place du Nouvel-Oupeye. Michel and Josette Morgand sell everything in this hardware shop and they know all there is to know about the region.

WHERE TO STAY

Campsites

🛖 **Camping Les Roches**: in Caroual Village, opposite the large Plage de Caroual. Access via the D786 between Erquy and Val-André. ☎ and fax: 02-96-72-32-90. Open from April to mid-September. A pitch costs 15F and the price per adult is 17F. A well-located and reasonably priced two-star campsite. Mini-golf (free), table tennis, volleyball, and so on. A good welcome is guaranteed. Mobile homes are also available for rent, costing 1,200–2,400F per week.

🛖 **Camping Les Pins**: on the road to Le Guen. ☎ and fax: 02-96-72-31-12. Open from mid-April to mid-

September. A pitch costs 18F and there's a charge of 18F per car and 25F per person. Located in a pine forest on the cliff. Suitable for those who want peace and quiet rather than proximity to the beach. Tennis court and pool on site. The comfort and facilities of a three-star campsite.

🛏 **Camping Le Vieux Moulin**: rue des Moulins. ☎ 02-96-72-34-23 and 06-11-30-81-87. Fax: 02-96-72-36-63. Open from April to September. Recommended four-star site with 175 spaces, with heated pool and tennis court.

☆–☆☆ Budget to Moderate

🛏 **Le Reflet de la Mer**: *see below* 'Where To Eat'.

🛏 ✕ **Hôtel Beauséjour**: 21 rue de la Corniche. ☎ 02-96-72-30-39. Fax: 02-96-72-16-30. Restaurant closed Monday out of season. On an overhang, just 100 metres from the harbour. Small, traditional holiday hotel in a quiet area. Well-kept rooms, from 250F to 320F with shower and toilet. Attractively priced half board from 285–335F per person, compulsory from mid-July to the end of August. Copious and delicious set menus from 85F to 172F, including such delicacies as scallop kebabs in a crab sauce

(*brochettes de St-Jacques au coulis d'étrilles*) and seafood sauerkraut (*choucroute du pêcheur*).

🛏 ✕ **Hôtel-restaurant Le Relais**: 60 rue du Port. ☎ 02-96-72-32-60. Fax: 02-96-72-19-57. Closed Wednesday evening and Thursday out of season; also closed late November to early December, and during the February school holidays. Quite a friendly hotel with a sea view (just a few metres from the harbour), completely refurbished and well maintained. Double rooms from 300F (shower) to 350F (bath, balcony, TV). Also a restaurant with a set menu for 78F.

🛏 **Chambres d'hôte Les Bruyères**: route des Hôpitaux. Leaving the town centre, head towards Les Hôpitaux; after about 1.5 kilometres, turn left and follow the signs. ☎ 02-96-72-31-59. Fax: 02-96-72-04-68. Aline and Prosper will give you a warm welcome all year round to the three guest rooms in their home, one of which has a terrace and balcony. Two adjoining rooms can accommodate a family of four. Self-catering possible. Garden and play area. The closest beach is 1.5 kilometres away. Expect to pay 280F for a double room out of season and 340F in season, including a generous breakfast.

WHERE TO EAT

✕ **Le Roof**: at the opening to the harbour. ☎ 02-96-72-16-11. Open from February to mid-November, daily during school holidays, otherwise only at the weekend. Karine has taken over the running of this 'bar-*crêperie*-ice-cream parlour' with a marine decor and a beautiful terrace facing the sea and harbour, and gives a friendly and informal welcome. Her *galette* specialities include the 'Côtes-d'Armor' and the 'Nazado', made with scallops

from the bay. The *galette au beurre* (with butter) costs from 13F. The waffles (*gauffres*) are also very good. For dessert, you'll be spoiled for choice with 35 different ice-cream dishes. Everything here is homemade from traditional recipes and Karine is carrying on the family tradition started by her mother and grandmother. It's a small community where everyone knows everyone else, and Karine's husband manages the Sables-d'Or tennis courts.

CÔTES-D'ARMOR

✕ 🏠 **Crêperie and rooms to rent,
Le Reflet de la Mer**: 18 rue du
Port. ☎ 02-96-72-00-95. Open
from April to September. Closed Friday out of season. Facing the Plage
du Centre, a little place with authentic and delicious traditional *galettes*
from 12F to 40F, which can be
enjoyed either on the terrace or in
the all blue-and-white dining room.
Also, seven plain but clean guest
rooms with basin and bidet (all
other facilities on the landing) for
170F, and six ground-floor rooms
looking out on a peaceful garden
full of flowers, for a terrific price of
140F. This is a good little place with
a simple and friendly atmosphere.

✕ **Restaurant Le Nelumbo**: 5 rue
de l'Église. ☎ 02-96-72-31-31.
Closed Sunday evening and Monday out of season and public holidays, plus at the end of February
and the last two weeks of November. In the town centre. Set menus
for 78F (weekdays) to 160F, and the
Formule St-Jacques (with scallops)
for 120F. They serve a wide range of
fish and seafood dishes, including
monkfish roasted in olive oil (*gigot
de lotte rôti à l'huile d'olive*) and king
prawns in a cheese sauce (*queues
de langoustines gratinées*).

✕ **Restaurant La Cassolette**: 6
rue de la Saline. ☎ 02-96-72-13-
08. Just 50 metres from the beach,
where it's convenient to park outside, and not far from the place de la
Poste. Closed Thursday and Friday
lunchtime out of season, and in
December and January. They serve
a decent lunchtime set menu with

main course and dessert for 68F
and five other set menus from 79F
to 235F. Expect to spend 250F if
eating à la carte. The people of
Erquy are very lucky to have two
really good restaurants in such a
small place: this one and L'Escurial
(*see below*). Here the up-and-coming young chef, with lots of experience working in some of the top
restaurants, is allowed to show off
his talents under the care of the lady
owner. Seafood is the house speciality – not surprising with the sea so
close at hand. The menu is filled with
mouth-watering items such as scallops in pastry (*ravioles de Saint-
Jacques*) and king prawns in orange
sauce (*cassolette de langoustines à
l'orange*). The desserts are every bit
as exotic. The setting is also very
attractive – a little dining room decorated in rustic style, with a large
fireplace. There's a terrace and
garden for eating outside in fine
weather. First-class service and a
good welcome.

✕ **Restaurant L'Escurial**: boulevard de la Mer. ☎ 02-96-72-31-56.
Closed Sunday evening and Monday. Open daily in August. One of
the best restaurants in the region.
View of the open sea from the dining
room, which has comfortable,
green-and-white leather armchairs.
Set menu for 110F, with other
menus from 160F to 260F. Seafood
specialities include John Dory with
foie gras and tagliatelle (*St-Pierre
poêlé au foie gras et tagliatelles*).
Good value for money is guaranteed, so it's advisable to book.

SWEET TREATS

– **Pâtisserie Le Jardin de Ker Étienne**: 1 rue de la Corniche. ☎ 02-96-72-
09-61. Local sweet delicacies, including *Noix de St-Jacques*.

WHERE TO STAY AND EAT IN THE AREA

🛏 **Chambres d'hôte with M. and Mme Balan**: 1 rue du 3-Août-1944, La Couture; 4 kilometres (2.5 miles) from Erquy on the road from Pléneuf to St-Brieuc. ☎ 02-96-72-38-58. Open from June to September. The house is charming, the garden is full of flowers and there are three delightful and impeccably clean rooms that cost 250–270F including breakfast. A friendly welcome and outside access to the rooms. The only fly in the ointment is this beautiful granite house's location – at the crossroads of two main roads (the 786 and the D34). Earplugs are indispensable for light sleepers, but otherwise the place cannot be faulted.

🛏 ✕ **Auberge La Bonnaie**: 2 kilometres (1 mile) from La Bouillie, on the road to Pléneuf-Val-André, the D17. ☎ 02-96-31-51-71. Closed Sunday evening and Monday out of season; also closed in October. An old farmhouse right out in the countryside which has been made into a small neighbourhood restaurant. If you book in advance, you will be served hotpot, guinea fowl (*pintade*), or rib-steak cooked over a wood fire (*entrecôte cuite au feu de bois*). Also homemade tarts and a delicious *far breton* (traditional Breton cake). A copious set menu for only 97F, guest rooms for 220F, and half board for 190F. A good welcome is guaranteed.

✕ **Relais St-Aubin**: 3 kilometres (2 miles) from Erquy, on the D68 (heading towards La Bouillie), signposted from the main road (the D34). ☎ 02-96-72-13-22. Closed Monday, Tuesday out of season, and during the February school holidays. Reservations essential in high season, and all year round at weekends. Located in a hamlet, this characterful old house with a large garden was formerly a 17th-century priory, and offers complete peace and quiet. A delightfully rustic and romantic spot. Gorgeous dining room with beams, antique furniture and a huge granite fireplace, and eating on the terrace in summer. There are various set menus, including one for 80F (weekday lunchtime), and from 118F to 190F (three courses plus scallops) in the evening. Attractively priced dish of the day posted on the slate (about 80F). Dishes from the à la carte menu include monkfish stewed in cider (*marmite de joues de lotte infusées au cidre*) and mussel fricassée with bacon in cider (*fricassée de moules au lard et au cidre*). There's something to suit every budget and appetite, in an exceptional setting with a welcome to match. Extremely good service. An excellent house wine: the *menetou-salon* (red or white).

WHERE TO GO FOR A DRINK

🍸 **Pub-pizzeria Les Salines**: on the main road (the *nationale*), in the town centre. ☎ 02-96-72-31-73. Closed Monday and Friday lunchtime out of season. A young people's bar with delicious and generous pizzas and salads. The cheapest set menu costs 55F (lunchtime only). Billiards and video games.

CÔTES-D'ARMOR

WHAT TO SEE AND DO IN AND AROUND ERQUY

★ **Cap d'Erquy**: this place has offered exceptionally good walks since the preservation of the Garenne d'Erquy woodland began. It's a rocky promontory, with magnificent pink sandstone cliffs, and covered with moorland and heather. Erquy sandstone (*le grès d'Erquy*) was actually used to construct a part of the Arc de Triomphe in the French capital, and is even found in the paving stones of Lisbon in Portugal. The 170 hectares (425 acres) now belong to the Conservatoire du Littoral (national body for the preservation of the coastline), and so the narrow coastal paths leading to small, unspoiled beaches are once again open to exploration by careful visitors. On the Pointe des Trois-Pierres, which, along with the headland, borders the beautiful Anse (cove) de Port-Blanc, the vestiges remain of an 18th-century foundry, where cannonballs were heated to red-hot before being shot at enemy ships. A *chemin de douanier* (customs officers' path) leads to the Plage de Lourtuais, enjoyed by naturists, then to the Plage de Portuais. At low tide, Sables-d'Or can be reached via the beach.

– On the point in summer, there are **visites à thèmes** (themed tours). Details from the tourist office. ☎ 02-96-72-30-12.

– **Boat trip on the Sainte-Jeanne**: exploration of the coastline in a delightful old sailing ship. Costs 150F for a half-day. Details from the tourist office.

– **Randonnée pédestre** (hike): 14 kilometres (9 miles) long. Allow about 3 hours 30 minutes for the return journey without any stops. A fairly easy loop starting from the car park at the Plage d'Erquy, 35 kilometres (22 miles) east of St-Brieuc. Markers: white and red markers of the GR34 hiking path, and blue. Map: IGN 1015 Sud (south).

A panoramic landscape with views of jagged cliffs, moorland in bloom and the fine sand of the Plage de Caroual. The land fortifications date back to Roman times.

Starting at the car park, the GR34 footpath runs along the Cap d'Erquy and rises above the Plage du Lourtuais. Along the way, the cannonball foundry and the Camp de César are worth a visit. The *oppidum* (Roman hillfort) at Cap d'Erquy, or the Camp de César as it is called, is on the site of a hillfort dating from the Iron Age. Dating from a few thousand years earlier, two trench systems are visible: the Fossé Catuelan, which cuts off the tip of the Cap d'Erquy from north to south, and the Fossé de Pleine-Garenne. Many traces of the era are discernible beneath the grass.

The route along the cliffs overlooks the sea, offering some very beautiful panoramic views. At the Domaine de Lanruen on the Plage du Guen, a blue marker indicates a path heading south as far as the dolmen of La Ville-Hamon. Not long afterwards, another path crosses it, still with a blue marker, and follows the old railway line. Return via the Plage de Caroual south of Erquy and the GR34 hiking path, which takes you back to the car park.

The tourist office can supply a little booklet that gives detailed descriptions of all the walks that can be done in and around Erquy.

– Every day in July, August and September, the tourist office for the 'Caps' organizes trips and expeditions that focus on everything from nature and history to culture and the local economy. Ask for the leaflet called *D'un cap à l'autre* at the tourist office.

★ **Château de Bienassis**: a stone's throw from the D34, between Erquy and Pléneuf-Val-André. ☎ 02-96-72-22-03. From mid-June to mid-September, guided tours 10.30am–12.30pm and 2–6.30pm, except Sunday morning; the rest of the year, by appointment only for groups. Admission charge 25F (15F for children aged 7 and over, students and groups of 20 people or more). Beautiful 15th- and 17th-century fortified edifice, with fine Breton Renaissance furniture and formal French gardens. The castle has belonged to the same family since 1880.

FESTIVALS AND EVENTS

– **La Fête de la Coquille** (scallop festival): celebration of the *coquille St-Jacques*, which happens every third year, in rotation with similar events at Saint-Quay-Portrieux and Loguivy-de-la-Mer. The next one should take place here in early April 2002. Everything there is to know about the *coquille St-Jacques*, from catching and farming them, to eating them. There is also a scallop-opening competition – the record is 50 in 4 minutes.

– **Concerts**: free concerts take place every Tuesday evening in summer.

PLÉNEUF-VAL-ANDRÉ
(*PLENEG-NANTRAEZH*) 22370   (Pop: 3,771)

Built in 1888, this resort has retained the quaint charm of the early 20th century. As a concession to modernization, there is an immense seawall with an esplanade which runs along the beautiful, fine sand of the Plage de Val-André for a distance of 2.5 kilometres (1.5 miles). Around Val-André, which is classed as a yachting centre, are the village of Pléneuf and the port of Dahouët, once the home port where fisherman going to Icelandic waters registered their boats. Located at the far end of a bottle-shaped inlet surrounded by steep hills, and with its 400 floating docks, it is a safe haven for pleasure boats.

USEFUL ADDRESSES

🏠 **Office du tourisme**: cours Winston-Churchill, beside the casino. ☎ 02-96-72-20-55. Fax: 02-96-63-00-34. Email: pleneuf@clubinternet.fr. Open Monday to Saturday 9am–1pm and 2–7pm, and Sunday (April to September) and public holidays 10am–12.30pm and 4–6pm.

■ **Centre nautique de Dahouët** (sailing school): ☎ 02-96-72-95-28. Sailing school for residential and day courses. Sand-yachting is available.

■ **Golf**: Plage des Vallées. ☎ 02-96-63-01-12. A recently built 18-hole golf course in a very pretty location. Highly rated by golfers.

■ **Tennis**: parc de l'Amirauté at Le Val-André. A number of hard courts are available. Each year in early August a major national tournament takes place here.

■ **Promenades en bateau** (boat trips): on *La Pauline*, a former yacht. ☎ 02-96-63-10-99. Costs 130F for 2 hours.

■ **Randonnées au clair de lune** (moonlight walks): walks by night are held, one in July and one in August, either going in the direction of Hillion and the bay or in the direction of Erquy. Details are available from the tourist office.

■ **Casino**: on the seafront, behind the tourist office. ☎ 02-96-72-85-06. Open all year round, 10am–3am (4am on Saturday). Everything from slot machines to roulette. Quite small and not at all upmarket, with stakes beginning at 1F.

■ **Markets**: every Tuesday at Pléneuf there's a market spread out all around the church. It's a great place, where, if you fancy it, you can stroll around and look at the stalls while munching a sausage-filled *galette*. The best snacks are to be had from Charpentier, who parks his van on place de l'Église opposite the Hôtel de France. In summer, there's also a Friday market at Le Val-André.

WHERE TO STAY

⌂ There are three equally good **campsites** (all three-star); **La-Ville-Berneuf** is nearest to the sea. ☎ 02-96-72-28-20. Open from March to October.

⌂ **Hôtel de la Mer**: 63 rue Amiral-Charner. In the centre of Val-André, on the road that runs parallel with the sea. ☎ 02-96-72-20-44. Fax: 02-96-72-85-72. Closed in January. A two-star hotel, with a pleasant welcome and well-kept rooms. From 210F for a double, rising up to 350F. Good food (*see also* 'Where To Eat'). Half board compulsory in July and August

⌂ **Hôtel Printania**: 34 rue Charles-Cotard. ☎ 02-96-72-20-51. Open from Easter to mid-October. Single rooms from 140F; double rooms from 160F to 320F. Breakfast is extra (30F). Very well placed and in a quiet location close to the centre of town, on a street overlooking the beach, this large early 20th-century bourgeois house fits in well with the style of the resort. Run by a German gentleman, it is clean and tidy.

⌂ **Chambres d'hôte Le Clos Fontaine**: 5 rue de la Corderie. ☎ and fax: 02-96-63-08-53. Open April to November and out of season by reservation. ☎ 06-68-10-12-05. Double rooms cost 250F and there's a family room with kitchen for 290F with a supplement of 70F per extra person. Breakfast is included. This nicely restored and flower-covered building is just 3 minutes' walk from the village of Pléneuf and 10 minutes' walk from the beach. The owner, Maud Le Nai-Meheut, lavishes plenty of care and attention on her visitors. The bedrooms are spotlessly clean; the decor is attractive and each room has a theme. One of the two 'rooms' is in fact a split-level apartment, with a double bed up top and two singles down below, plus a kitchen and dining area. It also has its own entrance. This is ideal for a family, and there's even a nappy-changing table. An excellent place.

⌂ **Rooms and apartments for rent, Chez Max**: for details, *see below* 'Where To Go for a Drink'. Just 150 metres from the beach. Prices range from 1,500F per week for a double room to 1,800F per week for an apartment with three bedrooms. Max also rents rooms for shorter periods at very reasonable rates (about 200F per day). These rooms are either above or next door to his bar and have all been tastefully redecorated, using bright, lively colours that give the place character, unlike so many hotels. Breakfast is also available.

🔒 *See also* the entry on **Le Panoramic**, the restaurant at the Grand Hôtel, under 'Where To Eat'.

🔒 **Chalets in the Vallée du Préto**: at Le Feu de Noël, 2 kilometres (1 mile) from the village on the road to Erquy. ☎ and fax: 02-96-63-19-79. Email: philippe.barthelemy4@wana doo.fr. ♿ Prices range from 1,800F per week in low season through to 2,500F in mid-season, rising to 3,200F in high season, with heating and washing included. It's also possible to rent accommodation for the weekend. There are 15 fully equipped chalet-bungalows, laid out around a large pond in an attractive and peaceful setting.

WHERE TO EAT

✕ **Restaurant du Golf**: Plage des Vallées. ☎ 02-96-63-01-12. Open at lunchtime, daily except Tuesday. Closed in January. There's a simple à la carte menu, and set price menus range from 62F to 120F. This is by no means a gastronomic staging-post, but people do come here for the incredible view of the ocean.

✕ **Restaurant de l'Hôtel de la Mer**: 63 rue Amiral-Charner. ☎ 02-96-72-20-44. Set menu (weekdays only) for 95F. Wide range of menus, including the chef's menu at excellent value for money, the *Nouvelle Vague* menu for 135F with two courses of your choice, and a delicious gastronomic menu that is more expensive. Something for every budget, with fine food and extremely good service.

✕ 🔒 **Le Panoramic**, **restaurant du Grand Hôtel du Val-André**: 80 rue Amiral-Charner. ☎ 02-96-72-20-56. Fax: 02-96-63-00-24. Open from mid-March to mid-November, evenings only except Sunday and public holidays. Worth trying for its beautiful dining room looking out over the sea and its competitively priced menus. Set menus: *Verdelet* for 95F, *Val-André* for 130F and *Grand Large* for 160F. Sunday and public holidays there is an 'all you can eat' seafood buffet for 160F (not including drinks and dessert). Wide choice of homemade delicacies. A well-run establishment financed by the town council. Accommodation available: 495F for a double room facing the sea and 405F for one overlooking the car park. Although they are all equally comfortable, the newest rooms are the best, as the others are rather gloomy.

✕ **Le Zef**: by the harbour in Dahouët. ☎ 02-96-72-96-62. For those who want to experience the real world of seafaring fishermen. Run by a characterful local lady, it serves mussels, *crêpes* and good rib steaks.

✕ **Dahouët en France**, **Art et Saveur** (art and flavours): 28 quai des Terre-Neuvas, by the harbour in Dahouët. ☎ 02-96-63-19-17. Open 10am until the evening meal, daily in season and during school holidays; Saturday to Tuesday for the rest of the year. Closed in March and for the last two weeks in November. You can get a substantial, filling meal for 30–60F. A hundred years ago, this house was used as a sail-loft by one M. Le Péchon, a shipowner, who lived in the grand house that adjoins it. He had a fleet of schooners that sailed the waters of Nova Scotia and Iceland. Today, the building is used not to mend sails but to show works of art on canvas. The proprietor started out by placing a few tables on the pavement outside, to make the place seem friendlier, and it seems to have done the trick, as people no longer pass on by but stop for a drink or to try one

CÔTES-D'ARMOR

of the dishes. The location is great, right opposite the harbour, and the place is stylishly decorated with antique furniture, some of it from the house itself, including the original counter. Concerts and themed musical evenings are held from time to time. It's an excellent idea that works extremely well.

✗ **Restaurant Le Haut-Guen**: 46 rue de la Plage des Vallées. ☎ 02-96-72-25-07. Open daily in July and August; closed Tuesday evening and Wednesday in May, June and September; open lunchtime only from November to May; also closed in February and October. Set menus cost from 78F to 195F. This little restaurant faces the sea and the water almost touches its door at high tide. Although the decor is rather nondescript, the cuisine – mainly seafood – is carefully prepared and well served. Specialities include fricassée of shrimps in whisky and sea-bass with fennel (*bar au fenouil*).

✗ **Restaurant Au Biniou**: 121 rue Clemenceau; near the beach. ☎ 02-96-72-24-35. Closed Tuesday evening and Wednesday except during school holidays; also closed in February. In high season, it's wise to reserve. Set menus from 98F to 220F. Allow 250F to eat à la carte. This is a traditional restaurant that is very popular with locals. The setting is elegant, and the chef-owner has shown himself to be really good at his job, offering a number of seafood dishes such as king prawns and scallops in vermouth (*fricassée de langoustines et Saint-Jacques au Noilly*). After your meal it's good to take a stroll on the vast expanse of beach, or along one of the many footpaths in the vicinity.

WHERE TO STAY AND EAT IN THE AREA

🛏 **Chambres d'hôte Le Pré Mancel**: on the road to Erquy, 4 kilometres (2.5 miles) from Pléneuf; at the roundabout, on the left, head towards the Plage de la Ville Berneuf; in the countryside, 1 kilometre from the beach. ☎ 02-96-72-95-12. Open all year round. An ideal location with impeccable guest rooms costing 240F with bathroom, including breakfast. A friendly welcome is an added bonus.

🛏 **Ferme de Malido**: in St-Alban. ☎ 02-96-32-94-74. Fax: 02-96-32-92-67. Take the road for St-Brieuc and the farm is signposted on the left. M. and Mme Le Grand run a comfortably refurbished and modern farm with a garden, play park and kitchen area. Five guest rooms from 220F to 260F for two people, 320F for three and 390F for four. Also a double room with balcony for 300F. Breakfast included. Prices change out of season. Groups can also be accommodated.

✗ **La Moulerie de la Baie**: on the Grève de Jospinet at Planguenoual; from Val-André, go to Dahouët then take the little road that goes behind the unattractive building at the marina, then follow signs for La Cotentin and Jospinet. ☎ 02-96-32-82-22. Open from Easter to 1 November, daily except Tuesday lunchtime in July, August and the first week of September; the rest of the year, open Friday and Saturday evening, and lunchtime and evening on Sunday and public holidays. This very simple little restaurant is run by mussel- and oyster-farmers, who are basically here to sell what they farm. A really good place. If you're here at low tide, go and take a look over the end of the slipway, where you can inspect the mussel beds close up.

✗ **Auberge du Poirier**: at the Le Poirier roundabout, beside the petrol station, in St-Alban. ☎ 02-96-32-96-21. Closed Sunday evening and Monday out of season. Olivier Termet, who learned his trade in larger, more famous establishments, is now able to demonstrate his youthful talent in a place of his own. Early recognition of his skill as a chef has allowed him to extend the restaurant, so there is now a very elegant dining room. The cheapest set menu, with a main course, dessert, wine and coffee, costs 75F (served Tuesday to Saturday lunchtime); others range from 95F up to 200F, and the dishes are changed four times a year according to the seasons. Each dish is perfect, and an unqualified success, making it one of the top places to eat in the region. It is, of course, wise to reserve.

WHERE TO GO FOR A DRINK

♟ **Chez Max**: 4–6 rue de Lamballe, at the end of the main road in Val-André in the direction of Dahouët. ☎ 02-96-72-22-78. Open 9am–1am in summer and 5pm–1am weekends only in winter. It's now several years since Max took over this former hotel and turned it into the best bar in Pléneuf-Val-André. The interior looks good, with a 1930s feel about it. There's a decent range of draught beers, including Guinness, Kilkenny and Warsteiner, which he keeps very well, and some good music to be heard – mainly jazz and blues. Max is German, but speaks English as well as French. As you might expect, there's a *Biergarten* (beer garden), great in summer, where you can listen to music and eat simple food in a convivial, slightly Bohemian atmosphere. The food is good in winter too.

♟ In Val-André there are a number of lively bars in the summer, such as the **Bar du Casino** and the **Gatsby Pub** (beside the Biniou). There's also **La Petite Dune** and **Le Swing**. Many of them offer live music and happy hours in high season.

♟ *See also* the entry on **Dahouët en France** under 'Where To Eat'.

WHERE TO LISTEN TO MUSIC

– **Jazz à l'Amirauté**: every Tuesday in high season, free concerts in the parc de l'Amirauté, and live entertainment on Thursday in the streets of the resort.

FESTIVALS

– **Fête de la Mer**: on the quayside at Dahouët, every year in mid-August. This is a festival to celebrate the sea, and you can hear sea shanties, watch folk-dancing and see old sailing ships.

– **Pardon de Notre-Dame-de-la-Garde**: this Breton *pardon* takes place at Dahouët in August. The procession goes from the chapel down to the quay, where prayers of blessing are said and flowers are cast into the sea.

WHAT TO SEE

★ **Dahouët en France**: by the harbour in Dahouët. Small café and a very nice art gallery, staging a wide variety of exhibitions (*see also* 'Where To Eat').

★ **La cidrerie des vergers** (orchard and cider-making): on the D786, after the Le Poirier roundabout. ☎ 02-96-32-94-98. Tours from April to September daily except Sunday, 8.30am–noon and 2–7.30pm. The Monvoisin family runs an orchard of 7,000 apple trees, and will tell you all there is to know about cider. Guided tour, cider for sale and the chance to sample *crêpes* with apple jelly. In July and August, daily 5–8.30pm, a **farmers' market** is held here. You can buy produce from about 10 local growers and drinks and snacks are also available.

★ If you are passing by Pléneuf when there is a *grande marée* or spring tide, visit the **Réserve Ornithologique du Verdelet** (bird sanctuary). During an hour-long walk around the reserve you should see many of the wild bird species of the region. Details from the tourist office.

★ **La Ferme du Vaumadeuc**: on the D786 heading towards St-Brieuc. ☎ 02-96-72-85-82. Open daily except Sunday, by appointment. Tours of the farm with commentary, including milking at 6pm. Farm produce for sale and tastings, including *tomme au lait cru* (a delicious cheese made with unpasteurized milk).

★ **La Ferme du Laboureur**: at Le Clos Villéon. Take the D786 towards St-Brieuc until you get to Planguenoual, from there, it's about 2 kilometres (1 mile), signposted on the left as you leave the village. ☎ 02-96-32-76-92 or 02-96-63-02-93. Open April, May, June, September and October, Sunday 2–6pm, July and August, Wednesday–Friday and Sunday 2–6pm. Groups can visit all year round. A guided tour lasts about two hours. Admission charge 20F (10F for children aged 8–14). This is a life-size reconstruction of a typical farm of the region at the turn of the 20th century. Old ways and traditions are brought to life and presented enthusiastically by members of the older generation who actually lived and worked on neighbouring farms. Exhibits cover everything from the livestock and machinery to the customs of the day and the home life of the workers. It's a fascinating display and a rewarding place to visit.

LAMBALLE (*LAMBAL*) 22400 (Pop: 11,187)

As the commercial crossroads of the area, the capital of the Penthièvre region has lost some of its medieval character. The town is closely linked with the memory of Mme de Lamballe. After the death of her husband, the Prince de Lamballe, she served as lady-in-waiting to Marie-Antoinette for 20 years. During the French Revolution, she fell victim to the massacres of September 1792, and the sight of her head being paraded through the streets on a pike remained one of the most powerful images of that period.

USEFUL ADDRESSES

Ⓑ Office du tourisme: on the ground floor of a listed building, la Maison du Bourreau, place du Martray. ☎ 02-96-31-05-38. Fax: 02-96-50-01-96. Email: otsi.lamballe@netcourrier.com. Open July and August, Monday to Saturday 9.30am–6.30pm and Sunday and public holidays 10am–noon; in April, May, June and September, Monday to Saturday 10am–12.30pm and 2–6pm; from October to the end of March, Monday to Saturday 10am–12.30pm and 2–5pm. The staff are very efficient and have lots of documentation available. Guided tours of the town are organized from 15 June to 15 September, every day except Sunday and Monday at 10.30am and 3pm.

🚃 Gare SNCF (train station): boulevard Jobert. ☎ 08-36-35-35-35 (premium rate) or 02-96-31-01-22.

🚌 Cars C.A.T. (buses): between Lamballe, St-Brieuc and the beaches. ☎ 02-96-68-31-20.

WHERE TO STAY AND EAT

🛏 Chambres d'hôte with M. et Mme Le Teno: 14 rue Notre-Dame (behind the place du Martray). ☎ and fax: 02-96-31-00-41. Closed in January. This 18th-century house has the distinction of being the birthplace of the well-known Breton painter Mathurin Méheut. The owner is a delightful lady and the interior has a certain charm. From 225F to 280F per night, including breakfast. The five guest rooms have a private bathroom. Kitchen for the use of guests. Pleasant garden.

🛏 ✕ Hôtel La Tour d'Argent: 2 rue du Docteur-Lavergne. ☎ 02-96-31-01-37. Fax: 02-96-31-37-59. ✕ Double rooms cost 250–380F. Right in the centre of town. This is a standard Logis de France hotel with the level of comfort that you would expect, but it has no special charm. The restaurant has a wide range of dishes and offers a set menu (weekdays) at 60F and other menus up to 165F.

✕ Crêperie Ty-Coz: 35 place du Champ-de-Foire. ☎ 02-96-31-03-58. Closed Wednesday all year round, Sunday lunchtime in winter; also closed for the last two weeks in December. Set menus are available on weekday lunchtimes for 44F and 54F, and another menu at 76F evenings and weekends. This place is run by a nice young couple, who produce excellent *galettes* and *crêpes* that you can eat in a pleasant environment with Celtic music playing in the background. One of the specialities on the menu is a delicious caramelized apple dish.

✕ Le Boeuf d'Or: 12 rue du Docteur-Calmette; near the museum and the place du Marché. ☎ 02-96-31-31-31. Closed Sunday and Wednesday evening all year round, Sunday out of season; also closed September and November. Lunchtime three-course set menu for 52F (except on Sunday), and other menus for 76F to 115F. This little restaurant is popular with local people and displays works of art by a Breton artist.

✕ Le Connétable: 9 rue Paul-Langevin, 200 metres from the place du Martray. ☎ 02-96-31-03-50. Closed Sunday evening and Monday. Lunchtime set menu for 60F during the week, as well as menus from 82F to 195F. This is *the* place for gourmets in Lamballe. The comfortable setting and the successful, classic cooking have won over the local community and its popularity is assured. The chef likes to cook with fish from the Bay of St-Brieuc, which are freshly bought each morning from the fishermen of Erquy and vary according to the season. Booking at the weekend is essential.

WHAT TO SEE

★ **Place du Martray**: square surrounded by a few old houses. The most beautiful is the **Maison du Bourreau** (the tourist office is located here) with its striking facade. Inside are two museums. First is the **Musée d'Art Populaire du Pays de Lamballe** (museum of popular arts and crafts from the Lamballe area): ☎ 02-96-34-77-63. Open July and August, 9.30am–6.30pm; from April to June and in September, daily except Sunday and public holidays 10am–12.30pm and 2–6pm; from October to March, 10am–12.30pm and 2–5pm. Admission charge 10F. Groups are welcome, by appointment. Popular arts and crafts and traditions, including tools, traditional dress, pottery and household objects, plus a fascinating model of the town in feudal times. The second is the **Musée Mathurin Méheut**: ☎ 02-96-31-19-99. Open during the spring holidays 10am–noon and 2.30–5pm daily except Sunday and public holidays; until 6pm from June to September and afternoons only, closing at 5pm, for the rest of the year. Closed in January. Admission charge 15F. Displays the works of this painter, a native of the town – a sizeable body of drawings, paintings and ceramics bequeathed by Méheut which accurately reflect the social and cultural life of Brittany in the first half of the 20th century.

If you're passing through Dinan, don't miss the **Maison d'Artiste de la Grande Vigne**, now a gallery, which belonged to Yvonne Jean-Haffen, the artist's patron and muse. Several of Méheut's canvases can be seen there (*see* Dinan: 'What To See').

★ **Collégiale Notre-Dame**: at the top of the rue Notre-Dame. ☎ 02-96-31-05-38 (tourist office) or 02-96-31-02-55 (presbytery). Guided tours in July and August, Monday to Saturday 10am–12.30pm and 2.30–6pm. Fortress-like Gothic collegiate church with some Romanesque parts, such as the superb left (or north) portal. Huge nave also with Gothic arches descending to friezes adorned with plants. An unusual feature on the right-hand side is the harmonious combination of a 15th-century rood screen in the Flamboyant style and a finely carved organ case.

★ **Église St-Jean**: church in a corner of place du Martray, with three interesting altarpieces in the apse.

★ **Église St-Martin**: at the end of rue St-Martin (beginning at the place du Champ-de-Foire). This church has a Romanesque porch topped by a very original canopy with an unusual shaped 16th-century slate roof. To visit the church, ask the lady next door for the key.

★ **Haras national** (stud farm): place du Champ-de-Foire; in the town centre. ☎ 02-96-50-06-98. Guided tours are available from 15 June to 15 September 10am–noon and 2–5.45pm; the rest of the year open on Wednesday, Saturday and Sunday afternoon. Admission charge 25F; 15F for children under 12. Of interest to all horse lovers, this stud farm has bred a large number of draught horses. Tour of the stables, harness rooms, riding school, main saddle room, forge, and other areas.

– At the end of January, just before the riding season starts, the stud farm shows its stallions. The event attracts 300–400 breeders, and is a colourful sight for spectators. A competition, where Breton stallions are also sold, takes place at the end of September.

IN THE AREA

★ **Abbaye de Boquen**: 20 kilometres (12.5 miles) south of Lamballe. Founded in 1137, this abbey was neglected and used as a stone quarry during the French Revolution. Between 1936 and 1965, Dom Alexis Presse, a monk of the Cistercian Order, courageously rebuilt the abbey. Since 1976, a contemplative community of the nuns of Bethlehem, of the Assumption of the Virgin and of St Bruno, live and pray here in silence and solitude. The abbey itself is very beautiful, 72 metres (234 feet) in length. The gossamer-like wooden framework forming the nave was made by the Compagnons du Devoir et du Tour de France (an organization of highly skilled artisans and craftsmen who travelled throughout France after completing their apprenticeship, and whose work was highly prized). In the south transept, there is a 15th-century statue of the Virgin Mary carved in wood. In the north transept lie two reliquaries containing the bones of the founding saints of Breton monasteries. The church is open to all those who knock on the monastery door. A few days' hospitality in silence and solitude may be offered to those who request it. Guests are permitted to participate in the liturgical celebrations.

★ **Jugon-les-Lacs**: 16 kilometres (10 miles) east of Lamballe. Very pretty village on the edge of a small man-made lake, with numerous old houses such as the **Maison Sevoy**, built in 1634. The main square is lined with houses from the same period, including the **Hôtel de l'Écu**. Campsite. A new tourist office is now based here. ☎ 02-96-31-70-75.

ST-BRIEUC (*SANT-BRIEG*) 22000 (Pop: 48,895)

At first glance, the capital of Côtes-d'Armor does not possess enormous charm. With almost no artistic or architectural works of art, it is first and foremost an administrative, industrial and commercial centre. However, the town has undergone changes and is a brighter, more attractive place than it once was, especially the area around its interesting cathedral, the rue Fardel. And on closer inspection, St-Brieuc has much else to offer – a dynamic cultural life, for example, which stems from a solid literary tradition; a number of well-known French writers were either born here or attended the town's *lycée*.

Some might find 'St-Broc' (as the local youngsters call it) too quiet. Certainly, this is not the case during the *Festival Art Rock*, which takes place during the last weekend in May. In addition, the arts centre, La Passerelle, also has an active programme, and few French towns of the same size are privileged to have such an institution. Finally, during the *Été en Fête* (summer festival), musicians and all sorts of performers liven up the streets on Thursday and Friday during July and August.

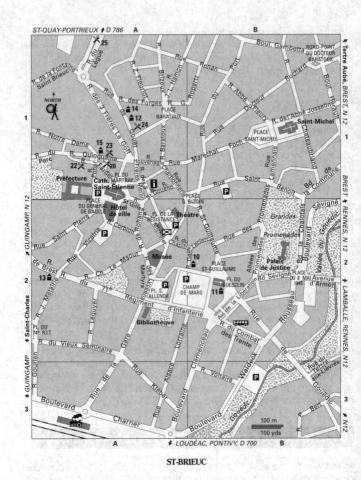

ST-BRIEUC

■ **Useful Addresses**

🛈 Office du tourisme

🚂 Gare SNCF (train station)

🏠 **Where To Stay**

10 Hôtel du Champ-de-Mars
11 Hôtel Duguesclin
12 Le Ker-Izel
13 Au Pot d'Étain
14 Hôtel de Clisson

15 Chambres d'hôte: M. and Mme.
    de Fonclare

✕ **Where To Eat**

20 Crêperie-saladerie Le Ribeault
22 Le Chaudron
23 Le Madure
24 L'Amadeus
25 Aux Pesked

Traffic in St-Brieuc is a real headache. When you arrive, park your car and walk – it's much quicker.

USEFUL ADDRESSES AND INFORMATION

▇ Office du tourisme (A1 on the map): 7 rue St-Gouéno. ☎ 02-96-33-32-50. Fax: 02-96-61-42-16. Website: www.mairie-saintbrieuc.fr or www.bretagne-4villes.com. Open Monday to Saturday 9am–noon and 1.30–6pm; in summer, Monday to Saturday 9am–7pm and Sunday 10am–1pm. In the town centre, a stone's throw from the cathedral. Guided tours of the town are organized in summer, visiting the cathedral and the Old Town every day and the parcours Louis-Guilloux every Friday at 10.30am and 3pm. In low season, tours are available by reservation.
– There is another tourist office at the Yffiniac rest area, 5 kilometres (3 miles) before St-Brieuc, on the motorway to Lamballe. ☎ 02-96-72-59-81. Open from 1 June to 15 September and holiday weekends in April and May.
▅ Gare SNCF (train station) (A3 on the map): Paris–Brest service. ☎ 08-36-35-35-35. Takes 3 hours from Paris on the TGV (high-speed train).
◐ Airport: ☎ 02-96-94-95-00. Paris is one hour away; also flights to Jersey.
▭ Gare routière (bus station): rue du Combat-des-Trente. (B2 on the map) and car park at the gare SNCF (train station) (A3 on the map). Regular service between Lamballe, St-Brieuc and the beaches. ☎ 02-96-68-31-20.
■ **Car rental**: **Hertz**, 53 rue de la Gare. ☎ 02-96-94-25-89. Perfect for those who arrive by train and want to visit the region. Other companies are also to be found close by.
– **Market**: place de la Poste and all around the cathedral. An open-air market on Saturday and Wednesday mornings. Don't miss the Charpentier van selling sausage-filled *galettes*, which is usually to be found on place de la Cathédrale outside the old fish market building.

WHERE TO STAY

Campsites

▟ To the northeast of St-Brieuc, in the district (*commune*) of Plérin (round St-Laurent, Martin-Plage and Ville-Hery), there are at least five campsites. The peaceful and green **Camping des Vallées** is the nearest (close to the parc des Expositions and the sports ground). ☎ 02-96-94-05-05.

☆ Budget

▟ **Auberge de jeunesse** (youth hostel): Manoir de la Ville-Guyomard, Les Villages. ☎ 02-96-78-70-70. Fax: 02-96-78-27-47. Open all year round except for the last week in December. Located 3 kilometres (2 miles) from the town centre, near the shopping centre *Géant* (well signposted from the station). Reservation strongly recommended. Set in a superb 15th-century Breton manor house. Rooms with from one to four beds. Expect to pay 72F per night, with breakfast extra. Meals from 55F. Mountain bike rental. Excellent welcome.
▟ **Au Pot d'Étain** (A2, **13** on the map): 3 rue de Brest. ☎ 02-96-68-17-89. Friendly, very clean and centrally located hotel with nine small, recently redecorated rooms. Expect

to pay 195F for a double room. Also a room without a shower for 145F. Breakfast is extra (27F). All rooms overlook the inner courtyard, which is also a free car park, and have a toilet, telephone and TV. Inexpensive restaurant, also open on weekday lunchtimes, but closed during August, although half board or full-board are still available.

☆☆–☆☆☆ Moderate to Chic

⌂ **Chambres d'hôte: M. and Mme de Fonclare** (A1, **15** on the map): 20 *bis* rue Quinquaine. ☎ 02-96-33-27-33. There's a double room for 250F, or 280F including breakfast; also a child's room if needed. In the old part of St-Brieuc, this vast house looks out over the pretty place Louis-Guiloux. Everything is very well kept. The de Fonclares are very welcoming and the guest room is colourful with a decent bathroom. There's also a large garden and parking is available in the courtyard of the house.

⌂ **Hôtel du Champ-de-Mars** (A2, **10** on the map): 13 avenue du Général-Leclerc; in the town centre. ☎ 02-96-33-60-99. Fax: 02-96-33-60-05. Closed between Christmas and New Year. This well-kept and pleasant hotel, with all the mod cons expected of a two-star place including lift, TV and telephone, is also quite inexpensive, costing from

270F to 300F for a double room, with breakfast an extra 38F. The husband and wife owners are welcoming and pleasant.

⌂ ✕ **Hôtel Duguesclin** (B2, **11** on the map): 2 place Du-Guesclin. ☎ 02-96-33-11-58. Fax: 02-96-52-01-18. Centrally located and completely refurbished, the Duguesclin has bright and comfortable rooms. Double room with shower, toilet and TV costs 270F. Also a restaurant with a weekday lunchtime menu for 60F and other menus from 92F and 172F. Specialities include scallop mousse (*mousseline de coquilles St-Jacques*), grilled bass in fennel (*bar grillé au fenouil*) and the chef's own smoked fish dishes (*poissons fumés maison*).

⌂ **Le Ker-Izel** (A1, **12** on the map): 20 rue du Gouët, in the historic town centre. ☎ 02-96-33-46-29. Fax: 02-96-61-86-12. Warm and welcoming old house. Quite elegant and comfortable rooms, from 225F to 320F.

⌂ **Hôtel de Clisson** (A1, **14** on the map): 36–38 rue du Gouët, in the town centre. ☎ 02-96-62-19-29. Fax: 02-96-61-06-95. ♿ Open all year round. An extremely comfortable hotel offering double rooms from 350F to 440F. Some rooms even have a jacuzzi, plus cable TV and video recorder. There is private parking.

WHERE TO EAT

☆ Budget

✕ **Crêperie Bleu-Marine** (A3, off the map): 28 *bis* rue Aristide-Briand, a little out of the centre, in the Robien district, behind the station. From place du Champ-de-Mars, go up boulevard Clemenceau then right just after the bridge and the road to Robien is on the left. After that, it's about 400 metres until you reach

the junction with rue Aristide-Briand. Closed Sunday and Monday, plus the last week of July and the first two weeks of August. ☎ 02-96-94-26-73. This is an excellent and popular little neighbourhood *crêperie* where *galettes* cost from 8F to 35F and *crêpes* are from 9F to 26F. The owner selects her flour with great care, from Plénée-Jugon, and all the pastries are made on the premises. The results are delicious: her light, tasty *galettes* are among the best to be had in St-Brieuc, using simple fillings with a base of ham, eggs, cheese, sausage, tomatoes or mushrooms. Anyone with a sweet tooth will not be disappointed by the *crêpes*, and there's also an excellent Fouesnant cider that is fruity and not too gassy. There's a strong local clientele and a welcoming atmosphere.

✗ **Crêperie-saladerie Le Ribeault** (A1, **20** on the map): 8 and 10 rue Fardel; 30 metres from the place du Martray. ☎ 02-96-33-44-79. Closed Sunday lunchtime except during school holidays. A small, friendly dining room with a welcoming atmosphere. Good *crêpes*. Menus from 38F at lunchtime and 45F in the evening.

☆☆ Moderate

✗ **Le Sympatic** (A3, off the map): 9 boulevard Carnot; just behind the train station: take boulevard Clemenceau and turn right after the railway line. ☎ 02-96-94-04-76. Closed Saturday lunchtime and Sunday, and the first three weeks in August. Service until 11pm. Good humour and good grilled meat (on vine leaves) complement each other at this popular local restaurant. The decor is also attractive, with exposed beams and stone walls. The place lives up to its name, with its warm and friendly atmosphere and cheerful, efficient service. Large platefuls are served with vegetables and chips, the produce is good quality, and the bill is fairly small. Six fixed-price menus from 68F to 250F, plus an à la carte menu.

✗ **Entre Terre et Mer** (A2, off the map): 5 rue Palasme-de-Champeaux. From place Général-de-Gaulle, go up rue St-Pierre, cross rue de Brest, and opposite, take the rue des Capucins and go to the far

end. Go across the crossroads and the restaurant is in the second road on the left. ☎ 02-96-94-50-74. Closed Sunday and Monday (except for groups, by reservation). A two-course meal can be had at lunchtime for 60F and a full meal costs 90F lunchtime or evening. Allow about 130F if you're eating à la carte. The decor inspires confidence, with its discreet white-clothed tables, stone walls and big fireplace, and the cuisine lives up to expectation. A number of dishes of the day are on offer, depending on the season, and the excellent menu seems like real value for money. The chef's speciality is fish, but the slate lists various good meat dishes including braised leg of lamb with garlic and rosemary (*jarret d'agneau braisé à l'ail et au romarin*) and deliciously tender fillet steaks. The food is well presented and the portions are generous. This is an establishment of quality that won't damage the budget.

✗ **Le Chaudron** (A1, **22** on the map): 19 rue Fardel. ☎ 02-96-33-01-72. Fax: 02-96-61-34-08. Closed Wednesday lunchtime and Sunday. Menu of the day for 75F at lunchtime, and a variety of specialities such as *fondue* (*savoyarde* with cheese, from 78F to 85F; *bourguignonne*, with meat; and *du pêcheur*, with seafood), *reblochonnade* (made with cheese from the Savoie region of France), *raclette* (melted cheese prepared at the table under a special grill, with potatoes and cold meats) and meats grilled on a hot stone. Very popular because of its warm and friendly atmosphere. Expect to pay about 150F à la carte.

✗ **Le Madure** (A1, **23** on the map): 14 rue Quinquaine. ☎ 02-96-61-21-07. Closed Sunday and Monday, and the last two weeks in August. In old St-Brieuc, not far from the cathedral. Very pleasant, rustic

ST-BRIEUC

decor. Delicious terrines and salads, dish of the day for 70F and, in particular, generous portions of excellent and tender meat grilled over a wood fire.

☆☆☆ Chic

✕ **L'Amadeus** (A1, **24** on the map): 22 rue du Gouët. ☎ 02-96-33-92-44. Closed Monday lunchtime and Sunday; also closed in the February school holidays and the last two weeks in August. Always highly rated for its cosy setting and pleasant atmosphere. Its wonderful dishes include fried fresh duck's liver (*foie frais de canard poêlé*) or lamb with garlic and thyme (*tian d'agneau à l'ail et au thym*), as well as some excellent fish and seafood specialities. Set menus for 115F (weekdays only), 160, 240 and 260F. The menu changes every two months.

✕ **Aux Pesked** (A1, **25** on the map): 59 rue du Légué. ☎ 02-96-33-34-65. Closed Sunday evening and Monday, and during the Christmas holidays. This gastronomic establishment is now the unanimous first choice in St-Brieuc. It has modern, restrained and elegant decor, a superb view of the Vallée du Légué and exquisite, enjoyable and not overly rich fare. Set menus for 110F during the week and 145F at the weekend, and the highly recommended and filling *menu surprise* for 190F (two starters, main course, dessert, appetizer), another at 290F and a seven-course gourmet menu at 390F. Very nice wine list with a wide choice.

WHERE TO STAY AND EAT IN THE AREA

🛌 **Chambres d'hôte, Le Pré Péan**: with Mme Gaubert, 22590 Pordic; 9 kilometres (5.5 miles) north of St-Brieuc. ☎ 02-96-79-00-32. Open all year round. Three guest rooms for 230F, including breakfast; an extra bed costs 70F. Set in a 14th-century farm in the middle of the countryside. Breakfast is served at the large kitchen table with the scent of warm milk coming from the farmyard as an added bonus.

🛌 **Le Clos Laurentais**: 1 rue Jean-Bart, 22190 St-Laurent-de-la-Mer; 6 kilometres (4 miles) north of St-Brieuc. ☎ 02-96-73-03-38. Fax: 02-96-73-11-79. Closed at the end of September and the end of March; also closed Tuesday out of season. This village bar, hotel, tobacconist and bookshop all rolled into one (you can even buy your lottery ticket here) offers clean and quite spacious rooms for less than 150F, with a small discount if you stay three nights or more. Some rooms have sea views. Private parking.

Beautiful and little-known beach nearby.

✕ **Le Buchon**: 12 rue de Brest, 22440 Trémuson; 6 kilometres (4 miles) west of St-Brieuc heading towards Trémuson. ☎ 02-96-94-85-84. Closed in the evening. An unpretentious little roadside inn, offering feasts of fish, lobster, crab and other seafood. Freshness is guaranteed and the preparation is faultless. Cheapest set menu for 88F – unbeatable value for money with, for example, spider crab with mayonnaise (*araignée mayonnaise*), delicious fillet of duck breast, and then a dessert; additional menus for 125F and 165F. Superb seafood platters, as you would expect.

✕ **Crêperie des Grèves**: 23 rue des Grèves, 22360 Langueux; on the RN12, 6 kilometres (4 miles) east of St-Brieuc. ☎ 02-96-72-56-96. ♿ In July and August, open daily except Sunday and Monday lunchtime; the rest of the year, open lunchtime from Wednesday to

Friday, and Friday, Saturday and Sunday evening. Closed for two weeks in February and the last two weeks in September. Located in the *marais* (marshland), this is a nice little *crêperie* run by a devotee of the region – the menus are even written in Breton. The *crêpes*, sweet and savoury, are made with organic flour and regional products such as cockles (*coques de baie*) and smoked sausage (*saucisse fumée*). Set menu for 71F and a 'discovery' menu for 89F, which includes a special *digestif* – a Ruzé Bréhat. Children's menu for 56F.

✕ **Les Quatre Saisons**: 61 chemin des Courses, Cesson. ☎ 02-96-33-20-38. Fax: 02-96-33-77-38. Email: manoirlequatresaisons @hotmail.com. From St-Brieuc, head towards Le Légué, and turn right at the roundabout just before the motorway bridge; then go straight on for about 2 kilometres (1 mile) and follow the signposts. Closed Sunday and Monday evening, and for two weeks in March and October. Choice food in a rather secluded, traditional Breton house with cosy little dining rooms. Plain, simple cooking with plenty of character includes, for example, king prawn salad with *galettes* or an oyster casserole. Four very good set menus from 110F to 277F. Expect to pay about 350F if you're eating à la carte.

WHERE TO GO FOR A DRINK

To be honest, St-Brieuc's nightlife leaves something to be desired, but it *is* possible to find places with quite a lot of action – if you know where to look.

♟ **La Passerelle** (A1–A2 on the map): place de la Résistance. ☎ 02-96-68-18-40. From September to June, theatre, music and dancing are on the programme in two auditoriums. One is a small, hundred-year-old Italian theatre, all red velvet and chandeliers – well worth seeing. Open to the public all year. Guided tour free of charge on request.

♟ **Place du Chai**: near the cathedral, an unusual pedestrian square, which is a bizarre, brightly coloured and very modern design placed in an old setting. Contemporary shopfronts and restaurants merge harmoniously with old granite dwellings. A pleasant place to have a drink in a pavement café at lunchtime or late in the evening. Especially lively on market days (Wednesday and Saturday morning).

♟ **Chez Rollais** (A2–B2 on the map): 26 rue du Général-Leclerc; in the town centre. ☎ 02-96-61-23-03. Open 9am–10pm (1am Friday and Saturday). Closed on Sunday and public holidays. This wine bar has been fashionable since 1912. The decor doesn't seem to have changed since then, and yet the place is still in vogue. Little old men rub shoulders with trendy young people over a good bottle of wine, and the owner, a first-rate wine connoisseur, serves only good-quality wine, selected from inexpensive and choice local producers.

♟ **Le Piano Bleu** (A1 on the map): 4 rue Fardel; a stone's throw from the cathedral. ☎ 02-96-33-41-62. Closed Sunday. A cheerful concert café where accomplished artistes entertain the customers. Open-air show in the summer.

♟ **L'Illiade**: 5 rue du Légué; north of the town centre (from the place de la Grille, head for the harbour). ☎ 02-96-33-46-99. Open 8pm–3am in summer and 6pm–3am in winter.

Closed Sunday. Rock music and a lively atmosphere.

♀ In addition, there are some lively **bars** in the summer in Binic, 12 kilometres (7.5 miles) to the north, such as **Le Miramar** and **Le Radeau**, the oldest nightclub in the Côtes-d'Armor.

WHAT TO BUY

Wine

🔒 **Cave Victor' Inn**: I rue Saint-Vincent-de-Paul, between the place de la Grille and place St-Michel. ☎ 02-96-61-36-35. Open 10am–12.30pm and 3–7.30pm. Closed Monday and Sunday afternoon. The proprietor here has two passions – wine and whisky. He keeps an excellent cellar, and knows his trade very well, having started out as a wine waiter. In stock is a range of well-chosen bottles, from unknown vineyards all the way through to the big names. Also 200 whiskies to choose from.

🔒 **Au Petit Récoltant**: 2 rue Pierre-Le-Gorrec. ☎ 02-96-68-28-72. Closed Sunday and Monday morning. This is one of the best wine stockists in St-Brieuc; the owner has a number of good contacts with winegrowers who produce excellent wines in small quantities. You will find labels here that you probably won't see anywhere else.

Souvenirs

🔒 **Aux Arts Bretons**: 5 rue St-Gilles. ☎ 02-96-62-17-18. Good quality Breton souvenirs and gifts are sold here, from badges and flags to jewellery, pewterware or Quimper pottery. Everything is authentically made in the region.

WHAT TO SEE

★ **Cathédrale St-Étienne** (A1 on the map): built around 1350 by the bishop and feudal lord of the town (who was also a great warrior), which explains its fortified appearance. Like so many other cathedrals, during the French Revolution its name and purpose were changed and it became a stable and then an armoury. Within its tranquil interior there is a Romanesque vault in the nave, which becomes Gothic in the choir, and an elegant triforium. The cathedral's masterpiece is undoubtedly the baroque large carved wooden altarpiece by Yves Corlay (1745), carefully hidden in a haystack during the Revolution. Its style is as dazzling as the chapel which houses it, also baroque, especially in the early afternoon, when the sun streams through the windows.

There is a very beautiful 16th-century organ case and, in the bays, old tombstones of the cathedral canons. In the south transept is a splendid stained-glass window in the Flamboyant style and an interesting modern *Stations of the Cross*.

★ **Place du Martray** (A1 on the map): the town's marketplace, with a brightly coloured, metal-sheathed shopping centre that serves as a covered market. Not very beautiful.

★ **St-Brieuc Old Town** (A1 on the map): although not very big, old St-Brieuc does have several examples of medieval houses in a few small squares and lanes. Take a stroll along the main shopping street, the rue St-Guillaume, and through the old rues Quinquaine, Pohel, Fardel (look out for the superb Maison Fardel) and places Louis-Guilloux, au Lin, and so on. In the rue Notre-Dame is the Fontaine St-Brieuc, a fountain sheltered by a fine 15th-century porch. It was here that Brieuc, a Welsh evangelist monk, established his first chapel in the sixth century.

★ **Musée d'Art et d'Histoire des Côtes-d'Armor**: rue des Lycéens-Martyrs. ☎ 02-96-62-55-20. Open 9.30–11.45am and 1.30–5.45pm. Closed Monday and Sunday morning. Admission charge 21F. This museum, housed in a former police barracks, is very well laid out. The whole history of the *département* since the French Revolution is displayed thematically: fishing, maritime history (with some outstanding models), life in the ports, agriculture, the development of crafts and industry (especially the evolution of the spinning mills, with an impressive collection of looms), social and religious life, in addition to many more cultural collections (furniture, clothing, household objects, tools). Also interesting temporary exhibitions.

FESTIVAL

– **Festival Art Rock**: takes place on the first weekend of June. Established almost 20 years ago, this festival seems to broaden its scope with every year and attracts an ever-increasing crowd, with the result that St-Brieuc is positively heaving for three days and three nights. The programme includes music, drama, dance, visual arts and video, with big names from France and beyond. Imagine a bill that includes Blur and Miles Davis. For information, call Wildrose: ☎ 02-96-68-18-40. Website: www.artrock.org

WHAT TO SEE IN THE AREA

★ **La Maison de la Baie**: rue Étoile-Hillion, in Hillion, 15 kilometres (9.5 miles) east of St-Brieuc. ☎ 02-96-32-27-98. Visitor centre for the discovery of the natural and economic environment of the bay, with demonstrations and exhibitions about the natural marine environment throughout the year. Also a seawater aquarium.

★ **Plérin**: the **Plage des Rosaires** is popular with the inhabitants of St-Brieuc. The seaside resort, said to have been created by Lucien Rosengart, the automobile industrialist of the inter-war period and designer of the Targa-Florio, has a very busy sailing school. The sea here doesn't recede quite as far as elsewhere in the Baie de St-Brieuc. Fine examples of classic, pre-war villas can still be found along the beach. Don't miss the beautiful panoramic view from the Pointe du Roselier. The end of the beach near St-Laurent is popular with nudists (when the wind isn't blowing too hard – which often happens!).

ST-BRIEUC

Towards 'L'Argoat' – Inland Brittany

QUINTIN (*KINTIN*) 22800 (Pop: 2,930)

Located 19 kilometres (12 miles) from St-Brieuc and dominated by an imposing castle, this small characterful town is a pleasant place to stop. In the 17th and 18th centuries it was an important centre for the production of linen cloth. Although a variety of small businesses has now replaced the traditional linen industry, a fine collection of prestigious half-timbered houses and mansions remains from that period. With a beautiful lake at the castle, this is a very nice little town.

USEFUL ADDRESS

Office du tourisme: place 1830. ☎ 02-96-74-01-51. Fax: 02-96-74-06-82. Email: otsi.pays-de-quintin@wanadoo.fr. Open July and August, Monday to Saturday 9am–12.30pm and 2–6pm, Sunday 10am–12.30pm and 2–5.30pm; the rest of the year, Tuesday to Saturday 9am–noon and 2–5pm. Run by Mme de Bagneux, a lady 'to the manner born', with a real knack for sharing her love of the region. You can also find out about all the little castles in the vicinity of Quintin, many of which are worth a look and some are open to visitors.

WHERE TO STAY AND EAT

Camping Municipal: next to the velodrome. ☎ 02-96-74-92-54. Fax: 02-96-74-06-53. This campsite is open from Easter to the end of October.

Hôtel du Commerce: 2 rue Rochenen. ☎ 02-96-74-94-67. Fax: 02-96-74-00-94. Closed Sunday evening and Monday out of season; also closed for three weeks from Christmas to mid-January and two weeks in March. Small, ivy-covered hotel and restaurant in the town centre. Guaranteed peace and quiet. Rooms from 270F to 330F. Set menus from 75F to 190F. Superb medieval dining room and cuisine of an excellent quality. Try the breast of duck in ginger and wild honey (*magret de canard au gingembre et miel sauvage*).

Hôtel de la Gare: 8 rue de la Gare, in St-Brandan, 1 kilometre away. ☎ 02-96-74-84-27. Fax: 02-96-79-60-88. Restaurant closed Friday evening and Saturday lunchtime, and 1–20 August. After the roundabout, head towards the station. A very small hotel with a friendly, down-to-earth atmosphere. Acceptable rooms for 120F. Set menu from 52F (lunchtimes during the week), with cheese and dessert and a small carafe of wine, and others from 80–155F. Half board for 160F.

Chambres d'hôte Le Clos du Prince: 10 rue des Croix-Jarrots. ☎ and fax: 02-96-74-93-03. From the town hall, take the rue des Douves, then rue des Forges, then rue St-Yves, which takes you to the rue des Croix-Jarrots. Double rooms here cost 350F or 380F, with singles at 270F, breakfast included. One room can sleep three, with a supplement of 150F for the third person (a child over seven years). This is a haven of peace in a very elegant townhouse with an interior courtyard-garden planted with 100-year-old trees, including an incredible sequoia. The owner gives a lively, smiling welcome. She runs an antiques shop on the ground floor, so the rooms are furnished with style and taste. Each one is different, and all are pretty and quite comfortable.

â **Chambres d'hôte and gîtes with Marie-Hélène Leroux**: in the village of St-Eutrope, just 1.5 kilometres from Quintin. ☎ and fax: 02-96-74-87-56. Double rooms cost 220–240F with a generous breakfast included. One room can sleep an extra person, for a supplement of 60F. This is another haven, in a large granite house that looks out over the countryside. The rooms are pretty and very well looked after, and there's no doubt at all that Mme Leroux looks after her guests very well. The breakfast is extremely appetizing, with homemade jams and

crêpes as well as all the usual fare, and liberal quantities of tea, coffee and hot chocolate. In the evenings, use of the kitchen is also possible. Mme Leroux has also created two fully equipped *gîtes* in the next-door barn, which has been well converted. One sleeps three and the other sleeps four plus a child, with the cost varying from 1,300F to 2,500F per week, according to the season. The highest rate for the smaller one is 2,000F. There's a free tennis court a couple of kilometres away, and several good fishing spots close by.

✕ **Crêperie du Château**: 16 rue Vau-de-Gouët. ☎ 02-96-74-92-39. Closed on Monday and for three weeks end of October to early November. This is a pleasant little village *crêperie* run by a very nice couple, Pierrick and Martine Jégo, whose *crêpes* and *galettes* are quite special. They also serve decent pizzas and bar meals, with a good choice of salads and meat dishes. In summer, you can eat on a terrace looking onto the pavement. Prices offer excellent value for money.

✕ There's also the **château** (*see* 'What To See').

WHAT TO SEE

★ **Château**: entrance on the place 1830. ☎ 02-96-74-94-79. Fax: 02-96-74-98-64. Open June to September, daily 10.30am–12.30pm and 1.30–6.30pm; May, 1–15 June and 15–30 September, 2–5.30pm; the rest of the year, Saturday and Sunday only, 2–5.30pm. Admission 30F (including the audio-visual show). Guided tours. The castle may open in addition to the stated times for groups (reservation only). Restaurant facilities on site, with menu from 90F, including drinks (also for groups and by reservation only).

The main wing of the castle dates from 1645 and the buildings north of the courtyard from 1775. For several centuries, it has belonged to the Bagneux family, who have carried out extensive renovation work in order to open a part of the castle to the public. On display are the hall, sitting room, dining room and six additional rooms with period furniture and objects (particularly from the 17th and 18th centuries). Head-dresses, wind-up toys, pipes, pieces of porcelain, a collection of fans and baby bottles are just some of the items that have been discovered over the years. In one room, there is an exhibition of priceless original manuscripts, including letters written by François I and Louis XIV, decrees by the parliament of Brittany, a document written by Napoleon Bonaparte when he was a Premier Consul of France, a Papal bull from 1655 and an old account book. The oldest piece dates from 1322. There is also a display on the history of canvas in Quintin and a *potager* (granite oven). Three rooms have recently opened, containing donations from private collections. These include glassware, head-dresses and christening robes.

A 10-minute audio-visual show tells the history of the castle and the region. There is also an exhibition of porcelain, with more than 750 pieces on display.

★ **Musée-atelier des toiles de Quintin** (Quintin museum and sailcloth workshop): rue des Degrés. ☎ 02-96-74-01-51. Open early June to early September, Tuesday–Sunday 1.30–6.30pm; in the morning by appointment. Admission charge 15F. Guided tour, lasting about one hour. The production of linen and the resulting trade in sailcloth established Quintin's prosperity in the 17th and 18th centuries, and a number of elegant dwellings in the town date from this time. Some of what was produced was sold in Spain and in South America. This little museum recreates this prosperous period in the town's history, demonstrating the various crafts associated with the production of canvas and linen. Interesting demonstrations also take place.

★ **Atelier de vitraux** (stained glass workshop): at the edge of the town centre and the bois de la Perche. ☎ 02-96-74-92-28. Open Monday to Friday 8.30am–noon and 2–6.30pm. Admission free. It's essential to telephone in advance, to check that the man in charge is available to show you around. This is a workshop in which about ten craftsmen work at restoring old pieces of stained glass as well as making new pieces. The space is quite breathtaking, with a huge stained-glass window and a mezzanine floor. When the workshop first opened, in 1947, it was located in one of the towers of the chateau.

★ **Quintin Old Town**: begin the tour of old Quintin in the Grand-Rue, starting at the place 1830. There are a number of beautiful half-timbered houses, some with decorative carving, and elegant granite buildings. In the place du Martray stand the splendid Maison du Changeur (money changer's house) (1728), and the town hall (1740). Two magnificent corbelled buildings mark the entrance to the rue au Lait (the tourist office is in one of them). The rue des Degrés is also picturesque.

– **Rue de la Basilique**: the Maison des Chanoines (canons' house) has sculpted porches Opposite is a fountain from the crypt of the Chapelle Notre-Dame-d'Entre-les-Portes, with a painted stone statue of Notre-Dame-des-Vertus (Our Lady of the Virtues), which looks a little faded.

– **Basilique Notre-Dame-de-Délivrance**: completed in 1887, on the site of the castle chapel, which, in 1250, received a relic said to come from the Virgin Mary's belt. The new neo-Gothic building is 76 metres (247 feet) long and 28 metres (91 feet) wide, with a vault 16 metres (52 feet) high; the weathercock on the bell tower is 75 metres (244 feet) above the ground. Inside, the silver reliquary contains a thin piece of closely woven linen.

FESTIVALS

– **Pardon**: the local religious festival takes place on the second Sunday in May.

– **St-Jean**: on 24 June. This is a *son-et-lumière* spectacle.

– **Festival de chant choral** (choral singing): third week in July.

– **Fête des Tisserands** (weavers' festival): at the beginning of August. This is a festival that celebrates the craft of weaving and linen production, involving music-making and folk dancing, plus demonstrations of the old crafts.

– **Festival des chanteurs de rue** (street-singing festival): in early November.

IN THE AREA

★ **Lanfains**: village located south of Quintin, on the side of a hill 325 metres (1,056 feet) high, right on the watershed between the English Channel and the Atlantic Ocean. Don't miss the Manoir de la Porte-Fraboulet and its superb arched entry porch. There are also some typical farms (Ste-Marie, la Moinerie).

❢ **Le Petit Village**: to get there, follow the signposts from Lanfains. ☎ 02-96-32-44-39. A *bar-cabaret* in the stable of an attractively converted farm, with music on Saturday evening from 10pm to 5am. Run by a farmer trying to reconcile his passion for music and motorcycles with his work. His other aim is to meet new people, escape from the daily grind and bring a bit of excitement back to a rural area that is suffering from the general drift away from agriculture. His place is now well known all over the region. Every year at the end of August, there is a large *fest-noz* (traditional music festival).

★ **Château de Beaumanoir**: at Le Leslay. Take the D7 in the direction of Châteaulaudren. It's signposted on the left, about 2 kilometres (1 mile) out of Quintin. ☎ 02-96-58-17-86. Email: hspierre@wanadoo.fr. Open June to mid-September, daily 2–7pm. This fine castle dates from the 15th century. It was abandoned during the French Revolution and reoccupied in the 19th century. A few remains of the original castle can still be seen, including a tower with a staircase and the guardroom fireplace. Also to be viewed are the stables and saddlery, the courtyard and vegetable garden, and there is a pleasant park with a pool.

★ **Boqueho**: small isolated village in the 'mountains', where the Templars used to hold a large horse fair. Four breeders and a blacksmith still carry on the tradition.

– On 15 August, the feast of the Assumption, the *Pardon de Notre-Dame de la Pitié* is a simple and authentic religious festival.

★ **Uzel**: 15 kilometres (9.5 miles) to the south, halfway between Quintin and Loudéac. A little village perched up on a hill, Uzel, like Quintin, was a significant place for linen production. It was also the birthplace of the inventor Fulgence Bienvenüe, whose name can be found on the Paris Métro station name Montparnasse-Bienvenüe.

MONCONTOUR-DE-BRETAGNE (*MONKONTOUR*) 22510 (Pop: 873)

One of the most important towns in Brittany during the Middle Ages – coins were minted here in the 14th century – Moncontour-de-Bretagne now enjoys the status of a 'Cîté d'Europe'. Many an attempt was made to gain control of the town and to exploit its position high on a hill dominating all the major regional roads. Later, it was completely forgotten. The sole alteration made to it in the last five centuries was the partial demolition of its ramparts, ordered by Richelieu, leaving intact a small but immensely charming town of character. The most beautiful view of the site can be seen coming from Quessoy (on the D1). In summer, Moncontour comes alive again, with numerous activities such as a medieval festival, knights' tournaments and concerts.

USEFUL ADDRESS

🏢 **Office du tourisme**: 4 place de la Carrière. ☎ 02-96-73-50-50. Open 1 June–13 July, daily 10am–12.30pm and 2.30–6.30pm; 14 July–31 August, 10am–6.30pm; September, 10am–12.30pm and 2–6pm; out of season, contact ☎ 02-96-73-44-92. Fax: 02-96-73-53-78. Friendly staff, with a list of chambres d'hôte and a programme of summer activities. On the first floor, there is the Museum of the Chouan Uprising (*see* 'What To See and Do, Maison de la Chouannerie').

WHERE TO STAY

🛏 **Camping municipal**: in the hamlet of Moulin-St-Michel, 100 metres from the ramparts. In season: ☎ 02-96-73-50-50; the rest of the year, apply to the town hall. A two-star campsite run by the tourist office. Only about 20 spaces.

🛏 **Chambres d'hôte Le Ray Christiane:** 10 place Penthièvre. ☎ and fax: 02-96-73-52-18. Excellent location in the heart of Moncontour, a few minutes from the Église St-Mathurin. This 16th-century house has four charming, spacious and clean guest rooms, each decorated in the style of a particular period: *Louis-Philippe*, *Belle Époque*, *Bretonne* and *Rêves de Jeunesse* ('dreams of youth'). Large beds, beams, tapestries and a fireplace, in addition to a fantastic terrace for breakfast. From 250F to 450F, including breakfast. Table

d'hôte for 95F, including drinks. Excellent welcome.

🛏 **Chambres d'hôte, with Mme Rouillé**: 1.5 kilometres out of town on the road to St-Brieuc (D765), opposite the Renault garage. ☎ 02-96-73-40-82. With two guest rooms for 200F; **with Mme Henaff**, in Les Grands-Moulins, also on the D765, opposite the previous address. ☎ 02-96-73-57-58. Just one guest room for two people for 200F, including breakfast; **with Mme Gouélou**, in La Vallée, at the bottom of Moncontour, heading towards Lamballe. ☎ 02-96-73-55-12. Two guest rooms for 200F for two people, including breakfast; or in Quessoy, 8 kilometres (5 miles) further north, *gîtes* and meals at the **Orangerie du Château de Bogard** ☎ 02-96-42-38-25 or 02-96-42-30-02.

WHERE TO EAT

✕ **Crêperie-pizzeria Au Coin du Feu**: place Penthièvre. ☎ 02-96-73-50-56. Closed Monday out of season. A granite fireplace in each of the two dining rooms explains the name – 'the fireside *crêperie*' – of this friendly place, where food is served on Quimper pottery. The menu has a good choice of savoury *crêpes*, which all come with a green salad. *Complète* (with Gruyère cheese, ham and a fried egg) only costs 28F; for big eaters, the *super complète* or the *Forestière* for 32F. A complete meal washed down with a bowl of cider won't cost more than 55F.

✕ **Le Chaudron Magique**: 1 place de la Carrière; right in the centre of town, near the tourist office. ☎ 02-96-73-40-34. Closed Sunday even-

ing in season and Monday from October to May; also closed for two weeks in October. Menus from 67F to 145F. The menus include certain medieval dishes, including nettle soup (*soupe d'orty et herbe*) or snails with black peppercorns (*limassons aux poyvres noirs*), and *douceurs de la Reine* for dessert, all brought to the table by waiters in period costume. Customers are also provided with clothing inspired by the Middle Ages. A few good modern wines are offered to accompany the banquet, but more authentic are the *Framboculum* (sweet strawberry wine), the *Ypocras* (the best-known of the spice-flavoured medieval wines), or the *Clairet* (white wine with spices and honey).

WHERE TO EAT IN THE AREA

✕ **Le Fournil**: Le Coudray, in Plémy, 5 kilometres (3 miles) along the road to Ploeuc-sur-Lié. ☎ 02-96-60-20-37. Open Tuesday to Saturday. This country inn still has the authentic feel of an old Breton house in spite of the restoration work that has been done. There's a weekday lunchtime set menu for 80F and two evening menus, for 102F and 133F, which vary with the seasons but always include delicious traditional recipes made with fresh produce (vegetables from the kitchen garden). The chef comes from Alsace and his menu includes such rich specialities as chicken in Riesling (*coq au riesling*), duck conserve (*confit de canard*), or chicken in cider (*poulet au cidre*). Children's menu 51F. Seafood platter by special order, with 48 hours' notice. Very reasonably priced wine list. It is wise to reserve to be sure of getting what is on the menu for that day. To help you digest this copious regional cuisine, you can always have a game of *boules* after your meal.

WHAT TO SEE AND DO

★ **Église St-Mathurin**: dating from the 16th century, with a baroque facade added in the 18th century. In 1902, the church tower was embellished with an unusual belfry, which fitted perfectly into the architecture of the town and gave it a touch of originality. Inside, lovers of stained-glass windows will be moved by some of the most beautiful groups of windows in Brittany. The three windows to the left of the nave and two on the right, plus the large window of the choir, all date from the time when the church was first built, and represent a priceless set of jewels. The second on the right, depicting the *Tree of Jesse*, has bright colours and wonderful blue tones. The one in the choir recounts the childhood of Christ. There is also a granite baptismal font, a superb 16th-century *pietà*, choir balustrade cast in the Vaublanc forges and polychrome marble high altar (1768).

★ **Château**: during the summer holidays, you can visit the remnants of the medieval fortress demolished during the reign of Louis XIII. Ramparts, dungeons, oubliettes.

★ **Maison de la Chouannerie**: in the tourist office (*see* 'Useful Address'). Same opening times. Admission charge 15F. On three floors, reconstructed scenes of secret Masses and official meetings of the Chouan Uprising in the region. Numerous documents and some fine costumes. A short film about Moncontour and the surrounding area.

★ **Stroll through the town**: as you wander round Moncontour's streets and alleyways, look out for half-timbered houses, granite mansions, vestiges of city gates, Renaissance porches and small niche statues of the Virgin Mary. Many of the lanes have lovely names – the beautiful **rue des Hautes-Folies** is in the form of a stairway (access via the rue de la Pompe), and there is even a little street called Hors-Voie ('off-road'), which nevertheless does lead somewhere. Above all, don't miss the 40 humorous signs created by Gilles Bizien. They can be made to order by applying to Papegault, 4 rue de la Porte-d'en-Haut. ☎ 02-96-73-48-14.

FESTIVALS

– **Grand pardon de St-Mathurin**: religious festival for the patron saint of the sick, at Whitsuntide. On Saturday afternoon, the *pardon des malades* (ceremony for the sick) takes place. At about 9pm, the torchlight procession sets off to the bonfire. On Sunday, there is a procession with the saint's relics and, on Monday, other festivities.

– **Fête médiévale**: a medieval festival during the second two weeks of August. Highlight of the summer festivities, with local residents in period costumes, folk groups, troubadours, stalls with regional products, music and dancing. Smaller than Dinan's medieval ramparts festival, but more accurate historically – like stepping back in time.

IN THE AREA

★ There are numerous **chateaux** in the region, most of which are private and cannot be visited. However, the most important one, **Château de la Touche-Trébry**, located 5 kilometres (3 miles) east of Moncontour, on the D6, the road to Collinée, is open to the public. Tours in July and August, Monday to Saturday and public holidays, 2–6pm. Admission charge. Beautiful 16th-century fortified dwelling, with great architectural unity and a style entirely representative of the Breton Renaissance.

★ **Site du Bel-Air**: south of Moncontour, a 'divine hill' on the watershed line. Once a Celtic place of worship dedicated to Bellenos (the sun god); a star-shaped arrangement of trees remains from this period. The hill, which is the highest point in the Côtes-d'Armor at 339 metres (1,102 feet), was Christianized with a very mediocre chapel planted on its summit. Mysterious rites continue to be performed there but the hill has no great interest for the uninitiated, apart from offering a superb view of the Baie de St-Brieuc and the region of Loudéac. Annual *pardon* (religious festival) on 16 July.

'L'Argoat' – Inland Brittany

Inland from Moncontour lies the 'real' Brittany. Here is a harsh terrain of ridges worn down by thousands of years of erosion, a landscape whose contours are being continually and randomly rearranged. This is a country of dreams and legend, the enchanted land of the fairy Morgane, with moors of heather and gorse dominating green valleys, hikes, swimming in the lakes and fishing. Along the way, the visitor can pass via St-Gilles-du-Méné, in the district of Collinée, close to the Menez moors (for some beautiful walks, *see* 'Loudéac, In the Area'), and the Abbaye de Boquen (*see* 'Lamballe, In the Area'). You will find information about the Méné region at the Pays d'Accueil (reception centre, ☎ 02-96-34-47-58). Then the route either returns to Loudéac or, for those who can't wait to see the sea again, goes straight to the Côte du Goëlo.

LOUDÉAC (*LOUDIEG*) 22600   (Pop: 10,134)

Compared to the *département* as a whole, this small commercial and industrial town is of no great interest to the tourist. Its 18th-century church looks best when lit up at night.

However, the **Forêt de Loudéac**, which covers 2,500 hectares (6,250 acres), and the **Landes du Mené** (Méné moors) are quite close. Unfortunately, this magnificent forested area was badly damaged during the 1987 hurricane. Every year since 1914, on the four Sundays before Easter, the inhabitants of the town have presented a Passion Play before thousands of spectators.

'Loudia', as it is known locally, also goes horse mad every summer in mid-August, when 220 animals, mostly post horses and Breton draught horses, along with about 30 horse teams, gather together to enjoy equestrian displays, a competition to choose the best lady rider, brass bands, and agricultural work. The whole event has a general atmosphere of bygone days.

USEFUL ADDRESSES

🛈 **Pointe Info Tourisme** (tourist office): 1 rue St-Joseph. ☎ 02-96-28-25-17. Fax: 02-96-28-25-33. Website: www.ville-loudeac.fr. Open July and August, Monday–Saturday 10am–12.30pm and 2–7pm; mid-June to mid-September, 11am–noon and 2–6pm. At other times, open afternoons only.

🛈 **Pays d'accueil de Loudéac** (information centre for the Loudéac area): 4 rue St-Joseph. ☎ 02-96-66-09-09. Fax: 02-96-66-09-08. Not open to the public. Information requested and provided by post.

🚌 **Buses**: information at the train station in St-Brieuc. ☎ 02-96-01-61-33. Services to Rennes, Carhaix, Pontivy and Auray.

WHERE TO STAY AND EAT

â **Camping du Val de Landrouët Loisirs, Vacances, Tourisme**: 22230 Merdrignac. ☎ 02-96-28-47-98. Fax: 02-96-26-55-44. The campsite is open from June to mid-September. Reservation recommended. Two-star campsite, with 60 spaces. Surrounded by greenery and overlooking a lake. Brand-new sanitary block. Lots of activities: pool, mini-golf, archery, windsurfing.

â ✕ **Hôtel-restaurant des Voyageurs**: 10 rue de Cadélac; near the church. ☎ 02-96-28-00-47. Fax: 02-96-28-22-30. Open all year round. Well-maintained modern and comfortable hotel. Rooms from 225F to 300F. Restaurant offering good value for money. Menus from 80F to 225F.

✕ **Le Cheval Blanc**: 6 place de l'Église. ☎ 02-96-28-00-31. Fax: 02-96-28-23-96. Closed Sunday evening and Monday; also closed in November and February. This place has an intimate yet casual atmosphere and the decor is country style. It's not *haute cuisine* but the food is well prepared; there's a good à la carte menu and a wide choice of set menus starting from 49F during the week. The welcome is warm.

✕ **Crêperie-pizzeria La Belle Époque**: 16 rue de Pontivy. ☎ 02-96-28-34-98. Open daily except Sunday lunchtime. Good value for money and efficient service. Delicious *pizza océane* (with seafood) and copious meat portions.

WHAT TO SEE

★ **Marché à la Ferme**: at Le Bout-de-la-Lande, 5 kilometres (3 miles) from Loudéac on the road to Mur-de-Bretagne. The farmers' market takes place every Thursday, 5–8.30pm.

IN THE AREA

★ **La Chèze**: very pretty flower-bedecked village with a stream running through it, 10 kilometres (6 miles) southeast of Loudéac. Ruins of a 13th-century castle and an interesting Musée Régional des Métiers about trades and professions in Brittany. ☎ 02-96-26-63-16. Open July and August, 10am–noon and 2–6pm; in May, June and September, afternoons only; out of season, telephone for details. Admission charge 20F. Guided tour and choice of video. Visit the milliner's workrooms, and view the consulting rooms and diverse (and alarming) equipment used by dentists in the 1950s. The equipment will be demonstrated on request!

– Take a look at the wonderful wooden clogs of M. Aubry, 54 rue de la Madeleine (the main street).

– On the last Saturday in September, there is an amusing *foire aux chevaux* (horse market) and sampling of typical dishes amid the atmosphere of a village fête.

★ **Landes du Mené** (Mené moors): to the southeast of the Forêt de Loudéac. A walk through a quite picturesque but irregular landscape takes you to two old villages. Due to the roughness of the terrain, this was once *the* place for *la chouannerie* (Royalist insurgency during the French Revolution).

★ **Les Aquatides**: at Les Livaudières. ☎ 02-96-66-14-40. Water park with jacuzzis, water rides, 70-metre (227-foot) slide and a paddling pool for very small children. Admission charge 29F.

★ **St-Lubin**: 16th-century listed village. Approach via the road to La Prénessaye to appreciate the beautiful unity of this rural architecture. Sturdy sandstone farmhouses; massive church; old sculpted fountain on the road to Vaublanc.

★ **Le Vaublanc**: a former metalworking complex, deep in a small and remote valley, on the edge of the Forêt de Loudéac. Another pretty village here. Noteworthy architecture of the forges, which were in use from 1672 to 1871. Nowadays, some very nice *gîtes* as well, from 1600F to 2000F per week (☎ 02-96-25-68-83). Opposite the lake are a fine building and old 17th-century granary with a roof coming down to the level of the road.

★ **Lac de Bosméléac**: The lake, which covers 76 hectares (190 acres), is part of a system of lakes and rivers rich in fish.

🏠 **Camping du Lac de Bosméléac**: ☎ 02-96-28-87-88. Fax: 02-96-28-80-97. Open mid-June to mid-September. A very beautiful, brand-new and well-located three-star campsite with a lake, kayaking, and a waterfall, and a refreshment room and *crêperie*. Just 16F per space.

★ **Rigole d'Hilvern**: west of Loudéac, along the River Oust. This mini-canal runs between the dam at Bosméléac and Hilvern. These are actually only 20 kilometres (12 miles) apart, although the canal is 62.5 kilometres (39 miles) long. Dug between 1828 and 1838, the canal used to feed into the Nantes–Brest canal. The task required about 400 labourers, many of whom were former weavers whose source of employment had dried up. Nowadays, the mini-canal no longer feeds the larger canal, but it does offer romantic walking and riding paths. Ask at the tourist office for information on the best places to go. For information, contact the Hilvern conservation society (Association pour le sauvegarde de la Rigole d'Hilvern) at the town hall at St-Gonnery, 56920.

★ **Haute Vallée de l'Oust** (high valley of the Oust): among the interesting and unusual sights in this area are granite houses with workshops, called *maisons de toileux* ('clothmakers' houses'), which belonged to shopkeepers in the 17th and 18th centuries. They can be seen particularly in the villages of Uzel, Le Quilio and Merléac.

★ **Le Quilio**: beautiful listed parish, 10 kilometres (6 miles) northwest of Loudéac. Not far from the village is the site of **Notre-Dame-de-Lorette**, with its chapel and megaliths, from which there is a splendid panoramic view. It is even possible to see as far as Vannes on a clear day.

★ **St-Thélo**: just before you reach Le Quilio. This was an extremely important settlement at the time when sailmaking was at its height. A number of old houses can still be seen.

The Guerlédan and Korong Region

This is the sort of place about which lovers of green countryside and rambling enthusiasts dream. It has a lake covering 400 hectares (1,000 acres), forests and, in the south, the remote moorland of the Lande de Gouvello. There are numerous small Breton houses scattered about in the wilds, some of which serve as stopovers to welcome weary hikers. The tourist office in Mur-de-Bretagne can provide detailed maps of the footpaths that criss-cross the region, as well as information about renting mountain bikes or horses.

MUR-DE-BRETAGNE (*MUR*) 22530 (Pop: 2,136)

If you are coming from the north, take the D63, which crosses the Gorges de Poulancre, to reach this small town on the edge of the Lac de Guerlédan and the Forêt de Quénécan. North of the town, visit the 15th-century Chapelle Ste-Suzanne with its 18th-century bell-tower. Inside the chapel, there are paintings decorating wood panelling and altarpieces with interesting statues. The *base d'activités nautiques* (watersports centre) is located 2 kilometres (1 mile) from Mur, at the roundabout by the lake. Unsupervised bathing is possible here.

USEFUL ADDRESSES

🛈 **Maison du Tourisme de la Région du Lac de Guerlédan** (tourist office for the Lac du Guerlédan region): place de l'Église. ☎ 02-96-28-51-41 or 02-96-26-31-37 (town hall). Open from Easter to 15 September, daily except Sunday afternoon, 10am–12.30pm and 2–7pm; the rest of the year, office at the town hall.

★ **Watersports on the lake**: information from the *base départemen-* *tale de plein air* (departmental centre for outdoor activities), located at the roundabout for the lake. ☎ 02-96-67-12-22. In summer only.

★ **Sailboat, windboard, canoe and mountain bike rental: club F.F.C.K. Kayak Guerlédan**, on the Plage du Rond-Point, ☎ 02-96-26-30-52, and **BSA**, ☎ 02-96-26-30-94, on the same beach.

WHERE TO STAY AND EAT

🛏 ✕ **La Perrière**: 2 rue des Ardoisiers; behind the church. ☎ 02-96-26-08-63. Closed for one week over Christmas. An unpretentious stopover hotel, bar and restaurant. Double rooms cost from 150F to 230F. There are eight rooms, six with shared shower at the lower price and two others, with individual shower, for 230F. No. 7, a little apartment in itself, is the best. Everything is clean and the restaurant has an economy-priced evening menu and a set menu of the day.

☆☆–☆☆☆ Moderate to Chic

🛏 ✕ **Auberge Grand-Maison**: 1 rue Léon-Le-Cerf. ☎ 02-96-28-51-10. Fax: 02-96-28-52-30. In the town, near the church. Closed

Sunday evening and Monday, also closed for the first two weeks in March and three weeks in October. *Affaires* ('bargain') set menu at lunchtime for 170F (except Sunday), prepared by Jacques Guillo, master chef of France and one of the best in the *département*. A range of menus on offer: *Tradition* for 210F (except Sunday), *Réjouissance* for 250F, and *Émotion* and *Fête* for 400F. Children's menu for 100F. Just reading through the menu is enough to make your mouth water: think about the *foie gras* profiteroles in a truffle sauce or the Roquefort in a ginger flaky pastry . . . quite a gourmet establishment. Also, nine magnificent rooms which have been very tastefully decorated, from 320F (two rooms) to 650F. Breakfast costs 90F but is a complete meal in itself. Attractive price for half board in this exceptional place.

WHERE TO STAY AND EAT IN THE AREA

🛏 ✕ **Auberge de jeunesse André Le Provost** (youth hostel): at St-Guen (pronounced 'gwan'), located 3 kilometres (2 miles) north of Mur, on the D35 heading toward Le Quillio. ☎ 02-96-28-54-34. Fax: 02-96-26-01-56. Open April to the end of October. FUAJ card required. A wonderful youth hostel, as nice as they come and done up like new. Wonderfully equipped kitchen. Very clean and brightly coloured rooms with four to six beds. Spotless bathrooms and toilets. It really is surprising to find a youth hostel like this in such a small place right out in the sticks. A bed costs 45F per night. Breakfast costs 19F, a meal is 50Fand half board is 114F per person. Inner courtyard with tables outside in the summer. Peace and quiet guaranteed. You can also camp here, for 25F per pitch.

☆☆ – ☆☆☆ Moderate to Chic

🛏 ✕ **Le Relais du Lac**: in Caurel, 5 kilometres (3 miles) west of Mur. ☎ 02-96-67-11-00. Fax: 02-96-67-11-09. Closed Sunday and Monday evening out of season; also closed for the first two weeks in January and the last two weeks in November. Completely restored former coaching inn, with rooms costing from 230F to 270F. A complete menu for 58F (except Sunday), and additional menus from 65F to 130F. Attractively priced half board.

🛏 ✕ **Hôtel-restaurant Beau Rivage**: in Beau Rivage (south of Caurel). ☎ 02-96-28-52-15. Closed Sunday and Monday evening and Tuesday out of season; also closed for two weeks in October and during the February school holidays. Modern but really lovely little hotel at the edge of the lake, with eight comfortable rooms from 270F to 320F. Ask for Nos. 1, 2 or 3, which have a view of the lake. In the dining room with its panoramic windows, or at a table outside overlooking the lake, you will be offered a veritable feast, starting at 90F (except Saturday evening and Sunday). There are additional set menus going up to 170F. and among the specialities, you may find prawn gratin (*gratin de langoustines*), pigeon with wine sauce (*suprême de pigeon sauce vineuse*), warm oysters (*huîtres chaudes*), and to finish with, delicious *crêpes* filled with hot apples and caramel sauce (*l'aumônière de crêpes aux pommes chaudes, sauce caramel*). With such excellent food in so marvellous a setting, you'll be sorry to leave here.

✕ The **Crêperie du Rohic** is actually in Morbihan, in Malvan-en-St-Aignan, but it's only a very short distance from the Lac de Guerlédan: ☎ 02-97-27-51-72.

FESTIVALS

– **Festival des Arts traditionnels**: held every year around about 14 July, this festival offers a showcase of music and traditional dance from all over the world.

– **Fête du Lac**: on 15 August, this festival takes the form of a triathlon and a Breton *fest-noz*.

IN THE AREA

★ **Lac de Guerlédan** (lake): unsupervised bathing in Beau-Rivage, a place where you can rent small boats and pedaloes, with the possibility of water-skiing (☎ 02-96-26-02-18 in season) or a mini-cruise (departures from the restaurant L'Embarcadère, in Beau-Rivage, for trips lasting 1 hour 30 minutes or 3 hours, with the option of a meal on board; ☎ 02-96-28-52-64).

★ **Laniscat**: the **Église St-Gildas** (1667) still has one of the few remaining carillon wheels in Brittany. Large classical altarpiece by Olivier Martinet from Laval.

– Go looking for that lost nugget with Dominique Giraudet, who will introduce you to the art of *orpaillage* (panning for gold). Weekend package including accommodation and meals; information at the tourist office in Mur.

GOUAREC (*GWAREG*) 22570 (Pop: 1,058)

A peaceful village still surrounded by a green and undulating landscape, places to discover and lovely walks. The Abbaye de Bon-Repos and the Forges-les-Salles should not be missed. Then, after a day exploring, you can relax with a dip in the pool.

WHERE TO STAY AND EAT OR GO FOR A DRINK

🏠 **Camping**: a very peaceful campsite beside the canal. ☎ 02-96-24-85-42.

🏠 ✕ **Hôtel-restaurant du Blavet**: RN164, 22570 Gouarec. ☎ 02-96-24-90-03. Fax: 02-96-24-84-85. Email: louis.le-loir@wanadoo.fr. Hotel closed at Christmas and in February; restaurant closed Sunday evening and Monday out of season. Large stone house on the banks of the River Blavet, with a relaxed atmosphere which is Breton through and through. Mahogany wardrobes, a view of the beautiful Blavet and a pleasant dining room. The chef-owner offers fine, tradi-tional cooking through a wide choice of menus from 85F (during the week) to 250F. The rooms are attractive and comfortable, costing from 190F to 280F. For an extra 45F, you'll be able to enjoy the sauna. No. 6 (with canopy bed and view of the river) is more expensive at 350F.

✕ ❢ **Crêperie-bar du Bon-Repos**: right beside the main road, just past the abbey. ☎ 02-96-24-86-56. Closed Monday and from mid-September to mid-October.

❢ **Café de l'Abbaye**: an old lock-keeper's house right beside the Blavet. An extra-special little café where the local viscount and other locals meet up to discuss the weather. P'tite Anne serves all her customers unaffectedly and with good humour. She has a pot-bellied stove too.

☗ Tavarn du Daoulas: at the edge of the road, just before the Abbaye du Bon-Repos. ☎ 02-96-24-90-37. Irish pub atmosphere. Good rock and blues music. Canoe and kayak rental.

WHAT TO SEE AND DO IN THE AREA

★ **Abbaye Cistercienne du Bon-Repos** (Cistercian abbey): the ruins of this 12th-century abbey lie on a very beautiful site overlooking the Lac de Guerlédan. Founded in 1184 by Alain III, Vicomte de Rohan, the Abbaye du Bon-Repos was occupied by Cistercian monks until the French Revolution, during which it was totally pillaged. The ruins, now being restored, date for the most part from the 14th and 18th centuries. Fine view of the main building from the old, ivy-covered bridge. Self-guided tour. During the second week in August there is a big sound and light show about the history of the region, with the participation of 400 unpaid volunteers. Reservations: ☎ 02-96-24-85-28.

★ **Les Forges-les-Salles**: take an enjoyable stroll through the forest, from Bon-Repos to Les Forges-les-Salles, one of the oldest metalworking centres in Brittany. Guided tours weekends out of season, daily in July and August, 2–6.30pm. Admission 20F. ☎ 02-96-24-90-12. Built in the 17th century, this is one of the best-preserved sites of its type. A homogenous architectural grouping in a magnificent setting, particularly the long row of 18th-century workers' houses. There is also a castle with outbuildings and terraced gardens. A victim of competition from overseas, the forge closed down in the middle of the 19th century.

– **Bathing** in St-Gelven, at Roc'h Tregnanton.

– **Mountain-bike rental**: in Bon-Repos. Information at the Bar de l'Abbaye or at the Daoulas.

– **Piscine municipale Aquadelis** (public swimming pool): Attractive greenery creates an exotic atmosphere and contributes to an ecologically friendly heating system. Canoe rental.

The Fisel Region

ROSTRENEN (*ROSTRENENN*) 22110 (Pop: 3,925)

This large village is a stopping-off place on the road between Rennes and Châteaulin, right in the heart of the Fisel region. It has a certain architectural unity but few monuments typical of the area. The church, in a patchwork architectural style, is dedicated to Notre-Dame-du-Roncier (*see* 'Josselin'). All that remains of the 15th-century structure are the four enormous pillars in front of the choir. The central nave dates from the 19th century. There is an interesting porch with polychrome statues of the Apostles. A narrow street beside the church leads to a fine 16th-century fountain. At the *Poterie de Trémargat*, near the church, you will find some interesting ceramics.

USEFUL ADDRESS

fl Syndicat d'initiative (tourist office): 4 place de la République. ☎ 02-96-29-02-72. Open daily in high season, 10am–12.30pm and 2–7pm. Out of season, call the town hall: ☎ 02-96-57-42-00. Information available about walks, including the GR37 footpath.

– **Bike hire**: at the Maison de la Presse, next door to the tourist office.

WHERE TO STAY AND EAT

🛏 ✕ Hôtel-restaurant Henri IV: in the hamlet of Kerbanel, as you leave Rostrenen (beside the road), heading towards Glomel. ☎ 02-96-29-15-17. Fax: 02-96-29-26-67. Closed January. Modern hotel without any charm, but one of the few in the area, and offering good value for money. Recently redecorated and really comfortable rooms from 220F to 240F. The establishment has two restaurants – a traditional one, the **Henri IV**, where menus begin at 70F, and a gastronomic one, **Le Médicis**, with menus from 140F to 240F.

✕ Coeur de Breizh: 14 rue Abbé-Gibert, in the town centre. ☎ 02-96-29-18-33. Closed Wednesday and from 15 November to 10 December. Weekday lunchtime menu for 80F and other menus at 98F and 149F. The à la carte menu prices are also very reasonable. This is an excellent address right in the middle of town, identifiable by its large yellow building. The owners, Anne-Laure and Roger, encouraged by their many friends and regulars who were always telling them to expand their bar into a restaurant, did so by borrowing a small sum from each. It paid off, as everything is first-class. The environment is very attractive, with exposed stone walls and Breton country-style decor. Roger makes a charming and relaxed host, while Anne-Laure, a tremendous self-taught chef, manages her kitchen with panache. All the fare is made with quality products, many of them organic, chosen carefully from local suppliers. Everything is completely fresh, and each dish is generously served. The desserts are delicious, too. Last orders at 10pm during the week and 11pm at weekends.

✕ Pizzeria Le Kumquat: 8 place du Martray. ☎ 02-96-29-30-01. Closed Sunday, and in November. In an old house with exposed stonework and beams, and a relaxed atmosphere. Good pizzas made with organic flour and baked in a wood-burning oven, and a variety of salads. Dishes of the day include such items as chilli con carne and curried chicken (*poulet au curry*). Lunchtime menu for 55F, with the dish of the day for 52F. Order half a pizza for the children, from 25–35F. It's a good idea to book.

TRADITIONAL FESTIVALS

– **Pardon de Notre-Dame de Rostrenen**: takes place on 14 and 15 August. This *pardon* has been celebrated since the 14th century. As part of the religious festival, the statue of the Virgin Mary, discovered around 1300 under a bed of roses in the middle of winter, is carried in a torchlight procession up the Montagne du Minou.

– **Festival de Danses Fisel**: festival of regional dances held during the last weekend in August in the village hall.

GLOMEL (*GRONVEL*) 22110   (Pop: 1,502)

A large village 8 kilometres (5 miles) west of Rostrenen, which has grown up between two lakes, one of which is the Korong. A good place for activities on the water, as the Nantes–Brest canal passes nearby. Kayaking is one of the favourite sports among the locals. Another object of interest (mainly because of its size) is the tallest menhir in the Côtes-d'Armor.

WHERE TO STAY AND EAT

☖ **Camping de l'Étang du Korong**: ☎ 02-96-29-84-20. Open mid-June to mid-September. Well-equipped campsite costing 20F per night per person. Offers a range of water-based activities (windsurfing, fishing, bathing, pedaloes, and so on). Stop-over point for walkers as well.

☖ ✕ **Hôtel-restaurant La Cascade**: 5 Grande-Rue (the main street). ☎ 02-96-29-60-44. Open at lunchtime during the week. Double rooms cost from 160F to 180F, or 220F with a third person. This very pleasant little country hotel offers four pretty rooms, each with nice, personal touches and equipped with TVs. Everything is totally clean, there's a warm welcome and the prices are reasonable. On the restaurant side, they offer a set menu for 55F, but in the evening and at weekends, you need to book if you're not staying at the hotel.

☖ ✕ **Ferme-auberge Le Manoir de St-Péran**: on the road to Paule, the D85, just after Glomel. ☎ 02-96-29-60-04. Fax: 02-96-29-86-34. Meals need to be booked in advance. In the middle of the countryside, a large building joined onto a medieval tower. The most surprising feature is a large lawn with an imposing collection of palm trees. Comfortable rooms for 220F, with shower and toilet, as well as TV, radio-alarm and telephone. Breakfast for 35F. Half board is available for 205F per person. Farmhouse meals based on the house specialities of chicken, hotpot and *crêpes*. Set menus from 75F to 120F. Children's menu for 40F. After eating, you can stroll along the nearby Nantes–Brest canal. On Friday and Saturday, home-produced cooked meats, old-fashioned pâté and sausage meats are on sale.

☖ **Chambres d'hôte Canal Chouette**: at Kergérard, 2 kilometres (1 mile) out of town. It's well sign-posted once you're at the food-store and bakery in the town centre. ☎ 02-96-29-81-44. Double rooms cost 250F and a single is 180F, including breakfast. Dinner is available, for less than 50F per person, but you have to book. This little establishment is right next to the Nantes–Brest canal, out in the country in a peaceful location. There are four rooms on offer, all of which are modern and extremely well kept, plus a large sitting room with a big window overlooking the canal. Excellent welcome.

WHAT TO SEE

★ **Menhir de Glomel**: not easy to find, as it is (fortunately) not as much of a tourist attraction as the stones at Carnac. As you leave the village (heading towards the canal), the menhir ('long stone') stands in the middle of a group of houses. Signposted from the centre; then up a little path on the left (not signposted). Obelix would have appreciated this one – it's 14 metres (46 feet) high.

★ **La Maison de la Nature**: at Coatrennec, about 4 kilometres (2.5 miles) from Glomel and indicated with little blue signs on the left as you go along the Rostrenen road. ☎ 02-96-29-15-93. Fax: 02-96-29-10-87. Open daily, 2–6pm. Closed Tuesday out of season as well as in December and January. Admission charge 25F. Within an enormous modern building that is nevertheless quite well integrated into its environment, this nature study centre explains its subject using all kinds of displays. The first section covers the transformation of the countryside over the centuries with the development of agriculture. The next section undertakes to explain the relevance of environmental factors to local places. Finally, there is an exhibition on the various types of rock to be found in this part of Brittany. The subject is fascinating and the displays are well conceived.

– A number of themed **walks** around the region are organized by the Maison de la Nature.

WHAT TO DO

– **Kayaking**: the canal has 21 gates for canoeing enthusiasts to negotiate. Details from the CASCK association. ☎ 02-96-29-65-01.

FESTIVAL

– **Rencontres Internationales de Clarinette Populaire** (international clarinet festival): in May, during Ascension weekend. This festival has, without really trying, become one of the biggest musical events in the *département*. Programme: ☎ 02-96-29-69-26.

IN THE AREA

★ **Château de Coat-Couraval**: 5 kilometres (3 miles) south of Glomel on the D85, on the other side of the lake. Superb 15th-century building set in green terraced gardens. Open from 1 July to 1 September. ☎ 02-96-29-30-46.

★ **Walk along the banks of the Nantes–Brest canal**: between 1825 and 1836, a trench was dug in the shale near Glomel by thousands of workmen (including a large number of convicts from the prison in Brest). Many perished on the job. To compensate for the elevation of the site, the canal trench reaches a depth of 35 metres (114 feet) in places. Between Rostrenen and Glomel is the canal's *bief de partage* (watershed), at 184 metres (598 feet) above sea level.

★ **Étang du Korong**: lake created during the reign of Napoleon I to channel water into the canal. Unsupervised bathing, and a watersports centre, with sailing, windsurfing, canoeing, tennis, rock climbing, archery and mountain biking. ☎ 02-96-29-60-51.

KERGRIST-MOËLOU (*KERGRIST-MOELOÙ*) 22110 (Pop: 711)

This village, 9 kilometres (5.5 miles) north of Rostrenen, gets its name from *kergrist* ('village of Christ') and *moëlou* (*moyeu* or 'wheel hub', which denotes a good-quality wood found in the surrounding area and used to make this essential part of a wheel). There is a great archaeological harmony here, as well as the most beautiful parish close in the Côtes-d'Armor.

WHAT TO SEE

★ **Église de la Sainte-Trinité**: built at the start of the 16th century, this church is one of the most fascinating examples of the great Flamboyant Gothic period in Brittany. A striking group of buildings with, on the same side as the close, a calvary, a superb porch, a delicate ossuary, and a massive 40-metre (130-foot) high tower with balustrades. There are endless unusual architectural details, particularly the gargoyles, and, beneath their finely sculpted canopies, the polychrome statues of the porch. You enter the church via a large, 16th-century wooden door, whose carving is almost completely worn away (you can barely make out St Peter and his large key now). Some statues are worth looking at, like the superb Virgin and Child by the altar on the right (both the Virgin and Child are holding a curious sphere in their hands) and, on the other side, Sainte Anne and the Virgin.

★ **The Calvary**: the most important calvary in the Côtes-d'Armor, inspired by the one in Plougonven and erected in 1578. It suffered considerable damage during the French Revolution and was restored in the 19th century. Bizarrely, all the scenes were muddled up when the reconstruction took place. Have a special look at the 'entombment', the only scene to be spared in 1793, which radiates great strength of feeling. It shows a rather plump St John, a dignified Holy Virgin and a thin Christ on a shroud with long folds. In the close, some very old tombs remain.

★ Grouped all around the close are 16th- and 17th-century **houses** with austere granite facades.

TRÉMARGAT (*TREMARGAD*) 22110 (Pop: 174)

This ancient village is one of the most emotive of the region. It seems frozen in its past, unaware of the crazy modern world surrounding it. Many of its old granite houses now lie empty.

WHAT TO SEE

★ **Church**: low and modest, in keeping with the size of the village, but not without some architectural points of interest (gargoyles, a sculpted portal, and a small ossuary which still contains some bones). Inside the church, there is an anachronistic Way of the Cross. The Apostles look like members of the Resistance from 1940 and the Roman soldiers are carrying submachine guns.

THE TOUL-GOULIC GORGES AND THE HAUTE VALLÉE DU BLAVET

The River Blavet rises a bit to the north of the lake – good for fishing – which bears its name, near the village of St-Norgan. A little further down, following the valley, the *Chaire des druides* ('druids' pulpit') is an impressive mass of rocks not far from the farm which once belonged to the writer Villiers de l'Isle-Adam. One huge rock has been completely entwined by the roots of a tree. The *Lac Artificiel* (artificial lake) *de Kerné Uhel* in Peumerit-Quintin offers bathing, pedaloes and fishing.

The road from Trémargat to Lanrivain is a pretty one. En route, there is an unusual and poetic sight in a remarkable setting: the Chapelle St-Antoine (from the 15th century), and then, suddenly, by the roadside, a wonderful 17th-century calvary. It was probably built as a protection against the plague, judging by the buboes adorning the column.

A little road (the D110) then leads to the surprising Gorges de Toul-Goulic – a fantastic and chaotic mass of enormous round rocks covering almost 400 metres, with the River Blavet rumbling below. From the car park there is a narrow marked path, which is a little steep but not difficult; it would take a family barely five minutes to reach the rocks.

North of the Fisel Region, Towards Guingamp

LANRIVAIN (*LARRUEN*) 22480   (Pop: 535)

Lanrivain is another village worthy of note. Its church has been reconstructed, but has retained some original features, such as the 16th-century porch. Mostly, the interior has little of interest, but the very old ossuary, on the other hand, is still full of skulls and leg bones. The calvary is from 1548 (broken in 1793 but restored in 1866) – its *Mise au tombeau* (entombment) has figures that are abnormally large for a traditional calvary.

WHAT TO SEE IN THE AREA

★ **Chapelle Notre-Dame-du-Guiaudet**: less than 2 kilometres (1 mile) away. A beautiful, tree-lined avenue leads to this 17th-century chapel with bell-tower. Inside the chapel, there are old commemorative processional banners, a gilded wooden altarpiece and a very rare reclining Virgin nursing Jesus. In the close is a fountain with two basins.

★ **Chapelle de Lannégan**: restored. Fleur-de-lys windows.

ST-NICOLAS-DU-PÉLEM
(SANT-NIKOLAZ-AR-PELEM) 22480 (Pop: 1,917)

This pleasant flower-bedecked village is on the border between the 'regrouped' and the 'non-regrouped' regions; to the south, the communities have suffered more than those to the north. In the church, in the window of the chevet, a stained-glass window from 1470 depicts the *Passion of Christ* in 24 very realistic panels. Beside the church, the elegant 17th-century **Fontaine St-Nicolas** has a niche with two small columns. About 1 kilometre to the southeast stands the little 15th-century **Chapelle St-Éloi**.

The St-Brieuc tourist office (*see* 'St-Brieuc, Useful Addresses') publishes details of a *Parcours du Patrimoine* (heritage tour) of the area, where there is much to see, including windmills, old wells and stone farms.

USEFUL ADDRESS

🏢 **Syndicat d'initiative** (tourist office): place du Kreisker. ☎ 02-96-29-52-51.

WHERE TO STAY AND EAT

🛏 ✕ **L'Auberge du Kreisker**: 11 place du Kreisker. ☎ 02-96-29-51-20. Fax: 02-96-29-53-70. Closed Sunday evening and occasionally Monday out of season. Double rooms from 180F to 260F. Rustic dining room with very good regional cooking. Specialities include homemade pâté, warm Trémurgat goat's cheese (*chèvre chaud de Trémurgat*) and chocolate mousse. Set menus from 72F to 156F.

IN THE AREA

★ **Musée de l'école de Bothoa** (school museum): at Bothoa, 3 kilometres (2 miles) north of St-Nicolas-du-Pélem. As you leave the village heading north. ☎ 02-96-29-73-95. Open 15 June to 15 September, Tuesday to Sunday 2–6pm. Admission charge 20F. A really charming museum set up in a 1930s school building, with displays about the old Bothoa school and a chance to visit the schoolmaster's house and the classroom itself. Visitors can have a try at writing with pen and ink. Note that there's a dictation session every Tuesday at 3pm.

ST-GILLES-PLIGEAUX
(*SANT-JILI-PLIJO*) 22480   (Pop: 309)

Another charming little village dating back to the 14th century and with some interesting buildings, notably a remarkable combination of church and chapel, which will appeal to all photographers. The 16th-century church has a pretty domed tower and balustrade (added later), a 17th-century altarpiece and a sinister catalfaque. The delightful Chapelle St-Laurent has a magnificently worked Renaissance doorway. In particular, don't miss, below the church, the two beautiful twin fountains hemmed in by their stone enclosure. You can reach them via two time-worn little stairways. Such a monument is rare in the region.

IN THE AREA

★ **Kerpert**: this old village is worth a detour for its 16th-century church alone. Situated on a little hillock surrounded by a stone wall, it has been eaten away by lichen. Its porch and belfry represent a noble and rugged style of architecture. Small ossuary in the cemetery.

★ **Abbaye de Coatmalouen**: only some ruins remain near a large farm, a few kilometres to the northeast. Its large facade is open to the sky and it seems to have remained standing only by a miracle. At the far end are the remains of the chapel with sculpted tomb.

★ **St-Connan**: very old village, on a little road heading for Quintin. A delightful group of typical old granite houses surrounds the village church. Despite the protection of large, round rocks, the community is now largely deserted, and today has a serene and rather poignant charm.

★ **Senven-Léhart**: north of St-Connan, this is another timeless village. The church dates from the 19th century, but still possesses a 16th-century calvary.

★ **Corlay**: village in the heart of Brittany, with a long tradition of horse-racing. Its own racecourse, the Hippodrome du Petit-Paris, hosts races in June and on 4 and 14 July. The Corlay breed (not to be confused with the *bidet breton*, or Breton pony, *see* 'Callac') was very closely related to the English thoroughbred, and was bred for racing.

The 12th-century **feudal castle**, destroyed during the Hundred Years' War and then rebuilt in the 15th century, today houses in its ruins the Maison du Cheval, for those who are interested in horses. ☎ 02-96-29-42-90. Tours from 15 June to 15 September, 10.30am–12.30pm and 2–6pm. Tourist office in the castle courtyard.

BOURBRIAC (*BOULVRIAG*) 22390   (Pop: 2,337)

This village, with its church as big as a cathedral, tries very hard to make itself attractive to tourists, with flowers and floodlighting on its lake. The church is open all day; its crypt dates from the 10th century and the bell-tower was completed in the 19th century, so traces of many different styles can be found. The organ, however, is brand new.

You should also visit the Chapelle Notre-Dame-du-Daouet, once a very popular pilgrimage destination, which retains a beautiful 14th-century window. In the neighbouring district of Plesidy are the Menhir de Kailouan (11 metres/36 feet high), some very pretty 16th-century Breton manor houses (*Toul An Golet*) and a number of chapels.

USEFUL ADDRESS

❸ Syndicat d'initiative du pays de Bourbriac (tourist office for the Bourriac region): in the place de l'Église, on the corner of the rue du Télégraphe. ☎ 02-96-43-46-03. In high season, open Monday to Friday 9am–12.30pm and 1.30–5pm and Saturday 9am–12.30pm; out of season, open Monday, Wednesday and Friday 9am–12.30pm. Friendly, helpful staff. Every Monday in July and August, free tastings of *kir breton* (a local aperitif), served with local cakes.

WHERE TO EAT IN THE AREA

✗ **Auberge Pierr'an Daol**: in the hamlet of Crec'h-Cant. Located 6 kilometres (4 miles) from Bourbriac, 9 kilometres (5.5 miles) from Guingamp. ☎ 02-96-21-81-02. Open all year round at weekends both lunchtime and evening; in July and August, open every evening except Monday. Take the D63 from Bourbriac as far as Coadout; the *auberge* is signposted to the right as you leave Coadout. You will find it at the end of a road dotted with old farms decked with flowers. Meat is cooked to order over a hot stone. Set menus for 85F, 88F and 100F. Attentive staff.

BULAT-PESTIVIEN
(*BULAD-PESTIVIEN*) 22160   (Pop: 443)

Just off the road halfway between Guingamp and Carhaix, the village of Bulat-Pestivien has one of the most remarkable churches in the whole region. The drive here is also delightful, on a network of country roads, via countless villages that reflect long-forgotten traditions and ways of life.

WHERE TO STAY

⌂ **Camping municipal**: in the hamlet of C'horonk, 500 metres from the village on the D50 heading towards Maël. ☎ 02-96-45-76-86 or 02-96-45-72-00 (town hall). Fax: 02-96-45-75-56. Open from 1 May to 31 August. Not expensive.

WHAT TO SEE

★ It is amazing that such a modest village could possess such a **church**. Its porch is a real masterpiece. In the middle, a column sculpted with vines supports a splendid Flamboyant tympanum surmounted by a profusion of plants. In their niches, the Apostles stand under a delicately sculpted canopy. Beneath the 66-metre (215-foot) high tower and spire, the main portal is flanked by two figures holding manuscripts; lichen gives them strange contours and colouring. The front and sides of the church are covered in picturesque but disturbing sculptures of gargoyles, animals, grotesque figures, scallop shells, and more. The omnipresent figure of *Ankou* (the Breton Grim Reaper) is depicted in a series of grimacing characters; one of them, brandishing bones, appears to be screaming. Inside the church is a curious lectern in the form of a peasant in local costume, and a large offertory table from 1583, sculpted in stone with geometric figures. In the sacristy is a macabre frieze.

★ In the cemetery, the **fountain** at the far end resembles a kind of swimming pool. Two other interesting fountains, those of the *Coq* and the *Sept Saints*, can be seen on the road to Callac, as you leave the village.

★ Located 1 kilometre to the north is the charming little **enclos de Pestivien** (the close), with a chapel and a calvary. Note the desperate and contorted writhing of the two thieves carved on the latter.

IN THE AREA

★ **Chapelle de Burtulet**: about 5 kilometres (3 miles) to the south, the chapel rises up, completely on its own on a pine-covered hill. A very romantic spot.

CALLAC (*KALLAG*) 22160   (Pop: 2,509)

Nothing remains in Callac – once an area of glory and prosperity – of the feudal castle that was razed to the ground in 1619 on the orders of Richelieu. In front of the village's stud farm is a statue of the famous stallion *Naous*, sculpted by Guyot. This draught-horse embodies the line of the *bidet breton* (Breton pony), different from the post-horse of Landivisiau.

USEFUL ADDRESS

🄱 **Syndicat d'initiative** (tourist office): place du Centre. ☎ 02-96-45-59-34.

WHERE TO STAY AND EAT

🛏 ✕ **Gîte d'étape de la ferme-manoir de Kerauffret**: in Maël-Pestivien. ☎ 02-96-45-75-28. Walkers' stopover open all year round, managed and recommended by the FUAJ (youth hostel association). In an early 19th-century noble building, dormitory accommodation is 41F per night. Breakfast for 20F and meals can be ordered for 60F. Run by an enthusiastic man who even bakes his own bread.

♠ ✕ Les Fous Anglais: Pen ar Vern, in Carnoët. From Callac, 7 kilometres (4.5 miles) heading towards Carhaix. ☎ and fax: 02-96-21-52-32. Closed Wednesday and at the end of November. Out in the middle of the countryside, a lovely inn situated in an old Argoat mansion. The place is so successful that it is advisable to book in advance in high season. The inn is restful, with a family atmosphere, and offers good fresh food. Set menus for 50F (lunchtime only), then from 58F to 85F. Specialities are meat grilled over a wood fire, and tasty home-made desserts. Children's menu. Patio and play area. Three *gîtes* in the courtyard of the manor house for 1,500F, 2,500F and 3,500F per week. Swimming pool and bric-a-brac shop.

SHOPPING

🔒 Café-Quincaillerie: 4 rue des Martyrs, in the Old Town. Closed Sunday afternoon. You can get coffee in this old-style hardware shop, overfilled with stock you rarely see nowadays. In the middle of all the jumble you find a worn old counter . . . and a lady proprietor with a lively character.

🔒 Le Comptoir de Campagne: 2 rue des Portes, in the Old Town. ☎ 02-96-45-51-06. Open 9.30am–noon and 2.30–7pm. Closed Sunday, and Monday out of season. This family business started in 1913 but moved across the road to the existing premises in 1927. Today, it's a cross between a hardware store, a corner shop and a household goods shop, but either way, it still has plenty of old-fashioned charm. You can buy everything from nails to small items of furniture, from underwear to fishing and hunting tackle. The atmosphere is extraordinary, as there are wooden floors, a lofty ceiling and the owner's office is at the back inside a 'cage', just as it was in the old days.

WHAT TO SEE

★ **La tannerie de Callac**: on the Z.A. de Kerguiniou (industrial estate). ☎ 02-96-45-50-68. A tannery specializing in fish skins! Visits possible, and some nice souvenirs for sale, such as bracelets and even novelty pocket ashtrays.

IN THE AREA

★ **Lac de la Vallée-Verte**, the **Pont-à-Vaux** and the **Chapelle Ste-Barbe** – site of a lake, bridge and chapel.

★ In **St-Tréfin**: 15th-century chapel and tumulus.

★ **La Chapelle-Neuve**: between Callac and Belle-Isle-en-Terre. An organization called La Maison de la Forêt et du Bocage organizes numerous guided nature walks in this pretty part of inland Brittany. ☎ 02-96-21-60-31.

★ **Plougonver**: between Callac and Belle-Isle-en-Terre. Stop off at the *café-alimentation* (grocer's shop and café in one) in the village square, not far from the pretty little 15th-century church. In the quaint setting of the grocer's shop, amid brooms and bicycle wheels, Lucie Riou serves coffee in cider bowls while recounting tales of village life. Make the most of it; in a few years, these kind of places will have disappeared.

★ Foodies should try to make another stop at Kerbriand, to have a taste of the homemade preserves at **Les Merveilles de Tante Alice**. ☎ 02-96-21-62-11. It's best to telephone first. You'll find it about 4 kilometres (2.5 miles) east of Plougonver in the direction of Gurunhuel.

PLOURAC'H (*PLOURAC'H*) 22160 (Pop: 383)

Right on the border with Finistère, about 10 kilometres (6 miles) west of Callac, this village, off the main tourist track, is a real find.

WHAT TO SEE

★ **Enclos paroissial** (parish close): one of the most beautiful and most complete rural parish closes you'll see anywhere. The 15th-century **church** has a splendid Breton Renaissance porch, and its sides are adorned with fantastic gargoyles and coats of arms. The belfry has a balustrade and round turret. On the calvary, admire the *pietà*, whose severe, almost grotesque features reflect the harsh nature of the region.

LOC-ENVEL (*LOKENVEL*) 22810 (Pop: 76)

Located 4 kilometres (2.5 miles) south of Belle-Isle-en-Terre and the Guingamp to Morlaix road, Loc-Envel is a natural pause on any tour of upper Cornouaille and the Trégor region. This tiny hill-top village has typical Breton architecture and one of the finest churches in Brittany.

WHAT TO SEE

★ **Church**: from the outside, this church has little to distinguish it from others in the region. It clings to its hill, like the village, and has a small bell-tower and gargoyles in the form of bizarre animals. It is the interior of the church, however, that is striking in its splendour. Near the entrance stands an amazing Flamboyant carved wooden rood screen, dating from the 16th century and ornamented with foliage, arabesques and birds. The lower part of the gallery is carved with vine branches to create a veritable lacework in wood. The best work, though, is the fabulous display of multicoloured purlins, *blochets* (pieces of wood linking beams and panelling) and *engoulants* (beam ends) which adorn the nave and choir. The detail is extraordinary. One of the purlins shows a terror-stricken figure being devoured by a dragon, and other comical figures, at once religious and secular, are also on view. The *engoulants* are also remarkable – monstrous animal heads that appear to swallow up the beams. The *blochets* are adorned with strange figures. The vaulting rests on a central purlin which is completely covered in carving (this is quite rare). At each rib, there is an object symbolizing an instrument of the Passion (hammer, nail, crown, and so on). The most beautiful piece, at the crossing of the transept and the choir, is the large, sculpted keystone symbolizing the Trinity. In the four corners are the Evangelists. Another keystone, behind the altar, personifies Christ in majesty.

The 16th-century stone altar was sculpted from a single block. The altarpiece, composed of five panels depicting the Passion, dates from the 17th century. There is a superb main window.

As you retrace your steps back to the main entrance, note the three little windows on the left, which allowed lepers to follow the Mass without entering the church.

BELLE-ISLE-EN-TERRE
(BENAC'H) 22810   (Pop: 1,115)

A very pretty road leads through woods to Belle-Isle-en-Terre, a large, peaceful and pretty village. Here, there are remains of galleries from the silver-bearing lead mines of Toul Al Lutun, as well as the castle of Lady Mond, a poor local girl who, in 1922, married the 'nickel king'.

The little Chapelle Locmaria is 1.5 kilometres to the north. Its gallery is a former 16th-century rood screen.

USEFUL ADDRESS

⊟ Office du Tourisme: 15 rue de Chrec'h Ugen, in the Old Town, opposite the chateau. ☎ 02-96-43-01-71. Fax: 02-96-43-31-00. Website: www. qualite-info.fr/belleisle. In season, open Monday–Friday 9.30am–12.30pm and 1.30–6pm, Saturday 9.30am–1pm; out of season, open Monday–Friday 9am–12.30pm. The staff are efficient and friendly.

WHERE TO STAY AND EAT

≜ ✕ Le Relais de l'Argoat: 9 rue du Guic; near the post office. ☎ 02-96-43-00-34. Fax: 02-96-43-00-76. Closed Sunday evening and Monday (except in July and August), as well as in January. Very comfortable rooms for 250F. Half board starts at 280F per person sharing a double room. Menus from 85F (weekday lunchtime) and from 120F to 280F evenings and weekends. Specialities include lobster, turbot in cider and fillet of beef en croute.

≜ Gîte d'étape (walkers' stopover): 5 rue des Tilleuls. See Mme Derrien (☎ 02-96-43-08-95) or ask at the town hall (☎ 02-96-43-30-38).
✕ Crêperie Ty ar C'hrampouz: place de l'Église. ☎ 02-96-43-00-01. Closed Monday except during school holidays. There's a family atmosphere in this nice little *crêperie*, and it has a good local reputation, perhaps because they only use organic flour. Allow about 60F to eat à la carte.

WHERE TO STAY AND EAT IN THE AREA

🛏 ✕ **L'Ancien Presbytère**: opposite the church in Trégrom, 7 kilometres (4.5 miles) north of Belle-Isle, leaving the N12 at Louargat or Belle-Isle-en-Terre and heading for Trégrom. ☎ and fax: 02-96-47-94-15. In a charming building dating from the 17th, 18th and 19th centuries, Nicole de Morchoven has converted this former presbytery into a *gîte* for six people (around 3,500F per week) and three guest rooms (300F, including breakfast). A table d'hôte meal is offered in the evening, with just one menu for 125F, everything included (aperitif, food, wine, coffee). The setting is delightful and a warm welcome is guaranteed.

WHAT TO SEE AND DO

– Discover the River Léguer or go fishing, details from the **Centre d'initiation à la rivière** (centre for activities on the river): ☎ 02-96-43-08-39. ✕ The aquarium here is open Tuesday–Sunday 2–6pm in summer. The centre is located in the chateau that once belonged to Lady Mond. An aquarium of river life is the latest addition to the facilities and allows visitors to learn everything about rivers, all the way from the source down to the sea. There is much more than just fish to learn about and the displays are inviting as well as interesting and educational. Courses on ecology take place here throughout the year and, in addition, the centre also offers nature expeditions in the area in summer for a modest charge (20F).

– **Saboterie Kervoas**: place de l'Église. ☎ 02-96-43-30-13. Breton clogs are made and sold here – by the brother of the lady who runs the *crêperie*.

– **Biscuiterie des Îles**: 2 kilometres (1 mile) outside the town and well signposted. ☎ 02-96-43-30-03. Open all year round 9am–7pm (6.30pm out of season). This biscuit factory has been in existence since 1875 and sells buttery little *galette* biscuits made on the premises, as well as a number of products from the region. It's possible to do a 30-minute tour of the factory and see biscuits being made, Monday to Friday at 11am during the summer season, and you can taste the goods at the end. Apart from the simple butter kind, they also make delicious *galettes* with chocolate chips and coconut.

IN THE AREA

★ In **Plounevez-Moëdec**, 16th-century Église St-Pierre. The tower is ornamented with openwork, and there is a balustrade and several old tombs. Lovely houses all around, one of which has a large granite drinking trough.

★ In **Louargat**, on the road to Crec'h Even, is a *lec'h* or upright stone, pierced with 11 superposed cupules. After Louargat, you will see the **Menez-Bré**, which reaches a height of 301 metres (978 feet) and provides a beautiful panoramic view of the Trégor region. The Menez-Bré hill has always been a important place for esotericism and sorcery, and a source of inspiration and 'good vibrations'.

★ **Trégrom**: to the north of Belle-Isle-en-Terre before you reach Plouaret. Pretty and very quiet, this is a fisherman's paradise as the river Léguer is full of trout and salmon. The GR34 walkers' route passes close by.

– In the town, a little way below the church, there's a baker who makes organic bread the old-fashioned way, with a wood-fired oven. He only opens up two mornings a week, on Wednesday and Saturday from 9am to 12.30pm. It's worth the effort to catch him at work.

See also 'Where To Stay and Eat in the Area'.

PLOUARET (*PLOUARED*) 22420   (Pop: 2,160)

Anyone familiar with the train journey from Paris to Brittany using the Gare Montparnasse will recognize the name Plouaret, as it's here that most of the high-speed TGV trains stop on their way to Brest. A rather uninteresting small town, Plouaret has nothing to entice holidaymakers, who are, after all, on their way to the coast and the beaches. Nothing, that is, except possibly the *crêperie* with the best welcome in Brittany.

WHERE TO EAT

✗ **Crêperie Ty Yann**: 24 impasse des Vergers, just 50 metres away from the church. ☎ 02-96-38-93-22. Closed in October and January. Open daily in summer, noon–2pm and 7–11pm. From November to June, open Friday, Saturday and Sunday, and every evening during the Paris and Brittany school holidays. Despite the enormous number of *crêperies* in Cotes d'Armor, this is one of the best if not *the* best, and it's just about the only reason for stopping in Plouaret. The place is tucked away in a low little stone-built house and has only a few tables. A pretty decor and a warm, smiling welcome give a feeling of confidence and what they then serve confirms your impression. Using buckwheat from the Moulin de la Fatigue mill at Vitré, and adding a variety of first-class fillings, Yann, who is the owner as well as the chef, manages to satisfy the most demanding of palates. Try, for example, the *Bigouden*, which mixes savoury and sweet. Leave some room for a *crêpe*, too – perhaps an *antillaise*, which is a feast to look at as well as to eat. Even the prices are reasonable.

CULINARY TREATS

🔒 **Foie Gras Tommy**: at Kerbridou Vian, 2 kilometres (1 mile) north of Plouaret on the road to Lannion. ☎ 02-96-38-85-44. This farm shop is open 9am–noon and 2–7pm. Closed Sunday. You may think of *foie gras* as being a speciality of southwest France but, in his field, Tommy has snatched awards from under the noses of his Gascon colleagues. He sells not only *foie gras* but also a variety of pâtés, *rillettes* (potted pork), *gésiers* (gizzards), *magrets* (duck breasts) and other regional products. It's possible to tour the breeding pens.

From Plouaret to the Côte du Trégor

If you aren't in a hurry, take time to explore the tangle of charming little country roads that criss-cross this area of small fields and hedgerows.

★ **Armoripark**: to the right of the D767 between Guingamp and Lannion. An amusement park for young and old, with a play pool, zoo and various other enjoyable attractions.

GUINGAMP (*GWENGAMP*) 22200   (Pop: 8,830)

A town at the crossroads between the Goëlo and Trégor regions, and close to the border between the Breton-speaking and Gallo-speaking regions. Follow the cleverly signposted tours (medieval and Renaissance) to discover the lovely old districts of the town. Its beautiful basilica was the first of the Renaissance period in Brittany. Guingamp has been a university town since 1993, and is therefore a lively home to many young people and bars.

USEFUL ADDRESSES

🛈 Office du tourisme: place Champ-au-Roy (opposite the park). ☎ 02-96-43-73-89. Fax: 02-96-40-01-95. Open Monday–Saturday 10am–12.30pm and 1.30–6pm, Sunday 10am–1pm. Closed Sunday and Monday out of season.

🚆 Gare SNCF (train station): ☎ 08-36-35-35-35 (premium rate). On the Paris–Brest line, with connections for Paimpol, Carhaix and Lannion.

WHERE TO STAY

🛏 Camping de Milin Kerhé: in Pabu, 2.5 kilometres (1.5 miles) to the north. Well signposted. ☎ 02-96-43-77-94 or 02-96-44-05-79 (in high season). Fax: 02-96-44-04-27. Open mid-June to mid-September. Not expensive – allow about 50F for two people.

🛏 Hôtel d'Armor: 44–46 boulevard Clemenceau. ☎ 02-96-43-76-16. Fax: 02-96-43-89-62. Email: hotel armor.guingamp@wanadoo.fr. 50 metres from the station. Open all year round. Recently built, modern (with satellite TV), although the rooms are rather dull. A double room costs

300–330F, with shower or bath. Very welcoming. Half board arrangement with *L'Express* restaurant.

☆☆☆ Chic

🛏 Demeure de la Ville-Blanche: 5 rue du Général-de-Gaulle, near the place du Centre. ☎ 02-96-44-28-53. Fax: 02-96-44-98-90. Closed in January. Double rooms cost 340–430F, with an extra bed at 80F; the weekly rate is 1,550–1,950F. Breakfast costs 42F. This is a very proud 17th-century gentleman's residence where a likeable couple, Françoise and Patrick Solo, are offering some excellent and very comfortable rooms. The whole place has a refined air and there is antique furniture throughout. The rooms all have telephone, TV, video, and a hi-fi system, and the suites have fully equipped kitchens. Guests can also use the large sitting room on the ground floor, as well as the garden. A room has been set aside and kitted out for guests to organize their stay, with a good supply of brochures, magazines, maps and books about the region. Plenty of advice is also on offer. This is a great place – and it's relaxed despite its elegance.

☆☆☆☆ Très Chic

🛏 ✕ **Le Relais du Roy**: 42 place du Centre. ☎ 02-96-44-76-62. Fax: 02-96-44-08-01. Closed over Christmas and Sunday between mid-November and the beginning of April. A double room costs 650F, which seems a bit expensive. Set menus cost 125–220F, but there's a weekday lunchtime two-course menu for 85F. Half board costs 1,000F for two people. This very old house is Guingamp's best address. A superb granite staircase leads up to the bedrooms, which are very comfortable but lack the charm of the Demeure de la Ville-Blanche. The restaurant has an excellent local reputation and you can dine in style in a very elegant dining room where everything is meticulously chosen, from the curtains to the napkins. The welcome is excellent and the service attentive.

WHERE TO EAT

✕ **Crêperie Saint-Yves**: rue St-Yves, very close to the place du Centre. ☎ 02-96-44-31-18. 🦽 Closed Monday in July, Sunday evening and Monday out of season, as well as two weeks in May and November. Good *crêpes* and *galettes*. Set menu for 48F and à la carte. Specialities include savoury buckwheat pancake (*galette de blé noir L'Armor*) and savoury plain flour pancake (*galette de froment L'Aumônière*). This very friendly place is great, but remember to book in advance as the dining room is tiny.

✕ **L'Express**: 26 boulevard Clemenceau. ☎ 02-96-43-72-19. 🦽 Closed Sunday evening out of season and Saturday lunchtime throughout the year. Next to the Hôtel d'Armor. This brasserie is possibly the best value for money in Guingamp, with very reasonably priced weekday lunchtime menus. Good, traditional cuisine and lots of customers both inside and outside.

Dish of the day for 50F, set menus from 85F to 155F.

✕ **La Roseraie**: parc Styvel. ☎ 02-96-21-06-35. Open 7–11pm. Closed Monday evening out of season. Barely 1 kilometre from the centre of Guingamp, on the road to Tréguier; the restaurant is signposted on the right. In a beautiful, bourgeois residence in the middle of its own grounds, this restaurant has one of the nicest situations imaginable. The dining rooms are pleasant and the food is tasty, with pride of place going to grills and seafood. Quite simply, a real treat. Expect to pay from 100F to 150F. Definitely advisable to book in advance.

✕ **Le Clos de la Fontaine**: 9 rue du Général-de-Gaulle, very close to the place du Centre. ☎ 02-96-21-33-63. Five set menus are available, from 78F to 230F, plus à la carte. This restaurant serves good, traditional fare in a pleasant room with exposed stone walls, and there's a terrace too. Specialities include scallop salad and fresh *foie gras* with apple, although the menu changes according to the season.

✕ **Le Relais du Roy**: *see* 'Where To Stay'.

WHERE TO GO FOR A DRINK

🍸 **Campbell's Pub**: place St-Michel. ☎ 02-96-43-85-32. Open daily from 11am (4pm on Sunday in winter, 5pm on Sunday in summer) to 1am (2am on Friday and Saturday). The trendiest bar in town, frequented by all the local young people; very lively atmosphere on Saturday nights and when the local football team comes to celebrate a victory.

🍸 **L'Épave**, just along the road in rue de la Trinité, is a café with music that is often packed with customers. Also in rue de la Trinité is **Le Nosey Parker**, where there's live music and a young ambiance. **La Glycine**, rue du Grand-Trotrieux, is a little pub that is plain but friendly.

WHERE TO BUY WINE

Cave Victor'Inn: place du Centre. Under the same ownership as the one in St-Brieuc. *See* 'What To Buy' in 'St-Brieuc'.

WHAT TO SEE

★ **Basilique Notre-Dame-du-Bon-Secours**: begun in the 13th century and built on to an old Romanesque church. The basilica was constructed in the Gothic style, but still retains Romanesque elements, such as the arches where the transept crosses the choir. In 1535, the tower, the side aisle and the west portal collapsed. In planning its reconstruction, the architect Jean Le Moal took a daring and unexpected decision: to rebuild in the Renaissance style, which was still practically unknown at that time. As a result, a view of the building from the street reveals a style that is pure Gothic, while, from the garden, the visitor sees an original mixture of Gothic and Renaissance (with some Romanesque elements still remaining in the oldest part).

There are beautiful Renaissance **windows** in the side walls, and the west **portal** is a Renaissance masterpiece with an abundance of decoration. Look carefully at the arches. The secular elements greatly outnumber the religious ones. Admire the three **towers**: the Tour de la Flèche, 57 metres (185 feet) high; the Tour de l'Horloge, a fortified clock tower crowned by a roof with four panels; and the flat tower known as the Tour des Cloches. The chapel is situated on the street side, closed off by grillwork to protect the **statue of Notre-Dame du Bon-Secours**. On the first Saturday in July, there is a great religious *pardon* with a torchlight procession and bonfire.

Inside the church, the same mix of Gothic and Renaissance styles is evident, with the dividing line virtually down the middle. Very elegant Renaissance **triforium** (high gallery running the length of the nave). The presence of such huge pillars in the middle of the church, breaking up the space, is unusual. There are very few original furnishings (the French Revolution saw to that), but the wooden multicoloured **high relief** at the far end of the choir (scenes of the Passion) is worthy of note. Next to it is the *Vierge de l'Annonciation* (Annunciation to the Virgin).

★ **Place du Centre**: the heart of the town, this square is reserved for pedestrians. It is surrounded by noble houses and mansions with tall granite chimneys, and some facades are timber-framed or clad in slate. Pretty Renaissance **doorways**, such as the one on the same side as the Hôtel du Relais du Roy and the one at No. 1 rue Olivier-Ollivro. Beautiful turreted **house** on the corner of the rue Jean-Le-Moal (next to the basilica). Splendid Renaissance fountain, known as *la Plomée*, with three basins.

★ **Hôtel de Ville** (town hall): housed in the old Hôtel-Dieu (hospital), the town hall has an elegant Italian baroque facade, and you can see the remains of the cloisters of an Augustinian monastery (from the end of the 17th century). In the hall, where the municipal offices are to be found, you can see two large paintings by Paul Sérusier (1904): *L'Annonciation* (the Annunciation) and *Moïse devant le buisson ardent* (Moses and the burning bush). In passing, note the monumental fireplace and the equally impressive 18th-century staircase.

★ **Place du Vally**: standing in this square are the remains of the ramparts, demolished on the orders of Richelieu. Three of the four mid-15th-century towers of the castle of Pierre II, Count of Guingamp and later Duke of Brittany, are still standing. There is a picturesque view of the towers from the rue du Grand-Trotrieux.

CELEBRATIONS AND FESTIVALS

– **Fête de la St-Loup**: begins on the Sunday of the week of 15 August and lasts for one week. Folk dances and the famous *dérobée de Guingamp*, a kind of great farandole with dancing figures.

– **Festival de danses bretonnes exécutées par des enfants,** *Bugale Vreizh*: a festival featuring Breton dances performed by children, on the first Sunday in July.

– **Open-air concerts** take place every Thursday in July and August, on the bandstand in the public park. Information from the tourist office.

CHÂTELAUDREN (*KASTELLAODREN*) 22170   (Pop: 948)

Almost exactly halfway between Guingamp and St-Brieuc – from Guingamp, take the N12 towards St-Brieuc, then go left on the D7. Châtelaudren is a small characterful village, the former capital of the Goëlo region and once the fief of the soldiers of the Republic during the French Revolution. In its **Chapelle Notre-Dame-du-Tertre** there is a wonderful and unusual group of paintings on wood panels dating from 1460. There are no fewer than 96 in the choir alone, depicting scenes from the Old and New Testaments, and about 40 others in the **Chapelle Ste-Marguerite**, recounting the martyrdom of the eponymous saint. The beautiful colours of the group have been skilfully restored, especially the red and gold backgrounds. The drawings are impressive, with sumptuous details in the demeanour and clothing of the figures, for example, halfway between illumination and naïve art. Definitely not to be missed.

At the top of the village is a lake in a charming setting. In the village itself, the **Église St-Magloire** has interesting altarpieces by Yves Corlay. Take a pleasant walk around the little streets and the place de la République to view the old houses, near the waterfall by the old printing works of the *Petit Écho de la Mode* newspaper. These old buildings are at the centre of an important project in the cultural life of the area. The idea is to turn the place into a multi-disciplinary centre, covering everything from music and drama to economics, geography and various branches of science and technology. It is already in use for conferences.

USEFUL ADDRESS

🖫 **Syndicat d'Initiative au Pays de Châtelaudren** (tourist office for the Châtelaudren area): 1 place du Leff. ☎ 02-96-74-12-02 or 02-96-79-51-05 (fax/voicemail). In summer, open Monday–Saturday 9.30am–12.30pm and 2.30–6.30pm, Sunday 10.30am–12.30pm. In winter, open Monday and Thursday 10am–noon and 3–6pm, Saturday 10am–noon. Welcoming staff and plenty of information about the area.

WHERE TO EAT

✕ **Le Relais du Leff**: place du Leff, opposite the tourist office. ☎ 02-96-74-10-33. This restaurant was opened fairly recently by a young chef who has worked in some of the best restaurants in the region, such as Crouzil at Plancoët. There's just one menu, which costs 57F.

WHERE TO STAY AND EAT IN THE AREA

✕ **Chambres d'hôte Les Écuries de la Magdeleine**: 5 kilometres (3 miles) to the south of Châtelaudren on the road towards Quintin and very well signposted from the road. If you're coming on the main road, leave at the Kertedevant-Châtelaudren-Quintin exit. ☎ and fax: 02-96-73-86-35 or 06-07-99-27-94. A double room costs 330F with breakfast included. This little chateau is perched on a hilltop in the peace of the open countryside. There's a warm welcome and a very relaxed atmosphere. The bedrooms are vast and are well laid out and functional, with good bathrooms. A kitchen is available and there's a sitting room with TV. The place operates as stables, so there's the opportunity to do a bit of horse-riding if you fancy it.

🛏 **Ferme-auberge Au Char à Bancs, chambres d'hôte La Ferme des Aïeux**: signposted from the village of Plélo, 3 kilometres (2 miles) northeast of Châtelaudren. ☎ 02-96-74-13-63. Fax: 02-96-74-13-03. Email: charabanc@wanadoo.fr. ✕ From mid-June to mid-September, open daily except Tuesday; the rest of the year, weekends only. Closed for the last two weeks of September. Book in advance in high season and at weekends. Basic set menu for 90F and other menus up to 170F. Almost 20 years ago, in this former watermill on the

River Leff, right on the border between the Gallo- and Breton-speaking areas, M. and Mme Lamour created one of the first *fermes-auberges* (farmhouse inns) in Brittany. The dining room sums up the country lifestyle: old stone walls, beams, wooden tables and a cauldron worthy of Asterix in the huge fireplace where their famous hotpot simmers away permanently. They also offer delicious savoury *crêpes* prepared in the traditional way. The perfect family day out is a meal here, followed by a visit to the park and the lake, to enjoy the pedaloes or ponies. About 400 metres from the mill, at the top of the property, is the Ferme des Aïeux, a former coaching inn said to date back to the 11th century. The Lamour family have turned it into a lovely little museum, with a forge, bakehouse, stables, barns, and so on (admission charge). Outside the farm complex, in a recently built annex, are five charming guest rooms (from 390F for a double room), one of which is a real gem with a bathroom in tradi-tional tiles, four-poster bed, small sitting room and rustic furniture. This beautiful room has even been featured on the front cover of the official *Gîtes de France* guide. There is also a traditional box bed, very popular with honeymooners. You can visit the little power station, which generates their electricity using the river's current.

✕ **Ferme-auberge de la Ville-Andon**: 22170 Plélo, on the road from Châtelaudren to Plourhan-St-Quay; signposted from the village. ☎ 02-96-74-21-77. Fax: 02-96-74-35-79. In summer, open daily except Monday; out of season, open weekends and during the school holidays. Specialities include *charcuterie* (cold meats), chicken in cider (*coq au cidre*) and duck with turnips, all served in a splendid rustic dining room where the food is prepared over an open fire. There's a set menu for 100F (children's menu for 50F) and it's a good idea to book. A very warm welcome is offered. There is usually an exhibition of paintings on the top floor.

WHAT TO SEE

★ **Terrarium de Kerdanet**: at Plouagat, 2 kilometres (1 mile) to the west of Châtelaudren. ☎ 02-96-32-64-49. ✦ Open mid-May to the end of September, on Wednesday, Saturday and Sunday 10am–noon and 2–6pm. Admission charge 26F (21F for children aged 5–12). Here you can take a close look at all sorts of amphibians – snakes, lizards, tortoises and toads – in a re-creation of their natural habitat. It's a fascinating place and very well presented. The guided tour takes about 1 hour, 30 minutes.

La Côte du Goëlo

The normal route from St-Brieuc to Paimpol takes you along the Goëlo coast. It has its holiday resorts as well as the fishing ports of Binic and St-Quay-Portrieux, but the wild cliff-faces at Plouha also make an interesting diversion.

Head inland, too, and discover the unspoiled paths and churches, some of which are real little works of art.

BINIC (*BINIG*) 22520   (Pop: 3,202)

This 'beauty spot on the Côtes d'Armor' (as described by the marketing material) is a nice seaside resort with a pretty seafront and lovely little harbour. It is a traditional weekend meeting place for the young Briochins (inhabitants of St-Brieuc). Believe it or not, Binic, a former deep-sea fishing port, was the largest of its kind in France in 1845. Today, pleasure-boating represents the main part of its maritime activity. Binic owes its charm to the fact that the marina and the town are so well integrated, and to its traditional harbour and beach hidden by the jetty.

USEFUL ADDRESS

🖪 Office du tourisme: L'Estran, avenue du Général-de-Gaulle, BP 37. ☎ 02-96-73-60-12. Fax: 02-96-73-35-23. Website: www.villebinic.fr. Open July to mid-September, daily 9am–12.30pm and 2–7pm; out of season, Monday to Saturday 9am–noon and 2–6pm. Boat trips are available, particularly to the Île de Bréhat.

WHERE TO STAY

🛏 ✕ Hôtel Benhuyc: 1 quai Jean-Bart. ☎ 02-96-73-39-00. Fax: 02-96-73-77-04. ♿ Closed in January. Restaurant closed in low season on Sunday evening and Monday lunchtime. Double rooms cost 295–430F and have TVs. In the restaurant, there's a lunchtime-only set menu for 68F and others from 95F to 220F. Specialities include seafood and a few Belgian dishes, as the proprietor comes from Belgium. The hotel is right in the centre of Binic looking out over the marina, and can be recommended. The rooms have recently been fitted out, and are comfortable, nicely decorated and very well kept. What's more, most of them face the marina or the beach. The cheaper rooms are quite small, but pleasant nevertheless. Attentive service.

WHERE TO EAT

✕ Au Vieux Logis: 7 place de l'Église. ☎ 02-96-73-35-56. Open daily in summer. Closed Monday lunchtime and Wednesday in winter. Set menus for 75F, 95F and 135F and a fun children's menu for 35F. In winter, there's a lunchtime menu for 60F. Built in 1679, this former coaching inn is the oldest building in Binic. The old stone walls, the granite flagstone floor and the traditional Breton furniture combine to make a warm, rustic environment and everything is arranged with care. The restaurant is run by a young couple sharing the workload, with Madame in the kitchen and Monsieur serving and dispensing jokes. Everything is freshly prepared and their buckwheat *galettes* are crispy and delicate. Specialities on the menu might include fricasséed veal with scallops and a variety of dishes originating in Alsace, where the couple came from. Recommended.

WHERE TO STAY AND EAT IN THE AREA

🏠 ✕ **Camping Les Madières**: in the hamlet of Le Vau Madec, 22590 Pordic. ☎ 02-96-79-02-48. Open from April to the end of September. Nice site, wooded in its highest part, 800 metres from the sea. A three-star campsite, comfortable and well organized. Reasonably priced. Bar and grocery shop. Good restaurant open to campers. Pony-trekking in the nearby countryside.

🏠 **Chambres d'hôte and gîte with Claudine Simon**: La Ville Morel, Plourhan, 22410 St-Quay-Portrieux. Just 4 kilometres (2.5 miles) from Binic, at the roundabout take the D21 towards Plourhan. ☎ 02-96-71-90-18. Fax: 02-96-71-43-90. Closed the first two weeks in October. There are four very nice guest rooms, one with wood panelling, bright and comfortable, with bathroom, for 200F for two people, including breakfast. Claudine Simon also offers accommodation in her *gîte* for walkers, large families and small groups (less than 10 people).

🏠 **Chambres d'hôte Le Pré Péan**: in Pordic. *See* 'St-Brieuc, Where To Stay and Eat in the Area'.

WHERE TO GO DANCING

– **Le Radeau**: by the harbour in Binic. Open every evening, in season. Out of season, open Friday and Saturday from 11pm. This is the oldest nightclub in the whole *département*, and is popular at weekends with the young Briochins. Admission 60F (including drink).

FESTIVAL

– **Fête de la Morue**: this festival – in celebration of the cod – happens either at Whitsun or around Ascension Day, depending on the tides. There's a gathering of old sailing ships, plus folk-dancing and singing . . . with cod being the main dish of the day.

WHAT TO SEE

★ **Musée de la Pêche et des Traditions** (museum of fishing and local traditions): next to the tourist office. Open from mid-April to the end of September, daily 2.30–6.30pm. Closed Tuesday out of season. Very small but interesting.

IN THE AREA

★ **Chapelle Notre-Dame-de-la-Cour**: 7 kilometres (4.5 miles) west of Binic, after the village of Lantic. Inside, the beautiful main window, dating from the 15th century, depicts the childhood of Christ and the life of the Holy Virgin.

★ **Le Jardin Zoologique de Bretagne** (Brittany zoo): about 6 kilometres (4 miles) west of Binic, right out in the country, on the road to Trégomeur; very well signposted. ☎ 02-96-79-01-07. In high season, open daily 10am–7pm; in winter (except Christmas) Wednesday and Sunday 2–6pm. Admission 55F (children 35F). Allow up to 2 hours. This zoo's priority is the saving of endangered species, and its director is regularly involved in exchanges with other European zoos, to encourage the reproduction of various rare species before eventually reintroducing them into the wild. There are no cages here (except for the tigers and lions). Zebras, ostriches, yaks, llamas, wild asses and wildebeest live in large enclosures, while sacred ibis, capuchin monkeys and ring-tailed lemurs make their home on little 'islands', and numerous species roam freely in the undergrowth. The 1-hour tour in this exotic setting is very pleasant. The only regrettable thing is the little tourist train (but it only runs in summer, luckily).

ST-QUAY-PORTRIEUX (*SANT-KE-PORZH-OLUED*) 22410 (Pop: 3,434)

Large and popular family seaside resort, with all sorts of activities to keep you busy – beautiful beaches, a casino, a saltwater swimming pool, marked footpaths, and so on. The sailors of St-Quay who, a long time ago, used to fish the waters as far afield as Newfoundland, would have difficulty in recognizing their little fishing port now, which has been enlarged to accommodate a thousand boats. There are nice views from the cliffs that overlook the resort.

– **Markets**: every Monday morning at the harbour and Friday morning at the church.

USEFUL ADDRESSES

🛈 **Office du tourisme**: 17 *bis* rue Jeanne-d'Arc. ☎ 02-96-70-40-64. Fax: 02-96-70-39-99. Website: www.saint-quay-portrieux.com. In high season, open Monday to Saturday 9am–12.30pm and 1.30–7.30pm, and Sunday and public holidays 10am–noon and 3–6pm; out of season, open Monday to Saturday 9am–12.30pm and 2–6.30pm. Very efficient staff, organizing excursions and selling tickets. Guided tours of the harbour and the fish auctions are available, if you book in advance.

🛈 **La Maison du Port**: esplanade du port d'Armor. ☎ 02-96-70-50-60. Open daily in July and August except Friday and Sunday morning.

WHERE TO STAY AND EAT

⛺ **Camping Bellevue**: 68 boulevard du Littoral. ☎ 02-96-70-41-84. Fax: 02-96-70-55-46. Open from 1 May to 15 September. Allow about 90F for two people. A three-star campsite, well situated and partly shaded. In the lower part, the gently sloping fields stretch as far as the cliffs overlooking the waters of the Golfe de St-Brieuc. You have the feeling of being surrounded by the sea. Clean sanitary block. Reservations advisable in summer. Part of the long-distance walkers' path, the *sentier des douaniers* runs alongside the campsite on the edge of the cliff and is ideal for a stroll.

⛺ **Chambres d'hôte Les Roches Douves**: 50 rue Jeanne-d'Arc. ☎ 02-96-70-93-43. A double room costs 200F or 250F. The proprietor, Mme Vérin, gives a very warm welcome and keeps her four rooms spotlessly clean. The location here is ideal as it's right in the centre of town, only 100 metres from the beach and close to the tourist office.

⌂ **Hôtel Le Commerce**: 4 rue Georges-Clemenceau, 50 metres from the harbour. ☎ 02-96-70-41-53. Closed on Tuesday and in January. A double room costs 250F and it's 350F for three or four people. Recently renovated, this little hotel is modest but good. The rooms all have bathrooms and have been nicely fitted out, with wood panelling. There's a bar on the ground floor, but there's no problem with noise as it closes quite early. Warm welcome.

⌂ ✕ **Le Gerbot d'Avoine**: 2 boulevard du Littoral; 100 metres from the main beach. ☎ 02-96-70-40-09. Fax: 02-96-70-34-06. Closed for three weeks in January and the last two weeks of November. Restaurant closed Sunday evening and Monday out of season. A pleasant and welcoming *Logis de France* with a nice, family boarding-house atmosphere. Popular with foreign tourists in the summer. Rooms from 270F to 340F; breakfast 42F. Half board obligatory in high season, from 300F per person. Good restaurant with traditional food. Set menus for 90F to 290F. Air-conditioned dining room.

✕ **Crêperie La Rosadèle**: place de l'Église; situated 150 metres from the tourist office. ☎ 02-96-70-96-25. Open all summer from noon to midnight. In winter, closed Tuesday evening and Wednesday; also closed for the first three weeks in December and two weeks in March. This *crêperie* takes its name from the old villa where it is located. Five menus to choose from, starting at 49F (drink included). Choice of about 40 à la carte specialities costing about 40F, from the *Super Paysanne* to the *Française* with Breton sausage, eggs and cheese. Children's menu for 40F. The sweet and savoury *crêpes* are exceptionally good and never prepared in advance. There's another comfortable dining room upstairs. The service is efficient and friendly, and customers usually leave well satisfied.

✕ **Crêperie Fleur de Blé Noir**: 9 rue du Commandant-Malbert (opposite the casino). ☎ 02-96-70-31-55. Fax: 02-96-71-91-64. Closed Monday and Tuesday, as well as January–March. Allow about 80F for a meal. A decent place to eat, which could be just another *crêperie* but for the fact that it turns out good food at good prices. Real old-fashioned savoury *crêpes* highly rated by the locals, which says it all. The *Iroise* and the *Gourmande* are recommended to food lovers. Complimentary house aperitif or coffee.

✕ **Le Mouton Blanc**: 52 quai de la République; by the harbour. ☎ 02-96-70-58-44. Closed Wednesday and Thursday, the last two weeks in November and 15–31 January. This restaurant has an excellent reputation in the region, due to the superb cuisine prepared by Patrice Bideau, the chef and owner, who learned his trade at another first-class establishment in Belle-Île-en-Mer. The set menus change with the seasons, but there is always a choice of fish or meat dishes. Menus from 96F to 180F, or reasonably priced dishes à la carte. Excellent choice of desserts. Eat upstairs if you want to enjoy the sea view.

☆☆☆ Chic

⌂ ✕ **Hôtel-restaurant Ker Moor**: 13 rue du Président-Le-Sénécal; up in the hills. ☎ 02-96-70-52-22. Fax: 02-96-70-50-49. Closed from 20 December to 5 January. Amazing Moorish house built in the 18th century by a Breton diplomat.

Professional staff and modern rooms with balcony and all mod cons. Rooms with sea view from 525F to 595F in high season. The prices are considerably lower in mid- and low season. Breakfast is 60F. Some rooms looking out on the garden are less expensive but in no way as interesting. Half board obligatory in July and August, and during school holidays. Good restaurant with set menus from 135F to 195F.

WHERE TO STAY IN THE AREA

🏠 **Camping L'Abri Côtier**: 4 rue de La Ville-es-Rouxel, in Étables-sur-Mer (neighbouring village, south of St-Quay). ☎ 02-96-70-61-57. Fax: 02-96-70-65-23. Open from the beginning of May to 20 September. Situated in a residential area. Costs 106F per night for two people in season and 88F in May, June and September. Mobile homes to let (four people) for 3,300F per week. Divided into two very quiet areas. Campsite shop. Swimming pool. Bar. Beach 500 metres away.

🏠 **La Ville-Hellio, chambres d'hôte with Mme Orhan**: in Plourhan; on the D9, between St-Quay-Portrieux and Lanvollon. ☎ 02-96-71-93-21. Large, very welcoming old farmhouse. Three rooms: toilet and bathroom on the first floor; 170F for two people, not including breakfast.

WHAT TO SEE AND DO

★ **The *sentier des douaniers*** (customs officers' path): picturesque corniche path leading from the harbour to the signal station. Beautiful panoramic view of the bay.

– **Boat trips to the Île de Bréhat**: from mid-June to mid-September. Details from the tourist office.

– **Mini-croisières** (cruises): cruises or fishing trips are available in a trawler. More information from the tourist office.

– **Cinéma**: if it rains, you can take refuge in the Arletty cinema, where there's lots of atmosphere.

– **Cinémathèque de Bretagne, Mémoire vivante de Bretagne**: esplanade du Port d'Armor. This is a branch of the Cinémathèque de Brest. Information from the tourist office, where you can also make bookings.

FESTIVAL

– **Fête de la Coquille-St-Jacques** (scallop festival): takes place every year but the venue rotates between St-Quay-Portrieux (next in 2003), Loguivy-de-la-Mer (2001) and Erquy (2002). Everything there is to know about the *coquille St-Jacques*, from catching and farming them, to eating them.

IN THE AREA

★ **Étables-sur-Mer**: located 5 kilometres (3 miles) to the south. Two beautiful beaches, the plage des Godelins and plage du Moulin. And, on the way, the pretty little Chapelle de Notre-Dame-de-la-Délivrance, perched on the cliff (stained-glass windows and tapestry). Don't miss the town's lovely church.

🛈 **Office du Tourisme**: 9 rue de la République. ☎ 02-96-70-65-41. They hold a list of people offering chambres d'hôte in the area.

★ **Tréveneuc**: 3 kilometres (2 miles) to the north, in the direction of Plouha. If you go down to the sea, to the grève St-Marc, there's a lovely chapel. Tréveneuc is a pretty mooring place used by a small number of boats. You can get a snack of oysters and mussels here. The *sentier des douaniers* walk begins at this point.

★ **Plouha** (22580): located 8 kilometres (5 miles) to the north. Large village nestled 70 metres (225 feet) above the sea. During World War II, Royal Navy officers came to plage Bonaparte to lift out British airmen who had landed on French soil. The cliffs at Plouha are thought to be the highest in Brittany and are certainly the most breathtaking. The best way to see them, coming from the town, is to go in the direction of the cemetery and then head towards Gwin Zegal. After about 3 kilometres (2 miles) you reach the sea, looking down onto Gwin Zegal harbour, which is one of only two harbours in Brittany (the other is at Porspoder in Finistère) where a curious array of tree trunks stick up out of the mud.

🛈 **Syndicat d'initiative** (tourist office): 5 avenue Laënnec. ☎ 02-96-20-24-73. Fax: 02-96-22-57-05. Email: o-t-plouha@wanadoo.fr

🛏 **Camping**: domaine de Keravel on the route de Port Moguer, 3 kilometres (2 miles) from Plouha and well signposted from the main road. ☎ 02-96-22-49-13. Fax: 02-96-22-47-13. Open from mid-May to the end of September. A pitch costs 49F. There are also apartments for rent in the manor house, which is open all year round. A luxury four-star site, appealing not only because of its beautiful location, but also because of its tennis courts and swimming pool.

★ **Lanvollon**: situated 12 kilometres (7.5 miles) to the west, on the road to Guingamp. In the heart of the Leff region, named after the little river which winds through it. Lots of walks in the area. The Viaduc de Blanchardeau (150 metres/487 feet long with 19 arches) is quite interesting and unusual. Constructed in 1905, it was closed just before World War II. Restored in 1993, it now carries a footpath.

🛈 **Office du tourisme du Leff** (Leff tourist office): place du Marché-au-Blé, in Lanvollon. ☎ 02-96-70-12-47. Open all year round. Very efficient staff will help you to discover the region and all its sporting and cultural activities. Guided tours and walks are arranged through this office.

🛏 ✖ **Lucotel**: parc Lannec, rue des Fontaines, as you enter Lanvollon going from St-Quay to Guingamp. ☎ 02-96-70-01-17. Fax: 02-96-70-08-84. Email: lucotel@wanadoo.fr. ♿ Closed Sunday evening and Monday lunchtime from September to March. Also closed in February and November. Recently built hotel, lacking charm, but well situated and offering all services and mod cons. Rooms for two cost from 280F to 310F; ask for a room on the garden side. Weekday set menus from 73F to 180F. Attentive staff. Tennis and mini-golf.

LANLOUP (*SANT-LOUP*) 22580 (Pop: 216)

Lanloup is a small village, as yet untouched by tourism, although that is changing. It has a gorgeous 15th-century church, with a remarkable porch with statues of the Apostles beneath their sculpted canopy. The harmonious group of church, calvary and preserved cemetery is very much in the Finistère style.

The Manoir de la Noé-Verte is 2 kilometres (1 mile) from the village. The beautiful 15th-century building is open to the public, with some rooms still furnished. You can have coffee in the grounds, surrounded by peacocks.

WHERE TO STAY AND EAT

🛌 ✕ **Studios de tourisme et crêperie St-Roch**: a few minutes from the church. ☎ 02-96-22-33-55 or 06-12-60-34-12 (mobile). Fax: 02-96-22-64-31. Open all year round except Monday. In a Breton house, formerly a smallholding, run by a very friendly person who organizes overnight accommodation for walkers (the GR34 footpath passes close by). Traditional Breton dinners organized on request. One night will cost 220F for two people out of season, 290F in high season. Special deal for hikers of 220F per day, per person. It is also possible to rent a studio for two, three or four people, fully equipped, for 1,400F per week for two people (out of season) and 2,200F (high season). Pleasant terrace on sunny days. Free swimming pool 300 metres away.

IN THE AREA

★ **Chapelle de Kermaria-an-Iskuit**: located 3 kilometres (2 miles) south of Lanloup via the D94; or take the D21 from Plouha. Built in the early 13th century and enlarged in the 15th and 16th centuries, the chapel has a beautiful ogive porch sheltering Apostles made of polychrome wood. The inside of the chapel is truly original, with several frescoes, including a strange *danse macabre* running the length of the nave, with around 50 figures, painted around 1490. Half of the figures are holding hands with a corpse. The detail in their clothing makes it possible to guess at the occupation – from peasant to bishop – or social condition of the deceased.

★ **'Temple' de Lanleff**: from Kermaria, take the D21 in the same direction and continue on through Pléhédel. A rather unique church, one of only two – the Église de Sainte-Croix in Quimperlé is the other – that are in circular form. Constructed in the 11th century in the most pure Romanesque style, the 'temple' is based on the plan of the Church of the Holy Sepulchre in Jerusalem. Although it has lost its dome, its sparseness and primitive coarseness mean that it remains impressive. It immediately makes you think of a small Roman temple. Well-preserved central rotunda with beautiful arches and some clumsily carved capitals.

★ **Bréhec**: located 3 kilometres (2 miles) north of Lanloup, this small harbour nestled in a cove is protected by the Pointe de la Tour on the right and on the left, by the Pointe de Berjule. The sea stretches away into the distance and the fishing boats lie beached on the shore which is rich in clams and other shellfish. A little seawall, built after World War II, shelters the beach and its visitors.

★ **Plouézec**: just 6 kilometres (3.5 miles) north of Lanloup in the direction of Paimpol. It's worth making a detour to see the tremendous view from the Pointe de Bilfot or the Pointe de Minard. Below the Pointe de Bilfot, you drive down to Port-Lazo then up again towards the Moulin de Craca. This windmill is the sole survivor of the many windmills that once turned on this stretch of the coast, and from here, there are incredible views towards the Pointe de Guilben, Ploubazlanec, Pors-Even and to the Île de Bréhat to the north. The windmill can be visited at certain times (details are available from the tourist office).

PAIMPOL (*PEMPOULL*) 22500   (Pop: 8,419)

The grand era of *Pem-Poull* in Breton (meaning 'the head of the pond'), when fishermen trawled the Icelandic waters, is long past. However, reminders of the heyday of the sailing ships remain in the lovely ship-owners' houses and the poignant sailors' cemeteries. Strolling through the small pedestrianized alleyways in the Old Town during July or August is a pleasant way to pass the time.

USEFUL ADDRESSES

🖪 **Office du tourisme**: place de la République. ☎ 02-96-20-83-16. Fax: 02-96-55-11-12. Out of season, open from Tuesday to Saturday 10am–12.30pm and 2.30–6pm; in high season, open from Monday to Saturday 9am–7.30pm, and Sunday and public holidays 10am–1pm.

■ **Maison des plaisanciers** (yachting): quai Neuf. ☎ 02-96-20-47-65
■ **Recorded Weather Forecast**: ☎ 08-36-68-02-22
🚆 **Gare SNCF** (train station): ☎ 02-96-20-81-22

WHERE TO STAY

Everything around the harbour is lively in the evenings and noisy at night.

🏠 Budget

🛏 **Camping Cruckin**: the nearest campsite to the town, in Kérity. ☎ 02-96-20-78-47. Open from Easter to 30 September.
🛏 **Hôtel Berthelot**: 1 rue du Port. ☎ 02-96-20-88-66. Plain house offering 12 rooms in this one-star, family run hotel. Rooms for two people from 160F to 240F, according to how well equipped they are. Breakfast for 27F. Parking in front of the hotel, along the harbour.

🏠🏠 – 🏠🏠🏠 Moderate to Chic

🛏 **Hôtel Le Terre-Neuvas**: 16 quai Duguay-Trouin, by the harbour. ☎ 02-96-55-14-14. Fax: 02-96-20-47-66. Double rooms cost 200–240F, with a small supplement for an extra person. Most of the rooms have a view of the harbour and have shower and WC, TV and telephone. Everything is nice and clean and there's a warm welcome. At the top of the house, there are two bedrooms and a bathroom, which is ideal for a family. You can also eat here: see 'Where To Eat'.

♠ **L'Origano**: 7 *bis* rue du Quai. ☎ 02-96-22-05-49. Open from Easter to 1 November. In a house typical of the old part of town, this hotel offers comfortable rooms costing 270F for two, 325F for three or 440F for five. Room No. 8 is particularly pleasant, with its old beams, fireplace and direct access to the small garden. There is also a family apartment for five people for 440F.

♠ **Hôtel K'Loys**: 21 quai Morand. ☎ 02-96-20-93-80. Fax: 02-96-20-72-68. Double rooms cost 395–695F and a room for four costs 795F. These two harbourside establishments under the same ownership both offer accommodation. The cheapest rooms are over the pub-restaurant called **L'Islandais**. Reached by a separate staircase, these rooms are both comfortable and attractive. At the far end of the restaurant, take a look up at the ceiling, which is cleverly constructed from an old ship's hull. Next door, in

an old ship-owner's house, is the **Hôtel K'Loys**, which has 11 superior rooms, all furnished and decorated with taste. Very little of the building's 19th-century appearance has been changed, making this a charming and elegant little hotel with an intimate atmosphere. The most expensive rooms have a view out over the harbour, and one even has its own sitting room and a bay window. One concession to modernity is the lift.

♠ **Le Repaire de Kerroc'h**: 29 quai Morand; by the marina. ☎ 02-96-20-50-13. Fax: 02-96-22-07-46. ♿ Restaurant closed Tuesday and Wednesday lunchtime. The hotel occupies a bourgeois stone residence, of the type typical of St-Malo, that dates back to 1793. It was built for a privateer who served under Napoleon. Offers 13 stylish rooms, spacious and spotless, from 290F to 580F, and a suite on two levels for 690F. Elegant dining room (see 'Where To Eat').

WHERE TO EAT

☆☆ Moderate

✕ **Crêperie-restaurant Chez M. Morel**: 11 place du Martray. ☎ 02-96-20-86-34. Open every day except Sunday out of season. Closed in November. In the town centre. A large, welcoming dining room which attracts lots of customers every day thanks to its delicious *crêpes*. Dish of the day for 45F. Excellent cider. As an aperitif, try the amazing *pommeau-des-menhirs*.

✕ **Le Terre-Neuvas**: (see above 'Where To Stay' for details). Four set menus are on offer, from 82F to 150F (children's menu at 42F). The first dining room as you enter looks out over the harbour. The restaurant specializes in fish, seafood and Breton dishes, and the menu includes

several dishes using cod, reflecting Paimpol's great fishing history, and various mussel recipes. The cuisine in this unpretentious little place is good, sometimes very inventive, and the fish in particular is well prepared and served.

☆☆☆ Chic

✕ **Restaurant de l'hôtel de la Marne**: 30 rue de la Marne; near the station. Private car park. ☎ 02-96-20-82-16. Fax: 02-96-20-92-07. Closed Sunday evening and Monday except for July and August and holiday weekends and during the February school holidays. A double room here costs 325F. Excellent set menu for 115F (except for public holidays), with cheese or dessert.

Additional set menus from 140F to 270F, which might include shelled lobster poached in chicken broth, king prawn *vinaigrette* or *foie gras* cooked in oil of truffles. There's an appetizing dessert menu, too. A 420F menu caters for real foodies (aperitif, wines and coffee included). Whatever your choice, you will understand why the motto on the menu is: 'Real happiness is attained when things taste of what they are.' Half-litre carafe of house wine for 46F, and a wine list with no fewer than 220 wines. Lovers of good food who want to prolong their pleasure can buy homemade *foie gras*, pâté, and so on, to take home. Guaranteed value for money, frequented mostly by locals.

✕ **La Vieille Tour**: 13 rue de l'Église; in the old part of Paimpol.

☎ 02-96-20-83-18. Closed Sunday evening and Wednesday except during school holidays. A friendly restaurant with set menus from 117F to 300F. Children's menu for 76F. Specialities include king prawn ravioli and skate with buttered cabbage. Could the owners be superstitious? Their address is No. 13, there are 13 tables in the dining room, 13 steps on the stairs and 13 letters in the name of the restaurant!

✕ **Le Repaire de Kerroc'h**: 29 quai Morand; on the harbour. ☎ 02-96-20-50-13. Closed Tuesday and Wednesday, and from mid-November to Christmas. Elegant dining room where you can treat yourself to traditional old recipes. Menus from 140F up to 495F (children's menu 85F). Rooms are also offered: *see* 'Where To Stay'.

WHERE TO STAY AND EAT IN THE AREA

🛏 ✕ **Chambres d'hôte at Ferme de Kerloury**: Kerloury, 22500 Paimpol. 2.5 kilometres (1.5 miles) from Paimpol. Leave by the road to Lézardrieux via Kergrist and turn right at the crossroads, 1 kilometre after the Leclerc shopping centre; signposted Kerloury-Landehy. ☎ 02-96-20-85-23. Family-style welcome to a pretty country house. Guest rooms for 240F (double), 300F (for three) or 380F (for four), with generous breakfast at the big kitchen table. The proprietor, Jeannette Le Goaster, gives tours of her garden to anyone who's interested, and will demonstrate her methods of growing plants from seeds and cuttings. Book in advance.

WHERE TO GO FOR A DRINK

– **Les Mardis du Port**: concerts and free entertainment at the harbour every Tuesday in summer.

🍸 **Bar-dancing Le Pub**: rue des Islandais. ☎ 02-96-20-82-31. On the corner of the quai Morand. Friendly pub playing rock or reggae.

🍸 **Le Corto Maltese**: 11 rue du Quai (behind Le Pub). ☎ 02-96-22-05-76. Open daily until midnight. Typical Breton bar – lively atmosphere guaranteed.

🍸 **La Ruelle**: 26 rue des Huit-Patriotes, in the old part of town. Late-night bar open every evening in high season, with the occasional gig at weekends.

🍸 **Le Cargo**: 15 rue des Huit-Patriotes. ☎ 02-96-20-72-46. Open until 1am (2am at weekends). This characterful café is done out in a marine theme, with an array of musical instruments fixed to the ceiling, and there are two concerts held every month. There's a good atmosphere and the place seems to be popular with local people of all ages. Dartboard.

WHAT TO SEE AND DO

★ **Paimpol Old Town**: **place du Martray**, and the little lanes all around it, have some beautiful examples of local architecture. On the corner of the square and the **rue de l'Église** is a superb Renaissance house which once belonged to a ship-owner, with square corner turret. Nearby is the rue Georges-Brassens, named after the French singer who holidayed in his house in Lézardrieux for more than 30 years. At No. 5 rue de l'Église, there is a half-timbered house with carvings. At No. 6 **rue des Huit-Patriotes** is an even older one, with figures on the corners.

★ **Musée du Costume**: rue Pellier. ☎ 02-96-20-83-16. Open daily in high season, 10.30am–1pm and 3–7pm. Admission charge 15F (8F for children). Traditional costumes from the area; here, you will find out the difference between the weekday head-dress, the *touken*, and the Sunday-best *capiole*.

★ **Musée de la Mer** (maritime museum): rue Labenne. Open from Easter to September, 10am–1pm and 3–7pm. Admission charge 25F (13F for children). Installed in a former cod-drying plant, a fascinating reminder of the region's marine heritage (and, notably, of the days when deep-sea fishing was done in the waters off Iceland), by means of models, photos, ropes and cables, buoys, sails and various implements.

– **Boat trips**: on the *Vieux-Copain*, a tuna boat dating from 1940 which is a listed historic monument. Call M. Le Joliff: ☎ 02-96-20-59-30. Daily in July and August, weekends only during the rest of the year. Day-long cruises and training courses from one to seven days, from 1 April to 31 October; accommodation for up to 30 people.

– **Le Trieux à toute vapeur** (steam train ride): steam train trips run along the Trieux valley between Paimpol and Pontrieux. ☎ 02-96-20-52-06. The return trip costs 120F (half-price for children under 11). It's a good idea to book as this is a busy tourist attraction.

SHOPPING

🔒 **Marine clothing**: in the maritime cooperative, avenue du Général-de-Gaulle, or in **Dalmard Marine**, place du Martray. Family business founded in 1922, creator of the famous *Kabic* waterproof fleece jacket and formerly supplier to the fishermen who fished off Newfoundland.

IN THE AREA

★ **Abbaye de Beauport**: on the road to St-Brieuc, after Kérity. ☎ 02-96-20-97-69. Open from 15 June to 15 September, daily 10am–7pm; the rest of the year, 10am–noon and 2–5pm. An abbey dating from the beginning of the 13th century, partially destroyed in 1789. Listed as an historic monument in 1862, it now belongs to the Conservatoire National du Littoral (national body for the preservation of the coastline). You can visit the abbey, the pretty chapter room, the beautiful storeroom and the remains of the cloister, set in 35 hectares (nearly 90 acres) of pastoral parkland by the sea. Exhibitions, classical concerts and Thursday evening story-telling events are hosted in high season.

– Paimpol is the starting-off point for a long *circuit pédestre*, an excellent circular walking tour of the peninsula via Porz-Even, the Pointe de l'Arcouest and Loguivy, along little country roads and uneven coastal paths. Details from the tourist office in Paimpol.

– An unusual **train journey**: the railway line from Paimpol to Guingamp follows the right bank of the Trieux as far as Pontrieux. From the train you can see a ruined house, then the Lande de Lancerf (Lancerf moor), where Alain Barbe-Torte finally drove back the Norman chief Incon and his Vikings in 931. *See above* 'Le Trieux à toute vapeur'.

After that, you should catch sight of the manor house that belonged to Pierre Quéméneur, whose unexplained disappearance resulted in a prison term of 22 years for Joseph-Marie Seznec in 1924. After crossing the Leff at the Frynaudour stop, the Château de La Roche-Jagu comes into view (*see* 'Pontrieux, What To See in the Area').

– In summer, you can also go up the Trieux **by boat** as far as La Roche-Jagu. Departures from l'Arcouest or from Bréhat. Information is available from the tourist office. (*see* 'Pointe de l'Arcouest').

PLOUBAZLANEC
(*PLAERANEG*) 22620   (Pop: 3,460)

This village to the north of Paimpol has a very moving sailors' cemetery.

WHERE TO STAY AND EAT

♠ ✗ Pension Bocher: 44 rue Pierre-Loti; main street in Pors-Even (the lower part of Ploubazlanec). ☎ 02-96-55-84-16. Closed from 1 November to 1 April. In a traditional building for the area, covered in ivy, pleasant rooms from 160F (washbasin) to 300F. Set menus from 90F and children's menus for 50F and 60F. Half board from 290F to 310F per person. Fish specialities, including lobster with cream sauce (*homard à la crème*) and seafood. A good place to eat.

♠ Motel Nuit et Jour: as you enter Ploubazlanec coming from Paimpol. ☎ 02-96-20-97-97. Open all year round, 24 hours a day. Not ideally situated (by the side of the road, like all good motels, and not near a beach), but that is its only fault. Small, clean and comfortable wooden bungalows. Bathroom, TV, telephone and double-glazed windows. Double rooms from 235F to 355F; some have a kitchenette. Family rooms as well with mezzanine costing 395F for four people. Breakfast for 37F. For chess enthusiasts there is an outside board, 4 metres square. Very friendly young owner.

✗ Le Café du Port: by the harbour in Pors-Even. ☎ 02-96-55-83-51. Open daily in summer; out of season Friday, Saturday and Sunday on reservation. Ideal for a drink or perhaps a plate of oysters, a bowl of mussels or a sausage-filled savoury *crêpe* on the outside terrace. There's lots of local atmosphere, very reasonable prices, and a good view over the harbour and the bay.

SWEET TREATS

✗ **Boulangerie-pâtisserie Ferchaux**: in the centre of town, on the left on the main road as you come in from Paimpol. Open daily 7am–8pm in summer. Closed on Wednesday in winter. Here you can taste one of the culinary specialities of Goëlo and Le Trégor – rice pudding (*le riz au lait*), which they sell an excellent version of by the ladleful, along with tremendous *crêpes* and a mouth-watering array of cakes.

WHAT TO SEE

★ **Le cimetière marin** (sailors' cemetery): on a long wall, plaques remind visitors of the ultimate price paid by those local people who fished the Icelandic waters. Simple wooden boards, painted black, bear the names of all those lost at sea recorded in faltering handwriting. More than 100 schooners went down, and some two thousand men were lost. The Icelandic campaign began in the middle of the 19th century. At that time, boats had a crew of 20 men and were gone for six months at a time. The campaign reached its height in 1895, when 82 schooners left Brittany's shores. In 1935, only two boats embarked on the long (and final) voyage.

★ As you leave the village heading for Pors-Even, stop at the 18th-century **Chapelle de Perros-Hamon**, which has graceful sculptures on the facade. Under the porch is another poignant list of those lost at sea.

★ **Pors-Even** is a picturesque and quiet little harbour made famous by Pierre Loti, who discovered here the principal characters for his book *Pêcheur d'Islande* ('Fisherman of Iceland').

Follow the signs for the *Croix des Veuves* (widows' cross). At the end of the road, on a little knoll, is the spot where the fishermen's wives and mothers awaited the return of husbands and sons. Just before, there is a beautiful statue worn smooth by spray from the sea. From the spot where the cross stands, there is a wide panorama of the open sea, the islands and the reefs.

Still in Pors-Even, have a quick look at the *Dauphin* fish tanks, where you can shop for spider crabs, lobsters and magnificent crayfish – all fresh, of course.

LA POINTE DE L'ARCOUEST

Located 9 kilometres (5.5 miles) north of Paimpol, the Pointe de l'Arcouest is an embarkation point for the Île de Bréhat. This picturesque promontory, with a remarkable view of the archipelago, was a spot particularly prized by scientists. Pasteur, Frédéric and Irène Joliot-Curie, and the physicist and Nobel Prize-winner Jean Perrin were all frequent visitors.

WHERE TO STAY

⌂ **Camping Panorama du Rohou**: overlooking this beautiful landscape, well signposted as you come into the village. ☎ 02-96-55-87-22. Fax: 02-96-55-74-34. Allow about 70F for two people. Open all year round. Peaceful campsite with two-star comfort. The friendly owner runs boat trips to the islands.

WHAT TO DO

– **Boats trips to the Île de Bréhat**: crossing of the Chenal du Ferlas (Ferlas Channel) in 10 minutes (*see below*, 'Île de Bréhat'). Bicycles are only accepted up to 10am.

– **Boat trip up the River Trieux**: in operation 15 June to 10 September. Four-hour boat trip up the River Trieux leaving from the Arcouest landing stage (depending on the day – check in advance). Stops at the Château de La Roche-Jagu (*see* 'Pontrieux, What To See in the Area'). Returns around 6pm. Costs 100F for the full round-trip for adults and 70F for children. Details: ☎ 02-96-55-79-50.

ÎLE DE BRÉHAT
(*ENEZ-VRIAD*) 22870   (Pop: 424)

Unsurprisingly, as many as 300,000 tourists visit in high season, so the best time to explore the Île de Bréhat is in the spring, before the tourist invasion really begins.

It rains a lot less here than on the mainland, and a favourable microclimate has allowed an almost Mediterranean type of vegetation – with eucalyptus, palm trees, mimosa, fig trees, and so on – to flourish. Apparently, the island's hydrangea bushes can sometimes produce as many as 200 flowers. As a result, Bréhat has always attracted painters, including, in the past, Matisse and Foujita. About 3.5 kilometres (2.5 miles) at its widest point, the island is dotted with flower-bedecked villas and old stone mansions. There are no cars, apart from two emergency services vehicles, and it's a paradise for exploring on foot. The introduction of the latest tractor even made the headlines. On Bréhat, handcarts and bicycles predominate.

The **Plage du Guerzido** can be reached in 15 minutes via the cliff path from Port-Clos. A pebble and sand beach, it is safe and well protected. Situated 800 metres from Port-Clos is Le Bourg, the island's 'capital', with a delightful little square and 12th-century church altered in the 18th century. Inside, there is a beautiful Laval-style altarpiece, which, with the two side altars, forms a classical 17th-century grouping. The 18th-century lectern is said to have come from England. There is also a 16th-century pulpit supported by a caryatid, some statues and the model of a frigate, the *Reder-Mor*, donated by local man Admiral Cornic.

From the **Chapelle St-Michel** (1852), perched on a hillock, there is a vast panorama of the surrounding area. A stone's throw away is an old mill. The **Pont ar Prat**, a bridge built by Vauban, allows access to the north of the island, which is much more rugged than the south, with mostly moors and rocks. The **Phare du Rosédo** (lighthouse) is here, and the **Phare du Paon** is right at the furthest point. This is the wildest part of the island, where the coastline is fragmented into thousands of pieces of pink granite. At the foot of the lighthouse, you can imagine yourself in another world.

Legend has it that the Phare du Paon was the place for single young women to come to find out about their marriage prospects. Once a year, a girl could come to throw a stone down into the chasm behind the lighthouse. If the stone fell directly into the water without touching a rock, she would be married within the year. If, on the other hand, it bounced from rock to rock, she would have to wait for the same number of years as the stone had bounced.

GETTING THERE

– **Embarkation point for the Pointe de l'Arcouest**: car park (paying) with several hundred spaces (you won't be alone here in summer). Information: ☎ 02-96-55-79-50. Office open 8.30am–6.30pm from 1 April to 30 September. The return ticket is about 40F (34F for children from ages 4–11 inclusive). A dozen departures per day, 8.30am–7.30pm or 8pm. Only five departures in January. In summer you can also get to the island from Erquy, Pléneuf-Val-André, Binic or St-Quay-Portrieux. Details available from the relevant tourist offices. All the boats drop their passengers off at Port-Clos.

– **Tour of the Île de Bréhat**: it takes about 45 minutes to reach Bréhat, with time to visit the island, returning to the mainland by the regular service. Information: ☎ 02-96-55-79-50. Costs 70F.

USEFUL ADDRESSES

🚹 **Syndicat d'initiative** (tourist of-fice): in the village. ☎ 02-96-20-04-15. Fax: 02-96-20-06-94. Email: syndicatinitiative.brehat@wana-doo.fr. Open Monday–Saturday 10am–6pm (closed 1–2.30pm Monday and Saturday), 10am–1pm Sunday. Restricted opening hours out of season.

■ **Club nautique** (sailing club): ☎ 02-96-20-00-95.
■ **Bicycle rental**: in Port-Clos. ☎ 02-96-20-03-51. From the very helpful Rosine Dalibot, who runs a shop to the right of the Hôtel Belle-vue, at the little crossroads. There is another, more expensive place to rent bicycles to the right of the hotel.

WHERE TO STAY AND EAT

🏕 **Camping municipal**: ☎ 02-96-20-00-36 (town hall), or in season ☎ 02-96-20-02-46. Campsite over-looking the harbour.
🏕 Some **chambres d'hôte**: details from the tourist office.
Otherwise, the island has only three hotels (fortunately, for the peace and quiet of the inhabitants), which are always full in high season. The best is L'Allégoät.
🏕 **Chambres d'hôte L' Allégoät**: just 100 metres from the place du Bourg going towards La Chapelle

St-Michel. ☎ 02-96-20-03-48. A double room costs 300F in high season (a little less in low season), with breakfast at 25F. There are two rooms, sharing a bathroom. This curious house with its pointed roof is owned by a husband-and-wife team, an artist and a ceramicist, and their artistic influence shows everywhere. Examples of their work, carried out in their workshop at the end of the garden, are scat-tered through the bedrooms, which are comfortable and attractively presented. It's quite unlike any other B&B you'll ever see. What's more, they give a very warm welcome.

🛏 ✕ **Hôtel-restaurant Bellevue**: in Port-Clos, right in front of you as you leave the jetty. ☎ 02-96-20-00-05. Fax: 02-96-20-06-06. Email: hotelbellevue@wanadoo.fr. Closed from January to mid-February and the last two weeks of November. Large building that is fresh and pleasant, with modernized rooms with sea views. Always taken by storm by tourists who arrive off the boat, and therefore charges quite prohibitive prices: double rooms from 490F to 590F, and some larger rooms even more than that. Breakfast is extra (48F). Half board is obligatory at weekends, on public holidays and during all school holidays. Set menus from 135F up to 195F. The welcome is excellent.

✕ **Bar-restaurant La Potinière**: on the Plage de Guerzido, a five-minute walk from Port-Clos. ☎ 02-

96-20-00-29. ♿ Open from 1 May to the end of September. Quiet and very well situated. Large terrace outside in the shade of an ancient pine tree and dining room all in wood looking out over the sea. Mostly regular customers, some just there for a drink. Mussels and chips (*moules-frites*) for 60F or a dozen oysters for 90F, so it's not exactly *haute cuisine*.

✕ **Le Paradis Rose**: on the north of the island, not far from the Phare du Paon. Open daily from Easter to September, until 5pm or 6.30pm depending on the weather. This place is good, and not expensive, which is useful if you want to go round the island but don't want to bother carrying a packed lunch or a picnic. *Galettes* (10–25F) and *crêpes* (15–25F), plus chips and cold drinks, are all available from a counter in the garden and there are tables outside.

WHERE TO GO FOR A DRINK

The two best places on the island to have a drink are: **La Bouteille à la mer** and **Le Shamrock** on place du Bourg. If you study beers, you might want to know that they sell Coreff at La Bouteille à la Mer.

CULINARY TREATS

🔒 **Fromagerie Bio**: the best yoghurt on the island is undoubtedly made by Alain Louail. Equally good are his *tomme* cheese, *fromage frais*, *crème fraîche* and other organic dairy products. In summer, his products are on sale every morning up until 1pm at the market that takes place on the place du Bourg, and from 11am to 8pm at the *fromagerie*

itself, which is located on a farm on the north side of the island. It's on the left as you go up towards the Phare du Paon. ☎ 02-96-20-04-06. The goods are also on sale at La Salicorne (*see below*).

🔒 **La Salicorne**: in place du Bourg. This is a general food shop as well as a grocer and a cheese shop, selling a range of organic foods.

WHAT TO SEE

🔒 **Atelier Tourne la Terre** (artists' workshop): l'Allégoät, 100 metres from the place du Bourg in the direction of La Chapelle St-Michel (*see also* 'Where

To Stay and Eat'). This is an artist's studio-workshop, showing ceramics by Annick Argant and paintings by Jean-Claude Bréat, based at the end of the garden of the house with the pointed roof. Open 10am–12.30pm and 4–7pm. Out of season, it's best to telephone: ☎ 02-96-20-03-48.

– **Les Verreries de Bréhat**: a glass workshop set up in the castle that you see on the left-hand headland as you arrive by boat.

LOGUIVY-DE-LA-MER (*LOGUIVY-PLOUGRAZ*) 22620   (Pop: 1,014)

This busy little fishing port, nestling at the mouth of an inlet, has succeeded in preserving its authentic character. At low tide, or when the boats are coming in, it is always picturesque and colourful. On the left side (facing the sea), you can take in at a single glance the mouth of the River Trieux and all the islands. For those interested in Lenin's life story, the great theorist of the Russian Revolution took a break here from the class struggle in July 1902.

WHERE TO STAY AND EAT OR HAVE A DRINK

⌂ **Chambres d'hôte with Mme Armelle Riou**: 1 *bis* rue Le-Porjou. ☎ 02-96-20-42-47. Open from Easter to 15 September. Three comfortable guest rooms, two with communal shower room for 195F for two people, and one, with bathroom, for 280F. Unforgettable breakfast for 38F including, among other things, wonderful homemade jams. It's advisable to book in advance. Despite all this, it seems a bit expensive.

⌂ ✕ **Hôtel-restaurant Le Grand Large**: by the harbour. ☎ 02-96-20-90-18. Fax 02-96-20-87-10. Closed Sunday evening and Monday from the end of September to Easter; also closed in January and during the last two weeks in Novem-

ber. This hotel-restaurant is well positioned, facing the charming harbour and the Île de Bréhat. It has six comfortable and well-kept double rooms from 350F to 400F, although they are all quite small. Four of the rooms have a sea view. The staff are very welcoming. The restaurant dining room is bright, with white tablecloths – a good place to eat your shellfish looking out to sea. The first set menu costs 95F and there are others from 145F to 220F.

♟ **Le Café du Port**: just before you arrive in the harbour, it's on the right. This café is known locally as 'Chez Gaud'. It's a great experience just being in this real little Breton café and rubbing shoulders with sailors and old men that are full of character.

The Trégor Region

Situated between land and sea, sandwiched by the Argoat and the Goëlo coast in the east and the Côte du Granit Rose ('pink granite coast') in the west, the Trégor region is a true Breton hinterland that is full of history, with numerous castles and churches. It grew up around its two estuaries (the Jaudy and the Trieux), forming a strip of land that reached out to the open sea and became the unspoiled peninsula between La Roche-Derrien and

Pontrieux. The Trégor region was the birthplace of St Yves (Tréguier) and also the adopted homeland of legendary French singer George Brassens, who moored his boat *Les Copains d'Abord* ('Friends come first'), immortalized in song, in Lézardrieux.

The Trégor region was formerly much larger (stretching as far as the border with the present Finistère); here, we will limit our coverage quite arbitrarily to the peninsula and its surrounding area.

PONTRIEUX (*PONTREV*) 22260 (Pop: 1,273)

This pleasant little town, built on the flower-covered banks of the River Trieux (hence its name, which means 'bridge on the Trieux'), is still relatively free of tourists. Its delightful little central square has cobblestones and old houses; the half-timbered 16th-century Maison Eiffel immediately stands out with its blue-painted woodwork. Not far from the square, an unusual bridge with pink arches offers a lovely view of the riverside houses rising out of the water, and a small boat full of flowers on the river itself. Further on are the marina and, between two tree-lined banks, an area for beginners to learn to canoe. The Fête du Lavoir (details from the tourist office) and the famous little train that connects the town to Guingamp are interesting and unusual things to do. In summer, there's a steam train that takes visitors all the way to Paimpol. There are some nice *fermes-auberges* (farmhouse inns) in the area.

USEFUL ADDRESSES

🄱 **Syndicat d'initiative** (tourist office): in the Maison Eiffel, in the main square. ☎ and fax: 02-96-95-14-0. Website: www.ulys.com/pontrieux. In summer, open daily 10.30am–6.30pm. Out of season, open for limited periods only.

■ **Club de canoë-kayak**: by the harbour. ☎ 02-96-95-17-20. Very friendly and helpful. Boat-hire, plus courses, lessons or trips on the estuary, by kayak or canoe for 100F. Longer (two- or three-day) trips as well, going as far as the Bréhat archipelago, for 210F a day (meals not included), and to Les Sept-Îles and other places along the Pink Granite Coast. This official three-star French school of canoeing is one of the best.

WHERE TO STAY AND EAT

⌂ ✕ **Hôtel-restaurant Le Pontrev**: place de l'Hôtel-de-Ville. ☎ 02-96-95-60-22. Fax 02-96-95-68-94. Restaurant closed Friday, Saturday evening and Sunday out of season. Spacious, well-kept rooms with shower or bath and TV, from 170F to 210F. Half board from 230F to 250F, obligatory in August. Popular restaurant offering generous portions. Daily set menu for 55F (two starters, main course, salad, cheese and dessert), served every day except Saturday evening and Sunday. Additional menus for 85F and 125F. Specialities include filleted trout with a vermouth sauce and scallops in cream with saffron. Flower-decked terrace and garden bordering the River Trieux. The staff are genuinely friendly. A good, reliable place to eat.

✕ **La Sterne**: 40 rue du Port, opposite the canoeing school. ☎ 02-

96-95-19-55. Closed Monday evening out of season. A brasserie that is also a restaurant, offering set menus for 108F to 218F. Children's menu for 45F.

✕ **Les Jardins du Trieux**: 22 rue St-Yves, close to the little bridge. ☎ 02-96-95-06-07. Closed Monday out of season. Good *galettes* and *crêpes* to take away.

WHAT TO SEE AND DO

– **Balades en barque** (boat trips): every afternoon in summer you can take a boat trip, drifting along with the current, and one thing you will see is the 50 washing places along the river. Embarkation is from the public garden behind the church. There's a charge of 15F. Full details from the tourist office.

– **Circuits des Artisans d'art**: make a point of visiting the artists and craftsmen of the region in their studios and workshops. A brochure with all the names and addresses is available at the tourist office and those in town are well signposted. Work is also exhibited and sold every Friday morning in July and August on the place Le Trocquer.

– **Festival de musique mécanique**: on 14 July, every other year (in odd years, 2003 and 2005), there's a music festival where barrel organs and their owners congregate.

WHERE TO STAY AND EAT IN THE AREA

≜ **Chambres d'hôte at Ferme de Kerléo**: 22260 Ploëzal; 3 kilometres (2 miles) north of Pontrieux. On the D787, head for the Château de La Roche-Jagu. Signposted as you leave the village, as well as when you turn off for the Château de La Roche-Jagu. ☎ 02-96-95-65-78. Fax: 02-96-95-14-63. Open from Easter to the end of October. Situated on an old Breton farm near the castle, in a beautiful walking area. Four spacious, new guest rooms from 210F to 250F. Breakfast included.

≜ **Chambres d'hôte and gîtes ruraux with Marie-Thérèse Calvez**: in the hamlet of Kergadic, 22260 Quemper-Guézennec, 5 kilometres (3 miles) east of Pontrieux. ☎ 02-96-95-33-45. Open all year round. The three guest rooms have been recently redecorated – each room has a name: the 'Charme', the 'Rétro' and the 'Tournesol' (sunflower). Private shower rooms.

250F for two people, including a generous breakfast. The house is always filled with flowers. Tennis (free) and fishing in the village. Extremely friendly and an excellent place to stay.

≜ ✕ **Château Hôtel de Brélidy**: 22140 Brélidy; 8 kilometres (5 miles) south of Pontrieux on the D15, heading for Bégard. ☎ 02-96-95-69-38. Fax: 02-96-95-18-03. Open from Easter to 1 November. Offers 14 rooms from 390F to 820F, depending on the type of room and the season. Breakfast for 58F. Half board from 450F to 480F per person per day. The restaurant, open evenings, is set in a magnificent dining room. The set menus cost 150F and 195F. A really quiet and peaceful place to spend the night, deep in the Breton countryside, but a little pricey.

≜ ✕ **Ferme-auberge Le Marlec**: 1 Kerpruns, in Quemper-Guézennec 5 kilometres (3 miles) east of

Pontrieux. Signposted from the road. ☎ 02-96-95-66-47. Fax: 02-96-95-66-47. Reservations only; open every day except Monday lunchtime. Pretty flower-bedecked granite house, with two big dining rooms. Set menus begin at 75F with starter, chicken in tarragon (*poulet à l'estragon*) or roast pork, followed by dessert. Suckling pig (*cochon grillé*) available to order. Rooms with bathroom from 190F to 210F.

WHAT TO SEE IN THE AREA

★ **Château and Motte féodale de Brélidy**: 8 kilometres (5 miles) south of Pontrieux on the D15. ☎ 02-96-95-69-38. Telephone beforehand to arrange a visit (from Easter to 1 November). Dating from the 16th century, this feudal castle sits beside the remains of a 14th-century castle destroyed during the War of the Succession of Brittany. You can even spend the night here (*see* 'Where To Stay').

★ **Runan**: a nondescript little village that nevertheless possesses an interesting church, built between the 14th and 16th centuries. The construction is highlighted by four gables and a belfry with spire and balustrade. The porch is decorated with numerous figures and a carved lintel (with a *pietà* and an *Annunciation*). A dozen emblazoned bas-reliefs (with coats of arms) are strangely scattered about the facade. Small ossuary in the corner. Inside, in the chevet, is a beautiful stained-glass window dating from 1423 and 18th-century altarpieces. In front of the church is one of the few exterior pulpits still in existence in Brittany. Surmounted by a small calvary.

★ **Château de La Roche-Jagu**: situated about 10 kilometres (6 miles) southeast of Tréguier. ☎ 02-96-95-62-35. Open February to 1 November, daily 10.30am–noon and 2–6pm (10am–7pm in July and August). Admission to the grounds is free but a castle visit costs 25F. Built about 60 metres (195 feet) above the River Trieux, it occupies an exceptional strategic position in a beautiful setting. Constructed in the 15th century in a style halfway between a castle and a manor house. Elegant facade looking out on the courtyard. Inside, the visit includes the kitchen and the charming chapel. There are numerous sculpted fireplaces but, unfortunately, no furnishings. Temporary exhibitions are held here. The path round the walls offers a magnificent panorama of the meandering river.

✕ ❢ Within the castle perimeter there is a small bar-restaurant.

THE PRESQU'ÎLE SAUVAGE

The Presqu'Île Sauvage ('Wild Peninsula') is the tongue of land defined by its two estuaries, between Paimpol and Tréguier. It is 'wild', because it has no main towns, but also because of the isolated Talbert *sillon* (or 'fissure'), its incredible sandy point. You can do the tour by travelling from Pontrieux to La Roche-Derrien, taking the little D20 from Lézardrieux. Or, those with suitable shoes can take the famous GR34 footpath, which closely follows the coast and offers some beautiful panoramas.

USEFUL ADDRESS

🅱 **Maison de la Presqu'île (tourist office)**: at the Kerantour crossroads, in Pleudaniel. ☎ 02-96-22-16-45. Open daily in July and August, 9.30am–12.30pm and 2–7pm, and Monday to Friday 10am–noon and 2–5pm during the rest of the year, as well as Saturday mornings during the February and Easter holidays. Competent and friendly. Tourist information, rentals and exhibitions of local produce.

WHERE TO STAY AND EAT

Near Pleumeur-Gautier

🛏 **Kerpuns chambres d'hôte, with M. and Mme Jézéquel**: 22740 Pleumeur-Gautier. ☎ 02-96-22-16-10. Open all year round. Two kilometres (1 mile) from the D786, on the road from Paimpol to Tréguier, signposted from the hamlet of La Croix Neuve. An old renovated farm in a quiet location, with a house attached containing four guest rooms with bathrooms. Expect to pay 250F to 280F for a double room. There are rooms on the ground floor and another one upstairs with an attic roof; also a family room that sleeps four people. Breakfast included. Use of kitchen for guests. A possible stopover point for anyone travelling with horses, as there are horse boxes available.

At Pleubian

🛏 **Camping Port-la-Chaîne**: route de l'Armor. ☎ 02-96-22-92-38. Fax: 02-96-22-87-92. Website: www. portlachaine.com. ⅍ Open from April to the end of September. Mobile homes also available from 1,500F to 4,000F per week. This flower-bedecked, family-run three-star site was voted Campsite of the Year in 1991. Swimming pool.

At Lanmodez

🛏 **Gîte with M. Prigent**: at Keraniou. ☎ 02-96-22-83-51. About 1 kilometre from the town and only 10 metres from the sea. The *gîte* costs 3,500F per week in July and August and 1,800F in low season; weekend lets are possible. A really attractive place, this *gîte* can sleep up to seven people. It's nice and bright, with good furniture and a first-floor living room with a view of the sea. There's even an American-style kitchen and a simple garden.

Near Kerbors

🛏 ✕ **Maison d'hôte Troezel Vras with Françoise and Jean-Marie Maynier**: on the D786, between Tréguier and Paimpol. In Pleumeur-Gautier, go past the church on your right and then take the first right, heading for Kerbors. It is 2 kilometres (1 mile) from there, in a beautiful 17th-century Breton manor house. ☎ 02-96-22-89-68. Fax: 02-96-22-90-56. From April to the end of October they offer two family rooms, which are in fact small suites, at 400F for three people, 500F for four and 600F for five. Also three double rooms from 300F. In each of the tastefully decorated guest rooms you will find beautiful antique furniture. Table d'hôte in the evening if you request it, except for Sunday. The meals (95F) are served in the garden or by the fire, according to the season. After three years of restoration work, the Mayniers have breathed life into this manor house once more. A charming place to stay, in the heart of the peninsula, and not far from the sea. Use of a mountain bike is offered.

WHAT TO SEE AND DO

★ **Lézardrieux**: just as you come onto the Presqu'île Sauvage, 6 kilometres (4 miles) to the west of Paimpol on the banks of the River Trieux, Lézardrieux is a marina on an attractive bend in the river.

◘ **Office du tourisme**: place du Centre. ☎ 02-96-22-14-25. Open from June to the end of August. This excellent little tourist office can provide information about and take bookings for trips on old sailing ships.

★ **La Roche-Derrien**: there's a church combining Romanesque and Gothic styles, and old corbelled houses around the place du Martray.

– **Association Pays Touristique Trégor et Goëlo** (tourist association for the Trégor and Goëlo region): 9 place de l'Église, BP 18, 22450 La Roche-Derrien. ☎ 02-96-91-50-22. Fax: 02-96-91-31-07. Email: tourisme.tregor-goelo@wanadoo.fr. Open Monday–Friday 8.30am–noon. Offers lots of information about the area.

– **Stage de danse celtique** (Celtic dancing course): with Timmy Mac-Carthy, in Mantallot, 6 kilometres (4 miles) south of La Roche-Derrien, held in either July or August (telephone for details). ☎ 02-96-47-26-55 or 02-96-35-81-29. Expect to pay 200F for a weekend.

★ **Centre d'Étude et de Valorisation des Algues** (centre for the study and use of seaweed): in Larmor-Pleubian. ☎ 02-96-22-93-50. Visits possible in July and August, Sunday–Thursday 3–4.30pm only. Admission charge 25F (reductions for children). A technical and gastronomic tourist attraction – a laboratory that studies the growth and economic exploitation of the seaweed harvested on the huge expanse of flat rock between the coast and the Île de Bréhat. Seaweed is used in fertilizers, cosmetics, ice-cream, shoe polish, photographic film, mouldings, fish pies, soups and fabrics.

★ Right at the tip of the peninsula, at L'Armor, Tal-Benz, the **sillon de Talbert** (Talbert sandbar) is a unique geomorphologic feature of the coastline. It is a kind of natural tongue of sand and shingle, 3.5 kilometres (2.5 miles) long, patiently built up by the opposing currents of the Jaudy and Trieux rivers. (In July, there is a kite festival with a sound and laser show here.) Out to sea, the **Phare des Héaux**, at 45 metres (146 feet), is the tallest off-shore lighthouse in France.

★ **Pleubian**: the oldest exterior **pulpit** in Brittany (15th century) is to be found here. Tall and round, it is decorated with a magnificent sculpted frieze depicting the Passion. The figures are worn by weather and spray from the sea, of course, but the scenes (the Kiss of Judas, the Scourging, and so on) have retained an astonishing lifelike quality.

CÔTES-D'ARMOR

TRÉGUIER (*LANDREGER*) 22220   (Pop: 2,947)

The episcopal capital of the Trégor region, at the confluence of the Jaudy and the Guindy rivers, Tréguier is an official *petite cité de caractère* ('small town of character'). It is one of the prettiest towns in Brittany and was also one of the most important, up until the French Revolution. However, it is also very bourgeois, church-orientated and conservative. You won't see many down-and-outs here! Writer Ernest Renan's view of his native town was that 'it was a huge monastery where no outside sound ever penetrated.' Although Tréguier has lost all its privileges and is now nothing more than a small administrative centre for the diocese, it nevertheless retains a sense of its former greatness. There is something very noble, peaceful and even a bit strait-laced about it.

In summer, however, the *Mercredis en Fête* (festival Wednesdays) bring the old city to life. On the last three Wednesdays of July and August, from 8pm to midnight, the town is full of stalls, open-air restaurants (serving hog roast, seafood and mussels and chips) and music, in the place du Martray and the place des Halles. About 10 other festivals also take place during the summer. The highlight at the end of July is the performance of a baroque opera in the unusual setting of the Théâtre de l'Arche, an old neo-Byzantine chapel converted into an auditorium.

USEFUL ADDRESSES

🖬 **Office du tourisme du pays de Tréguier** (tourist office for the Tréguier area) (A1 on the map): 1 place du Général Leclerc , to the left of the cathedral. ☎ and fax: 02-96-92-22-33. Open Monday–Saturday 10am–12.30pm and 2–7pm (no lunchtime closure on Wednesday); Sunday 10am–1pm and 5–7pm. Limited opening hours out of season.

■ **Capitainerie du port de plaisance** (harbour master's office at the marina): ☎ 02-96-92-42-37 and 02-96-92-30-19 (town hall).
■ **Librairie Tanguy** (A1 on the map): opposite the cathedral, on the corner of the rue St-Yves. Bookshop specializing in books about Brittany.

WHERE TO STAY

⭐–⭐⭐ Budget to Moderate

🏠 **Hôtel Le St-Yves** (A1, **10** on the map): 4 rue Colvestre, a stone's throw from the cathedral, with an entrance next to the café of the same name. ☎ 02-96-92-33-49. Closed for three weeks at the end of September and beginning of October. Double rooms cost from 150F to 200F. There is also a tiny room for 110F. A splendid granite spiral staircase leads to

the three floors where seven rooms are located. Four have their own shower; three have been recently refurbished. The whole place is plain but very clean. Charming owners.
🏠 **Hôtel-restaurant L'Estuaire** (B1, **11** on the map): by the harbour. ☎ 02-96-92-30-25. Fax: 02-96-92-94-80. Double rooms cost from 140F to 250F. The place is nothing exceptional but it's one of the cheapest in town.

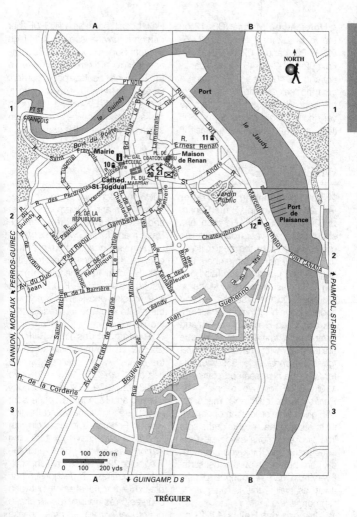

TRÉGUIER

🛏 Where To Stay

10 Hôtel Le St-Yves
11 Hôtel-restaurant L'Estuaire
12 Hôtel Aigue Marine and Restaurant des Trois Rivières

🍴 Where To Eat

20 La Poissonnerie du Trégor
21 Crêperie des Halles
22 Restaurant Le St-Bernard

⌂ **Hôtel Aigue Marine** (B2, **12** on the map): by the marina. ☎ 02-96-92-97-00 and 02-96-92-39-39. Fax: 02-96-92-44-48. Closed January and the first week in February. A nice modern building with a view of the boats in the harbour. Offers 48 very comfortable rooms from 380F (low season) to 520F (high season). Half board possible for 380F per person in low season, 440F in high season. Superb food (see 'Restaurant des Trois Rivières' in 'Where To Eat'). Lovely heated pool, garden, fitness room with sauna, jacuzzi and sun bed. Everything you need for a relaxing holiday, and even some palm trees in the garden.

WHERE TO EAT

✕ **La Poissonnerie du Trégor** (A1, **20** on the map): 2 rue Renan. ☎ 02-96-92-30-27. Fishmonger's shop open all year round; dining rooms open from the beginning of July to the end of September. This original and friendly place has been run for the last 30 years by Madame Moulinet. On the first and second floors, above his fishmonger's shop, her son, Jean-Pierre, offers fish and seafood in summer. Dishes include spider crab with mayonnaise (*araignée mayonnaise*) for 55F, mussels for 35F or a nice seafood platter for 110F (200F for two people). The *Petit Mousse* children's menu for 35F gives 'little sailors' an opportunity to sample the delights of the sea. The two enormous seascape frescoes make you think you are actually on board ship. No desserts. Everything can be bought to take away as well – this is, after all, a fishmonger's.

✕ **Crêperie des Halles** (A1, **21** on the map): 16 rue Renan. ☎ 02-96-92-39-15. Open daily. Perhaps the least touristy place in town, and probably the most authentic, frequented solely by locals. The gruff owner has received an award for the friendliest welcome in the Côtes-d'Armor (the jury clearly had a sense of humour). Arrive on time: between noon and 1pm and between 7pm and 8.30pm. His sweet and savoury *crêpes* are excellent. Basic menu for 65F with a *complète* (with gruyère cheese, ham and fried egg), and a sweet *crêpe* to finish with. His cider from the town of Ys is just how it should be. In addition, he is a scholar who knows everything there is to know about Tréguier and the Trégor region.

✕ **Restaurant des Trois Rivières** (B2, **12** on the map): restaurant of the Hôtel Aigue Marine, by the harbour. ☎ 02-96-92-97-00 and 02-96-92-39-39. Closed Sunday evening and Monday out of season; also closed in January and the first week in February. Menus begin with the *Jaudy* (weekdays) for 115F, the *Armor Passion* for 160F and the *Trégor* for 220F with monkfish, scallops (*coquilles St-Jacques*), *trou breton* (a traditional drink between courses), red mullet (*papillonnade de rouget-barbet*), *tomme* cheese in pastry shells (*croustades à la tomme fermière*) and *Trégorois*, a dessert made by the talented young chef, Olivier, whose aim it is to make the best use of local products. Prices are very reasonable in view of the quality of the cuisine. The children's set menu costs 60F.

WHERE TO STAY AND EAT IN THE AREA

☐ **Crech Choupot**, **chambres d'hôte** with M. et Mme Keramoal: 22220 Trédarzec; on the road to Paimpol (D 786), 3 kilometres (2 miles) from Tréguier. ☎ 02-96-92-40-49. Website: www. perso.wanadoo.fr/jacques.keramoal. Open from April to October. In this pretty house typical of the area, the owners offer three guest rooms with bathroom for 250F, breakfast included. The room named *Lys* ('lily') on the ground floor is decorated all in white, while two styles of furniture give their name to *Bretonne* and *Rétro*, on the first floor. Pretty garden and vegetable plot. Extremely welcoming.

☐ ✕ **Kastell Dinec'h**: 1.5 kilometres from Tréguier on the road to Lannion (N786), set back from the road surrounded by trees. ☎ 02-96-92-49-39. Fax: 02-96-92-34-03. Email: kastell@club-internet.fr.

Open from the end of April to mid-November. Closed Tuesday and Wednesday out of season. Elegant Breton manor house converted into a hotel-restaurant, which has retained its period furniture and intimate atmosphere. Swimming pool in the garden. Offers 15 pleasant rooms from 470F to 490F; the dearer rooms can accommodate three people. Breakfast costs 60F. From mid-September to the end of June, 15 per cent reduction in the price of rooms during the week. Half board is required from 14 July to 20 August and costs 500F per day per person. You will not regret it, as the food is excellent and the service attentive. Menus (evening only) for 135F, 240F or 330F with, for example, on the first menu, a *galette* with queen scallops (*pétoncles*) cooked in a garlic and parsley sauce or salmon in a citrus sauce.

SHOPPING

☐ **La Copér' marine**: leaving Tréguier heading for Trédarzec, just after the Canada Bridge, on the right. ☎ 02-96-92-35-72. If you want to buy sailors' clothing or equipment, visit this well-stocked typical chandlery, with a nice smell of boat tar.

WHERE TO HAVE A DRINK

☐ **Brasserie artisanale du Trégor**: in the industrial estate (the Z.A. or *zone artisanale*) on the Lannion road as you leave Tréguier; the brasserie is behind the Casino supermarket. ☎ 02-96-92-43-66. Open daily, 9am–5pm. One beer is now appearing in Breton bars everywhere, and that's Dremmwell, which is made here. You can get a 15-minute tour with an opportunity to taste the goods at the end. The tour is free of charge on Wednesday in July and August from 5.30–7pm. Inevitably, there's a sales counter too.

WHAT TO SEE

★ **Cathédrale St-Tugdual**: one of the masterpieces of Breton religious architecture. The cathedral has three towers: a round turret, a Romanesque square tower (12th century), a Gothic square tower (15th century) and a 63-metre (205-foot) 18th-century spire. Four types of stone (schist, stone from

Caen, pink granite and grey granite) contribute to the brilliant display of form and colour (which changes according to the intensity of the sunlight). Its construction, begun in 1339, took 150 years to complete, incorporating elements of the old Romanesque cathedral. In 1794, it was pillaged by almost a thousand soldiers of the Republic from the Étampes battalion. The exterior presents a wonderful facade and splendid porches. The main porch is surmounted by a long opening in the Flamboyant style.

The interior is similar to that of Chartres – as soon as you enter, the 40-metre high (130-foot) vaulting literally carries you heavenward. There are beautiful arches with Gothic coving in the choir, and a triforium surmounted by a balustrade gallery. The ribbed vaulting, ending in grotesque figures, helps to create an almost perfect harmony of style.

In the middle of the church is a rather heavy-looking and overworked copy of the mausoleum of St Yves, built in the 15th century and destroyed during the French Revolution. The remarkable **choir stalls** date from 1509. Look closely at the detail: the wood-carvers have displayed an incredible freedom of expression and a surprising touch of realism.

The cathedral treasures include old statues, reliquaries, religious furnishings, and so on, as well as a head of St Yves (in a shrine normally kept in the large reliquary).

Just before the cloisters, a heavy Romanesque pillar with six columns holding up two semicircular arches has splendid **capitals** sculpted with interlaced, stylized flowers. Beside the entrance to the cloisters, the altar of the Virgin has a remarkably beautiful sculpture.

The magnificent **cloister** in the Gothic Flamboyant style is the best-preserved in Brittany, and the most original. There are numerous tombs. To see the treasures or visit the cloisters, there are guided tours 10am–noon and 2–6pm. It costs about 14F for both. There's also an exhibition of art and local traditions, including *coiffes* and other costumes.

From the corner opposite the entrance, there is a fine perspective of the whole cathedral, with its different periods clearly visible.

★ **Tréguier Old Town**: the only way to explore all the streets and alleyways around the cathedral in old Tréguier is on foot. Leave your car by the harbour and go up towards the cathedral via the rue Ernest-Renan; or leave it in the place de la République opposite the school and go down into the town via the rue Kercoz. In the **rue Colvestre** there is a fine wood-framed house, and noble granite residences. Go up as far as the **rue Marie-Perrot** to admire the Gothic porch and spiral staircase of the **former bishop's house**. The **rue St-Yves** is a charming little street leading off from the cathedral square. Guided tours of the Old Town every Friday in high season. Meet at 3pm on the square in front of the cathedral. Information from an organization called A.C.P. (*art, culture et patrimoine* or 'art, culture and heritage') ☎ 02-96-92-27-54. Try not to miss the 17th-century Augustine **monastery**, open in season every day from 3–6pm.

★ **Maison natale d'Ernest Renan** (birthplace of Ernest Renan): 20 rue Ernest-Renan. ☎ 02-96-92-45-63. In July and August, open daily 10am–1pm and 2.30–6.30pm; in April, May, June and September, open Wednesday to Sunday 10am–noon and 2–6pm. Admission 25F (student reductions and free for under-18s). Ernest Renan was born and lived in this house, and always returned here for holidays. This elegant half-timbered building contains a small museum devoted to the great philosopher and historian, with various mementoes and a reproduction of his study at the Collège de France. On the ground floor is the room where he was born, and on the top floor the room where he slept and studied as a schoolboy. A 20-minute audio-visual presentation recounts his life.

FESTIVAL

– **Le grand pardon de St-Yves**: takes place each year on the third Sunday in May. One of the most fervent *pardons* in Brittany, when the shrine containing the head of St Yves is carried in a procession. St Yves was for a long time an ecclesiastical judge, and acquired a reputation for integrity and kindness which attracted huge crowds. He took in the poor and sick, fasted three days a week and slept with a rock for a pillow. He died exhausted on 19 May 1303. He is considered to be the patron saint of lawyers and the guardian of the poor.

La Côte de Granit Rose (The Pink Granite Coast)

After Tréguier, you reach a very famous stretch of coastline that is justifiably beloved of tourists. The Côte de Granit Rose ('pink granite coast') has a mild climate, wide sandy beaches protected by pine trees and creeks concealed behind piles of strangely shaped pink rocks. Its many assets have favoured the development of large seaside resorts such as Perros-Guirec. All kinds of watersports and numerous walks are available, and lively evenings are guaranteed in the port towns. If you prefer more peace and quiet, stay on the Côte des Ajoncs, between Plougrescant and Port-Blanc.

Near Perros, the Côte des Ajoncs

This is possibly the most beautiful stretch of the Côte de Granit Rose – just before the large seaside resorts full of tourists, a piece of coastline still relatively free of construction. The moors stretch down towards the coast, forming a gentle, almost homely landscape, in stark contrast to the jagged coastline with its unruly mass of rocks and numerous islets. The area's incredibly narrow little roads lead everywhere and nowhere, but always to a charming viewpoint. Late afternoon offers the best views: contours become more pronounced, and the hamlets and small fishing ports bask in soft colours and tones.

PLOUGRESCANT
(*PLOUGOUSKANT*) 22820 (Pop: 1,431)

A lovely peninsula lined with a string of islands and islets, many of which are inhabited. The winds and the tides make this a constantly changing landscape.

WHERE TO STAY AND EAT IN THE AREA

☆–☆☆ Budget–Moderate

🛖 **Camping municipal de Plougrescant**: Beg-ar-Vilin, 2 kilometres (1 mile) from the village. ☎ 02-96-92-56-15. Open from the beginning of June to mid-September. Not expensive, but there are better campsites in the area.

🛖 **Camping du Gouffre**: in Crec'h Kermorvan, 2.5 kilometres (1.5 miles) from Plougrescant, heading for Le Gouffre. ☎ 02-96-92-02-95. 🍴 Just 700 metres from the beach. Open from the beginning of April to the end of September. One of the best campsites in the region, offering maximum comfort and impeccable sanitary blocks. Site plus car: 25F, then 18F per person.

🛖 ✕ **Auberge de Penn-Ar-Feunten**: on the road to Penvenan. ☎ 02-96-92-51-02. Closed Sunday. Simple and rustic, but welcoming and inexpensive. Menu for 58F (lunchtime, and in the evening by reservation during the week). Double rooms from 110F (washbasin) to 130F (shower). Half board for 170F per person.

🛖 **Chambres d'hôte and gîtes with Marie-Claude Janvier**: on the road to Le Gouffre, 1 kilometre from Plougrescant. ☎ and fax: 02-96-92-52-67. Open all year round. The house is easy to spot, with its European flag; they also speak Breton! Flower-filled garden. The well-kept interior has three guest rooms with bathroom for 260F, and another with TV for 290F. Good breakfast included. Bicycles can be rented here for 30F per day.

🛖 **Chambres d'hôte and gîtes ruraux du Tourot with M. and Mme Gilles Le Bourdonnec**: 2 Kervoazec Hent Tourot. ☎ and fax: 02-96-92-50-20. On the tour of the Côte des Ajoncs, 300 metres from the sea and 2 kilometres (1 mile) from the village of Plougrescant. Go right at the leaning belfry, and continue for 2 kilometres (1 mile) in the direction of the campsite until you reach a pink granite stele; go left there for about 300 metres and it's the first farm on the right. The four guest rooms, all with bathroom and toilet, have a sea view and look out over a large garden with dovecote. Expect to pay 250F for a double room including a generous breakfast served in the large farmhouse dining room. There is a kitchen at guests' disposal, as well as a small living room. Nearby are the little port of Le Castel, from which the *Marie-Georgette* boat departs, the sea kayak base in Beg Vilin, and the starting-off point for the *sentier des douaniers* (customs officers' path) and the tour of the Côte des Ajoncs (*Circuit des Ajoncs*).

✕ **Crêperie du Castel**: in Le Castel. In Plougrescant, take the road on the right behind the Chapelle St-Gonery and continue for 2 kilometres (1 mile); you will arrive in the port of Le Castel, facing the Île Loaven. The *crêperie* is in a former fisherman's house. ☎ 02-96-92-59-65. Open from February to September, plus weekends and school holidays, from noon each day. Essential to book for evenings. Very good savoury *crêpes* made with organic buckwheat flour. The specialities cost 42F and there is a big choice. On the dessert menu, there are 15 kinds of sweet *crêpe*. Try the apple, caramel and almond *crêpe* (*pomme cuite maison, caramel et amandes*). Oyster tasting at any time. The garden and little terrace overlooking the sea are exceptional. If the weather is dismal, there are two dining rooms inside. Credit cards not accepted.

☆☆☆ Chic

🏠 **Manoir de Kergrec'h, chambres d'hôte**: 800 metres from the village. Signposted from the Chapelle de Plougrescant. ☎ 02-96-99-59-15. Fax: 02-96-92-51-27. Open all year round. Wonderful 17th-century turreted mansion, in huge grounds stretching to the shoreline 300 metres away. A warm welcome from the young lady owner. Spacious, elegant guest rooms with antique furniture and superb bathrooms. Expect to pay 600F night, including a real gastronomic breakfast. An excellent place to stay in this price range.

WHERE TO GET A DRINK

♥ Café Pesked: at the Roche-Jaune harbour, below the coast road, just 3 kilometres (2 miles) out of Plougrescant in the direction of Tréguier. ☎ 02-96-92-01-82. The café is in an old fisherman's cottage on the harbour in a pretty setting. The decor is bright and colourful and is in very good taste. A good family atmosphere prevails and it's very peaceful. Oysters and mussels are available.

WHAT TO SEE

★ **Chapelle de St-Gonéry**: the chapel's steeple, 'perched aslant like a slightly tipsy astrologer's hat' according to Florian Lerry, attracts the attention of all visitors as they arrive in Plougrescant. From the road, the fortified Romanesque part, dating from the 10th century, is visible. The rest is from the 15th century. The leaning steeple dates from 1612. Within the grounds is a 16th-century octagonal **pulpit**. To visit the church, ask for the key in the shop opposite.

Inside, the ceiling is in the form of an upturned boat (made, incidentally, by boat builders), with an exceptional series of **frescoes** from the late 15th and 18th centuries. The very naïve, almost clumsy but imaginative drawings have retained their fresh colours, and display a certain sense of design. The strip cartoon on the doorway wall shows, from left to right, the Creation, the animals, Adam and Eve, and so on. In fact, the whole of the *Book of Genesis* and the *New Testament* is here.

Below the belfry is the 17th-century **tomb of St Gonéry**, an Irish monk renowned for healing fevers. In the past, sailors would take a handful of soil from the tomb with them on their boats. An alabaster statue of the Virgin dates from the 16th century, as does the tomb of a bishop of Tréguier. Above here, and near the superb piece of furniture in the sacristy, there are beautiful carved purlins (one of them depicting the Seven Deadly Sins).

– **Fête de St-Gonéry**: festival on Easter Monday. The saint's skull is also carried in a procession on the fourth Sunday in July.

WHAT TO DO

– **Boat trip**: If you are a good sailor, set off with the young Pascal Jeusset aboard his boat the *Marie-Georgette* based in Le Castel-en-Plougrescant; he is often to be found in the Café Arvag, ☎ 02-96-92-51-03. You can also book by telephone: ☎ 02-96-92-58-83. For 200F, this day-long trip on board a 9-metre (29-foot) wooden sailing boat is worth a little seasickness, if only for the superb views of the coastline.

IN THE AREA

★ **Beg-Ar-Vilin**: peninsula stretching out into the estuary of the River Jaudy, facing the Île Loaven. Here you can still see the oratory dedicated to St Gonéry's mother.

★ The superb **Anse de Gouermel** (cove) at high tide is no more than a narrow strip of white sand. The 16th-century **Chapelle St-Nicolas** has a very old calvary.

★ In **Pors-Scarff** is another pretty little bay, with a wonderful jumble of rocks to the right of the harbour. The road follows the coast, weaving its way through fields, little pine woods, cultivated land and piles of rocks, before finally emerging at the magnificent **Pointe du Château,** with its enormous blocks of granite.

★ **Castel-Meur**: on stormy days the waves crash into the **Gouffre de Castel-Meur** (a chasm barely 15 minutes away on foot). Here, you can see 'that instant when the sea comes to do battle with the shoreline', as described by writer Xavier Grall.

The **Petite Maison de Plougrescant**, situated in the sheltered site of Castel-Meur, is a gorgeous house wedged between two rocks on its own islet, as if in defiance of the ocean. A favourite subject of postcards, it has also appeared on the front cover of a telephone directory, and has been featured in a Paris-based advertising campaign aiming to entice holiday-makers to visit the 'new generation' Brittany. The owner is pretty fed up with all of this – one day she even found a Japanese tourist being photographed on her roof! She rarely visits the cottage now, and has decided to take to court any photographer who tries to use a picture of her house for commercial purposes.

★ **Buguélès**: a charming little harbour, with a small slipway, boats lying on the sand at low tide, rocks, children fishing on the beach, all adding up to a picture-book image of this stretch of the Brittany coast.

PORT-BLANC 22710 (Pop: 2,491)

This small fishing port and pleasantly discreet and modest seaside resort has several fine, sandy beaches. In the middle, there is a large rock with a small oratory. The poet Anatole le Braz lived here, as did Lindbergh, and Nobel Prize-winner for medicine, Alexis Carrel. The *Torrey Canyon* disaster of 1967 is now just a bad memory.

USEFUL ADDRESSES

🛈 **Syndicat d'initiative** (tourist office): ☎ 02-96-92-81-09. In season open 9.30am–noon and 3–6pm.

■ **Capitainerie et école de voile** (harbour master and sailing school): ☎ 02-96-92-64-96.

WHERE TO STAY AND EAT

🛏 ✗ **Grand Hôtel du Port-Blanc**: boulevard de la Mer, opposite the beach. ☎ 02-96-92-66-52. Fax: 02-96-92-81-57. Closed from 5 November to 15 March. Double rooms cost from 230F to 270F. This is a 'Grand Hotel' reminiscent of bygone days, with a tall, white frontage facing the ocean. The rooms overlooking the sea have a splendid view. Tennis court. The restaurant is worth a visit, with menus from 80F to 210F. Half board is available.

✗ **Crêperie Les Embruns**: at the top of the town by the main road. ☎ 02-96-92-68-70. Closed from mid-September to 1 April and Wednesday out of season. Allow about 65F for a meal à la carte. Pleasant service and surroundings and superb view from the dining room overlooking the coast. In addition, good savoury *crêpes* and cider at a good price.

WHAT TO SEE

★ Pretty 16th-century **chapel** in the hamlet, with a roof that almost reaches the ground. Inside, there are semicircular arches and a chancel in wood ornamented with openwork. There is a 17th-century calvary in the close. In high season there is a free guided tour that includes a history of the region, daily from 10.30am–noon and 3–6pm. ☎ 02-96-92-62-35 for further information. Another source of information is the Tréguier A.C.P., who are in attendance every Wednesday at 5pm. ☎ 02-96-92-27-54.

★ The *sentier* **des douaniers** (customs officers' path) from Port-Blanc to Buguélès is very picturesque.

TRÉVOU-TRÉGUIGNEC (*AN TREVOÙ*) 22660   (Pop: 1,186)

At a distance of 3.5 kilometres (2.5 miles) from Port-Blanc going towards Perros-Guirec, there's a little hamlet, several good beaches and a bar.

🍷 **Gwenojenn**: on the road that goes down towards the plage du Royau. ☎ 02-96-23-71-36. Open 11am to 1am at weekends and during school holidays; 3pm to 1am the rest of the time. Closed Tuesday and Wednesday except during school holidays; also closed in early October. This well-known Breton bar is to be found in a large, white house typical of the region – don't mistake it for an Irish pub or one of those cafés done up in pseudo-nautical style. This is somewhere where you can see Bretons at home in their natural environment, but don't expect to go and stare – there's a very mixed clientele, every one of them in tune with the 'Gwenojenn' way of thinking.

This temple of Breton culture is run by its high-priestess, Sylvie Bouder, who is a painter and a militant member of the UDB (Breton democratic union). A brightly coloured and studiedly chaotic decor gives the whole place a strongly Breton feel. There's an ox-roast every Tuesday evening in summer and on the second Sunday and the last Friday of the month out of season. Storytelling evenings happen on Monday and Wednesday in summer and once a month out of season. Exhibitions of art also take place regularly. It's an amazing bar.

PERROS-GUIREC
(*PERROZ-GIREG*) 22700   (Pop: 7,890)

The village of *Pen-Ros*, meaning 'top of the mound' in Breton, was evangelized in the 17th century by the Welsh abbot Guirec, and given the name that it has today. Famous since the invasion of the first striped bathing costumes in the early 20th century, this upmarket seaside resort naturally attracts many tourists. The official population of just over 7,500 apparently welcomes 40,000 holidaymakers in the summer. The setting, with all its cliffs, is superb, and the village has something of the Côte d'Azur about it. The downside is that the authentic spirit and character of the Côtes d'Armor might be a little lacking.

The resort is spread over several kilometres with distinct districts: beaches, town centre, luxurious marina, La Clarté, Ploumanac'h (*see below*). Sheltered beaches include those of Trestraou, Trestrignel, St-Guirec, plus the Plage du Château and the Plage des Arcades, to the east. Those who have nightmares about overcrowded beaches will prefer Port-Blanc.

USEFUL ADDRESSES

🛈 Office du tourisme: 21 place de l'Hôtel-de-Ville. ☎ 02-96-23-21-15. Fax: 02-96-23-04-72. In high season, open Monday–Friday 9am–7.30pm, 10am–12.30pm and 4–7pm Sunday and public holidays; out of season, open 9am–12.30pm and 2–6.30pm. An efficient office, run by the person in charge of tourism in all of Brittany.

■ **Location de vélos** (bicycle hire): 14 boulevard Aristide-Briant. ☎ and fax: 02-96-23-13-08.

■ **Port de plaisance** (marina): a floating dock. Harbour master:

☎ 02-96-49-80-50. Regatta society: ☎ 02-96-91-12-65. Sailing school: ☎ 02-96-49-81-21.

■ **Station météo** (weather station): recorded weather forecast. ☎ 08-36-68-02-22. In the same building as the sailing centre.

■ **Casino**: Plage du Trestraou. ☎ 02-96-23-20-51. Free admission. Slot machines, boule, roulette.

– A programme of all the events going on in the area is printed in the weekly newspaper, *Le Trégor*, which comes out on Thursday.

WHERE TO STAY

Campsites

♠ **La Claire Fontaine**: rue du Pont-Hélé. ☎ 02-96-23-03-55. Fax: 02-96-49-06-19. About 800 metres from the Plage du Trestraou. Signposted as you enter Perros. Open from mid-April to September. A pitch with car costs 20F plus 35F per person, including use of showers. 180 spaces and recently built bungalows. Food store, for emergency supplies.

♠ **West Camping**: 105 rue Gabriel-Vicaire, at Ploumanac'h. ☎ and fax: 02-96-91-43-82. Open from Easter to the end of September. Allow 90F in season for a pitch with car and two people. This is a three-star site that's quieter than La Claire Fontaine, with only 50 spaces. Swimming pool.

☆ – ☆☆ Budget to Moderate

♠ ✕ **Le Suroît**: 81 rue Ernest-Renan. ☎ 02-96-23-23-83. Fax: 02-96-91-18-32. By the harbour. Closed Sunday evening and Monday out of season; also closed in February and October. The old wood panelling gives the place a cosy feel. Rooms cost from 170F to 230F and in the restaurant, set menus are available at 92F, 134F and 218F. Chef's speciality is spicy seafood couscous (*couscous de la mer aux aromates*). Good value for money.

♠ ✕ **Les Violettes**: 19 rue du Calvaire. ☎ 02-96-23-21-33. Closed at weekends in low season and for the last two weeks in December. Double rooms cost 170F to 220F in high season and from 140F to 190F in low season. This is an unpretentious little family-run hotel with a warm atmosphere, offering an excellent welcome. Half board is available. The restaurant offers simple but nicely packaged meals, with set menus for 55F to 98F, with other meat and fish dishes to be chosen à la carte. Seafood is available to order and the desserts are home-made.

♠ ✕ **Hôtel-restaurant Le Gulf Stream**: 26 rue des Sept-îles, in the centre of town, at the beginning of the road leading down to the plage de Trestraou. ☎ 02-96-23-21-86. Fax: 02-96-49-06-61. Closed Wednesday and Thursday out of season; also closed in January. Double rooms cost from 165F to 350F, with triples from 350F to 400F. There's a weekday set menu in the restaurant for 98F, with other menus at 150F and 225F; à la carte is also available. This is a charming hotel-restaurant with a very pleasant early 20th-century atmosphere and a superb view of the open sea, although not all the rooms have a view. The rooms are simple but attractive and very well kept; the cheapest rooms have shared facilities. You can tell that the proprietors really enjoy what they do from their warm manner, and you'll be equally welcome if you're a walker or a biker, as they own a garage too. The restaurant has a good atmosphere: the tables are elegantly laid and well spaced, there are plenty of plants, decent background music and another tremendous view of the sea. The house speciality is fish and seafood, with such dishes as scallops with leeks and grilled lobster. The wine list is well chosen, too.

♠ **Chambres d'hôte with Madame Razavet**: 60 boulevard Clemenceau. ☎ 02-96-91-01-68. Located right on the bend by the viewpoint of the coast and the islands. Spectacular setting. The three guest rooms on offer for 300F (July, August, September) or 250F (the rest of the year) are impeccable, functional and spotless. Double-glazed windows effectively cut out the outside noise. Two ground-floor studios can be rented by the week. An excellent place to stay and open all year round.

🛏 **Chambres d'hôte with Marie-Clo Biarnès**: 41 rue de la Petite-Corniche. ☎ 02-96-23-28-08. Fax: 02-96-23-28-23. Email: guy.biarnes@wanadoo.fr. Coming from Lannion, head for the town centre via the corniche and go up the boulevard de la Mer for about 1 kilometre; the rue de la Petite-Corniche is on the left by the signs, and the house is about 300 metres from the boulevard de la Mer. Closed at Christmas. Marie-Clo offers her guests two beautifully decorated bedrooms with adjoining shower room and a living room with bay windows looking out over the sea. There is also a garden for deckchair sessions. Expect to pay 300F, including breakfast, in high season, and 250F for the rest of the year. The Plage de Trestrignel and the harbour are 15 minutes away. Guaranteed parking spaces. Also a *gîte*, which starts at 2,200F per week.

WHERE TO EAT

✗ **Hôtel-restaurant Le Gulf Stream** (*see* 'Where To Stay').

✗ **Crêperie Hamon**: 36 rue de la Salle. ☎ 02-96-23-28-82. Open evenings only, 7.15pm and 9.15pm in high season, around 7pm out of season. Closed Monday. Booking is essential. Allow 75F à la carte. This local institution has been in existence since 1960. Situated opposite the car park of the bassin de Linkin, in a steep little street. A 'well-kept secret' (except that the address is known for miles around), appreciated for its rustic setting and good-humoured atmosphere (smiling is compulsory), and for the spectacle of the owner tossing excellent *crêpes* that are caught by the waitress and then served straight to customers.

✗ **Crêperie du Trestraou**: 20 boulevard Thalassa. ☎ 02-96-23-04-34. Closed Monday evening and Thursday; also closed 15 November to 15 December. Sweet and savoury *crêpe* menu for 75F. À la carte, gastronomic savoury *crêpes* from 55 to 75F with the *Poulet en Chemise*, the *Impériale*, the *Reine des Mers.* Nice choice of mixed salads and sweet *crêpes* (some flambéed). Meat dishes as well. Full of tourists, of course, and the decor has suffered accordingly, but customers always enjoy what is served up on their plate.

WHERE TO STAY AND EAT IN THE AREA

🛏 ✗ **La Bonne Auberge**: place de la Chapelle, in La Clarté. ☎ 02-96-91-46-05. Fax: 02-96-91-62-88. On the higher ground between Perros and Ploumanac'h. Restaurant closed Saturday lunchtime from 1 October to 1 May except during school holidays. Very welcoming and charming surroundings, with a wood fire, a piano, and comfortable sofas. Small and plain rooms from 160F to 220F, all with showers, toilet and TV. Nos. 1, 2 and 3 have a distant sea view. Half board (210F to 240F per person) obligatory in July and August, and during long weekends. There is also a restaurant with terrace. Set menu for 75F on weekday lunchtimes. Additional menus for 105F, 135F and 160F. Fish and seafood specialities – the owner, Michel, is also a fishmonger. A nice place to stay; authentic and inexpensive in an area where reasonable prices are becoming more difficult to find.

WHERE TO GO FOR A DRINK

Tavarn An Dremmwell: 87 rue du Maréchal-Joffre, in the road that goes down on the right as you face the church. ☎ 02-96-23-17-82. Open 11am–2pm and 5pm–1am. Closed Monday and Tuesday except during school holidays. This is where to come for the kind of real bar atmosphere that makes all the other places in Perros seem overdone by comparison. This welcoming bar has opened up in what was an old antique dealers' shop with a beautiful window. The place still has an antique feel, as the proprietors have invested in old Breton country furniture – you can sit down inside what was a cupboard (minus its doors, of course) and part of the bar is made up from pieces of an old box-bed (*lit-clos*). A ship's rudder is put to use in the bottom of the staircase, there's an array of old coffee-pots strung up on the ceiling and books and comics are scattered all around. The owner, Sébastien, only stocks Breton beers, including Coreff and the entire Dremmwell range from Tréguier. One of their draught beers, Dremmig, was specially commissioned when this bar opened. It's on the cards that beer will soon be brewed on site. Storytelling evenings take place on Tuesday and there's an ox-roast on Thursday. An excellent place – one of the best.

Pub Brittania: 19 boulevard de la Mer. ☎ 02-96-91-01-10. British-style pub, with a good range of pure malts.

Le Clem's: Plage du Trestraou, next to the casino. Hang-out for the post-grunge or neo-whatever youth, but neat and tidy. Typical little bar-pub where it is easy to meet people.

La Taverne: rue des Écoles, 22700 Louannec, 1.5 kilometres east of Perros-Guirec. Closed Thursday. It is definitely worth making the effort to go to Louannec to visit this café, which offers a variety of music, a local clientele and a relaxed atmosphere. Very good Irish coffee made by the friendly owner and good food on Wednesday and Sunday evenings, with stews for 60F including wine. Good, plain home cooking.

FESTIVALS

– **Festival de la Bande dessinée**: a cartoon and comics festival takes place in the first two weeks of April.

– **Les Jeudis du Trestraou**: the 'Trestraou Thursdays' happen in the summer and there are concerts, storytelling sessions and other events too.

– **Fête folklorique des Hortensias**: a festival to celebrate the hydrangea takes place during the first two weeks of August.

– **Festival 'Place aux Mômes'**: there's a 'Room for the Kids' festival once a week during the season, on the beach at Trestraou. It's completely free, and children and their families are welcome. More details from the tourist office.

WHAT TO SEE AND DO

Day or night, you will never be bored in Perros. Enjoy seawater therapy, gamble away your holiday budget in the casino or count the pink rocks which are now the property of the Conservatoire National du Littoral (national body for the preservation of the coastline).

★ The **Église St-Jacques** (a listed historic monument) possesses a large and unique belfry with openwork balustrade and octagonal dome. Inside, a Romanesque nave coexists with a Gothic nave and choir. The altarpiece dates from the 17th century and has carved panels and polychrome statues.

★ **Chapelle de Notre-Dame de La Clarté**: halfway between Perros-Guirec and Ploumanac'h. This is a fine chapel, built in 1445, with a bell-tower and spire added in the 17th century. The entrance has a wooden Renaissance door. The porch is decorated with fine painted wooden statues and above is a sculpted lintel with a *Pietà* on the left and the Annunciation on the right. There is a rather curious 15th-century stoup, made of granite and with several carved faces. A large altarpiece dates from the 17th century. Three model ships form a panel of thanksgiving erected by the sailors to testify to their gratitude for the Virgin's saving grace.

– Fairly recently **craftsmen** have installed themselves in this quiet part and you can find a picture framer opposite the chapel, a sculptor up on the hill and a potter near the crossroads.

★ **Musée de Cire** (wax museum): at the marina. ☎ 02-96-91-23-45. Open every day from April to October and during the school holidays, with a 30-minute guided tour. The scenes on view are mainly re-creations of historic scenes connected with revolutionary wars in the region.

★ **Boat trip to the Sept-Îles**: on board the *Armor Découverte*. ☎ 02-96-91-10-00. From March to October and during the school holidays, a trip of two to three hours. The trips start from 99F and the boat may or may not stop off at the Île aux Moines, depending on the tide. The archipelago of the Sept-Îles, including the Île aux Moines, which has just been acquired by the Conservatoire National du Littoral (national body for the preservation of the coastline), is part of the largest seabird sanctuary in France. Its mascot is the puffin. There are also many gannets and a colony of seals.

– **Boat trips**: on board *L'Arjentilez*, with an introduction to traditional sailing ships. Details from the Centre Nautique. ☎ 02-96-49-81-29.

– **Sea trips**: you can go out on a catamaran, the *Bugel Ar Mor*, either to sail up the River Léguer or the River Jaudy, or out for a seaweed observation trip. Tickets are obtainable in one corner of the maritime station at Trestraou. ☎ 02-96-23-32-32 or 06-85-92-60-61 (mobile). Tickets also available from the tourist office in Lannion, at the new harbour at Trébeurden (☎ 02-96-37-23-48) and at Trégastel at the plage de Coz-Pors, near the Forum de la Mer ☎ 06-85-92-60-61.

– There are also **trips out on old sailing ships**: on the *Sant C'hireg*, which leaves from Trégastel or Perros-Guirec.

– **Jardin des Mers**: at the Centre Nautique, plage de Trestraou. ☎ 02-96-49-81-21. A good place for children under eight, this nautical centre gives kids a full induction into the ways of the sea.

– **Voyages et Taxis Petretti**: ☎ 02-96-23-20-35. Excursions round Brittany in a 20-seater minibus are organized by this company.

DIVING

The Pink Granite Coast has a number of treats in store of a non-terrestrial kind. One glance under the waters, especially around the Sept-Îles, and you will find a haven for all manner of species that is only accessible during the summer months. The diving clubs can give you information about the currents. Don't forget to get hold of a tidetable.

– **Émotion Sub**: 26 boulevard du Sémaphore, 22700 Perros-Guirec. ☎ 02-96-91-67-20. Open from 15 March to 15 November. Here you can dive with a group (12 maximum), under the leadership of Johann Ross, the friendly owner of this diving school who has a fast boat. You can choose from a number of locations to explore without too much of a crush, and they can handle anyone from beginners up to level III. All the equipment is available for hire. Reserving two weeks ahead is advisable in the summer. Discounts on accommodation are also possible.

The Best Places To Dive

La réserve naturelle des Sept-Îles: about 30 minutes off the coast, this peaceful little group of islands is famous for awe-inspiring cliffs and for its seal colony, whose graceful, timid members live in the crystal-clear waters. Visibility is good for up to 15 metres (50 feet), so you could well get the chance to swim alongside one of these creatures as they slide through the feathery weed. There are several good spots for diving, namely the *Cerf* ('stag'), the *Congre* ('conger') and the *Four* ('oven'), which plunge down to about 40 metres (130 feet). At that depth, you get to be dazzled by the colourful abundance of gorgonia (sea-fans), sea roses and hydras that show up under your flashlight beam. It's quite common to come across lobsters and crayfish in the mating season, as well as edible 'sea beans' (*haricots de mer*). The wreck of the *Pierre-Jean* can be explored, at a depth of 20 metres (65 feet). This old petrol tanker now houses a fascinating collection of new tenants – strapping lobsters and conger eels. It's also possible to go down at night. Level I ability.

Porzh Kamor: starting out from the shore, this is a dive to 30 metres (98 feet) in a cove where there's an SNSM lifeboat. There's a wonderfully varied seascape, with rocks, sand chasms, caves and whole forests of laminaria fronds. Be careful of the strong currents as you come out of the cove, and of dangerous undertow on days of heavy swell. You will hear an underwater siren blast if the lifeboat goes out. Suitable for all levels of ability.

Around L'Île Tomé: to the southwest, if you dive down to the *Bilzic*, at a depth of 15–20 metres (50–75 feet), you can see two cannons and a large anchor: level I ability. Nearby, at a site known as 'Les Couillons de Tomé', there's a very rich variety of fauna to see, including sponges, sea anemones, crabs and fish.

SHOPPING

🔒 **Les cartes postales d'Éric Besnard**: exhibition of postcards at **Photo Armor** (Plage de Trestraou, 116 avenue du Casino). Works of art to send to 'special' friends.

PLOUMANAC'H 22700

Part of the administrative area of Perros-Guirec, and sharing the same tourist office, but a seaside resort in its own right, Ploumanac'h is quite different from Perros because of its less sophisticated atmosphere and unique setting. It began as a fishing village built on the site of a Gallic city, which later became a Roman hillfort.

USEFUL ADDRESS

– **La Maison du Littoral** ('display about the coast') on the *sentier des douaniers* (customs officers' path) at Ploumanac'h, opposite the lighthouse. ☎ 02-96-91-62-77. Open from 15 June to 15 September 11am–7pm; the rest of the year open by request. Free admission. This is an exhibition that describes how the famous rocks at Ploumanac'h were formed. Guided tours are available on request, on such topics as flora, fauna, geology, etc.

WHERE TO STAY AND EAT

🛏 **Camping Le Ranolien**: chemin du Ranolien. Reached via the boulevard du Sémaphore. ☎ 02-96-91-43-58. Fax: 02-96-91-41-90. Closed from 15 November to 15 March. The price of a pitch and charges for two people range from 75F to 130F according to the season. Very well situated, by the *sentier des douaniers* (customs officers' path) and not far from the little Plage de Pors-Rolland. Peaceful and quite isolated. All mod cons. Superb pool, tennis court, mini-golf. Quite expensive but a four-star campsite and one of the best in Brittany. You won't be lonely here, though, as the campsite has 500 spaces.

🛏 **Hôtel Pen Ar Guer**: 115 rue de St-Guirec. ☎ and fax: 02-96-91-40-71. Closed from the end of October to one week before Easter. A double room costs 170–230F, and the cheapest of these have shared washing facilities. There are a few family rooms large enough for four or five people, costing 300F. Breakfast is extra (30F). Situated just 150 metres from the plage de St-Guirec and the old harbour. A modest but extremely well kept place and the bedding is of very good quality. The proprietor gives a very warm welcome and the whole place has a pleasant family atmosphere. Add to that the excellent location and it's not hard to see why there are so many regular customers. Booking is essential.

🛏 ✗ **Hôtel-restaurant Le Parc**: by the car park in Ploumanac'h, not far from the sea. ☎ 02-96-91-40-80. Fax: 02-96-91-60-48. Email: hotel.-duparc@libertysurf.fr. Closed Sunday evening and Monday from 1 October to mid-November; also closed mid-November to 30 March. A small, unpretentious stone house. Set menus cost from 78F to 158F (children's menus for 46F); allow about 130F to eat à la carte. Clean, pleasant rooms from 245F to 260F. Half board is available, from 270F per person. Specialities include sea-food tagliatelle (*tagliatelles aux fruits de mer*) and fresh *foie gras* with tiger prawns (*foie gras fraix aux langoustines*). Friendly staff.

WHERE TO GET A DRINK

♀ **Curragh's**: 120 rue St-Guirec. ☎ 02-96-91-45-26. In the centre of Ploumanac'h, just 150 metres from the plage St-Guirec and the old harbour. A really good Irish pub, with the sort of atmosphere and decor that you'd expect in such a place. Live music – the Celtic kind.

WHAT TO SEE AND DO

★ Don't miss the chance to take a **walk** through the most famous piles of pink rock. Leave the village from the **Plage de St-Guirec** (with its small oratory) and follow the charming *sentier des douaniers* (customs officers' path) around the peninsula. Discover the fascinating **rock formations** with their most unusual and eccentric shapes. On summer evenings, the colours become more luminous and the pinks are set alight. There are many things to see along the way, including the **lighthouse** and the **Cap Ar-Skevell**, and even the town park is a pretty place to let your imagination run riot.

★ **Le Parc de Sculptures Christian Gad**: as you arrive in Ploumanac'h coming from the centre of Perros. This little open-air sculpture park contains some very large granite sculptures by Christian Gad.

IN THE AREA

★ **Walk: Ploumanac'h to Perros-Guirec** via the sentier des douaniers (customs officers' path): a three-hour round trip on foot, best taken at high tide. This marked path follows the cliff and goes through the *parc municipal*. Large rocks shaped by the water and wind over the course of centuries lie scattered everywhere. En route, visit the **Maison du Littoral** (*see above*). This walk can also be done in the opposite direction, from Perros-Guirec to Ploumanac'h. In Perros-Guirec, the path begins near the Plage de Trestraou.

★ **Vallée des Traouïero**: stretches from Ploumanac'h to Trégastel, with several starting-off points along the way. Impressive pile of granite rocks and a 14th-century tidal mill that houses exhibitions.

TRÉGASTEL (*TREGASTELL*) 22730 (Pop: 2,291)

One of the most famous seaside resorts in Brittany, and rightly so, with its wonderful, fine sandy beaches and piles of rocks. Of course, you won't be alone in enjoying it.

USEFUL ADDRESSES

🏛 **Office du tourisme**: place Ste-Anne. ☎ 02-96-15-38-38. Fax: 02-96-23-85-97. In July and August, open 9am–7pm (10am–12.30pm Sundays and public holidays); the rest of the year, open Monday to Saturday 9am–noon and 2–6pm. A small guidebook to walks in the area is available. Post office opposite.

WHERE TO STAY AND EAT

A list of **chambres d'hôte** is available from the tourist office.

🛏 **Camping Tourony**: 105 rue de Poul-Palud. Near the Plage du Tourony. Very well situated. On the outskirts of Perros-Guirec. ☎ 02-96-23-86-61. Open from Easter to the end of September. On site are fishing, sailing and mountain-bike rental. Three-star campsite.

🛏 **Hôtel des Bains**: boulevard de Coz-Pors, opposite the beach. ☎ 02-96-23-88-09. Fax: 02-96-15-33-86. Closed in December and January. This hotel consists of two white buildings around a large courtyard. The rooms are clean and reasonably priced for the area; 15 of them have been renovated and have TV and telephone. Double room prices range from 210F to 305F . Reductions in price are offered according to season. Picnic lunches can be prepared for walkers (48F). A half board arrangement is offered, in conjunction with a neighbouring restaurant (300 metres away), costing from 230F to 280F per person.

🛏 ✕ **Hôtel de la Corniche**: 38 rue Charles-Le-Goffic. ☎ 02-96-23-88-15. Fax: 02-96-23-47-89. In the centre of town, not far from the beaches. A double room costs from 170F to 320F according to the facilities. Closed Sunday evening and Monday out of season; also closed for two weeks in October and three weeks in January. The decor is bright and welcoming. Restaurant with set menus from 85F. Half board costs from 200F to 300F per

person and is obligatory in July and August.

🛏 ✕ **Hôtel Beauséjour**: plage du Coz-Pors. ☎ 02-96-23-88-02. Fax: 02-96-23-49-73. Closed in December and January except on public holidays. Of the 16 rooms with shower or bath, 10 have a sea view (from 330F to 360F in July and August, otherwise between 250F and 340F). Breakfast for 40F. Also a low-cost room with bathroom for 150F. Half board from 340F to 380F per person sharing a double room. Restaurant called *Le Roof*, with menus starting at 85F.

🛏 **Chambres d'hôte**: at the house of Michel Le Cun, 8 rue de la Ferme-de-Kervadic, at Guéradur. Just 4.5 kilometres (2.5 miles) out of town going towards Lannion on the D11. ☎ 02-96-23-93-77. A double room in this attractive farmhouse costs 140F with a double bed or 180F with twin beds. Breakfast is 25F.

✕ **Auberge de la Vieille Église**: place de l'Église, in Trégastel Old Town, on the Lannion road, 2.5km (1.5 miles) from the beach. ☎ 02-96-23-88-31. Closed Sunday evening and Tuesday evening plus Monday out of season; also closed during the February school holidays. This was once a workers' restaurant and it has been superbly converted. The facade is covered with flowers. Well known in the area and run by the same family since 1962, with a wonderful range of set menus, from 85F at lunchtimes (except

Sunday and public holidays). Other menus for 120F and 220F. The latter might include unforgettable home-smoked salmon, monkfish in cider with apples (*fricassée de lotte au cidre et aux pommes*), and apple caramel ring (*couronne de pommes caramelisées*). Specialities include might fish sauerkraut (*choucroute de poisson*) and seafood stew (*pot-au-feu de la mer*). Allow about 200F without wine if you're eating à la carte. The cuisine is of exceptional quality, the service attentive, and the decor and table settings a great success. Book in advance for evening meals in high season and at weekends. Car park.

WHERE TO GO FOR A DRINK AND SOME MUSIC

♥ **Pub Toucouleur**: in the hamlet of Poul Palud, as you leave Trégastel heading for Perros. ☎ 02-96-23-46-26. Breton and Irish music in a pub frequented by local young people. Concerts in summer on Tuesday, Thursday, Friday and Saturday. On Tuesday, concert with aperitif at 6.30pm.

WHAT TO SEE

★ **Aquarium Marin** (seawater aquarium): boulevard du Coz-Pors. Quite unique, situated as it is beneath thousands of tons of large rocks which appear to have been prehistoric cave dwellings. ☎ 02-96-23-48-58. In high season (from 15 June to 15 September), open daily 10am–6pm (8pm in July and August); the rest of the year, open during school holidays at varying times. Admission 28F. All varieties of fish from Breton waters and a large and very ingenious model of Trégastel, about 30 square metres (325 square feet) in size, which shows the movement of the tides. Fine view from the top of the building of the mass of rocks all around.

★ **Beaches and rocks**: many people come here for these alone – with some justification. Imaginative observers will see all kinds of fantastical shapes in the rocks, especially animals. From south to north you will discover in turn the *grève des Curés* (priests' beach), *grève Rose* (pink beach), the wonderful rocky piles of the *chaos rocheux de l'Île aux Lapins* and the *grève Blanche* (white beach). Take the *sentier des douaniers* (customs officers' path) to get to the plage de Coz-Pors (the favourite tourist beach), then pass by the *Rocher des Tortues* and the *Rocher de la Tête de Mort* (turtles' and Death's head rocks), before arriving at the peninsula of the Presqu'île Rénot, and the long Toul-Drez beach. This is an extremely enjoyable walk. Don't miss the **panoramic viewing table**.

WHAT TO DO

– **Boat trips to the Sept-Îles**: from mid-June to the end of August, you can take a 2 hour 30 minute trip from Trégastel to the Sept-Îles bird sanctuary, where you will see cormorants and gannets and, with a little luck, puffins or even seals. Costs 96F for adults. You can also do this trip on a traditional sailing ship (full-day or half-day excursions). Details and prices are available at the tourist office.

– **Forum de Trégastel**: plage de Coz-Pors. Huge thermal seawater complex with water at 28°C (82°F). A Roman-style activity centre, with sauna, jacuzzi, Turkish steam bath and other baths, but modern and up-to-date as well, with a fitness room, sun beds, and a paddling pool for the little ones. The seawater swimming pool is also heated.

IN THE AREA

★ By the side of the road to Trébeurden, just as you leave Pleumeur-Bodou, is the beautiful **allée couverte de Kerguntuil** (covered walkway) and dolmen.

★ **Le menhir de St-Uzec**: near Penvern, before the crossroads with the road to Pleumeur-Bodou. This giant 'long stone' engraved with symbols and surmounted by a cross is a fine example of a Christianized menhir.

TRÉBEURDEN
(*TREBEURDEN*) 22560 (Pop: 3,540)

This is a family seaside resort split between the Old Town perched up on the cliffs and, down below, the beaches and a new marina. The building of the marina caused quite a stir in the 1990s, and even though everything might have been more attractive left as it was, the new development has fitted into the townscape much better than anyone expected, and certainly better than other examples of its type.

Fortunately, there are still some beautiful beaches on either side of the rocky Pointe du Castel, particularly the **plage de Pors-Termen** and the large **plage de Tresmeur**. After the Pointe de Bihit, don't miss the **plage de Pors-Mabo**.

On the corniche is a grey wooden dome resembling a flying saucer. This igloo, invented by the architect Jean-Paul Rizzoni, can revolve through 360 degrees thanks to a home-automated power station and a platform mounted on wheels. It can protect from the wind or derive maximum benefit from the sun. This little masterpiece of a biotic habitat cannot be visited, but if you are seriously interested in having such a house, it is possible to make an appointment: ☎ 02-96-23-65-09.

USEFUL ADDRESSES

◪ **Office du tourisme**: place de Crec'h-Héry. ☎ 02-96-23-51-64. Fax: 02-96-15-44-87. Website: www.perso.wanadoo.fr/trebeurden. Open Monday–Saturday 9am–7pm and Sunday morning; in winter open Monday–Saturday 9am–noon and 2–6pm. The staff are efficient, and can offer documentation on the whole region. Themed tours are also handled here, on such topics as the megaliths in the area and the Quellen marshes. In summer, it's worth getting their brochure on arranged outdoor activities (*Les espaces naturels s'animent*).

■ **Centre activité plongée** (scuba-diving centre): ☎ 02-96-23-66-71.
■ **École de voile** (sailing school): in Tresmeur. ☎ 02-96-23-51-35.
■ **Kayak de mer** (sea kayaking): on the plage de Tresmeur. ☎ 06-85-09-96-60.

WHERE TO STAY AND EAT

⌂ **Camping Armor-Loisirs**: above the plage de Pors-Mabo, in rue de Kernevez. ☎ 02-96-23-52-31. Fax: 02-96-15-40-36. ♿ Open from Easter to the end of September. Three-star campsite rather like an English-style garden, with a games room, volleyball court, and *boules*. Themed evenings, activities and outdoor concerts in a covered space. Snack bar and provisions shop.

⌂ **Auberge de jeunesse** (youth hostel): in Le Toëno, 2 kilometres (1 mile) north of the town. A stone's throw from the sea, in pretty surroundings. ☎ 02-96-23-52-22. Fax: 02-96-15-44-34. Open all year round. A modern building, which seems rather incongruous, but in one of the best-located youth hostels in the whole of Brittany. No curfew. Costs 49F per night in dormitories sleeping from 4 to 12 people. Breakfast 19F. Botanical path all around and underwater diving nearby. Camping is also possible at a cost of 29F per person. Musical evenings.

⌂ **Hôtel de la Plage**: at the end of the plage de Goas-Trez (signposted to the right as you head for the town centre). ☎ 02-96-23-55-96. Open from April to the end of October. The least expensive and best-situated hotel in the resort, with a good welcome. Half the rooms have a superb view of the beach and the coastline, and there's a garden with terrace overlooking the sea. Rooms have a minimum standard of mod cons (communal shower and toilet) but are clean. Costs 160F (courtyard side) and 170F (facing the sea and garden). Very peaceful.

⌂ **Chambres d'hôte with Mme Le Guillouzic**: 19 *bis* rue de Kerwenet. ☎ 02-96-23-59-01 or 02-96-23-51-64. A double guest room costs 200F in high season and 180F in low season. Breakfast is 20F extra. Situated in a quiet street near the town centre, this is an attractive new house built partly of wood. There is one comfortable and pleasant room with bathroom and everything is nice and clean. The garden has a small terrace. Excellent welcome.

⌂ ✕ **Hôtel-restaurant Le Molène**: 1 rue de Bihit (by the roundabout in the town, near the church). ☎ 02-96-23-66-06. ♿ Open from April to the end of October. The chef is now the owner. A nice, inexpensive little place to eat. Welcoming and cheap, with good traditional home cooking that is uncomplicated but well presented. The cheapest set menu (59F) is perfectly acceptable. Very cheap rooms as well, starting at 120F. Nos. 4, 6, 7 and 8 are the quietest.

☆☆☆ Chic

⌂ ✕ **Hôtel-restaurant Ker An Nod**: rue de Porz-Termen. ☎ 02-96-23-50-21. Fax: 02-96-23-63-30. Email: keranod@infonie.fr. Closed from the beginning of January to the end of March. Quiet hotel facing the Île Millau, with 20 rooms, 14 of which have a sea view. The vast sandy beach is only minutes away. Run by a nice young couple. The rooms, costing from 290F to 420F according to the view and the season, are bright and comfortable, and some have lovely bay windows. Pleasant dining room, serving lots of fish and seafood, and house specialities include warmed oysters in Muscadet butter and chicken 'Trégor', with king prawns. The set menus cost from 90F to 185F.

✕ **La Tourelle**: 45 rue du Trouzoul, facing the harbour. ☎ 02-96-23-62-73. This hotel is on the first floor of a modern new building. Closed on Wednesday out of season; also closed in January, during the February school holidays and for the first three weeks of December. Five set menus are on offer, ranging from 89F to 245F, at this decent harbour-side restaurant with good views. The cuisine is well prepared and the house speciality is fish and seafood, although there are excellent meat dishes too.

WHERE TO HAVE A DRINK

❢ Bambous: between the harbour and the beach. This bar is where local youngsters meet up before moving on to a club. There's a good atmosphere.

WHAT TO DO

– **Sea trips**: for trips out on the *Bugel ar Mor*, *see* 'Perros-Guirec'.

FESTIVALS AND EVENTS

– **Fête des battages**: the first weekend in August. A traditional threshing season festival, starting with a Celtic evening and finishing up with a *fest-noz* (music festival) in a field.

– **Les mercredi soirs du Castel**: the 'Le Castel Wednesdays' take place every Wednesday evening during the summer, in the harbour, when there's music and theatre and all the elements of a *fest-noz* music festival.

– **Sorties en calèche**: trips out in a horse and carriage are available on Wednesday and Friday from 14 July to 20 August. Details from the tourist office.

IN THE AREA

★ **Île Milliau**: the island, 350 metres (1,150 feet) wide and covering 23 hectares (58 acres), has a high point of 52 metres (170 feet) and supports 270 plant species, half of which are exposed to the winds off the sea, and the other half to winds coming from the mainland. It is a botanical museum for specialists, accessible on foot at exceptionally low tides. Be careful – the site is a protected one. Guided tours are organized in July and August. Details from the tourist office. The little Île Molène, nearby, has a huge three-ton rock. For more detailed information, contact M. Beauge: ☎ 06-81-04-97-81.

★ **Le Marais du Quellen** (Le Quellen marshland): behind the plage de Goas-Trez. This area of marshland covering 22 hectares (55 acres) is a secretive place full of various forms of life, such as snipe, grebe and teal, and many plant species. Tours are organized both by Mme Porcher (☎ 02-96-05-82-56) and by the *Ligue pour la Protection des Oiseaux* (bird protection league). ☎ 02-96-91-91-40.

★ **Île Grande**: about 5 kilometres (3 miles) north of Trébeurden. This 'island' is, in fact, a peninsula. Joined to the mainland by a bridge, the parish belongs to the administrative area of Pleumeur-Bodou. It remained relatively free of buildings for a long time but is now being slowly taken over by villas and housing developments. The writer Joseph Conrad lived on the island for several years. There are beaches all around, and a footpath. The island's centre for ornithology (☎ 02-96-91-92-10), signposted when you arrive, presents exhibitions, videos, slide shows and talks about the birdlife. It also organizes walking tours to observe the wildlife (binoculars supplied) and boat trips. There's a large municipal campsite by the sea. The **camping du Dolmen** is situated in a quiet spot. Excellent watersports centre and sailing school. ☎ 02-96-91-92-10.

★ **Cosmopolis**: in Pleumeur-Bodou. In high season, open daily10am–7pm; out of season, open until 5.30pm, and closed Saturday. Admission 65F. Tickets on sale at the Musée des Télécommunications or at the planetarium. Times vary for guided tours (of the planetarium and the radar dome), but they take place every 60 or 90 minutes (check first). The famous *radôme* (or *radio-dôme*) is recognizable from miles around because of its huge white dome. In its immediate surroundings are the Centre de Télécommunications par Satellites (satellite telecommunications centre), a field of eight corollas, and parabolic reflector antennae pointed at their own satellites, like sunflowers turned towards the sun. They receive and emit signals for geostationary satellites 36,000 kilometres (22,500 miles) away. The tele-communications centre itself cannot be visited, but the dome, the adjoining telecommunications museum and the planetarium, a little further on, have all been brought together under the name of Cosmopolis. The entry ticket gives access to all three sites.

Pleumeur-Bodou was chosen in the early 1960s as the site of the antenna which, on 11 July 1962, at 12.37am, made it possible for the first-ever intercontinental satellite link in history to take place, between the USA and France via the Telstar satellite. As a result, television viewers were able to see live pictures of Man's first step on the moon. All this impressive technology in fact owes very little to French genius. The design and construction of both antennae and satellite are entirely American (although this fact isn't really made clear when you visit), and all the pieces of the dome were simply put together in Pleumeur.

– **Musée des Télécommunications**: ☎ 02-96-46-63-80 (programme) and 02-96-46-63-81 (reservations). Near the radar dome, a white delta-shaped wing 2,500 square metres (27,000 square feet) long houses the memorabilia of 150 years of technological adventure. Divided into eight thematic areas, this very interesting and modern museum presents all the great moments in the history of telecommunications, from Bell's prototype to the video phones of tomorrow, via large cupboards from the 1930s or 1950s full of con-nections and the boats that laid endless underwater networks of cables connecting islands and continents. There's a brand new 20-minute hi-tech show about the history of communication, full of lasers and sound effects. The whole thing is very interesting.

– **Radôme** (the radar dome): reached via the Musée des Télécommunica-tions, to which it is joined. Enormous dome, 50 metres (162 feet) high and 64 metres (208 feet) wide, inflated a few millibars higher than the outside to maintain its shape. Its purpose is quite simply to protect the antenna, a 60-metre (195-foot) long piece of technology. Original and interesting sound and light presentation, with a film projected on to the *cornet*, or 'ear', as the dome is sometimes called, recounting the amazing advances in satellite communication.

– **Planetarium de Bretagne**: close to the radar dome (on the left as you enter Cosmopolis). ☎ 02-96-15-80-30. ♿ Open daily from mid-April to September; the rest of the year closed Wednesday and Saturday. Admission charge 40F (30F for children aged 5–17 and students). A family ticket costs 120F for two adults and two children, and then 20F for each extra child. The Trégor planetarium depicts the celestial universe by themes to encourage understanding of the planets, satellites, stars, galaxies, and so on. The countless unknown worlds, unimaginable distances and time scales are presented in a show (in an overly air-conditioned room – bring a sweater), which puts human existence into perspective. Telephone for times of shows.

– **The village of Meem le Gaulois**: in Cosmopolis, opposite the planetarium. ☎ 02-96-91-83-95. Open from Easter to the end of September, daily 2–6pm (in July and August, 10am–7pm). Admission 15F (20F in July and August). Reduction for children. In an original and generous scheme, the humanitarian organization MEEM has, since 1985, organized this working site for young people from all over the world, who have built the village and put on shows and events here. The profits are redistributed to sub-Saharan Africa to help with the running of village schools. The revenue for the initiative is essentially derived from visitors. In the village there are traditional Gaulish and African houses. Boat trips (in summer) and pony-trekking are organized; cider and *crêpes* are on sale.

LANNION (*LANNUON*) 22300 (Pop: 19,351)

Lannion is the second-largest town in the Côtes d'Armor and the regional centre for electronics and telecommunications. Thanks to technological developments, it has enjoyed an economic boom, but it has managed to preserve the friendly atmosphere of a provincial town, with, here and there, superb old houses and picturesque little lanes. The tranquil River Léguer with its flower-covered banks and the proud Église de Brélévenez contribute to the pleasant atmosphere. In high season, organ recitals are given, within the framework of the Trégor area festival, and summer photography courses are organized.

USEFUL ADDRESSES

🚪 **Office du tourisme** (A2 on the map): quai d'Aiguillon. on the bank of the River Léguer, near the post office. ☎ 02-96-46-41-00. Fax: 02-96-37-19-64. Email: tourisme.lannion@wanadoo.fr. In July and August, open 9am–7pm (Sunday and public holidays, 10am–1pm); out of season, open 9.30am–12.30pm and 2–6pm, closed Sunday. Full range of brochures and ticket distribution. Excellent staff.

🚆 **Gare SNCF** (train station) (A3 on the map): ☎ 08-36-35-35-35. Paris via Guingamp, or direct in the summer (one train a day).

🚌 **Gare routière** (bus station) (A3 on the map): CAT, 28 avenue du Général-de-Gaulle. Opposite the train station. ☎ 02-96-46-76-70.

➕ **Airport**: ☎ 02-96-05-82-22. Head for Trégastel. Lannion–Paris service provided by Air Liberté. ☎ 08-03-80-58-05.

■ **Librairie Gwalarn**: 15 rue des Chapeliers. Bookshop located in the historic centre of town. A huge range of books, with one section entirely devoted to Brittany.

■ **Voyelles**: 13 rue Duguesclin. ☎ 02-96-46-35-95. Closed Sunday and Monday except in summer. Old books and works about Brittany.

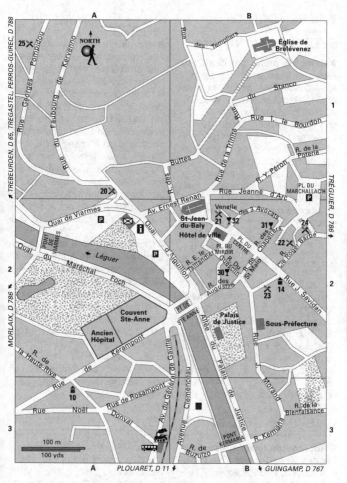

LANNION

■ **Useful Addresses**

- 🛈 Office du tourisme (tourist office)
- 🚃 Gare SNCF (train station) and
- 🚌 Gare routière (bus station)

🛏 **Where To Stay**

- 10 Auberge de jeunesse Les Korri-gans
- 14 Chambres d'hôte with Maryse Lantoine

✕ **Where To Eat**

- 20 Le Serpolet
- 21 Le Refuge
- 22 La Sabotière
- 23 Le Tire Bouchon
- 24 La Gourmandine

🍷 **Where To Go for a Drink**

- 30 Le Zen et Le Comptoir des Indes
- 31 Le Chapelier

WHERE TO STAY

☆–☆☆ Budget to Moderate

≜ Camping municipal des Deux Rives: on the road to Guingamp, 1 kilometre from the station. ☎ 02-96-46-31-40; out of season: ☎ 02-96-46-64-22. Open from April to the end of September. Cheap (16F for a pitch and 16F per person) and well situated on the banks of the River Léguer (connected by a small bridge) and beside a kayaking club. 110 spaces and some bungalows and chalets to rent.

≜ Auberge de jeunesse Les Korrigans (A3, **10** on the map): 6 rue du 73e-Territorial. ☎ 02-96-37-91-28. Fax: 02-96-37-02-06. Email: lannion@fuaj.org. Open all year round. No curfew. Just a couple of hundred metres from the station and from the town centre. This youth hostel is part of the national federation of youth hostels (the FUAJ), so you will need a membership card. The charge is 52F per night; breakfast costs 22F extra. Half board is also available, for 122F, in the summer. Recently renovated in bright colours, it has rooms for two or four

people (each with bathroom), and fully equipped kitchen. Very friendly staff organize a host of artistic and sporting activities – bird-watching, walking, boomerang club, Breton dancing, archery, acrobatic kite flying, and so on – and will provide all kinds of information about what there is to do and see in the area. There's a bar-restaurant and occasional live music, making this one of the liveliest youth hostels around. (korrigans, by the way, are Breton gnomes who come out at night to watch over . . . or disturb your sleep.

≜ Chambres d'hôte with Maryse Lantoine (B2, **14** on the map): 14 rue Jean-Savidan. ☎ 02-96-46-40-12. ♿ Open all year round. A double room costs 230F including breakfast (free for children under 12). This pretty little house, built of stone with half-timbering, is in the heart of the historic centre. The owner is an artist and provides three lovely rooms, all with bathrooms, plus use of a kitchen. There's a lovely quiet courtyard garden.

WHERE TO STAY IN THE AREA

≜ Auberge de jeunesse de Beg-Léguer: where the plage de Gwalagorn begins, in Beg-Léguer, 7 kilometres (4.5 miles) northwest of Lannion. ☎ 02-96-47-24-86. Inexpensive, at 35F per night. An annex of Les Korrigans (see above). Closed in low season. In summer, there is a bus from Lannion. A tiny youth hostel with one 12-bed dormitory – mattresses thrown side by side on the floor – and a shower which isn't always warm, but still a wonderful place with a great atmosphere. It is literally on the beach, but well away from the crowds. There is a kitchen, and a fire in the

fireplace. Right next door there is a little bar-crêperie run by a laid-back West Indian.

≜ Camping à la Ferme de Kroaz-Min: in Servel; 2 kilometres (1 mile) from Lannion, heading for Pleumeur-Bodou. ☎ 02-96-47-22-21. Fax: 02-96-47-26-22. Open from 15 June to the end of August. A pitch costs 18F, or 12F for a small tent, plus 14F per adult. Quiet and cheap, with a clean sanitary block. Run by a friendly young couple. Volleyball, table tennis, boules and farm products.

≜ Camping: in Beg-Léguer, about 7 kilometres (4.5 miles) west of

Lannion, after Servel. ☎ 02-96-47-25-00. Fax: 02-96-43-08-72. Open from April to the end of September. A pitch costs 25F, plus 15F for a car and 24F per adult. Run by two very energetic people. Near the sea and with all mod cons (three-star). Swimming pool and two tennis courts. Provisions shop.

⌂ **Hôtel Arcadia**: on the road to Perros, near the airport and the industrial estate, 3 kilometres (2 miles) from the centre of Lannion. ☎ 02-96-48-45-65. Fax: 02-96-48-15-68. ⌘ Open all year round except Christmas and New Year. A kind of motel with 20 plain but functional rooms costing 350F in high season and 290F in low season. Maisonette for two to four people from 360F to 460F in high

season. Buffet breakfast for 38F. This establishment has the added advantage of a small, heated indoor pool, ideal when the weather prevents you from enjoying the sea 3 kilometres (2 miles) away.

⌂ **Hôtel-bar-restaurant Ar Vro**: in the village of Le Yaudet, 8 kilometres (5 miles) southwest of Lannion, via Ploulec'h. ☎ 02-96-46-48-80. Fax: 02-96-46-48-86. Closed Sunday evening and Monday out of season; also closed 30 October to 15 December and from 1 January to Easter. Small, quiet, well-run hotel with a cosy atmosphere. Double rooms with shower, toilet, TV and telephone for 265F and half board for 295F per person. Menus from 107F to 177F (local produce, fish and seafood).

WHERE TO EAT

☆–☆☆ Budget to Moderate

✗ **La Sabotière** (B2, **22** on the map): 13 rue Compagnie-Roger-Barbé. ☎ 02-96-37-45-09. Out of season, closed at lunchtime on Wednesday and Sunday. Set menus start at 47F with a savoury *crêpe* of ham, cheese and fried egg, a chocolate *crêpe*, a glass of cider or *lait ribot* (a drink made from whey). On the savoury *crêpe* menu, 13 specialities, including the *Ginkgo aux St-Jacques et à la fondue aux poireaux* (with scallops and buttered leeks) for 43F. Equally big choice on the sweet *crêpe* menu. Alternatively, try one of the mountain specialities with cheese (*fondue, raclette, tartiflette*), as a reminder of your last skiing holiday. The owner comes from the Savoy region in the French Alps, which explains why there is a pair of skis in the dining room.

✗ **Le Tire Bouchon** (B2, **23** on the map): 8 rue de Keriavily. ☎ 02-96-46-71-88. Closed Sunday. The sign

on the door, which says 'no chips, no ketchup', is a real incentive to go in. You won't be disappointed. The atmosphere in the dining room is convivial and the decor is eclectic. Lunchtime set menu with dish of the day or a mixed salad, dessert and coffee for 65F (not including drinks). The dishes are all displayed on a board on the wall, ranging in price from 40F to 90F. They vary according to the season but among those always on offer are snails in garlic pastry (*escargots au feuilleté d'ail*), warm goat's cheese and apple (*chèvre chaud et pommes*), Périgord salad (*salade périgourdine*), or frogs' legs, duck conserve with honey (*confit de canard au miel*) and scallops in mead (*St-Jacques au chouchen*). About 15 desserts to choose from. Wine from the barrel.

✗ **La Gourmandine** (B2, **24** on the map): 23 rue Compagnie-Roger-Barbé. ☎ 02-96-46-40-55. Closed Saturday lunchtime and all day Monday. Set menus from 55F to 120F. The dining room is pleasant, with a large fireplace. This restaurant specializes in grilled meat. Knuckle of pork and *kig sal* (very lean bacon) are grilled over the open fire of this 16th-century house. A good place to come if you have overdosed on seafood. There is also a menu with sweet and savoury *crêpes* and a range of salads including the *Lannionnaise* with *foie gras* and smoked fillet of goose, and the *Salade Surprise*, which is a meal on its own.

✕ **La Flambée**: (A1, **25** on the map): 67 rue Georges-Pompidou. ☎ 02-96-48-04-85. Closed Monday out of season. Set menus cost from 105F to 149F. Unanimously held by local people to be the best restaurant in Lannion, where you can eat in a pleasant dining room with old stone walls and a maritime decor. The food they serve consists of local produce, fish and seafood, including Plougrescant fish and warm oysters from the La Roche-Jaune beds Plouguiel and it's excellent value for money. Specialities include turbot in cider, 'sea sauerkraut' and a monkfish casserole with little vegetables; for dessert there's a very special zabaglione. All in all, the food is simple and flavoursome.

✕ **Le Serpolet** (A2, **20** on the map): 1 rue Félix-Le-Dantec. ☎ 02-96-46-50-23. Closed Sunday evening and Monday out of season; also closed for one week at the end of December. In a setting that is supposed to be medieval (or is it pirate?), there is a whole range of set menus from 85F up to 198F. The composition of the menus varies according to the season, but the chef likes to include ostrich and kangaroo as well as more traditional fare.

✕ **Le Refuge** (B2, **21** on the map): 4 venelle des Trois-Avocats. ☎ 02-96-37-23-72. Closed Saturday lunchtime and Sunday, plus one week in September. Lunchtime-only set menus for 55F and 62F; expect to pay 130F for a good à la carte meal. If you're always dreaming of Alpine pastures or ski slopes, look no further than Le Refuge, with its pairs of skis on the ceiling and *raclette* on its plates. Friendly surroundings and attentive service are offered, as well as various kebabs, grills, *fondues* and *tartiflettes*, not to mention the *braserades* (meat cooked over glowing embers).

☆☆☆ Chic

✕ **La Ville Blanche**: 6 kilometres (4 miles) from Lannion, on the road to Tréguier, near Rospez. ☎ 02-96-37-04-28. Fax: 02-96-46-57-82. ⚹ Closed Sunday and Wednesday evening except in July and August, and Monday, as well as from mid-December to mid-February and the third week in October. Essential to book in advance. Cuisine fit for a king prepared by two brothers who have returned to their roots. They may even show you their aromatic herb garden. The cheapest set menu is 130F (Tuesday to Friday). Additional menus from 210F to 380F. Specialities include brie roasted in rhubarb (*brie rôti à la rhubarbe*), millefeuille pastry with caramelized apples (*millefeuille aux pommes caramélisées*). First-rate fare accompanied by excellent wines, which – and this is rare – can be bought by the glass.

WHERE TO GO FOR A DRINK

☂ Le Zen (B2, **30** on the map): 6 rue Duguesclin. ☎ 02-96-46-42-00. Open Tuesday, Wednesday and Thursday 6–10pm, Friday and Saturday 11am–10pm and Sunday 2–10pm. Closed Monday and for the month of September. Sophie, the owner, has hung up her rucksack here and set up a little café to welcome fellow travellers. Her bar-café with its Zen decor offers little-known beers, gins, writers' favourite drinks (Pagnol's and Kerouac's, among others), various teas, and chocolate from Angelina's. Stop off here and browse through the books that are provided for customers to read while enjoying a sandwich or a slice of homemade cake.

☂ Pub Chez Jacques: a nice little bistrot tucked away in a small lane behind the Église St-Yves, between the rue de la Mairie and the avenue Ernest-Renan. Former 17th-century inn with exposed stone walls and beams. Tiny little rooms, cosy and warm, make this the perfect hide-away!

☂ Le Flambart: 7 place du Général-Leclerc. Open until 1am or 2am at weekends. A great little bar with a relaxed atmosphere and regular live music. They serve a good range of Breton beers, including some by Bernard Lancelot and the Dremm-well brewery in Tréguier.

☂ Le Chapelier (B2, **31** on the map): 16 rue des Chapeliers (pedestrianized area in the town centre). ☎ 02-96-37-17-14. The Chap' is very well known. A young people's bar where the owner is a fan of 1960s and 1970s rock.

☂ Le Comptoir des Indes (B2, **30** on the map): 19 rue des Augustins, in the centre. Café with terrace where the whole of Lannion comes to see and be seen, and a lively bar as well. Live rock some weekends.

WHAT TO SEE AND DO

★ **Place du Général-Leclerc and the surrounding streets**: this 'long' square is otherwise known as the place du Centre. Among its uneven numbers, three wonderfully typical buildings stand side by side; the modern blends very successfully with the old and the restored. Some houses are gabled, some are corbelled and some have slate facades. There are beautiful houses at Nos. 1 and 3 **rue Jean-Savidan** as well. No. 5 is a granite townhouse. **Rue des Chapeliers** has a row of several half-timbered houses. The picturesque **rue St-Malo** leads down to the river.

★ **Église St-Jean-de-Baly**: a stone's throw from the place du Général-Leclerc. Built in the 16th century, the church has a large tower with an ornate balustrade. Very little of note inside, apart from the hollow pillar on the left side of the nave, which led to an old rood screen.

★ **Église de Brélévenez**: reached via a picturesque granite staircase of 140 steps, bordered by pretty, flower-bedecked houses. To get here, take the rue de la Trinité as far as the rue des Buttes-du-Stanco. There is a fine view of the town from the top. The church was built by the Templars in the 12th century. A beautiful Romanesque porch and the chevet still remain from this period. Loopholes and buttresses show that it was fortified because of its strategic site. Belfry with spire and double gallery dating from the 15th century. Inside, 12th-century stoup, formerly used to measure wheat. In the choir, interesting 17th-century altarpiece.

★ On the other side of the River Léguer, beyond the Pont Ste-Anne, rise the buildings of the former **Couvent des Augustines Hospitalières** (Augustine convent). In the rue Kérampont, at No. 19, is a superb 16th-century **mansion** with tower.

★ **Markets**: the Lannion market is held all day every Thursday in the place du Centre, the pedestrian streets and the quai d'Aiguillon. It is one of the liveliest in the area and a real attraction. In addition, in the beautiful Halle aux Poissons, place du Miroir, fishmongers sell fresh fish from their stalls every morning from Tuesday to Saturday.

★ **Stade d'Eau Vive**: on the River Léguer, in the town centre. ☎ 02-96-37-43-90. Or, in July and August, phone the canoeing club in Lannion. ☎ 02-96-37-05-46. A unique installation providing kayaking, rafting and canoeing in inflatable craft all year round. The river's tidal water means that visitors can practise all disciplines (rafting right in the centre of the town, and canoeing on the river or sea kayaking) whatever the weather – even during dry spells – and whatever your level, beginner or expert.

★ **Sea trips**: for trips out on the *Bugel ar Mor*, *see* 'Perros-Guirec'.

★ **Plane trips**: the Lannion flying club offers excursion flights. ☎ 02-96-48-47-42.

★ **Breton whisky:** to discover the mysteries of the Celtic spirit and of Breton whisky, visit the Warenghem distillery, on the road to Guingamp. ☎ 02-96-37-00-08. Tours, tasting and a shop from mid-June to the end of August, Monday 3–6pm, Tuesday–Friday 10am–noon and 3–6pm, Saturday 10am–noon.

★ **Banks of the River Léguer**: take a lovely walk along the right bank on the towpath, or along the left bank towards the Promontoire du Yaudet. Lovers will enjoy the romantic Allée des Soupirs or 'lane of sighs', on the left bank, starting from the Pont de Kermaria.

★ **Chapelle de Loguivy-lès-Lannion**: 1 kilometre to the west, on the banks of the River Léguer. A quite remarkable chapel group that is not to be missed. Enter the close through a gateway in the Flamboyant style. In the cemetery, there is a Renaissance fountain. At the foot of the steps is another fountain with the statue of St Ivy. The church was built in 1450, and there is a belfry wall with a staircase on the side. Inside is a splendid 17th-century altarpiece of the Three Kings.

FESTIVALS

– Many different festivals and events take place here in the summer, including: **Les Estivales photographiques** (photography), **le Festival d'orgue et de musique du Trégor** (Trégor organ and music festival), **les Tardives** (four days of shows and other musical events), **le Marché des loisirs** (leisure activities), **les Journées Terroir et Patrimoine** (celebration of the local heritage), **Foire aux puces** (flea-market). Details on all of these are available from the tourist office.

IN THE AREA

★ **La Ferme Enchantée** (Magic Farm): 2 kilometres (1 mile) from Lannion, at Convenant-Goalès. Head for Tréguier, then left towards Convenant; it's the second house on the left. ☎ 02-96-37-03-05. ☂ Open from July to September 2.30–7pm, also during the Easter holidays and Sunday and public holidays from Easter to July; the rest of the year, open by appointment in the afternoon. Admission charge 30F for adults (20F for children). Learn all about the very friendly resident donkeys: how to harness them and put on a packsaddle. Rent them for walks or even buy them.

★ **Crique de Mez-an-Aod**: this beautiful sandy beach surrounded by pale-coloured granite is the northernmost haven in France for naturists. Reached via Beg-Léguer and Servel to the left of the Lannion-Trébeurden road.

★ **Le Yaudet**: 8 kilometres (5 miles) southwest of Lannion, via Ploulec'h. Reached via a wonderful corniche road, through an absolutely serene landscape. Your car will slow down all by itself to take in the splendid panorama of the Léguer estuary and the bay, especially at sunset. Across the bay, the granite houses of the characterful and charming village of Le Yaudet huddle against each other and cling to the hillside. Visiting the chapel is a must, to see the curious reclining Virgin. The Virgin is stretched out on a small bed with the Infant Jesus, amid an abundance of lacework. At the foot of the bed, God the Father appears to be reading them an old Breton tale. Beautiful polychrome altarpiece with garlands.

Le Yaudet is also none other than the village of Astérix. According to the British newspaper *The Independent*, archaeologists have uncovered all the proof needed to confirm that this is indeed the village described by Goscinny and Uderzo in the *Astérix* books: same era (Iron Age), same location (the one enlarged under a microscope on the inside cover of every book) and same mementoes. Coins have been discovered on Le Yaudet's Gallo-Roman site representing wild boar – the favourite food of Astérix and his fellow Gauls.

★ **Locquémeau**: little fishing port, where the locals formerly fished for sardines. The 16th-century church has a turreted wall-belfry and a Flamboyant-style gateway. Inside, there are pretty carvings. The walk to the Pointe du Dourven is enjoyable and on easy paths. This area, listed as an *espace naturel sensible* (fragile natural area), is protected. Nearby, a Maison Départementale serves as a gallery of contemporary art.

🏠 **Camping**: near the sea. ☎ 02-96-35-26-44 (Kéravilin-Locquémeau). Open from April to October. Inexpensive.

🏠 ✗ **Hôtel de la Baie**: 22 rue du Port. ☎ and fax: 02-96-35-23-11. ☂ Closed in October and Wednesday and Sunday out of season. Small family hotel-restaurant, quiet and inexpensive, with 10 rooms from 130F (wash-basin) to 230F (shower and toilet). Cheapest menu for 80F and half board for 260F. Children's menu for 50F. They have just opened a *crêperie* as well. Less than a couple of hundred metres from the sea, although you can't see it.

– On the harbour there's a decent fish and seafood restaurant, **Les Filets Bleus**.

★ **Trédrez**: south of Locquémeau, by St-Michel-en-Grève. Don't miss this peaceful little village with its wonderful parish close. If it's closed, ask for the key in the town hall opposite (during office hours). St Yves was the parish priest here for seven years. The early 15th-century church has a small belfry with steeple, turrets and Flamboyant balustrades. The interior has a granite font surmounted by a polychrome canopy reputed to be the oldest in Brittany. Beautiful carved purlins; the Tree of Jesse has been magnificently restored. Ancient processional banner and, on the left, an altarpiece from St Laurent. Very old statue of the Virgin with the Infant Jesus and St Anne.

– It is possible to do an exhilarating tour of the cliffs from Trédrez as far as the Pointe de Séhar.

🛏 ✕ **Auberge St-Erwan**: in Trédrez, in front of the church. ☎ 02-96-35-72-51. Open all year round. This pretty, flower-bedecked little house is timeless in its appeal and offers four plain rooms for 140F per night. They serve set menus from 44F to 119F and offer excellent *crêpes* and *galettes*, substantial grills and interesting paella, all at very low prices. This is a very friendly establishment, and a cosy atmosphere prevails, with stone walls and an open fireplace in the dining room. There's also a little garden. Try the house speciality from the bar: a *kir de Trédrez*, made from blackberry juice and cider with a splash of Calvados to give it some tang.

Along the Vallée du Léguer

★ **Calvaire de Ploubezre**: 3 kilometres (2 miles) south of Lannion, on the road to Plouaret. Calvary consisting of five crosses, a reminder of a 14th-century battle between five inhabitants of Ploubezre (victorious) and five Englishmen (vanquished). The crosses were probably not all erected at the same time, and the wide-tipped one appears to be the oldest. In the village, the Église St-Pierre-et-St-Paul possesses 12th-century capitals, 14th-century windows and a wall-belfry from 1577. Working watermill in Keguiniou.

★ **Chapelle de Kerfons**: directly above the River Léguer, 4 kilometres (2.5 miles) from Ploubezre, the chapels stands in one of the most peaceful and pastoral settings you could ever hope to find. ☎ 02-96-47-15-51. Open from 15 June to 15 September 10am–6.30pm; the rest of the year, ask for the key at the town hall. One of the most fascinating chapels in the Trégor region. Gothic construction but with splendid Renaissance decoration. One portal has curved ornamental mouldings, and another has columns. An elegant turret is decorated with figures. Small 15th-century calvary on a huge pedestal. The inside is delightful. The rood screen is one of the most beautiful in Brittany, with wonderful polychrome wood delicately carved in the Flamboyant style. Among the 15 figures, the 12 Apostles are recognizable by their symbols. Note the fine engravings on the columns. The painted wood altarpiece on the main altar is in a very naïve style.

★ **Château de Tonquédec**: rejoin the D31 after Kerfons. Open in April, May, June and September, 3–7pm; in July and August, 10am–8pm. ☎ 02-96-54-60-70. Out of season, open on demand (☎ 02-96-47-18-47). Admission 20F. Superbly situated, with its 11 towers overlooking the Léguer Valley. All that remains of the castle, which was rebuilt in 1406 by Roland IV de Coëtmen before his (fateful) departure for the Crusades, is the seignorial dwelling and a chapel in the east wall of the ramparts. Jean II had fortified it in 1577, but the castle, having become a Huguenot hide-out during the wars of the League, was razed by order of Richelieu around 1626. Nevertheless, it still bears proud witness to feudal architecture in Brittany.

★ **Château de Kergrist**: on the road to Plouaret 7 kilometres (4 miles) south of Ploubezre, after you pass the calvary. ☎ 02-96-38-91-44. Open from Easter to May, 2–6pm and June to October, 11am–6.30pm. Admission charge, with reductions for groups. Built in 1427, the castle was altered several times, and now combines strength and elegance. Formal gardens in the French style. If you visit out of season, you can still admire one of the facades through the gate.

★ **Les Sept-Saints**: a hamlet to the north of Le Vieux-Marché. Chapel dating from the early 18th century, built on top of a dolmen (which you can see through a small grill on the ground floor). Today, it stands as a symbol of the dialogue between Christians and Muslims, thanks to Louis Massignon, an Orientalist of the Collège de France, who discovered common links between the origins of the Breton *pardon des Sept-Saints* and the cult of the Seven Sleepers from Ephesus in Turkey. A joint festival and *pardon* is held on the last Sunday in July.

WHERE TO STAY AND EAT OR HAVE A DRINK IN THE AREA

⌂ **Manoir de Coat-Nizan**: near Pluzunet. ☎ 02-96-35-81-72. Two kilometres (1 mile) from Cavan and 4.5 kilometres (3 miles) from Bégard, on the D767; take the D33 towards Pluzunet, then follow the signs. Closed 15 December to end January. This place is completely hidden away in wild countryside – you couldn't imagine a more secret and romantic manor house. It was built in the 19th century using stones from the 1286 castle, which was abandoned during the French Revolution and turned into a quarry. When you arrive, having crossed the old moats, you will be greeted by a gaggle of geese on the lawn leading up to the manor house. Beautiful, sturdy house offering *gîtes* with old-fashioned furniture and all equipped with bathroom, toilet and kitchen (from 1,500F per week for one to six people out of season and 2,200F per week in July and August). Can also be rented for the weekend (except in July and August) for 900F. Large dining room with fireplace. The surrounding countryside is ideal for walks.

✕ **Chambres d'hôte and crêperie Le Queffiou**: at Tonquédec on the road to the chateau. ☎ and fax: 02-96-35-84-50. Closed October to March. In summer, the *crêperie* is open lunchtime and evening daily; closed Tuesday in winter. A double room costs 360F with a generous breakfast included. This is a large house surrounded by a lovely tree-filled park, dating from the turn of the 20th century. The owner, a lady called Odette, is able to offer four rooms with huge private bathrooms. While there is no table d'hôte, there is a good *crêperie* also in the house, run by Odette's daughter. The dining room here is bright and attractive. Only fresh produce is used and you can get excellent *galettes* and mixed salads. It's a good idea to book in summer.

✕ **Au Coin Fleuri**: 4 rue du Général-de-Gaulle, at Cavan. ☎ 02-96-35-86-16. Closed Saturday lunchtime. Booking is essential. This restaurant in an old, ivy-clad house offers an inexpensive set menu for 60F (weekday lunchtime only) and additional menus from 85F to 140F. Good traditional cuisine, offering such things as scallop salad (*salade de St-Jacques*).

♥ Chez Janot: on the D31, 3.5 kilometres (2 miles) north of Tonquédec in the hamlet of Kerbrunec. Janot, the owner of this bar-bookshop-foodstore, is a real character and this is a local hostelry with a real Breton feel.

The Southwest, towards Finistère

★ **St-Michel-en-Grève**: 11 kilometres (7 miles) from Lannion, on the D786. Nice little seaside resort looking out on the magnificent Grève de St-Michel. Very few buildings spoil the view of this huge sheltered beach, which is 4 kilometres (2.5 miles) long, and known locally as the 'Lieue de Grève'. At the far end, the Grand Rocher offers a pleasant little climb up to the viewpoint, from which there is a superb panorama. From St-Michel to Trédrez, a fairly steep *sentier des douaniers* (customs officers' path) is part of the GR34 hiking path.

At St-Michel, there's a pretty **church** with sailors' cemetery that overlooks the sea.

🖪 Syndicat d'initiative (tourist office): ☎ 02-96-35-74-87. Open all day from 15 June to 15 September, except Sunday afternoon; in winter open mornings only.

🏠 Le Relais des Voiles with Mme Boulanger: 46 avenue de la Lieue-Grève, 22310 Plestin-les-Grèves. At St-Efflam, 5 kilometres (3 miles) west of St-Michel, over the restaurant 'Le Rafiot'. ☎ 02-96-35-64-88. Closed during the February school holidays. Looking out over the bay, this little hotel has five rooms costing from 195F to 250F. Breakfast is extra (32F), served in the room.

🏠 Chambres d'hôte with Mme Pastol: on the road to Kerivoal. ☎ 02-96-35-74-32. Starting from the church, go towards the harbour. After you turn left to the harbour, turn immediately right and drive for about half a kilometre. Open from April to the end of September. A double room costs 160–180F, with breakfast extra at 25F. This is an imposing farmhouse and manor house out in the country, with rooms decorated in a rustic style with plenty of Breton furniture. Guests are offered the use of the garden and the barbecue. Mme Pastol gives a very warm welcome; she can also offer a small house suitable for three people, available by the week.

♥ Voile de Cuir-Café artisanal: 20 côtes-des-Bruyères (the main road in St-Michel-en-Grève). ☎ 02-96-35-79-72. Open noon–1am. Closed Monday. The owner, one Jean-Christophe Gondouin-Muzellec is nothing less than a saddler, shoemaker and repairer who also runs a café. He set out to make it a welcoming place and has certainly succeeded. One side of the shop is for his leatherwork and the café occupies the other side. It's hard to describe exactly what it is about this place that's so good – but it certainly has something special, even more so in the evening, when local people of all ages meet up here. There's a chess night on Wednesday, an ox-roast on Friday and occasional storytelling evenings too.

★ **Thermes Gallo-Romains du Hogolo** (Gallo-Roman thermal baths): in **Plestin-les-Grèves**. Restored and beautifully set off by the pastoral area and landscaped surroundings, the baths date from the first and second centuries AD. They are the only ones of their kind in Brittany.

★ **Plouzélambre**: after St-Michel-en-Grève, go left on the D22 for 4 kilometres (2.5 miles) and then turn left. This small village possesses one of the few complete parish closes in the Côtes d'Armor. It is a charming grouping, with a Gothic church with Renaissance ornamentation, a small calvary, and an ossuary with trefoil arches and a doorway with a pointed arch.

★ **Château de Rosanbo**: situated near Lanvellec, between Plouaret and St-Michel-en-Grève. ☎ 02-96-35-18-77. Open daily in July and August, 11am–6.30pm; in April, May, June, daily 2–5pm; in September and October, Sunday only 2–5pm. Guided tours of the apartments, lasting about 45 minutes. Adults: 30F. Children: 18F. One of the largest castles in Brittany, built in the 14th century by the Knights of Coaskaër and continuously inhabited by the same family. In 1988, the Marquis of Rosanbo celebrated the 1,000-year anniversary of his family line.

Visitors can see the Breton room, with its beautiful furniture, the dining room, with its India Company china tableware, the former kitchen, and the library containing 8,000 volumes, which belonged to Le Peletier, former finance minister to Louis XIV.

– Free picnic area near the old stables. Three hectares (7.5 acres) of grounds with formal French-style gardens to be enjoyed, and several tree-lined walks, one of which is one of the longest in Europe.

★ **Orgue de Lanvellec** (organ): in the small neighbouring village of Rosanbo. This instrument must be heard to be appreciated properly. One of the two oldest in Brittany, it was made in 1653 by the organ builder Dalam, who was of English extraction. Since its restoration, it has been delighting music lovers who attend the festival of baroque music every autumn. Details: ☎ 02-96-35-14-14. Fax: 02-96-35-13-72.

CÔTES-D'ARMOR

North Finistère

Finistère, or *Pen ar Bed*, meaning 'the end of the earth' (you will have to get used to the bilingual road signs), is a patchwork quilt of smaller regions. In the north, there is Brest, the Iroise region and the deep Aber estuaries. After that, there is the historic province of Léon, within which is the upper Léon region and the area that contains the walled parish closes (*enclos paroissiaux*). Finally, there is the Trégor region in the east, which touches the Côtes-d'Armor, and the Monts d'Arrée.

In short, Finistère is a land that offers an extraordinary number of different landscapes in relatively close proximity. The jagged coastline forms a framework for wide expanses of fields, moors and woodland. This land contains some of the most densely populated areas in France while, just a short distance away, are areas that are virtually uninhabited.

Both North and South Finistère have largely succeeded in keeping at bay any ill-considered redevelopment of its tourist sites, and can offer the visitor completely unspoiled areas, where time really does appear to have stood still. The whole area is like a fine museum dedicated to stonework, with some of the most beautiful calvaries, wonderful parish closes and magnificent 'country cathedrals'. Although it is a region that has long attracted tourists, it is amazing how free of traffic jams and cheap souvenir shops its towns, villages and tourist sites still are.

USEFUL ADDRESSES

BREST

🛈 **Comité départemental du tourisme du Finistère** (Finistère regional tourist office): 11 rue Théodore-Le-Hars, BP 1419, 29104 Quimper Cedex. ☎ 02-98-76-24-77. Fax: 02-98-52-19-19. The regional tourist association has invented the term *clé vacances* ('the key to a good holiday') to denote furnished rental accommodation and chambres d'hôte of good quality.

🛈 **Union départementale des offices du tourisme et des syndicats d'initiative** (regional headquarters for all tourist information offices): 11 rue Théodore-Le-Hars, BP 1154, 29101 Quimper Cedex ☎ 02-98-76-23-25.

■ **Relais départemental des gîtes de France** (regional headquarters for Gîtes de France): 5 allée Sully, 29322 Quimper Cedex. ☎ 02-98-52-48-00. Fax: 02-98-52-48-44.

BREST 29200 (Pop: 156,217)

In an exceptional location at the mouth of a 150-kilometre (95-mile) long 'harbour', at the confluence of the Élorn and Aulne rivers, Brest has always had a maritime vocation. The lighthouses and beacons of Brest constitute the largest concentration of navigational markers in France, with no fewer than 23 lighthouses, 63 beacons, 14 radio navigation stations and 258 buoys. These automated markers (none of which can be visited) help to guide sailors off the coast of Brittany in a zone that is particularly busy and dangerous (*see also* the museum in Île d'Ouessant).

The Germans established a submarine base here during World War II. As a result, 98 per cent of Brest was destroyed by Allied bombing; it was rebuilt after the war on a geometric plan devised by the architect Mathon. Post-war architecture was not particularly exciting, but the walls of Brest's buildings are beginning to acquire a certain patina and a real effort has been made as far as green areas and lighting are concerned. Brest is most captivating for its harbour, its museums and the few areas, such as St-Martin and Recouvrance, which miraculously escaped the bombs.

The city also has a festive feel to it – this is reflected in the fact that there's at least one bar for every day of the year. The *Jeudis du Port* street festivals in summer and the jolly presence of so many sailing ships both contribute to the festive mood.

'*Tonnerre de Brest!*' (literally 'thunder of Brest', or 'Damn it all!') is a common expression in France. From 1650 to 1924, a cannon at the jail was fired twice a day, at 7am and 7pm. It was one way of keeping the time, but it was also used every time a convict escaped from the prison, or for sounding the alarm and warning the population of danger. Its boom (*tonnerre*) could be heard 20 kilometres (12.5 miles) away.

Having accommodated more than 70,000 people between 1750 and 1858, Brest's jails were razed to the ground in 1947. Today, they are no more than an unpleasant memory.

History

The Romans were the first to see the defensive possibilities of this attractive site, and traces of their camp have been found within the perimeter walls of the castle. Coveted throughout the Middle Ages, the town belonged in turn to the French, the English and the Bretons. Under Richelieu, Brest acquired its importance, with the creation of a naval base and the arsenals. Later, Vauban completed the fortifications. The commercial port of Brest was created by Napoleon III.

In 1750, Brest prison was opened; it was not to close until a century later. The convicts, around 2,000 of them at a time, were branded with the letters 'TF', for *travaux forcés* (forced labour), and chained in pairs. Their labour was divided into 'heavy' and 'light' tasks, with the heavy tasks being reserved for the more rebellious among them. There was little leisure time, but the tradition of *veillées rouges* was retained. These were special evenings when the prisoners would sit in a circle and regale each other with the gruesome details of their exploits and crimes.

In 1944, the town had to endure more than 150 bombing raids and a siege that lasted 43 days. At the end of the war, the American liberators entered to find a city in ruins.

For a long time, Brest owed much of its importance to the presence of the French navy and the naval dockyards, where the nuclear aircraft carrier *Charles-de-Gaulle* was built. The livelihood of 8,000 people depended upon it, and for a long period the state supported more than half the population of Brest. Today, the town is feeling the full force of the policy of restructuring the dockyards following the end of the Cold War. The commercial port imports raw materials for animal fodder, wood and various

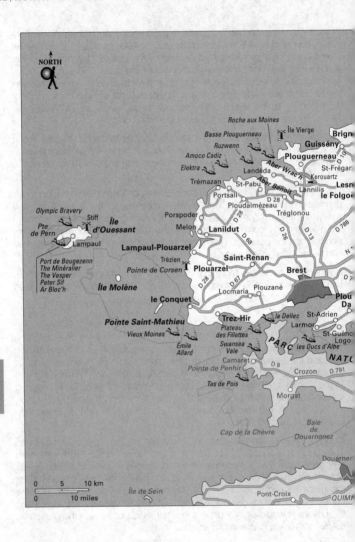

other materials. Investment has been heavy – perhaps too heavy – in the repairing of 550,000-ton super-tankers, which no longer suit the requirements of the world market.

USEFUL ADDRESSES

B Office du tourisme (B1 on the map): place de la Liberté. ☎ 02-98-44-24-96. Fax: 02-98-44-53-73. Email: office.de.tourisme.brest@ wanadoo.fr. Open mid-June to mid-September, Monday–Saturday

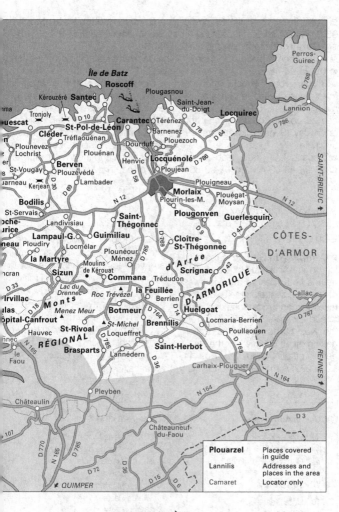

Plouarzel	Places covered in guide
Lannilis	Addresses and places in the area
Camaret	Locator only

BREST

NORTH FINISTÈRE

9.30am–12.30pm and 2–6.30pm, Sunday 10am–noon and 2–4pm; out of season open Monday–Saturday 10am–12.30pm and 2–6pm (closed Sunday). Located close to the town hall. Plenty of documentation; friendly and competent staff.

🚂 **Gare SNCF** (train station) (B2 on the map): ☎ 08-36-35-35-35 (pre-

mium rate). This station resembles an ocean liner and is a good example of pre-war architecture. It makes a great first impression of the town when you arrive by train. The TGV (high-speed train) for Paris via St-Brieuc and Rennes stops here.

✈ **Aéroport de Guipavas** (airport): ☎ 02-98-32-01-00. Air France:

☎ 0802-802-802. Finist-Air: ☎ 02-98-84-64-87 (for Île d'Ouessant).

🚌 **Gare routière** (bus station) (B2 on the map): place du 19e-R.I. ☎ 02-98-44-46-73.

■ **Bibus** (urban buses): departures from place de la Liberté (B2 on the map). ☎ 02-98-80-30-30. Tickets can be bought to last for one hour or all day. Season tickets are also available.

■ **Taxis**: 220 rue Jean-Jaurès. ☎ 02-98-80-43-43 or 02-98-801-801.

■ **Centre nautique du Moulin-Blanc** (sailing centre): ☎ 02-98-34-64-64.

■ **Capitainerie** (harbour master): ☎ 02-98-02-20-02.

■ **Centre culturel et des Congrès** (cultural and conference centre): avenue Georges-Clemenceau. Reservations: ☎ 02-98-33-70-70. Closed in summer. Ultra-modern centre, known as 'Le Quartz', between the train station and the tourist information office. They stage an excellent variety of shows.

WHERE TO STAY

Campsites

⛺ **Camping du Goulet**: in the hamlet of Ste-Anne-du-Portzic, 6 kilometres (3.5 miles) to the southwest of the town centre on the D789, then take the road to Ste-Anne on the left. ☎ and fax: 02-98-45-86-84. ♿ Take the No. 14 bus from the station, getting off at 'Cruguel', or the No. 7, getting off at 'Cosquer'; or Nos. 11, 12 or 26. Open all year round. Allow about 60F for two people, including a pitch and a vehicle. This is a quiet and well equipped campsite out in the countryside yet only 500 metres from the sea. Caravans and mobile homes are also available, but this is a site with plenty of regular visitors and is used by holiday companies, so there's not much room for casual callers. If you want to get in, book in advance.

■ **Useful Addresses**

🛈   Office du tourisme
🚌   Gare routière (bus station)
🚆   Gare SNCF (train station)

⌂ **Where To Stay**

10   Hôtel Pasteur
11   Hôtel Astoria
12   Hôtel Abalis
13   Hôtel de la Gare
14   Hôtel de la Paix
15   Relais Mercure Les Voyageurs
16   Auberge de jeunesse (youth hostel)
17   Hôtel Comoedia
18   Kelig Hôtel
19   Hôtel Bellevue

✕ **Where To Eat**

30   Crêperie Moderne
31   Le Voyage du Brendan
32   L'Abri des Flots
33   L'Espérance
34   Le Marrakech
35   La Pasta
36   Les Tables Savantes
37   Amour de Pomme de Terre
38   Le Tire-Bouchon
39   La Pensée Sauvage
40   Ma Petite Folie
41   Aux Trois Viandes

♟ **Where To Go for a Drink**

50   Les Quatre Vents
52   The Tara Inn
53   Le Vauban

BREST

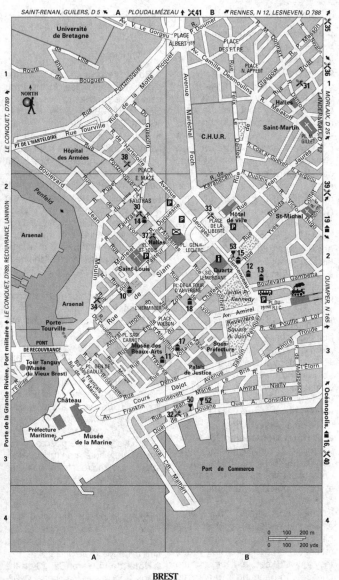

SAINT-RENAN, GUILERS, D 5 ↖ **A** PLOUDALMÉZEAU ↑ ✕**41** **B** ✈ RENNES, N 12, LESNEVEN, D 788 ↗

BREST

✪ Budget

♠ **Auberge de jeunesse** (youth hostel) (off B3, **16** on the map): Moulin-Blanc, 5 rue de Kerbriant. ☎ 02-98-41-90-41. Fax: 02-98-41-82-66. ♿ Open all year round. YHA card required. Try to arrive between 5pm and 8pm. About 2 kilometres (1 mile) from the station, the hostel is located in a modern building in a quiet spot within large wooded grounds. It's not far from the Plage du Moulin-Blanc, and about 300 metres from Océanopolis and the marina. From the station, take the No. 7 bus as far as 'Moulin-Blanc'. The rooms have four beds, and are almost luxurious, costing 72F per person per night, including breakfast. Set-menu meals for 49F.

♠ **Hôtel Pasteur** (A2, **10** on the map): 29 rue Louis-Pasteur. ☎ 02-98-46-08-73. Fax: 02-98-43-46-80. The type of hotel you would like to find in other large towns. No view, but high-quality service. A double room costs 190F during the week. The rooms are clean and comfortable (good-quality beds, double-glazed windows, TV), where only the sound insulation leaves something to be desired. A good hotel for those on a limited budget.

♠ ✗ **Hôtel Comoedia** (B3, **17** on the map): 21 rue d'Aiguillon. ☎ and fax: 02-98-46-54-82. Tucked away on a quiet little road in the centre of town, this hotel took its name from a cinema that used to be nearby. Rooms cost from 150F and, although the decor might seem a bit on the austere side, they have recently been done up. At any rate, they're well kept, and among the cheapest to be found in Brest. The simple restaurant occupies a light room where the walls are decorated with black-and-white movie stills. The dish of the day costs 45F and the set menu is 70F. You can also eat à la carte, based around a choice of three or four dishes.

✪✪ Moderate

♠ **Hôtel Astoria** (A3, **11** on the map): 9 rue Traverse. In the town centre, very close to the rue de Siam. ☎ 02-98-80-19-10. Fax: 02-98-80-52-41. Closed for the last two weeks of December and the first week of January. A hotel building like many others in Brest, but offers rare value for money, with a double room costing from 140F (with a basin) to between 240F and 290F with a bathroom. Parking costs extra, at 35F per day or 175F per week. Bright, colourful decor, and double-glazing in the rooms facing the street. Those at the back are quieter. All rooms have TV. An excellent place to stay, as much for its location (just a stone's throw from the commercial harbour) as for its friendly welcome. In July and August, the street festivals are only a 5-minute walk away.

♠ **Hôtel Abalis** (B2, **12** on the map): 7 avenue Georges-Clemenceau. ☎ 02-98-44-21-86. Fax: 02-98-43-68-32. Open all year round. Reception open 24 hours a day. Prices from 240F to 325F for two people, with a 10 per cent discount available weekdays from November to February. A handy hotel, centrally located, about 100 metres from both the station and the tourist office. All the rooms are well equipped, with double-glazed windows and TV, but they are a bit on the small side; Room 104 is not as nice as the others. Breakfast for 35F, available until midday for late risers!

♠ **Hôtel de la Gare** (B2, **13** on the map): 4 boulevard Gambetta. ☎ 02-98-44-47-01. Fax: 02-98-43-34-07. Email: info@hotelgare.com. Reception open 24 hours a day. Another nice hotel, opposite the station (as its name suggests) – in fact it's much nicer than most other hotels of the same name. Fine view of the harbour from the third floor. Double rooms cost from 285F to 305F.

â **Kelig Hôtel** (B2, **18** on the map): 12 rue de Lyon. ☎ 02-98-80-47-21. Fax: 02-98-43-28-00. Email: kelig.hotel@wanadoo.fr. Double rooms cost from 170F to 260F, with breakfast at 35F extra. Taken over quite recently by a charming young lady who is gradually bringing this rather faded little hotel back up to scratch.

â **Hôtel de la Paix** (A1, **14** on the map): 32 rue d'Algésiras. ☎ 02-98-80-12-97. Fax: 02-98-43-30-95. Website: www.oda.fr/aa/hotel.de.la.paix. Closed from 24 December to 6 January. A double room costs 290F to 320F. An affluent-looking hotel decorated in rather sombre colours, but the rooms are comfortable, clean and generally well kept, even offering such niceties as a trouser press, a safe and a hairdryer. If you can, go for rooms 2, 9, 16 and 23, which are the largest.

â **Hôtel Bellevue** (off B2, **19** on the map): 53 rue Victor-Hugo. ☎ 02-98-80-51-78. Fax: 02-98-46-02-84. Email: hbellevue@wanadoo.fr.

Open all year round. Double rooms cost from 180F to 270F. New owners have recently moved into what was always one of Brest's recommended hotels. Improvements to the decor have begun, and if the rooms develop along the same lines, it will continue to be a recommended address.

☆☆☆ Chic

â **Relais Mercure Les Voyageurs** (B2, **15** on the map): 2 rue Yves-Collet. ☎ 02-98-80-31-80. Fax: 02-98-46-52-98. Very central, at the junction of avenue Clemenceau and rue Yves-Collet, this three-star establishment stands out as much for its decor as for the comfort of the rooms. The hotel foyer has preserved its 1940s architecture. Open all year round. Rooms with all mod cons from 405F to 545F, all with attractive bathrooms. Breakfast costs 40F extra. Attentive and competent staff. Even though the breakfast room is dimly lit (perhaps to let you wake up slowly), the hotel remains the best in its category to be found in Brest.

WHERE TO EAT

☆ Budget

✗ **Crêperie Moderne** (A2, **30** on the map): 34 rue d'Algésiras. ☎ 02-98-44-44-36. Continuous service all year round 11.30am–10pm; closed Sunday lunchtime. In operation since 1922, serving delicious *crêpes* in fairly basic surroundings (despite the eye-catching yellow shopfront). House specialities include a wonderful *crêpe* with scallops in vermouth. A takeaway service is also offered.

✗ **Le Marrakech** (A2, **34** on the map): 44 rue Traverse. ☎ 02-98-46-45-14. Closed Wednesday lunch-time and Sunday, and from mid-July to mid-August. Subtle decor and sumptuous food – an excellent place to eat. Excellent *tajines* (Moroccan stews) and copious *couscous*, all very reasonably priced. Allow 100–120F if you eat à la carte. The cooking is delicate and aromatic, and spiced to perfection, with recipes that have been handed down from mother to daughter for generations. Lunchtime menus cost 61F or the dish of the day, such as *couscous* or lamb, costs 65F. Takeaway service as well. Highly recommended.

BREST

✗ **La Pasta** (off B1, **35** on the map): 2 bis rue Turenne, behind the Église St-Martin. ☎ 02-98-43-37-30. ✗ Closed Monday and Saturday lunchtimes and all day Sunday. Weekday lunchtime menu for 68F (children's menu for 36F). Expect to pay about 110F if you eat à la carte. This is an Italian restaurant just as they really should be. The freshness of the pasta is guaranteed, as it's cooked by the chef or his mother, and dishes include traditional *antipasti* as well as polenta, an excellent mixed pasta (*pasta mista*) and a good cannelloni. The decor is pleasant and the welcome typically Italian. A favourite haunt of the locals.

✗ **L'Espérance** (B2, **33** on the map): 6 place de la Liberté; under the arcades in the largest square in Brest, right next to the town hall. ☎ 02-98-44-25-29. Closed Sunday evening and Monday, and from 10 August to 10 September. This restaurant is halfway between being an up-market brasserie and a local eatery aimed at families. The cheapest menu costs 72F on weekdays, with others going up to 170F. The fare is traditional, with such eternal 'favourites' as calf's head in a vinaigrette sauce (*tête de veau ravigote*), a number of fish dishes and homemade desserts. The wine list is excellent.

☆☆ Moderate

✗ **Le Voyage du Brendan** (B1, **31** on the map): 27 rue Danton, about 300 metres from the Église St-Martin. ☎ 02-98-80-52-85. Closed Saturday lunchtime, Sunday, and during July and August. A tiny little restaurant (22 places) which takes some finding. Extremely friendly owner and first-rate traditional food using nothing but fresh produce. Menus at 58F and from 90F to 120F. Allow 110F if you eat à la carte. As a main course, try the

duck breast in cider (*magret de canard au cidre*) or the house speciality of seafood sauerkraut (*choucroute de la mer*). Small exhibitions of paintings by local artists change every two months, and there is also a permanent display. A wonderful small establishment.

✗ **Les Tables Savantes** (off B1, **36** on the map): 33 rue Navarin (place Guérin). ☎ 02-98-80-22-88. Fax: 02-98-44-08-29. Closed Sunday, Monday evening and from 15 August to 3 September. Located in a nice area, around the Église St-Martin, in the north of Brest, this quiet little restaurant offers meats, fish and salads. The weekday lunchtime dish of the day costs 42F, with other menus for 85F and 115F. Allow 110F to eat à la carte. Specialities include queen scallops in sweet wine (*noix de pétoncles au vin moelleux*) and filet mignon in two mustards. The desserts are stylish, such as chocolate fondant or iced nougat (*nougat glacé*). Good, reasonably priced wines. On sunny days, you can sit at tables outside in the square.

✗ **L'Abri des Flots** (B3, **32** on the map): 8 quai de la Douane. ☎ 02-98-44-07-31. Closed for the last two weeks of September. The set menu costs 115F. On the quayside of the commercial port. Run by a dynamic and friendly lady, the place has a convivial atmosphere, a good reputation and is popular with the locals. The restaurant dining room is quite intimate, with a lovely veranda and a pleasant terrace in the summer. Menus are based around seafood and fresh fish, with seafood couscous (*couscous de la mer*) a speciality. There's also a good list of *crêpes*.

✗ **Amour de Pomme de Terre** (A2, **37** on the map): 23 rue des Halles. ☎ 02-98-43-48-51. Fax: 02-98-43-61-88. Email: amourPDT@wanadoo.fr. ✗ Open daily until

11pm (10.30pm Sunday and Monday). Located behind the rue d'Algésiras and the Halles St-Louis. Set menus cost from 48F to 129F; allow 130F to eat à la carte. A restaurant that is unique in Brest – perhaps anywhere – as it's entirely dedicated to the potato. The spud devotee of an owner uses only one type, the 'Samba', which is well known for its qualities as a baking potato. The owner has even written potato poetry. Numerous variations are offered: it can come sprinkled with parsley, or baked with Roquefort or goat's cheese, or put into unusual (and almost untranslatable) dishes. The *Goémonier,* for example (*goémon* means 'seaweed') is best with a strong Belgian-type beer. The potatoes can be served with *charcuterie*, salads, meat, fish or seafood. The lunchtime menu concentrates more on local produce, with a stew with traditional Breton bacon flan (*pot-au-feu au kig ha farz*) on Thursday and other options on other days of the week. The desserts are all homemade and are guaranteed potato-free. Pleasant surroundings, with plenty of evidence on the walls of the virtues of the spud – and the owner's sense of humour. The place is almost always full and you can expect to eat packed in like sardines, which adds to the fun of this eating experience.

✕ **Le Tire-bouchon** (A1, **38** on the map): 20 rue de l'Observatoire; near the Lycée de l'Harteloire and the university. ☎ 02-98-44-15-18. Open daily until 10.15pm. Holiday closure period varies. Quite centrally located. The dining room has a warm, friendly, relaxed atmosphere, presided over by an ever-present and extremely welcoming boss with a big personality. The dish of the day costs 45F but allow 100F to eat à la carte. The fare is traditional and simple, but it's really quite good.

✕ **La Pensée Sauvage** (off B2, **39** on the map): 13 rue d'Aboville (and rue de Gasté), behind the Église St-Michel. ☎ 02-98-46-36-65. Closed Saturday lunchtime, Sunday and Monday, as well as from the end of July to mid-August. A restaurant well off the beaten track. Two small and plain but really cosy dining rooms. Worth a detour, for its copious and tasty food. The dish of the day costs 50F but allow 120F to eat à la carte. The menu includes such dishes as *cassoulet* and *confit de canard*, or prawns d'Ouessant-style (*langoustines à la mode d'Ouessant*). Excellent value for money, with doggy bags for unfinished food. Difficult place to find but top-rate.

✕ **Aux Trois Viandes** (off B1, **41** on the map): 48 rue Robespierre (on the corner of rue Henri-Barbusse). ☎ 02-98-03-55-11. ✗ Closed Sunday lunchtime and Monday. Allow 100–150F to eat à la carte. In a district some way from the town centre, right at the top of the Kérinou district. Small, clean dining room typical of the area, with a reputation for quality. Meat, and nothing but meat, is served here: leg of lamb (*gigot d'agneau*), rump steak (*pavé*), kebabs (*brochette*), beef ribs (*côte de boeuf*), chitterlings sausage (*andouillette*). Inexpensive wine list.

☆☆☆ Chic

✕ **Ma Petite Folie** (off B3, **40** on the map): Plage du Moulin-Blanc (beside the marina). Coming from Quimper, it's on the left after the bridge over the River Élorn. ☎ 02-98-42-44-42. Fax: 02-98-41-43-68. Closed Sunday. Just one set menu, at 110F, but allow at least 150F to eat à la carte. Rapidly becoming the best fish restaurant in Brest, located on a superb, sturdy *mauritanien*, a boat that brought back hundreds of tons of prawns from the fishing grounds off the African coast between 1952 and 1992. Today it has undergone a remarkable conversion, but has retained its charm and that feeling of having travelled the seas. Here, customers are warmly greeted and treated to some culinary delights, made with 100 per cent fresh ingredients; veal pâté with scallops (*terrine de veau et St-Jacques*), superb oysters, hake fillet in white butter sauce (*filet de lieu jaune au beurre blanc*), John Dory fillet in aniseed butter with fennel sauerkraut (*filet de St-Pierre au beurre d'anis et sa choucroute de fenouil*). Reservations are definitely advisable, and essential at the weekend. This is not a food production line: and there's usually only one sitting in the evenings, so that customers have time to savour their meal.

WHERE TO EAT IN THE AREA

✕ **Crêperies Blé Noir**: a branch in the Parc du Vallon du Stang-Alard. ☎ 02-98-41-84-66. Also at Bois de Kéroual, in Guilers. From Guilers, go south on the D105, as far as the red cross; then it's signposted. ☎ 02-98-07-57-40. Open daily, 12.30–9.30pm. Set menus from 58F to 70F. Both branches are in the two most beautiful green areas of the town, and the one at Bois de Kéroual is in an old windmill beside a pool. These stylish eating places serve delicious *crêpes* at very reasonable prices, with such speciality galettes as smoked salmon (*galette au saumon fumé*), and scallops (*galette aux noix de Saint-Jacques*).

Friendly service and the opportunity to walk off your meal in lovely natural surroundings.
✕ **Crêperie La Finette**: rue du Bois-Kerallenoc, 29850 Gouesnou. 8 kilometres (5 miles) north of Brest, on the D13. In the village, take the Kerallenoc road for 1 kilometre (it's signposted). ☎ 02-98-07-86-68. Closed Monday and Tuesday lunchtime. A beautiful old house, bordered by a small garden. The Breton decor is reminiscent of the sea – exposed stone interior and a fireplace. Very welcoming. Traditional and very tasty *crêpes*. Expect to pay 70F for a full meal. Reservations advisable.

WHERE TO GO FOR A DRINK

The port town of Brest has at least 365 bars and 10 nightclubs.

In the Quartier St-Martin

❢ **Le Café de la Plage**: 32 rue Massillon. ☎ 02-98-43-03-30. Closed Sunday. This is the place where people from every age group mingle and chat, including local workers, students and artists. Cabaret evenings on Tuesday.
❢ **Les Dubliners**: 28 rue Mathieu-Donnart. ☎ 02-98-46-04-98. Open every day 3pm–1am (5pm on Sunday). This little place lights up an otherwise uninteresting district. It's a real pub frequented by Brest's Irish community, where you can have your fill of Irish and Breton music on Thursday and Sunday evenings or learn Irish dancing on Monday evening.
❢ **La Convention**: 56 rue St-Marc. ☎ 02-98-80-69-35. Lots of good beers and whiskies in a popular student haunt with a pub atmosphere. On the first floor you can play chess, draughts and other board games.

By the Commercial Port and the Arsenal

Les Quatre Vents (B3, **50** on the map): 18 quai de la Douane. ☎ 02-98-44-42-84. ☖ Closed Sunday morning. Lively café run by its owner, Fifi, and frequented by a cheerful mix of young people, yachtsmen, tourists of all nationalities and locals. Elegant marine decor with lots of wood and a hull-shaped counter. They also serve snacks and there's a set menu for 30F. Allow 40F to eat à la carte (without a drink).

The Tara Inn (B3, **52** on the map): 1 rue Blaveau. ☎ 02-98-80-36-07.

Right by the quai de la Douane. This bar is a cross between a trendy café and an Irish pub. Long counter, stone floor, wood decor and large terrace for nice days.

If you don't fancy any of the above, try out the atmosphere, never the same from one night to the next, of the other places on the quai de la Douane: **Les Nations**, **Les Mouettes**, and so on. They are certainly worth visiting on the evenings of the 'Jeudis du Port' (*see below* under 'Festivals').

In the Town Centre

Le Vauban (plan B2, **53**): 17 avenue Clemenceau. ☎ 02-98-46-06-88. Le Vauban's glory days have been followed by years of lethargy. Today, only the retro charm of the brasserie and the concert room remain as a nostalgic reminder of the past. Every weekend, there is an old-time dance, and Le Vauban also stages all kinds of shows throughout the year (apart from July and August), with jazz, blues and comedy (maximum price for entry 110F). Black-and-white photographs of the artistes who have appeared here

adorn the walls of the ballroom and the brasserie. The brasserie offers a good range of draught beers.

Le Montparnasse: 16 rue Colbert. ☎ 02-98-44-35-48. Nice wine bar, with a friendly boss. Small outside terrace for eating toasted cheese sandwiches (*croques*), large salads and oysters.

La Madinina: place de la Gare. ☎ 02-98-44-44-22. Open until 1am. The new bar/ice-cream parlour/rum distillery of the restaurant La Calypso. Superb exotic decor for enjoying ice-creams and rum punch.

In Kérinou

This old district has been undergoing redevelopment since its brewery closed down. It isn't very lively in the evenings, but a few nice bars brighten the gloom.

Le Petit Bistrot Montmartre: 136 rue Robespierre (continuation of the rue Auguste-Kervern). ☎ 02-98-03-05-43. In high season, open 6pm–1am; out of season, 11am–1am. Closed Sunday. Another young people's pub, quite lively, with exhibitions of watercolours, and jazz and blues concerts every week from September to June, 7–10pm.

– **Le Manège:** 16 rue du Moulin-à-Poudre. ☎ 02-98-43-03-63. Closed in August. This is a good little no-frills sort of nightclub where there's an open-minded DJ who plays everything from reggae to soul to rock – no techno, though, which makes a change.

BREST

SWEET TREATS

– **Histoire de Chocolat** (A2 on the map): 60 rue de Siam. ☎ 02-98-44-66-09. Closed Sunday and Monday morning. The owner here is quite justifiably proud of his title of 'Best Chocolate-maker in France'. Apart from a stunning range of truly delicious 'normal' chocolates, there are such delicacies to be sampled as chocolate made with Breton honey, with caramel, with salted butter and . . . with seaweed.

WHAT TO SEE

Despite being almost totally destroyed in World War II, Brest still has some interesting streets and districts, particularly the cours Dajot, looking out over the harbour, the streets of Recouvrance (the oldest district in town), the old quartier St-Martin, and the famous rue de Siam. There is no real 'centre' to Brest, as it really has just two major streets: rue de Siam and the highly commercialized rue Jean-Jaurès, a very long, sloping street. Rue de Siam leads down to the River Penfeld. It's a straight road that is cut literally in half by the esplanade of the place de la Liberté.

Brest has the reputation (not entirely justified) of being a rain-sodden town. However, the poet Jacques Prévert's famous line, known to many students of 20th-century French literature, which goes: '*Il pleuvait sans cesse sur Brest*' ('It rained incessantly on Brest'), referred to the bombs that fell on the town, and not to the rain.

In the Town Centre

★ **Rue de Siam** (A2–B2 on the map): this street was given its name in 1686, when a group of Siamese ambassadors, in France to meet Louis XVI, paraded along it in style. The street was also immortalized for the French by Jacques Prévert, in his poem entitled 'Barbara'. A wide, straight street given over to commercial enterprises, the rue de Siam is a good example of exactly how the town was reconstructed after World War II. There are some fine contemporary fountains made of black granite.

★ **Musée des Beaux-Arts** (fine arts museum) (Musée Municipal; A3 on the map): 24 rue Traverse. ☎ 02-98-00-87-96. Open 10–11.45am and 2–6pm; on Sunday, 2–6pm. Closed on Sunday morning, Tuesday and public holidays. Admission charge (25F) except Sunday. Exhibition of paintings of the French, Italian and Flemish schools of the 17th and 18th centuries. Particularly notable is Pietro Della Vecchia's *Illumination de St François Borgia*, morbidly fascinating, with its decomposing face. There are also interesting works from the Pont-Aven school. Temporary exhibitions.

★ **Château de Brest** (A3 on the map): situated between the Recouvrance bridge and the cours Dajot (built by convicts in the 18th century). ☎ 02-98-22-12-39. The first building on the site was a Roman encampment, built in about AD 300, and some traces of this can still be seen in the chateau's foundations. A castle was built here in the 13th century, with modifications made during the 15th and 16th centuries, under Richelieu and Colbert, and the main gateway dates from the 15th century. It was eventually completed by Vauban, the military engineer, in the 17th century. The perimeter wall was nicely restored after World War II.

The chateau houses the harbour police (closed to the public) and the **Musée de la Marine** (maritime museum). ☎ 02-98-22-12-39. Open daily April–September 10am–6.30pm. Closed Tuesday morning. Out of season open daily except Tuesday, 10am–noon and 2–6pm. Closed mid-November to mid-December, Christmas Day, 1 January and 1 May. Admission charge (29F for adults; 19F for under 18s; free for under 8s). This museum houses a rich collection of maritime objects, including model sailing ships, pieces of wreckage, 17th-century figureheads plus old engravings and prints. Some of the more contemporary exhibits include captains' desks, small craft such as an S 622 midget submarine, a human torpedo and a boat used by refugee boat people.

★ **Cours Dajot** (A3–B3 on the map): this major promenade was commissioned in the 18th century and was built by conscripts. You can take an attractive walk underneath the plane trees down to the top end of the commercial port, passing in the centre an obelisk erected as a battle monument for American soldiers who fought here in World War II.

Recouvrance

The old district of Recouvrance (A2–A3 on the map) lies across the lifting bridge on the right bank of the Penfeld river. Left intact after the bombardment, Recouvrance now houses the oldest church in Brest, the 18th-century Église St-Sauveur. The river makes a natural division between Brest proper and this once lively part of town. The rue de la Porte and the rue Vauban were traditionally an area of streetwalkers, seedy bars, and sailors on leave, but the atmosphere has cooled down a great deal recently and on some evenings during the week, the district is virtually dead. However, if you climb the Madeleine steps off the rue St-Malo on a stormy night, stand on the sandstone cobbles, and close your eyes, you might be able to imagine how it once was.

★ **Tour de la Motte-Tanguy** (A3 on the map): in Recouvrance, to the left of the bridge as you cross over from Brest. ☎ 02-98-00-88-60. Open June to September, daily 10am–noon and 2–7pm; from October to May, open Wednesday and Thursday 2–5pm, as well as Saturday and Sunday and during some school holidays, 2–6pm. Free admission. This 14th-century tower, which controlled the mouth of the Penfeld river, houses the **Musée d'Histoire de Brest**, with models and dioramas that remind us that the town was not always built of white concrete.

★ **Arsenal de la Marine** (off A3 on the map): porte de la Grande-Rivière (coast road). ☎ 02-98-22-11-78. Open during the Easter holidays for tours at 10am and 2.30pm. Also open from 15 to 30 June and from 1 to 15 September 9–11am and 2–4pm. Open continuously from 1 July to 30 September 9–11am and 2–4pm. Only citizens of EU member states are freely admitted here, and you will still need to bring your passport for identification purposes. If you are not an EU citizen you should apply in advance, giving your full name and address, date and place of birth and passport number. Admission is free, although you should expect to give a tip to the guide. This is the operational base for the Atlantic squadron, for the training ship *Jeanne-d'Arc* and the underwater mine-clearance team. Nearby, under the Île Longue, is where the nuclear submarines are moored. The guided tour, which lasts between one-and-a-half and two hours, is in two parts. First comes a general explanation about the history of this naval arsenal and the submarine base. The uses of the various buildings on the military site are also explained. Then comes the chance to climb on board a warship, which might be a minesweeper, an advice-boat or a frigate. The whole thing is fascinating.

The St-Martin District

★ **Place Guérin** (B1 on the map): at the top of the town, not far from the Église St-Martin, the place Guérin remains one of the liveliest districts in town. It miraculously escaped the bombing during World War II, and certain buildings display the date of their construction (including No.1, the state school). Peaceful, narrow streets are lined with small blocks of flats, detached houses and pre-war bars. The long-standing residents of the area have been joined by artists and poets attracted by the 'good vibes'. In the afternoons, retired men emerge to play *boules* and mothers bring their children out for a stroll. In the evenings, the cafés and restaurants quickly fill up.

The Marina

★ **Port de plaisance du Moulin-Blanc** (marina): very pretty, nestled deep in the harbour. With a capacity among the largest in Brittany and the Atlantic coast, this marina is filled with boats as far as the eye can see. You can take a very pleasant stroll along the quays and perhaps have a drink or a bowl of mussels and chips at **Le Tour du Monde** (☎ 02-98-41-93-65). In the outer bay there's a large, sandy beach, the plage du Moulin-Blanc.

★ **Océanopolis** (off B3 on the map): Moulin-Blanc marina. ☎ 02-98-34-40-40. Fax: 02-98-34-40-69. Website: www.oceanopolis.com. Open June to September, daily 9am–7pm; October to May 9am–6pm. Admission charge (90F for adults; 70F for children aged 4–12). Take the No.7 bus from outside the tourist information office. Allow 1 hour 30 minutes for each of the park's pavilions, or a whole day to see everything.

Under an enormous futuristic pyramid (called 'the Crab' because of its shape), with 8,000 square metres (86,000 square feet) of exhibits, this is more than just a museum of the sea and certainly not a theme park. It describes itself as an 'ocean discovery park'. Océanopolis is the crossroads for all the latest scientific, technical and industrial discoveries connected with the marine world. Its main objective is educational. As a living museum, it is constantly evolving, developing various themes depending on their topicality or intrinsic interest. New exhibitions have included *La mer en mouvement* (the moving sea), *Les mammifères marins* (marine mammals), and *Les céphalopodes* (cephalopods: octopuses, cuttlefish, nautili). Video screens and interactive computer games illustrate the Brest estuary, the earth as seen from space, the importance of satellites, and the tides.

Océanopolis is made up of three enormous exhibition spaces, each containing aquariums representing a particular natural environment, using natural light, pebbles, vegetation, and the swell of the sea. In the **Pavillon Tempéré** ('temperate house'), the wealth of life in Atlantic waters can be examined at close quarters, including dancing sea anemones, prawns in a mud bank, a forest of oarweed, a flatfish nursery, and a seal pond with a plant known as *spaghetti des mers* (sea spaghetti). There is a superb ocean column for observing life on the sea bed, and at set times a diver goes down to feed the fish.

In the **Pavillon Polaire** ('Polar house') a multi-media show demonstrates how man has adapted to life in the Polar regions. There is a reconstruction of the Concordia Antarctic base and a presentation of the study of climate. On a lighter note, the Polar house accommodates a small colony of penguins, with examples of three different species, and an ice field where sea lions can be watched at play.

The **Pavillon Tropical** ('tropical house') houses a vast aquarium that contains a real coral reef – something that you normally have to travel thousands of miles to see.

★ **Parc du Vallon de Stang-Alard**: route du Stang-Alard. From the centre of town, head in the direction of Guipavas airport, on the D712, or take the D233 towards Quimper. By bus, take Nos. 3, 17, 25 or 27 and get off at 'Palaren'. This open space is Brest's 'green lung', with 40 hectares (99 acres) of greenery and many birds. A favourite place for family walks. Le Blé Noir (open daily), one of the best *crêperies* in Brest, is also here (*see* 'Where To Eat'). Some 22 hectares (54 acres) belong to the **Conservatoire Botanique**, which houses endangered species of plants from all over the world: 52 allée du Bot. ☎ 02-98-02-46-00. Open April to September 9am–8pm, October to March 9am–6pm. Free admission to the garden. Its 1,000 square metres (10,760 square feet) of greenhouses containing the rarest of plant species are open to the public (admission charge 22F for adults; half price for children); guided tours for groups on request; individuals can visit from 1 July to 15 September from Sunday to Thursday 2–5.30pm. Out of season, tours take place on Sunday at 4.30pm.

WHAT TO DO

■ **Boat trips**: around the harbour, the naval base and the commercial port. Fast connections to the Port du Fret on the Presqu'île de Crozon (peninsula). Information from: **Vedettes Armoricaines** in the commercial port. ☎ 02-98-44-44-04, or the **Société Azenor**, ☎ 02-98-41-46-23, at the Moulin-Blanc marina.

WHERE TO DIVE BETWEEN BREST AND CAMARET-SUR-MER

This location is exposed to strong westerly winds, and the whole area is permanently washed by fierce currents. These factors make diving here a technical exercise, and with visibility at about 5 metres (16 feet), divers go down as soon as the water becomes slack enough, using a compass for navigation. Solo diving is not advised and you need to proceed with care in these parts.

The waters around here contain a particularly large number of wrecks, with the most illustrious being the *Cordelière*, a vessel belonging to Anne of Brittany, the wife of Louis XII, which sank in 1512 during an affray with the English. Today, this wreck is the focus of a group researching into naval archaeology whose technique for examining the approaches to Brest includes the use of an electronic 'fish' pulled by a trawler. The research receives public funding and it is hoped that information gleaned from this wreck will shed new light on life at sea in the 16th century.

USEFUL ADDRESSES

■ **GMAP:** 1st pier, port de Commerce. ☎ 02-98-43-15-11. Open at weekends all year round; in the summer, closed Thursday and Sunday. This FFESSM club has two converted trawlers to take divers out to their chosen locations. All the instructors are state-approved and all equipment is supplied. Some free camping is available in summer.

■ **Scubaland Plongée:** 29 rue de l'Amiral-Troude. ☎ 02-98-43-01-10. Website: www.scubaland.fr. Open at weekends throughout the year and daily except Sunday in summer. A well-equipped little centre where the maximum num-ber in any group is 10 people. The qualified staff are all state-registered and the club has two fast boats to take you out to your chosen spots. Reductions are offered for five or ten dives, but it's essential to book.

■ **Club Léo Lagrange:** 2 rue du Stade, 29570 Camaret-sur-Mer. ☎ 02-98-27-90-49 or 02-98-27-92-20. Email: perso.wanadoo.fr/club.leolagrange. Open from Easter to mid-October and daily except Sunday in summer. The meeting place is at the quai Tephany, where you can go out in groups arranged according to ability on the club's five orange-and-black trawlers. The club leader knows these waters like the back of his hand and they offer dives from novice level up to level III ability. All the staff are state-registered and equipment is supplied. Reductions are offered for bookings of 10 dives or more. Booking is essential. Accommodation is also offered. This club attracts a lot of German and Dutch divers.

The Best Places To Dive

⚓ **Les Ducs d'Albe:** an exceptional dive that takes you down to a maximum of 18 metres (60 feet) where there are two huge concrete quays that were built to moor the battleship *Bismarck* during World War II. Today, its sides are encrusted with velvety halcyons, sponges and lush sea anemones that glow like jewels. The most spectacular part is on the inside (beware of pieces of rusted iron), where your beam of light will reveal a throng of fish and crabs. The north side is the best spot to go down. Level I ability.

⚓ **The *Reine de Léon*:** this is an all-time favourite dive down to the wreck of a little seaweed-gathering boat that sank in 40 metres (130 feet) of water in 1991. Today's crew are the fish, including enormous specimens of ling and tight shoals of shimmering whiting, which move in formation through the remains of the engine's framework. Level II ability confirmed.

⚓ **Le Plateau des Fillettes:** a good diving spot for fish-spotters around an impressive shelf at the harbour narrows. At a depth of anything from 3 to 28 metres (10 to 92 feet) you can observe vast numbers of fish finding their daily food among shimmering banks of kelp. They swirl about in all directions and you feel that they are barely aware of your presence. Bronze cannon can also be seen – the last remains of any number of shipwrecks brought about by this unexpected underwater shelf. The spot is very exposed. Level II ability confirmed.

The *Dellec*: the usual crowd of shiny whiting accompanies you down to this torpedo-tube, which sank in 1945 and lies at a depth of 12 metres (39 feet). Its original military purpose is now camouflaged by the brilliantly coloured sea anemones and the spirographs that coat its framework. Access to the hold is also possible. Watch out for the heavy swell from the west. Level I ability.

***Émile Allard*:** the front of this marker vessel, which was sunk by bombers in 1943, is dominated by a crane that still stands upright, thrusting through the shoals of gleaming whiting. From time to time you might glimpse a monkfish lurking on the sea bed as it watches the bubbles given off by visiting divers. Conger eels and the occasional wrasse are another noticeable presence. At the back of the ship, the enormous engines are still in place. This spot is only diveable in calm weather. Level II ability confirmed.

Les Vieux Moines: an orange buoy in front of the Pointe St-Matthieu marks the location of this rock.

The depth of the dive here never exceeds 20 metres (65 feet). Here, among the colonies of halcyons, the bones of a wrecked ship provide a hiding place for quantities of fish, but it's worth knowing that the banks of kelp conceal the opening of a fissure where you might find whiting and crabs. Dive here only when the sea is calm. Level II ability.

The *Swansea Vale*: this British cargo boat, which sank in 1918 lies in three pieces at a depth of 30 metres (98 feet). You might find giant conger eels curled up in among the rusty ironwork and girders, but they're peaceable enough. Fronds of kelp and brightly coloured halcyons decorate the scene and the whiting, as inquisitive as ever, are guaranteed to keep you company. Don't go inside the wreck. Level II ability confirmed.

Les Tas de Pois: this 'pile of peas', as the name suggests, are in fact four little islands lined up opposite the Pointe de Pen-Hir. The last island provides a drop of 25 metres (82 feet) that starts off with a forest of kelp. Then you pass into technicolour world, through a succession of sponges, downy halcyons, sea urchins and sea anemones in a brilliant array of colours. At the foot of this drop, a jumble of loose rocks provides the local whiting with a good meeting place. Close by, the *Basse des Lys* provides another excellent diving spot. Level I ability.

FESTIVALS

– **La Grande Fête des Bateaux**: this is a huge festival of the sea usually held every four years (next in 2004) in July. You can see old sailing ships, plus exhibitions on marine heritage (beacons, lighthouses, tidal mills, oyster-farming methods). The ships usually move on from Brest to elsewhere in Brittany. For information, contact the tourist information office.

– **Les Jeudis du Port**: huge free street festival held every Thursday evening in July and August. The aim for more than 10 years has been to re-create the atmosphere of the *bordées des marins* of yesteryear, when the sailors painted the town red and it echoed to the sound of sea shanties. Now, visitors and locals mill around, listening to big stars performing on stage, and enjoying street entertainers. In 1995, Joan Baez performed in front of a crowd of 40,000. Unbelievable atmosphere in the bars of the Quai de la Douane. The festival has succeeded in retaining a friendly and good-natured atmosphere.

– **St-Patrick** (mid-March): wonderful festival by the commercial port, emphasizing the links between the Bretons and the Irish. *Fest-noz* (traditional Breton music and dance), and Irish artists. Excellent beers.

– **Carnaval naval** (end of March): by the commercial port. For a whole Saturday, a carnival celebrating the sea. Festivities conclude with a dance open to the public. Details from the tourist information office.

LEAVING BREST

– **By bus**: there are numerous buses leaving Brest. **Cars CAT** (☎ 02-98-44-32-19) to Portsall and Quimper. **Cars St-Mathieu** (☎ 02-98-89-12-02) to Le Conquet. **Cars Bihan** (☎ 02-98-83-45-80) to Brignogan, Lesneven, Landereau, Roscoff and Kerlouan. **Cars Leroux** (☎ 02-98-84-23-23) to Lampaul and Plouarzel. **Cars Salaun** (☎ 02-98-27-56-00) to Le Faou and Crozon. For buses to Lilia, ask for details at the bus station in Brest: ☎ 02-98-44-46-73.

– **By boat**: to Île d'Ouessant and Molène (*see* 'Île d'Ouessant').

Le Pays d'Iroise

Not far away from Brest lies an area that seems to have remained unsullied by time. Miraculously protected from over-development, the area contains secluded beaches tucked away in small inlets, deep estuaries (*abers*) cut into the coastline, a number of fishing ports, and the lovely islands of Ouessant and Molène. The whole area is washed by the Iroise Sea. This stretch of water is considered to be the meeting point of the English Channel and the Atlantic Ocean, the actual dividing line being between the Île d'Ouessant and the Pointe de Corsen.

USEFUL ADDRESS

🛈 **Pays d'Iroise:** Kerlois (BP 78), 29290, St-Renan. ☎ 02-98-84-41-15. Fax: 02-98-32-43-37. Email: pays.iroise@wanadoo.fr. Website: www.pays-iroise.com. Open Monday–Friday 8.30am–noon and 2.30–5pm (4.30pm Friday). A good source of information on the Iroise region, including accommodation and activities.

SAINT-RENAN (*LOKOURNAN*) 29290 (Pop: 7,016)

This small town is less than 15km (9.5 miles) northwest of Brest, at a crossroads, in the heart of the Iroise region. Visitors usually pass quickly through it on their way to the coast, but its old town centre is worth a detour.

History

The town owes its name to Ronan, an Irish hermit who arrived to evangelize the area around AD 490. Enjoying the microclimate, he stayed for about 20 years before going to convert Cornouaille, finally dying in Locronan (where he is buried in the church).

In the 14th century, St-Renan was a town of some importance, with a law court administering 37 parishes (including Brest). In 1681, Colbert had the law court, and the civil and military administration transferred to Brest. Dispossessed, St-Renan sank into lethargy and developed no further. It did, however, enjoy a period of increased activity with the exploitation of the tin mines between 1957 and 1975.

After a row with her lover Victor Hugo, Juliette Drouet sought refuge with her sister here in the 1830s. Hugo, very much in love, made the long journey to St-Renan in 1834 in an attempt to patch things up. He seems to have been successful, as they subsequently returned to Paris together.

USEFUL ADDRESS

🛈 **Office du tourisme**: 22 rue St-Yves; near the place du Vieux-Marché. ☎ 02-98-84-23-78. Out of season, open Tuesday to Saturday 10am–noon and 2–5pm; in July and August, open from Monday to Saturday 9.30am–12.30pm and 2–7pm, Sunday 10.30am–12.30pm. Excellent documentation about the town, friendly staff and good advice. Free guided tour of the town every Thursday at 10am.

WHERE TO STAY AND EAT

⛺ **Camping municipal**: Lokournan, on the route de l'Aber. ☎ 02-98-84-37-67 in high season and 02-98-84-20-08 out of season. Fax: 02-98-32-43-20. Open from 1 June to 15 September. Located on the D27, the road to Lanildut. Signposted on the right after 2km (1 mile). A site for two people costs 40F. This is a quiet, shaded site by the side of a lake and a ten-minute walk to St-Renan, along a footpath.

⛺ ✕ **Hôtel-restaurant des Voyageurs**: 16 rue St-Yves. ☎ 02-98-84-21-14. Fax: 02-98-84-37-84. In the town centre. Reasonable, moderately priced double rooms with TV, for 300–350F, or family rooms to sleep four. Built of stone, the whole place has been refurbished by the fifth generation of the family concern. The restaurant has an excellent reputation, with menus from 80F (except Sunday) to 255F. Excellent seafood dishes including scallop casserole (*ragoût de St-Jacques*) and seafood stew (*pot-au-feu de la mer*). A very warm welcome is offered and this place is recommended, for both food and accommodation.

LE PAYS D'IROISE

✕ **Crêperie La Maison d'Autre-fois**: 7 rue de l'Église. ☎ 02-98-84-22-67. Closed on Sunday, Monday out of season and from mid-January to mid-February. Weekday lunchtime set menus cost 53F and 78F. Allow 75–100F to eat à la carte. This is a striking half-timbered house, with an interior that is just as beautiful as the facade. The stone walls and old furniture have been freshened up by blue-and-white tablecloths and fresh flowers. Traditional *crêpes* are served, such as the *Bretonne* (with scallops in a leek-and-cream sauce sizzled in Calvados) or the *Sauvage*, made with honey and caramel.

WHERE TO STAY IN THE AREA

🛏 **Chambres d'hôte with Marie Perrot**: at Lézavarn, 29280, Plouzané; on the D38 between St-Renan and Plouzané. ☎ 02-98-48-49-79. Open all year round. The farm is nothing special, but it *is* out in the countryside, with a lovely family atmosphere, good Breton beds and, above all, very reasonable prices. 230F for two people, including breakfast.

WHAT TO SEE

★ **Place du Vieux Marché**: bears witness to the town's prosperity at the time when it was the location for the law court and the royal administration. Above the café, a beautiful granite house dating from 1500 has a flower-bedecked Gothic accolade doorway and a pretty mansard roof with carved figures. Next to it is superb corbelled house from 1438 (with the *crêperie* on the ground floor). Note the grotesque polychrome figures beneath the corbelling. At No.2, at the corner of the square and the rue de l'Église, the building dates from 1450. On the other side of the square stands the Sabretache, the seneschal's house, dating from 1641. It has beautiful dormer windows.

★ **Église Notre-Dame-de-Liesse**: the church burned down in the 18th century, and was rebuilt, then enlarged in the 19th century. At that time, a Romanesque-style choir was added, a copy of the one in the former Abbaye de Landévennec. Although the interior no longer has much character, the carved altar front and especially the stoup in the small entrance on the left side of the nave are worth a look. All that remains of the previous church is the old baptismal font dating from 1235. Situated above it is a very pretty 15th-century polychrome statue of St Renan.

★ Around the church, there are some picturesque streets such as the curious **rue Casse-la-Foi** ('break the faith' road). Did its steep incline discourage people from going to church? The **impasse Notre-Dame** still has its original drainage channel and cobblestones. The **rue de la Fontaine** leads to the fountains and the old washing-place, where clothes were still being washed not all that long ago. Until 1927, when running water was first supplied, the women of St-Renan would come here regularly to carry out their domestic chores. Made of freestone, it is one of the most beautiful washing-places in Finistère.

★ **Musée d'Histoire Locale**: 16 rue St-Mathieu (off the place du Marché). ☎ 02-98-32-44-94. Open on Saturday 10.30am–noon. Open the rest of the year upon reservation for groups of at least four or five people. Admission charge (10F). Interesting collection of Breton head-dresses, clothes, house-hold objects and furniture from the Léon region. Numerous accounts of St-Renan in former times, its fairs and its tin mines.

★ **Galerie Notre-Dame** (art gallery): place du Vieux-Marché. Open Monday to Friday 2–6pm; Saturday 10am–noon and 2–6pm. In a beautiful old building. Interesting exhibitions of local artists, which take place three times a year, at Christmas, in spring and in summer. For exact dates, check with the tourist information office.

★ **Lac de Tycolo**: this watersports centre is located at a pretty little 14-hectare (34-acre) lake created by the flooding of a disused tin mine. Activities here are suitable for anyone over the age of eight. ☎ 02-98-84-30-93. Open from July to September, Monday to Friday 9am–5pm. Ideal if you fancy learning to sail without going out into the waves. Beginners' courses in windsurfing, sailing and kayaking. lasting from half a day to a full week.

★ **Menhir de Kerloas**: 4 kilometres (2.5 miles) to the northwest of St-Renan, on the D5 in the direction of Plouarzel. It's well signposted. Don't miss this impressive menhir, standing in a harsh landscape. At a height of 9.5 metres (31 feet), it is one of the tallest in Brittany. Legend has it that young married couples would come out here to rub the stone – for the young man it would bring a son, while the young woman believed it would bring her control in her own household.

FESTIVALS AND GATHERINGS

– **Saturday market**: one of the liveliest and most colourful markets in the region with a picturesque setting. In mid-July there is a medieval or folk festival, alternating from year to year. Don't miss the *samedis-traditions* ('traditional Saturdays'), which take place in mid-August, with traditional folk dances and food, such as *Fars Buan*.

– **Medieval festival:** held in mid-July, with a costumed procession and a medieval banquet.

LE TREZ-HIR-EN-PLOUGONVELIN (*PLOUGONVELEN*) 29217   (Pop: 2,919)

Situated about 20 kilometres (12.5 miles) from Brest is **Plougonvelin**, a large village with a number of walls painted with astonishing frescoes. Right next to it is **Trez-Hir**, a seaside resort favoured by the people of Brest because of its microclimate and its beautiful beach. As a result, it is very touristy and packed with people on sunny weekends. There is a nice walk as far as the **Rocher de Bertheaume**, a rock that rises to 60 metres (195 feet) above sea level. The rock is the starting point for a 2-hour walk along the coast as far as the **Pointe de St-Mathieu** 9 kilometres (5.5 miles) away, with views of rocky cliffs and panoramas of the Presqu'île de Crozon (peninsula), from the Pointe de Créac'h Meur and the Pointe St-Mathieu. On really clear days you can see as far as the Pointe du Raz and the Île de Sein.

LE PAYS D'IROISE

LE PAYS D'IROISE

GETTING THERE FROM BREST

– **Cars St-Mathieu** (buses): ☎ 02-98-89-12-02. There are five or six buses per day during the week and three on Sunday.

USEFUL ADDRESS

🛈 **Office du tourisme**: L'Hippocampe, boulevard de la Mer, Trez-Hir. ☎ 02-98-48-30-18. Fax: 02-98-48-25-94. Email: omt.plougonvelin@wanadoo.fr. Open all year round; in high season, Monday–Saturday 10am–12.30pm and 2–7pm, Sunday 10am–1pm; the rest of the year open Tuesday–Saturday 10am–noon and 2–5pm.

WHERE TO STAY AND EAT OR GO FOR A DRINK

🛖 **Camping de Bertheaume**: route de Perzel. In a cove and right next to the beach. ☎ 02-98-48-32-37. The charge is 60F for a pitch for two people. The campsite contains about a hundred spaces and there are mobile homes available for rent. Quite an unspoiled area.

🛖 ✕ **Hôtel Le Marianna**: Plage du Trez-Hir, route du Conquet. ☎ 02-98-48-30-02. Fax: 02-98-48-23-41. Closed from October to March. Tourist hotel on the seafront, the only one in Trez-Hir. Decent rooms for 250F for two people. In the restaurant, menus start at 55F (weekday lunchtimes) up to 98F.

🛖 **Parc de St-Yves**: 15 rue du Cléguer; in the centre of Trez-Hir and 400 metres from the beach. ☎ 02-98-48-32-11 in season. Out of season, contact the tourist office. Fax: 02-98-48-25-94. Open from 1 April to mid-November. This park offers mobile homes and chalets for four to six people and a week's hire costs from 1,500F to 2,900F. Sailing centre, shops and a coastal path nearby.

🍷 **Bar des Sports**: 1 rue de Pen-Ar-Bed. ☎ 02-98-48-34-10. Open all year round. Impossible to miss with its amusing fresco (actually representing the bar entrance). Nothing exceptional, but the friendly owner has succeeded in creating a nice atmosphere in this little village bar. Menu for 45F including coffee, served every day, plus a children's menu for 32F.

WHERE TO STAY AND EAT OR GO FOR A DRINK IN THE AREA

🛖 **Camping municipal de Portez:** plage de Portez, 29280 Locmaria-Plouzané. ☎ 02-98-48-49-85. Fax: 02-98-48-93-21. Open from 15 May to 15 September. A pitch for two people costs around 50F. This shady, terraced campsite offers a fantastic panoramic view over Bertheaume bay and the beach is only 100 metres away.

✕ **Crêperie La Cormandière:** plage de Trégana, 29280 Loc-maria-Plouzané. ☎ 02-98-48-92-53. Just 10 kilometres (6 miles) east of Trez-Hir on the D789 then turn right onto the route de Trégana. Open all year round. Allow 80F to eat à la carte. This restaurant in a picturesque little building has three separate dining rooms, from the ground floor up to the attics. For the best views you need to climb all the way up to the top floor. The decor is striking and the mood is created with Breton box beds, a fireplace, large wooden tables and suspended model ships. Very classy. The *crêpes* they serve are excellent (the sweet ones come artistically presented like traditional Breton lace *coiffes*), although the prices are not cheap. The place is very popular with the Brest student population, so it's best to book a table. Pleasant terrace for fine days.

¶ Bar du Minou: plage du Minou, 29280 Locmaria-Plouzané. ☎ 02-98-48-55.27. 15 kilometres (9 miles) from Trez-Hir on the D789 then turn right onto the D38 towards the pointe du Grand-Minou. This bar is tucked away in a marvellous spot on a little inlet below the point. It was once a little country hotel but has now been taken over by some young people from the area and turned into a really great beach bar. The walls are painted with psyche-delic waves and on the bar is an array of tractor seats. At Le Minou you might meet all sorts: surfers coming up from the beach, sales reps taking a short break, people from nearby Kanabeach or young people from the village itself. On Saturday nights there's a DJ and they play dub-cool-soul music on Sunday. If you feel you want to stay, there are a few rooms – basic but very cheap.

WHAT TO SEE

★ **Fort de Bertheaume**: in Plougonvelin, near Le Trez-Hir. ☎ 02-98-48-26-41 or 02-98-48-30-18 (tourist information office in Plougonvelin). Open April–October, daily 1.30–6.30pm, including public holidays. Admission charge (22F). *Son et lumière* every evening in July and August at 9pm (tickets 44F for adults; 25F for children aged 12–18). Joint tickets are available for the museum and the *son et lumière* together. The fort is situated on an island that was only accessible until 1835 by rowing boat. Originally a medieval castle, it was rebuilt by the 17th-century military engineer Vauban, but it was badly damaged during World War II. The Navy has recently given it over to the local community and it has now been restored for use as a cultural centre, and for a number of events. In the 19th-century blockhouse are displays including a slide show about the history of the site, a reconstruction of a ship called *La Cordelière*, which foundered offshore in 1512, and an amusing display showing a number of ways that the locals considered for linking the island to the mainland. An outdoor theatre houses occasional concerts and shows in a marvellous setting.

LA POINTE ST-MATHIEU 29217

This was once an important town, with as many as 36 streets in the Middle Ages. Situated at the end of the land, it is now only a small village overlooked by a lighthouse with a range of 60 kilometres (37 miles). It seems to rise up out of the ruins of an abbey church, where only the choir is intact. On stormy nights, wandering through the ruins, swept by the lighthouse beam, is surreal and rather moving.

WHERE TO STAY AND EAT

☆☆☆ Chic

🛏 ✗ **Hostellerie de la Pointe St-Mathieu**: opposite the lighthouse and the abbey ruins, in Plougonvelin. ☎ 02-98-89-00-19. Fax: 02-98-89-15-68. Closed Sunday evening out of season (except for residents). In a superb situation; the rooms have views either straight out to the lighthouse or the abbey ruins, or out to sea. Every one is different; some have porthole windows while others have a sitting area and a terrace. Double rooms from 310F to 660F according to season. There is a superb dining room where they serve brasserie-style food such as crispy cod (*croustillant de morue fraîche*), calf's trotters with mushrooms (*pied de veau aux champignons*) or saddle of rabbit stuffed with prunes (*râble de lapin farci aux pruneaux*). Set menus cost from 98F (except Sunday) up to 420F.

WHAT TO DO

–The **sentier des douaniers** (customs officers' path): 9 kilometres (5.5 miles); a round trip, without stops, of about two hours. Start from the car park loop at the Pointe St-Mathieu (24 kilometres/15 miles west of Brest), and follow the white and red markings of the GR34 footpath, then the yellow. Should be undertaken in good weather. Information from the tourist office in Le Conquet.

The coastal path of the Pointe St-Mathieu is the favourite walk of the inhabitants of Brest. There is a lovely smell of seaweed and an invigorating ocean breeze. Seaweed farming, once a rich source of income, has left its mark on the path. The *davied*, Breton for *pierres à goémon* or 'seaweed stones', are large, pierced slabs of rock at the edge of the cliff. They were formerly used for hauling the 'golden grass' up from the beach. Don't lean too far over the edge! Seaweed is now harvested by boat and tractor.

You will also see the lighthouse, with its revolving beam, the abbey ruins and a 17-metre (55-foot) memorial column with a Breton woman carved in granite.

From the car park (be careful if it's windy), look up towards the granite sculpture, near the abbey and the signal station. Following the coastal path, or GR34, you reach the Rochers des Rospects (rocks). The path continues alongside the Grève de Keryunan (beach) before branching off inland and towards St-Marzin and the melancholy Manoir de Pridic (manor house). Two menhirs surmounted by crosses, or *lechs*, stand isolated on Plougonvelin moor. They are nicknamed the *gibets aux moines* (monks' gallows). The path returns via the bottom of the village of St-Mathieu.

LE CONQUET (*KONK-LEON*) 29217 (Pop: 2,441)

This small fishing port has preserved much of its natural charm, and some old houses still have their Gothic doorways. At No.1 rue Aristide-Briand, the **Maison des Anglais** is the oldest (15th century). The port is an embarkation point for the Île d'Ouessant and the Île de Molène. On the road from the Pointe de St-Mathieu is the pretty **Plage de Porzliogan**.

For a picturesque walk, follow the coastal path around the Presqu'île (peninsula) de Kermovan. Pedestrian access is via the Passerelle (footbridge) du Croaë. Your reward at the end is the superb **plage des Blancs-Sablons**.

USEFUL ADDRESS

🄳 **Office du tourisme**: parc de Beauséjour. ☎ 98-89-11-31. Fax: 02-98-89-08-20. Open from 15 June to 15 September, daily except Sunday afternoon, 9am–12.30pm and 3–6.30pm; the rest of the year, from Tuesday to Saturday, 9am–noon and during the school holidays from 9am–noon and 3–6pm. Friendly staff. Lots of information about walks and accommodation in and around Le Conquet and Île d'Ouessant.
■ **Compagnie de cars de St-Mathieu** (bus company): ☎ 02-98-89-12-02.

WHERE TO STAY AND EAT

🛖 **Camping Le Theven**: Les Blancs-Sablons. ☎ 02-98-89-06-90. Fax: 02-98-89-12-17. About 5 kilometres (3 miles) from Le Conquet on the route des Blancs-Sablons. Open from April to September. A site costs about 50F for two people. This is a vast campsite, with 400 pitches and situated only 400 metres from the beach. It's quite well equipped, and has a food shop.
🛖 ✕ **Le Relais du Vieux Port**: 1 quai du Drellac'h. ☎ 02-98-89-15-91. ⚒ restaurant. Restaurant closed in January but continuous service the rest of the year. This hotel has a friendly atmosphere and a homely feel. Run by a family that really knows how to make people welcome. Wooden floors and white walls nicely brightened up by blue stencilled designs. Good-quality bedding. Each room is named after a Breton island. Five of the rooms have a view of the estuary and the room named 'Beniguet' has three windows. The least expensive, the 'Bannalec', is much smaller than the others. Rooms with shower and toilet very reasonably priced, from 220F to 350F. Generous breakfast for 35F, with bread and homemade jam laid out on a fine old wooden table. The restaurant is in a large room with a feature fireplace, and there are always paintings by local artists on show. There's a *crêperie* with a good choice of *crêpes*, offering a menu for 60F, although you should allow 80F to eat à la carte. In the restaurant, you can eat à la carte for about 100F. Their fish and seafood dishes include a scallop salad made to a local recipe (*salade iroise aux St-Jacques*) and monkfish in cider (*lotte au cidre*). Good wine list. In summer, musical evenings take place every Wednesday. Le Relais du Vieux Port is a front-runner among tourist hotels.
🛖 **Chambres d'hôte with M. and Mme Michel**: 24 chemin des Dames. ☎ 02-98-89-07-10. Open from April to October. At the *gendarmerie* (police station) in Le Conquet, take the first road on the left, follow the signs that say 'Route Touristique'; at the fourth sign, 'Route Touristique and Chemin des Dames', go right, and after 50 metres you're there. Well run, with an extremely warm welcome. 180F for a double guest room with shower and toilet. The rooms have a separate entrance and are equipped with

LE PAYS D'IROISE

TV, refrigerator and microwave. You get a generous breakfast for 25F. Phone if you get lost on the way there.

🛏 **Chambres d'hôte with Annick Pastouret**: 8 rue Amiral-Gueprat. ☎ 02-98-89-14-25 or 06-07-14-44-69. This *chambres d'hôte* is in a little street near the tourist office. Open all year round. Double rooms cost from 220F to 280F, with breakfast 30F extra. It's very close to the centre of town but in a quiet location – a pretty little house with a palm tree on either side of the front door and an attractive garden in front. At the back there's a terrace and another garden that slopes down to the estuary below. Some of the bedrooms look out to sea; they are all very pretty and full of family-style furniture and trinkets; in fact, it's full of decorating ideas that you might want to emulate back home. Only the largest room has its own bathroom; the other rooms share a bathroom and toilet. A relaxed family atmosphere reigns here and you feel as if you're staying with friends.

✕ ☝ **La Taverne du Port**: 18 rue St-Christophe. ☎ 02-98-89-10-90. Fax: 02-98-89-12-51. Closed Tuesday from October to March and most of January. The ground-floor bar is huge, with attractive decor with a maritime theme. The first-floor restaurant, with a terrace, specializes in seafood, with menus from 78F to 158F. Dishes include fish sauerkraut (*choucroute de poisson*) and scallops with salmon (*St-Jacques au saumon sur pierre*). The Taverne also offers breakfast, which you can get for 20F before you head off to Île d'Ouessant (the landing stage being only a stone's throw away). In the bar there are eight draught beers on offer, including Guinness and Coreff. There's a musical event every Wednesday in summer and occasionally in the winter.

WHAT TO SEE

★ **Church**: built in the 19th century, but retaining elements from the 15th century. Notably, on the facade, there are gargoyles in the form of lions and statues in niches. Above the portal is 'Christ in bonds'. Inside, there is a carved wood organ loft, and a 16th-century stained-glass window.

★ **Anse des Blancs-Sablons**: wild and picturesque cove, which, together with the Île de Molène offshore, offers enough space for naturists to coexist with clothed sunbathers.

FESTIVAL

– **Bénédiction de la mer** (blessing of the sea): mid-August.

ÎLE DE MOLÈNE (*MOLENEZ*) 29259 (Pop: 271)

This island is barely 1 kilometre long and 800 metres wide. Its name 'Molène' comes from *moal enez*, or 'bare island' in Breton – it is completely flat and treeless. The main activities on the island are lobster fishing and seaweed farming. Oddly, there are more fishermen here than on the larger Île d' Ouessant (*see below*), since Île de Molène has a more sheltered harbour.

LE PAYS D'IROISE

Traditionally, there is a reputed rivalry between the people of Île d'Ouessant and Île de Molène.

HOW TO GET THERE

By Boat

■ **Compagnie Penn Ar Bed:** at Brest, Le Conquet, Île de Molène and Île d'Ouessant. ☎ 02-98-80-80-80 (reservations). Fax: 02-98-33-10-08. The Brest–Île de Molène crossing via Le Conquet leaves Brest at 8.30am and Le Conquet at 9.45am (departures from Le Conquet also at 11.15am, 4.30pm and 5.45pm in high season). The crossing takes between 45 minutes and 1 hour. An adult return ticket costs from 120F to 140F.

■ **Compagnie Finist'Mer:** at Le Conquet. ☎ 02-98-89-16-78. Two departures daily from April to June and September to October, and seven departures daily in July and August. The crossing takes 30 minutes. Crossings also available from Camaret (☎ 02-98-27-88-44), with the Le Conquet–Île de Molène adult return ticket costing 115F.

WHERE TO STAY AND EAT

🛏 **Rooms in private homes**: information at the town hall. ☎ 02-98-07-39-05.
🛏 ✕ **Hôtel-restaurant Kastell An Daol:** on the harbour. ☎ 02-98-07-39-11. Fax: 02-98-07-39-92. Open daily. Closed from January until the school holidays in February. Ten recently renovated rooms, some with a sea view, cost 320F to 350F. Half board obligatory in July and August (340–360F per person). In the restaurant, seafood is the speciality, and everything is made with fresh local produce. The set menus cost from 98F to 139F. You are guaranteed a warm welcome at this hotel, which is on Greenwich Mean Time – two hours behind the mainland in the summer.

WHAT TO SEE

★ The little village is clustered around its church and the **signal station** (go up it for a fine view of the archipelago; open 11am–1pm and 3–5pm). At low tide, the unusual sight of islets and huge expanses of seaweed is uncovered.

★ **Musée du Drummond Castle**: behind the town hall. ☎ 02-98-07-39-05. Open from May to October: in June, July and August open daily from 2.30–6pm (3–5pm for the rest of the season). Admission charge (12F for adults; half-price for children). Museum devoted to one of the most heart-rending shipwrecks to have happened in these waters. On 16 June 1896, the *Drummond Castle*, an English steamship returning from a cruise sank in less than five minutes after striking the reefs. Only three of the 246 passengers survived.

ÎLE D'OUESSANT (*EUSA*) 29242   (Pop: 951)

'Qui voit Molène, voit sa peine. Qui voit Ouessant, voit son sang.' ('Whoever sees Molène, sees his suffering. Whoever sees Ouessant, sees his blood.') Does the proverb suggest that reaching Île d'Ouessant is rather hazardous? The name of Ouessant comes from the Breton *Enez Eussa*, 'the highest island', but it also has the nickname of the 'Île d'épouvante' (island of fear). With good reason: it regularly suffers dreadful storms and impenetrable fog, and has deadly reefs and currents, and an amazingly jagged coastline.

Île d'Ouessant is 8 kilometres (5 miles) long and 4 kilometres (2.5 miles) wide with around a thousand inhabitants and more or less the same number of sheep. The islanders view the mainland with haughty disdain, seeing themselves as rebellious children who have broken away from their family ties. It is hard to believe that in the past they were involved as much in farming as in fishing. There were once as many as 120 small farms here. Today, only one farmer remains, but there are 58,000 plots of land and five fishermen. In former times, when wives had to wait several months for any income from fishing, the saying was: 'In Ouessant, it's the man who earns the bread, but it's the woman who butters it.' Even though the mayor and the rural police officer are both female, Île d'Ouessant is no longer the island of women.

Tourism is becoming increasingly important, and is beginning, little by little, to rob the island and its inhabitants of their particular character. However, the same destruction has not happened here as in many other places. Now part of the Parc naturel régional d'Armorique (Armorican regional nature park), the island has managed to preserve most of its character and charm. Completely worn down by erosion over many thousands of years, its highest hill is only 60 metres (195 feet).

Climate and Fauna

Île d'Ouessant enjoys relatively mild temperatures throughout the year. There is no great difference between winter and summer, and rainfall is moderate. Only the wind lives up to its reputation, as well as the fog, which sometimes cuts off the island from the mainland for days at a time.

There are apparently no moles on Île d'Ouessant but it is a habitat for the pipistrelle (a small bat). Birdlife, on the other hand, is abundant. The nesting birds include blackbirds, song thrushes, collared doves, great tits, barn swallows, warblers, wheatears, pipits and wagtails. Only one bird of prey – a species of falcon – is present, and a rare crow (the chough). The seabirds include seagulls, shags, oyster catchers and stormy petrels. On the rocks small colonies of grey seals and puffins may be seen. The best places to observe the seabirds or the migrators (especially in September) are the Pointe de Pern and the Pointe de Penn ar Roch. At certain times of year there are brilliant displays of gannets, kittiwakes, fulmars, sandpipers, shore-dwelling birds and turnstones.

The Ouessant sheep is one of the smallest sheep in the world, standing no more than 48 centimetres (19 inches) high and weighing up to 18 kilograms (40 pounds). Only seven hardy pure-bred sheep remain, living in the open air and grazing the windswept moors. Traditionally, the dark brown wool was used, undyed, to make the *berlingue* fabric worn by the women of Île d'Ouessant, who always dressed in black.

Customs

The customs of the past, abandoned not so long ago, testify to the island's particular character. One example is the traditions of the *proëlla*, which disappeared only about 20 years ago. When a sailor drowned at sea, the family would make a small cross out of wax and place it on a white cloth next to the family table, together with some holy water and a photograph of the deceased. They would then pray all night. The next day, the wax cross would be carried in a procession to the church and, later, to the cemetery or to a mausoleum. There, you can still read these words: 'We place our *proëlla* crosses here in memory of our sailors who die far from their own shores, in wars, of illness and in shipwrecks.'

Warning

Île d'Ouessant is magnificent but, unfortunately, the rise of tourism has led to a fall in the standard of service in some cases. Be warned that some hotels charge prohibitive prices, and may make half board obligatory throughout the year. In one place, the 'welcome' was not at all acceptable. Also, it is worth pointing out that some visitors have apparently paid a deposit at their hotel for the boat trip, and have been unable to take the boat because it was full. In some instances, their deposits were not refunded. To avoid this, make a reservation for the boat at the same time as booking your hotel or room.

HOW TO GET THERE

By Boat

■ **Compagnie Penn Ar Bed:** Brest, Le Conquet. ☎ 02-98-80-80-80 (reservations). Fax: 02-98-33-10-08. Website: www.pen-ar-bed.fr. Tickets can be bought direct at the harbour station. The *Enez-Eussa III* and the *Fromveur* take about 1 hour between Le Conquet and the island, while the *André-Colin* makes the crossing in 30 minutes. There is a regular service every day of the year, leaving from the commercial port at **Brest** at 8.30am and from **Le Conquet** at 9.45am (departures from Le Conquet also at 11.15am, 4.30pm and 5.45pm in high season). An adult return ticket costs from 127F to 186F. Departures also from **Camaret** from May to September, with return tickets costing between 134F and 157F.

■ **Compagnie Finist'Mer:** at Le Conquet: ☎ 02-98-89-16-61. Fax: 02-98-89-16-78. At **Camaret:** ☎ 02-98-27-88-44; at **Lanildut:** ☎ 02-98-04-40-72. In low season, there are four departures from Le Conquet, of which two are direct to Île d'Ouessant, one via Camaret and one via Lanildut. In high season there are seven departures a day, of which five are direct to Île d'Ouessant. The boats are fast and a crossing takes 30–40 minutes. The Le Conquet–Île d'Ouessant adult return ticket costs 145F to 153F.

By Plane

■ **From Brest-Guipavas airport:** there are two daily return flights on **Finist'Air**, leaving Brest at 8.30am and 4.45pm and Île d'Ouessant at 9am and 5.15pm. Information from the airline: ☎ 02-98-84-64-87.

HOW TO GET AROUND ON ÎLE D'OUESSANT

– **by bike:** this is undoubtedly the best way to get around the island, but be aware that, contrary to what you hear, they do have cars here. They drive, of course, on the right. It's as well to know, too, that the road signs here are discreet to say the least (it *is* in the middle of a regional park) and while the map that they give out at the tourist office is good enough to get you around the various landmarks, you'll need a proper map if you really want to get to know the place. There are several bicycle hire companies to be found as you get off the boat. If, on the other hand, you would rather not slog up the steep hill out of Stiff harbour, you can also hire a bike at Lampaul. A bus to get you there costs only 10F. The charge is the same whichever company you go to: it costs 60F per day for a standard bike or 80F for a mountain bike.

– **on foot:** the island is a real walkers' paradise, with more than 60 kilometres (37 miles) of coastal footpaths where bikes are not allowed.

– **on horseback:** riding is another perfectly good way to explore the island. Details from the **Centre équestre Ty Crenn** (equestrian centre) at Stang-ar-Glann as you come into Lampaul. ☎ and fax: 02-98-48-83-58. Accommodation for walkers is also offered here at 89F per night, and there are a few furnished rooms.

– **by minibus:** a tour of the island, with commentary, is available, lasting 2 hours (including about 45 minutes on foot). The cost is 75F per person. Booking is essential in July and August: ☎ 06-07-90-07-43.

USEFUL ADDRESS

🇧 **Office du tourisme**: place de l'Église. ☎ 02-98-48-85-83. Fax: 02-98-48-87-09. Open Monday–Saturday 9.30am–1pm and 2.30–6pm, and Sunday 9.30am–1pm. Here you can get basic information on the island and a good map, which is indispensible if you're thinking of cycling.

WHERE TO STAY

Most visitors come to the island only for the day, which is a shame, because catching the island in the early-morning light is a wonderful experience. There are many guest rooms available but only a few are actually in the village. It is essential to book in July and August, and for long weekends.

⛺ **Camping municipal Pen ar Bed**: as you come into Lampaul, the 'capital' of the island. ☎ 02-98-48-84-65. Open from April to the end of September. A pitch costs about 50F for two people. Not a lot of shade but it's well protected from wind as the site is behind the perimeter walls of what used to be a colonial infantry barracks.

⛺ **Auberge de jeunesse** (youth hostel): at La Croix Rouge. ☎ 02-98-48-84-53. Fax: 02-98-48-87-42. ♿ Up in the heights of Lampaul. Bed and breakfast costs 70F. To use this hostel you need to be a member of the LFAJ, which is the 'other' youth hostelling federation in France. A year's membership costs 70F, but you can join on the day. The hostel, which opened its doors in 1999, is in a renovated old house. Rooms contain from between two to six beds, with basin. The showers and toilets are shared. No restaurant, but use of the kitchen is offered. Sheets are available for hire.

⛺ **Chambres d'hôte: Odile and Victor Le Guen**: Pen ar Land. ☎ 02-98-48-81-21 or 02-97-36-35-89. The house is about 4 kilometres (2.5 miles) from the village, opposite the plage d'Arland (one of the few beaches on the island) and near the landing stage. Two really nice guest rooms with a spacious shared bathroom. The decor is delightful and there are books about Île d'Ouessant at your disposal. Generous breakfast. Excellent service at a reasonable price: 200F with washbasin, not including breakfast (25F).

⛺ **Chambres d'hôte: Mme Jocelyne Gaillard**: Porsguen. ☎ and fax: 02-98-48-84-19. Friendly welcome. Guest rooms with shower, toilet and TV in a comfortable, detached house, costing 200F per night with breakfast extra (25F). Evening meal with the family for those who opt for half board: 70F per meal.

⛺ **Chambres d'hôte: Franck and Nathalie Peyrat**: Pen ar Land. ☎ 02-98-48-86-09 or 06-80-06-54-65. In a hamlet between Lampaul and Stiff harbour. This traditional house has three guest rooms on the first floor that are good value for money: 200F per night; breakfast for 25F. Shared bathroom on the ground floor.

⛺ **Chambres d'hôte: Dominique and Jean-Yves Moigne**: at the bottom of the village, near the church and opposite the little supermarket. ☎ 02-98-48-84-77. Fax: 02-98-48-81-59. Open all year round. Three quite small and ordinary guest rooms, each with bathroom. Expect to pay 220F per night, and 28F for breakfast. There's access to a kitchen and you can make your own meals at no additional charge.

⛺ **Chambres d'hôte: Jacqueline Avril**: at the bottom of the village and not far from Mme Moigne's (*see above*). ☎ 02-98-48-80-08 or 02-98-48-85-65. Impeccably clean and reasonably priced guest rooms.

☆☆ Moderate

⛺ **Ti Jan Ar C'hafé**: Kernigon. ☎ 02-98-48-82-64. Fax: 02-98-48-88-15. A little bit before you get to Lampaul, on the left if coming from Stiff. Closed in January and from 15 November to 15 December. A double room with shower costs 320F, or 420F for three people. This little house has been renovated from top to bottom and is a new listing that's halfway between a B&B and a hotel. The rooms are very attractive and tastefully decorated. There's also a sitting room in a similar vein and a peaceful terrace. Evening meals are available, usually based on the day's catch: Mme Thomas used to sell fish, so you can be confident of a well prepared meal.

LE PAYS D'IROISE

WHERE TO EAT

Most of the hotel-restaurants in town offer the celebrated *ragoût sous la motte*, which is an island speciality. In general the welcome is not very warm. The *crêperies* are OK, though.

✕ **Crêperie Ti a Dreuz**: in the village of Lampaul. ☎ 02-98-48-83-01. At the church, go down on the left. Closed from mid-September to Easter, except during the school holidays. Allow 80–100F to eat à la carte. *Ti a Dreuz* means 'The Leaning House' and, indeed, the freestone facade looks like it was built on a stormy day. This *crêperie*, with its pleasant and clean blue-and-white interior, is run well by a family of weavers. Large choice of *crêpes*: try the Camaret recipe with *fario* (sea trout). The dessert speciality is the *Joséphine*, a delicious combination of locally made lemon jam, bananas and vanilla ice cream.

✕ **Crêperie du Stang**: on the road to Stiff, near the village. ☎ 02-98-48-80-94. Fax: 02-98-48-86-40. Closed Sunday evening and Monday and from October to the end of March. *Crêperie* offering original and generously garnished sweet and savoury *crêpes* and *galettes*. Set menus start at 40F but allow 60–70F if you eat à la carte. Out of season the opening times are sporadic, and note that lunch is not served after 1.30pm.

WHERE TO GET A DRINK

❢ **Ty Korn**: in the centre of Lampaul. ☎ 02-98-48-87-33. A long bar that has more of a pub atmosphere except that they serve you at the bar only at the start of the evening. Seafood snacks are also sold. Set menus start from 75F but allow 160F to eat à la carte. A good place.

WHAT TO SEE AND DO

★ **Lampaul**: the island's 'capital' is situated 3 kilometres (2 miles) from the embarkation point at Stiff harbour. The houses are dazzling, with blue and green shutters, and there is a poignant sailors' cemetery. The church's bell tower was donated by Queen Victoria to thank the islanders for all their efforts when the *Drummond Castle* was shipwrecked.

For those who only have a few hours to spend here, this is the traditional tour:

★ **Pointe de Pern**: to get here, take a pleasant road meandering through the hamlets, past low drystone walls and *gwaskedou* (three-pronged, star-shaped shelters for sheep, made of stone and sods of earth). At the point, the jagged rocks – amazingly, all listed monuments – are pounded incessantly by the waves.

★ **Pointe de Créac'h**: on its cliff, the lighthouse commands the entrance to the English Channel and sees at least three hundred ships pass through each day. Built in 1862, it has a range of 50 kilometres (30 miles) and is one of five lighthouses positioned to protect ships from the currents off Île d'Ouessant.

★ **Musée des Phares et Balises** (lighthouses and beacons museum):

pointe de Créac'h. ☎ 02-98-48-80-70. Open from May to the end of September and during all school holidays, daily 10.30am–6.30pm and also 9–11pm from mid-July to the end of August; from 1 October to 30 April, open 2–4pm (6.30pm in April), closed on Monday. Admission charge (25F) and combined tickets with the Écomusée are also available.

The area of coastline around Brest has the largest concentration of lighthouses and beacons in the whole of France, with 23 lighthouses, 63 lights, 14 radionavigation stations and 258 buoys. These are all fully automated and provide important assistance to anyone navigating off the coast of Brittany, a stretch of water that is fraught with danger yet still very busy.

It seems fitting that the chosen location for this fascinating museum should be an old power station – an impressive building in its own right. The history of lighthouses and beacons is examined, showing how far back into antiquity this ancient technology can be traced. Models are on display of the first known lighthouses, including one of the Seven Wonders of the World, the 'Pharos' (lighthouse), built at Alexandria in the 3rd century BC. A number of documents show details of the construction of some of France's most important lighthouses, and trace the development of methods of lighting them, ranging from an oil lamp with a clockwork movement to an enormous 6,000-watt lightbulb.

On the way back, you pass close to the last windmill on the island, now restored (Karaes).

★ **Écomusée d'Ouessant** (open-air museum): Maison du Niou, in the hamlet of Niou-Huella. ☎ 02-98-48-86-37. Same opening times as the Musée des Phares et Balises and same admission charge (25F). A combined ticket is available. Guided tours of this traditional house take place every 30 minutes.

Two typical houses have been converted, to form what was France's first open-air museum. One of them appears exactly as it was at the end of the 18th century. There are two rooms, one at either end of the building. The first, known as the *penn ludu* or 'cinder end', was the room in which the occupants cooked, ate and slept, a practice common to many regions with a difficult climate. The ceiling is dark green in colour, painted that way so that it would not be blackened too quickly by the smoke. The furniture is also painted – since there are no trees on the island, much of the furniture was made from wood salvaged from shipwrecks, and the heavy decoration was used to disguise any imperfections. This absence of wood meant that what was burnt in the hearth would have been a combination of bracken, dried seaweed and cow dung. The table is positioned near the window in order to make best use of the light, for Île d'Ouessant got its first electricity supply as late as the 1950s. On the other side of the building is the *penn brao* or 'pretty end', where the family would entertain, embellished with the best of the pickings from shipwrecks.

★ **Le phare du Stiff** (lighthouse): in the eastern part of the island, on a direct road from Lampaul. At the island's furthest point is a lighthouse built by the military engineer Vauban. It is one of the oldest lighthouses in France and is still functioning. Right alongside it, the Navy has installed a 72-metre (234-foot) radar tower with a range of 90 kilometres (56 miles) to watch over the one-way system for ships entering the English Channel. A path leads from here to the Presqu'île de Cadoran (peninsula), with another picturesque view from there of the Baie de Beninou.

★ **Other walks**: to the **Pointe de Porz Yusin**, north of Lampaul, to go bird-watching. To the south, the **Presqu'île de Feunten Velen** (peninsula) and its cliffs. Nice view of the Pointe de Pern. In the middle of the island, archaeology enthusiasts will enjoy the ruins of an Iron Age Gallic village – Mez-Notariou – consisting of the foundations of around a hundred buildings separated by six streets. The sea is not visible from here.

DIVING

Diving conditions around Île d'Ouessant are known to be extreme, with strong currents and huge, sudden depths. The number of wrecks in these waters is too great to count, and more seem to be discovered with every new season. The visibility around this underwater graveyard is very good, at 15–20 metres (40–65 feet) and the area offers dives for all abilities, even beginners, although seasoned Level II or Level III divers will get the most out of the dives here. The most easily accessible spots are in the Baie de Lampaul, which has some shelter. You are advised to take great care: solo diving is not advisable.

Diving Club

■ **Ouessant Subaqua**: port de Lampaul (harbour). ☎ 02-98-48-83-84. Open at weekends from Easter to the end of September and daily in July and August. Here they take no chances at all on the safety front, and all the staff have plenty of experience of the diving conditions around the island, as well as being fully qualified. From the club a speedy inflatable boat takes you out to diving spots suitable for all levels of ability including beginners, all within five minutes of the harbour. You will be supplied with a full kit if required. It's essential to book in advance.

The Best Places To Dive

➷ **The *Peter Sif:*** this 95-metre-long (310 feet) Danish cargo vessel, which went down in 1979, lies at a depth of 50 metres (164 feet) with its cargo scattered all around it. The whole wreck adds up to quite a splendid sight, with such fine details as a fireplace bearing the company's coat of arms, cargo booms, a huge propeller and the bridge itself. The wreck is teeming with marine life and you can see some excellent plant specimens and living creatures tucked away. Level III ability.

➷ **Ar Bloc'h:** this is a crevice where you will be dazzled by the array of plant life. Down at a depth of 40 metres (130 feet) there's a real forest of laminaria kelp and big gorgonia, sea roses and lavish forests of halcyons and corynacties. Level I ability.

➷ **The *Vesper*:** this sizeable French cargo ship, which sank in 1903, lies at a depth of between 10 and 40 metres (33 and 130 feet) and is home to huge shoals of sea bass and coley that have reached a considerable size. The remains of this ship – the boiler, propeller housings and various bits of ironwork – are scattered around, although everything is slowly disappearing beneath an impressive curtain of seaweed. You could say that Mother Nature was reclaiming the sea bed here. Level I ability.

⚓ **The *Minéralier:*** this unidentified cargo ship lies upside down at a depth of 40 metres (130 feet) and houses a large colony of gorgonia and halcyons. Alongside it lie piles of minerals – the ship's spilled cargo. Also nearby is a magnificent chasm, rich with giant laminaria kelp and brilliantly coloured corynacties. Level II ability.

⚓ **Port de Bougezenn** (harbour): a quiet little harbour with slightly shallower waters (10–30 metres/ 33–100 feet), so this is the place to come if you want to get back on form. Throngs of fish and crustaceans live here (particularly spider crabs and common crabs) and

there is also a lovely little cave. It's fun to snap your fingers in front of the spirographs and watch their instant reaction. Nearby you can catch sight of three anchors and two cannon among the kelp – these seem to be the last remains of the *Atlas*, a French vessel that sank some time in the 18th century. Level I ability.

⚓ ***Olympic Bravery:*** this Greek super-tanker foundered on the rocks to the north of the island in 1976 and is the largest wreck to be found in 10 metres (33 feet) of water anywhere in Europe. It's absolutely monstrous. This is quite a tricky dive, with very strong currents. Level II ability.

EVENT

– **Salon international du livre insulaire:** at the end of August. This newly established literary festival (the first one was in 1999) brings together writers who either live on or write about islands. There's the usual round of workshops and talks, and plenty of opportunity to meet the writers. Details from the tourist office.

LEAVING ÎLE D'OUESSANT

– **To Le Conquet and Brest** (stopping at Île de Molène): crossings all year round with the company **Penn Ar Bed**: ☎ 02-98-80-80-80.

– **To Le Conquet or Camaret** (in season): contact **Finist'Mer:** ☎ 02-98-89-16-61.

– **To Brest-Guivapas airport:** Departures at 9am and 5.15pm. Contact **Finist'Air:** ☎ 02-98-84-64-87.

PLOUARZEL (*PLOUARZHEL*) 29810 (Pop: 2,519)

Plouarzel is a quiet little town in the Breton interior. Its 19th-century church includes an interesting ossuary chapel dating back to the 18th century.

WHERE TO EAT

✗ **Crêperie Ty-Forn:** at Kervourt. ☎ 02-98-89-65-77. Open daily in season. Closed Tuesday from 11

November to the February school holidays. Allow a minimum of 75F for a meal. This excellent eatery in a long stone building has been open for 20 years. In that time they have built up a reputation for good food with a difference, namely that their buckwheat *galettes* are made with mashed potato, although they are very tasty. The *crêpes* and *galettes* come with a good choice of imaginative fillings, including artichoke hearts, and a sausage and leek fondue. Plentiful use is made of organic produce from Brittany and the sorbets and ice creams are locally made.

WHAT TO SEE IN THE AREA

★ **Pointe de Corsen:** 6 kilometres (3.5 miles) southwest of Plouarzel. A cliff standing 30 metres (98 feet) high marks the end of what is the most westerly point of mainland France and therefore the actual 'Finistère' ('land's end'). It is also the point held to mark the boundary between the English Channel and the Atlantic Ocean. The area shelters a number of small villages nestled away in the valleys, but the number of closed-up or ruined houses and farms is a sure sign of the harshness of life in these parts. In many ways you feel as if you are in a foreign country here.

Go back to **Porsmorguer** and on to the **anse de Porsmorguer** (bay), which has a lovely sheltered beach. Take the coastal path, below the cliffs, for a 45-minute walk back to the **pointe de Corsen**, where the occasional creek gives you a thin strip of fine sand with good shelter. From here Britanny's largest signal station can be seen, at Cross-Corsen. Don't get excited about viewing it, though, as it's used by the military for sea traffic surveillance. Going on to the **grève de Trézien** (beach), where there's a creek that is popular with nudists.

★ **Phare de Trézien:** this lighthouse is northeast of the pointe de Corsen and 5 kilometres (3 miles) west of Plouarzel. Open to visitors daily in July and August 3.30–6pm. Also open to groups all year round, by appointment only. Information from the tourist office: ☎ 02-98-89-69-46. A climb of 182 steps takes you to a worthwhile view at the top.

LAMPAUL-PLOUARZEL
(*LAMBAOL-BLOUARZHEL*) 29810 (Pop: 1,784)

A little holiday resort with a pretty white-sand beach. Further on, at **Kerriou**, there are excellent waves for anyone wanting to surf or bodyboard. Nearby is the **grève de Gouérou**, a place noted for its seaweed ovens, and the little harbour at **Porspol**. This is a quiet spot for most of the year, although it sees an inevitable influx of tourists during the summer months.

USEFUL ADDRESS

🅱 **Office du tourisme:** 7 rue de la Mairie. ☎ 02-98-84-04-74. Open from mid-June to the end of August, daily except Sunday afternoon, 10am–12.30pm (noon in June) and 1.30–4.30pm. The first two weeks in September, open Monday–Friday 10am–noon. Out of season open Tuesday–Thursday 9am–noon.

WHERE TO STAY AND EAT

🛏 **Chambres d'hôte: M. and Mme Jézégou:** 19 rue de Mol-ène. ☎ 02-98-84-06-11. After the church, turn left along the road that leads down to Porspol harbour. Open all year round. Double rooms start at 190F with breakfast extra (30F). This place offers two rooms in quite a basic outbuilding, but they're adequate, the welcome is good and it's not at all expensive. The beach is 1 kilometre away.

✕ **La Chaloupe:** port de Porspol (harbour). ☎ 02-98-84-01-19. 👟 Closed Monday out of season. Set menus cost from 65F (weekdays only) up to 245F in this peaceful little restaurant. They give excellent value for money with generous portions, although the dining room itself is rather uninteresting. There's a basic set menu available during the week, but if you can bear to pay a bit more, you can have specialities such as scallops in cream (*feuilleté de Saint-Jacques à la crème*), breast of duck (*magret de canard au chouchen*), or a decent seafood salad (*salade croquante de la mer*).

THE ABER-ILDUT AND LANILDUT (*LANNILDUD*) 29840 (Pop: 855)

★ **The Aber-Ildut**: this is the smallest of the three estuaries that you will cross if you follow the coastline between Le Conquet and Roscoff, and it's probably best seen on foot (roughly 1.5 kilometres). A small path leaves from Pont-Reur (on the D28) linking it to Brelès (on the D27). If you love country manor houses, make a little detour of less than 2 kilometres (1 mile) to see the elegant, slightly austere looking grey granite **Manoir de Kergroadès**. (The well-renowned local granite is pink; it was used for the base of the obelisk in the place de la Concorde in Paris.) In **Brelès**, there is a 16th-century church whose cemetery is entered through a curious archway.

★ **Lanildut**: pretty little village on a steep bank of the estuary, where there are some fine examples of 17th- and 18th-century houses hidden away behind high walls of grey granite. Full of charm. A small road leads to the **Rocher du Crapaud**, where there is a fine viewpoint.

Although the industry is hardly visible, Lanildut is Europe's leading port for the processing of seaweed (*see* 'Background'). France's most important seaweed beds are located offshore from the *abers* and around the Île de Molène. As many as 370 different kinds of seaweed are to be found here, and supplies are gathered in between mid-March and mid-October.

Modern boats are used nowadays, and the old-style hand guillotines have been superseded by a kind of mechanical arm that is able to cut the weed along the sea bottom. One relic of the old way of doing things is still in existence in the shape of a seaweed oven at the water's edge, in which the stuff was once burned in order to extract iodine. It consists of a 6-metre-long (20 feet) trench lined with flat stones that retained the heat.

In the surrounding area, some butchers make a delicious ham smoked with seaweed. The simple recipe involves putting the ham in boiling water (with no added ingredients) and boiling for one-and-a-half hours. Serve with boiled potatoes and, perhaps, a vinaigrette dressing.

USEFUL ADDRESS

🖪 **Point info tourisme:** on the harbour at Lanildut. ☎ 02-98-04-31-62. Open July and August 10.30am–12.30pm and 4–7pm (5–7pm Monday). Closed Sunday. There is an exhibition relating to seaweed production, plus activities and excursions.

From the Aber-Ildut to Portsall

Don't miss out on this tiny little coastal road which meanders from fishing port to fishing port. Wonderful sunsets are a certainty.

★ **Melon** and **Porspoder**: Melon, with its gorgeous little natural harbour, looks good enough to eat. Porspoder, on the other hand, is a family holiday resort with more tourists. The village has a beautiful setting in a bay, with rocks and coastal paths.

★ **Trémazan**: from Argenton to Trémazan, the coastline is much gentler, and this is one of the nicest stretches, unspoiled by urban development. Lawns of green grass reach down and touch the sea, which is fringed by a simple rocky edge. An adorable little chapel and large granite cross make the sunsets something to remember. In Trémazan, there is a picturesque and imposing ivy-clad feudal castle. It still possesses its large square 12th-century keep. The tides kept the moat full.

★ **Portsall**: charming fishing village that would have preferred not to have taken its place in history – on 16 March 1978, the tanker *Amoco-Cadiz* ran aground. Fortunately, no traces remain of the 230,000 tons of oil that were spilled all along the coastline here, although the village had to wait until 1992 to receive 115 thousand million francs worth of compensation. The tanker's anchor lies as a reminder (if one were needed) by the harbour.

WHERE TO STAY AND EAT IN THE AREA

✕ **Crêperie La Salamandre**: place du Général-de-Gaulle, Ploudalmézeau, on the way out of town in the direction of Portsall. ☎ 02-98-48-14-00. ⅋ Open daily from April to September, and at weekends during the school holidays (except Wednesday) during the rest of the year. Closed from mid-November to mid-December. A *crêperie* handed down from father to son, he and his wife run this pleasant *crêperie* with a refreshing approach. Everything is done to make children welcome and the *crêpes* are tasty. Allow

yourself to be tempted by the *St-Jacques aux petits légumes* (scallops with vegetables) for 31F, or by the *Bigouden* (chitterling with fried potatoes and cream). Expect to pay around 80F to eat à la carte.
✕ **Crêperie du Château d'Eau**: as you leave Ploudalmézeau on the road to Brest. ☎ 02-98-48-15-88. Fax: 02-98-48-03-67. ⅋ Open from 15 February to 15 November; out of season, open at weekends and during the school holidays. Set menu from 85F. Allow about 85F to eat à la carte. The restaurant is

located in a local curiosity – a water tower 112 metres (364 feet) above sea level. There is a lift to reach the dining room, with a panoramic view that is the main purpose of the visit, or you can climb the 278 steps. The place is rather touristy, as you might expect.

The Côte des Abers

The *abers* are estuaries that penetrate deep inland. From Le Conquet towards Roscoff, the superb coastline has its fair share of little corners that remain as yet untouched by mass tourism. It is still known as the 'Côte des Naufrageurs' ('shipwreckers' coast') because, in former times, peasants would sometimes light fires to mislead the ships, and then pillage them after they had run aground.

USEFUL ADDRESS

🛈 **Pays des Abers Côte des Légendes** ('the *Aber* region – coast of legends'): BP 35, 29830 Ploudalmézeau. ☎ 02-98-89-78-44. This tourist office offers information by post or by telephone on every aspect of the area.

THE ABER-BENOÎT AND THE ABER-WRAC'H

The **Aber-Benoît** estuary cuts inland for about 8 kilometres (5 miles), flanked by fields and forest. At low tide substantial mud banks are exposed, which provide an environment attractive to certain kinds of bird. The *aber* can be explored along several marked footpaths and there is a good walk of about 7 kilometres (4.5 miles), which takes just over two hours, along the vallée des Moulins ('valley of windmills'). At the turn of the 20th century, the number of windmills in the valley amounted to more than a hundred. Several oyster beds can be seen on the right bank and there is an attractive little harbour at St-Pabu. At the mouth of the *aber* are some good beaches, including one at the bay of Béniguet, which is more of a lagoon, and a long beach at Corn ar Gazel.

The **Aber-Wrac'h** is much deeper, reaching 32 kilometres (20 miles) inland, and is wider and grander than the Aber-Benoît. A superb panorama of the estuary can be had from the pont de Paluden (bridge), which is on the D13 between Lannilis and Plouguerneau. On the south bank of the Aber-Wrac'h, 2.5 kilometres (1.5 miles) from Lannilis, stands the 15th-century **Château de Kerouartz**, a fine example of Breton Renaissance architecture. It is not open to the public, but you can admire it from the outside. It has been in the same family for 300 years. At the mouth of the *aber*, where l'Aber-Wrac'h harbour lies tucked away, and the delightful little beach at the baie des Anges, the Ste-Marguerite peninsula closes it off in the southwest. The beach is vast, a windswept stretch of fine sand lined with dunes planted with beachgrass. The countryside around here is wonderful – and still pretty wild, though it is hardly a haven of peace in the summer months.

THE CÔTE DES ABERS

USEFUL ADDRESS

🄱 **Aber-Tourisme** (tourist office): 1 place de l'Église, 29870 Lannilis. ☎ 02-98-04-05-43. Fax: 02-98-04-12-47. Website: www.abers-tourisme.com. Open in July and August 9.30am–12.30pm and 2–7pm Monday–Saturday and 10am–12.30pm Sunday. Out of season open Monday–Friday 9.30am–noon. This tourist office has plenty of good literature about this fascinating region. A brochure that describes a number of possible walks is available.

WHERE TO STAY IN THE AREA

⚓ **Camping des Abers:** dunes de Ste-Marguerite, 51 Toull Treaz, 29870 Landéda. ☎ 02-98-04-93-35. Fax: 02-98-04-84-35. Website: www.abers-tourisme.com. Open from Easter to 24 September. In season, a pitch costs about 70F for two. This campsite is in a superb location, between l'Aber-Wrac'h and l'Aber-Benoît at the end of the Ste-Marguerite penin-sula. It is bounded by a long beach of fine sand and there is decent hedging to protect the site from the sea winds. A good welcome is offered and everything is spotlessly clean. Mobile homes are also available.

⚓ **Chambres d'hôte des Abers:** 150 Kérizak, 29870 Landéda. ☎ 02-98-04-84-61. This B&B is in a residential part of the village, about 2 kilometres (1 mile) from l'Aber-Wrac'h harbour and the beaches at Ste-Marguerite. Open all year round. A double room costs 270F including breakfast, with a reduction if you stay more than three nights. The hosts in this modern house are very hospitable and the rooms are OK.

⚓ **Manoir de Trouzilit:** in Trouzilit, 29870 Tréglonou, signposted off the D28 between Tréglonou and Ploudalmezeau, in the open coun-tryside and quite near the Aber-Benoît river. ☎ 02-98-04-01-20.

Fax: 02-98-04-17-14. Open all year round. Just about every kind of accommodation can be found at this huge 16th-century manor house, from *gîtes* sleeping two to twelve people (costing 1,300–2,200F per week for a *gîte* for five), to guest rooms with sloping ceilings costing 260F for two people. Break-fast is included. Dormitory accom-modation costs 50F per night. There's also a *crêperie*, which is open daily in season (out of season open weekends only), plus minigolf and pony rides. Friendly welcome guaranteed.

☆☆☆☆ Très Chic

⚓ **Hôtel de la Baie des Anges**: 350 route des Anges, port de l'Aber-Wrac'h, 29870 Landéda. ☎ 02-98-04-90-04. Fax: 02-98-04-92-27. ♿ This is a charming early 20th-century hotel facing the plage de la Baie des Anges. The proprietor is justly proud of his hotel, which is every bit as good as it boasts. It offers tastefully decorated and very comfortable rooms from 420F to 560F, some benefiting from the as-tonishing sea view and the lovely sunsets. The breakfast costs 60F and is worth every centime, with a good choice of coffees, pastries and excellent bread. The terrace is de-lightful.

WHERE TO EAT

✗ **Cap'tain:** port de l'Aber-Wrac'h, 29870 Landéda. ☎ 02-98-04-82-03. Closed Monday and Tuesday out of season and December to mid-February. The dish of the day costs 44F, or 64F with either a starter or a dessert, and the set menu costs 89F. The wood-panelled dining room has a maritime feel, with painted tables and large windows looking out at the sea view. Efficient service and a warm welcome are given and the cuisine has some nice surprises – fish cooked exactly right, excellent *crêpes* and huge salads that are big enough for a meal in themselves. Recommended.

✗ **Crêperie de l'Aber-Benoît**: Pors ar-Vilin, 29830 St-Pabu. ☎ 02-98-89-86-26. ♿ Right at the end of the village, by the little pocket-sized harbour. Open evenings on Friday, Saturday, Sunday and during school holidays; and lunchtime and evening in season. Closed in January. Pretty stone house with a garden,

and a charming Breton interior. Good reputation for its *crêpes*. Specialities include *Coquille St-Jacques* (scallops), the *Gwelle* (egg, ham, cheese, mushrooms, tomatoes), and the *Paysanne*. The sweet *crêpes* and the ice cream are also excellent.

☆☆☆☆ Très Chic

✗ **Le Brennig**: St-Antoine, port de l'Aber-Wrac'h, 29870 Landéda. ☎ 02-98-04-81-12. Closed Tuesday. Large house facing the harbour, offering particularly elegant surroundings with a 'yacht-club' feel about it. Modern, stylish and welcoming, with efficient service and a warm atmosphere. Ask for a table in the bay window if you want to dine with a sea view. Excellent reputation in the area for exquisite food that's completely fresh, and amazingly good value for money – probably the best in the area. Menus cost from 98F to 196F.

WHERE TO BUY GOOD FOOD

🔒 **La Maison du Boulanger:** 3 rue des Marchands, 29870 Lannilis. ☎ 02-98-04-48-05. Closed Thursday and Sunday afternoon. In the centre of the village. An attractive shop selling bread made the way it used to be, all cooked in a wood-oven. As well as their rye bread and unleavened bread, they make a rustic loaf that keeps so well that local sailors take it to sea with them.

🔒 **Huîtres Prat-Ar-Coum:** Prat-Ar-Coum, 29870 Lannilis. ☎ 02-98-04-00-12. On the right bank of

l'Aber-Benoît and very well signposted. The shop is open daily except Sunday but the restaurant is open in July and August only. The Madec family has been farming oysters in the baie de Carantec and the beds of this *aber* since the end of the 19th century. Like those produced around Belon, these oysters have a slightly nutty flavour. They are sold here, as well as a range of other seafoods, and in summer you can do your tasting at tables looking out across the *aber*. Allow about 190F.

WHERE TO DIVE IN THE AREA

The rich inlets of l'Aber-Wrac'h and l'Aber-Benoît deserve a detailed exploration. The visibility is not wonderful but improves offshore, where you find astonishing lengths of kelp – probably the longest off French shores. This stretch is fairly sheltered although the wind from the northwest is fierce.

Diving Clubs

■ **Abersub**: port de l'aber Wrac'h, 29870 Landéda. ☎ 02-98-04-81-22. Email: abersub.chapon@wanadoo.fr. Open all year round and open every day in high season. Up anchor on board the *Imprévu*, one of the club's two boats, with Eric Chapon and his team of state-qualified coaches, who can guide you to some familiar-sounding wrecks. A wide programme is on offer, ranging from beginner's dives to trips suitable for Level IV ability and you can do short courses, underwater orientation and diving at greater depths. Anyone over the age of eight is welcome. Price reductions are offered for either six or ten expeditions, and reservation is always advisable. Discount-priced lodging is also available.

■ **Aber-Benoît Plongée**: quai du Stellac'h, BP 68, 29830 St-Pabu. ☎ 02-98-89-75-66. Fax: 02-98-04-46-60. Email: a.b.p.@wanadoo.fr. Open from Easter to the end of October; daily in the summer. This club is a far cry from the diving clubs that operate on a production line. A well-equipped centre, the club offers dives in small groups only, with a maximum of 16 people, on the theory that this helps you to get closer to nature. The two very likeable proprietors, Catherine and François Leroy, are both state-qualified and take you out in their fast boat to the best locations in the area, with dives suitable for all levels including beginners. Children over the age of eight years are welcome. Discounts are available for five or ten dives and booking is advisable.

The Best Places To Dive

⚓ **The *Amoco-Cadiz***: it is now more than 20 years since the *Amoco-Cadiz* disaster, which produced the biggest oil slick of all time. The wreck of the massive oil-tanker now lies broken apart, at depths varying from 6 metres to 32 metres (19–105 feet), with the plantlife of the ocean disguising its shape with increasing speed as the years pass. Diving here is best done at slack water. Level II ability.

⚓ **The *Elektra***: why not forget all about the *Amoco-Cadiz* and opt for exploring the *Elektra*, a pretty little Greek cargo boat that sank in 1963 in 20 metres (65 feet) of water. The wreck is draped in kelp

and brown marine algae and you can even get hold of the wheel and act out steering the ship. Slack water diving is recommended. Level I ability.

⚓ **La Roche aux Moines:** this rock sticks up out of the sea by the edge of the Aber Wrac'h channel, in 20 metres (65 feet) of water. The rock is home to an array of brown and green sea anemones, flame-coloured sponges, shrimps and other small crustaceans and the whole area seems to be keenly supervised by a shoal of massive coley. Level I ability.

⚓ **Basse Plouguerneau:** a fissure along the Aber Wrac'h channel, ranging from 10 to 40 metres (30 to 130 feet) in depth. From about 25 metres (82 feet) down, the rocks are literally smothered in 'sea plums', which look like little orange gourds, and there are two splendid anchors to be seen. Level II ability. There's another excellent dive, with cannon to be seen, on the other side of the channel at **Les Trépieds**. Here an underwater rock-slide gives shelter to a number of species of fish and other creatures at depths ranging from 15 to 50 metres (49 to 164 feet). Level II ability.

◄ **Le Tombant des Oeillets:** in the Aber Benoît channel is this pebble-like rock covered in white sea carnations at a depth of 20 metres (65 feet), alongside a whole colony of lobsters and conger eels living quietly together in the spot-light provided by divers' lamps. Level I ability. As you leave the channel, the **Ruzwenn**, at a depth ranging from 6 to 40 metres (20 to 130 feet), provides a massive array of kelp to swim through and some interesting crevices to explore. Level II ability.

PLOUGUERNEAU
(*PLOUGERNE*) 29232   (Pop: 5,708)

This pleasant village is said to stand on the site of Tolente, a mythical town that had its moment of glory during the ninth century, and then disappeared after being pillaged by the Normans. It is the gateway to the magnificent **Plage de Lilia** and **Plage de St-Michel**, which both have beautiful clean sand dotted with polished rocks. Visit the **Phare de l'Île Vierge** (lighthouse).

– To get there: daily bus service Brest–Plouguerneau–Lilia. Information: Les Cars des Abers, ☎ 02-98-04-70-02.

USEFUL ADDRESS

🏢 **Office du tourisme**: place de l'Europe, BP 23. ☎ 02-98-04-70-93. Fax: 02-98-04-58-75. Email: ot.plouguerneau@wanadoo.fr. Open all year round, Monday–Saturday, 9.15am–12.15pm and 1.30–5pm. In July and August, open until 7pm daily and also open Sunday 10am–1pm.

WHERE TO STAY AND EAT

🏕 **Camping du Vougot**: plage du Vougot. Well signposted. ☎ 02-98-25-61-51. Open from Easter to Oc-tober. A nice, quiet campsite, in an unspoiled area, just 300 metres from the beach, surrounded and protected by a tall hedge of conifers. A friendly welcome, spotless sani-tary blocks, and wide spaces for caravans and mobile homes. It costs about 60F for two people with a vehicle. Children's play area.

Advisable to book from mid-July to mid-August.
🏕 **Camping municipal La Grève Blanche** at St-Michel. ☎ 02-98-04-70-35. Fax: 02-98-04-63-97. ♿ About 3 kilometres (2 miles) from the town centre and 5 minutes from the Grève Blanche beach. Open from the beginning of June to the end of September. The cost for two people with a vehicle is about 45F and there's an extra charge for use of

the showers. Night-time security. Decent facilities, with an on-site grocer, a chip-shop and volleyball court.

✗ **Restaurant Trouz Ar Mor**: place du Corréjou, heading for St-Michel. ☎ 02-98-04-71-61. Open all year round. Closed Monday evening and Wednesday evening out of season. Traditional rustic decor in a bright dining room overlooking the sea. The cuisine is traditional too, with a good range of set menus costing from 89F (weekday lunchtime) to 210F. Generous portions are served and the menus offer plenty of choice of fish and seafood. Terrace outside for nice days.

✗ **Crêperie Lizen**: route de St-Michel in Plouguerneau. ☎ 02-98-04-62-23. Closed in November. Open all day. Allow 80F for a meal à la carte. Stop off for a quick *crêpe* in this pretty little place with a thatched roof and you may end up spending the whole evening. The little renovated cottage, which dates from the early 19th century, is like something out of a fairytale. The menus are presented in school exercise books and written with a quill pen and the cider is kept cool in . . . beach buckets. The place has quite a personality, probably due to the owner, who looks like a latterday d'Artagnan from *The Three Musketeers*. Pleasant terrace. The *crêpes* are OK, too. Credit cards are not accepted.

WHAT TO SEE

★ **Musée des Goémoniers** (seaweed harvesters' museum): route de St-Michel. ☎ 02-98-04-60-30. Open June to August daily, 2.30–6.30pm; open September, Friday–Sunday 2.30–5.30pm. Other times by appointment only. Admission charge (15F). This little museum is the place to find out all about the Aber coast and its main source of wealth – seaweed. The museum has a great deal of archival documentation about the seaweed farmers, and the old boats that were used to collect the seaweed, as well as videos on the gathering and treatment of seaweed, naval signalling, underwater archaeology and the natural marine habitat. There is a permanent exhibition about the modern uses of seaweed. You can even have a trip aboard a former seaweed harvester's boat. One-day cookery courses are held regularly. Groups of ten or more people may request a guided tour of the different sites of the open-air museum.

IN THE AREA

★ **Ruins of Iliz Koz**: take the road towards St-Michel from Plouguerneau and turn left (signposted) after 2 kilometres (1 mile). ☎ 02-98-04-71-84. Open mid-June to mid-September Tuesday–Sunday, 2.30–6pm. Admission charge (15F). These are the substantial ruins of the old parish church of Tremenec'h. The story goes that the parish close disappeared under the sand back at the beginning of the 18th century when three young men out for a lark tried to get a blind priest to baptize a black cat. The cat started to howl and the panicking priest put a curse on the boys and the whole place. The boys died instantly and the church was swallowed by the sands. Rediscovered in 1970, the site now contains the ruins of the church and an interesting medieval burial chamber containing more than a hundred tombs of merchants, sailors, knights and priests. The decoration on each headstone gives a good idea of funerary art in medieval Brittany.

★ **La Grève Blanche:** to the west of Iliz Koz. This is a great place for anyone who likes sand dunes and great stretches of white sand. In the direction of Guisseny, the **Grève du Zorn** is another splendid wild beach.

★ **Phare de l'Île Vierge** (lighthouse): opposite the pretty harbour at Lilia, this granite lighthouse tower was built between 1897 and 1902. It stands 77 metres (253 feet) high and is the tallest lighthouse in Europe. It is also one of the last to be still manned. Inside, the floor is made from irridescent opaline. A total of 397 steps take you to the top but it's worth it for the view. The island can be reached from the harbour at Perros with the company **Vedette des Abers** (☎ 02-98-04-74-94). It's as well to be aware that the lighthouse is only open to the public in July and August 11am–noon and 3–6pm and the number of visitors has to be limited.

GUISSÉNY (*GWISENI*) 29249 (Pop: 1,180)

Between Guissény and Brignogan, you find yourself in the heart of the *pays païen* (pagan country), as the place and its people were called by Irish missionaries in the fifth century. The pagans were formidable and efficient wreckers, capable of emptying a boat run aground of its cargo in one night. For this extremely impoverished population, a shipwreck represented months of survival.

You will still find little unspoiled areas between Guissény and Brignogan. Near Plouguerneau, the **Grève de Zorn** is a very attractive beach. In Guissény, see the **church** and its beautiful 17th-century bell tower, with superposed balconies. Four crosses mark the entrance to the cemetery. There is a superb **altarpiece** in the Chapelle de l'Immaculée-Conception. Above all, be sure to visit Menez-Ham (*see below*).

WHERE TO STAY AND EAT IN THE AREA

🛏 ✗ **Ferme-auberge de Keraloret**, **with M. and Mme Yvinec**: at Keraloret, 4 kilometres (2.5 miles) southeast of Guissény on the D10 in the direction of Plouguerneau then left along a minor road. It's well signposted. ☎ 02-98-25-60-37. Fax: 02-98-25-69-88. Guest room accommodation available throughout the year, restaurant open only from May to October. This farm with accommodation is attractively located in a group of old buildings out in the countryside. There's a friendly welcome and they offer pleasant rooms for 290F for two people, including breakfast. Camping allowed. Good substantial country food. Set menus for 85F and 100F, but reserve ahead. Excellent bottled cider. The main speciality is the *kig ha farz* (traditional Breton bacon flan), on Tuesday and Saturday evenings. Must be ordered the day before or early in the morning. A nice place to eat.

WHAT TO SEE

★ **The village of Menez-Ham**: take the D10 for 6 kilometres (3.5 miles) to the northeast of Guissény and in Kerlouan you reach the village along a narrow road that leads down to the coast. On a slightly elevated site, with a wide panorama of the sea and coastline, Menez-Ham is a fishermen's village whose roofs have long since disappeared under the constant battering by wind and storms. The village is currently being restored, and may be opened to the public. Two thatched houses have miraculously survived intact. Among the ruins, there is a fireplace in every room. In one case, a fireplace more like those found in town dwellings stands out against its rustic surroundings. In each case, the size of the rooms and the simplicity of the architecture prove that this was not a rich village. Notice the ovens set apart from the dwellings. The one farthest away is the most interesting.

In the area immediately around the village, the ground was obviously once cultivated. The fishermen were engaged in three activities: as well as fishing, they worked at farming and harvesting seaweed.

The scenery around here is stunning. On windy days – of which there are many – the light is constantly changing, and the rocks take on evocative shapes (some look amazingly like fish). The jewel in the crown is a tiny stone-built coastguard's house, nestled right in the middle of a mass of rock, sheltered from the wind, and just a few steps from the sea. Even the roof is made of stone. Climb up on the rocks for a magnificent view – but take care. While you're here, it's worth pressing on as far as Ménéham, where the beach is rather wild, with a spectacular pile of rocks and fine sand.

BRIGNOGAN-PLAGE
(*BRIGNOGAN*) 29890 (Pop: 870)

A family seaside resort, which is rapidly becoming more built up. The surrounding area is famous for its piles of rocks; on one of the beaches, they look rather like toads. Don't miss the **Anse du Phare de Pontusval** (Pontusval lighthouse cove), with its long beach of white sand, and the charming **Chapelle Pol**, a little chapel built among the rocks, 2.5 kilometres (1.5 miles) north of Brignogan.

On the road to the chapel is a curious Christianized **menhir**, which is almost 8 metres (26 feet) high and surmounted by a cross.

USEFUL ADDRESS

🄷 **Office du tourisme**: in the village. ☎ 02-98-83-41-08. In July and August, open Monday 11am–7.30pm, Tuesday to Saturday 10am–7.30pm and Sunday 10am–1pm; from September to June, open Tuesday–Saturday 10.30am–12.30pm and 4–6pm.

WHERE TO STAY AND EAT

🛏 ✕ **Hôtel Ar-Reder-Mor**: 35 avenue du Général-de-Gaulle. In the centre of the village. ☎ 02-98-83-40-09. Fax: 02-98-83-56-11. Restaurant open 1 June to 20 September. This place is a little old-fashioned and is nothing special, but nevertheless it's a decent family-run hotel in the main street. Double rooms cost from 190F to 305F. In August, half board is obligatory

(280F per person). They do food as well (menus from 80F to 210F), with predictable specialities such as seafood salad (*salade du pêcheur*) and salmon with sorrel (*saumon à l'oseille*).

IN THE AREA

⛺ **Camping municipal:** at Kérurus, 29890 Plouénour-Trez; in the nearby village, 4 kilometres (2.5 miles) southeast of Brigognan and just a stone's throw from the sea. ☎ 02-98-83-41-87. Open from 15 June to 15 September.

SPORT AND LEISURE

– **Char à voile** (sand-yachting): hire from **Évasion pour tous**, Le Menhir, 29890 Plouénour-Trey. ☎ 02-98-83-59-13. They also offer sea- and river-kayaking, mountain-bikes and archery.

GOULVEN (*GOULC'HEN*) 29890   (Pop: 455)

Nestled at the end of a large bay and with a huge beach that stretches for several kilometres. Superb photographs are guaranteed when the sun shines from behind the clouds.

WHERE TO EAT

✗ **Crêperie de St-Goulven Ar Pitilig**: in the village of Kerargroaz, on the road to Kerlouan in the direction of Brigognan. ☎ 02-98-83-55-76. ✗ Closed Monday to Thursday except during the school holidays; also closed in January and February. Allow 65F to eat à la carte. This is a *crêperie* set up in a flower-decked farmhouse. The *crêpe* menu is tasty and specialities include regional dishes such as *kig ha farz* (Breton bacon flan), potatoes with bacon (*patates au lard*) and chicken in cider (*poulet au cidre*). Photo exhibition. Friendly staff.

WHERE TO STAY IN THE AREA

⛺ **Camping municipal d'Ode Vras**: at Ode-Vraz, 29430 Plounevez-Lochrist. About 6 kilometres (3.5 miles) east of Goulven on the D10. ☎ 02-98-61-65-17. Open from 15 June to 15 September. Not far from the sea, just 300 metres from the baie de Kernic.

⛺ **Camping municipal de Keremma**: Keremma, 29430 Tréflez. About 4 kilometres (2.5 miles) east of Goulven on the D10. ☎ 02-98-61-62-79. Open from the last week-end in June to the end of August. The campsite is right next to the famous Keremma dunes and near the beach.

⛺ ✗ **Chambres d'hôte: Claudine Roué:** at Kerséhen, 29260 Plouider. Just 5 kilometres (3 miles) to the southwest of Goulven on the D125. ☎ 02-98-25-40-41 or 06-81-04-10-87. Three comfortable double guest rooms from 230–250F. Tasteful decor in a modern house. Very welcoming. Table d'hôte on reservation, with one set menu for 90F including wine. Bicycle hire also.

WHAT TO SEE

★ **The church** in Goulven is one of the most beautiful along the coastline. The 16th-century belfry is in the same style as Notre-Dame-du-Kreisker at St-Pol-de-Léon. To the right of the Renaissance porch is a superb doorway in the Flamboyant Gothic style. The remarkable altar is carved in grey granite. In front of it, there is another, smaller altar with carved and polychrome naive scenes. Former 16th-century rood screen used as an organ loft.

★ Heading for Plouescat along the coast and 3 kilometres (2 miles) east of Goulven on the D10, you go past the famous **dunes de Keremma** (sand dunes), which are in the careful hands of the Conservatoire du littoral (national body for the preservation of the coastline). **La Maison des Dunes** (☎ 02-98-61-69-69) offers thematic nature walks in July and August through these superb but fragile, wild expanses of dunes. Horse-riding is also an option. An attractive beach runs the length of the dunes and there is another acceptable beach at St-Guevroc.

LESNEVEN (*LESNEVEN*) 29260 (Pop: 6,931)

An important commercial centre in the Léon region, situated at the hub of a network of roads, and famous for the quality of its cakes and pastries. Who could have imagined that this quiet little town would turn out to be the birthplace of Auguste Le Breton, the highly successful author known to the French for his thrillers and for his use of slang?

USEFUL ADDRESS

🚹 **Office du tourisme:** 14 place du Général-Le-Flô. ☎ 02-98-83-01-47. Fax: 02-98-83-09-93. Open in the summer on Monday 9.30am–6.30pm and Tuesday to Saturday 9.30am–12.30pm and 2–6.30pm; Sunday 10.30am–noon. The rest of the year open Monday to Saturday 9.30am–noon and 2–6pm. Closed Sunday. You can pick up a brochure that's full of information about the town.

– **Market:** every Monday 9am–7pm.

WHERE TO EAT

✕ **Couleur Pays**: 11 place du Château. ☎ 02-98-83-30-90. Closed Wednesday and Thursday plus two weeks in August, one week in March and one week in June. The dish of the day costs 49F, or 65F with dessert and 85F with wine and coffee. A *crêpe* menu is served for 70F lunchtime only, and there's a set menu for 110F. You can't miss this restaurant-*crêperie* on one of the squares in the centre of town – the front is painted in bright colours and in summer there are geraniums at every window. The atmosphere is convivial in the two spacious and attractive dining rooms, which are separated by a massive fireplace, and local people gather here to eat at the wooden tables, each decorated with a painted local landscape. As well as the *crêpes* there's an excellent selection of fish and seafood dishes, all simply done and attractively served.

WHERE TO EAT IN THE AREA

✕ **Restaurant Breton**: 29260 St-Frégant, a village 5 kilometres (3 miles) northwest of Lesneven on the D25. Situated in the centre of the village opposite the church. ☎ 02-98-83-05-33. Meals available lunchtime only. Closed Sunday and the first three weeks in August. A small, plain-looking restaurant with a deceptively spacious dining room; good food, generous portions, and not expensive: the only set menu is 60F. On Thursday (reservations only) the food is either typically Breton *(kig ha farz*, or Breton bacon flan*)*, or exotic (couscous). Arrive just before noon if you want to be sure of a table. Friendly staff, a lively atmosphere, and not many tourists.

WHAT TO SEE

★ Although the town of Lesneven itself does not possess any great charm, there are nevertheless some fine old houses, and a very interesting museum, the **Musée du Léon**: 12 rue de la Marne, located in the Maison d'Accueil, a former Ursuline convent. ☎ 02-98-21-17-18. Open 2–6pm. Closed on Tuesday; also closed on Friday between October and the end of April. Admission charge (15F for adults; free to under-12s). The museum covers a wide range of things, from prehistory to the Gallo-Roman period, plus religious art. There are some beautiful pieces of furniture and examples of traditional crafts and costumes.

LE FOLGOËT (*AR FOLGOAD*) 29260 (Pop: 3,188)

Situated 2 kilometres (1 mile) from Lesneven on the D788, Le Folgoët is the site of the second-largest **pilgrimage** in Brittany, which attracts thousands of people on the Sunday nearest to 8 September. It is strange to think that such a little village in the heart of the countryside should possess such an impressive basilica, almost a cathedral. It is certainly one of the most beautiful churches in Brittany.

History and Legend

Around 1315, a poor lad named Salaün lived in the trunk of an old tree. He would constantly repeat the words '*ave Maria, ave Maria*', and spent his time begging for bread and going to Mass. The people gave him the nickname *Fol Goat*, the 'fool of the wood'. When he finally died, they buried him like a dog, without prayers or priest, rather than taking him to the cemetery. God caused a white lily to grow on the grave. Its petals formed the words '*ave Maria*' in letters of gold. The miracle lasted for several weeks, attracting people from all over Brittany, and it was decided to build a chapel on the spot.

Jean IV, Duke of Brittany, having vowed to construct a basilica to the Virgin, decided to build it at Le Folgoët, on the site of the miracle. He laid the first stone, went off and forgot all about it. Six years later, Jean V remembered his father's vow and had the work completed. It was in Le Folgoët that Kersanton granite was first used; this type of stone was later to become famous in Breton architecture. The basilica was completed around 1460.

The basilica has had a chequered past. The rather small-minded Louis XIV, who disliked the Breton people, reduced the basilica to the status of chapel. Fires and the excesses of the French Revolution (during which the Apostles in the porch were guillotined!), followed by social change (the church was transformed into a pigsty, then a barracks), meant that the building was in real danger of falling into ruin. The writer Prosper Mérimée, then Inspector General of Historic Monuments, saved Le Folgoët in 1835 by submitting a report that favoured its restoration.

WHAT TO SEE

★ **The basilica**: flanked by two towers, one of which reaches a height of 56 metres (182 feet), this is considered to be one of Brittany's finest. Its beautiful south portal is in the Flamboyant style. Just opposite is the calvary. Inside the basilica is the rood screen, a masterpiece of medieval sculpture. Carved in Kersanton granite and finely proportioned, with three elegant columns supporting three arches surmounted by pointed ogives. There is a remarkable rose window in the choir, and numerous 15th-century granite altars.

★ **The deanery**: opposite the basilica. A 16th-century turreted mansion, now used as the presbytery.

★ **Maison du Patrimoine** (heritage centre) and **Musée Notre-Dame**: open daily 10am–12.30pm and 2.30–6.30pm. Closed Sunday morning. Admission charge. Located in the Hôtel des Pèlerins ('pilgrims' inn'), housing statues from various eras and medieval furniture including a box bed (*lit-clos*). The centre was built only 50 years ago but in a neo-Gothic style, ensuring that the group of monuments in Le Folgoët retains a fine sense of unity.

FESTIVAL

– **Grand Pardon de Notre-Dame-du-Folgoët**: one of the best and most Breton of all the *pardons*, taking place on the Sunday nearest to 8 September.

Haut Léon

Léon is one of Finistère's most historic regions, second only to Cornouaille. Its name came from the place where the first settlers originated from – the city of Caerleon in South Wales. Due to the warm waters of the Gulf Stream, the climate of this region has become milder and the northernmost part of Léon, known as Haut (or 'upper') Léon, has become the market garden for Finistère, if not for the whole of France. It is the country's leading supplier of artichokes, cauliflowers and potatoes, visible in that the countryside is dotted with greenhouses and the roads are often rutted by heavy tractors. This huge region is also blessed with marvellous beaches and the garden-island of Batz.

USEFUL ADDRESS

🅑 Pays du haut-Léon (tourist office): place de l'Évêché, 29250 St-Pol-de-Léon. ☎ 02-98-29-09-09. Fax: 02-98-29-00-98. This tourist office has everything you need to know about the region.

PLOUESCAT (*PLOUESKAD*) 29430 (Pop: 3,775)

This large farming community is known for growing tulips and cauliflowers. The modern market is held under a 16th-century covered market with fine wooden beams, and is now the area's main attraction since the business of the *Zizi de pépé* ('grandpa's willie'). This large phallic rock (whose shape was indeed unmistakable) had succeeded for centuries in provoking nothing but crude jokes. In 1987, the town council of Plouescat, in line with a certain wave of moralism at the time, quite simply blew it up. In revenge, local artists, armed with red paint, daubed the smoothest and most well-rounded rocks with a number of *Fesses de mémé* ('grandma's buttocks')!

There are superb **beaches** around here, particularly the **Plages de Pors-Meur** and **de Pors-Guen** with their endless expanse of fine white sand, and attractive piles of granite rocks. This is paradise for windsurfers and sand yachters.

WHERE TO STAY

♙ Hôtel Roc'h ar Mor: 18 rue Armor, Plage de Pors-Meur. ☎ 02-98-69-63-01. Fax: 02-98-61-91-26. About 3 kilometres (1.5 miles) from the town. Open from Easter to the end of September. This is a modest but good little hotel with eight simple but well-kept double rooms costing from 140F to 160F. Pleasant and friendly, with a decent bar.

BERVEN 29225

This tiny village in the middle of nowhere has an interesting **parish close**, entered through a Renaissance triumphal gateway with three semicircular arches (the old entrance to the cemetery), which gives the impression of being unfinished. The quite austere-looking 16th-century **Chapelle Notre-Dame** has a bell tower with openwork lantern turrets and balustrades, and some interesting gargoyles. In front of the facade is the entrance to the close with elegant scroll-like ornamentation. Inside there are beautiful carved purlins and beams, and a remarkable choir enclosure in stone and wood.

WHERE TO STAY AND EAT IN THE AREA

⌂ **Hôtel Le Goff**: 6 rue St-Hervé, 29430 Lanhouarneau. ☎ 02-98-61-48-06. Ten kilometres (6 miles) southwest of Berven on the D788. Double rooms from 165F to 190F. This little hotel from another era is in the main street. It's a grocer and general store with first-floor rooms that are hardly the height of luxury but have an old-fashioned charm nevertheless. Everywhere is spotlessly clean and the prices are as good as the welcome. Parking is free.

⌂ ✗ **Hôtel des Voyageurs**: 1 rue St-Pol-de-Léon, 29440 Plouzévédé. ☎ 02-98-69-98-17. Fax: 02-98-29-55-91. ✗ Two kilometres (1 mile) to the south of Berven on the D33 and right in the centre of the village. Restaurant open every day. Expect to pay 280F for a double room. Set menus from 56F (weekday lunchtime) to 180F. The bar has been open since 1851 and is in a very beautiful stone building that has recently been refurbished by the new owners. The decor nowadays has a classy rustic feel, rather like an English club. A total re-vamp of the rooms has given them added comfort and in the restaurant they serve cuisine that is beginning to acquire a good local reputation.

✗ **Crêperie du Château**: Kerfao, 29440 St-Vougay. Situated 200 metres from the Château de Kerjean. ☎ and fax: 02-98-69-93-09. ✗ Open from Easter to the end of September, daily except Tuesday, and weekends in winter. Set menus for 75F; allow 80F to eat à la carte. In a nicely renovated farm in the middle of a prize-winning flower-filled park, this friendly *crêperie* serves delicious pancakes made with farm produce and also offers *kig ha farz* (Breton bacon flan).

✗ **Moulin de Kerguiduff**: allée du Meunier, 29440 Tréflaouénan. ☎ 02-98-29-51-20. ✗ Clearly signposted in Tréflaouénan. Closed on Monday in season, and every evening except weekends out of season. This restaurant is in a pretty little spot out in the countryside and right next to a stream. The miller has made way for a restaurateur who offers sound menus for 68F to 110F. Traditional cuisine. One of the chef's specialities is a scallop casserole (*cassolette de St-Jacques*).

IN THE AREA

★ **Château de Kerjean**: at St-Vougay, 5 kilometres (3 miles) southwest of Berven). ☎ 02-98-69-93-69. Fax: 02-98-29-50-17. Open daily in July and August 10am–7pm. In June and September open 10am–6pm and closed on Tuesday. Out of season, telephone for information. Admission charge (25F). This is the most beautiful castle in the Léon region, now the property of the state and managed by the *département*. Built during the second half of the 16th century, this castle is a happy blend of fortress and splendid Romanesque architecture. Composed of an outer perimeter, a square courtyard and three wings, its interior has huge fireplaces and beautiful Breton furniture (box beds, dowry chests, trunks, wardrobes). Around it, the grounds are splendid, with columns, a fountain and a 16th-century dovecote. As well as castle tours, there are temporary exhibitions and shows.

★ **Ferme-musée du Léon** (farm museum of the Léon region): at Lanquéran, between Plouzévédé and Tréflaouénan, to the north of Berven.

☎ 02-98-29-53-07. Open daily from 1 May to 30 September, weekends out of season, 10am–noon and 2–7pm. You might think the museum is rather tucked away but it's well signposted on the many roads in the area. It's an authentic thatched farm building turned into a museum showing rural life in the Léon region in the early 20th century. Numerous activities in summer connected with the various types of farm work. Friendly staff.

★ **Chapelle de Lambader**: south of St-Pol, on the D69 in the direction of Landerneau, one of the prettiest chapels you will see, surrounded by old houses in the most pastoral setting imaginable. Open 9am–7pm all year round. Its spire and four pinnacle turrets soar heavenwards to a height of 58 metres (188 feet), and it has a belfry porch with trefoil balustrade and sculpted cornice. Each year during a July weekend there are spectacles retracing Brittany's past, from its origins to the present day. The history of a North Finistère village is re-created, and shows the harshness of peasant life. More than 500 volunteers take part in this spectacle, which sets itself a high standard. Information from the organizers (Association AVEL Lambader): ☎ 02-98-61-01-04.

CLÉDER (*KLEDER*) 29233 (Pop: 3,723)

Rather characterless Léon village, whose surroundings are authentically rural, and reveal some architectural treasures. Along the coastal road, there is a seaweed oven nestled in the dunes, as well as beautiful inlets, a coastguard's house and amazing ruins buried deep in the greenery.

USEFUL ADDRESS

🄳 **Office du tourisme**: 2 rue Plouescat, BP 5. ☎ 02-98-69-43-01. Open all year round.

WHERE TO STAY AND EAT

⌂ **Camping municipal de Poulennou**: at Poulennou, by the sea. ☎ 02-98-69-48-37 or 02-98-69-40-09 (town hall). Fax: 02-98-69-47-99. ♿ Open from 15 June to 15 September.

⌂ **Chambres d'hôte Kerliviry, with M. and Mme Ponthieux**. In the village. ☎ 02-98-61-99-37. A double room costs from 320F to 350F including breakfast. They offer two double rooms with bathroom and a family room, on a mezzanine floor, with its own washing facilities. The breakfast is generous, and offers lots of local produce, cereals and cheeses, as well as homemade

jams. Everything is peaceful at this restored manor house in the middle of the countryside, and children and adults alike will have fun with the farm animals that share the space with family and visitors.

⌂ **Chambres à la ferme de Kernevez: with Marceline and François Grall**, in Kernevez, 2.5 kilometres (1.5 miles) from Cléder. ☎ 02-98-69-41-14. Near the Manoir de Tronjoly, in a charming Léon farmhouse. Two guest rooms with shared bathroom and two rooms with their own bathrooms. From 200F to 250F for two people, including a delicious Breton breakfast. You will be made extremely welcome.

✕ **Entre Terre et Mer**: 9 rue de l'Armorique. ☎ 02-98-19-53-22. Closed Monday and Tuesday evenings from June to September and Monday and Tuesday all day out of season. There's just one set menu, at 110F. The charming service and an excellent cuisine that offers really good value for money far outweigh the rather uninteresting decor here. Specialities include spicy pig's cheek (*joues de cochons aux épices*), gurnard (*rouget grondin*) and, for dessert, shortbread biscuit with strawberries (*sablé breton aux fraises*). The chef is a young man who has a good way with all the first-class local produce that this part of Léon provides (hence the name 'Entre Terre et Mer' or 'between the land and the sea'). In fact, the combination of these factors makes this little place deserve a strong recommendation, and it can hold its own against much bigger fish.

WHERE TO STAY AND EAT IN THE AREA

🛖 **Camping municipal Bois de la Palud**: at Palue, 29250 Plougoulm. ☎ 02-98-29-81-82. Fax: 02-98-29-92-26. Situated 4 kilometres (2.5 miles) to the northeast of Cléder. Open from 15 June to 15 September. Very nice view of the sea.

🛖 ✕ **Hôtel-restaurant La Marine**: port de Moguériec, 29250 Sibiril. Take the D10 out of Cléder to the northeast, a distance of about 7 kilometres (4 miles). At Sibiril, between Plouescat and St-Pol-de-Léon, turn left onto the D69. ☎ 02-98-29-99-52. Fax: 02-98-29-89-18. ✕ restaurant. Closed on Monday out of season. Friendly little hotel, looking directly out over the harbour. Decent rooms with or without bathroom, from 165F to 275F, although the decor is a bit of a 1970s time-warp. Good healthy food and generous menus from 98F to 220F. Specialities include seafood (the owner is a former fishmonger), and grilled lobster (*homard grillé*). The bar specializes in whisky, with around two hundred brands.

WHAT TO SEE AROUND CLÉDER

★ **Manoir de Tronjoly** (manor house): as you leave Cléder on the D10, going towards Plouescat and the Parc des Amiets. Only the grounds and the chapel are open to the public. Charming 16th-century manor house, hidden away in a hollow. In the middle of the courtyard is a beautiful monolithic basin.

★ **Château de Kerouzéré**: in Sibiril, 3 kilometres (2 miles) west of Cléder on the D10. The outside can be visited free of charge. To visit the interior, afternoons only, telephone: ☎ 02-98-29-96-05. Admission charge (20F; half-price for children aged 11 and over; free for under-10s). Guided tours. This is an impressive 15th-century fortified castle with a strongly medieval feel, especially on the north side, evidenced by its crenellated walls and rampart walk. In summer visitors can see the guard room, which has a massive fireplace, and the main hall, with its impressive roof structure.

SANTEC (*SANTEG*) 29250 (Pop: 2,204)

This little village is typical of the Léon region, where carrots are the main crop. A number of good beaches are close by, including one of the best along this stretch of coast, the **plage du Dossen**, which is very long and a popular haunt for sand-yachting devotees. It is flanked by forest and faces the little Île de Sieck, which can be reached on foot at low tide.

WHERE TO STAY AND EAT

â**Chambres d'hôte: Claudette and Jean-François Grall**: 207 route du Dossen. ☎ 02-98-29-78-49. A double room costs 250F including breakfast. This B&B is in a residential district just five minutes from the beach and offers two pleasant rooms in a quite modern house. The garden has a barbecue and a nice little arbour where you can sit and eat. Evening meals are also available on request. There's also a fully equipped studio flat on the ground floor. Excellent welcome.

✕ **Le Bistrot à Crêpes:** at Méchouroux, between the village and the plage du Dossen. ☎ 02-98-29-73-92. Closed on Wednesday and for the month of November. You get a really good welcome at this little eatery. They serve mind-numbingly powerful cocktails as well as an excellent range of *crêpes*. Friday is the day for the Breton bacon flan *kig ha farz* (you need to book ahead for this). The decor isn't wonderful here, but it doesn't matter as the food is good.

ROSCOFF (*ROSKO*) 29680 (Pop: 3,688)

Roscoff is the archetypal Breton port with a flourishing economy. It has also managed to retain all its charm and architectural unity. The new port was built a little further along the coast so as not to upstage the old harbour. The lovely seafront is overlooked by the unusual baroque tower of Notre-Dame-de-Kroaz-Batz. At the end of the 19th century, Roscoff's mild and invigorating climate made it the number one centre for rest and relaxation and for recuperation from illnesses such as tuberculosis. As a departure point for travelling to Great Britain and Ireland, from the port of Bloscon, Roscoff is today a dynamic platform for foreign trade and a busy tourist destination.

History

A former pirates' stronghold, Roscoff was always at odds with the English, the true traditional enemy, and many naval battles were fought off its shore. In 1548, six-year-old Mary Stuart landed here, having been despatched to become engaged to the *dauphin*. In 1746, after the Battle of Culloden, which saw the Scots defeated at the hands of the expansionist English, it was in Roscoff that Bonnie Prince Charlie, heir to the Scottish throne, sought refuge.

Up until the French Revolution, Roscoff was one of the most prosperous ports in France. In 1828, Henri Ollivier had the bright idea of crossing the

Channel to sell his surplus of pink onions from the Léon region to English housewives. It proved to be such a successful venture that in 1930 almost 1,500 hawkers, called 'Johnnies' by their English customers, were plying their trade across the water with their bicycles and strings of pink onions. Since then, the market in fruit and vegetables has seen considerable progress. Another business success story of more recent years is that of former farmers' union activist Alexis Gourvennec, who created Brittany Ferries.

USEFUL ADDRESSES

🛈 Maison du tourisme: 46 rue Gambetta, by the old harbour. ☎ 02-98-61-12-13. In July and August, open Monday to Saturday 9am–12.30pm and 1.30–7pm, and Sunday and public holidays 10am–12.30pm; the rest of the year, open Monday to Saturday 9am–noon, and 2–6pm. Offers boat trips up to the Baie de Morlaix and tours to the Île de Batz. From June to September there are one-day train-and-boat excursions with a guide, leaving from Morlaix or Roscoff: **Léon à Fer et à Flot** ☎ 02-98-62-07-52. The cost is 100F; half-price for children.

■ **Bicycle rental**: Desbordes, 13 rue Brizeux. ☎ 02-98-69-72-44.

WHERE TO STAY

Campsites

⛺ Camping municipal: on the Pointe de Perharidy, heading towards Santec. ☎ 02-98-69-70-86. Fax: 02-98-61-15-74. ♿ Open from Easter to the end of September. This campsite is reasonably well equipped and has a good location, right next to the beach. The cost in season is about 45F for two people with a vehicle. Also bungalows for rent.

☆ Budget

⛺ Auberge de jeunesse (youth hostel): on the Île de Batz. ☎ 02-98-61-77-69. Fax: 02-98-61-78-85. Departures from Roscoff. For a description, see Île-de-Batz, Where To Stay'.

☆☆ Moderate

⛺ Hôtel Les Tamaris: 49 rue Édouard-Corbière. ☎ 02-98-61-22-99. Fax: 02-98-69-74-36. ♿ Closed from 15 November to 15 March. Well situated and separated from the sea by the rocky promontory, this hotel looks out at the Île-de-Batz. Bright, comfortable rooms and the constant spectacle of the tides for those with a sea view. Double rooms with shower or bath and toilet from 260F to 350F. Breakfast for 35F. No restaurant, but one of the friendliest welcomes in the whole of the Léon region.

⛺ Hôtel des Chardons Bleus: 4 rue de l'Amiral-Réveillère. ☎ 02-98-69-72-03. Fax: 02-98-61-27-86. Closed Thursday (except in July and August) and Sunday evening in winter. Situated near the church and in one of the liveliest streets in the town, the hotel is also only 500 metres from the beaches. Very well-run, offering excellent value for money, with modern rooms costing from 280–300F. The bed linen is decent and they have double-glazing to the front. Set menus for 65F (weekday lunchtime), and evening menus up to 215F. The cuisine is traditional and everything is very flavoursome. A warm welcome.

☆☆☆ Chic

⚓ **Hôtel Talabardon**: place de l'Église. ☎ 02-98-61-24-95. Fax: 02-98-61-10-54. Closed from March to October. Restaurant closed on Sunday evening, except for full board or half board guests. This hotel is full of character, and right at the water's edge. In 1966, the ground floor was partially destroyed by a storm. Bright, clean rooms from 380F up to 590F in high season; surcharge of 80F for a sea view. Parking costs an extra 50F. All the rooms have been re-cently renovated and three of them have balconies. The decor is yellow and blue, or yellow and green (the three colours of Brittany). Generous breakfast buffet for 58F served in a pleasant dining room. The cooking draws on the abundant produce of the sea, which is right on the door-step. The menu varies according to the season and delivery. Set menus for 100F (weekdays) up to 280F; children's menu for 60F. Attractive wine list. An excellent place to go for its charm, the freshness of its fish and the quality of the welcome.

WHERE TO EAT

☆ Budget

✗ **Crêperie Ti Saozon**: 30 rue Gambetta. ☎ 02-98-69-70-89. Open evening only, from 6.30pm. Closed Sunday and Monday, and from mid-November to mid-December and mid-January to mid-March except during school holidays. Allow 70F to eat à la carte. A tiny little *crêperie*, full of character, near the old harbour. Cosy and welcoming. The batter is beaten by hand. Specialities include the *complète forest-ière* (with ham, cheese and a fried egg), *coquille St-Jacques sauce beurre blanc* (with scallops and white butter sauce), *andouille et oignon* (with chitterlings sausage and onion), and *fond d'artichaut crème d'algues* (with artichoke hearts in seaweed cream sauce). Be sure to reserve in advance. By the way, it's a no-smoking establishment.

✗ **Restaurant l'Amiral**: 18 rue Amiral-Reveillère. ☎ 02-98-61-19-04. Ⴟ Closed on Monday evening and Tuesday (except in July and August); also closed in October and January. Set menus from 60F to 98F. A pleasant and very welcoming restaurant offering a good welcome, with two dining rooms painted in warm colours. The food is very good value for money for Roscoff. Nice juicy meats cooked to perfection.

☆☆ Moderate

✗ **Les Korrigans**: 31 rue de l'Amiral-Courbet. ☎ 02-98-61-22-15. Fax: 02-98-69-78-96. Closed from the end of November to the beginning of February. From the outside, this restaurant-*crêperie* looks very different from the other shop fronts in the town, as it's all contemporary with large windows. Still, there is a warm welcome inside from a professional young couple who have established a reputation over a number of years. Some of the *crêpes* are quite expensive (there is a definite tendency in the town to hike the prices). The *complète* (with ham, cheese and a fried egg) is reasonable, but you will have to shell out for the *Océane* (with mus-sels, scallops, cockles and prawns in white butter sauce). The fresh fish and seafood are good value for money. Set menus for 75F, 97F and 130F. Allow 100F to eat à la carte. Overall, the restaurant is probably better value than the *crêperie*. There is an excellent dessert *crêpe* flambéed in Grand Marnier.

☆☆☆ Chic

✕ **L'Écume des Jours**: quai d' Auxerre. ☎02-98-61-22-83. Closed on Wednesday lunchtime in season and on Tuesday evening and Wednesday out of season, as well as in December and January. In a fine granite house (almost certainly the former residence of a ship-owner), this address is becoming increasingly well known in the Léon region. The restaurant is comfortable, welcoming and quiet, with a large fireplace. The chef combines local produce from both sea and land in a uniquely inspired way. Set menu at lunchtime during the week for 95F and other menus from 130F to 230F. À la carte offers lots of wonderful little dishes, such as braised scallops (*poêlée de pétoncles*) or fillet of duck breast with stuffed potatoes (*magret de canard et pommes de terres farcies*).

WHAT TO SEE

★ **Église Notre-Dame-de-Croatz-Batz**: open daily 9am–noon and 2–7pm. Volunteers give guided tours from April to September; details from the tourist information office. Built in the 16th century in the Gothic Flamboyant style, with remarkable outer dimensions. The amazing Renaissance turret belfry looks like a cactus. In the church close, two ossuaries date from the same time. The outer walls are adorned with reliefs of tritons, sea creatures and ships. Inside, as in many 'maritime' churches, the ceiling is in the shape of an upturned boat, and there are carved beams and purlins. The magnificent baroque altarpiece is made of wood with a tabernacle supported by caryatids, beautiful canopied cathedra, 17th-century carved organ gallery, and a 17th-century baptistery. In the chapel on the right, note the Ascension of Christ and the Passion in alabaster (of English origin, 15th-century).

In the square, opposite the chevet at No. 23, is a superb house with unusual windows.

★ **Musée-aquarium**: place Georges-Teissier (a stone's throw from the church). ☎ 02-98-29-23-25. Open daily from Easter to October, 10am–noon and 1–6pm (1–7pm from 14 July–20 August). Admission charge (26F; students 22F; children aged 6–12 13F). In about 40 different aquariums you can trace the development of, among others, torpedo rays, seahorses, gorgonia, through to spirographis, octopuses, squid, giant conger eels and echinoderms (sea urchins, brittle-stars, starfish and holothurians). Interesting themed exhibitions too.

★ **Tour of the old houses**: around the church, in the avenue Albert-de-Mun, the rue Armand-Rousseau (the oldest street) and the rue de l'Amiral-Réveillère stood the superb townhouses of rich ship-owners. Many remain, with decorated facades, sculpted skylights and spiral staircases. Opposite the Chapelle St-Ninien, in the rue de l'Amiral-Réveillère, two houses vie for the distinction of being Mary Stuart's house. However, despite the claims that she stayed there, in truth both were built shortly after her visit. Nearby is a beautiful watchtower, a remnant of the ancient ramparts.

Right at the far end of the harbour, towards the fish tanks, is the small **Chapelle Sainte-Barbe**.

★ **The Roscoff fig tree**: the first town guidebook (1908) read as follows: 'In a beautiful private property (a former Capuchin convent), you can admire a giant fig tree, planted, it is said, in 1621. The branches spread horizontally on both sides of a small wall which supports the trunk. The tree covers a surface area of 600 metres (1,950 feet), and is supported by a large number of pillars. What is really interesting from a botanical point of view is that the whole tree has grown from a single trunk whose offshoots spread horizontally for a certain distance almost at ground level before curving back down to the soil and taking root. Thus new trunks were formed from the original, to which they remained connected by what amounts to huge vertical roots.'

Don't bother to go in search of this botanical wonder. It was cut down in 1987 to make way for a building. If you mention the tree to the locals, they will stare at their feet. Some were concerned about the developer's plans, and quickly sought a preservation order, but it arrived two days after the 'crime'.

★ **La maison des Johnnies**: a little museum set up in the Chapelle Sainte-Anne, next door to the tourist office. Same telephone number as the tourist office (☎ 02-98-61-12-13). Open from mid-June to mid-September 10am–noon and 3–6pm (closed Tuesday). Admission charge (10F). As you might guess, this museum is dedicated to the 19th-century Breton onion-sellers, known as 'Johnnies', who used to travel across to England and Wales to sell their onions door-to-door. Display panels give information about this astonishing phenomenon and describe the way of life of the travelling salesmen and how they crossed the sea. There's a fascinating collection of old photographs donated by the descendents of the onion men, as well as some video footage including one made by the BBC in 1954.

★ **Le Jardin exotique** (botanic garden): a 20-minute walk from the town centre. From the harbour, head for the car-ferry port and casino. ☎ 02-98-61-29-19; out of season: ☎ 02-50-75-84-69. Fax: 02-98-61-12-34. In summer, open 10am–7pm; out of season, 10am–noon and 2–6pm. In November, December and February open 2–5.30pm only. Closed Tuesday from November to March; also closed in January. Admission charge (25F for adults; 20F for students and children over 12; 15F for children under 12). More than 2,000 varieties of plants from the four corners of the earth bloom here by the sea, notably one of the largest collections of Southern Hemisphere plants, a palm grove, giant ferns and a waterfall. An interesting change of scenery.

★ **Le comptoir des Algues**: rue Victor-Hugo. ☎ 02-98-69-77-05. Website: www.thalado.fr. Open all year round, Monday–Saturday 9am–noon and 2–7pm. Admission free. It's worth telephoning to get details of what's going on, as programmes vary according to the tides and you can make an advance booking. Situated near the spa and only 300 metres from the church, this new museum tells the story of the seaweed that is so abundant (800 different kinds) off the north coast of Brittany. There are display panels about the kind of occupations that historically were linked to seaweed, slide shows about local marine seaweed and its current uses, and talks twice a week.

FESTIVALS

– **Pardon de Sainte-Barbe**: religious festival held on the third Sunday in July.

– **Gouel Rosko:** history and folklore festival, held at the end of June.

LEAVING ROSCOFF

There are plenty of buses and local trains to St-Pol-de-Léon and Morlaix.

By Boat

For the inhabitants of Brittany, Roscoff is the most convenient port for travelling to England and Ireland.

– **For Plymouth:** boats leave two or three times daily in high season for the six-hour crossing.

– **For Cork:** in high season there are two boats per week and the crossing takes 15 hours. A number of discounts are available.

• **Brittany Ferries**: reservations and brochures: ☎ 0803-828-828. Fax: 02-98-29-28-91. Website: www.brittany-ferries.com

• **Irish Ferries**: harbour station. ☎ 02-98-61-17-17. One or two crossings per week to Rosslare, in June, one on alternate weeks in July and one per week in August.

ÎLE DE BATZ (*ENEZ-VAZ*) 29253   (Pop: 596)

Lovely little island just 3.5 kilometres (2.5 miles) long and 1.5 kilometres (1 mile) wide, offshore from Roscoff; it's a 15-minute journey away by boat. There are few cars but 60 tractors have taken over from horses on the 35 or so tiny farms. A wonderful microclimate supports an almost Mediterranean-style vegetation. The 700 inhabitants earn their living from tourism, fishing and the growing of early fruit and vegetables, as well as from harvesting seaweed. This microclimate allowed Georges Delaselle to create a *jardin colonial* (botanic garden) in 1899 on the island's eastern point – in other words, sheltered from the wind. The park, abandoned in 1937 and allowed to revert to fallow land, has now been restored and is open to the public. With the exotic sights and smells, you could really believe yourself to be in the West Indies!

It is possible to tour the island in three hours. Heading west, you will arrive at the **Fort de Beg Seac'h**, then the **Toul ar Zarpant** (the 'hole' or 'monster's lair), a mass of rocks where St Pol Aurélien is said to have drowned a dragon that was terrorizing the island. Since then, it is said, the sea has made a strange inexplicable rumbling noise.

The lighthouse, built in 1836, is unfortunately no longer open to the public. On the nearby rocks of Roc'h ar Mor, grow succulent plants such as *Ficus* and *Dracaena*.

In the west of the island, on the superb **grève Blanche** – 800 metres of fine sand – you may disturb curlews or terns. In the south, there are numerous fine sandy beaches.

GETTING THERE

– **Compagnie de Transport maritime Armein**: ☎ 02-98-61-77-75 and 02-98-61-75-47. From the end of June until mid-September, boats leave every 30 minutes in both directions, from the old harbour at high tide and from the landing stage at low tide. Departures from Roscoff, 8am–8pm. Departures from Batz, 7am–7.30pm. In winter, boats leave approximately every two hours. They also run guided trips with commentary around the Baie de Morlaix and a tour round the Île de Batz: in summer every day except Sunday at 2.15pm; out of season, group tours are available by arrangement. The return trip from Roscoff to the Île de Batz costs 34F.

– **Les Vedettes CFTM**: ☎ 02-98-61-79-66. This company offers the same service as above.

USEFUL ADDRESSES

🄸 **Office du tourisme**: at the pier. ☎ 02-98-61-75-70. In July and August, open Monday–Saturday, 10.30am–12.30pm and 2.30–5pm; the remainder of the year, phone or write for information.

■ **Bicycle rental**: from **Jean-Yves Le Saoût** at Le Rhû. ☎ 02-98-61-77-65. Fax: 02-98-61-78-78. Open from April to October. Bicycles can be rented for a half-day or full day. Or from **M. Prigent**. ☎ 02-98-61-76-91 or 02-98-61-75-25.

WHERE TO STAY AND EAT

🄰 **Auberge de jeunesse Île-de-Batz** (youth hostel): at Creach ar Bolloc'h. ☎ 02-98-61-77-69 and 02-98-41-90-41. Fax: 02-98-61-78-85. Open April to September (for members). Sailing school in July and August. Five little houses, in a superb situation overlooking the sea and the rocks, with sleeping quarters that closely resemble cabins. Costs 49F per night (sharing a room), breakfast for 20F, meals for 49F. In summer, 32 spaces are available in large tents. Kitchen for use by individual guests. The hostel also organizes sailing courses, sea-kayaking and trips to the island.

🄰 ✕ **Hôtel-restaurant Roch Ar Mor**: by the landing stage for the Île de Batz. ☎ 02-98-61-78-28. Open daily from mid-March to October. Small, plain well-maintained hotel. Rooms (some with sea view) for 225F, although breakfast is quite expensive. The modern dining room serves a cuisine based on fish and seafood, with set menus from 50F to 150F.

🄰 **Chambres d'hôte: Marie-Pierre Prigent**: Ti Va Zadou, in the village. ☎ 02-98-61-76-91. Open from 1 March to 20 November. Just 200 metres from the landing stage for boats coming from Roscoff. Go up the little street towards the church, then turn right just before reaching it. The windows of the large old granite house look out over sloping fields and, not very far away, lies the main port of the island. Very welcoming and tastefully decorated. Pretty wooden box bed in the room on the right-hand side of the ground floor. Guest rooms on the first floor with a superb view. Peaceful nights guaranteed. Costs 300F (including breakfast) for two, and between 300 and 420F for a family room with three or four people. Excellent place to stay. Essential to reserve in advance in summer.

🛏 ✕ **Grand Hôtel Morvan**: by the harbour. ☎ and fax: 02-98-61-78-06. Closed from 1 December to 15 February. Plain, bright rooms from 210F (with washbasin) to 230F (with shower and toilet). Half board for 255F per day, per person. The restaurant has a rather pleasant 1950s decor, with menus from 85F (weekdays) to 150F and specializing in fish and seafood. This is a family-run hotel with an old-fashioned charm.

✕ **La Crêpe d'Or**: very close to the harbour and the beach, in a little street which goes up to the right after the Grand Hôtel. ☎ 02-98-61-77-49. Open in July and August only. Allow 70–80F to eat à la carte. The name is a reminder of the druid in the Astérix books, and his golden sickle (*serpe d'or*). A good place to eat at lunchtime as well as evenings. The *crêpes* are worth an extra bicycle ride. Inside, a very simple dining room extended by a veranda looks out over a lovely exotic garden nestling behind the house. The profusion of near-tropical plants and flowers, not usually found on the north coast of Finistère, owe their success to the island's microclimate. The *crêpes* are above average; the buckwheat *crêpe* with mushrooms in butter sprinkled with chopped parsley (*blé noir avec des champignons au beurre persillé*) is rarely served in *crêperies*.

WHAT TO SEE

★ **Jardin Exotique Georges-Delaselle** (botanic garden): in the eastern part of the island. ☎ 02-98-61-75-65. In October, open weekends only 2–6pm; in April, May, June and September, open daily except Tuesday 2–6pm; in July and August, open daily 1pm–6pm. Closed from November until the first weekend in April. Admission charge (23F). Guided tours from April to October, every Sunday at 3pm. Beautiful exotic garden in the heart of Brittany, created by Georges Delaselle. He fell in love with the spot and began digging the earth in order to protect his trees from the wind. Financially ruined by this labour of love, he had to sell the garden during the 1930s. Recently, thanks to an active association, the sand has been cleared from the palm trees and the magnificent garden restored.

★ **The lighthouse**: open from July to mid-September 1–5.30pm; in June and the last two weeks of September open daily 2–5pm except Wednesday. There's a tour of the lighthouse (*phare*), with an admission charge (10F). Group bookings are also possible (☎ 02-98-61-75-70). From the top, there's an excellent view of the surrounding area, the island, Roscoff and the open sea.

FESTIVALS

– **Quatorze Juillet** (14 July or 'Bastille Day'): horse races on the beach. Breton games such as *lever de la perche* (see 'Background, Traditional Breton Sports') and other entertainments.

– **Pardon de Ste-Anne**: religious festival on the last Sunday in July. Fireworks display in the dunes, in the east of the island, near the ruined chapel.

– **Fête de la Mer** (festival of the sea): mid-August.

– **Fête du Cheval** (equestrian festival): on 10 August.

ST-POL-DE-LÉON
(*KASTELL-PAOL*) 29250   (Pop: 7,400)

It was Welsh immigrants who were first attracted to the site of this settlement, one of whom, Pol Aurélien, was to become the first bishop of the area.

Today, the village is the capital of the Breton artichoke (brought from Italy in the 15th century) and of the *prince de Bretagne* cauliflower. The proximity of the market in Kérisnel makes St-Pol France's most important export centre for early fruit and vegetables. The town has some interesting architecture and there are also a few good beaches.

USEFUL ADDRESS

🛈 **Office du tourisme**: next to the cathedral in the place de l'Évêché. ☎ 02-98-69-05-69. Open all year round from Monday to Saturday 8.45am–noon and 1.30–7pm (6pm on Saturday in summer and 5pm in winter); also open Sunday 10am–noon in high season. Welcoming staff.

WHERE TO STAY AND EAT

🛏 **Camping Ar Kleguer**: rue de la Grève-du-Man, Le Vrennit. ☎ 02-98-69-18-81 or 05-39. Fax: 02-98-29-12-84. ✕ Open from April to September. Three-star campsite with tennis court and swimming pool. Cost of a pitch for two people in July and August is 90F.

🛏 ✕ **Hôtel-restaurant Le Passiflore**: 28 rue Pen-ar-Pont (near the train station). ☎ 02-98-69-00-52. Open all year round except for one week at Christmas. Closed on Sunday evening. A really nice little hotel. Conventional, unpretentious, but offering pleasant rooms for 200F (two people). The warm welcome is worth a mention and especially the excellent restaurant, **Les Routiers**, situated on the ground floor. At lunchtime it is chock-a-block and

the 'workman's lunch' is very popular, at 55F (weekdays only); other menus cost up to 180F.

🛏 ✕ **Hôtel-restaurant de Kerisnel**: on the road to Plouenan, near the market, just 2 kilometres (1 mile) to the northwest of the town centre on the D75. It's well signposted although almost out in the country. ☎ 02-98-29-05-60. Fax: 02-98-29-11-26. Website: www.hotel-kerisnel.com. ✕ Restaurant closed Saturday lunchtime and Sunday. A large double room will cost from 200F to 250F. Family rooms (for three people, with mezzanine) for 380F. There are also studios with kitchen, to rent (320F – sleeping four people). The restaurant has set menus ranging from 55F to 180F. This is a huge building without much character, almost facing the market. Next to it are curious-looking chalets with pointed roofs, and this is where the family rooms are located. The welcome is excellent and the cuisine is decent, so this makes a good place to stay if you're catching the ferry.

✗ **Crêperie Les Fromentines**: 18 rue Cadiou. ☎ 02-98-69-23-52. ♿ Closed Thursday (except for July and August); one week in February and June and three weeks in October. In the shadow of the famous spire of the Kreisker church, tasty *crêpes* such as the *Léonarde* (with artichokes and Roquefort cream sauce) and other original and delicious specialities. Dish of the day as well. Set menu for 58F, but allow 80F to eat à la carte. Salads and ice cream. Friendly owner, who also offers accommodation a couple of kilometres away, costing 220F including breakfast.

✗ **Crêperie-snack Ty Korn**: 17 rue des Minimes, a road running parallel to the main street. ☎ 02-98-69-25-14. Open daily in summer. Closed Monday evening and Tuesday in winter, annual holidays in January. Allow 80F to eat à la carte. The atmosphere here is quite pleasant and they offer good *crêpe* specialities, notably the *Lutine* (special house recipe with fish) and the *Spountus* (with caramelized apples,

cinammon-flavoured ice-cream and sugared almonds). On Thursday there is *kig ha farz* (traditional Breton bacon flan), and *tartiflette* (potatoes, onions, bacon and cheese) on Wednesday.

☆☆ Moderate

🛏 **Hôtel de France**: 29 rue des Minimes. ☎ 02-98-29-14-14. Fax: 02-98-29-10-57. Double rooms cost 230F to 300F, with some larger rooms also available. Only minutes from the town centre but this is a large house set in its own grounds, so it's very quiet. Renovated in 1999, the house has a family atmosphere and the rooms are pleasant.

✗ **La Pomme d'Api**: 49 rue Venderel. ☎ 02-98-69-04-36. In a street at right angles to the rue du Général-Leclerc. Closed Sunday evening and Monday in low season, the last two weeks in November and for two weeks during the February school holidays. In a very pretty stone house dating from the middle of the 14th century, this restaurant enjoys a genuinely charming Breton setting. Decor in wood and stone, and a beautiful monumental fireplace. The cuisine is excellent (the best reputation in town). Set menus for 85F (lunchtime on weekdays) up to 225F.

WHERE TO STAY IN THE AREA

🛏 **Chambres d'hôte: Alain and Sylvie Cazuc**: in Lopréden, 29420 Plouenan, 8 kilometres (5 miles) to the south of St-Pol-de-Léon on the D75. ☎ 02-98-69-50-62. Fax: 02-98-69-50-02. Open from March to October. Three guest rooms (shower and toilet) for 240F. Facilities for cooking your own meals. Very welcoming.

WHAT TO SEE

★ **Chapelle Notre-Dame-du-Kreisker**: construction of this chapel began in the 14th century, and it was superbly renovated in 1993. Its spectacular Gothic belfry has the tallest spire in Brittany, at 78 metres (254 feet). It is a masterpiece of light and balance and a wonderful sculpture, with openwork pinnacle turrets, balustrades and almost a hundred gargoyles. Interesting north porch in the Gothic Flamboyant style, with a host of decorative features. On the west side, a wonderful semi-circular stained-glass window and 14th-century rose window. Also a 17th-century oak altarpiece.

★ **Cathedral**: rebuilt from the 12th century ruins of a Romanesque church destroyed by the Danes. Free guided tours in July and August. Its imposing towers rise 55 metres (179 feet). Choir in the Flamboyant style with around 60 superbly carved stalls dating from the 16th century. Note the finely embossed backs of the stalls, the work of goldsmiths. Above are polychrome canopies.

★ **The old town**: lots of picturesque old houses from the 16th and 17th centuries, notably in the rue du Général-Leclerc (Nos. 9, 12, 30 and 31), the rue Rosière (Nos. 6 and 9) and the rue du Petit-Collège (Hôtel de Keroulas, with a beautiful Gothic porch). Free guided tours of old St-Pol on Thursday in July and August, including the town hall in the former episcopal palace and, in the place du Petit-Cloître, the prebendal house dating from the 16th century, which has exhibitions of painting and sculpture all year round.

★ **Marché au Cadran:** guided tours of the market are available from July to September on Fridays from 9.30am. The cost is 30F per person. Full details from the tourist office. This is a good way to get an insight into the production of vegetables – the region's main commercial activity. You can see inside a greenhouse and a packing centre, as well as finding out how mushrooms are grown.

WHAT TO SEE IN THE AREA

★ **Dried flowers**: at Ty Nevez, 29670 Henvic. ☎ 02-98-62-83-21. Located 8 kilometres (5 miles) southeast of St-Pol, on the D58 in the direction of Morlaix. Mme Marie-Michèle Stéphan is a flower grower who invites visitors into her garden and to see her attic, which is filled with hundreds of bouquets. The bouquets and flower arrangements are for sale, and they can also be found in local markets, especially the one at Morlaix.

CARANTEC (*KARANTEG*) 29660   (Pop: 2,818)

This rather stylish seaside resort (sometimes called 'North Finistère's answer to Beverley Hills') sits perched up on a promontory overlooking the Baie de St-Pol-de-Léon. The site is well sheltered, protected in the east by the Pointe du Diben, and in the west by the Pointe de Roscoff.

The superb Plage du Kelenn is overlooked by the famous *chaise du curé* (priest's chair), a rocky outcrop which offers a lovely panorama of the bay and the Pointe de Roscoff. The parish priests used to come here to gaze out at the sea and meditate. There are many other beaches along the point, which stretches out in front of you. Naturally, the area is very busy in summer.

Before arriving at the Île de Callot, you will be able to spot the **Château du Taureau**. Built in 1544 as a defence against perfidious Albion (the name given to Great Britain since the second century AD), it became first a prison and then a nautical centre. It now stands empty, although the authorities are seeking a use for it, which they will finance. They need to act quickly, as its rescue is now an urgent matter.

The **Île de Callot** is easily reached at low tide, with fine sandy beaches and a little 16th-century chapel that is listed as an historic monument: a *pardon* takes place here on 15 August. Take a pleasant stroll around the verdant Pointe de Pen Al Lann. The **Île Louet**, not very far from the Château du Taureau, has many interesting tourist attractions.

USEFUL ADDRESS

🛈 **Office du tourisme**: 4 rue Pasteur. ☎ 02-98-67-00-43. Open all year round; during high season, Monday to Saturday 9am–7pm (also 9am–1pm on Sunday during July and August); out of season, open 9am–noon and 2–6pm. They keep plenty of information about the town and can offer a useful map that helps you to stroll round the many little streets without getting lost. You can also get details of an interesting walk, a round-trip of about 15 kilometres (9 miles). They also organize boat trips around the Baie de Morlaix and the Île de Batz.

WHERE TO STAY

🛏 **Chambres d'hôte at Le Manoir de Kervézec**: as you come into Carantec and well signposted. ☎ and fax: 02-98-67-00-26. This lovely townhouse has wonderful guest rooms, all furnished in a very individual style, ranging from 280 to 380F (high season), including breakfast. The affluent Bohic family have opened up their home and give a very warm welcome. There is a terrace where you can relax and enjoy the view of the sea, and wooded grounds, where horses and llamas graze.

🛏 **Hôtel-restaurant Le Relais**: 17 rue Albert-Louppe; in the town centre. ☎ 02-98-67-00-42. Fax: 02-98-78-30-58. Open all year round. The rooms are plain but clean and well kept, and inexpensive too, costing from 145F to 205F (with shower and toilet). Half board is obligatory in high season, and prices start from 245F per person. Set menus cost 57F (weekday lunchtime) and 75F.

The cuisine is traditional and reasonably priced.

🛏 ✕ **Hôtel du Pors-Pol**: 7 rue Surcouf. ☎ 02-98-67-00-52. Fax: 02-98-67-02-17. Open from Easter to the end of September. A double room costs 265F to 290F. In a quiet mainly residential part of town, this is a large holiday hotel with a timeless sort of charm. It's near the beach, which you reach along a pleasant footpath. Plenty of regular customers come here and the welcome is very warm. The rooms are decorated in conventional style but they are well maintained.

🛏 **Camping Les Mouettes**: route de la Grande-Grève. ☎ 02-98-67-02-46. Fax: 02-98-78-31-46. Open from May to mid-September; mobile home rental is offered (1,500–3,600F per week) from Easter to mid-September. This large four-star campsite near the sea is superbly equipped and run. A pitch for two costs from 105F to 150F.

WHERE TO EAT

✕ **La Cambusec – Le Cabestan**: by the harbour. ☎ 02-98-67-01-87. Fax: 02-98-67-90-49. Closed on Tuesday in season and on Monday and Tuesday out of season. Set menus at Le Cabestan cost 120F, 180F and 225F. At **La Cambusec**, allow at least 200F to eat à la carte. Here you have two restaurants in the one place – choose one or the other, depending on your mood. Same chef, but two teams and two very different atmospheres. La Cambusec is a cross between a brasserie, a bar and a tavern. Very lively in summer, it is even boisterous, and positively torrid some weekends, with deafening rock or Irish music. A favourite with holidaymakers, locals and 'rough diamonds' of all nationalities, all attracted by the atmosphere and reputation of the food, which is generous and reasonably priced: 12 oysters for 66F, garlic sausage, curried lamb, salt-cod, and so on. Next door, **Le Cabestan** is calmer, even peaceful, with linen tablecloths, quiet customers, and lovers exchanging gentle words over a nice fillet of sole or sea bass with seaweed.

✕ **La Chaise du Curé**: 3 place de la République. ☎ 02-98-78-33-27. Closed on Wednesday, Thursday lunchtime and the month of February. Set menus cost from 95F to 165F. Right in the town centre, this restaurant has two pleasant and bright little dining rooms offering interesting menus based on local produce. You might get such dishes as chicken in cider (*poulet fermier au cidre*) or salmon in a buckwheat pancake (*rouleaux de saumon en crêpes de sarrasin*). The Breton bacon flan speciality *kig ha farz* is available to order. There's a nice family atmosphere and the staff are charming.

WHERE TO GO FOR A DRINK

♟ **Le Bar des Sports**: ☎ 02-98-67-01-83. Frequented by young people and sailing enthusiasts. Lively atmosphere in the evenings.

♟ **Le Bar du Club de Tennis de Pen-Al-Lann**: this tennis club bar hosts enthusiasts of other sports too. Music.

♟ **Bar Le Petit Relais**: Plage du Kelenn. ☎ and fax: 02-98-78-30-03. Bar open every day from April to September, brasserie open only in high season. In August they hold all kinds of musical evenings, from 10pm. Mussels (*moules*) are a speciality.

FESTIVALS

– **Fête de la Moisson** (harvest festival): the first Sunday in August. *Fest-noz.*

– **Fête de la Mer** (festival of the sea): mid-August.

LOCQUÉNOLÉ (*LOKENOLE*) 29670   (Pop: 751)

This delightful little village nestling in the green countryside is 7 kilometres (4.5 miles) from Morlaix, heading towards Carantec. The 17th-century church with its openwork belfry and small walled parish close, the calvary, the fountain and the little square, with its old café, present a harmonious grouping. An *arbre de la liberté* ('freedom tree', planted to commemorate Bastille Day on 14 July 1789, which effectively signalled the beginning of the French Revolution) still grows there. Beautiful view across to the port of Dourduff.

WHERE TO STAY AND EAT

✕ **L'Auberge du Vieux Chêne**: 12 place de la Liberté. ☎ 02-98-72-24-27. Fax: 02-98-72-25-56. ⚒ Closed Tuesday evening and Wednesday out of season. In a charming little square, opposite the church. Modern but pleasant dining room, serving decent traditional food with imaginative touches. Set menus from 98F to 165F. Dishes from the menu include monkfish in cider (*pavé de lotte au cidre*), smoked duck and nut salad (*salade de magret fumé aux noix*), marinated salmon with pink peppercorns (*saumon mariné aux baies roses*), and duck conserve (*confit de canard*).

MORLAIX (*MONTROULEZ*) 29600 (Pop: 16,978)

A pleasant town and port, Morlaix is situated at a geographical, historical and human crossroads. To the east is the Trégor region, with its as yet unspoiled countryside; to the west are the market gardens of the Léon region; to the north lies the English Channel; and to the south, the Monts d'Arrée. Morlaix has a quite unique setting amid three hills, and old houses rise in tiers on both sides of the River Morlaix. The colossal viaduct that divides the town in two gives it a kind of third dimension.

This town was the birthplace of French poet Tristan Corbière (*Les Amours jaunes*), referred to by fellow writer Verlaine as the *poète maudit*, or 'cursed poet'. Also born here were Fanch Gourvil, an expert in the Breton language and on Brittany, and Albert Le Grand, author of the famous *Vie des Saints en Bretagne* ('Lives of the Breton Saints').

Morlaix is a middle-class town that grew wealthy through maritime trading, particularly in the linen that was cultivated and woven in the hinterland. Its motto – '*S'ils te mordent, mords-les!*' ('If they bite you, bite them back!') – with its play on words (*mords-les* is pronounced the same as 'Morlaix') dates from the 16th century, when the English fleet suffered a severe thrashing. Having taken Morlaix by surprise, the English troops, much the worse for wear after their visit to the wine cellars of the town, were massacred that same evening by the inhabitants of Morlaix.

The tobacco industry is no longer the success it once was, but the service industry, shops and the hospital help to maintain Morlaix's position as the third most important town in Finistère. Yet Morlaix still seems to be searching for its true identity in the new millennium.

USEFUL ADDRESSES

🛈 Office du tourisme (A1 on the map): place des Otages. Under the viaduct, in the centre of town. ☎ 02- 98-62-14-94. In July and August, open from Monday to Saturday 9am–7pm and Sunday 10.30am–

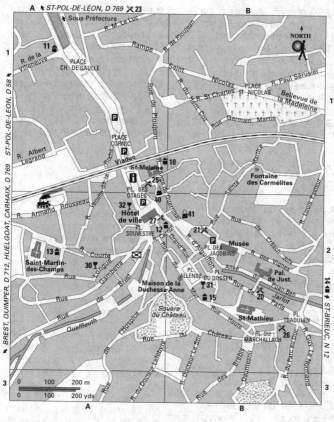

MORLAIX

- **Useful Addresses**

  - ☐ Office du tourisme
  - ☒ Poste centrale (main post office)
  - 🚂 Gare SNCF (train station)

- **Where To Stay**

  - **10** Hôtel St-Melaine
  - **11** Hôtel du Port
  - **12** Hôtel de l'Europe
  - **13** Greenwood Café Hôtel
  - **15** Chambres d'hôte (M. and Mme Brezillon)

- **Where To Eat**

  - **20** Les Bains-Douches

- **21** Crêperie Ar Bilig
- **23** Le Tempo
- **25** Le Marée Bleue
- **26** Brocéliande
- **27** Brasserie Le Lof

- **Where To Go For a Drink**

  - **30** Les Danseurs de Lune
  - **31** Ty Coz
  - **32** Café de la Terrasse

- **Shopping**

  - **40** Au Four St-Melaine
  - **41** Maison des Vins

12.30pm; open the rest of the year 9am–noon and 2–6pm. Friendly staff and lots of information available. The M.J.C. offers theatrical guided tours, a novel way of discovering the town's rich maritime history.

⊠ **Poste centrale** (main post office) (A2 on the map): rue de Brest. At the back of the town hall.

🚄 **Gare SNCF** (train station) (A2 on the map): rue Armand-Rousseau.

☎ 08-36-35-35-35 (premium rate). Built in 1864, the station has the most modern signalling system in France, but the 25 million francs that this cost seems to be reflected in the ticket prices.

⊕ **Aérodrome Morlaix-Ploujean** (Morlaix-Ploujean airport): ☎ 02-98-62-16-09. Head office of the company **Brit Air**: ☎ 02-98-62-10-22.

■ **Radio-taxis**: ☎ 02-98-88-36-42.

WHERE TO STAY

☆ Budget

⬥ **Auberge de jeunesse** (youth hostel) (off B2, **14** on the map): 3 route de Paris. ☎ 02-98-88-13-63. Fax: 02-98-88-81-82. Open all year round for members of the youth hostel association. A 20-minute walk from the station. 49F per night. Breakfast for 20F. Meals for 49F.

⬥ **Hôtel St-Melaine** (A1–B1, **10** on the map): 75–77 rue Ange-de-Guernisac. ☎ 02-98-88-08-79. Closed on Sunday from 20 December to 2 January, as well as for two weeks in May. Under the viaduct. Take the St-Melaine exit to get to this small family hotel, on a quiet street. Very friendly owner. Plain rooms, some with rather old furniture, but generally well kept. Expect to pay 150F or 160F for two people (for a room with shower and toilet). Difficult to find anything less expensive. Good traditional food and a set menu for 60F with a good buffet of starters. Another menu for 85F.

☆☆ Moderate

⬥ **Hôtel du Port** (A1, **11** on the map): 3 quai de Léon, not far from the viaduct, on the left bank of the marina. ☎ 02-98-88-07-54. Fax: 02-98-88-43-80. Open all year round. Closes at midnight. Rooms are modern, bright and impeccable

(although a bit small), and range in price from 210F to 230F. TV in every room. Very welcoming and excellent value for money.

⬥ **Chambres d'hôte with M. and Mme Brezillon** (B2, **15** on the map): 14 rue Haute. ☎ 02-98-88-05-52. Right in the heart of old Morlaix. Open all year round. There is just one double guest room (at 280F including breakfast) available in this charming 17th-century half-timbered house where they give a warm welcome. Bunk beds are available, and you can use the kitchen if you are staying for several days.

⬥ **Greenwood Café Hôtel** (A2, **13** on the map): 25 place St-Martin. ☎ 02-98-88-03-29. Fax: 02-98-63-97-80. This place is near the Église St-Martin, so it's a little way out of the centre. Open all year round. A double room costs 250F. It's basically a local bistrot with a pub name, but the first-floor accommodation is good value for money.

☆☆☆☆ Très Chic

⬥ **Hôtel de l'Europe** (A2–B2, **12** on the map): 1 rue d'Aiguillon. ☎ 02-98-62-11-99. Fax: 02-98-88-83-38. Website: www.hotel-europe-com.fr. ✗ Open all year round. An affluent-looking building right in the heart of town, the hotel boasts a beautiful, tastefully renovated staircase with wood panelling dating from the 17th century. Some of the rooms have been refurbished and these are nice and bright, with smart decor. Other rooms awaiting transformation are rather dated. Room prices are 320F to 340F with shower or bath and toilet.

WHERE TO EAT

☆ Budget

✕ **Les Bains-Douches** (B2, **20** on the map): 45 allée du Poan-Ben, opposite the Palais de Justice (law courts). ☎ 02-98-63-83-83. ✄ Closed Saturday lunchtime and Sunday evening. One of the most original restaurants in town. Worth visiting just for its walkway and the tiles and stained-glass windows of the former public baths, which date from 1904. The original decor has been tastefully preserved. The friendly atmosphere is a combination of Celtic and Parisian and the café food on offer is decent and reasonably priced. Weekday lunchtime set menu for 67F, with another menu for 135F. Allow 150F to eat à la carte.

✕ **Crêperie Ar Bilig** (B2, **21** on the map): 6 rue Au-Fil; between place des Jacobins and place des Viarmes. ☎ 02-98-88-50-51. Closed Sunday and Monday as well as end of September to early October. Annual holidays in October. The decor isn't exactly wonderful, but this is a very good, inexpensive *crêperie*. There's a menu for 50F offering three *crêpes*, but allow 50–60F to eat à la carte. Milk and cream directly from the farm.

✕ **Le Tempo** (off A1, **23** on the map): bassin à Flot, cours Beaumont (opposite the factory on the Trégor side of town). ☎ 02-98-63-29-11. Open all year round. Closed Saturday lunchtime and Sunday. Allow 100F to eat à la carte. Delicious savoury pies, generous salads. The decor changes according to the exhibitions. Relaxed atmosphere, and a very lively bar in the evenings. Tables outside with a view of the boat masts.

☆☆–☆☆☆ Moderate to Chic

✕ **La Marée Bleue** (A1, **25** on the map): 3 rampe St-Melaine (in a street at right angles to place des Otages). ☎ 02-98-63-24-21. Closed Monday and Sunday evening out of season; also closed for three weeks in October. Set menus from 80F (not Sunday) to 235F – or expect to pay 190F to eat à la carte. This place enjoys a good reputation – specializing in fish and seafood, so it attracts a well-heeled clientele. Still, the staff are genuinely friendly. Very elegant, with lots of wood and stone, on two levels. The prawns and seafood are wonderfully fresh and the meat exceptionally tender.

✕ **Brocéliande** (B2, **26** on the map): 5 rue des Bouchers. ☎ 02-98-88-73-78. ✄ Open all year round, evening only. Closed on Tuesday and the month of November. From the place des Halles, go up the rue Haute and then down again to the rue des Bouchers. This small and unique restaurant is in a nice district. The warm decor is reminiscent of a traditional bourgeois provincial apartment. It's a place where you feel at ease. Good food, which might include steak with stewed rhubarb (*filet mignon à la compote de rhubarbe*) or mussels stuffed with honeyed butter (*moules farcies au beurre de miel*). One set menu for 130F. Very welcoming.

✕ **Brasserie Le Lof** (A2, **27** on the map): place Émile Souvestre. ☎ 02-98-88-81-15. Open all year round.

Set menus for 85F and 158F. This brasserie is in the same building as the Hôtel de l'Europe (see 'Where To Stay') but the decor is in a different style altogether. There are two levels, linked by a modern walk-way and contemporary art can be seen on the walls. The cuisine is excellent, with specialities such as salmon and scallops in tartare sauce with sesame seeds, and a good version of the local *kig ha farz*.

WHERE TO STAY AND EAT IN THE AREA

♠ **Chambres d'hôte Kérélisa**: in St-Martin-des-Champs, 3 kilometres (2 miles) to the northwest of Morlaix. ☎ 02-98-88-27-18. Open all year round. The farmer-owners have completely renovated a family mansion. The six superb and very comfortable guest rooms are all equipped with shower or bath, basin and toilet. Expect to pay 240F for a double room with breakfast included. Very friendly welcome guaranteed. As well as a kitchen, a large garden is also at the guests' disposal, and in May and June you can even pick strawberries here.

♠ **Chambres à la ferme: Le Pillion**: 29600 Plourin-lès-Morlaix; leaving from the place Traoulen (B2 on the map), take the road towards Plourin for 2 kilometres (1.5 miles) and then turn left where it's signposted. ☎ 02-98-88-18-54. Open in July and August. The first floor of a private house has been turned into guest accommodation and there are three pleasant rooms with a communal bathroom, for 220F for two people, including a generous Breton breakfast (with farm-fresh products). Farm visit possible. Warm welcome and tips on good walks in the area.

♠ **Camping at Croas Men farm**: Croas Men, 29610 Plouigneau. ☒ This campsite is near Garlan, 7 kilometres (4.5 miles) to the east of Morlaix. Follow the signs. ☎ 02-98-79-11-50. Open all year round. The cost is 22F per pitch. Farm products for sale, activities, exhibitions. Slide shows about the running of the old farm.

♠ **Chambres à la ferme: J. and Y. Laviec**: Penavern, 29600 Plourin-lès-Morlaix. ☎ 02-98-72-52-78. Open only in July and August. Very welcoming. A beautiful white and grey Breton house with granite window and door frames. Spacious guest rooms (communal bathroom). Costs 200F for two people, including a real Breton breakfast.

☆☆☆☆ Très Chic

♠ ✕ **Chambres d'hôte: Domaine de Lanhéric**: 29410 Lanhéric Plouneour-Menez. ☎ 02-98-78-01-53. From Morlaix, head towards Pleyber-Christ; 2 kilometres (1.5 miles) after Pleyber, turn right, then right again (follow the sign for 'Domaine de Lanhéric'). Quite difficult to find, but well worth the effort. In the heart of this lovely quiet spot stands a wonderful granite house, with two quite expensive guest rooms (300–350F with breakfast included). Each of the spotlessly clean rooms has a separate bathroom. The decor is rustic with wood panelling and old furniture. The surroundings are equally interesting: a first-floor living room provides books and games; on the ground floor there is a monumental fireplace in front of which you have breakfast – and what a breakfast White and brown bread, homemade marmalade and jam, *crêpes*, *fars* (Breton custard tart), homemade yoghurt, cereals, and other meals (book in advance) with farm-fresh ingredients. The grounds are superb, with vegetable plots and flower beds – the owner is a landscape gardener. This is a great place to stay.

⌂ **Chambres d'hôte: Manoir de Lanleya:** 29610 Plouigneau. ☎ and fax: 02-98-79-94-15. Open all year. This little hamlet full of character, where the owner, André Marrec, has literally resurrected a superb 16th-century manor house, is surrounded by unspoiled nature. Situated about 9 kilometres (5.5 miles) east of Morlaix, and about the same distance from Locquirec. It's 3.5 kilometres (2 miles) north from the Plouigneau turn-off, and well signposted. Charming interior with old furniture that blends perfectly with the elegant architecture. A delightful spiral staircase leads to the guest rooms, which themselves are reached through granite arches. Five romantic rooms are only 360F for two people, and breakfast is included. There is even a room in a picturesque turret. The welcome equals the quality of the accommodation. There are also three well-equipped and reasonably priced

gîtes to rent. A stay in the Manoir de Lanleya would get any trip to Finistère off to the best possible start.

⌂ **Chambres d'hôte: Manoir de Roch ar Brini:** 29600 Ploujean-Morlaix. ☎ 02-98-72-01-44. Fax: 02-98-72-01-44. Website: www.brittanyguesthouse.com. Just 3 kilometres northeast of Morlaix on the road that follows the line of the river, in the direction of Dourduff, then signposted off to the right. A double room costs up to 430F depending on the season, including breakfast. Here is a superb, huge late 19th-century mansion in its own park up on the heights overlooking the river at Morlaix. It originally belonged to the shipowner Edouard Corbière, who was a writer and father of the poet Tristan Corbière. There are two lovely rooms, both very spacious and with good-sized bathrooms. The welcome is relaxed and casual. Recommended.
– For other accommodation at Dourduff and Plougonven, *see also* 'Where To Stay' in 'The Trégor and Léon Regions'.

WHERE TO GO FOR A DRINK OR A SWEET TREAT

♟ **Les Danseurs de Lune** (A2, **30** on the map): 29–31 rue Longue. ☎ 02-98-88-54-79. Open 6.30pm–1am at the weekend. Closed Sunday. In the heart of the old town. This long-established café has a young and friendly, family atmosphere. It has a tiny bar, a huge fireplace and various little rooms that somehow seem to make every huddle of students look like a gang of conspirators. Rock music is played, giving an excellent atmosphere. Warm welcome.
♟ **Ty Coz** (B2, **31** on the map): 10 venelle Au-Beurre; near the place des Halles (place Allende). ☎ 02-98-88-07-65. Open every day ex-

cept Thursday, until 1am. Open Sunday from 7pm. Annual holidays from 20 May to 5 June and the month of September. On the first floor, those who are keen on darts and billiards will enjoy the Breton-speaking atmosphere of this pub whose recently restored interior dates from the 15th century and boasts a 600-year-old fireplace
♟ **Café de la Terrasse** (A2, **32** on the map): in the place des Otages. ☎ 02-98-88-20-25. Open all year round 7am–midnight (1am in summer). Allow 85F to eat à la carte. Superb café dating from the early 1900s, with an amazing spiral staircase. It was a stopover

point for the very first Tour de France cycling race. From its terrace customers can enjoy the beautiful sight of Morlaix bathed in the first sunlight of the day. Brasserie meals with a reasonable reputation.

♥ In the St-Mathieu district (B2 on the map), there are pubs and lively nightclubs. Near the place du Marchallach, there's **La Cabane,** which is halfway between a bar and a club, and **La Selle,** which is altogether quieter.

THE CALMING EFFECTS OF COREFF

In 1985, an extraordinary event took place for all genuine beer drinkers (at least in Brittany): a Breton beer called Coreff was born.

The following information about the beer is reproduced courtesy of the magazine *Ar Men*.

Unlike almost all French and German beers, Coreff is a high-fermentation beer (like Guinness, British bitter beers and those made by Belgian Trappist monks). No carbon dioxide is added to cool it or filter it – that happens naturally. Likewise, none is needed to draught it. That takes place automatically when a hand pump is used. The ingredients are chosen rigorously, and include malted barley from Valenciennes, hops from Bourgogne and Bavaria, and English brewers' yeast. Coreff, with its black label, is a bitter that is neither filtered nor pasteurized, whether it's the light ale, at 4.5°, or the brown ale, at 7.5°.

Supply is limited to café owners who are able to provide very precise storage and draught conditions. This restriction will guarantee that Coreff remains a traditional beer for a long time to come. Today, fewer than a hundred cafés in Finistère-Nord and the Côtes-d'Armor sell the beer. According to one owner: 'Coreff contains a high level of hops, whose soothing properties are well known, and we have observed that our customers have been much calmer since they started to drink it!'

You can visit the brewery – the brewing, fermentation and bottling rooms – and sample the product as you leave.

■ **Brasserie des Deux-Rivières**: 1 place de la Madeleine. ☎ 02-98-63-41-92. Free tours in July and August every weekday at 11am and 2pm. Telephone to arrange a visit out of season.

WHAT TO SEE

★ **Circuit des venelles** (tour of the alleyways): first, go to the tourist information office and buy a brochure (5F) describing the various tours that will help you discover some of Morlaix's wonderful townhouses. Look out for carved wood and statues on the corners. For those with limited time to spend, the most interesting streets are place des Viarmes and rue Ange-de-Guernisac, where there are 15th-century houses with slate-lined walls. **Église St-Melaine**, dating from the 16th century, is in Flamboyant Gothic style. If you take the venelle aux Prêtres or the venelle du Créou, you will come to the Esplanade du Calvaire (next to the viaduct), with its panorama of the town, and you can 'straddle' the place des Otages by passing over the first level of the viaduct.

The venelle de La Roche on the slope opposite the Église St-Melaine leads you to Notre-Dame-des-Anges, where there are nice views. From there, go back to the **rue Longue** via the **rue Courte** (in other words, go back to the 'long street' via the 'short street') to see some beautiful 17th-century houses.

★ **Maisons à Lanterne**: Morlaix possesses one particular style of house that is quite unique and about ten of these lovely *maisons à lanterne* or 'skylight houses' are still standing. Built between the 15th and early 18th centuries, the houses are arranged with all the rooms leading off a central glazed atrium through which a spiral staircase twists to the top. The highly ornamented carved handrails are sometimes known as *ponts d'allée* (or '*pond allez*'), from which comes the other name for these houses, the *maisons à Pondalez*. Some stairway beams were rescued during the demolition of one of these houses and can be seen at the **Maison à Pondalez** (*see below*). Some of these houses can be visited:

– **Maison de la Duchesse Anne** (Duchess Anne's house) (B2 on the map): 33 rue du Mur. ☎ 02-98-88-23-26. In July and August open 10am–6.30pm; in April and September open 10am–noon and 2.30–5pm; in May and June open 10am–noon and 2–6pm. Closed Sunday and public holidays. Admission charge (10F). This property is one of the most beautiful mansions in Morlaix.

– **Maison à Pondalez** (B2 on the map): 9 Grand-Rue. ☎ 02-98-88-03-57. Telephone for exact opening times. Maximum of 16 people at a time. Admission charge (20F); combined ticket option with the **Musée des Jacobins**.

– **Maison des Vins:** 1 rue Ange-de-Guernisac (*see below* under 'Shopping').

★ Other **ancient dwellings** can be found in the place des Halles (place Allende: B2 on the map) and in the Grand-Rue, the central artery of the old town. As you enter the Grand-Rue, you will see an exhausted looking gentleman who has been holding up corbelling for the past 300 years.

★ The continuation of the rue du Mur, and the rue Haute and rue Basse are equally picturesque. In the rue Basse, all that is left of the original **Église St-Mathieu** (B2 on the map) is its 16th-century tower. Inside is a real jewel: a 15th-century statue of the Virgin which opens up. Inside are painted panels.

★ **The viaduct**: you really can't miss it. The imposing mass of its wide supports allows the railway to cross the Dossen at a height of 58 metres (188 feet). Begun in 1861, its construction was completed in 1863. It measures 292 metres (950 feet) in length. If you want to walk over it, you could take the venelle de La Roche and return via the venelle aux Prêtres. The English tried to bomb the viaduct during World War II, but missed, and destroyed many old houses instead. It was a heavy toll, especially since dozens of the houses, including some of the finest, had already disappeared during the construction of the viaduct. A little further downstream, the road viaduct of the RN12, with its four lanes, measures almost 1 kilometre in length but does not possess the same elegance.

★ **Musée des Jacobins** (B2 on the map): place des Jacobins. ☎ 02-98-88-68-88. From November to Easter, open 10am–noon and 2–5pm (6pm on Sunday); closed Tuesday and Saturday morning; from Easter to the end of

June, and in September and October, open daily except Tuesday and Saturday morning, 10am–noon and 2–6pm; in July and August, open daily 10am–12.30pm and 2–6.30pm. Admission charge (26F). Interesting regional museum of history, ethnography and fine arts, housed in a former 13th-century church. On display are maritime mementoes, old engravings, paintings of old Morlaix, beautiful statues from surrounding chapels and stair columns. One of them, dating from 1557, measures almost 11 metres (36 feet) and was carved from a single piece of oak. Note the surviving wooden **spoon-holders**, which were lowered by means of a pulley. Numerous rural household objects (churns, spinning wheels, hackles) and farm implements. Some noteworthy paintings include a landscape by Hippolyte Lebas, and the works of local artist, Charles Penther, who painted sleazy bars. In *Une porte s'ouvrit* ('A Door Opens'), silhouettes mill about behind a haze of smoke. There is also a recent collection of contemporary art. Very interesting temporary exhibitions throughout the year.

★ **Le Télégramme de Brest**: 7 voie d'accès au port, BP 243, 29205 Morlaix. You can visit this large newspaper company from Monday to Friday morning. Telephone to arrange a visit (only for groups of 10–20 people). ☎ 02-98-62-11-33. The paper was founded in 1944, and has a circulation of around 210,000.

FESTIVAL

– **Festival les Arts dans la Rue** (street arts festival): from mid-July to mid-August, from 5pm to midnight every Wednesday, the town becomes completely caught up in a celebration of music, entertainment, food and folklore. A free-spirited feast for the senses that is both beautiful and creative.

SHOPPING

Au Four St-Melaine (A1–A2, **40** on the map): 1 venelle du Four. ☎ 02-98-88-10-22. Closed Monday and Sunday out of season, as well as two weeks in February. This is the oldest *boulangerie* in the town and has a strong reputation for its excellent Breton cakes, including *far*, *kouign amann* and the house speciality, known as *l'Armoricain*, whose recipe is a closely guarded secret.

Maison des Vins (B2, **41** on the map): 1 rue Ange-de-Guernisac. ☎ 02-98-88-72-43. Closed Monday. Admission is free. In a superb *maison à lanterne* (*see* 'What To See' *above*), this wine shop provides a place to admire the beauty of a typical old Morlaix house as well as somewhere to choose a good vintage wine. An interior staircase is lit by an opening in the roof. Notice the statue right up high and the rather Dalí-esque fireplace hanging at first-floor level. The partition wall at the far end is actually the cliff face, which means that the temperature remains constant – and cool – and the wine matures slowly. You are welcome to go in and have a look around.

DIVING

The silt of the Morlaix river tends to cloud the waters in the southern part of the Baie de Morlaix, although this is still rich territory for divers, with a number of glorious fissures to explore. In particular there are two good places to dive a little further out. The best way to get a clear view is at slack water.

Diving Clubs

■ **Groupe subaquatique Morlaix Trégor**: 18 route de Kernelehen at Plouhezoc'h (about 200 metres before you reach the megalith), 29252 or BP 145, 29204 Morlaix Cedex. ☎ 02-98-79-50-95 or 06-11-08-02-78. Open from March to October, 9am–5pm every day in summer, weekends only in September. You can go out on one of the club's two fast barges; each of which can hold up to 18 divers. The club is FFESSM registered and a team of fully qualified instructors offers everything from beginner sessions to level III dives, as well as courses and expeditions that will leave you with some astonishing memories. Reservation is essential and all equipment is provided. Discounts are offered for five or ten dives.

The Best Places To Dive

The **Aboukir Bay:** the story of the wreck of this three-masted English vessel, which went down in 1893, is well known in the region. The town mayor at the time of the wreck refused to allow the bodies of 19 sailors to be laid to rest in the cemetery, objecting to the fact that they were Protestants. Many of the local people were highly indignant about this and the mayor was sent packing. A new cemetery was created and strong ties of friendship developed between the townspeople and the sailors' families. You can now dive down to a depth of 30 metres (98 feet) to inspect the ship's rusting skeleton. The anchor is still in its place and the housing is open. Nowadays, however, the ship is crewed by a different band of creatures altogether – there are solitary conger eels, shoals of whiting and a few predatory bass. This is a very exposed location. Level II ability.

Les Trépieds: in the northern part of the Baie de Morlaix, this is one of the best diving locations in the area. The water up here is often clear, so it is possible to go down between 15 and 50 metres (50 and 165 feet) to explore the fantastic crevasses and fissures, which are smothered with brightly coloured corynacties. If you take a decent torch it's possible to go in search of the many creatures that live in among the fronds of kelp. This is a very exposed location. Suitable for all levels of ability.

The Trégor Region of Finistère

Although the Trégor region is now split administratively between the two *départements* of Finistère and Côtes d'Armor, its historic boundary was the river Morlaix. There are still very few visitors coming into this pretty landscape with the Monts d'Arrée as a backdrop. Here there is pleasant strolling along the wild stretch of coastline between Morlaix and Locquirec.

The coast from Morlaix to Locuirec

★ **Réserve Ornithologique de la Baie de Morlaix** (bird sanctuary of the Bay of Morlaix): run by the society for the study and protection of nature in Brittany, the sanctuary shelters the most beautiful colony of terns in Europe, with more than a thousand pairs. It is forbidden to approach the islands but you will see lots of birds diving for fish in the bay. In winter there are barnacle geese, sandpipers, godwits, curlews, and so on.

★ **Dourduff and Plouézoc'h**: 6 kilometres (4 miles) from Morlaix. From Plouézoc'h, there is a pretty view of the estuary. Interesting church with openwork tower and turret – Pardon de St-Antoine in early August. After-wards, you come to the charming little port of Dourduff. The pretty road follows the east bank of the River Morlaix.

★ **Grand cairn de Barnenez** (tumulus): ☎ 02-98-67-24-73. Open all year round: 10am–12.30pm (1pm in July and August) and 2–6pm from April to the end of September, and 10am–noon and 2–5pm from October until the end of March. Closed on some public holidays. Admission charge (25F). Although it is 7,000 years old and one of the most important megalithic sites in France, the cairn came within a whisker of ending up as building material for the local road system. A quarry was even opened up, despite the discovery of several intact chambers of considerable archaeological import-ance. Only the stubborn determination of some journalists and research workers from the CNRS (national organization for scientific research) prevented the exploitation of the quarry. The clearing and restoration work took 13 years, and the end result is superb (even though a minister of the Fifth Republic refused to be the guest of honour at the inauguration because the work had begun under the Fourth Republic!).

Situated on a promontory, the tumulus overlooks the bay like a Greek monument. From a distance, the harmonious proportions of its graded terraces create an aesthetically pleasing effect. With a length of 80 metres (260 feet) and a height of 10 metres (32 feet), it is built entirely of drystone. The funeral chambers are made from dolmens aligned to form a corridor. Numbering 11 in all, some are open to the public.

★ **From Térénez to St-Jean-du-Doigt**: this part of the region is hardly developed at all and there are a number of isolated farmhouses surrounded by a network of narrow roads.

Plougasnou has an interesting 16th-century church with a spire adorned with four pinnacle turrets, and a Renaissance porch. Tourist information office: ☎ 02-98-67-31-88. The picturesque **Pointe de Primel** is a jumble of pink rocks, and after the point there is a succession of little ports, such as **Le Diben**, hidden away among the jagged granite blocks. **St-Samson** has a wide beach. The whole region is still quite rural, with isolated farms in a network of narrow roads.

Térénez is the little port on the other side of Barnenez; from here, you will see gorgeous sunsets over the Baie de Morlaix, its islands and the Château du Taureau at its mouth.

★ **St-Jean-du-Doigt**: follow the pretty coastal road, via Poul-Roudou, from Locquirec to St-Jean-du-Doigt, which lies in a little valley. Its **church** has a picturesque cemetery, an ossuary, a monumental gateway in the Flamboyant style, a baroque fountain, a calvary and a remarkable 16th-century chapel with carved woodwork. The relic of the saint's finger (*doigt*), which has been preserved in the church since the 15th century, is said to be responsible for numerous miraculous cures. A great *pardon* takes place on the Sunday after the Fête de la St-Jean, when a large bonfire (*tantad*) is lit.

It is possible to do a short walking tour starting from the church. About 6 kilometres (4 miles) in length, it will take you through pretty countryside, past old windmills, and so on. Details from the tourist information office in Plougasnou (☎ 02-98-67-31-88) or the town hall (☎ 02-98-67-30-06).

From St-Jean-du-Doigt to Locquirec, you can follow a pretty coastal route that takes you through Poul-Roudou.

WHERE TO STAY IN THE AREA

☖ ✕ **Hôtel Roc'h Velen**: St-Samson, 29630 Plougasnou. ☎ 02-98-72-30-58. Fax: 02-98-72-44-57. Email: roch.velen@wanadoo.fr. This hotel is well signposted, on a road leading down to the sea. Closed on Sunday night out of season; also closed for two weeks in January. Small hotel at the entrance to the Baie de Morlaix, with 10 rooms. The rooms (with bath or shower, toilet and telephone) are each named after one of the Ponant islands, and some enjoy a sea view. Prices range from 220F out of season to 310F in July and August. The restaurant offers seafood dishes, with set menus at 90F and 120F. In summer, the Roc'h Velen features a local singer once a week.

☖ ✕ **Hôtel L'Abbesse**: 20 rue de l'Abbesse, Le Diben, 29630 Plougasnou. ☎ 02-98-72-32-43. Fax: 02-98-72-41-99. ⚓ Closed from 1 November to Easter. A double room costs 240F to 280F according to the season. Half board costs 240F to 285F per person and is obligatory in July and August. Set menus range from 86F up to 285F. This is a rather smart hotel right in the centre of the little harbour of Le Diben. The rooms are tastefully decorated and very comfortable; some have sea views. Excellent salt-water swimming pool, sauna and fitness centre. Warm

welcome. In the restaurant, seafood is the speciality, with fish and shell-fish brought straight to the kitchens from the holding tanks across the way.

✕ **Crêperie au Goûter Breton**: 6 rue du Grand-Large, Primel-Tregastel, 29630 Plougasnou. ☎ 02-98-72-34-62. Open noon–10pm all year round on Friday, Saturday, Sunday, public holidays and during school holidays. Allow 70–80F to eat à la carte. Right in the centre of this little resort town with its old world charm. The outside makes the place look like a Mexican saloon bar while the inside has more of a Breton maritime feel, with model ships, fishing nets and so on. Excellent *galettes* and a warm welcome.

✕ **Le Café du Port**: 10 route du Port, Dourduff, 29252 Plouézoc'h. ☎ 02-98-67-22-40. On the harbour, as you might have guessed. This little place has a good terrace where you can eat straightforward shellfish dishes in a very pleasant atmosphere. It gets very busy here.

Campsites

☖ **Camping de la Baie de Térénez**: 29252 Plouézoc'h. ☎ and fax: 02-98-67-26-80. ⚓ Just 3 kilometres (2 miles) out of town, between Plouézoc'h and Térénez. Closed from the end of September

440 | **NORTH FINISTÈRE**

until Easter. Comfortable. A pitch for two people costs about 90F and they also offer mobile homes. Small grocery shop. Restaurant/bar, swimming pool.

☎ **Camping de Kerven**: Le Diben, 29630 Plougasnou. ☎ and fax: 02-98-72-41-22. Open from Easter to October. Mobile homes also available for hire by the week (1,500–2,500F).

☎ There are three other **campsites** near Plougasnou: the municipal campsite is the one at **Milin Ar Mesqueau** (☎ 02-98-67-37-45), which is quite a nice place, well equipped and next to water. It costs about 50F for a pitch for two people. In the same price group, there's also **Le Trégor** (☎ 02-98-67-37-64), and another municipal site ☎ 02-98-72-37-06.

LOCQUIREC (*LOKIREG*) 29241   (Pop: 1,326)

Locquirec is a charming little port on the boundary of the Côtes-d'Armor, enjoying an exceptionally beautiful setting. The village, with its fine architectural unity, stretches over a rocky promontory which offers the holiday-maker no fewer than nine beaches. Within the short distances on this tiny peninsula, a variety of sunbathing locations can be explored in the same day. In addition, Locquirec, being well protected from the prevailing winds, enjoys a mild and iodized climate. To the north are the superb Plages des Sables-Blancs (white-sand beaches). At low tide, one of the most beautiful beaches in Finistère stretches out opposite the harbour; it is a paradise for seashell enthusiasts.

The village has a 17th-century church with a turreted bell tower. Inside, there are Flamboyant arches and, at the transept crossing, painted panelling dating from 1712. The artist who sculpted the polychrome figures of the altarpiece at the high altar clearly had a joyous and naïve talent.

A *sentier des douaniers* (customs officers' path) makes it possible to do a tour of the peninsula on foot.

USEFUL ADDRESS

🚹 **Office du tourisme**: by the harbour. ☎ 02-98-67-40-83. Fax: 02-98-79-32-50. From April to September, open Monday to Saturday 9am–12.30pm and 2–7pm, and Sunday 10.30am–12.30pm and 3–6pm; from October to March, open 10am–noon and 2–4pm, closed Wednesday, Saturday afternoon and Sunday.

WHERE TO STAY AND EAT

☎ **Camping municipal**: this municipal campsite is 1 kilometre from the town, on the road to Plestin-les-Grèves. ☎ 02-98-67-40-85. By the sea and not expensive.

☎ ✗ **Hôtel Les Sables-Blancs**: 15 rue des Sables-Blancs. ☎ 02-98-67-42-07. Fax: 02-98-79-33-25.

Well signposted from the D64. Closed Wednesday, Tuesday in mid-season only and from January to mid-March. Small hotel nestled in the sand dunes of the Plage des Sables-Blancs, looking out over the Baie de Lannion, in a wild and imposing setting. Double rooms from 220F to 250F (Nos. 1, 2, 3, 4 and 6 have a beautiful sea view). Friendly and welcoming. *Crêperie* and salad bar on the veranda, with a set menu for 60F: mussels in mead (*moules au chouchen*), or excellent chitterlings sausage crêpe (*crêpe super andouille*). Oyster tasting at any time.

☆☆☆☆ **Très Chic**

≜ ✕ **Le Grand Hôtel des Bains**: 15 *bis* rue de l'Église. ☎ 02-98-67-41-02. Fax: 02-98-67-44-60. E-mail: hotel.des.bains@wanadoo.fr. ✗ Open all year round. Luxury hotel-restaurant with 36 rooms, some with patio. This large building, one of the few seafront hotels in Finistère, has a magnificent formal French-style garden. The decor of the rooms is reminiscent of an early 20th-century seaside resort with wooden panelling, painted furniture and wicker chairs. Huge and pleasant bay windows fill the large, flower-filled sitting room with light. Double rooms from 550–1,000F depending on the season and whether or not they have a sea view. Half board for 700F. The restaurant offers set menus for 150F, 200F and 295F. Specialities include Breton lobster cooked in a *court-bouillon* of Sauternes flavoured with ginger and served with vegetables (*homard breton à la nage de sauternes parfumé au gingembre et ses petits légumes*), or seafood stew with prawn cream sauce (*ragoût de fruits de mer à la crème de langoustine*). Good choice of wines. Heated indoor pool, sauna and jacuzzi. A quality address for those who can afford it.

THE TRÉGOR REGION

WHERE TO EAT OR GO FOR A DRINK IN THE AREA

♟ **Caplan and Co**: Poul-Rodou, 29620 Guimaëc. 2 kilometres (1.5 miles) from Guimaëc heading for Plougasnou, at the third crossroads. ☎ 02-98-67-58-98. Fax: 02-98-67-65-49. Open every day in summer from noon until midnight. Open in winter on Saturday 3–9pm and on Sunday noon–9pm. Set menu for 58F. Buffeted by the wind and drenched by the sea spray, the Caplan stands at the end of the road as if defying the elements. Those who push open the door to shelter from the storm are seduced by a warm and friendly atmosphere. This combination of café and bookshop is virtually unique in France, and a wonderfully successful alliance, with soul. The rows of books have been carefully chosen by the owners, who both used to work for publishing houses. The range is very varied. This remarkable place also offers one substantial Greek dish served with Greek wine each day.

FESTIVAL

– **Pardon de St-Jacques et Fête de la Mer** (St-Jacques *pardon* and festival of the sea): last Sunday in July.

WHAT TO SEE IN THE AREA

★ **Le domaine de Kervéguen** (cider factory): 29620 Guimaëc. ☎ 02-98-67-50-02. Fax: 02-98-67-58-95. 9 kilometres (5.5 miles) to the northwest of Locquirec on the D64. Open every day except Sunday in July and August 10.30am–6.30pm; in April, May, June and September and during the school holidays, open every day except Sunday 2.30–6.30pm; from October to March except for school holidays, open every Saturday 2.30–6pm or by appointment. Free cellar visit and wine tasting in an old-fashioned cider factory where the product is aged in oak barrels. Located in a former 15th-century farm building. Beside it is a beautiful dovecote as well as an authentic cowshed still equipped with the large shale slabs that separated the animals. The estate is the supplier of cider to the French government.

PLOUGONVEN
(PLOUGONVEN) 29640   (Pop: 3,164)

This village about 10 kilometres (6 miles) southeast of Morlaix on the D9 possesses a remarkable **parish close**, paradoxically one of the least well known. The church is in the Flamboyant style with galleried belfry and turret, with particularly interesting gargoyles representing grotesque, sniggering figures. The very impressive **calvary**, on an octagonal base, is reputed to be the second-oldest in Brittany (1554). On the first level are all the classic scenes from the life of Christ before the Crucifixion. On the second, the Scourging, the Crown of Thorns, and so on. Apart from Christ and the Virgin, all the other characters are wearing middle-class or peasants' clothing of the 16th century; one of the guards is even armed with an ancient gun. The **ossuary** has beautiful windows with trefoil arcades. In the interior of the church are three naves with barrel vaulting, and a panelled ceiling. The carved oak lectern on the left dates from 1673. The interesting statues include St Yves, St Barbe, a large Christ with the Virgin and Mary Magdalene, and the polychrome *pietà* is very primitively carved.

WHERE TO STAY AND EAT IN THE AREA

♠ ✕ **La Grange de Coatélan**: Kersahet, 29640 Plougonven. This *crêperie*-inn is on a farm 5 kilometres (3 miles) northwest of Plougonven and well signposted off the D109. ☎ and fax: 02-98-72-60-16. ✗ Reservation only. Three lovely guest rooms are available, including one in a barn. Closed at Christmas and for the first two weeks in January. Food every evening except Wednesday. A beautiful 16th-century weaver's house renovated with style and originality, with sumptuous double rooms from 250F to 350F including breakfast. The food includes meat grilled over the open fire, traditional dishes prepared from farm produce and homemade desserts; à la carte for about 125F. The

owner exhibits his own paintings on the walls of the dining room (which fills up rapidly, with only six tables). Very welcoming. No credit cards.

♠ **Chambres d'hôte: Cécile and Alain Travel-Chaumet**: Trovoas, 29640 Plougonven. 8 kilometres (5 miles) to the northwest of Plougonven on the D9. About 4 kilometres (2.5 miles) before you reach Morlaix, look out for a little signpost on the left. ☎ 02-98-88-15-84. A double room costs from 270F to 300F including breakfast, with an 80F supplement for a third person. Out in the countryside in a quiet little hamlet, this 19th-century house with a steeply sloping roof has a marvellous, slightly eccentric garden with a babbling brook, making it a really lovely spot. The guest room, which is in a separate building, has a large bay window that looks out over open country, so it almost feels like sleeping out of doors. All the decor, including the bathroom, is turn-of-the-century, giving a strong period feel. Also a *gîte* that sleeps four people in two rooms (one has a box bed); it also has a kitchen. This can be hired by the night out of season. The owners are very laid-back and have plenty of useful information to offer about restaurants and decent walks in the area.

â **Camping municipal de Kervoazou**: for information on this campsite ☎ 02-98-78-64-04.

WHAT TO DO

– The 'Jarlot', a **walking or cycle route**, passes close to Plougonven. Quite a novelty, it is the former railway line from Morlaix to Carhaix, cleverly transformed into a path.

– **Bicycle hire:** try **Espaces verts et bleus** at Kerdavid (in the direction of St-Eutrope), 29640 Plougonven. ☎ 02-98-78-65-85.

GUERLESQUIN
(*GWERLISKIN*) 29650   (Pop: 1,650)

In the rural district of the Armorican regional nature park lies the large village of Guerlesquin, off the beaten track but well worth a detour. Situated 24 kilometres (15 miles) from Morlaix and about 10 kilometres (6 miles) from Plougonven, it presents exceptional architectural harmony and gives an accurate idea of what a Breton village would have looked like in the past. It is basically arranged around a very wide street, lined by houses full of character. In the middle, various public buildings fit harmoniously into the architectural logic. The place du Martray, the large park, the old covered market, and then the *présidial*, a curious square building from the 17th century adorned with elegant cornerstone turrets, which formerly served as a prison, all stretch away into the distance past the church. In front of the *présidial* stands the wheat measure from 1539 known as *Men Gaou* or 'lying stone'. The grain market here was controlled by the feudal lord.

The **Église St-Ténénan** dates from the 16th century. It was rebuilt in the 19th century but the original tower and a large part of the facade survived. It has a pretty belfry with a balustrade in the Flamboyant style, 'rosette' pinnacles and spire. There is a turret on the side, as well as beautiful gargoyles.

Another characteristic of the region is that it depends economically, and in an almost exclusive way, on the Tilly abattoirs. For many of the families who live here, the abattoirs offer the only opportunities for work. Each day, several hundred thousand chickens meet their end here: 55 per cent of the production is exported to the Middle East, 30 per cent within Europe and the rest to the French overseas departments and territories.

USEFUL ADDRESSES

El Syndicat d'initiative (tourist information office): in the place du Martray (opposite the church). ☎ 02-98-72-84-20. Open July and August, 9.30am–12.30pm and 2–7pm (Sunday 10am–12.30pm and 2–4.30pm).

■ **Mairie** (town hall): ☎ 02-98-72-81-79.

WHERE TO STAY AND EAT OR GO FOR A DRINK

⚑ ✕ **Hôtel des Monts d'Arrée**: 14 rue du Docteur-Quéré. ☎ 02-98-72-80-44 and 64. Fax: 02-98-72-81-50. Closed Sunday evening, public holidays and for two weeks at Christmas. A beautiful granite house in the main street. The hotel has almost all been renovated and double rooms are offered from 255F to 285F. Good restaurant, popular with the locals, with set menus for 60F (weekdays) up to 155F. You can book your evening meal by paying half board (255F per person).

⚑ ✕ **Gîte d'étape Hent Melin Cove** (walkers' stopover): 50 metres from the post office, turn left (into a courtyard). ☎ 02-98-72-80-58. Offers 15 places. Closed Monday afternoon and the first two weeks in September. Expect to pay 45F per night. Meals available.

✕ **Crêperie du Martray**: in the place de l'Église. ☎ 02-98-72-83-21. Closed Tuesday and Sunday lunchtime except during school holidays. Allow 80F to eat à la carte. Dining room with Breton decor (exposed stone walls and a fireplace). Arrive early, as the dining room fills up rapidly. Delicious *crêpes*, with a good choice: *complète bacon* (bacon, cheese and a fried egg), *M. Seguin* (warm goat's cheese, bacon, lettuce), *guerlesquinaise* (egg, ham, cheese, mushrooms).

♀ Bar an Toll-toul: opposite the *présidial*. ☎ 02-98-72-81-96. Closed Tuesday and the first three weeks of September. Very friendly Breton café, with a warm welcome; a favourite with young locals.

WHERE TO STAY AND EAT IN THE AREA

⚑ **Chambres à la ferme** (rooms in a farm): in Kerviniou, 29610 Plouigneau. ☎ 02-98-79-20-58. Open all year round. Signposted from the turn-off on the motorway from St-Brieuc to Morlaix. Located 12 kilometres (7.5 miles) from Morlaix. One room with toilet for 200F and two other rooms with shared bathroom and toilet for 220F, all with a generous breakfast included.

✕ **Ferme-auberge de Pen an Neac'h** (farm-inn): Pen an Neac'h, 29650 Plouégat-Moysan. Located 6 kilometres (4 miles) north of Guer-lesquin, in the direction of Le Ponthou. ☎ 02-98-79-20-15. Fax: 02-98-79-22-73. ⅃ In high season, open every day except Tuesday; open weekends only in low season. Always reserve in advance. Excellent sweet and savoury *crêpes* (especially the *super charolaise extra*, with minced beef, paprika, onions, tomatoes, egg, cheese and fresh cream), *côte de boeuf* for two, Breton salads. Set menus for 70F, 85F and 125F. Delicious beef stew (*pot-au-feu*) for 80F (book the previous evening for a minimum of six people). *Kig ha farz* (traditional bacon flan) on Friday and Saturday lunchtime and *bara kig* (breaded pork) on Sunday evening. Exhibition of regional products.

WHAT TO SEE

★ **Musée des Machines Agricoles Miniatures**: place du Présidial. ☎ 02-98-72-84-20. Open every day in July and August; out of season open on request – ask at the town hall (☎ 02-98-72-81-79). Admission is free. Remarkable exhibition of the work of a local artist who made working miniatures of farm machines.

WHAT TO DO

– **Footpaths**: walks to the Kerellou menhir (12 kilometres/7.5 miles) and the pond at Le Guic (13 kilometres/8 miles). Details at the *syndicat d'initiative* (tourist information office): ☎ 02-98-72-84-20; or at the town hall: ☎ 02-98-72-81-79.

IN THE AREA

★ **Le plan d'eau du Guic**: lake open in July and August, 9am–noon and 1.30–7pm. Sailing, windsurfing, boardsailing, canoeing. Information: ☎ 02-98-72-85-21; out of season: ☎ 02-98-72-81-79.

â **Camping municipal**: a stone's throw from the lake, this municipal campsite is cheap and well equipped. Open only in July and August. Details during July and August from the Bar du Guic: ☎ 02-98-72-88-94; outside these dates: ☎ 02-98-72-81-79 (town hall). Fax: 02-98-72-90-64.

The Monts d'Arrée

Covering most of the Parc naturel régional d'Armorique (Armorican regional nature park), the area around the Monts d'Arrée is a Brittany that remains off the beaten track and almost untouched. For a long time it was a land of witchcraft. When the soul of the deceased refused to leave a house, a priest was summoned to perform a certain ritual. The spirit was apparently exorcized by being made to enter the body of a black dog, which was then hastily drowned. These Breton 'mountain people' have clung to their traditions, and they still dance *hander-dro* or gavottes to the sound of the *biniou-koz* (bagpipes) and the diatonic accordion.

The word 'mountains' may be something of an exaggeration – the highest point is 334 metres (1,085 feet) – but, without being steep, the contours are genuine and the hills offer beautiful panoramas. In this land of contrasts, green fields alternate with areas of gorse and heather, and *menez* (sandstone hillocks worn down by erosion) with *roc'h* (bare summits covered with jagged rocks of schist).

This is a mysterious region, full of interest. With poor soil and a harsh climate, it is very sparsely populated, with barely 40 people per square kilometre. It

THE MONTS D'ARRÉE

could truly be described as 'wild', and is able to support some rare wildlife –
10 beavers introduced to the banks of the River Ellez in 1968 have happily
proliferated here, undisturbed.

The Parc Naturel Regional D'Armorique (Armorican Regional Nature Park)

Created in November 1969, the Armorican regional nature park covers 39
communes (rural districts), and 172,000 hectares (430,000 square miles) of
central Finistère, with a population of 56,000. Around the park, there are a
number of museums and other exhibits that will tell you whatever you might
want to know about the local agrarian economy and the traditions of the
area. Shared accommodation is available in Commana, Le Mougau, St-Éloy
and Bannalec.

Information is available at the **Maison du Parc**: 15 place aux Foires, BP 27,
29590 Le Faou. ☎ 02-98-81-90-08. Fax: 02-98-81-90-09.

LE CLOÎTRE-ST-THÉGONNEC
(AR C'HLOASTR-PLOURIN) 29410   (Pop: 581)

This village, about 12 kilometres (7.5 miles) from Morlaix, is laid out around two small squares. Its very plain 17th-century church has a font carved from a menhir.

WHERE TO STAY

⌂ **Camping des Bruyères**: in Kergollot. Less than 1 kilometre west of Cloître-St-Thégonnec. ☎ 02-98-79-71-76. Open in July and August. Basic in terms of comfort but a magnificent situation and run by a charming British lady.

WHAT TO SEE

★ **Musée du Loup** (museum of the wolf): in the village. ☎ 02-98-79-70-36. Open every day in July and August, and Sunday until mid-December, afternoons only 2–6pm. Admission charge. Unique in France, this museum aims to make finding out about wolves, both legendary and real, an enjoyable experience. Part of the experience takes you into an amazing cave and a fireplace to sit round while listening to tales and legends. There is also a panorama of the surrounding Monts d'Arrée. Equally suitable for adults and children, the museum also has a superb herbarium devoted to the plants found in Brittany.

WHAT TO DO

– The Société d'Étude et Protection de la Nature en Bretagne (SEPNB) (society for the study and protection of nature in Brittany) organizes guided tours of the **Réserve Biologique du Cragou** (Le Cragou nature reserve). Information at the museum. The society is conducting an experiment in the management of moorland which supports a unique fauna. Dartmoor ponies occupy a huge enclosure covering 60 hectares (150 acres).

WHAT TO SEE IN THE AREA

★ **Abbaye du Relecq**: 5 kilometres (3 miles) southwest of Cloître-St-Thégonnec on the D111. The only remains of the Cistercian abbey built in the 12th century are an austere Romanesque church (currently being renovated), a large fountain and a few ruins. Guided tours are available from May to September on Sunday at 4pm, or by reservation during the rest of the year. A major *pardon* takes place here each year on 15 August. Concerts and exhibitions are held here on Sunday between May and September (information from ☎ 02-98-78-05-97; website: www.abbayedurelecq.com). A choral music festival takes place here every September.

THE MONTS D'ARRÉE

– The three-hour *Circuit du Relecq* (12 kilometres/7.5 miles) is a nice walk. Leave from the Abbaye du Relecq, and follow the partial marking of a variant of the GR380 footpath through charming little villages, past calvaries, and along a Roman road.

SCRIGNAC (*SKRIGNEG*) 29640　　　(Pop: 906)

This village is in the foothills of the Monts d'Arrée, as it rises on a little hill to a height of 210m (682ft). A pretty road goes to Scrignac from Guerlesquin, another village in the regional park, which is surrounded by beautiful countryside. Several kilometres to the west are the **moors** and the **rocks of Le Cragou**, an interesting destination for walkers. The area is sparsely populated, but extremely rich in fauna. You can go back up towards Plougonven via the **Jarlot**, a pleasant footpath that passes 2km (1.5 miles) north of Scrignac.

USEFUL ADDRESS

■ To find out what is happening in the area, ask at the **town hall**. ☎ 02-98-78-20-15.

WHERE TO STAY AND EAT OR GO FOR A DRINK

🛏 ✕ **Hôtel-restaurant Le Sénéchal**: in the main square. ☎ 02-98-78-23-13. Closed Sunday evening out of season, and from 20 January to 20 February. Simple rooms with washbasin, plain and clean, for 160F. Nice choice of set menus from 79F (weekdays) to 210F. You can eat well with even the cheapest lunchtime menu, but this place serves an excellent cuisine and it may be worth spending a little more to get the full benefit. Specialities include snail stew in red wine from the Touraine region (*ragoût d'escargots au bourgueil*), monkfish with oyster mushrooms (*gigot de lotte aux pleurotes*), skate in seaweed (*raie aux algues*). If you are in the area in the autumn, call in for their game menu.

🛏 **Camping municipal**: ☎ 02-98-78-20-15 (town hall). This campsite is open all year round and has a tennis court next door.

WHAT TO SEE

★ **Maison de la Faune Sauvage et de la Chasse** (wildlife and hunting museum): ☎ 02-98-78-25-00. Open from 15 May to 30 September, 10am–noon and 2–6pm. Closed Tuesday. Admission charge (15F). The museum is in the former train station in Scrignac-Berrien. Small exhibition, nicely done, with videos and more than 50 stuffed animals – foxes, snipe, sparrowhawks, and so on.

WHAT TO SEE IN THE AREA

★ **Berrien**: about 10 kilometres (6 miles) to the southwest of Scrignac, this village on the Huelgoat to Morlaix road (the D769) is the capital of Breton wrestling (*gouren*) in Finistère. Surrounded by wild and pretty protected countryside, of undulating hills, moors and small fields interspersed with copses. A little piece of the true Brittany, Berrien should, in theory, be popular with feminists and agnostics. A long time ago, the women of the village furiously resisted the brainwashing of the Christian missionaries. They were regularly greeted with stone-throwing, and their teachings were blamed for causing a loss of libido among the village men.

Interesting **church** from the 15th and 16th centuries, with a Renaissance porch. Numerous megalithic remains and tumuli all around the village. **Annual festival** during the first weekend in July. Tourist information from the town hall: ☎ 02-98-99-01-14.

HUELGOAT (*AN UHELGOAD*) 29690 (Pop: 1,707)

A combination of forest and piles of rocks, and an almost unique vegetation, this area is an integral part of the Armorican regional nature park, and a marvellous place for walking. Numerous paths criss-cross the forest, which always seems to be bathed in a golden light.

The existence of these curious piles of boulders is, inevitably, explained away by local legend. The story goes that, a long time ago, the inhabitants of Plouyé and Berrien hated each other so much that they continually threw stones at one another. As their hatred increased, so did the pile of stones, which inevitably fell in the middle, on Huelgoat. In truth, the scenery owes its appearance to the differential erosion of the rocks, subjected first of all to a tropical climate and then to a partial Ice Age. After that, the rotten and crumbling materials were, quite simply, washed away.

USEFUL ADDRESS

🄳 **Office du tourisme**: place de la Mairie. ☎ 02-98-99-72-32 or 02-98-99-71-55 (town hall). In July and August, open every day: 9am–noon and 2–5.30pm; the rest of the year, open Monday to Saturday 11am–noon and 2–4pm.

WHERE TO STAY AND EAT

🛏 ✕ **Hôtel-restaurant du Lac**: 9 rue du Général-de-Gaulle. ☎ 02-98-99-71-14. Fax: 02-98-99-70-91. Closed from November to mid-January. The hotel benefits from being in a central location and it's the only hotel in town, which may mean that it rather trades on its position. The rooms are comfortable enough, and most look out over the lake. Still, the place lacks a personal touch. Double rooms cost 280–320F. In the restaurant, the dining room has wood panelling and a crackling fire. Grilled food is on offer, although it's nothing special. Set menus from 75F (weekday lunchtime) up to 140F.

THE MONTS D'ARRÉE

⌂ **Camping municipal du Lac**: 700 metres from the centre. ☎ 02-98-99-78-80. Fax: 02-98-99-75-72. Open 15 June to 15 September. Very well situated. All mod cons. Swimming pool; tennis court. Costs around 60F for a pitch for two people.

⌂ **Camping la Rivière d'Argent** at La Coudraie. ☎ 02-98-99-72-50. Fax: 02-98-99-90-61. Located on a riverbank at the edge of the national forest of Huelgoat. Family campsite at a meeting point of two of the *grande randonnée* footpaths, the GR37 from Guerlédan to Douarnenez and the GR380 from Plouegat-Moysan to Douarnenez. There are 80 sites (60F per site). Impeccably clean. Swimming pool; tennis court.

✕ **Crêperie de l'Argoat**: 12 rue du Lac. ☎ 02-98-99-71-72. ♿ Closed on Tuesday and in January. Allow 60F to eat à la carte. The *crêpes* here are delicious and not at all expensive. What's more, there's a very warm welcome, and they stay open late into the evening. The little terrace looks right out onto the lake.

✕ **Crêperie des Myrtilles**: 26 place Aristide-Briand, on the main square. ☎ 02-98-99-72-66. Closed Monday out of season, as well as November to December. Very good sweet or savoury *crêpes*. Set menus from 52 to 92F. You can eat outside on sunny days.

WHERE TO STAY AND EAT IN THE AREA

⌂ ✕ **Chambres d'hôte les Tilleuls**: Goasvennou, 29246 Poullaouën. ☎ 02-98-93-57-63 or 02-98-93-53-88. Take the D769 towards Poullaouën-Carhaix, then continue for 1 kilometre along the D114 towards Bolazec. Follow signs for ULM then look for '*chambres d'hôte*' signs. A double room costs 250F including breakfast and table d'hôte meals are available for 80F. This pretty little house is tucked away in the middle of nowhere, so peace and quiet are guaranteed. It has a large, flower-filled garden with a pond, and the family offer four attractive rooms, each individually decorated. Warm welcome.

WHERE TO GO FOR A DRINK

♟ **Ty Élise**: at Plouyé. ☎ 02-98-99-96-44. In high season, open Monday–Friday 2pm–midnight (open at noon at the weekend and until 1am from June to September); out of season, closed Monday and Tuesday. In a lovely little village 7 kilometres (4.5 miles) from St-Herbot and Huelgoat, in the middle of nowhere, you will find one of the best watering holes in the whole of Brittany. The owner Bryn, a colourful and talkative Welshman, gives the place an engaging quality. The decor and surroundings have changed little since the revolt of the *Bonnets Rouges*: big traditional fireplace, wooden bar top that's big enough to sit on, and old beer pumps with Kriek, Coreff and Guinness, which is pulled perfectly for customers.

WHAT TO SEE

★ **Moulin du Chaos**: rue des Cendres. ☎ 02-98-99-77-83. Same opening hours as the tourist office. Owned by the Armorican regional nature park, this converted windmill is the place to find out about the region, with exhibits on archaeology, geology, fauna and flora.

★ **Jardin de l'Argoat:** impasse des Fontaines. ☎ 02-98-99-71-63. Open daily 10am–6pm from June to September; closes 5pm October to May. Admission charge (20F for the garden only and 40F for the garden and the arboretum). Curiously, it's possible to walk around here without paying, if you come outside opening hours. A small and very pleasant garden originally put together for the occupants of the nearby retirement home and now open to the public. Some of the vegetation has a tropical feel and more than a thousand different plant species can be seen here. Guided tours are offered.

– The tourist information office has a useful little brochure giving details of **walks** in the region, including times and distances. Make good use of it, but do ask for advice first, as certain trails are no longer very interesting because of re-afforestation taking place.

First of all, approach the **Chaos du Moulin**, a huge pile of rocks, followed by the **Grotte du Diable** (Devil's Grotto), and then an open-air grassy theatre. From here, turn left towards the river to reach the **Roche Tremblante**. This rock, weighing some 100 tons, moves if it is pushed in a certain place. The **Ménage de la Vierge** (Virgin's Kitchen), a picturesque mass of rocks, comes next. Then the Chemin Violette path follows the left bank of the River Argent and leads to the road to Carhaix.

The whole walking tour of the forest lasts about three hours. Along the way, you can see the **Saut du Gouffre** (a quite spectacular waterfall on the River Argent), the **Promenade du Fer à Cheval** (horseshoe walk), the **Mare aux Sangliers** (boars' pool), the **Grotte d'Artus** (a cave where King Arthur is said to have slept), and the **Camp d'Artus** (the largest Gallic area of fortification in the region). Off the path leading to the **Roche Tremblante**, you can go and visit an apiary and sample the honey. ☎ 02-98-99-94-36.

WHAT TO DO IN THE AREA

★ **Kerguévarec:** on the C2 heading for Plouyé. Small group of farms that are more than 200 years old, with ancient wells.

★ **Locmaria-Berrien**: sleepy little village in an undulating landscape just off the D769 in the direction of Carhaix. Of the many characterful houses, some are closed up or in ruins, testifying to the population exodus from the region. Lovely **church** with a very low roof and an amazing blue ceiling strewn with gilded stars. In front, there are huge trees with split trunks.

– **Roulottes de Bretagne** (Breton horse-drawn caravans): ☎ 02-98-99-73-28. From April to mid-October, trips by horse-drawn caravan, carriage or stagecoach, for a weekend, five days, a week or longer. Explore the banks of the River Aulne using the towpath, or the Monts d'Arrée by following the old railway line. Point of departure is the old station in Locmaria-Berrien, 6 kilometres (4 miles) from Huelgoat. Saddle horses can be rented as well.

★ **Poullaouen**: on the beautiful tourist route from Huelgoat to Carhaix (the D769), another village typical of the Argoat region. Well known for having the largest silver-bearing lead mines in France until the early 20th century, and also famous for excellent traditional *fest-noz* dancers and singers. The four Goadec Sisters, old ladies who were very popular singers during the 1970s, came from here. At the top of the village is a beautiful Renaissance church,

THE MONTS D'ARRÉE

which has a quite original facade, with large, elegant stone scrolls on the sides. There are superposed columns and a pretty balustrade above the porch. A microlight centre is also based here (☎ 02-98-93-51-19).

ST-HERBOT 29530

In the Middle Ages, they didn't just dream about building; they went ahead and did it. St-Herbot is one result of such activity – a mini-cathedral right out in the middle of the countryside.

Built between the 14th and 16th centuries, in the Flamboyant Gothic style, in a wild setting 6 kilometres (4 miles) from Huelgoat, this 'chapel' is one of the architectural gems of Finistère, and not to be missed. You are struck first of all by the huge tower 30 metres (97 feet) high, inspired by the one in Quimper. Here, very wide openings give the tower a certain grace and levity. Right at the top, there is a Flamboyant balustrade. At its base, the entry porch is a real marvel. The large Gothic arch has delicately sculpted foliage and a double basket-handle door separated by a cabled column. Above, the **statue of St Herbot** is framed by two angels. On the road side is an elegant horseshoe staircase. The part facing the calvary also possesses a beautiful accolade porch with delicate sculptures. Inside, on either side, stand the classic Apostles in serried ranks.

The **calvary** was constructed in 1571, with figures sculpted in Kersanton granite. The group, which is quite compact, comprises numerous original features. Look at the faces of Christ and the thieves, with their heavy eyelids and rather puffed-up features. The approach is surprisingly modern, and uses an artistic licence bordering on caricature that is unique in Cornouaille.

Inside the church, there are magnificent furnishings, including a 16th-century **chancel** in carved wood under a large crucifix, and 15 finely carved **stalls** from the same period, surmounted by a canopy with evangelists and prophets.

Note the polychrome *pietà*, where Christ appears tiny in the Virgin's arms – simply a tearful mother holding her child in her arms? In the month of May, the farmers used to come here to place a pat of butter on one of the two stone tables, and on the other some hair from the tails of their cows, in honour of St Herbot (patron saint of horned cattle). In the chevet, a large 16th-century **stained-glass window** depicting the Passion contains remarkable colours.

IN THE AREA

★ **Loqueffret** (29530): almost 3 kilometres (2 miles) southwest of St-Herbot on the D14. The 16th-century **church** has a very low roof. The **calvary** was erected in 1576, although the thieves have now disappeared. Accolade windows and interesting gargoyles. Visit the **Maison du Recteur** in the former presbytery. Open in July and August Tuesday to Sunday, 10am–noon and 2–6pm. Information: ☎ 02-98-26-44-50. Here you will find retraced the history of the *pilhaouerien*, rag-and-bone men from the Monts d'Arrée, poor itinerant peasants who collected rags, bits of metal and rabbit skins. Lots of popular songs tell of their exploits; these were intended to frighten children into behaving themselves.

★ **Lannédern** (29190): village is 3.5 kilometres (2.5 miles) southwest of Loqueffret on the D14. A virtually complete **parish close** with cemetery, ossuary, calvary and church. Between the last two, the Menez Sant-Mikael can be seen in the distance. On the facade of the ossuary is a skull and crossbones. *Ankou* (Death) is to be seen in the window to the left of the church porch, with a sardonic smile, hollow eye sockets and an arrow. On the calvary, St Edern is riding a stag. In the church, a beautiful large stained-glass window illustrates the Passion (with, on the left, St Edern again on a stag). Finally, there is a baroque altarpiece. Recumbent statue of St Edern. In the nave, on the left, six bas-reliefs recount his life.

Around Le Yeun Elez

The Yeun Elez is a wide bowl hollowed out of the central Monts d'Arrée. The River Elez has its source on the hillside at St-Michel-de-Brasparts (although some say it's at Rivoal) and spreads out in the enormous tract of peat marsh that has become a feeder lake for the local power station. The whole place has an awesome feel, sometimes even rather mournful, if you happen to be there when it is hung with a ghostly mist. Local legend has it that this is the gateway to Hell – at any rate, it's a desolate landscape with very few trees – the film *Planet of the Apes* was filmed here. However, if you take a stroll through the marshland and the bogs, there's every chance of seeing birds in their flocks: teals and divers, kingfishers and curlews.

This savagely beautiful place is criss-crossed with more than 100 kilometres (60 miles) of marked paths, which make it more easily accessible. Still, don't venture in without waterproof shoes. Perhaps the best is the *Circuit du Yeun* (16 kilometres/10 miles) or the *landes et tourbières* (marsh and peat bogs) path (14 kilometres/8.5 miles). Try to get a copy of the park's own leaflet *Circuits de petite randonnée autour du Yeun Elez*, which is very useful.

THE MONTS D'ARRÉE

BRASPARTS (*BRASPARZH*) 29190 (Pop: 1,039)

According to an old Breton saying, *Tri dra zo dic'hallus da Zoue: Kompezan Brasparz!* ('Three things are impossible for God to achieve, and the first is to flatten Brasparts!').

This charming village, surrounded by wooded hills, peat bogs, cultivated land and rich pasture, and celebrated in poetry by Max Jacob, merits a visit at any time.

– **Market**: first Monday of every month.

USEFUL ADDRESS

🅱 **Office du tourisme**: ☎ 02-98-81-47-06. Open July–August, Monday to Saturday, 9am–noon and 3–7pm, and Sunday 9am–12.30pm. Open all year round.

WHERE TO STAY AND EAT

♠ In the village district, there are about ten **gîtes ruraux** and other holiday accommodation rooms for rent. They tend to be invaded in season, so book as early as possible. Between 1,500–2,000F per week in July and August (900F in low season). For details, contact the tourist information office or the town hall.

♠ **Chambres d'hôte: Le Village de Garz ar Bik**. ☎ 02-98-81-47-14. Half a kilometre to the north of the village on the D785. Open all year round. A superb set-up, with three luxury *gîtes* that sleep up to six people (1,000–2,600F), and two guest rooms, and a great deal of character. A lover of old pieces of furniture, the owner has decorated the rooms delightfully, down to the last detail. CDs and a CD player, walking maps and a kitchen are at the disposal of customers staying in the guest rooms. Expect to pay 260F for two people, including a generous breakfast. The owner is also passionate about her local area. She knows the Monts d'Arrée like the back of her hand and has a great talent for recounting local tales. There is a small stream below, and a large courtyard in the middle. No restaurant but the owner will point you in the direction of some quality establishments.

♠ **Chambres d'hôte: Romy Chaussy**: domaine de Rugornou Vras. ☎ 02-98-81-46-27. Fax: 02-98-81-47-99. Two kilometres (1.5 miles) outside the village to the north, on the D785. Open all year round. A double room costs 260F including breakfast and table d'hôte meals cost 90F with drinks thrown in. Right out in the countryside, this establishment is an old farm brought back to useful life by an energetic young woman (daughter of Marie-Christine Chaussy at the previous establishment, so it's obviously in the blood). The before-and-after photographs prove just how much work has been done to turn this into the charming place that it has become. It offers four rooms separate from the main house in what was the stable block, and they come with all mod cons yet a lovely country feel, with exposed beams and plenty of ancient furniture. Breakfast is served downstairs, in a comfortable big room with stone walls and on the menu are Breton dishes, made with farm produce, much of it organic.

WHAT TO SEE AND DO

★ The **parish close** offers some interesting and sometimes original elements. It looks out over the valley which, in the evening, when the relief of the countryside is no longer diminished by the bright light of day, reveals some quite astonishing shades of green.

The **calvary**, erected at the beginning of the 16th century, deserves to be studied in some detail. Angels collect the blood of Christ, in a probable reference to the Holy Grail, the famous receptacle of Celtic legend. The thief, who has survived the ravages of time, is literally bent backwards on the cross. Above, St Michael is slaying the dragon. Most remarkable of all is the *pietà*, which is a masterpiece: three women standing (quite a rare position), their faces hard and impassive, staring into the void. The undulating folds in the garments, and the rhythm of the legs and fingers of Christ, contrast strongly with the stiffness of the figures.

The **church** also has a remarkable porch with three turrets and diagonal buttresses plus the 12 Apostles. Inside, are a beautiful altarpiece and some wooden statues, for example the Notre-Dame-de-la-Pitié, which is notable for its great dignity and the beauty of its costume. To the left of the choir is a 16th-century window. Note as well a strange sculpture: a horned creature with a woman's breasts and serpent's tail. Some people believe it is Morgane, the legendary goddess of water.

The **ossuary**, in the Flamboyant style, possesses, for its part, two representations of *Ankou*, both threatening, one with a scythe and the other with an arrow.

– **Centre culturel des Monts d'Arrée**: 22 rue St-Michel. ☎ 02-98-81-49-43. Open all year round 3–7pm; closed Monday and Tuesday. This cultural centre has a bookshop run by artists specializing in all things Celtic, Druid and, of course, Breton. Permanent exhibition of local artists' work.

– **Cahin-Cahâne**: Tromarc'h, 29190 Brasparts. ☎ 02-98-81-47-45. Open all year round; booking required. Self-guided, well-planned walking tours with a mule and saddlebags. This brave and docile companion, which will carry children and baggage, can be rented for a whole day or longer.

FESTIVALS

– **Fête du village**: 15 August, lasting for three days.

– **Grand rassemblement druidique** (gathering of druids): on the third Sunday in July. Details from the cultural centre. ☎ 02-98-81-49-43.

IN THE AREA

★ **Site Archéologique Ti Ar Boudiged** (archaeological site): follow the signs to 'Sépulture en V (dolmen)'. This megalithic dolmen dating from 3000 BC is partly buried under a tumulus and covered by three stone slabs. One of them weighs more then 30 tons.

★ **Mont St-Michel** (*Menez Sant-Mikael*): reached via the D785, the Mont St-Michel is one of the highest points of the Monts d'Arrée, at 380 metres (1,250 feet). The view from the top is stupendous, and on a clear day you can see all the way to the clocher du Kreisker at St-Pol-de-Léon. Up there is a pretty little chapel, used until the end of the 19th century by shepherds seeking refuge from wolves.

ST-RIVOAL (*SANT-RIWAL*) 29190 (Pop: 170)

This pretty village is reached via delightful roads (the D42 and D30) that pass through undulating countryside. Arriving here at the end of a beautiful afternoon is a wonderful moment of peace and tranquillity. You have the impression that somewhere, time is standing still, caught and held in passing by the jagged schist. Along the way is St-Cadou, totally peaceful and almost deserted. Incidentally, legend has it that a girl from St-Cadou would never marry a boy from St-Rivoal!

WHERE TO EAT

✕ **Crêperie du Menez**: in front of the town hall. ☎ 02-98-81-45-63. Pretty Breton house. Good buckwheat and plain flour *crêpes*.

WHAT TO SEE

★ **Écomusée des Monts d'Arrée** (museum of rural culture): ☎ 02-98-68-87-76 or 02-98-81-40-99 (in season). Moulins de Kerouat open mid-March to end May and in September 10am–6pm (Sunday 2–6pm). Closed Saturday. In June, open 10am–6pm every day; in July and August, open 11am–7pm every day. The Maison Cornec is open in June 2–6pm, 11am–7pm in July and August and 2–6pm for the first two weeks in September (closed Saturday). Admission charge (27F for adults, 14F for children for the windmills and 18F for adults; 12F for children for Maison Cornec). This folk museum has been installed in the Maison Cornec, an 18th-century country house with an authentic beaten-earth floor. It has a stone staircase and an *apoteiz*, the protruding wing so characteristic of buildings in the Monts d'Arrée. The living conditions of an 18th-century peasant have been recreated here, and there is plenty of original furniture, arranged as it would have been, as well as a bread oven and a cowshed. Fifteen separate buildings make up the Village des Moulins, which grew up in the 17th century.

★ Scenic **viewpoints** from three summits, with nice walks up to them: the **Pen-ar-Favot** (over the Vallée de Nivot), the **Pen-ar-Guer** (over the Vallée des Moulins) and the **Montagne St-Michel**. Local tourist brochures are most indignant that the latter is attributed to a neighbouring village, Brasparts, when it is actually in their area.

WHAT TO DO IN THE AREA

★ **Parc Animalier de Menez-Meur** (wildlife park): ☎ 02-98-68-81-71. From June to August, open every day 10am–7pm; in September open 10am–6pm, closed Saturday; the rest of the year, open Wednesday, Sunday and public holidays 10am–noon and 1–6pm. During the school holidays, open every day except Saturday, 10.30am–noon and 1–6pm. Closed in January. Admission charge (20F). This little park is part of the Armorican regional nature park; there are a number of walks allowing the opportunity to observe various wild animals, including mouflons, wild boar, stags, fallow deer and foxes. The **Maison du Cheval Breton** highlights the importance of the horse in traditional rural Breton society.

BOTMEUR (*BONEUR*) 29690 (Pop: 219)

A small village completely off the beaten track and well away from the tourist routes, on the pretty road to La Feuillée-St-Rivoal. Overlooking the myster-ious Marais du Yeun Elez (marshland), the source of so many legends. Beavers have been introduced into the local rivers, the Elez, the Roudouhir and the Roudoudour. Discovery trails organized by the SEPNB. ☎ 02-98-49-07-18. Fax: 02-98-49-95-80.

WHERE TO STAY

⌂ **Chambre d'hôte and gîtes with Marie-Thérèse Solliec**: Kreisker, 29690 Botmeur. ☎ and fax: 02-98-99-63-02. Email: msol@club-inter net.fr. Open all year round. Coming from Commana, go through Botmeur in the direction of La Feuillée and it's on the right (down an unpaved road). Traditional stone house, with one wood-panelled guest room, with pretty soft furnishings. Friendly welcome. Also to rent, two very well-equipped *gîtes* in authentic little Breton houses (2,200F per week in season). Large living area, two bedrooms, washing machine, dishwasher. Reasonably priced (250F per night for two people, including breakfast).

⌂ **Camping municipal**: the municipal campsite is open in July and August. ☎ 02-98-99-63-06.

WHAT TO SEE IN THE AREA

★ **La chaîne des Monts d'Arrée** (the Monts d'Arrée range): older even than the French Alps, the Monts d'Arrée range stretches out from Botmeur and Commana. The D785 runs through it in a straight line and provides a good place to stroll in this ancient and craggy environment. The **Roc'h Trévézel** at 370 metres (1,210 feet) high, is often hidden in winter, and even occasionally in summer, by fog and mists. When the weather is fine, the views from the top are marvellous. A bit further on, on the **Roc'h Trédudon** stands a television mast that was famously blown up in the 1970s by the Breton Liberation Front, an act that deprived the people of Brittany of any television for several months. Apparently this had the (temporary) effect of reviving local activities and bringing back a feeling of community spirit – which is food for thought.

LA FEUILLÉE (*AR FOUILHEZ*) 29690 (Pop: 617)

Another picturesque village in the Monts d'Arrée, one of the highest in Brittany. Formerly the site of one of the largest livestock fairs in Finistère, nowadays it is an ordinary little village with an austere charm. Remains of a Templar commandery. Good *festoù-noz* (festivals of traditional Breton dancing). Tourist information from the town hall: ☎ 02-98-99-61-52.

WHERE TO STAY

⌂ **Camping de Tal ar Hoat**: route de Kerbargain. ☎ 02-98-99-61-52 (town hall). Fax: 02-98-99-68-55. Email: mairielafeuillee@wanadoo.fr. A well shaded little campsite that is quiet and not expensive, at 35F per night for two people.

WHAT TO DO

– **Randonnées à la découverte des castors** (walking tours to observe beavers): these creatures were introduced into the River Elez in 1969 and leave visible traces with their dams. Taking one of these walking tours is a

THE MONTS D'ARRÉE

good way to see this part of the Argoat region. Walks start in Brennilis in front of the nature reserve lodge, every Thursday and Saturday in July and August at 3pm.

– **Randonnées à la découverte des chevreuils** (walking tours to observe deer): organized by the SEPNB. ☎ 02-98-79-71-98 or 02-98-49-07-18. Tours leave from the Abbaye du Relecq Thursday at 7.30pm, in July and August.

– **Walking tours** around the marshland at Le Cragou take place on Friday at 3pm, also organized by the SEPNB (same telephone number as above). Meet at the Musée du Loup at the Cloître St-Thégonnec.

IN THE AREA

★ **Trédudon**: only a couple of kilometres to the northeast of La Feuillée, on the southern slope of the Monts d'Arrée, this very pretty village with its typical rural architecture is hidden away among moors and fields. During World War II, Trédudon was the first village in France to resist the occupying forces. Unfortunately, the soil is not rich here, and the winters are long and harsh, and the village has emptied over the years. Time has stood still and the noble granite houses are slowly decaying. Only a few stubborn young farmers remain, and the old folk, who sit resignedly outside their front doors.

🛏 ✗ **La Ferme de Porz-Kloz**: Trédudon-Le-Moine, 29690 Berrien. ☎ 02-98-99-61-65. Fax: 02-98-99-67-36. Email: porz-kloz@libertysurf.fr. ♿ Open evenings only. Closed Tuesday and from December to March. Reservation obligatory. In a hamlet near Trédudon. An enterprising farming couple opened this farm-inn a few years ago in an attempt to breathe new life into the hamlet. Nine gorgeous rooms (including a very pleasant family attic room) are on offer for those who love peace and quiet and authentic surroundings. Rooms for two people with shower and toilet, from 260F to 400F. Telephone in every room. Breakfast is extra (40F). Delicious home cooking, which might include tomato mousse (*mousse de tomates*), goat's cheese with cumin in puff pastry (*chèvre au cumin en croûte*), lamb with leeks in cream sauce (*épaule d'agneau aux poireaux à la crème*), cheeses and lovely desserts. Evening meal for residents only. A friendly and genuine place to stay. The seventh night is free. One menu only for 120F. Half board from 270F to 340F. Bagpipe serenade at dawn – on request!

BRENNILIS (*BRENNILIZ*) 29690   (Pop: 471)

Known particularly for its nuclear power plant, which pioneered atomic power 30 years ago and is now permanently closed down because of non-profitability. It has been converted into a factory making ham and pâté. The village overlooks the Lac de Nestavel (also known as the Reservoir de St-Michel) and the Yeun Elez where, Celtic legend has it, the entrance to Hell is to be found. **Church** surmounted by a pretty openwork belfry. Inside, interesting polychrome panels on the main altar. **Calvary** with *pietà*, very sober but not devoid of feeling. For once, the figures radiate serenity and not pain.

WHERE TO STAY

â **Camping municipal de Nestavel**: at the Nestavel-Bras leisure park (*base de loisirs*). ☎ 02-98-99-66-57. Open from 15 June to 15 September. This municipal campsite was set up quite recently by the side of a lake. Absolutely charming. The best spaces, with a view of the lake, are normally reserved for caravans. But if you arrive late in the season, you may be able to put your tent up there. Little grocery shop for emergencies.

WHAT TO SEE

★ **Musée-expo Youdig** (or 'The Dream at the Gates of Hell'): in Kerveguenet. ☎ 02-98-99-62-36. Signposted from Brennilis. Open every day, all year round; telephone beforehand if possible. Admission charge (30F). In her husband's former mechanic's workshop, Annick Le Lann has reconstructed in minute detail a miniature village (50 square metres/540 square feet) typical of the Monts d'Arrée. *Youdig* is the diminutive of Yeun Elez. To retain the colours of the area, she collected thousands of little pieces of slate from the old slate quarries of Maël-Carhaix. The figures are made of wool and wire, and there are plenty of authentic details such as milestones and piles of manure (apparently a measure of wealth). Around the village is a remarkable collection of box beds, regional head-dresses, clothes from Quimper or Vannes and traditional tools. The tour is guided enthusiastically by Annik.

Annick's husband organizes dawn hikes across the moor; a unique way of discovering this desolate countryside with its yellowed grass.

â ✕ **Chambres d'hôte:** it is possible to get accommodation here and make your own meals: a *chambre d'hôte* costs 220F per night for two people, with breakfast extra (25F). You can eat at the **Auberge de Youdig**, which serves *crêpes* and various traditional Breton dishes including *kig ha farz* if you book ahead. Set menu for 75F. It's a bit touristy but not a bad place.

Tour of the enclos paroissiaux (parish closes)

The region between Landerneau and Morlaix, to the north of the Monts d'Arrée, has the highest concentration of architectural and sculptural masterpieces in Brittany. A journey around this area, from one parish close to the next, is fascinating.

WHAT ARE THE *ENCLOS*?

The *enclos paroissial* – or walled parish close – usually consists of a gateway or monumental arch and an outer wall, a calvary, a funeral chapel or ossuary, and a church. In spite of the variety of purpose of the buildings, the close presents a harmonious and almost theatrical whole.

The name of the gateway, *porz a Maro* ('gateway of Death'), the presence of the ossuary, and of the *Ankou*, the strange female character that symbolizes death and suffering who often adorns it in the form of a skeleton holding a scythe or a bow and arrow, might suggest that Brittany's former inhabitants

THE MONTS D'ARRÉE

possessed a profoundly morbid vision of their own existence. Far from it. In line with their Celtic heritage, they practised instead a kind of phantasmal co-existence with death.

The parish close is, above all, the place where the dead and the living come together. Here, death is not hidden, but accepted, in a relationship that is clearly imbued with the supernatural, and represented through allegory and poetry.

ORIGINS OF THE PARISH CLOSE

In the 16th and 17th centuries, Brittany had both wealth and religious fervour. These two elements were very much at the origin of the proliferation of the parish close. A prosperous maritime trade (in 1553, in Antwerp, the largest commercial port of the time, more than 800 of the 1,000 vessels registered were from Brittany), and the population's adaptation to the increased use of buckwheat (which grew well in poor soil), permitted the export of rye and wheat. However, the product that yielded the most profit in those days was linen, which was woven into cloth and exported in huge quantities to England (hence the growth of the port of Morlaix), Spain and Portugal. The weavers, who were both farmers and craftsmen, soon became a well-to-do section of society. Finally, there was also the production of paper, mainly for export (numerous paper mills in the Léon and Trégor regions).

The parishes, in addition to their revenue from farms and properties, benefited from this prosperity. After Mass, substantial gifts in kind (pieces of cloth, animals, and so on) would be given to the members of the church council (notables who were elected each year to manage the parish finances). Auctions were often held in front of the church immediately after Mass, and brought in a great deal of money. With the support of the faithful, the wealthy parishes began to construct their parish closes – an outward manifestation of wealth, dedicated to the glory of God.

Soon, towns and villages began to try to emulate or outdo each other in their building, and this rivalry became something of a phenomenon. Poor peasants took as much pride in possessing the finest church in the region as did the local noblemen. The nobles, having invested so much money, felt that their sin – of being rich – was forgiven. This state of affairs encouraged parishes to escalate the size and magnificence of their buildings, which explains why small villages often have parish closes that are built on a disproportionately grand architectural scale. It often happened that a par-ticular parish, jealous of another's church, copied and erected the same tower some years later, but made it higher and more richly decorated.

It was Louis XIV who hastened the decline of Breton art, by causing Brittany's economy to crash. In order to develop 'national production' and trade in French woollen cloth, Colbert placed a hefty tax on woollen cloth from overseas. In retaliation, the English stopped buying Breton cloth, and Brittany plunged into a dramatic economic crisis. (This taxation was surely not without a political ulterior motive, and Louis XIV and his central government were not displeased to witness the weakening of Brittany.) Afterwards, the wars against England put an end to all trade. By the time peace returned, England had developed its own industry and found other markets, and Brittany had seen its financial resources dwindle considerably. The final nail in the coffin was a royal decree in 1645 forbidding any new building work without prior permission from the central government. Breton artists and craftsmen were no longer able to produce anything on a large scale, and St-Thégonnec thus became Brittany's artistic swansong.

COMMANA (*KOMMANNA*) 29450   (Pop: 1,050)

Commana is a charming village on a little hill at the foot of the Roc'h Trévezel, and another fully fledged member of the parish close tour. The velvety countryside directly around it offers a nice contrast with the brown mass of the Monts d'Arrée, which act as its backdrop.

If you are coming from Plounéour-Menez (where there is also a small parish close) or from Guimiliau, avoid the main departmental roads (the D11 and the D785). Stay on the smaller roads that meander between farms with their attractive rural architecture and rows of dwarf oaks.

WHERE TO STAY AND EAT

â **Chambres d'hôte: Danielle Le Signor**: in Kerfornédic, 2 kilometres (1.5 miles) southwest of the Drennec dam. ☎ 02-98-78-06-26. On the southerly slopes of the Monts d'Arrée, on a small road linking Commana with St-Cadou. Hamlet with a few houses in the middle of countryside. For those who really want to escape. In a tastefully renovated house typical of the Monts d'Arrée, there are two very nice, well-equipped guest rooms, scented with the fragrance of the wildflowers that decorate the whole house. A double room costs 320F including a generous breakfast using good pro-

duce. Minimum stay is two nights (three nights in June, July and August). A marvellous base for exploring the Monts d'Arrée. The *Sentier des crêtes* (ridgeway path) passes close by. Superb *gîte* to rent (for four adults and one child), from 1,800F to 2,700F per week (electricity is extra).

â **Camping municipal Milin Nevez**: ☎ 02-98-78-05-57. Open from mid-June to the beginning of September. Excellent level of comfort. Shaded site by a river offering 50 spaces. Games and services. Definitely to be recommended and not expensive.

WHAT TO SEE

★ **Église St-Derrien**: the church is approached through a monumental turreted gateway. It dates from the end of the 16th century and the close still has its cemetery with two calvaries. The impressive belfry, 57 metres (185 feet) high, gives an impression of severity and austerity. Perhaps it was intended to echo the jagged rocks of the Monts d'Arrée? Right at the top, the cockerel is the highest in Brittany. To the belfry's height must be added the 261.99-metre (851-foot) hill (this very precise measurement is inscribed in stone at the foot of the belfry).

The admirable Renaissance porch is modelled on the one in the St-Houardon church in Landerneau. Everything here is harmonious and balanced. The angled buttresses on either side of the portal, adorned with elegant sculptures, give a superb effect of relief and perspective. For once, the 12 Apostles on the interior of the porch, traditionally greeting the faithful from their niches, were not destroyed during the French Revolution. Quite simply, they never existed! The parish was never able to purchase them, as their finances had been bled dry by the small fortune it cost to build the church.

Several gems await you inside the church: a beautiful polychrome carved baptistery from the 17th century, with graceful statuettes symbolizing the great Virtues (Justice, Temperance, Faith, Charity, Hope). To the left of the altar, the **retable de Ste-Anne** (altarpiece) is a real showstopper; its exuberant baroque style will leave you breathless. It would take two pages of eulogy to describe it properly. One important historical detail helps to explain its quality. In 1675, there was a great revolt against the taxes levied by Louis XIV. The peasants of Commana suspected their parish priest of conniving with the government, and seized him. Statements were made by witnesses to the authorities: 'They dragged him from his house, pulling him and trampling on him, beat him again and again, left him bare-headed in the sun, knocked him down three or four times, until he was reduced to asking for the Extreme Unction, which he was unlikely to receive, some saying that he should be stoned and others that he should be hung from his door, and yet others that he should be taken up to the top of the belfry and thrown off with a stone round his neck.' The priest finally managed to crawl away, and escaped to Morlaix, where he was looked after. His parishioners repented, he withdrew his complaint against them and, in gratitude to the church, they bled themselves white to donate the marvellous altarpiece, around 1682. Each panel is decorated differently, with a profusion of medallions, garlands of flowers, cherubs, and so on. The whole altarpiece is unbelievably ornate, and perhaps the most beautiful in Brittany.

Also interesting is the **retable des Cinq Plaies** (altarpiece of the Five Wounds), next to it. It shows a serene Christ displaying his wounds and crowned with flowers by the angels. The superb **pulpit** is carved in the same style as the large rustic chests of the time.

The **ossuary** bears, on its side and carved in the stone, the names of the *fabriciens* (patrons of the building work).

★ **Les poupées de Pascaline** (doll collection): 4 place de l'Église. ☎ 02-98-78-01-80. Open all year round, 9am–noon and 2–7pm. Closed Monday out of season. Admission charge (20F). Guided 20-minute tour around a mini village, with scenes of life in bygone days animated by little wax dolls and about 30 automatons.

WHAT TO DO

– **Centre Nautique de l'Arrée**: ☎ 02-98-78-92-91. Affiliated to the FFV (French yachting federation), offering courses in sailing, windsurfing and kayaking.

THE MONTS D'ARRÉE

FAIR

– **Foire de Commana**: end of September. This fair is for buying and selling horses, ponies, sheep, rabbits and all kinds of poultry.

IN THE AREA

★ **Allée couverte du Mougau-Bihan** (megalithic covered walkway): called *al lia ven* in Breton ('the stone loggia'), this is one of the most significant megalithic structures in the region. Situated in a little hamlet less than 2 kilometres (1.5 miles) south of Commana, in very pretty countryside. The tomb measures 14 metres (45 feet) in length and is said to date from between 3000 and 2500 BC. Inside, there are some faint carvings in the stone. According to legend, it is a giant's tomb.

🛏 It is possible to spend the night in a *gîte d'étape* (walkers' stopover) run by the Armorican regional nature park. ☎ 02-98-81-90-08. Fax: 02-98-81-90-09.

★ **Le lac du Drennec**: a lake about 3 kilometres (2 miles) from Commana. Lovely walk of about 2 kilometres (1.5 miles) around the perimeter of this lake created by the dam, with, en route, some picturesque old houses and scenic viewpoints. Water activities, campsite. Mountain-bike rental.

★ **Moulins de Kérouat** (open-air museum): ☎ 02-98-68-87-76. Open from Monday to Friday, from mid-March to the end of October and during school holidays, 10am–6pm, and Sunday and public holidays 2–6pm; closed Saturday off season, except in June; in July and August, open 11am–7pm. Admission charge (27F). Very pretty setting, 4 kilometres (2.5 miles) west of Commana, this little hamlet consists of 15 buildings constructed between the 17th and 20th centuries, lived in by five generations of millers, farmworkers, and, more recently, horse-breeders. Restored by the Armorican regional nature park, this open-air museum gives a good idea of the activities and traditions of the region in past times. There are two windmills, a barn, two bread ovens, a dwelling house with typical furniture, and farm outbuildings.

★ About 2 kilometres (1.5 miles) south of the Moulins de Kérouat, be sure to visit the **Expo Art et Nature**, in the small village of Kervelly. From mid-July to the end of August, open every day 10am–6pm; the rest of the year, Sunday from 2pm to dusk. Booking required for groups: ☎ 02-98-78-03-43. Guided tour (1 hour 30 minutes). Admission charge (40F for adults; 25F for children). Presentation of the flora and fauna of the Monts d'Arrée, with animals running wild (including badgers, wild boar, peacocks and pheasants), and several displays, covering birds, deer and the forest. Waterfalls and ponds to visit, too.

SIZUN (*SIZUN*) 29450   (Pop: 1,911)

This peaceful village, a gateway to the Monts d'Arrée, has one of the most beautiful parish closes. Curiously, however, there is no calvary, just a cross over the main entrance.

THE MONTS D'ARRÉE

USEFUL ADDRESS

🛈 Office du tourisme des Monts d'Arrée: 3 rue de l'Argoat. ☎ 02-98-68-88-40. Open from Easter to the end of September; in July and August open Monday to Friday 9am–12.30pm and 2.30–7pm and Sunday 10am–12.30pm. For the rest of the year, tourist information is available at Landivisiau (☎ 02-98-68-33-33).

WHERE TO STAY AND EAT

🛏 Camping municipal Le Gollen: ☎ 02-98-24-11-43; out of season: ☎ 02-98-68-80-13. Fax: 02-98-68-86-56. Open from Easter to the end of September. Situated by a river. Clean and reasonably priced (about 45F). Hot showers, washbasins and toilets.

🛏 ✕ Le Clos des Quatre Saisons: 2 rue de la Paix. ☎ 02-98-68-80-19. Fax: 02-98-24-11-93. Email: jr.gilette@wanadoo.fr. As you come into Sizun. Closed the first week of September. A double room costs from 150F to 200F depending on the facilities. Set menus from 69F to 139F. The rooms in this house with garden all around it are simple but pleasant. The restaurant across the road serves decent traditional cuisine with an excellent choice of dishes. Restaurant closed Friday, Saturday and Sunday evenings out of season.

🛏 ✕ Hôtel des Voyageurs: 2 rue de l'Argoat. Next to the parish close. ☎ 02-98-68-80-35. Fax: 02-98-24-11-49. 🍴 Closed for the month of September and Saturday and Sunday evenings out of season. Small provincial hotel, plain but respectable. Rooms 280F. So-so restaurant with menus from 78F (weekdays) to 155F. Homemade pâtés and cakes. Half board from 210–255F per day.

WHERE TO STAY AND EAT IN THE AREA

🛏 ✕ Chambres d'hôte: Elisabeth Soubigou: at Mescouez. ☎ 02-98-68-86-79. Fax: 02-98-68-83-39. From Sizun, head for Landerneau on the D764. After approximately 4 kilometres (2.5 miles), turn left. It's signposted. Go on for a further 1.5 kilometres (1 mile). The owners are Bretons who enjoy sharing their love for the region. Their beautiful house contains five charming guest rooms, cosily arranged with rustic decoration, bright colours and old furniture. 275F for two people, including breakfast (with homemade cake). On the first floor, a pretty mannequin wears a 1930s dress that belonged to a great-great-aunt. Table d'hôte meals (95F) are available if you book (except between 15 July and 15 August). Good home cooking. *Gîtes* to rent as well in the old buildings which surround an interior courtyard (about 2,300F per week in summer). The kitchens are equipped with refrigerators. Undercover parking.

WHAT TO SEE

★ The close is entered through the most impressive monumental **gateway** in Finistère. It is 15 metres (50 feet) long, pierced by three archways and surmounted by a turreted balustrade. Unfortunately, the war memorial rather spoils the historic harmony of the site.

★ Right next to it, the **ossuary** is in the same style as the gateway and dates from the same time (1585). A typical example of the Breton Renaissance style, it has semicircular arches, adorned with spirals and caryatids, and Corinthian columns. The 12 Apostles are in little niches, and not under the porch – for once. Inside is a small museum of local arts and culture (**Musée d'Arts et Traditions Populaires**), which is open at Easter and from May to September, every day from 9am–7pm. ☎ 02-98-68-87-60. Admission free. Contains beautiful old statues, regional costumes, a Breton box bed and dresser, pretty embroidery. Items for sale as well.

★ The **porch belfry** has a slender spire, constructed in the 18th century and modelled on the Kreisker church in St-Pol-de-Léon. The interior has interesting altarpieces and beautiful carved beams and purlins.

★ **Maison de la Rivière, de l'Eau et de la Pêche** (centre for rivers, waterways and fishing): in the Moulin de Vergraon (mill). ☎ 02-98-68-86-33. Below the village, it's signposted. Open every day in summer 10am–6.30pm, and during the school holidays 2–5.30pm, except Saturday; the rest of the year, open 10am–noon and 2–5pm. Admission charge (25F). For children and teenagers, lively educational presentation using texts, models and various documentation on everything to do with water: fish, angling, flora, conservation, ecology, and so on. Re-creation of riverbanks, aquariums, and an outside trail. Note the glass opening where you can see the trout swimming by – Brittany is the main trout-breeding area of France.

– **Milin Kerroch**: 1 kilometre from Sizun, a small recreation area near a pond, for families. ☎ 02-98-68-81-56. In an old restored windmill, a bar-crêperie-grill. Pedal boats, fishing and outdoor bowling.

– **Horse-riding**: you can go trekking on horseback, going from one gîte to the next, from anything from half a day to several days. Great fun. Information from **Rando Loisirs** at Kerinizan, 29450 Sizun. ☎ 02-98-68-89-98.

FESTIVALS

– **Fête de la Moisson**: harvest festival held on 14 July.

– **Pardon de Loc-Ildut**: religious festival on the last Sunday in July.

ST-THÉGONNEC
(*SANT-TEGONEG*) 29410   (Pop: 2,316)

This village has perhaps the most impressive of all the parish closes, the apogee of 17th-century Breton art. It is a fusion of Renaissance style and early baroque influence from Italy. The name Thégonnec was derived from the Welsh Connog, one of the monks who fled from Wales in the 6th century before the advancing Scots and Angles. The complete close took almost 200 years to build, from the first stone to the final part of the altarpiece inside the church. It is entered through a monumental gateway (1587), essentially constructed in a style borrowed from the Renaissance, notably the upper part with its two lantern turrets.

THE MONTS D'ARRÉE

USEFUL ADDRESSES

■ **Mairie de St-Thégonnec** (town hall): ☎ 02-98-79-61-06. Contact them for all kinds of information. Open in July and August.

■ Contact the **SPREV** (Sauvegarde du patrimoine religieux en vie):

☎ 02-98-79-61-06. Supports the protection of the living religious heritage in the region. Organizes free guided tours of religious monuments in July and August. Programme sent on request.

WHERE TO STAY AND EAT

🛏 ✕ **Chambres d'hôte Ar Prespital Coz, with M. and Mme Prigent**: 18 rue Lividic. ☎ 02-98-79-45-62. Fax: 02-98-79-48-47. In St-Thégonnec, follow the signposts. In the former presbytery of St-Thégonnec. Six spacious and comfortable guest rooms, particularly welcoming to people who are interested in parish closes. 270F for two people, including breakfast. Table d'hôte for 95F.

🛏 **Chambres d'hôte: Marie-José Boderiou**: 1A rue des Genêts, 400 metres from the church. ☎ 02-98-79-43-14. Open all year round. On the circuit of parish closes (GR380 footpath). An attractive, welcoming house. Two guest rooms with communal shower room and toilet. 200F for two people, including breakfast. Guaranteed parking spaces and large garden behind the house.

🛏 **Chambres d'hôte: Mme Kergadallan**: 20 avenue Kerizella (entrance on rue des Cyprès). ☎ 02-98-79-65-30 and 02-98-79-63-86. ⚒ Three guest rooms with all mod cons, two with a communal lounge. 220F for two people, including breakfast. Facilities for preparing cold meals. The owners also own the shop *An Ty Korn*, which sells Celtic jewellery and local crafts.

🛏 **Chambres d'hôte au Moulin de Kerlaviou with M. and Mme Cornily**: ☎ 02-98-79-60-57. Open from Easter until 1 November. Leaving St-Thégonnec, take the D712 for Landivisiau, and it's signposted on

the left. Attractive setting in a small farm by the river, beside an old mill, in countryside full of flowers. Double guest rooms with bath for 260F, including breakfast. Reservation recommended. No pets.

✕ **Restaurant du Commerce**: 1 rue de Paris. ☎ 02-98-79-61-07. Closed Saturday and Sunday, as well as three weeks in August. A stone's throw from the parish close. Open lunchtime on weekdays, a good, generous and inexpensive set menu (60F) with soup, starter, main course, cheese and dessert. Drinks are included for 'workers' but not for 'those passing through', according to the menu. Children's menu for 35F. Specialities include beef and vegetable stew (*pot-au-feu*), *kig ha farz* (traditional Breton bacon flan), and couscous. Possibility of breakfast as well (20F). Pleasant dining room with drystone wall. Lively atmosphere.

✕ **Crêperie Steredenn**: 6 rue de la Gare. ☎ 02-98-79-43-34. Fax: 02-98-79-40-89. ⚒ Open 11.30am–10pm. Closed Monday and Tuesday and December to January. Friendly welcome, wood fire and 150 different *crêpes* that are good and inexpensive. Favourites include the *Douarnenez* (sardine butter with green pepper), the *St-Thégonnec* (onions, tomatoes, cheese, ham, curry), and the *Druidique* (marmalade, almonds, Grand Marnier). Set menus from 61F to 70F. They also sell homemade cider.

☆☆☆ Chic

⚓ ✕ **L'Auberge de St-Thégon-nec**: 6 place de la Mairie. ☎ 02-98-79-61-18. Fax: 02-98-62-71-10. Email: auberge@wanadoo.fr. ⚓ Service lunchtimes and evenings until 9pm. Closed Sunday evening and Monday from mid-September to mid-June; also closed from 20 December to 10 January. Reservation essential in high season. Elegant and refined atmosphere, and impeccable service. If you eat à la carte, the bill will hit the roof rather quickly (allow 300F), but the chef has had the good sense to offer delicious 120F menus (not including drinks) with, among other things, curried squid in puff pastry (*feuilleté d'encornets au curry*), Barbary duck sautéed in wine (*canette de Barbarie sautée à la vigneronne*) or hake in white wine (*mironton de lieu au gamay de Touraine*). Other menus cost up to 250F. This really is one of the best places to eat in the whole of Finistère. The place also offers very nice rooms with all mod cons for 380F to 450F, and breakfast is served in a comfortable lounge.

WHERE TO STAY IN THE AREA

⚓ **Chambres d'hôte and gîtes ruraux** with Jean and Annie Martin: Ty-Dreux, 29410 Loc-Éguiner-St-Thégonnec. Take the D18, then the D111 (which goes to Plounéour-Menez). ☎ 02-98-78-08-21. Right off the beaten track, about 10 kilometres (6 miles) south of St-Thégonnec, is Ty-Dreux, a former weavers' village. In a blissfully quiet setting, Jean and Annie extend the warmest welcome to their farm, where they have converted two charming guest rooms. Double room with shower or bath and toilet 270F, including breakfast. Three comfortable *gîtes* (for six people) to rent as well, with Breton furniture and large stone fireplaces. From 1,490F to 3,200F per week according to the season. Lots of walks in the surrounding area (the GR380 footpath goes right past the farm) and, in the distance, the Roc Trévezel beckons romantically. This is convivial Brittany, unpretentious and just as it should be.

WHAT TO SEE AND DO

★ **Church**: built in a more austere style than the ossuary. The bell tower is the oldest part (1565), and the imposing sacristy dates from 1690. Inside are a polychrome carved wooden choir, a splendid pulpit, clearly demonstrating the importance of the spoken word towards the end of the 17th century, and a large **retable du Rosaire** (altarpiece) where the Virgin is giving a rosary to St Catherine and St Dominique. On one of the columns is a niche with a **statue of St Thégonnec**. On the right-hand side of the nave, above the entrance, is another niche with a remarkable **Virgin** enthroned in a Tree of Jesse. This church has witnessed some strange events: during a typhus epidemic between 1740 and 1743, 750 bodies were buried beneath its stone slabs.

★ **Ossuary**: probably the most beautiful and impressively monumental in France, built between 1676 and 1682. The composition and ornamentation on the outside wall are rich and perfectly harmonious, with Corinthian columns, shell-shaped niches, and so on. Inside, under the crypt, is an **Entombment** carved in wood, the work of Lespagnol, a sculptor from Morlaix (also responsible for the retable du Rosaire).

★ **Calvary**: one of the last great Breton calvaries, erected in 1610. The base depicts nine scenes from the Passion. The style of the characters dressed in the clothes of the time appears rather naïve, while the faces and demeanour of the active characters are more expressive. Of the two evil individuals who are whipping Jesus, one is sticking out his tongue like an idiot. Look out for the sorrowful expression on the face of Veronica as she holds Christ's head, and of the women beside her.

– **Walk**: St-Thégonnec is on the GR380 hiking path, from Lampaul-Guimiliau to Morlaix.

GUIMILIAU (*GWIMILIO*) 29400   (Pop: 836)

The site of one of the four most important parish closes in Finistère, the village of Guimiliau owes its name to St Miliau, who was descended from the ancient kings of Brittany. In some ways, its close is more spectacular than that of St-Thégonnec, because the surroundings are less obviously connected with tourism. As you approach you become aware, little by little, of all the elements that make up the whole: the monumental gateway, the church, the calvary and the ossuary.

WHERE TO STAY

🛏 **Chambres d'hôte: Christiane Croguennec**: at Croas-Avel. ☎ 02-98-68-70-72. Double rooms cost 250F including a copious breakfast with *crêpes*. The accommodation is very simple, although spotlessly clean, but what makes it all worthwhile is the incredibly warm and lively welcome from the owner of this large house not far from the town centre.

WHAT TO SEE

★ After the **triumphal gateway** the great **calvary** rises up. Built between 1581 and 1588, it includes over 200 figures, representing all sorts of characters and full of energy. It is easy to become disorientated and lost in the scenes, which are finer and more polished than in St-Thégonnec. Several of them are admirable, particularly the **Entombment**, which shows a very original Virgin wearing the clothes and traditional head-dress of the wife of a nobleman of the time. The moving **Deposition**, with a figure of Christ bent double, is modern in style and rhythm. Finally, note the scene known as *La Gueule de l'Enfer* (the 'mouth of Hell'), which incorporates the symbolism of the leviathan, or monster, swallowing men, and a local tale about Katell (Catherine) Gollet, who was said to have taken a lover who turned out to be the Devil. She can be seen, with a look of despair on her face, a rope around her neck, being threatened with a large fork. Her ample bare breasts are there to remind the observer about the nature of her transgression. . . .

★ **Church**: in the Gothic Flamboyant style, with Renaissance overtones. Very ornate facade with one of the most beautiful porches in Finistère. Two arched doorways at the entrance, with a font in the middle surrounded by a fine group of **Apostles** beneath a Flamboyant canopy. Easily recognizable are Peter with his great key; James the Elder (St-Jacques), covered in shells; and John, the only one without a beard. Notice the delicate carving of the folds of their clothes.

The inside is every bit as impressive as the outside. First, the magnificent carved wood **baptistery** is a stunning baroque work of art dating from 1675, displaying expert craftsmanship. Eight cabled columns support an elegant canopy. The **pulpit** dates from the same time as the baptistery and is equally rich in carved decoration. In passing, note the remarkable **choir balustrade** and the **lectern**. On the right, the polychrome **altarpiece** is sumptuous. The **processional banners**, embroidered in gold thread, date from the 17th century. Finally, beneath the vaulted roof, there are beautiful, finely carved beams and purlins representing animals and scenes of peasant life. The **organ**, built by Thomas Dallan in 1677, had fallen into disrepair, and had been dismantled and stored in the attic of the town hall. It has now re-taken its place after three years of restoration work costing 20 million francs. Gérard Guillemin, an organ builder from Malaucène, put his heart and soul into the work. Hearing such a voice in such a superb setting once again completes the appreciation of Sunday Mass.

★ **Ossuary**: this little masterpiece of classicism and harmony houses a shop and store. Opposite, you can see the large sacristy in the form of an apse, which was added, as was often the case with Breton churches, at the end of the 17th century (at the time of the Counter-Reformation).

LAMPAUL-GUIMILIAU (*LAMBAOL-GWIMILIO*) 29400 (Pop: 2,076)

Less spectacular than those of St-Thégonnec or Guimiliau, with a calvary of less significance, the parish close of Lampaul-Guimiliau has, nevertheless, a character all of its own and a more richly decorated church interior. It is the most ancient of the series of parish closes. Again, all of the elements of a close are here: triumphal gateway, calvary, church and ossuary. The architects also saw to it that all the elements could be clearly seen through the archway.

The bell tower once supported a 70-metre (227-foot) spire, which was brought down by a lightning strike in 1809. The Gothic porch is very similar to the one in Guimiliau; this is not unusual, as the architects and artists of the day would copy their neighbours and attempt to outdo them. However, the one in Lampaul is 70 years older. The 12 apostles are surmounted by Gothic canopies.

★ The **church** is one of the oldest (1553) you will find and also one of the most uniform, with very harmonious proportions. It is certainly special. Inside, across the choir, is one of the most beautiful **rood beams** in the whole of Finistère, with a painted wooden **crucifix**. The Virgin, to the left, seems, with her eyes, to be imploring the faithful, and John has a look of religious

THE MONTS D'ARRÉE

ecstasy. The naïvety and vigour of the frieze runs across the beam. Notice the extreme violence of the scourger on the right.

The beautiful polychrome **baptistery** is less attractive than the one in Guimiliau, which is later and was built by parishioners who wanted it to outshine all previous versions. Here, the emphasis is on simplicity, tinged with fervour.

In passing, notice the beautiful 17th-century stalls and balustrade. Even more remarkable are the altarpieces, notably the one on the left, the *autel de la Passion*, which is interesting for its feeling for detail and the delicate execution of the painting (note the soldier giving Christ a kick). One unusual panel shows a **Nativity** with the Virgin lying down. There are about a dozen of these in Brittany.

In the centre of the church, on the left, is a 16th-century **pietà**, carved from a single piece of wood. Further on, there is a beautiful stone **Entombment**.

FESTIVAL

– **Grand Pardon de Ste-Anne**: religious festival on the second to last Sunday in August.

IN THE AREA

★ **Locmélar** (*Lokmelar*, 29400): 8 kilometres (5 miles) south of Lampaul-Guimiliau. The parish close here is worth the detour. In the cemetery is a very pretty 16th-century double cross. The bell tower has a balustrade gallery. In the chevet, the 'sacristie-sanction' dates from the time of the Counter-Reformation. Renaissance porch with the 12 Apostles, with, once again, one figure drawing his sword. Beautiful **altarpieces** inside. In the charming composition dedicated to St Hervé, showing the saint in the company of a wolf that he has tamed, observant visitors will spot the spelling mistakes. Finally, have a good look at the 16th-century banners embroidered with gold, the pulpit, the baptistery and the *Vierge de Pitié*.

★ **Landivisiau** (*Landivizio*, 29400): apart from being the birthplace of poet and journalist Xavier Grall, this large town has little of interest. The new church, built in the 19th century, has no real charm but has nevertheless retained its predecessor's fine 16th-century porch. The frame of the double door is extremely delicate. From the place de l'Église, the little rue St-Thivisiau leads to a very old fountain decorated with *bas-reliefs*, also dating from the 16th century. Continue on to an old washhouse which has been nicely restored, and further on still (near the library) stands the statue of Xavier Grall. Finally, the 16th-century ossuary dedicated to St Anne has been completely rebuilt in the town cemetery.

For a long time, Landivisiau has been an important breeding centre for the Breton post-horse. There is a large horse fair in spring and autumn. Most activity nowadays is centred around an air and sea military base.

THE MONTS D'ARRÉE

USEFUL ADDRESSES

▐ Tourist information: ☎ 02-98-24-60-01.

✕ Le Terminus: 94 avenue Foch, on the road to Morlaix, as you leave the town. ☎ 02-98-68-02-00. Open all year round. Closed Sunday evening, Friday evening and Saturday lunchtime. One of the best truck stops in Finistère, with a generous 'workers' menu' for 60F, made up of two starters (including seafood), a main course with as many vegetables as you want, salad, cheese, dessert, coffee, and a whole litre of red wine on the table! The number of lorries in the car park testifies to the unbeatable value. Otherwise, there is a restaurant dining room next door with traditional menus for 80F and 110F, and a seafood platter for 120F. Modest rooms are also available, costing 130–190F.

BODILIS (*BODILIZ*) 29400   (Pop: 1,396)

The **church** in this tiny village a few kilometres north of Landivisiau is one of the most appealing in the Léon region. You are first struck by the enormous bell tower in the Flamboyant style, then by the harmonious proportions of the church itself, and finally by the wonderful **porch** (possibly even more beautiful than the one in Guimiliau, and that's saying something). The use of Kersanton stone means that there are beautiful colours and tints in certain parts of the building and in the statues. On either side of the portal, with its Romanesque lines, are the Holy Virgin and the Archangel Gabriel. On the interior of the porch are the traditional 12 Apostles under their canopies. Magnificent friezes and scenes on the lower part combine symbols and Christian and esoteric signs. Look closely at the intriguing mass of detail – one is a woman entwined by a man-serpent. Elsewhere in the church, there are other notable items, particularly mysterious medallions and strange gargoyles. The beautiful sacristy was added in the 17th century, the work of the same architect who built the Sacristie de La Martyre.

Inside, the vaulted ceiling is in the form of an up-turned boat. There are numerous carved beams, particularly in the nave on the right-hand side. Wonderful **altarpieces** (especially that of the main altar) by the same artist who designed the pulpit in St-Thégonnec. The representation of the Holy Family shows the child Jesus taking his parents' hand to cross the street. Finally, on the right-hand side, beside a list of those who lost their lives in World War I, is a superb polychrome **Entombment**. The baptistery is in local stone.

IN THE AREA

★ **St-Servais:** on the D30 about 4 kilometres (2.5 miles) south of Bodilis. This village also has an 18th-century parish enclosure, attractively renovated, with the usual arrangement of ossuary, calvary and graveyard. It has a splendid tall clock tower that stands 36 metres (118 feet) high and has been frequently copied in the surrounding area. The door is superb, painted in polychrome at the end of the 16th century – in the panel on the left a man is

THE MONTS D'ARRÉE

being plunged into a cauldron of water, and since this was the period of the Inquisition, no further explanation is needed. The work of the St-Servais artist Yan' d'Argent hangs in every part of the parish enclosure and the ossuary houses a large, slightly macabre triptych. There is a small **museum** dedicated to his work: open July–September daily 2–6pm (mornings by appointment). ☎ 02-98-68-15-21 or 02-98-68-10-72. Admission charge (15F). A guided tour is available of the museum and the parish, given by the curator. Yan' d'Argent started out as a draughtsman with a railway company but gave this up in 1850 in order to become a full-time artist. Despite regular exhibitions, it took him until 1861 to make his name. Around 1870 he began the decoration of churches in Brittany and he spent six years painting the side chapels in the cathedral at Quimper. A fresh exhibition of his work (drawings, canvases and sketchbooks – mostly Brittany-inspired) is held here each summer.

LA ROCHE-MAURICE
(*AR ROC'H-MORVAN*) 29800   (Pop: 1,738)

As you approach this village, which has a magnificent setting, you first come across the ruins of a 12th-century castle, whose purpose was to keep watch over the Vallée de l'Élorn. Afterwards, you see the **Église St-Yves**, architecturally very plain, with a sloping roof that seems to make it merge with the ground, and a superb belfry. The portal is a harmonious blend of Gothic and Renaissance styles. However, the real beauty of the church is to be found inside. A Renaissance **rood screen** served to separate the nave from the choir, and certain readings were conducted from the gallery. Made entirely from painted oak, it is one of the most beautiful in Finistère. Note the small arches on the Corinthian capitals with their picturesque decoration, and the superb panels on the choir side. Coffered ceiling. Above the rood screen is Christ on the cross with the Virgin and St John. Take time to look at all the detail on the sculptures, where there is a profusion of figures and symbols, and sumptuous colours. Beautiful carved purlins and 17th-century pulpit. Alcove shows St Yves between a pauper and a rich man. Admirable **stained-glass window** in the choir, with the arms of the Rohan family, depicting, in brilliant colours, no fewer than 14 scenes from the Passion. Begin at the bottom left with Palm Sunday.

In the parish close there is a harmoniously proportioned **ossuary** with delicate sculptures. Before the first window, above the font, *Ankou* (Death) threatens us with its arrow: 'Death comes to you all'.

WHERE TO EAT

✗ **Crêperie Milin An Elorn**: on the D712 heading towards Landivisiau, just after La Roche-Maurice. ☎ 02-98-20-41-46. Closed Monday. In a rustic setting near a watermill on the River Élorn. Wood fire, old stone walls, very good crêpes.

✗ **L'Auberge du Vieux Château**: 4 Grand-Place. ☎ 02-98-20-40-52. Fax: 02-98-20-50-17. ♿ Open lunchtime and weekend evenings; open for group reservations (ten or more) only on weekday evenings. This is an excellent restaurant, offering the best value for money in the Landernau region and is located on the village square close to the church and the ruins of the 11th-century castle. The weekday lunch-time menu (58F) attracts all sorts – farmers, sales reps, businessmen and ordinary workers. In the evening, other speciality fish menus cost up to 150F.

LA MARTYRE
(AR MERZHER-SALAUN) 29800   (Pop: 608)

About 10 kilometres (6 miles) from Landerneau, the pretty, flower-bedecked village of La Martyre jealously protects its original parish close, the oldest one in the Léon region, and a real jewel. There are few clues to the origin of the name 'Martyre', although historians record the martyrdom in the church during the ninth century of a king of Brittany by the name of Salomon (hence the name of the church – the Église St-Salomon). What is known for certain is that the village hosted a large cloth fair during the Middle Ages, with buyers coming from Holland, England and Ireland. A Dutchman, Fons De Kort, who loves La Martyre and the area's parish closes, has discovered a reference in a Shakespearean play to *daoulas*, a renowned cloth made near La Martyre. It is thought that Shakespeare's father, who was a cloth merchant, often travelled to the fair in La Martyre.

WHERE TO STAY

🛏 **Camping du Bois-Noir**: ☎ 02-98-25-13-19 (town hall). Fax: 02-98-25-14-02. Open all year round. Six spaces.

WHAT TO SEE

★ **The monumental arch**: in the middle of a high wall, with three rather lopsided gateways, but adorned with a balustrade in the Flamboyant style. The close is so small that the calvary has also been perched here.

★ **The church**: admirable 15th-century porch, one of the oldest in Finistère. Constructed from Kersanton stone, it has acquired over the centuries a soft patina and many subtle colours and tones. It seems also to be sinking into the ground a little on one side. Richly decorated, it has a curious **Nativity** on the tympanum – unusually, the Virgin is lying on a bed. The kidnapper of Léon has struck again here, and the infant Jesus has disappeared, as well as the Virgin's ample breasts, removed by the hammer blows of some particularly repressed parish priest.

Under the porch, *Ankou* (Death) is found in the form of a font, apparently strangling someone.

Considered as a whole, the church gives a pleasing impression of a rather haphazard style of architecture, with bits and pieces added over the years. Behind the church stands the superb **sacristy**, built by Kerandel between 1697 and 1699, with a dome on a square base with tangential circles.

THE MONTS D'ARRÉE

Inside, in the nave, on the left, there is interesting woodwork with polychrome carved beams and purlins. Of the 16th-century stained-glass windows, the most beautiful was a model for dozens of churches in Finistère. The eight columns of the rood screen support an arch crowned by Christ on the cross. The panelling on the ceiling is being renovated. For once, the modern altar at the front of the choir does not destroy the harmony of the whole.

★ **The ossuary**: built in 1619. Note the strange dead female figure in the form of a caryatid and bound up like a mummy. The Breton inscription reads 'Death, Judgement, Cold Hell. Man should tremble when he thinks of it. Foolish is he who does not accept that we must all depart this life.' (Interestingly, Bretons never used the metaphor of the flames of Hell, but rather refer to the Celtic mythology of icy sea waters and misty lakes to represent Purgatory.)

IN THE AREA

★ **Ploudiry**: the church (rebuilt in the 19th century) is less interesting than the one in La Martyre, but possesses a porch worthy of note, with beautiful carved coving. The ossuary, erected in 1635, again carries an *Ankou* (Death), aggressively brandishing an enormous arrow. Above the openings are five quite delicately sculpted figures, representing all social classes and symbolizing the equality of everyone in the face of Death.

LANDERNEAU (*LANDERNE*) 29800 (Pop: 15,141)

Landerneau is a large market town at a crossroads on the River Élorn, straddling the two regions of Léon and Cornouaille. According to a local saying, the inhabitants have 'their nose in Léon, and another appendage in Cornouaille'.

In Roman times Landerneau was an important port of call and during the 16th and 17th centuries it was one of the most important ports in Brittany. During the French Revolution, it became the administrative centre for Finistère. In the early part of the 20th century, agriculture and commerce took over from the textile industry and Landerneau became the centre of the largest agricultural co-operative in France. It is not surprising, then, that this town with a history of business was the birthplace of one of the most unusual commercial adventures of the last 50 years – the huge Leclerc supermarket chain, owned by Édouard Leclerc, also known as the 'grocer of Landerneau'.

There are many representations of the moon throughout the town – on the church and in the place St-Thomas, for example – and this motif has its origins in a Landerneau legend. Having achieved a certain fame, the Prince de Rohan was invited to Versailles by Louis XIV (the Sun King). The de Rohan coat of arms contained the sun and the moon, and de Rohan, bowing to the king's superiority, offered the king the sun, the brighter symbol. He would keep the moon, he said: 'Unable to be king, not deigning to be prince, Rohan I remain.' His people were unhappy, however, and soon began to complain: 'The moon of Landerneau is all we have left.'

USEFUL ADDRESS

⌂ Office du tourisme: pont de Rohan. ☎ 02-98-85-13-09. Open all year round Monday–Friday 9am–12.30pm and 1–7pm, Saturday 9am–noon and 2–7pm; also open Sunday and public holidays in season 10am–1pm. Closed Sunday out of season. Open in June, September and during school holidays on Monday afternoon 2–6pm, Tuesday–Friday 9.45am–12.30pm and 2–6pm, Saturday 9.45am–12.15pm and 2–6pm. The rest of the year, open Monday afternoon 2–5pm, Tuesday–Friday 9.30am–12.15pm and 2–5pm, Saturday 9.30am–12.15pm.

WHERE TO STAY AND EAT

✿ Budget

✗ **Le Guantanamera**: 11 rue de Brest. ☎ 02-98-21-41-00. ♿ Open every day except Sunday (but open Sunday evening from June to September). As its name suggests, the chef offers South American or Creole dishes, in a convivial and exotic setting. Set menu of the day for 56F, but allow 100F to eat à la carte, where dishes include salads, pizzas and mussels with chips. Also a take-away service.

✗ **Crêperie L'Épi d'Or**: 4 rue de la Libération. ☎ 02-98-85-09-86. Open 11.30am–9pm. Closed Sunday lunchtime and Monday (except public holidays). Allow 50–60F to eat à la carte. Very friendly staff. Ideal for a bite to eat between visiting parish closes, as the service is quick. Decent prices.

✗ **Restaurant de la Mairie**: 9 rue de La-Tour-d'Auvergne. On the quay opposite the town hall. ☎ 02-98-85-01-83. Fax: 02-98-85-37-07. ♿ Open all year round except Tuesday evening. Friendly bar-restaurant, with a warm decor of glass, red carpeting and luxuriant plants. The lady owner has run this establishment with infectious enthusiasm for the past 30 years or so. Set menus for 59F (weekday lunchtime) to 185F, with a dish of the day available lunchtime and evening for 59F. Allow 120F to eat à la carte. Among the specialities, the *marmite Nep-tune* is worth its weight in gold: scallops, monkfish, shrimps and prawns are expertly simmered in cream and cognac and covered with a soufflé. It takes half an hour to prepare this dish. Apart from this, there are also mussels and a variety of other good value-for-money dishes on the menu. Wine by the glass. Very friendly staff.

✗ **La Duchesse Anne**: place du Général-de-Gaulle, near the pont de Rohan. ☎ 02-98-85-12-19. Closed Sunday. Splendid setting in the 17th-century Maison de la Sénéchaussée. Weekday lunchtime menus for 60F and 70F and set evening menus from 100F to 200F. Simple, decent fare.

✿✿ – ✿✿✿ Moderate to Chic

🛏 ✗ **Hôtel-restaurant L'Amandier**: 53–55 rue de Brest. ☎ 02-98-83-10-89. Fax: 02-98-85-34-14. Hotel closed Sunday evening; restaurant closed Sunday and Monday evening. Coming down the street from the station, go right at the first set of traffic lights. This hotel represents amazingly good value for money. Very elegant surroundings, with beautiful paintings, decor and furnishings. Rooms are particularly pleasant and extremely comfortable. Double rooms 270–300F. Evening meal plus room for 310F. Renowned for its traditional regional cuisine with some delightful new touches.

Weekdays at lunchtime, dish of the day for 55F, with other set menus from 105F to 180F.

▦▦▦▦ Très Chic

🔔 ✗ **Le Clos du Pontic**: rue du Pontic. ☎ 02-98-21-50-91. Fax: 02-98-21-34-33. Email: clos.pontic@wanadoo.fr. ✗ Restaurant closed on Friday, Saturday lunchtime and Sunday evening (except for guests) out of season and on Friday and Saturday lunchtime in high season. Reservation essential. In a street at right-angles to the River Élorn on the Cornouaille side (on the right coming from Quimper). Large affluent-looking villa in the middle of its own grounds. Comfortable double rooms for 340F with shower and toilet. Set menus start at 95F (except Sunday) going up to 230F. Specialities include chitterlings and potatoes in cider vinegar (*rosace d'andouille et pommes de terre au vinaigre de cidre*) and soufflé with Williams pears (*soufflé léger à la poire Williams*).

WHERE TO STAY IN THE AREA

🔔 **Aire naturelle de camping Coat-Bihan**: Guerrus, 29800 La Forest-Landerneau. 4 kilometres (2.5 miles) south of Landerneau. ☎ 02-98-20-26-49. Fax: 02-98-20-24-39. Take the road towards Brest, then turn directly south towards Relecq-Kerluhon. Nicely situated in the Vallée de l'Élorn, right beside a forest. The cost is about 40F for two people with a car.

WHAT TO SEE AND DO

★ **Pont de Rohan**: bridge constructed in 1510 to cross the River Élorn. This is the best example of Europe's seven remaining inhabited bridges. One of the houses, the Maison Gillart, dates from 1639. Morning is the best time to capture the bridge's most photogenic side from upstream.

★ **The old houses**: on the south side of the river, at the corner of the place Poul-Ar-Stang and the rue St-Thomas, are a number of beautiful medieval houses, including the Maison Notre-Dame de Rumengol (1668), a former inn. Opposite is a wood-framed house from 1670. Not far away are the 16th-century Église St-Thomas, and the ossuary.

On the north side of the river, in the place du Général-de-Gaulle (formerly the place du Marché), is the superb **Maison de la Sénéchaussée** or Maison de la Duchesse Anne (1664). There are other beautiful houses in the rue Fontaine-Blanche. The rue du Commerce, which also has some picturesque old houses, starts in front of the Monoprix store (itself a former 18th-century mansion).

★ Also worth seeing are the Domaine des Ursulines (previously a convent, now a secondary school), the Chapelle des Capucins and the Manoir de Kéranden.

★ **Église St-Houardon**: church rebuilt in 1860, but retaining a remarkable Renaissance porch from 1604 which served as a model for many other churches in the region. Also worth seeing is the church of St-Thomas (for Thomas à Becket of Canterbury), rebuilt in the 17th century.

– **Comptoir des produits bretons**: 3 quai de Cornouaille. ☎ 02-98-21-35-93. Exhibition and sale of regional arts and crafts, and a gallery of paintings.

– **Boat trips**: whole-day trips to the Glénan islands, from June to September. Information from the Gouelia association: 6 rue Jean-Baptiste Bousquet, 29000 Quimper. ☎ 02-98-65-10-00. They offer weekends on the Île de Groix with a trip on an old sailing boat. You can also go with the Notre-Dame-Rumengol (*An Test* association). Information at the tourist office.

IN THE AREA

★ **Pencran**: this little village 2 kilometres (1.5 miles) south of Landerneau possesses a beautiful parish close. On the original calvary, the two statues are separated from the central cross, and frame the entrance to the close, which is made up with rounded stones, which you have to step over. The drape of the folds of cloth on the figure of Mary Magdalene, below the cross, is beautifully carved. The **church** has a belfry with a double balcony, a porch (1552) with the 12 Apostles on, and vaulting with a hanging quoin. Underneath is a delicately carved canopy in the Gothic Flamboyant style. The porch has a basket-handle arch surmounted by a pediment with curved ornamental mouldings, and a fragment of the Nativity in the tympanum. Delicate little figures adorn the framework of the doorway. The ossuary, dating from 1594, has been subjected to change on more than one occasion. It has been, in turn, a school, a tobacconist's and a dwelling; it now serves as a burial vault for the Rosmorduc family.

The Presqu'Île de Plougastel

Stretching into the sea like the fingers of a hand, the Plougastel peninsula is reached via a beautiful new cable-stayed bridge 400 metres (1,300 feet) long, with pylons standing 114 metres (370 feet) high. Perhaps because the peninsula is too close to Brest, or perhaps because of its lack of well-known or fashionable beaches, most visitors head further south towards the Crozon peninsula. If you do have time, explore the countryside around Plougastel – it is full of tiny square fields and hedges on an incredible tangle of roads no wider than your car, which lead ultimately to delightful little ports. The peninsula is famous for its strawberries, which have been grown here since the 18th century, as well as for its numerous chapels, which demonstrate the strong Christian faith of the region.

PLOUGASTEL-DAOULAS
(*PLOUGASTELL-DAOULAZ*) 29470 (Pop: 12,471)

This small town suffered extensive bomb damage during World War II due to its proximity to Brest, and the rebuilt town has lost its charm of bygone days.

Plougastel-Daoulas remains well known for its **calvary**, which has more than 150 figures; its restoration was financed by the American airmen who were responsible for the bombing. It was built in 1602 and modelled on the calvary in Guimiliau, to give thanks for the fact that the plague had not killed everyone in the area. Its *kroaziou ar vossen* (plague cross) is recognizable by the balls that can be seen on the body of the cross, symbolizing the buboes of the illness. As in Guimiliau, the legend of Katell (Catherine) Gollet is sculpted in the stone (*see also* 'Guimiliau'). The two different tones of the stone appear rather strange, but are probably due to the use of both Kersanton granite and ochre stone during the restoration.

Regrettably, a shopping centre was recently built not far from the calvary. A favourable court decision in Quimper has managed to ward off the worst, however.

USEFUL ADDRESS

🛈 **Office du tourisme**: place du Calvaire. ☎ 02-98-40-34-98. Fax: 02-98-40-68-85. Open all year round; in July and August, from Monday to Saturday 9am–12.30pm and 2.30–7pm, and on Sunday 10am–noon. Out of season, open Tuesday to Saturday 9am–noon and 2–6pm.

WHERE TO STAY AND EAT

⌂ **Camping St-Jean**: in the town. ☎ 02-98-40-32-90. Fax: 02-98-04-23-11. Open all year round, this campsite on the bank of the River Élorn costs about 80F for a site for two people. It has a covered, heated swimming pool and a bar serving snacks. Mobile homes are also available.

✕ **Crêperie de Kertanguy**: 22 rue du Champ-de-Foire, Croix de Kertanguy, 80 metres from the town. ☎ and fax: 02-98-40-33-48. Closed on Monday out of season and in October. Set menu for 74F (40F for children) but allow 80F to eat à la carte. More than a hundred kinds of *crêpes* on the menu, although some are rather inconsistent in quality, to eat in a rustic setting. Specialities include the *Ogresse*, the *Pâturage*, the *Exotique*, and there's a *crêpe* made with Plougastel strawberries. Also mixed salads, ice-cream.

✕ **Le Chevalier de l'Auberlac'h**: 5 rue Mathurin-Thomas; 400 metres from the calvary. ☎ 02-98-40-54-56. Fax: 02-98-40-65-16. Closed on Sunday and Monday evening. The best restaurant on the peninsula and the large dining room is quite pleasant, with a rather stylish rustic decor. Among the specialities are the fish sauerkraut (*choucroute de poisson*) and the duck foie gras (*foie gras de canard au torchon*) have pride of place. Good homemade desserts. Lunchtimes only during the week, menu for 78F; other menus cost up to 180F.

WHERE TO EAT IN THE AREA

✕ **Crêperie An ty Coz:** Ty Floch, pointe de l'Armorique, 29470 Plougastel-Daoulas. ☎ 02-98-40-56-47. Open every day, all year round. It's advisable to book at weekends and in the summer. In a little village just before the point, this restaurant is in an attractively decorated house with a verandah and garden shaded by weeping willows. This provides a very pleasant setting if you want to eat a *crêpe* made with Plougastel strawberries. The welcome, though, is rather variable.

THE PRESQU'ÎLE DE PLOUGASTEL

WHAT TO SEE

★ **Musée du Patrimoine** (heritage museum): rue Louis-Nicole. ☎ 02-98-40-21-18. From June to September, open from Monday to Friday 10am–12.30pm and 2–6.30pm, and on Saturday and Sunday, afternoons only; in April, May, October and during the school holidays, open from Tuesday to Sunday 2–6pm; open all year round during the week for groups by reservation. Admission charge (25F). This museum is devoted to the peninsula's heritage, covered via different themes such as history, habitat, costumes and local economy. Within the museum there is also a cultural centre (library), with a new exhibition area devoted to the history of the strawberry from the 14th to the 20th century.

IN THE AREA

★ **Chapelle Ste-Christine**: about 4 kilometres (2.5 miles) from the village, on the road towards the pointe de l'Armoric and Caro bay, this is a pretty 15th-century chapel. The saint is represented with a millstone round her neck. Inside, there are beautiful polychrome wooden statues. A very popular *pardon* takes place on the last Sunday in July.

★ **Chapelle St-Adrien**: at the end of the baie de Lauberlac'h. This chapel has calvaries dating from the 16th century. The interior offers very rich furniture. A highly festive *pardon* happens on the second Sunday in May.

If you ask the way often enough, you will finally get directions to the delightful little port of **Lauberlac'h.**

★ **Chapelle St-Guénolé**, on the other side of the baie du Lauberlac'h. This is a 16th-century chapel beside a pool, with a fine polychrome altarpiece made of wood. Climb up to the **Point de vue du Keramenez** (viewpoint) to enjoy a panorama of most of the peninsula, Brest harbour and Crozon. Pretty drive to the little port of **Tinduff**.

★ **Chapelle St-Claude**: to the east of Plougastel, below the anse de Pensoul. This 16th-century chapel has a small leaning belfry.

★ **Chapelle de la Fontaine-Blanche**: dating from the 15th century. A major *pardon* takes place here on 15 August and is well known for its traditional costumes. The chapel has double semicircular doorways and a little lantern bell tower. The majestic presbytery nearby is, sadly, falling into ruin.

★ **Chapelle St-Jean:** to the north of the town on the banks of the River Élorn. This chapel dates from the 15th century. Its one astonishing feature is that all the statuary is painted white.

★ **Pointe de l'Armorique**: at the tip of the peninsula. With military terrain to one side and private properties on the other, it isn't possible to actually get there. If you're looking for views, the best you'll get are the ones at Kerdéniel and Keramenez (*see above*).

DAOULAS (*DAOULAZ*) 29460   (Pop: 1,840)

Situated about 20 kilometres (12.5 miles) south of Brest, this village enjoyed considerable fame in the Middle Ages thanks to the manufacture of *daoulas*, a fine cloth that was highly sought after by buyers from every corner of Europe. William Shakespeare's father, who was a draper, was one regular customer. Today, visitors come to see the ruins of the abbey, founded in AD 500, and the Romanesque cloister, unique in Brittany.

USEFUL ADDRESS

🖪 **Information point**: place du Valy. Open in July and August.

WHERE TO EAT AND GET A DRINK

✕ **La Ferme du Cloître**: in the hamlet of Le Cras, about 300 metres beyond the abbey. ☎ 02-98-25-80-56. Closed on Monday afternoon and Tuesday out of season, as well as from mid-November to mid-December. Allow about 60–70F to eat à la carte. There's a good welcome in this *crêperie* set in an old farm building. The environment is suitably rustic, with exposed beams and a large fireplace. They serve all kinds of Breton snacks as well as excellent *crêpes*.

♟ **Café Paul**: 1 route de Quimper. ☎ 02-98-25-85-41. On the corner of the road leading to the abbey. This place is not at the forefront of fashion, just a plain little *bistrot* full of regulars where the atmosphere is comfortable and welcoming and you soon feel at home. You know the kind of thing: a bar counter that gets crowded on market days, with just a few tables and chairs on a wooden floor, and a very welcoming proprietress. The terrace, which looks out over the River Mignonne, has a more up-to-date feel.

WHAT TO SEE

★ **Cemetery gateway**: this monumental 16th-century gateway, formerly the south porch of the church, is something of a rarity. Admire the beauty of the sculptures. At the back of the cemetery is a very old calvary. Viewed together with the picturesque 15th- and 17th-century buildings all around, it paints a harmonious and moving picture.

★ **Church**: constructed in the 12th century, with a long nave without a transept, this church is a fine example of Romanesque Breton architecture. The ochre stone used to build the church gives it an unusual warmth. The harmonious proportions of the vaulted columns – strong and graceful – are evident. In the chevet, the former ossuary is today used as a sacristy. Further down is the Renaissance Chapelle Ste-Anne (open every day).

★ **Cloister**: the only complete example of a Romanesque cloister in Finistère, with 32 small-columned arches, with delicately sculpted foliage on the capitals. In the middle is a washbasin decorated with heads and geometric motifs. There are annual exhibitions (admission fee).

★ High-quality seasonal exhibitions are also held in the **Centre Culturel**. ☎ 02-98-25-84-39. Open all year round, with a break of at least one month in low season so it's advisable to telephone beforehand. In high season, open every day when an exhibition is being shown 10am–7pm; in low season, from Monday to Friday 10am–noon and 1.30–5.30pm, and at weekends and on public holidays 2–6pm. Admission charge (35F).

– **The market in Daoulas**: a pleasant Sunday morning market is held on place St-Yves, near the River Daoulas. Everything is sold here, including very pretty bouquets of dried flowers at competitive prices, and no fewer than 500 varieties of medicinal plants.

IRVILLAC (*IRVILHAG*) 29460   (Pop: 1,030)

Situated 4 kilometres (2.5 miles) from Daoulas, the village of Irvillac has an interesting Gothic and Renaissance church.

WHERE TO EAT

✗ **Ti Lannig**: in the main street. ☎ 02-98-25-83-62. Open lunchtime only, from Monday to Saturday (Saturday lunchtime reservations only). Closed Monday and Wednesday afternoon and during the first week in August. This restaurant attracts a good clientele with its 58F (weekday) workers' menu. Additional menus for up to 285F, offering simple and tasty food, in generous portions. Friendly staff.

WHAT TO SEE

★ **Church**: the interior may be nothing exceptional (apart from a moving 15th-century *pietà*), but the exterior offers a curious buttress belfry adorned with baroque-style turrets. Struck by lightning in the 18th century, it was rebuilt by Italian workmen, which perhaps explains its exuberant aspect.

★ **Chapelle Notre-Dame-de-Lorette**: 3 kilometres (2 miles) to the south-west. To get there, take the road to Hanvec as far as the crossroads in Malenty (about 2 kilometres/1.5 miles). From there, a little path leads to the chapel. The calvary here is almost unique in Brittany, being in the shape of a stylized ship's anchor (although some people see it as a kind of stone tree). On the fountain beneath the calvary, the feet of the Virgin with Child are crushing a serpent woman.

L'HÔPITAL-CAMFROUT
(*AN OSPITAL*) 29460   (Pop: 1,700)

Halfway between Daoulas and Le Faou, this unattractive little village inherited its strange name from the leprosy hospital that existed here in the Middle Ages.

WHERE TO EAT

✗ **Restaurant Haméry-Les Routiers**: 68 rue Émile-Salaün. ☎ 02-98-20-01-21. Fax: 02-98-20-06-20. Closed in the evening except Saturday; also closed for one week in mid-February and the last two weeks in October. On the main road that runs through the town, this typical *restaurant routier* (transport café) offers a traditional cheap set menu (61F) on weekday lunchtimes as well as a variety of decent menus with a good choice for up to180F. Warm welcome.

WHERE TO STAY IN THE AREA

🛏 ✗ **Le Moulin de Poul-Hanol**: Poulhanol, 29460 Hanvec. About 3 kilometres (2 miles) out of town on the D770 in the direction of Le Faou, just after L'Hôpital-Camfrout, in the village of Hanvec. It's on the right and is signposted. Former mill by the anse de Kérouse (cove). ☎ 02-98-20-02-10. Restaurant closed on Monday out of season (Monday lunchtime only in July and August). Advisable to book in advance. In one of the most beautiful little corners of the region, this exquisitely restored old mill has eight gorgeous little rooms decorated in the local style (most with bathroom). Very reasonable prices, from 120F to 200F. In the pleasant dining room, you can sample the delicious home-made *crêpes*. Menus from 70F to 120F.

🛏 **Camping municipal**: Roz, 29460 Logonna-Daoulas. ☎ 02-98-20-67-86. Fax: 02-98-20-68-59. Situated 5 kilometres (3 miles) to the southwest of L'Hôpital-Camfrout. Open from mid-June to mid-September. Good sanitary facilities. The campsite is by the sea so there's a nice natural setting and the sites are adequate. Lovely walks all around in the direction of the Pointe and the Îles du Bendy.

WHAT TO DO

– **Walks with a pack-mule:** contact the Association Bretâne, Coat Forest, 29460 Hanvec. ☎ 02-98-21-91-04. This could be one way to get to see the natural side of Brittany, with a pack-mule for company who will carry your bags. This costs 200F per day or 350F for a weekend, with a 50F initial association membership fee. They also offer campsites, *chambres d'hôte*, *table d'hôte* meals and walkers' shelters (*gîtes d'étape*).

Understanding the Menu

During your stay you are sure to have a few meals out in a restaurant – after all, what would a trip to France be without sampling the cuisine? This list has been compiled to help you understand the menu and enjoy your meal. Bon appétit!

À point medium rare
Abats offal
Abricot apricot
Acarne sea-bream
Affiné(e) improve, ripen, mature (common term with cheese)
Africaine (à l') african style: with aubergines, tomatoes, ceps
Agneau lamb
Agrumes citrus fruits
Aigre-doux sweet-sour
Aiguillette thin slice
Ail garlic
Aile (Aileron) wing (winglet)
Aïoli mayonnaise, garlic, olive oil
Algues seaweed
Aligot purée of potatoes, cream, garlic, butter and fresh Tomme de Cantal (or Laguiole) cheese
Allemande (à l') German style: with sauerkraut and sausages
Alsacienne (à l') Alsace style: with sauerkraut, sausages and sometimes foie gras
Amande almond
Amandine almond-flavoured
Amer bitter
Américaine (à l'), Armoricaine (à l') sauce with dry white wine, cognac, tomatoes, shallots
Amuse-gueule appetizer
Ananas pineapple
Anchoiade anchovy crust
Anchois anchovy
Ancienne (à l') in the old style
Andouille smoked tripe sausage
Andouillette small chitterling (tripe) sausage
Aneth dill
Anglaise (à l') plain boiled
Anguille eel
Anis aniseed
Arachide peanut
Arc-en-ciel rainbow trout

Artichaud artichoke
Asperge asparagus
Assaisonné flavoured or seasoned with; to dress a salad
Assiette (de) plate (of)
Aubergine aubergine, eggplant
Aumônière pancake drawn up into shape of beggar's purse
Auvergnate (à l') Auvergne style: with cabbage, sausage and bacon
Avocat avocado pear
Baba au rhum sponge dessert with rum syrup
Baguette long bread loaf
Baie berry
Baigné bathed or lying in
Banane banana
Bar sea-bass
Barbeau de mer red mullet
Barbue brill
Basilic basil
Basquaise (à la) Basque style: Bayonne ham, rice and peppers
Baudroie monkfish, anglerfish
Bavette skirt of beef
Béarnaise thick sauce with egg yolks, shallots, butter, white wine and tarragon vinegar
Béchamel creamy white sauce
Beignet fritter
Belle Hélène poached pear with ice cream and chocolate sauce
Berrichonne bordelaise sauce
Betterave beetroot
Beurre (échiré) butter (finest butter from Poitou-Charentes)
Beurre blanc sauce with butter, shallots, wine vinegar and sometimes dry white wine
Beurre noir sauce with brown butter, vinegar, parsley
Bière à la pression beer on tap
Bière en bouteille bottled beer

Bifteck steak
Bigarade (à la) orange sauce
Bisque shellfish soup
Blanc (de volaille) white breast (of chicken); can also describe white fish fillet or white vegetables
Blanchaille whitebait
Blanquette white stew
Blé corn or wheat
Blettes swiss chard
Blinis small, thick pancakes
Boeuf à la mode beef braised in red wine
Boeuf Stroganoff beef, sour cream, onions, mushrooms
Bombe ice-cream
Bonne femme (à la) white wine sauce, shallots, mushrooms
Bordelaise (à la) Bordeaux style: brown sauce with shallots, red wine, beef bone marrow
Boudin sausage-shaped mixture
Boudin blanc white coloured mixture; pork and sometimes chicken
Boudin noir black pudding
Bouillabaisse Mediterranean fish stew and soup
Bouillon broth, light consommé
Bouquet garni bunch of herbs used for flavouring
Bourguignonne (à la) Burgundy style: red wine, onions, bacon and mushrooms
Bourride creamy fish soup with aioli
Brandade de morue salt cod
Bretonne sauce with celery, leeks, beans and mushrooms
Brioche sweet yeast bread
Brochet pike
Brochette (de) meat or fish on a skewer
Brouillé scrambled
Brûlé(e) toasted
Bruxelloise sauce with asparagus, butter and eggs
Cabillaud cod
Cacahouète roasted peanut
Cacao cocoa
Café coffee
Caille quail

Cajou cashew nut
Calmar (Calamar) inkfish, squid
Campagne country style
Canard duck
Caneton (Canette) duckling
Cannelle cinnamon
Carbonnade braised beef in beer, onions and bacon
Carré chop
Casse-croûte snack
Cassis blackcurrant
Cassolette small pan
Cassoulet casserole of beans, sausage and/or pork, goose, duck
Cèpe fine, delicate mushroom
Cerise (noire) cherry (black)
Cerneau walnut
Cervelas pork garlic sausage
Cervelle brains
Champignons (des bois) mushrooms (from the woods)
Chanterelle apricot coloured mushroom
Chantilly whipped cream sugar
Charcuterie cold meat cuts
Charcutière sauce with onions, white wine, gherkins
Chasseur sauce with white wine, mushrooms, shallots
Chateaubriand thick fillet steak
Chaussons pastry turnover
Chemise (en) pastry covering
Chicon chicory
Chicorée curly endive
Chipiron see Calmar
Choix (au) a choice of
Chou (vert) cabbage
Choucroute souring of vegetables, usually with cabbage (sauerkraut), peppercorns, boiled ham, potatoes and Strasbourg sausages
Chou-fleur cauliflower
Chou rouge red cabbage
Choux (pâte à) pastry
Ciboule spring onions
Cidre cider
Ciboulette chive
Citron (vert) lemon (lime)
Citronelle lemon grass

Civet stew

Clafoutis cherries in pancake batter

Clou de girofle clove (spice)

Cochon pig

Cochonailles pork products

Cocotte (en) cooking pot

Coeur (de) heart (of)

Coing quince

Colin hake

Compote stewed fruit

Concassé(e) coarsely chopped

Concombre cucumber

Confit(e) preserved or candied

Confiture jam

Confiture d'orange marmalade

Consommé clear soup

Coq (au vin) chicken in red wine sauce (or name of wine)

Coque (à la) soft-boiled or served in shell

Coquillage shellfish

Coquille St-Jacques scallop

Coriandre coriander

Cornichon gherkin

Côte d'agneau lamb chop

Côte de boeuf side of beef

Côte de veau veal chop

Côtelette chop

Coulis de thick sauce (of)

Courge pumpkin

Couscous crushed semolina

Crabe crab

Crécy with carrots and rice

Crème cream

Crème anglaise light custard sauce

Crème brûlée same, less sugar and cream, with praline (*see* Brûlée)

Crème pâtissière custard filling

Crêpe thin pancake

Crêpe Suzette sweet pancake with orange liqueur sauce

Cresson watercress

Crevette grise shrimp

Crevette rose prawn

Croque Madame toasted cheese or ham sandwich with an egg on top

Croque Monsieur toasted cheese or ham sandwich

Croustade small pastry mould with various fillings

Croûte (en) pastry crust (in)

Cru raw

Crudité raw vegetable

Crustacés shell fish

Cuisse (de) leg (of)

Cuissot (de) haunch (of)

Cuit cooked

Datte date

Daube stew (various types)

Daurade sea-bream

Décaféiné decaffeinated coffee

Dégustation tasting

Diane (á la) pepper cream sauce

Dieppoise (à la) Dieppe style: white wine, cream, mussels, shrimps

Dijonaise (à la) with mustard sauce

Dinde young hen turkey

Dindon turkey

Dorade sea-bream

Doux (douce) sweet

Échalotte shallot

Écrevisse freshwater crayfish

Émincé thinly sliced

Encre squid ink, used in sauces

Endive chicory

Entrecôte entrecôte, rib steak

Entremets sweets

Épaule shoulder

Épice spice

Épinard spinach

Escabèche fish (or poultry) marinated in court-bouillon; cold

Escalope thinly cut (meat or fish)

Escargot snail

Espadon swordfish

Estouffade stew with onions, herbs, mushrooms, red or white wine (perhaps garlic)

Estragon tarragon flavoured

Farci(e) stuffed

Farine flour

Faux-filet sirloin steak

Fenouil fennel

Fermière mixture of onions, carrots, turnips, celery, etc.

Feuille de vigne vine leaf

Feuilleté light flaky pastry

Fève broad bean

Ficelle (à la) tied in a string
Ficelles thin loaves of bread
Figue fig
Filet fillet
Financière (à la) Madeira sauce with truffles
Fine de claire oyster (*see* Huîtres)
Fines herbes mixture of parsley, chives, tarragon, etc.
Flageolet kidney bean
Flamande (à la) Flemish style: bacon, carrots, cabbage, potatoes and turnips
Flambée flamed
Flamiche puff pastry tart
Foie liver
Foie de veau calf's liver
Foie gras goose liver
Fond d'artichaut artichoke heart
Fondu(e) (de fromage) melted cheese with wine
Forestière bacon and mushrooms
Four (au) baked in oven
Fourré stuffed
Frais fresh or cool
Fraise strawberry
Fraise des bois wild strawberry
Framboise raspberry
Frappé frozen or ice cold
Friandise sweets (petits fours)
Fricassée braised in sauce or butter, egg yolks and cream
Frisé(e) curly
Frit fried
Frites chips/french fries
Friture small fried fish
Fromage cheese
Fromage de tête brawn
Fruit de la passion passion fruit
Fruits confits crystallized fruit
Fruits de mer seafood
Fumé smoked
Galette pastry, pancake or cake
Gamba large prawn
Ganache chocolate and crème fraîche mixture used to fill cakes
Garbure (Garbue) vegetable soup
Gâteau cake
Gauffre waffle
Gelée aspic gelly
Genièvre juniper
Gésier gizzard

Gibelotte *see* Fricassée
Gibier game
Gigot (de) leg of lamb; can describe other meat or fish
Gingembre ginger
Girofle clove
Glacé(e) iced, crystallized, glazed
Glace ice-cream
Gougère round-shaped, egg and cheese choux pastry
Goujon gudgeon
Goujonnettes (de) small fried pieces (of)
Gourmandises sweetmeats; can describe fruits de mer
Graisse fat
Gratin browned
Gratin Dauphinois potato dish with cheese, cream and garlic
Gratin Savoyard potato dish with cheese and butter
Gratiné(e) sauced dish browned with butter, cheese, breadcrumbs, etc.
Gravette oyster (*see* Huîtres)
Grenouille (cuisses de grenouilles) frog (frogs' legs)
Gribiche mayonnaise sauce with gherkins, capers, hardboiled egg yolks and herbs
Grillade grilled meat
Grillé(e) grilled
Griotte (Griottine) bitter red cherry
Gros sel coarse rock or sea salt
Groseille à maquereau gooseberry
Groseille noire blackcurrant
Groseille rouge redcurrant
Gruyère hard, mild cheese
Hachis minced or chopped-up
Hareng herring
  à l'huile cured in oil
  fumé kippered
  salé bloater
  saur smoked
Haricot bean
Haricot blanc dried white bean
Haricot vert green/French bean
Hollandaise sauce with butter, egg yolk and lemon juice
Homard lobster

Hongroise (à la) Hungarian style: sauce with tomato and paprika
Huile oil
Huîtres oysters
Les claires: the oyster-fattening beds in Marennes terrain (part of the Charente estuary, between Royan and Rochefort, in Poitou-Charentes).
Flat-shelled oysters: *Belons* (from the River Belon in Brittany); *Gravettes:* from Arcachon in the South West);
both the above are cultivated in their home oyster beds.
Marennes are those transferred from Brittany and Arcachon to les claires, where they finish their growth.
Dished oysters (sometimes called *portugaises*):
these breed mainly in the Gironde and Charentes estuaries; they mature at Marennes.
Fines de claires and *spéciales* are the largest; *huîtres de parc* are standard sized.
All this lavish care covers a time span of two to four years.
Hure (de) head (of); brawn, jellied
Île flottante unmoulded soufflé of beaten egg with white sugar
Imam bayeldi aubergine with rice, onions, and sautéed tomatoes
Infusion herb tea
Italienne (à l') Italian style: artichokes, mushrooms, pasta
Jalousie latticed fruit or jam tart
Jambon ham
Jambonneau knuckle of pork
Jambonnette boned and stuffed (knuckle of ham or poultry)
Jarret de veau stew of shin of veal
Jarreton cooked pork knuckle
Jerez sherry
Joue (de) cheek (of)
Julienne thinly-cut vegetables: also ling (cod family)
Jus juice
Lait milk
Laitue lettuce
Lamproie lamprey

Langouste spiny lobster or crayfish
Langoustine Dublin Bay prawn
Langue tongue
Lapereau young rabbit
Lapin rabbit
Lard bacon
Lardons strips of fatty bacon
Laurier bay-laurel, sweet bay leaf
Léger (Légère) light
Légume vegetable
Lièvre hare
Limaçon snail
Limande lemon sole
Limon lime
Lit bed
Lotte de mer monkfish, anglerfish
Loup de mer sea-bass
Louvine (Loubine) grey mullet, like a sea-bass (Basque name)
Lyonnaise (à la) Lyonnais style: sauce with wine, onions, vinegar
Mâche lamb's lettuce; small dark green leaf
Madeleine tiny sponge cake
Madère sauce *demi-glace* and Madeira wine
Magret (de canard) breast (of duck); now used for other poultry
Maïs maize flour
Maison (de) of the restaurant
Maître d'hôtel sauce with butter, parsley and lemon
Manchons *see* Goujonnettes
Mangetout edible peas and pods
Mangue mango
Manière (de) style (of)
Maquereau mackerel
Maraîchère (à la) market-gardener style; velouté sauce with vegetables
Marais marsh or market garden
Marbré marbled
Marc pure spirit
Marcassin young wild boar
Marché market
Marchand de vin sauce with red wine, chopped shallots
Marengo tomatoes, mushrooms, olive oil, white wine, garlic, herbs
Marennes (blanches) flat-shelled oysters (*see* Huîtres)

Marennes (vertes) green shell oysters

Marinières *see* Moules

Marmite stewpot

Marrons chestnuts

Médaillon (de) round piece (of)

Mélange mixture or blend

Ménagère (à la) housewife style: onions, potatoes, peas, turnips and carrots

Mendiant (fruits de) mixture of figs, almonds and raisins

Menthe mint

Merguez spicy grilled sausage

Merlan whiting (in Provence the word is used for hake)

Merlu hake

Merluche dried cod

Mesclum mixture of salad leaves

Meunière sauce with butter, parsley, lemon (sometimes oil)

Meurette red wine sauce

Miel honey

Mignon (de) small round piece

Mignonnette coarsely ground white pepper

Mijoté(e) cooked slowly in water

Milanaise (à la) Milan style: dipped in breadcrumbs, egg, cheese

Millefeuille puff pastry with numerous thin layers

Mirabeau anchovies, olives

Mirabelle golden plums

Mitonée (de) soup (of)

Mode (à la) in the manner of

Moelle beef marrow

Moelleux au chocolat chocolate dessert (cake)

Montmorency with cherries

Morilles edible, dark brown, honeycombed fungi

Mornay cheese sauce

Morue cod

Moules mussels

Moules marinières mussels cooked in white wine and shallots

Mousseline hollandaise sauce with whipped cream

Moutarde mustard

Mouton mutton

Mûre mulberry

Mûre sauvage (de ronce) blackberry

Muscade nutmeg

Museau de porc (de boeuf) sliced muzzle of pork (beef) with shallots and parsley with vinaigrette

Myrtille bilberry (blueberry)

Mystère a meringue dessert with ice-cream and chocolate; also cone-shaped ice-cream

Nature plain

Navarin stew (usually lamb)

Navets turnips

Nid nest

Noilly sauce based on vermouth

Noisette hazelnut

Noisette sauce of lightly browned butter

Noisette (de) round piece (of)

Noix nuts

Noix de veau topside of leg (veal)

Normande (à la) Normandy style: fish sauce with mussels, shrimps, mushrooms, eggs and cream

Nouille noodle

Nouveau (Nouvelle) new or young

Noyau sweet liqueur from crushed stones (usually cherries)

Oeufs à la coque soft-boiled eggs

Oeufs à la neige *see* Île flottante

Oeufs à la poêle fried eggs

Oeufs brouillés scrambled eggs

Oeufs en cocotte eggs cooked in individual dishes in a bain-marie

Oeufs durs hard-boiled eggs

Oeufs moulés poached eggs

Oie goose

Oignon onion

Ombrine fish, like sea-bass

Onglet flank of beef

Oreille (de porc) ear (pig's)

Oreillette sweet fritter, flavoured with orange flower water

Origan oregano (herb)

Orléannaise Orléans style: chicory and potatoes

Ortie nettle

Os bone

Osso bucco à la niçoise veal braised with orange zest, tomatoes, onions and garlic
Pain bread
Pain de campagne round white loaf
Pain d'épice spiced honey cake
Pain de mie square white loaf
Pain de seigle rye bread
Pain complet/entier wholemeal
Pain grillé toast
Pain doré/Pain perdu bread soaked in milk and eggs and fried
Paleron shoulder
Palmier palm-shaped sweet puff pastry
Palmier (coeur de) palm (heart)
Palombe wood pigeon
Palomête fish, like sea-bass
Palourde clam
Pamplemousse grapefruit
Panaché mixed
Pané(e) breadcrumbed
Papillote (en) cooked in oiled paper or foil
Paquets (en) parcels
Parfait (de) mousse (of)
Paris-Brest cake of *choux* pastry, filled with butter cream and almonds
Parisienne (à la) leeks, potatoes
Parmentier potatoes
Pastèque watermelon
Pastis (sauce au) aniseed based
Pâte pastry, dough or batter
Pâte à choux cream puff pastry
Pâte brisée short crust pastry
Pâté en croûte baked in pastry crust
Pâtes fraîches fresh pasta
Pâtisserie pastry
Paupiettes thin slices of meat or fish, used to wrap fillings
Pavé (de) thick slice (of)
Pavot (graines de) poppy seeds
Paysan(ne) (à la) country style
Peau (de) skin (of)
Pêche peach
Pêcheur fisherman
Pèlerine scallop
Perche perch

Perdreau young partridge
Perdrix partridge
Périgourdine (à la) goose liver and sauce Périgueux
Périgueux sauce with truffles and Madeira
Persil parsley
Persillade mixture of chopped parsley and garlic
Petit gris small snail
Pétoncle small scallop
Picholine large green table olives
Pied de cheval large oyster
Pied de mouton blanc cream coloured mushroom
Pied de porc pig's trotter
Pigeonneau young pigeon
Pignon pine nut
Piment (doux) pepper (sweet)
Pintade (pintadeau) guinea fowl (young guinea fowl)
Piperade omelette or scrambled eggs with tomatoes, peppers, onions and sometimes ham
Piquante (sauce) sharp tasting sauce with shallots, capers and wine
Pissenlit dandelion leaf
Pistache green pistachio nut
Pistou vegetable soup bound with *pommade* (thick smooth paste)
Plateau (de) plate (of)
Pleurote mushroom
Poché(e), pochade poached
Poêlé fried
Poire pear
Poireau leek
Pois pea
Poisson fish
Poitrine breast
Poitrine fumée smoked bacon
Poitrine salée unsmoked bacon
Poivre noir black pepper
Poivron (doux) pepper (sweet)
Polonaise Polish style: with buttered breadcrumbs, parsley, hard-boiled eggs
Pomme apple
Pommes de terre potatoes
    dauphine croquettes
    château roast
    frites chips

gratinées browned with cheese
Lyonnaise sautéed with onions
vapeur boiled
Porc (carré de) loin of pork
Porc (côte de) loin of pork
Porcelet suckling pig
Porto (au) port
Portugaise (à la) Portuguese style: fried onions and tomatoes
Portugaises oysters with long, deep shells (*see* Huîtres)
Potage thick soup
Pot-au-feu clear meat broth served with the meat
Potimarron pumpkin
Poularde large hen
Poulet chicken
Poulet à la broche spit-roasted chicken
Poulpe octopus
Poussin small baby chicken
Pré-salé (agneau de) lamb raised on salt marshes
Primeur young vegetable
Profiterole puffs of *choux* pastry, filled with custard
Provençale (à la) Provençal style: tomatoes, garlic, olive oil, etc.
Prune plum
Pruneau prune
Quenelle light dumpling of fish or poultry
Queue tail
Queue de boeuf oxtail
Quiche lorraine open flan of cheese, ham or bacon
Raclette scrapings from specially-made and heated cheese
Radis radish
Ragoût stew, usually meat but can describe other ingredients
Raie (bouclée) skate (type of)
Raifort horseradish
Raisin grape
Ramier wood pigeon
Rapé(e) grated or shredded
Rascasse scorpion fish
Ratatouille aubergines, onions, courgettes, garlic, red peppers and tomatoes in olive oil
Réglisse liquorice
Reine-Claude greengage

Rémoulade sauce of mayonnaise, mustard, capers, herbs, anchovy
Rillettes (d'oie) potted pork (goose)
Ris d'agneau lamb sweetbreads
Ris de veau veal sweetbreads
Riz rice
Robe de chambre jacket potato
Rognon kidney
Romarin rosemary
Rôti roast
Rouget red mullet
Rouget barbet red mullet
Rouille orange-coloured sauce with peppers, garlic and saffron
Roulade (de) roll (of)
Roulé(e) rolled (usually crêpe)
Sabayon sauce of egg yolks, wine
Sablé shortbread
Safran saffron
Saignant(e) underdone, rare
St-Jaques (coquille) scallop
St-Pierre John Dory
Salade niçoise tomatoes, beans, potatoes, black olives, anchovy, lettuce, olive oil, perhaps tuna
Salade panachée mixed salad
Salade verte green salad
Salé salted
Salmis red wine sauce
Salsifis salsify (vegetable)
Sandre freshwater fish, like perch
Sang blood
Sanglier wild boar
Saucisse freshly-made sausage
Saucisson large, dry sausage
Saucisson cervelas saveloy
Sauge sage
Saumon salmon
Saumon fumé smoked salmon
Sauvage wild
Scipion cuttlefish
Sel salt
Soja (pousse de) soy bean (soy bean sprout)
Soja (sauce de) soy sauce
Soubise onion sauce
Sucre sugar
Tapenade olive spread
Tartare raw minced beef

Tartare (sauce) sauce with mayonnaise, onions, capers, herbs

Tarte open flan

Tarte Tatin upside down tart of caramelized apples and pastry

Terrine container in which mixed meats/fish are baked; served cold

Tête de veau vinaigrette calf's head vinaigrette

Thé tea

Thermidor grilled lobster with browned béchamel sauce

Thon tuna fish

Thym thyme

Tiède mild or lukewarm

Tilleul lime tree

Tomate tomato

Topinambour Jerusalem artichoke

Torte sweet-filled flan

Tortue turtle

Tournedos fillet steak (small end)

Touron a cake, pastry or loaf made from almond paste and filled with candied fruits and nuts

Tourte (Tourtière) covered savoury tart

Tourteau large crab

Tranche slice

Tranche de boeuf steak

Traver de porc spare rib of pork

Tripoux stuffed mutton tripe

Truffade a huge sautéed pancake or galette with bacon, garlic and Cantal cheese

Truffe truffle; black, exotic fungus

Truite trout

Truite saumonée salmon trout

Turbot (turbotin) turbot

Vacherin ice-cream, meringue, cream

Vapeur (à la) steamed

Veau veal

Veau pané (escalope de) thin slice of veal in flour, eggs and breadcrumbs

Venaison venison

Verveine verbena

Viande meat

Vichyssoise creamy potato and leek soup, served cold

Viennoise coated with egg and breadcrumbs, fried (usually veal)

Vierge literally virgin (best olive oil, the first pressing)

Vierge (sauce) olive oil sauce

Vinaigre (de) wine vinegar or vinegar of named fruit

Vinaigrette (à la) French dressing with wine vinegar, oil, etc.

Volaille poultry

Yaourt yogurt

©Richard Binns

Index

Note: Page numbers in *italics* refer to maps

Abbaye de Beauport 312
Abbaye de Boquen 259
Abbaye Cistercienne du Bon-
  Repos 281
Abbaye de Coatmalouen 288
Abbaye de Relecq 447
Abbaye de Saint-Magloire 229
Aber-Benoît 399–403
Aber-Ildut 397–9
Aber-Wrac'h 399–403
Abers, Côte des 399–410
Aboville, Gérard d' 87
accommodation 27–31
  see also individual places
Aff, River 127
agriculture 85
air travel 13–21
Ajoncs, Côte des 329
ambulances 47
Ankou 92
Anne of Brittany 79, 103, 155,
  206
Aquatides 277
Arcouest, La Pointe de l' 314–15
l'Argoat 275
Armorique, Pointe de l' 479
Arrée, Monts d' 445–77, 446
  range 457
Arthur, King 92, 131
Arthurian legends 92, 131, 134,
  135
Astérix 88
au pairs 76
auberges 28
  see also individual places
Aubert, Bishop of Avranches
  186–7

Baie de Morlaix, Réserve
  Ornithologique de la 438
Ballue, Château de la 144
Balzac, Honoré de 201
Baguer-Morvan 184
Barenton, Fontaine de 134
Barnenez, grand cairn de 438
Barrage Jean-Descottes, Lac du
  135
bars 37
  see also individual places
Batz, Île de 86, 420–3
Beaumanoir, Château de 271
Beauport, Abbaye de 312
Beauvoir 191–2
Bécassine 88
Bécherel 137–9
Bédée 136
beer 434
Beg Seac'h, Fort de 421
Beg-Ar-Vilin 332
Bel-Air, Site du 274–5
Belle-Isle-en-Terre 293–5
Benedictines 187, 188
Berrien 449
Bertheaume, Fort de 383
Berven 411–13
Bétineuc, Base de loisirs de 230
Bienassis, Château de 251
Bienvenüe, Fulgence 87, 88, 271
Binic 302–4

Blanchardeau, Viaduc de 307
Blanche, La Grève 405
Blancs-Sablons, Plage des 385
Blavet Valley 286
boarding 159
Bobet, Louison, museum 137
Bodilis 471
Boël, Moulin de 124
Bon-Repos, Abbaye Cistercienne
  du 281
Boquého 271
Boquen, Abbaye de 259
Bosméléac 277
Botmeur 456–7
La Bouëxière 124
Bourbansais, Zoo-Château de la
  143–4
Bourbriac 288–9
Bourg-des-Comptes 124–5
Brasparts 453–5
Brassens, Georges 319
Bréhat, Île de 306, 315–18
Bréhec 308–9
Brélidy, Château and Motte
  féodale de 321
Brelès 397
Brélévy, Château and Motte
  féodale de 321
Brennilis 458–9
BREST 360–78, 365
  accommodation 364–7
  Arsenal de la Marine 373–4
  bars 370–1
  boat trips 375
  Château de Brest 372–3
  Conservatoire Botanique 375
  Cours Dajot 373
  diving 375–7
  eating places 367–70
  festivals 377–8
  history 361–2
  leaving 378
  Marina 374–5
  Musée des Beaux-Arts 372
  Musée de la Marine 373
  naval dockyards 361–2
  navigational markers 360
  Océanopolis 374
  Parc du Vallon de Stang-Alard
    375
  Place Guérin 374
  Port de plaisance du Mouli-
    Blanc 374
  Recouvrance 372, 373–4
  Rue Jean-Jaurès 372
  Rue de Siam 372
  St-Martin district 372, 374
  sweet treats 372
  Tour de la Motte-Tanguy 373
  useful addresses 362–4
Brétigny, Treaty of 179
Briant, Théophile 162
Brieg, St 81
Brignogan-Plage 406–7
Brittany:
  emblems 79–80
  flag 79
  nationalism 78–9
  Welsh connection 80–2
Brocéliande Forest 131
Broualan 184

Broussais, Dr 146
Bruz 124
budget 31
Buguélès 332
Bulat-Pestivien 289–90
Burtulet, Chapelle de 290
buses 75

Cado, St 81
cafés 37
  see also individual places
Callac 290–1
Callot, Île de 426
camping 30
  see also individual places
canal trips 65
Canards, Vallée des 124
Cancale 86, 172–8
canoeing, sea 159
canoes, rental 126
car hire 74
car travel 24–5
  driving 74
  vocabulary 52
Caradeuc, Château de 230
Carantec 245–7
Carrel, Alexis 332
Cartier, Jacques 146, 155, 156,
  162
Castel-Meur 332
Caulnes 230
Celtic Cross 80
Centre d'Etude et de Valorisation
  des Algues 323
Cézembre, Île de 161
Chambre au Loup, Vallon de la
  134
chambres d'hôte 28
Champ-Dolent, Menhir du 184
Champeaux 206–7
La Chapelle-Neuve 291
Charles VIII 103, 206
  Château, Pointe de 332
Chateaubriand, Pont 230–1
Chateaubriand, René de 146,
  155, 156, 161, 234
Châteaugiron 122–3
Châtelaudren 299–301
Châtelet 234
Chausey islands 179
Chère, River 127
Cherrueix 185–6
Chevet, Pointe de 234
Chevré, Etang de 206
La Chèze 276
Childebert, King 187
children, eating out with 39
Chrétien, Jean-Loup 79
Christianity 80
cider 242, 256
Cisterciens 259
Cléder 413–14
climate 31–3
Le Cloître-St-Thégonnec 447–8
clothing 33
  sizes 34
coaches 25–6
Coat-Couravel, Château de 284
Coatmalouen, Abbaye de 288

INDEX